REVIEW TEXT IN WORLD HISTORY

(Revised, 1973)

by IRVING L. GORDON

Department of History and Economics
Midwood High School
Brooklyn, New York

Dedicated to serving

AMSCO

our nation's youth

When ordering this book, please specify:

either **R 48 P**

or REVIEW TEXT IN WORLD HISTORY

AMSCO SCHOOL PUBLICATIONS, Inc.

315 Hudson Street   New York, N. Y. 10013

PREFACE

Americans today are increasingly affected by world affairs. In the years since the beginning of World War II, we have witnessed great tides of change: independence for almost all African and Asian peoples, the advent of nuclear energy, the growth of Soviet power, and the emergence of the United States as the leader of free nations. Americans, consequently, need an understanding of the men and forces that have helped shape our world.

High school students are afforded an opportunity to secure such understanding by a course in world history. However, because of the vast quantity of historical information, high school students need a concise text that may be used by itself, as a supplement to a more elaborate text, or as a review for examinations.

To meet these needs, *Review Text in World History* contains the following features:

1. It is a history of the entire world. Although European developments predominate, increasing attention is paid to the non-European aspects of world history. The major Asian nations—India, China, and Japan—are portrayed from earliest times. The problems facing Africa and Asia today are fully discussed.

2. The text is organized to focus attention upon significant facts and concepts. Nonessential and irrelevant data have been eliminated.

3. The text has an up-to-date perspective. Considerable attention has been given to the discussion of recent world affairs, and the past is viewed in terms of current forces and problems.

4. The text has been carefully graded to the comprehension level of high school pupils. Difficult terms and concepts are explained at length. Every effort has been made to assure crisp, clear, and varied language so as to facilitate understanding and maintain interest.

5. The text contains much illustrative material—maps, pictures, charts, and cartoons. The maps help relate geographic factors to historical events. The pictures illustrate cultural developments. The charts and cartoons, mostly pertaining to recent times, help encourage critical thinking about world problems.

6. The text contains many test questions, arranged by topic and placed after the appropriate subject matter. Carefully graded, the tests probe significant information and enable the pupil to measure his mastery of the content. Many questions require logical reasoning and mature understanding—major objectives of social studies teaching.

—I. L. G.

CONTENTS

Page

UNIT IX. DEVELOPMENTS IN INDUSTRY, SCIENCE, AND CULTURE

UNIT X. IMPERIALISM AND COLONIAL NATIONALISM

UNIT XI. WORLD WARS AND DICTATORSHIPS IN A TROUBLED WORLD

Introduction to the Study of History

WHAT IS HISTORY?

History is the story of man's past. History systematically records and explains what man has thought, said, and done. History deals with political, economic, and social matters.

1. **Political**—pertaining to *government*.
2. **Economic**—relating to *agriculture, industry,* and *trade.*
3. **Social**—referring to *everyday life* and *culture.*

These three aspects of history are interrelated; a development in one phase usually affects the others.

History describes man's efforts to improve his world. It recounts his achievements and setbacks in the long, uphill climb toward a high level of civilization.

Le Pelley in The Christian Science Monitor

"Hello, I don't believe we've met socially."

What world challenges face students before graduation? After graduation? Are they friendly? Hostile? Formidable?

1

WHY STUDY HISTORY?

1. For Knowledge. We study history to understand (*a*) our way of life and its development, (*b*) today's world problems by comparing them with relevant past situations, and (*c*) the interdependence of nations.

2. For Skills. History helps us sharpen our ability to (*a*) comprehend books, newspapers, and radio and television programs, (*b*) interpret maps and graphs, (*c*) separate fact from opinion, (*d*) analyze problems, gather and evaluate evidence, and arrive at conclusions, and (*e*) discuss vital current issues.

3. For Attitudes. As we study history, we learn that (*a*) we owe a debt to other peoples for their contributions to civilization, (*b*) we have an obligation, as civilized persons, to seek peaceful settlement of differences, and (*c*) we have the duties, as American citizens, to protect and preserve our democracy.

Section One. Ancient History

UNIT I. MANKIND: FROM PRIMITIVE LIFE TO EARLY CIVILIZATIONS

Part 1. Primitive Man Emerges

MAN APPEARS AND SURVIVES DURING THE ICE AGE

About a million years ago, the earth entered a geologic period called the *Ice Age*. Four times during the Ice Age, tremendous sheets of ice (*glaciers*) advanced southward from the north polar region, covered large portions of the Northern Hemisphere, and then receded. The last retreat of the ice occurred about 15,000 years ago. Today, the earth is in its fourth postglacial, or warm, period.

Earliest man appeared on earth during the first half of the Ice Age. Man survived the intense cold and other hardships because he had (1) a *brain* to reason and learn from experience, (2) the *power of speech* to communicate, (3) *hands* with which to grasp objects and make tools and weapons, and (4) an *upright posture*, which enabled him to use his hands freely.

These characteristics not only enabled man to survive but also to progress and create complex civilizations.

THE AGES OF MAN: CLASSIFIED BY MATERIALS USED IN IMPLEMENTS

1. **The Old Stone Age, or Paleolithic Age (500,000-8000 b.c.).** Early man shaped *rough* or *chipped stone* into crude tools and weapons, such as fist hatchets, knives, spearheads, arrowheads, and chisels. He also made implements of wood and bone. Man lived as a nomad, wandering from place to place in search of food. Man learned to (*a*) live in small groups and cooperate in hunting and fighting, (*b*) sew clothes of animal skins, (*c*) seek shelter in caves, (*d*) paint pictures on cave walls, and (*e*) make fire.

Late in the Old Stone Age, several types of man existed, each for many thousands of years. Notable were the *Neanderthal* man—short, stocky, and low-browed—and later the *Cro-Magnon* man—taller and more intelligent. Cro-Magnon man is classified as being of the same species as modern man, *Homo sapiens*.

3

2. The New Stone Age, or Neolithic Age (8000-4000 B.C.). Man *ground* and *polished stone* into sharper implements. He settled in small communities and secured food by farming. Man learned to (a) plow the soil and domesticate animals, (b) use the wheel and axle for transportation, (c) weave plant fibers into cloth, and (d) mold clay pottery.

3. The Copper and Bronze Age (4000-1000 B.C.). Man used metals—first *copper*, which is comparatively soft, and later, *bronze*, a harder metal—to form more serviceable implements: daggers, swords, axes, and hammers. Man built the first civilizations. He (a) organized government, (b) built cities, (c) developed industry, (d) established trade, and (e) kept written records.

4. The Iron Age (Starting 1000 B.C.). Man forged *iron*—a harder, more durable metal than bronze—into stronger tools and weapons. Because today's complex industrial civilization depends on iron (and *steel*, an alloy of iron), we may still consider man as living in the Iron Age.

THE AGES OF MAN: CLASSIFIED BY TYPES OF HISTORICAL EVIDENCE

1. The Prehistoric Period (Before 4000 B.C.). Not having learned to write, prehistoric man left no written records. Our knowledge of this period comes from *material remains:* bones, tools, weapons, utensils, cave paintings, cloth, pottery, and buildings. Material remains are unearthed and studied by *archaeologists.*

Since prehistoric remains lack inscriptions, they cannot provide an exact *chronology.* The dating of events in the Prehistoric and early Ancient Periods remains approximate.

2. The Historic Period (Since 4000 B.C.). Having learned to write, man left not only material remains, but also *written records.* These include stone inscriptions, tablets, scrolls, letters, diaries, newspapers, and books.

More accurate dating of events began with written records. During the Historic Period, as the use of writing spread, chronology became more nearly precise.

For chronological convenience, the history of Western civilization is usually subdivided as follows:

a. *Ancient History*—4000 B.C. to 500 A.D.

b. *Medieval History*—500 A.D. to 1400 A.D.

c. *Modern History*—1400 A.D. to the present.

The earliest written records describe man's first civilizations. These arose in the Middle East—Egypt and the Fertile Crescent.

Part 2. Ancient Egypt: Man's First Civilization

FAVORABLE GEOGRAPHIC CONDITIONS

1. **The Nile.** Ancient Egypt, located in northeast Africa, was a narrow strip of land about 550 miles long. It extended 15 miles on each side of the Nile River. Each summer, the Nile overflowed. The rich soil it deposited on the adjacent fields could produce as many as four crops per year. This fertility encouraged the nomadic people of the region to settle permanently on farms.

Because the land would be a desert without Nile waters, Egypt was called "the gift of the Nile."

2. **Natural Boundaries.** Egypt was partially protected by natural barriers: deserts, mountains, and seas. (See the map below.) Thus shielded, the early Egyptians devoted themselves chiefly to peaceful pursuits.

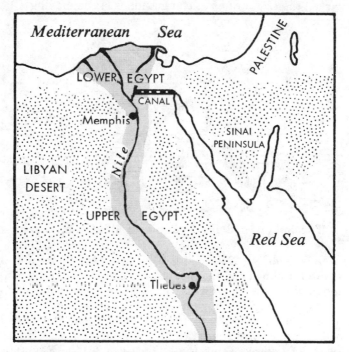

Ancient Egypt: "Gift of the Nile"
After the canal was built in 1900 B.C., the Red Sea receded, and the canal was extended southward.

HISTORY OF ANCIENT EGYPT

1. Early Governments. Governments evolved in ancient Egypt to regulate the Nile. The people needed (*a*) *dikes* and *reservoirs* to control the annual flooding of the Nile Valley, and (*b*) *canals* to irrigate the dry farmlands. These major projects required group effort, which led to local governments, usually chiefdoms.

Through war and marriage, these chiefdoms eventually combined into two large kingdoms: (*a*) **Lower Egypt,** the northern part of the Nile Valley, including the river's mouth, or delta, and (*b*) **Upper Egypt,** the central part of the Nile Valley. About 3100 B.C., *Menes,* ruler of Upper Egypt, conquered Lower Egypt and united the country. He became the first *Pharaoh,* or King.

2. The Old Kingdom (3100-2200 B.C.). The "Old Kingdom," with its capital at *Memphis,* lasted about 1,000 years. The Pharaohs of this period erected huge stone pyramids to serve as their tombs. *Khufu* (2900 B.C.) kept 100,000 men toiling over 20 years to build the famous *Great Pyramid* at Gizeh. *Khafre* (2850 B.C.) constructed another imposing pyramid at Gizeh and also carved the *Great Sphinx,* a tremendous statue having a lion's body and a man's face.

The Sphinx and the Pyramid of Khafre at Gizeh

3. The Age of Nobles (2200-1730 B.C.). During the "Age of Nobles," the Pharaoh's power declined and that of the nobles increased. Egypt experienced disunity and civil wars. Nevertheless, some Pharaohs accomplished great engineering feats, building (*a*) huge irrigation projects, and (*b*) a ship canal that, together with the Nile, connected the Mediterranean and Red Seas.

In 1730 B.C. Egypt was almost completely conquered by invaders from western Asia, the *Hyksos.* From these fierce people, the Egyptians learned to fight on horseback and use war chariots. Egypt was ruled by the Hyksos for about 160 years.

4. The Empire (1570-1100 B.C.). A strong Egyptian leader finally drove out the Hyksos. The "Empire" that arose, with its capital at *Thebes*, lasted about 470 years.

During this period, ambitious Pharaohs assembled large armies and organized great war fleets. They conquered Nubia (Ethiopia) to the south, and Palestine and Syria to the northeast. They built huge stone statues of themselves as well as splendid temples. The most famous, near Thebes, is the *Temple of Karnak.*

The best-known Pharaohs of the Empire were the military leaders *Thutmose III* and *Rameses II;* and the religious reformer *Amenhotep IV* (see page 8).

About 1100 B.C. Egypt began to decline militarily. Ruled thereafter by successive foreign invaders, Egypt did not regain national independence until the 20th century A.D.

ASPECTS OF EGYPTIAN LIFE

1. Absolute Monarchy. The *Pharaoh* was the absolute ruler, worshipped as the gods' earthly representative. He made laws, maintained courts, waged war, collected taxes, and owned all land. The Pharaoh was assisted by the (*a*) *nobles,* who served as local governors, tax collectors, and military commanders, and (*b*) *priests,* who were concerned with religious matters.

2. Wide Class Distinctions. The privileged aristocracy consisted of the Pharaoh, his royal family, the nobles, and the priests. These dominant classes lived luxuriously.

The unprivileged masses included (*a*) *freemen,* who were scribes (public writers), city merchants, and skilled craftsmen, (*b*) *peasants,* who worked the farms, and (*c*) *slaves,* the manual laborers who dug irrigation ditches and built temples. The unprivileged classes could not participate in government. While the freemen enjoyed some wealth and comforts, the peasants and slaves suffered hardship and poverty.

3. Economic Activities. The Egyptians depended chiefly on agriculture. They plowed the land; grew wheat, barley, and flax; and raised sheep and cattle. In the cities, they developed such industries as construction, glassblowing, metalworking, cloth weaving, and pottery. They also engaged in foreign trade, exporting glassware, linen cloth, and clay vases; and importing ivory, spices, and copper.

To support the Pharaoh's government, the Egyptians paid heavy taxes in either labor or products.

4. Religious Beliefs. The Egyptians worshipped many gods. A belief in many gods is called *polytheism.* The chief gods of the Egyptians were *Re,* the sun god; *Amen,* god of Thebes; and *Osiris,* judge of the dead. The Egyptians hoped for life after death. Only those who could prove they had led a good life were granted immortality by Osiris. In preparation for judgment, deceased Egyptians were entombed with the *Book of the Dead*, a collection of religious hymns, magical terms, and moral principles. The Egyptians chemically preserved (embalmed) the bodies of important persons to give the soul a permanent resting-place. A body so preserved is called a *mummy*.

In 1375 B.C. Pharaoh Amenhotep IV, known as *Ikhnaton*, introduced the worship of a single god, the new sun god *Aton*. A belief in one god is called *monotheism*. Ikhnaton was opposed by the priests, who feared the loss of their power; and by the people, who feared the wrath of their traditional gods. After Ikhnaton's death, the Egyptians restored polytheism.

CONTRIBUTIONS TO CIVILIZATION

1. Architecture and Engineering. The Egyptians excelled in working with stone (stonemasonry), and constructed gigantic pyramids and temples. These temples featured vast halls lined by massive *colonnades* (rows of columns). Egyptian engineers also built dams and irrigation canals.

2. Art. The Egyptians were accomplished sculptors who created huge stone statues. On the stone walls of temples and tombs, artists carved and painted domestic and historical scenes. Egyptian craftsmen skillfully designed delicate metal jewelry, elaborate wood furniture, and beautiful pottery.

3. Hieroglyphic Writing. The Egyptians developed one of the first systems of writing, *hieroglyphics*, meaning sacred carvings or priestly writings. Hiero-

The Temple at Karnak: Columns With Hieroglyphics

glyphics are picture symbols that represent objects, ideas, or sounds. First inscribed on stone, these symbols were later written in ink on specially prepared plant material called *papyrus* (the origin of our word "paper"). To house their papyrus scrolls, the Egyptians established the first libraries.

The key to the translation of hieroglyphics is the *Rosetta Stone*. This slab was unearthed in 1799 by one of Napoleon's soldiers. The Rosetta Stone bears the same inscription in both Egyptian hieroglyphics and Greek letters. In 1822 *Jean Champollion*, a French scholar, used his knowledge of Greek to decipher the hieroglyphics.

4. Science

a. Solar-Year Calendar. The Egyptians, excellent astronomers, devised the first calendar that divided the year into *365 days*. It was more accurate than the *lunar* calendar, based on the revolutions of the moon around the earth. Introduced about 4200 B.C., the Egyptian solar-year calendar is the basis of the calendar we use today.

b. Other Scientific Achievements. The Egyptians acquired considerable knowledge of practical science. In their construction projects, Egyptian engineers calculated weight by simple arithmetical operations. They surveyed land and computed area by geometrical formulas. In preparing mummies, Egyptian embalmers used chemical processes. Egyptian healers, though relying primarily on magic, set broken bones, recognized disease symptoms, and prescribed drugs.

MULTIPLE-CHOICE QUESTIONS

Select the number preceding the word or expression that best completes the statement.

1. The *least* important reason for studying history is to learn (1) to avoid mistakes made in the past (2) to distinguish fact from opinion (3) historical dates (4) how our present civilization has developed.
2. Prehistoric man had the advantage over animals in his (1) matchless strength (2) superior resistance to heat and cold (3) ability to think and to use his hands freely (4) power of communication through writing.
3. In the Old Stone Age, man knew how to (1) make fire (2) mold clay (3) use wheels (4) domesticate horses.
4. The first metal weapons were made from (1) tin (2) copper (3) iron (4) silver.
5. The beginning of the Historic Period corresponds to the beginning of the (1) Old Stone Age (2) New Stone Age (3) Copper and Bronze Age (4) Iron Age.
6. An archaeologist is a specialist in (1) building stone bridges and roads (2) painting and sculpting (3) studying habits of birds (4) studying remains of past civilizations.
7. A person living about 500 B.C. would consider his own times as (1) prehistoric (2) ancient (3) medieval (4) modern.
8. Egypt is said to be "the gift of the Nile" because the Nile (1) flows through the center of Egypt (2) overflows each spring, fertilizing the lowlands (3) provides a means of transportation (4) protected the Egyptians against invasions.

9. The pyramids of ancient Egypt were (1) tombs (2) forts (3) storehouses for treasure (4) temples.
10. The government of ancient Egypt was (1) a democracy (2) a dictatorship (3) a city-state (4) a republic.
11. The ancient Egyptians worshipped (1) many gods (2) only Aton (3) the pyramids (4) fire.
12. *Not* characteristic of farming in ancient Egypt was (1) irrigation (2) the use of artificial fertilizer (3) slave labor (4) cultivation of wheat and barley.
13. A contribution of the ancient Egyptians to architecture was the (1) column (2) arch (3) stained-glass window (4) rounded dome.
14. The Rosetta Stone was (1) a symbol of the Pharaoh's authority (2) the keystone in the Great Pyramid at Gizeh (3) an island in the Nile delta (4) the key to translating hieroglyphics.
15. A major contribution of the ancient Egyptians was in the field of (1) law (2) printing (3) the calendar (4) philosophy.
16. Egypt was a major power in the ancient world for about (1) 100 (2) 500 (3) 1,000 (4) 2,000   years.

MATCHING QUESTIONS

Match the items in column *A* with those in column *B*.

Column A	*Column B*
1. Menes	*a.* Introduced religious reforms
2. Khufu	*b.* Deciphered hieroglyphics
3. Ikhnaton	*c.* Built the Great Pyramid at Gizeh
4. Hyksos	*d.* Wrote the Book of the Dead
5. Champollion	*e.* United ancient Egypt
	f. Conquered ancient Egypt
	g. Constructed a canal connecting the Mediterranean and Red Seas

Part 3. Other Early Civilizations of the Middle East

THE FERTILE CRESCENT

While Egyptian civilization was developing in northeastern Africa, other civilizations were evolving in nearby southwestern Asia, chiefly in the *Fertile Crescent*. This region was so named because of its rich soil and half-moon shape. The Fertile Crescent was divided into (1) the eastern portion, consisting of the *Tigris* and *Euphrates* river valleys, called *Mesopotamia* (land between the rivers), and (2) the western, or Mediterranean portion. (See map, page 11.)

GEOGRAPHIC FACTORS INFLUENCING THE FERTILE CRESCENT

1. The Tigris and Euphrates Rivers. The waters of these rivers enriched the land in Mesopotamia, thereby encouraging nomads to settle and farm. As in Egypt, the need for dikes to control floods and for canals to irrigate farms led to the establishment of governments.

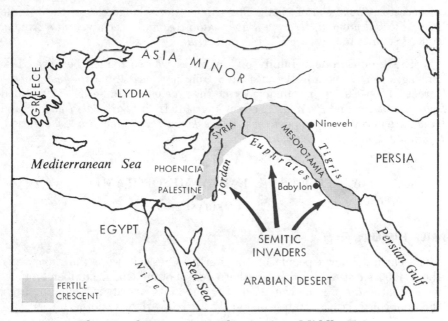

The Fertile Crescent: The Ancient Middle East

2. Mediterranean Coastline. As seaports developed along the Mediterranean coast, the people became seafarers. They built ships and traded throughout the Mediterranean area.

3. Lack of Stone. Lacking stone, the people used clay bricks for construction and clay tablets for writing.

4. Low Level Plains. The Mesopotamian plain and the Mediterranean coastal plain afforded no natural barrier against invasion. The inhabitants were therefore conquered repeatedly by invaders from the adjoining mountains and deserts. These newcomers remained in the region and contributed to its civilization.

LANGUAGES OF THE MIDDLE EAST

By analyzing sounds and their meanings, linguistic experts compare languages. They classify related languages into distinct families on the assumption that these languages probably evolved from one common (usually unrecorded) parent tongue. Linguists have classified most of the languages of the Middle East as either *Semitic* or *Indo-European*.

1. The Semitic family of languages was so named because the ancient peoples speaking these languages supposedly descended from a single Biblical ancestor, *Shem,* son of Noah. The chief Semitic languages of the Middle East were *Babylonian, Hebrew, Phoenician, Aramaic,* and *Assyrian.* Among modern Semitic tongues are *Hebrew* and *Arabic.*

2. The Indo-European family of languages was so named because these languages were spoken in the vast area from northern India to westernmost Europe. Indo-European languages of the ancient Middle East included *Lydian, Hittite,* and *Persian.* The languages of India, *Sanskrit, Bengali,* and *Hindi,* are also Indo-European, as are *Greek, Latin, French, Spanish, Italian, Russian, German,* and *English.*

A. PEOPLES OF EARLY MESOPOTAMIA

1. Sumerians

BRIEF HISTORY

The earliest-known people of the Fertile Crescent were the *Sumerians.* About 4000 B.C. they lived in southern Mesopotamia in a number of independent *city-states.* Each consisted of a small city and its surrounding area. The rulers of these city-states constantly warred with one another.

CONTRIBUTIONS TO CIVILIZATION

1. Cuneiform Writing. The Sumerians developed *cuneiform,* a system of writing about as old as Egyptian hieroglyphics. The Sumerians employed a sharp-pointed instrument (a *stylus*) to inscribe wedge-shaped characters on clay tablets. Reading and writing in cuneiform were difficult because the

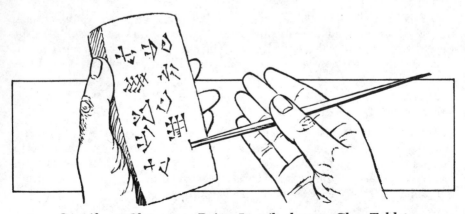

Cuneiform Characters Being Inscribed on a Clay Tablet With a Stylus

alphabet consisted of a great number of characters, about 550. Nevertheless, cuneiform was widely used in the Middle East for thousands of years.

The key to the deciphering of cuneiform was the *Behistun Rock,* which contains inscriptions in both cuneiform and Persian. The cuneiform was translated in 1846 by an Englishman, *Sir Henry Rawlinson.*

2. System of Numbers. The Sumerians developed a number system based on the unit 60. Today, we use this unit in telling time.

3. Architecture. The Sumerians invented the *arch* and built temple towers, or *ziggurats.* A ziggurat was a pyramidlike structure consisting of progressively set-back floors, the highest of which contained a shrine to the chief god.

2. Babylonians

BRIEF HISTORY

Semitic-speaking invaders from the Arabian Desert entered southern Mesopotamia (1900 B.C.) and captured the city-state of Babylon. About 1750 B.C., led by their King, *Hammurabi,* they conquered the other city-states in the Tigris-Euphrates Valley and formed the *Babylonian Empire.* The *Babylonians* adopted and built upon the prevailing Sumerian culture. The Babylonian Empire lasted until 1700 B.C.

CONTRIBUTIONS TO CIVILIZATION

1. Code of Law. Guided by Hammurabi, the Babylonians recorded their laws and customs. This *Code of Hammurabi,* the oldest legal system known, reveals (a) a **stern sense of justice**—proclaiming the principle of "an eye for an eye" and demanding severe punishment for crimes, (b) a **sharp division of classes**—providing harsher punishment for an offense against a noble than for the same offense against a common person, (c) a **fair treatment of women**—permitting them to own property and engage in business, and (d) an **advanced business society**—establishing regulations for property protection, business contracts, interest on loans, and wages for workmen.

2. Astronomy. The Babylonians believed in *astrology,* the superstition that the movements of stars, planets, and other heavenly bodies directly affected the lives of men. However, by studying the heavens, they learned to recognize planets and to foretell eclipses, recording data later essential to *astronomy.*

3. Literature. The *Babylonian Epics,* which were partly based upon the Sumerian *Gilgamesh Legends,* describe the Creation, the first man, and the Great Flood. These stories resemble those in the Old Testament.

B. PEOPLES OF THE EASTERN MEDITERRANEAN

1. HEBREWS

BRIEF HISTORY

From 1400 to 1200 B.C. Semitic-speaking *Hebrews* from the Arabian Desert gradually invaded and settled Palestine. For about 500 years, the Hebrews maintained their independence. In 722 B.C. the Assyrians conquered the *Kingdom of Israel* in northern Palestine. In 586 B.C. the Chaldeans overran the *Kingdom of Judah* to the south and exiled many of the inhabitants to Babylon. In 539 B.C. the Persians captured Babylon and allowed the Hebrew exiles to return to their homeland. Later, Palestine was controlled by the Greeks and still later by the Romans. In 70 A.D. the Roman armies under *Titus* suppressed a Hebrew revolt for independence and drove the people from their land. This expulsion partly explains why the Hebrews, or *Jews*, are presently scattered throughout the world. (Many Jews have returned to Palestine in recent years, especially after 1948, when part of the land became the independent Jewish state of *Israel*.)

CONTRIBUTIONS TO CIVILIZATION

1. Monotheism. The Hebrews were the first people to accept the belief in a single God as the all-powerful Creator and Supreme Ruler of the Universe.

2. Old Testament. The Hebrews recorded their history and religious beliefs in the *Old Testament*, the Hebrew Bible. One of the greatest literary masterpieces, the Old Testament constitutes the first part of the Christian Bible.

3. High Moral Principles. Judaism, the religion of the Hebrews, embodies precepts of ethical behavior that were far advanced for the ancient world and that are applicable in our own times.

a. The **Mosaic Law** is found in the *Torah*, the first five books of the Old Testament. This Law of Moses teaches "Love thy neighbor as thyself." It includes the *Ten Commandments*. Some of its rules of conduct are: "Remember the Sabbath day, to keep it holy"; "Thou shalt not kill"; "Thou shalt not steal"; "Thou shalt not bear false witness"; and "Honor thy father and thy mother."

b. The **Hebrew prophets** of the Old Testament cried out for social righteousness and a better world. They denounced evil and oppression, and demanded justice for the poor and weak. The prophet *Isaiah* envisioned a time when nations "shall beat their swords into plowshares" and shall not learn war any more." The prophet *Micah* asked, "What doth the Lord require of thee, but to do justly, and to love mercy, and to walk humbly with thy God?"

The essence of Judaism, as summed up by the great teacher Hillel, who lived at about the time of Jesus, is the rule of conduct: "What is hateful unto thee do not do unto others."

In its emphasis on monotheism and high moral principles, Judaism influenced Christianity and Islam (Mohammedanism).

FAMOUS HEBREWS (AS RELATED IN THE OLD TESTAMENT)

(1) *Moses* led his people from servitude in Egypt and gave them the Ten Commandments. (2) *Saul* united the 12 Hebrew tribes, led them against the Philistines, and became the first Hebrew King. (3) *David* slew Goliath, the Philistine giant, and later succeeded Saul as King. David wrote many *psalms* (sacred songs). One of the most famous begins, "The Lord is my shepherd; I shall not want." (4) *Solomon,* son of David, was a King renowned for his wisdom. He also built the splendid Temple at Jerusalem, the capital.

2. PHOENICIANS

BRIEF HISTORY

From 1200 to 800 B.C. the Semitic-speaking *Phoenicians* lived and prospered on the Mediterranean coast north of Palestine. Their chief cities were *Tyre* and *Sidon.* The Phoenicians, highly skilled shipbuilders and navigators, were seafaring merchants. They traded throughout the Mediterranean and even ventured to the Atlantic coasts of Europe and Africa. They established many overseas colonies; the most important was *Carthage* in northern Africa (see page 51).

From a species of shellfish, the Phoenicians obtained their trademark: a purple dye. Known as *Tyrian purple,* this became the favorite color of royalty.

CONTRIBUTIONS TO CIVILIZATION

1. "Missionaries of Civilization." The Phoenicians served as "missionaries of civilization," bringing eastern Mediterranean products and culture to less advanced peoples.

2. The Alphabet. The Phoenicians replaced the cumbersome cuneiform alphabet with a phonetic alphabet of only 22 letters. After further improvement by the Greeks and Romans, this alphabet became the one we use today.

3. ARAMEANS

BRIEF HISTORY

Semitic-speaking *Arameans* occupied Syria about 1200 B.C. and established a number of independent city-states; the most important was *Damascus*. By overland caravans, the Aramean merchants traded throughout the Middle East. But in the 8th century B.C. the Aramean city-states fell to the Assyrians.

CONTRIBUTION TO CIVILIZATION

Language. Spread by Aramean merchants and diplomats, *Aramaic* was used as the international language throughout the Middle East for over 1000 years. It was spoken by Jesus Christ and used in many Christian and Jewish religious writings.

4. LYDIANS

BRIEF HISTORY

After 1000 B.C. the Indo-European-speaking *Lydians* lived in *Asia Minor*, a region directly northwest of the Fertile Crescent. Between 612 B.C. and 546 B.C. the Lydians enjoyed great power and prosperity as merchants. *Croesus,* their King, was reputed to be the wealthiest man of ancient times.

CONTRIBUTION TO CIVILIZATION

Coinage of Money. The Lydian government was the first to mint coins and guarantee their value. Because these coins simplified business transactions, they replaced money minted by private individuals.

C. EMPIRE BUILDERS

1. HITTITES

BRIEF HISTORY

About 2000 B.C. the Indo-European-speaking *Hittites* appeared in northern Asia Minor, a region rich in iron. In 1650 B.C. the Hittites began building a powerful Empire. They extended their control in Asia Minor, seized northern Syria from the Egyptians, and expanded into northern Mesopotamia. Hittite culture was greatly influenced by their contacts with the Babylonians. The Hittite Empire lasted about 450 years.

CONTRIBUTION TO CIVILIZATION

Use of Iron. The Hittites were the first to make iron tools and weapons. Their knowledge of ironwork soon spread throughout the Fertile Crescent and Egypt.

2. ASSYRIANS

BRIEF HISTORY

After 800 B.C. the Semitic-speaking *Assyrians* from northern Mesopotamia embarked on a policy of expansion. Having learned about iron from the Hittites, the Assyrians were the first to outfit armies entirely with iron weapons. To besiege cities, they devised new military equipment—movable towers and battering rams. The Assyrians terrorized their enemies by deliberately employing *cruelty* and *violence*. They conquered the Fertile Crescent and Egypt, and established a great Empire with its capital at *Nineveh*. The Assyrian Empire lasted over 150 years, finally being destroyed in 612 B.C.

CONTRIBUTIONS TO CIVILIZATION

1. Government. The Assyrians (*a*) divided their Empire into provinces, each administered by a governor responsible to the King, and (*b*) built military roads to move troops quickly to any part of the Empire.

2. The Library. *Assurbanipal*, an Assyrian King, built a great library at Nineveh containing many thousands of clay tablets. These documents have enabled scholars to accurately reconstruct life in the ancient Middle East.

3. CHALDEANS

BRIEF HISTORY

In 616 B.C. the Chaldeans, Semitic-speaking nomads from the Arabian Desert, seized Babylon. In 612 B.C. they (with the Medes) captured Nineveh and overthrew the Assyrian Empire. The Chaldeans then gained control of the entire Fertile Crescent and established the *Second Babylonian Empire*. In 539 B.C. this Empire was overthrown by the Persians.

CONTRIBUTIONS TO CIVILIZATION

1. Architecture. During the reign of *Nebuchadnezzar*, the Chaldeans constructed the famous *Hanging Gardens* of Babylon. These roof gardens were noted as one of the great wonders of the ancient world.

2. Astronomy. The Chaldeans continued the Babylonian practice of recording accurate observations of the heavens.

4. PERSIANS

BRIEF HISTORY

In 550 B.C. the Indo-European-speaking *Persians* lived east of the Fertile Crescent on the Plateau of *Iran*. Under *Cyrus the Great* (who ruled **559-529** B.C.), the Persians overthrew their kinsmen, the Medes, and ruled the entire Iranian Plateau. Thereafter, Cyrus conquered Lydia, Asia Minor, and the Fertile Crescent. Cyrus' son seized Egypt. Under *Darius* (521-486 B.C.), the Persians expanded their Empire eastward as far as the Indus River in northern India. (To the west, however, Darius failed to conquer the Greek city-states.)

The Persian Empire, the largest yet seen in the ancient world, extended **3,000** miles. (See map below.) The Empire flourished for **200** years, finally collapsing about 330 B.C. (see page 42).

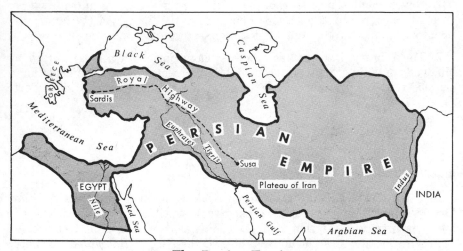

The Persian Empire

CONTRIBUTIONS TO CIVILIZATION

1. Government. The Persians (*a*) divided their Empire into provinces, each ruled by a *satrap* (governor) responsible to the King, (*b*) appointed special agents, the *King's eyes and ears*, to check upon the loyalty of the satraps, (*c*) built numerous roads to speed military movements and trade, and (*d*) treated subject peoples *humanely* to avert revolt.

2. Spread of Culture. By maintaining their vast Empire, the Persians stimulated cultural interchange among their many peoples. The Persians adopted many features of these civilizations. However, they remained faithful to their own religion, *Zoroastrianism*.

3. Religion. The Persians accepted the beliefs of their prophet *Zoroaster*, who preached that: (*a*) *Ahura-Mazda*, the god of light and goodness, was constantly fighting *Ahriman*, the spirit of darkness and evil. (*b*) Those supporting Ahura-Mazda by living virtuously will reach heaven; those following Ahriman will be punished in hell. (*c*) Goodness will eventually prevail, and the world will achieve eternal peace.

Zoroaster's teachings form the basis of the Persian bible, the *Avesta* or *Zend-Avesta*.

MULTIPLE-CHOICE QUESTIONS

1. The first civilization in the Fertile Crescent was developed by the (1) Assyrians (2) Arameans (3) Sumerians (4) Persians.
2. As the Nile was to Egypt, so were the Tigris and Euphrates to (1) Babylonia (2) Iran (3) Palestine (4) Asia Minor.
3. The chief building material used in the Fertile Crescent was (1) concrete (2) stone (3) clay brick (4) wood.
4. A Semitic language in modern use is (1) Greek (2) Assyrian (3) Hebrew (4) French.
5. Which of the following is *not* an Indo-European language? (1) Sanskrit (2) English (3) Persian (4) Arabic.
6. The Sumerians built ziggurats, which were (1) irrigation canals (2) religious shrines (3) royal palaces (4) large libraries.
7. The Babylonians are credited with having (1) possessed considerable legal and business ability (2) erected the largest buildings of ancient times (3) built a navy that dominated the Mediterranean (4) conquered India.
8. The Babylonians studied astrology because they believed that (1) man's fate was determined by the stars (2) other worlds existed (3) science was the basis of military power (4) the Old Testament required such study.
9. The Hebrew kingdom had a perilous existence because it (1) was situated between powerful rival states (2) was peopled by many different races (3) bore the brunt of the Greek attacks on Asia Minor (4) lacked a powerful navy.
10. The Hebrew capital and site of the famed Hebrew Temple was (1) Nineveh (2) Carthage (3) Damascus (4) Jerusalem.

11. The ancient conquerors who treated the Hebrews most humanely were the (1) Assyrians (2) Babylonians (3) Persians (4) Romans.

12. By predicting that nations "shall beat their swords into plowshares," the Hebrew prophet Isaiah was crying out for (1) more agriculture (2) government jobs for the unemployed (3) an era of world peace (4) greater effort to uncover mineral resources.

13. A Phoenician product particularly desired by monarchs was (1) purple dye (2) royal chariots (3) sundials (4) iron weapons.

14. The Aramaic language spread throughout the Middle East because of Aramean (1) military conquests (2) religious leaders (3) merchants (4) astrologers.

15. Assyrian rule of conquered peoples was characterized by (1) making them allies (2) cruelty (3) granting them local self-government (4) tolerance and justice.

16. The Assyrian practice of appointing governors to rule separate provinces was adopted later by the (1) Persians (2) Lydians (3) Egyptians (4) Sumerians.

17. The Zend-Avesta was the sacred book of the (1) Babylonians (2) Persians (3) Sumerians (4) Hebrews.

MATCHING QUESTIONS

Column A	Column B
1. Hammurabi	a. Translator of cuneiform
2. Nebuchadnezzar	b. Founder of Carthage
3. Zoroaster	c. Arranger of oldest known legal code
4. Moses	d. Lawgiver of Ten Commandments
5. Rawlinson	e. Founder of Persian Empire
6. Solomon	f. Persian god of light
7. Cyrus	g. Ruler renowned for wisdom
	h. Builder of Hanging Gardens
	i. Prophet of the Persians

IDENTIFICATION QUESTIONS

For each description below, select the name of the people to whom it best applies, making your selection from the following list:

Arameans	Hebrews	Persians
Assyrians	Hittites	Phoenicians
Babylonians	Lydians	Sumerians

1. We were the first people to accept monotheism, and our prophets denounced evil and injustice.

2. Although we were known for our military, not scholarly, pursuits, our extensive library has enabled modern scholars to reconstruct life in the ancient Middle East.

3. We developed cuneiform writing and also the number system still used in telling time.

4. A seafaring merchant people, we devised a simplified alphabet and were known as "missionaries of civilization."

5. We settled in Asia Minor, discovered iron ore deposits, and were the first people to make iron tools and weapons.

6. Our government was the first to mint coins, which replaced money minted by private individuals.

UNIT II. EARLY CIVILIZATIONS OF THE FAR EAST

Part 1. Introduction

The previous unit described the culture of the Egyptians and of other Middle Eastern peoples. From them evolved the Mediterranean-centered Greco-Roman civilization. This civilization, which later spread throughout Europe and the Americas, is the basis of our *Western*, or *Occidental*, cultures.

This unit will discuss developments in southern and eastern Asia, a region called the *Far East* by Europeans because it is farthest east of Europe. In India and China originated the *Far Eastern*, or *Oriental*, cultures.

Far Eastern history does not conform to the time periods of ancient, medieval, and modern history as used for the West. This book, however, will present the Far East within the framework of Western chronology to enable the reader to compare simultaneous developments in the Occidental and Oriental worlds.

During ancient and medieval times, the Far East and the West had relatively few contacts. Since the year 1500, however, relations between them have gradually expanded. Today, they influence each other considerably.

Part 2. Ancient India:
An Advanced Civilization in Southern Asia

GEOGRAPHIC FACTORS INFLUENCING ANCIENT INDIA

1. Location and Size. India (today constituting two nations, India and Pakistan) is located in southern Asia. It extends about 2,000 miles from north to south. Mainly a triangular peninsula, India is sometimes termed a *subcontinent* because its boundaries sharply separate it from the rest of Asia. (See map, page 22.)

2. Boundaries. Ancient India was protected against large-scale invasion (a) from the east, west, and south by the *Bay of Bengal*, the *Arabian Sea*, and the *Indian Ocean*, and (b) from the north by towering mountain ranges, chiefly the *Himalayas*. Nevertheless, a few mountain passes on the northwest border, such as the *Khyber Pass*, enabled ancient invaders to enter northern India.

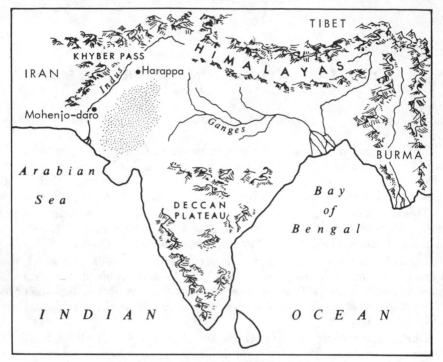

Ancient India: Geographic Factors

3. Topography. India consists chiefly of two regions:

a. In the North: The Plain of the Indus and Ganges. This fertile region is watered by two great river systems, both originating in the Himalayan Mountains. The *Indus River* flows southwest to the Arabian Sea, and the *Ganges River* flows southeast to the Bay of Bengal. The Indus Plain, directly accessible through the northwest mountain passes, attracted many invaders to India. (From the Indus River was derived the name India.)

b. In the South: The Deccan Plateau. This relatively inhospitable region, despite some good farmland, includes mountain ranges, tropical forest, and rocky soil. Although the Deccan was not impassable, usually little unity existed between northern and southern India.

HISTORY OF ANCIENT INDIA

1. The Early Indus River Valley Civilization (3000-1500 b.c.). Like the Nile in Egypt and the Tigris and Euphrates in Mesopotamia, the Indus River fostered the development of civilization. Archaeological excavations in the Indus Valley, at the ancient cities of *Harappa* and *Mohenjo-daro*, disclosed (*a*) well-planned cities containing extensive drainage systems and brick buildings with bathrooms, (*b*) highly productive farms with irrigation canals and domesticated animals, (*c*) pictographic writing (still undeciphered) on clay seals, and (*d*) cloth, jewelry, pottery, and implements of copper, and bronze. The resemblance between Indus and Sumerian pottery and implements indicates that these civilizations may have been related.

About 1500 B.C. the Indus civilization ended abruptly, destroyed (according to some scholars) by the invading *Aryans*.

2. The Aryan Conquests (2000-600 B.C.). The Indo-European-speaking *Aryans*, a light-skinned people probably related to the Persians, crossed the northwest mountain passes and invaded the Indus Plain. They conquered the inhabitants, the dark-skinned *Dravidians*. (Many Dravidians fled south, where their descendants still live.) By the 6th century B.C. the Aryans had subjugated the Ganges Valley and occupied the entire northern plain. They formed petty states that frequently warred amongst themselves.

Aryan history and culture are revealed chiefly by their religious writings, *Vedas*, of which the oldest is the *Rig-Veda*. During the Aryan period, sometimes called the *Vedic Age*, India's civilization began to assume its important characteristics. (*a*) The Aryans spoke *Sanskrit*, later the principal literary language of India. (*b*) The teachings of the Vedas later became part of the *Hindu religion* (see pages 25-26). (*c*) To prevent intermarriage and maintain supremacy, the Aryans placed the Dravidians into a separate, inferior class. This division was possibly the forerunner of the *caste system*.

3. Persian Rule in Northwest India (521-367 B.C.). Darius, King of Persia, annexed the Indus River region to his Empire. Persian rule stimulated cultural and commercial contacts between northwest India and the eastern Mediterranean area, including Greece.

4. Alexander of Greece Conquers Northwest India (326 B.C.). Alexander the Great (see page 42) mastered the Persian Empire and subdued the Indus River region. Although short-lived, Alexander's conquest increased Greek influence on India, particularly in art and politics.

5. The Maurya Empire (321-184 B.C.). The *Maurya*, an Indian family, established the country's first great Empire. Its outstanding rulers were Chandragupta and Asoka.

a. Chandragupta Maurya. Inspired by Alexander's military feats, Chandragupta drove out the Greek garrisons left by Alexander, won control of the northern plain, and founded the Maurya Empire. He established a highly centralized government modeled after Persian practice.

b. Asoka. Asoka, Chandragupta's grandson, continued the Maurya conquest southward until he ruled more than two-thirds of India. Rejecting war thereafter, he became a devout convert to the *Buddhist religion* (see page 26). He then promoted Buddhism within India and sent Buddhist missionaries to such countries as Ceylon and Burma.

Asoka's edicts, inscribed on stone pillars and large rocks, furnish considerable information about his activities and beliefs. A benevolent Emperor, he emphasized truth, justice, charity, religious tolerance, and nonviolence. Moreover, he restricted the slaughter of animals and urged vegetarianism. Asoka is often regarded as one of the world's noblest rulers.

After Asoka's death, the Maurya Empire declined. It was followed by five centuries of invasion, war, and disorder.

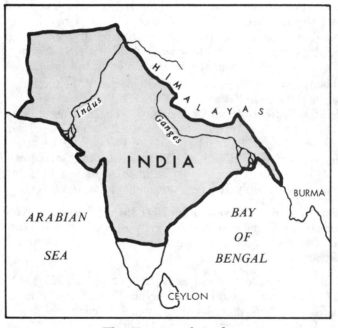

The Empire of Asoka

6. The Gupta Empire (320-535 A.D.). In the 4th century A.D. the *Gupta,* another native family, established an Empire embracing northern India. By restoring law and order, they revived prosperity. Their reign witnessed great achievements in literature, art, mathematics, and science. India became a center of learning, and her culture spread throughout eastern Asia. The Gupta period is sometimes called India's "golden age."

In the 6th century the Gupta government was overthrown by invaders from central Asia, the *White Huns.*

ANCIENT INDIA'S CONTRIBUTIONS TO CIVILIZATION

1. Religion and Philosophy

a. Hinduism (Brahmanism) and the Caste System

(1) *Caste in Daily Living.* About 1500 B.C. India began to develop rigid, increasingly complex social and economic class divisions called *castes.* (a) In order of importance, the four main castes were priests (Brahmans), rulers and warriors, landowners and merchants, and laborers and servants. These castes were further divided into several thousand subcastes. (b) Below the castes were millions of despised persons, the outcasts, or *untouchables.* (c) Each person remained in his own hereditary caste, was restricted in occupation, and was forbidden close contact with members of other castes. (d) A violator of caste rules became an outcast.

Thus, the outstanding feature of the caste system was strict segregation.

(2) *Hindu Beliefs and Caste.* Hinduism evolved into a complex religion. (a) The supreme universal soul assumes three forms: *Brahma* the creator, *Vishnu* the preserver, and *Siva* the destroyer. (b) To achieve union with the universal spirit, man must purify his soul by performing religious duties and living righteously. Religious duties include praying, respecting the Brahmans, and making pilgrimages to the sacred Ganges River. Righteous living consists of avoiding untruth and envy, seeking knowledge, granting

A Hindu Statue of the God Siva

charity, practicing nonviolence, and observing caste rules. (*c*) Since soul purification requires many lifetimes, each person's soul experiences rebirths, a process called *transmigration* or *reincarnation*. (*d*) Persons who disregarded Hindu precepts in a previous existence are punished by reincarnation into either a lower caste or an outcast, or even an animal. (Since animals may contain human souls, they may not be killed. Cows in particular are sacred.) (*e*) Persons who followed Hindu precepts in a previous existence are rewarded by reincarnation into a higher caste. (*f*) Through innumerable upward reincarnations, the soul will eventually be completely purified, freed from further rebirth into this sorrowful world, and united with the all-embracing spirit.

Today, Hinduism survives chiefly in the Republic of India, where it is practiced by the vast majority of the people. By stressing caste divisions and forbidding the slaughter of animals, Hinduism has delayed India's development into a prosperous modern nation.

b. Buddhism. In the 6th century B.C. *Gautama,* a nobleman, left his comfortable life for one of self-denial and meditation. He ultimately developed a philosophy that rejected the Hindu caste system but accepted the Hindu belief in reincarnation. As *Buddha,* the "Enlightened One," Gautama taught: (1) Man's life consists of suffering caused by desire. (2) Man can eliminate desire only by following the *eightfold path* of righteous living: renouncing material pleasure, controlling emotions, meditating selflessly, respecting all living creatures, acquiring knowledge, cultivating goodness, speaking truth, and acting generously. (3) By living righteously, man escapes endless reincarnations, and his soul enters a spiritual state of peace, *Nirvana.*

Buddhism battled Hinduism and the caste system for over 1,000 years. As certain Buddhist principles were absorbed by Hinduism, Buddhism disappeared in India. Today, Buddhism survives mainly in Ceylon, Thailand, Burma, China, Japan, and the nations of Indo-China.

2. Art and Architecture. Ancient India's art, revolving about Hinduism and Buddhism, stressed symbolic and ornate design. This style predominated in human and animal statues, cave-temple wall paintings, and temple construction. Indian architects used wood, brick, and stone in buildings featuring pointed domes, columns, and conical towers.

3. Literature. Ancient India produced an impressive literature, chiefly in Sanskrit. (*a*) The *Vedas* contain hymns, prayers, and religious principles. (*b*) The *Mahabharata* and the *Ramayana* are great epic poems, often compared with the Homeric epics of Greece (see page 35). (*c*) Hindu storytellers delighted in animal fables illustrating morals. These stories possibly provided the basis for Aesop's fables in Greece. (*d*) *Kalidasa,* a 5th-century A.D. poet and playwright, is sometimes called "India's Shakespeare."

4. Science and Technology. Indian physicians diagnosed major diseases, prescribed medicinal plants, and placed the sick in hospitals. They observed an ethical code similar to the Greek Hippocratic Oath (see page 45). The Indians applied chemical principles in dyeing cloth, tanning leather, manufacturing soap and glass, and refining iron ore. (Later, their process for purifying iron passed to the Arabs and then to medieval Europe.)

5. Mathematics. In mathematics, India was the most advanced of the ancient nations. Indian mathematicians devised the concept of zero, employed the decimal system, developed a rudimentary algebra, and created our modern written numbers. (Transmitted by the Arabs to medieval Europe, these symbols are misleadingly called *Arabic numerals.*)

Part 3. Ancient China: Development of an Inbred Civilization

GEOGRAPHIC FACTORS INFLUENCING ANCIENT CHINA

1. Location and Boundaries. China, a huge country in eastern Asia, comprises China proper and the outlying regions of Tibet, Sinkiang, Mongolia, and Manchuria. In ancient times, China proper was virtually isolated from the surrounding world by such natural barriers as the *Gobi Desert,* the *Tibetan mountain plateau* (sometimes called the "Roof of the World"), and the *Pacific Ocean.* (See the map below.) Little affected by outside cultures (except for India's Buddhism), China developed an inbred civilization.

Ancient China: Geographic Factors

2. Topography. China's mountains, plateaus, and hills constitute four-fifths of the country's land surface. The remaining one-fifth consists of coastal and river plains. Despite the mountainous terrain, the ancient Chinese migrated, spread their culture, and maintained a degree of cultural and political unity.

3. Important Rivers: Yangtze and Hwang Ho (Yellow River). Flowing several thousand miles eastward from the Tibetan highlands, the *Yangtze River* in central China and the *Hwang Ho* (Yellow River) in northern China both empty into the Pacific Ocean. These rivers drain China's heavily populated fertile plains. Because of its devastating floods, the Yellow River is often called "China's sorrow."

HISTORY OF ANCIENT CHINA

1. Early Yellow River Valley Civilization (4000-2000 B.C.). China's first civilization, like those of Egypt, Mesopotamia, and India, evolved from river valley conditions: fertile soil, uncertain rainfall, and disastrous floods. In the Yellow River region, the people raised agricultural produce, herded animals, used bows and spears, and made crude pottery. They lived in small, self-governing villages.

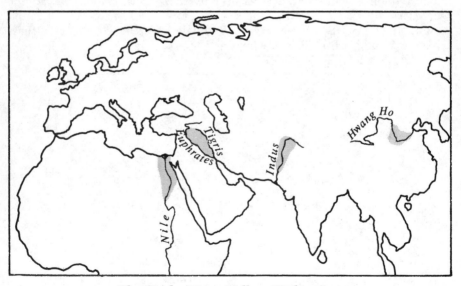

The Early River Valley Civilizations

2. Hsia Dynasty (2000-1500 B.C.). According to legend, *Hsia*, China's first *dynasty* (a succession of kings from the same family), ruled the eastern Yellow River city-states. During this period, the Chinese began casting bronze, cultivating silkworms, and, reputedly, writing.

3. Shang Dynasty (1500-1000 B.C.). The Shang Dynasty developed a highly organized state in the Hwang Ho Plain. To protect their domain, Shang warriors frequently fought frontier tribes. During this period, the Chinese produced artistic bronze implements and beautiful pottery; wrote on shells, metal, and wood; and began to worship their ancestors.

4. Chou Dynasty (1000-256 B.C.). The *Chou*, the longest-ruling dynasty, first overran Shang territory and then temporarily occupied part of the Yangtze Valley. Later Chou kings, unable to maintain authority, lost power to provincial nobles.

The Chou Period witnessed the introduction of iron implements, written laws, and metal coins. This era, China's "classical age," produced memorable literature and such renowned philosophers as *Lao-tse* and *Confucius* (see page 31).

5. Ch'in Dynasty (256-206 B.C.). The *Ch'in* was a short-lived but significant dynasty whose outstanding ruler was the self-named *Shih Huang Ti*, meaning the *First Emperor*. To bar northern invaders, he linked existing sectional fortifications into the 1,500-mile *Great Wall*. He expanded the Empire southward by annexing the Yangtze region and gaining nominal control of southern China.

Ch'in: The First Empire

Shih Huang Ti sought vigorously to unify the country (a) **politically**—by creating a strong centralized government, suppressing nobles, appointing provincial governors responsible to him, and enforcing a uniform legal code, (b) **physically**—by building roads, bridges, and canals, and (c) **culturally**— by simplifying and standardizing writing.

Also to provide unity, he attempted to eradicate knowledge of China's past political and cultural diversity by ordering the burning of most books.

From *Ch'in* was derived the name *China*.

· **6. Han Dynasty (206 B.C.-220 A.D.).** Han rulers (a) preserved political unity with a tightly centralized administration. (b) promoted Confucianism, even selecting government officials by tests on Confucian literature, (c) allowed Buddhism to be introduced from India, (d) established overland trade routes over which Chinese silks and spices reached the Roman-dominated Mediterranean world, and (e) expanded the Chinese Empire to Indo-China, central Asia, southern Manchuria, and northern Korea.

The Han Empire marked the height of ancient China's power, prosperity, and culture. Literature, art, science, and industry flourished as never before. The Chinese are so proud of this period that they often call themselves "the sons of Han."

The fall of the Han Dynasty was followed by four centuries of civil war, invasion, and political confusion. These turbulent years led many Chinese to accept Buddhism because it promised eternal peace (see page 26).

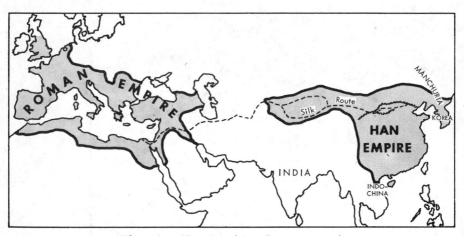

The Han Empire (1st Century A.D.)

ANCIENT CHINA'S CONTRIBUTIONS TO CIVILIZATION

1. Religion and Philosophy

a. Lao-tse (6th Century B.C.*).* For man to attain happiness, the philosopher Lao-tse taught: (1) Governments should minimize their controls over man. Since laws cannot improve man's condition, he should be permitted to conduct his own affairs. (2) Man should passively accept his lot in life. He can achieve peace of mind only by practicing humility and by renouncing wealth and prestige. He should live in a simple manner in harmony with *Tao,* "the way of nature."

Centuries later, Lao-tse's teachings, distorted by magic and combined with ideas of personal immortality, became part of the polytheistic religion *Taoism.*

b. Confucius (551-479 B.C.*).* To improve society and achieve good government, the great philosopher Confucius formulated a code of ethical conduct. He taught that man should be guided by the following "virtues": (1) Careful observance of ancient traditions. (2) Reverence for learning. (3) Cherishing of honesty. (4) Devotion to parents, family, and friends, and obedience to the rule "What you do not want done to you, do not do to others."

Whereas Lao-tse advocated a passive life for the individual and urged the least possible government, Confucius advocated man's active participation in society and recommended vigorous government action. He further believed that a ruler who practiced the Confucian virtues would govern as an influential, fatherly force. Unlike other Oriental philosophies, Confucianism placed little emphasis on the hereafter.

As *Confucianism* evolved, the original stress on tradition became associated with ancestor worship. For more than 2,000 years, Confucianism dominated Chinese daily life and politics. Confucian writings served as official school textbooks. By emphasizing tradition and ancestor worship, Confucianism stabilized society but retarded progress.

c. Intermingling Beliefs. The Chinese did not believe it illogical to live according to principles taken from different philosophies. While universally accepting Confucianism, many Chinese simultaneously practiced Buddhism and Taoism.

2. Strong Family Ties.
In keeping with Confucian teachings, the family —not the individual—became the basic unit of Chinese life. The family included all relatives. Living together or near one another, they sometimes constituted an entire village. The oldest male was the honored and obeyed family head. The family assumed responsibility for the livelihood and good conduct of its members. Marriage was not intended for individual happiness, but to perpetuate the family.

Intense family loyalty hampered the development of Chinese nationalism.

3. Written Language and Literature. Complex Chinese writing existed by 1500 B.C. Lacking an alphabet, it employed up to 40,000 characters (originally pictures), each representing a distinct idea or sound. The resulting difficulty in reading and writing sharply limited Chinese literacy. (Recently, attempts have been made to simplify Chinese writing by using a phonetic alphabet.)

Despite their complex written language, the Chinese created a noteworthy literature of poetry, history, and philosophy. The *Confucian Classics,* outstanding works, consist of (*a*) Confucius' collection of earlier writings, (*b*) Confucius' own sayings, the *Analects,* and (*c*) commentaries by later philosophers. The Imperial Library housed an extensive collection of books and manuscripts.

4. Art and Architecture. The ancient Chinese created elaborately decorated bronze and clay vases. They fashioned fine jewelry and figurines, using their most prized stone, *jade.* Chinese artists excelled in expressive, sym-

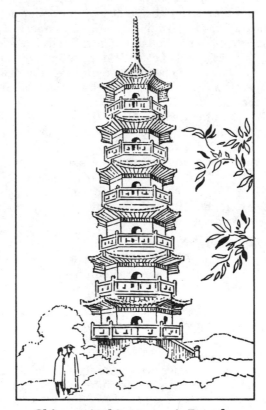

Chinese Architecture: A Pagoda

bolic landscape paintings. Chinese musicians developed an advanced music, different from that known in the Western world. Chinese architects, in designing palaces and pagodas, favored wood and stone columns, highly ornamented walls, and gaily colored tiled roofs. The most distinctive Chinese structure was the *pagoda*—a many-storied, tapered temple with a series of upward-curving roofs.

5. Science and Technology. The Chinese invented sundials, water clocks, and instruments to detect earthquakes. Their astrologers contributed to astronomy by observing sunspots, studying eclipses, and devising a solar calendar of $365\frac{1}{4}$ days. Chinese farmers plowed the land, used fertilizer, and rotated crops. The Chinese also wove silk cloth and produced glazed pottery plates (chinaware). About 100 A.D. they discovered how to make paper.

MULTIPLE-CHOICE QUESTIONS

1. The Indian subcontinent is separated from the rest of Asia by the (1) Gobi Desert (2) Ganges River (3) Himalaya Mountains (4) Deccan Plateau.
2. Ancient invaders entered India from the northwest because (1) most invaders came from Europe (2) the northwest of India was unpopulated (3) the Khyber Pass provided an invasion route (4) the northwest of India consisted of open plains.
3. India's coasts are not washed by the (1) Indian Ocean (2) China Sea (3) Bay of Bengal (4) Arabian Ocean.
4. Two ancient cities, where excavations have revealed much of India's early civilization, were (1) Harappa and Delhi (2) Harappa and Mohenjo-daro (3) Delhi and Bombay (4) Mohenjo-daro and Bombay.
5. The Vedas were (1) religious writings (2) priests (3) iron swords (4) Hindu gods.
6. The Maurya Empire originated in (1) Ceylon (2) India's Deccan (3) India's northern plains (4) the plateau of Iran.
7. The period of disorder from the end of the Maurya Empire to the beginning of the Gupta Empire lasted approximately (1) 10 (2) 100 (3) 300 (4) 500   years.
8. The Gupta Period is sometimes called India's "golden age" because its (1) craftsmen sculpted many gold statues (2) writers, artists, scientists, and mathematicians brought forth great achievements (3) merchants secured much gold in exchange for exports of Indian goods (4) rulers conquered the rich gold mines of the Deccan.
9. The Brahmans, the highest Hindu caste, were (1) rulers and warriors (2) merchants (3) priests (4) farmers.
10. The caste system emphasized (1) national unity (2) local community cooperation (3) racial equality (4) strict segregation.
11. The Hindu belief that each person's soul experiences many rebirths is called (1) restitution (2) reincarnation (3) religion (4) evolution.
12. Gautama, the 6th-century B.C. philosopher, was entitled "Buddha," meaning the (1) great nobleman (2) enlightened teacher (3) stone heart (4) fierce warrior.
13. Hinduism and Buddhism both agree that man's life on earth (1) is one of sorrow (2) is preparation for immediate entrance to heaven (3) must conform to caste rules (4) is the same as his ultimate goal of Nirvana.
14. Today Buddhist influence is *least* evident in (1) India (2) Ceylon (3) Japan (4) Burma.
15. Kalidasa, who lived in the 5th century A.D., was a great (1) mathematician (2) ruler (3) playwright (4) religious reformer.

16. One achievement in ancient India *not* paralleled in ancient Greece was in (1) writing epic poems (2) relating animal fables (3) prescribing an ethical code for doctors (4) developing a simplified way of writing numbers.
17. Ancient China, in its natural boundaries and their effect upon China's civilization, most closely resembles (1) Egypt (2) Babylonia (3) northern India (4) Persia.
18. Hsia, China's first dynasty, is legendary, meaning that (1) its rulers were great warriors (2) its writers wrote imaginative novels (3) its existence has not been confirmed by archaeological evidence (4) its people worshipped many gods.
19. Ancient China's longest-ruling dynasty was the (1) Shang (2) Chou (3) Ch'in (4) Han.
20. The first Emperor of the Ch'in Dynasty, Shih Huang Ti, ordered the burning of books because he (1) feared that an educated people might revolt (2) feared that knowledge of China's past would hamper his efforts to establish a centralized government (3) wanted to combat monotheism (4) wanted scholars to produce original works.
21. While the Han Dynasty ruled in China, the Mediterranean world was dominated by (1) Egypt (2) Persia (3) Greece (4) Rome.
22. The philosopher Lao-tse taught that man could achieve happiness by (1) relying upon the government (2) accepting, with humility, his lot in life (3) pursuing wealth and giving it to the poor (4) reforming the evils of the world.
23. The philosopher Confucius formulated a code of conduct whose chief purpose was to (1) improve society and government (2) prepare man's soul for the hereafter (3) enable the Chou rulers to retain power (4) encourage the Chinese to conquer all of eastern Asia.
24. Confucianism encouraged the Chinese people to (1) learn from foreigners (2) experiment with new food crops (3) respect traditional ways of doing things (4) seek principles of science.
25. Confucianism encouraged a feeling of intense loyalty to the (1) family (2) province (3) neighboring warlord (4) nation.
26. Which was *not* an achievement of ancient China? (1) a solar calendar (2) glazed pottery (3) a phonetic alphabet (4) the making of paper.

COMPLETION QUESTIONS

Provide the word or expression that completes the statement correctly.

1. The earliest civilization in India developed in the valley of the _____ River.
2. The invading peoples who brought Sanskrit into India were the _____.
3. The European conqueror who in the 4th century B.C. extended his empire into northwest India was _____.
4. The great Maurya ruler who, after renouncing war, governed according to Buddhist ideals was _____.
5. The sacred river of the Hindu religion is the _____.
6. Early civilization in China developed in the valley of the _____ River.
7. Han rulers selected government officials by "civil service" examinations based upon a knowledge of the _____ Classics.
8. A major religious development during the Han Era was the introduction of _____.
9. The most distinctive Chinese structure, typified by a series of upward-curving roofs, is called a(an) _____.

UNIT III. THE CLASSICAL CIVILIZATION OF ANCIENT GREECE AND ROME

Part 1. Ancient Greece: Man's First Experiment With Democracy

THE CRETAN CIVILIZATION (3000-1400 B.C.)

The advanced *Cretan civilization* developed on *Crete,* an island near Greece in the eastern Mediterranean, and then spread to the Aegean Islands. (See map, page 36.) Poor soil and good harbors led the islanders to become seafaring merchants. Their rulers, the "Sea Kings of Crete," controlled the prosperous Mediterranean trade. By carrying Egyptian and other Middle Eastern learning to the backward Greek mainland, the Aegean world served as a cultural bridge.

Our knowledge of Cretan civilization derives chiefly from excavations of the palace at Crete's leading city, *Cnossus.* These ruins were unearthed starting in 1900 by the archaeologist *Sir Arthur Evans.* The Cretans devised excellent plumbing systems, using drains and tiled pipes. They enjoyed such sports as boxing and leaping over bulls. They made superb clay vases; bronze daggers decorated with enamel; gold cups; ivory carvings; and wall paintings. The Cretan civilization collapsed in 1400 B.C. when Cnossus was destroyed, possibly by the invading *Hellenes.*

THE HELLENIC INVASIONS OF GREECE (1500-1000 B.C.)

The *Hellenes,* Indo-European-speaking nomadic tribes of eastern Europe, migrated south to seek richer grasslands. These primitive people conquered Greece, Crete, and many Aegean islands. The Hellenes intermarried with the natives and evolved into a new people, the *Greeks.*

THE HOMERIC AGE (UNTIL 750 B.C.)

1. The Poems of Homer. Our knowledge of the early Greeks derives mainly from two long epic poems, the *Iliad* and the *Odyssey,* both by the blind Greek poet *Homer.* The *Iliad* relates the adventures of a Greek military expedition against the city of Troy on the coast of Asia Minor. The *Odyssey* describes the wanderings of the Greek hero Odysseus returning home from the Trojan War. People doubted the existence of Troy until its ruins were uncovered in the 1870's by the archaeologist *Heinrich Schliemann.*

2. Life During the Homeric Age. The Greeks lived primitively. They (*a*) were ruled by tribal chieftains or kings, (*b*) grew wheat, olives, and grapes and raised livestock, (*c*) warred constantly, and (*d*) believed that their gods actively intervened in human affairs.

GEOGRAPHIC FACTORS INFLUENCING GREEK DEVELOPMENT

1. Location. Greece is a peninsula in the northeastern Mediterranean within easy sailing distance of the Fertile Crescent and Egypt. The Greeks learned about writing, navigation, and the other achievements of these earlier civilizations from Cretan, Aegean, and Phoenician merchants.

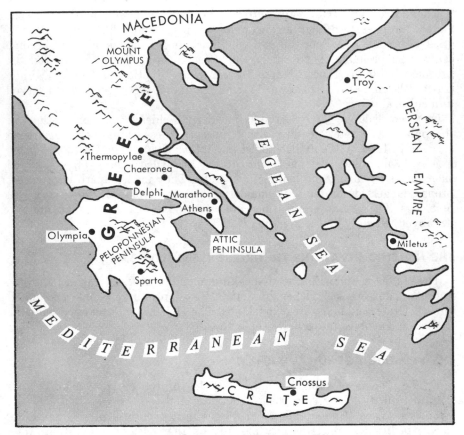

Crete and Greece in Ancient Times

2. Deep Harbors. Because Greece has numerous good harbors on its irregular coastline, many Greeks turned to the sea. They became merchants and traders who sailed the Black, Aegean, and Mediterranean Seas. The Greeks exported wine, olive oil, pottery, cloth, and metal implements; they imported foodstuffs, timber, hides, and metal ores.

3. Insufficient Farmland. Since Greece lacks sufficient farmland, many Greeks between 750 and 500 B.C. established colonies on the shores of the Mediterranean and Black Seas. (Greeks also emigrated to escape oppression by the nobility. See page 38.)

They founded important colonies at *Byzantium* (later called Constantinople) at the mouth of the Black Sea, *Naples* in Italy, *Syracuse* in Sicily, and *Marseilles* in France.

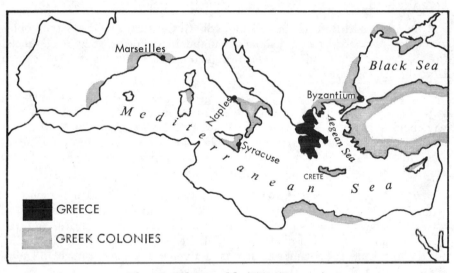

The Greek World (750-500 B.C.)

4. Mountains. Greece is a land of high mountain ranges enclosing fertile valleys. These valleys were isolated because transportation over the mountains was hazardous. Such geographic barriers led the Greeks to organize many independent *city-states* instead of a central government. Because the mountains helped cause political disunity, the first loyalty of each person was not to Greece as a nation, but to his own city-state.

ATHENS: DEVELOPMENT OF A DEMOCRATIC CITY-STATE

Athens, in east central Greece on the Attic Peninsula, was the leading Greek city-state. After 750 B.C. Athens slowly progressed from (1) **monarchy**

—rule by one man, the king, to (2) *aristocracy*—rule by a small group of nobles, to (3) *tyranny*—rule by one man, the tyrant, who generally favored the people, and finally to (4) *democracy*—rule by the people. Athenian democracy encouraged similar reforms in a number of Greek city-states.

1. Discontent in Athens (8th-7th Centuries B.C.)

a. Economic. The small farmers, unable to compete with low-priced grain imports, were poverty-stricken. They borrowed money from the wealthy nobles and mortgaged their land as security. When unable to pay their debts, these farmers (1) lost their land, and (2) were sometimes sold into slavery.

b. Political. The common people had no voice in the government. As the king lost power, control passed entirely into the hands of the aristocracy.

2. Leaders and Reforms in Athens (7th-5th Centuries B.C.).

As the nobles gradually responded to the people's demand for reforms, Athens advanced toward democracy. Leadership was provided by the following men, all drawn from the aristocratic class:

a. Draco in 621 B.C. *codified* (arranged systematically and set down in writing) the existing Athenian laws. Limited by this code, the judges, who were nobles, could no longer interpret unwritten laws to favor their own class at the expense of the common people. The code provided severe punishment for crimes; death was the penalty for even a minor offense. (From *Draco* comes our word *Draconic*, meaning "harsh" or "severe.")

b. Solon in 594 B.C. wrote the laws that (1) canceled mortgages on land, (2) freed persons enslaved for debt, (3) limited the amount of land owned by one person, (4) allowed all citizens to serve on juries, and (5) granted commoners the right to vote in the legislature, the *Assembly.* Thus, for the first time, the common man gained a voice in his government. (Today the word *Solon* means "a wise man" or "a lawmaker.")

Despite Solon's reforms, the wealthy retained control of the government. Only they could gain membership in the policy-making and administrative body, the *Council.* Only they could serve as chief executives.

c. Clisthenes in 508 B.C. expanded democracy by extending citizenship to more persons and permitting people of all economic classes to serve in the Council. Under Clisthenes' leadership, the Assembly adopted the practice of *ostracism,* banishing for 10 years any citizen deemed dangerous to the state. Ostracism was intended to prevent the rise of an Athenian dictator.

d. Pericles, from 461 to 429 B.C., headed the Athenian government. This great orator and popular statesman (1) removed the remaining restrictions on officeholding, thereby opening all government service to the common people, and (2) paid salaries to public officials, thus enabling poor citizens to accept jury duty and other government service.

The years of Pericles' leadership, the *Age of Pericles* or the *Golden Age of Athens,* marked the height of Athenian democracy. Arts and sciences thrived, manufacturing and trade prospered, and the city was beautified as never before. (See pages 43-45 for the Greek contributions to civilization during the Age of Pericles.)

TWO DEMOCRACIES: MAJOR DIFFERENCES

ANCIENT ATHENS	MODERN AMERICA
1. *Direct democracy*—citizens themselves were members of the legislature.	1. *Representative democracy*—the citizens elect legislators to represent them.
2. Citizenship based on Athenian ancestry. Generally denied to aliens.	2. Citizenship based on American birth. Granted also to immigrants following naturalization.
3. Women denied voting and other rights.	3. Women and men granted equal rights.
4. Slavery permitted.	4. Slavery prohibited.

SPARTA: AN ARISTOCRACY AND MILITARY CITY-STATE

Sparta was situated in southern Greece on the Peloponnesian Peninsula. Sparta's population consisted of (1) a small number of Spartan citizens, the landowning nobility, and (2) a large number of slaves (*helots*) who worked the land.

Fearing helot rebellions, the Spartans maintained an aristocracy in the belief that such a government could act more effectively than a democracy to suppress uprisings. The Spartans emphasized military prowess and made Sparta an armed camp. The government regulated all aspects of the people's lives. Spartan boys, taken from their homes at the age of seven, received a strict military education. Spartan girls underwent vigorous physical training to prepare for motherhood. Sparta exemplified the autocratic, or totalitarian, philosophy that the individual exists to serve the state.

The Spartans were the greatest warriors of ancient Greece. Their emphasis on militarism, however, caused them to neglect art, literature, and science.

BONDS UNITING THE GREEKS

Although divided into several hundred independent city-states, the Greeks were united by a common culture.

1. Language and Literature. The people spoke dialects of the Greek language and shared Greek literature, especially the stories of Homer.

2. Religion. The Greeks shared a polytheistic religion. Their most important deities were *Zeus*, the chief god; *Apollo*, the sun god; *Athena*, goddess of wisdom; and *Aphrodite*, goddess of love. These divine beings supposedly dwelt on top of *Mount Olympus*, in northeastern Greece.

The Greeks attributed human appearance and characteristics to their gods. The gods' personal lives, rivalries, and participation in human affairs are described in ever-popular Greek mythology.

The Greeks believed that priests could receive prophecies from the gods at holy places called *oracles*. People from all Greece sought advice at the famous oracle of Apollo at *Delphi*.

3. Olympic Games. The Greeks shared an interest in the Olympic games, held to honor the gods, especially Zeus. These athletic contests were conducted every four years at the city of Olympia and attracted many spectators. The finest Greek athletes competed in racing, jumping, discus throwing, boxing, and wrestling. All Greeks acclaimed the victors, often in songs and poems.

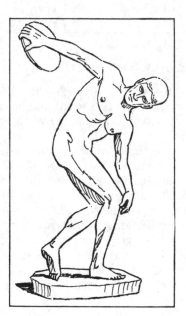

The *Discus Thrower*
by the Sculptor Myron

4. Fear of Persia. The Greeks feared that the mighty Persian Empire planned to conquer them. When the Persians attacked, most Greek city-states temporarily cooperated to preserve their freedom.

THE WAR AGAINST PERSIA (500-479 B.C.)

1. Outbreak of the War. The Persians controlled the entire Middle East (see page 18), including the Greek colonies on the coast of Asia Minor. In 500 B.C. these colonies revolted and received military aid from Athens. After suppressing the revolt, *Darius*, King of Persia, determined to punish Athens and annex all of Greece.

2. Major Events. In 490 B.C. Darius' huge army invaded Greece but was defeated by a smaller Athenian force at the *Battle of Marathon*. Carrying the glad news, a Greek messenger ran the 26 miles from Marathon to Athens. (Today, the word *marathon* means "a long-distance race" or "an endurance contest.")

Led by *Themistocles*, Athens prepared to repel further Persian attacks. Themistocles (a) added 200 warships (*triremes*) to the Athenian navy, and (b) organized most Greek city-states, including Sparta, into a defensive alliance.

In 480 B.C. King *Xerxes*, the son of Darius, launched another Persian invasion. At the *Pass of Thermopylae* in northern Greece, the Persians overwhelmed a small band of gallant Spartan warriors led by King *Leonidas*. The Persians then marched southward and captured Athens. Although Greece seemed doomed, the Greeks rallied their forces to win great naval engagements off *Salamis* (480 B.C.) and *Mycale* (479 B.C.), and a land battle at *Plataea* (479 B.C.). The Persians withdrew and Greece was saved.

3. Significance. By repelling the Persian forces, the Greeks preserved their political independence and individual freedom. Unlike Persian autocracy, Greek democracy, typified by Athens, permitted the individual to develop his abilities and interests. With the Persian threat removed, the Greeks directed their energies to building a rich and varied civilization.

THE PERSIAN WAR IS FOLLOWED BY GREEK DISUNITY

After the Persian War, Athens and Sparta bitterly vied for control of Greece. Athens dominated a city-state alliance, the *Delian League*. Sparta headed an opposing alliance, the *Peloponnesian League*.

The *Peloponnesian War* (431-404 B.C.) was a long, costly struggle between Athens and Sparta in which Sparta triumphed. The war so weakened Sparta, however, that she could not unite Greece.

PHILIP OF MACEDON UNITES GREECE

The *Macedonians*, living north of Greece, were a semicivilized people related to the Greeks. In 359 B.C. *Philip*, an admirer of Greek culture, became King of Macedonia. He formed a powerful army and resolved to unify the

Greek city-states by force. Because he threatened Greek independence, Philip was often denounced by an Athenian orator, *Demosthenes*. However, Demosthenes' warnings to the Greek city-states went unheeded. (Our word *philippic*, derived from these speeches against Philip, means "a bitter verbal attack.")

Philip conquered the city-states at the *Battle of Chaeronea* (338 B.C.), united them militarily (excepting Sparta), and planned to attack Persia. Before Philip could proceed, he was assassinated. His throne, his armies, and his ambitions were inherited by his 20-year-old son, *Alexander*.

CONQUESTS OF ALEXANDER THE GREAT (336-323 B.C.)

Alexander, leading Macedonian and Greek troops, won great victories at the *Granicus River, Issus,* and *Arbela.* He conquered the entire Persian Empire: Asia Minor, Egypt, the Fertile Crescent, and Persia. He then subjugated the Indus River region in India. Alexander's Empire, encompassing these territories plus Greece, was the greatest then known. (See the map below.) At age 33, Alexander the Great suddenly fell ill and died.

Alexander's achievements—so much in so little time by so young a man—make Alexander one of the most remarkable figures in world history. Within his Empire, he opened the way for a fusion of Greek and Middle Eastern cultures (see Hellenistic Period, pages 45-46); he also maintained peace and unity, ideals that later influenced the Romans (see Pax Romana, page 56).

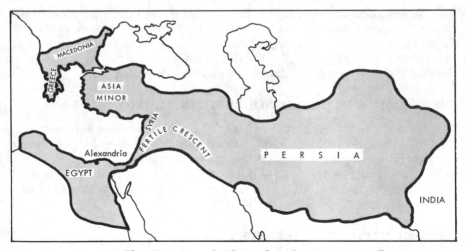

The Empire of Alexander the Great

ALEXANDER'S EMPIRE FALLS APART

After Alexander's death, his Empire was divided into three major king
doms, each ruled by one of his generals. (1) **Macedonia,** including part of
Greece, was governed by Antigonus. (2) **Syria,** including most of southwestern Asia, was governed by Seleucus. (3) **Egypt** was governed by Ptolemy.

These kingdoms maintained their independent existence until, in the 2nd
and 1st centuries B.C., they fell under the rule of Rome.

GREEK CONTRIBUTIONS TO CIVILIZATION: THE HELLENIC PERIOD

The *Hellenic Period* refers approximately to the five centuries preceding
the conquests of Alexander the Great. Hellenic culture reached its height in
Athens during the Age of Pericles (461-429 B.C.). Athenians boasted that
Athens was the educator of Greece, the *school of Hellas.*

1. Theater. Greek dramas, produced in outdoor amphitheaters, employed
little scenery and used a chorus to help relate the story.

The outstanding Greek writers of tragic drama were Aeschylus, Sophocles,
and Euripides; the outstanding writer of comic drama was Aristophanes.

a. Aeschylus (525-456 B.C.) wrote *Agamemnon, Prometheus Bound,* and
The Persians. He argued that the gods ultimately provide human justice.

b. Sophocles (495-406 B.C.) wrote *Oedipus Rex, Antigone,* and *Electra,*
highly dramatic plays dealing with the conflict between man's will and fate.

c. Euripides (480-406 B.C.) wrote *Medea* and *Orestes.* He realistically
examined social and political ideas and vigorously criticized war, prejudice,
hypocrisy, and greed.

d. Aristophanes (446-385 B.C.) satirized the political and cultural leadership of Athens in his plays *Lysistrata* and *The Frogs.*

2. Poetry

a. Homer (9th century B.C.) wrote the *Iliad* and the *Odyssey.*

b. Hesiod (750-700 B.C.) wrote poems about farm life and hard labor.

c. Sappho (600 B.C.), a poetess, wrote beautiful lyric love poems.

d. Pindar (522-443 B.C.), the great lyric poet, wrote odes honoring the
victorious athletes at the Olympic games.   •

3. Philosophy. Philosophers seek to understand man in his relationship
with God, nature, and other men, and to uncover the meaning of such
human ideals as justice, morals, and success. The outstanding Greek philosophers were Socrates, Plato, and Aristotle.

a. Socrates (469-399 B.C.) advocated the maxim "Know thyself." He sought truth through the "Socratic Method" of persistent questioning. Condemned for corrupting the minds of youth, Socrates was put to death by poison. Socrates left no written works. His philosophy is contained in the writings of his students, especially Plato.

b. Plato (427-347 B.C.) wrote many *Dialogues*, which were fascinating discussions of ethics, religion, beauty, and logic. In the dialogue *The Republic,* Plato described his ideal government—not democracy, but aristocracy of intelligence. His most famous student was Aristotle.

c. Aristotle (384-322 B.C.) wrote learned treatises on philosophy, science, government, and literature. His encyclopedic works strongly influenced European thinking for almost 2,000 years. Among his important books were *Logic* and *Politics*. Aristotle served as personal tutor to the young Alexander and stimulated the future leader's interest in Greek culture.

The Greeks practiced the philosophy of "a sound mind in a sound body." The individual's mental and physical faculties they considered to be essential to a happy and useful life.

4. Historical Writing

a. Herodotus (484-424 B.C.), the "father of history," described the Persian invasions of Greece. He embellished facts with fable, superstition, and hearsay.

b. Thucydides (471-400 B.C.), the "first scientific historian," wrote an accurate and impartial account of the Peloponnesian War.

Ruins of the Parthenon on the Acropolis in Athens

5. Architecture. The *Parthenon,* the most famous building of ancient Greece, was a magnificent marble temple to the goddess Athena. Erected during the Age of Pericles on the *Acropolis,* a hilltop in Athens, the Parthenon is considered one of the world's most beautiful structures.

Many modern public buildings imitate the three great styles of Greek columns: *Doric*—simple; *Ionic*—more decorative; and *Corinthian*—most elaborate.

DORIC   IONIC   CORINTHIAN

The Three Orders of Greek Columns

6. Sculpture

a. Phidias (500-432 B.C.), the greatest sculptor of ancient Greece, carved the majestic statue of the goddess Athena for the Parthenon and the marble frieze (ornamental band) that extends along the Parthenon's walls.

b. Myron (about 450 B.C.) created the *Discus Thrower,* a statue portraying strength and motion.

c. Praxiteles (364-330 B.C.) carved lifelike statues of gods and goddesses.

7. Science and Mathematics

a. Pythagoras (582-507 B.C.) discovered important mathematical principles still studied in geometry.

b. Hippocrates (460-377 B.C.), the "father of medicine," attributed disease to natural, not supernatural, causes. The "Hippocratic Oath" to uphold medical standards is still taken by medical students upon graduation.

c. Democritus (460-362 B.C.) advanced the theory that all matter is composed of small, indivisible atoms.

GREEK CONTRIBUTIONS TO CIVILIZATION: THE HELLENISTIC PERIOD

The *Hellenistic Period* starts with the conquests of Alexander the Great and ends late in the 1st century B.C. Hellenistic culture fused Greek and Middle Eastern cultures.

In the lands he conquered, Alexander (1) introduced Greek language, literature, and art, and (2) founded many cities to serve as centers of Greek culture. In Egypt, he founded *Alexandria,* famed for its marble buildings, museum, and library. It was the greatest Hellenistic city.

1. Philosophy

a. Diogenes (412-323 B.C.), the leading *Cynic,* taught that, to achieve contentment, man should practice self-control and independence. He rejected society's accepted values—wealth, power, pleasure, social position, and patriotism. (Our word *cynic* describes "one who sneeringly distrusts people's motives, attributing their actions wholly to self-interest.")

b. Zeno (342-270 B.C.), the founder of *Stoicism,* urged that man should live according to reason and be indifferent to pleasure or pain. (Our word *stoic* means "one who calmly accepts pleasure without rejoicing and endures pain without flinching.")

c. Epicurus (341-270 B.C.) believed that man should seek pleasure and happiness. However, he emphasized that pleasures should be temperately chosen to help man attain a balanced, moral life. (Today, an *epicure* is "one who displays a highly refined taste in eating, drinking, and other pleasures.")

2. Sculpture.

Hellenistic sculptors carved realistic statues, including the *Venus de Milo,* the *Winged Victory of Samothrace,* the *Death of Laocoön,* and the *Dying Gaul.*

3. Science and Mathematics

a. Aristarchus (310-230 B.C.), an astronomer, concluded that the earth revolves about the sun.

b. Euclid (about 300 B.C.), a mathematician, systematized the subject matter of geometry.

c. Archimedes (287-212 B.C.), a mathematician and physicist, discovered important principles regarding the lever, the pulley, and specific gravity.

d. Eratosthenes (276-195 B.C), a geographer, believed the earth to be round and accurately estimated its circumference.

MULTIPLE-CHOICE QUESTIONS

1. Which Mediterranean country is most distant from Crete? (1) Greece (2) Palestine (3) Spain (4) Egypt.
2. As seafaring merchants and transmitters of culture, the Cretans most closely resemble the (1) Phoenicians (2) Persians (3) Aryans (4) Chinese of the Chou Dynasty.
3. In the nature of his work at Cnossus, Sir Arthur Evans may be most closely compared to (1) Champollion (2) Rawlinson (3) Euclid (4) Schliemann.
4. Between 1500 and 1000 B.C. Crete, Greece, and many of the Aegean islands were invaded by the (1) Assyrians (2) Hellenes (3) Spartans (4) Persians.

5. A city-state was (1) a city that performed all the functions of an independent nation (2) a city governed by a foreign nation (3) a capital of an Empire (4) the fortified section of a city.
6. A city-state in Greece that taught its boys absolute obedience to authority was (1) Thebes (2) Athens (3) Olympia (4) Sparta.
7. Athenian democracy resembled American democracy in that (1) women took no part in the government (2) few foreigners were granted citizenship (3) jury trials were common (4) the states joined together in forming a strong central government.
8. The Athenian practice of banishing a citizen considered dangerous to the welfare of the state is known as (1) tyranny (2) aristocracy (3) ostracism (4) welfare state.
9. Ancient Sparta was noted for its (1) talented sculptors (2) brave warriors (3) beautiful women (4) great writers.
10. A similarity between Athens and Sparta was that both (1) emphasized military training (2) were city-states (3) produced great art and drama (4) followed monotheism in religion.
11. The victor in the Peloponnesian War was (1) Sparta (2) Athens (3) Persia (4) Delphi.
12. The intellectual center of Greece about 450 B.C.—the "school of Hellas"—was (1) Sparta (2) Athens (3) Byzantium (4) Syracuse.
13. An important achievement of ancient Greece was the (1) introduction of algebra (2) development of philosophy (3) beginning of the alphabet (4) abolition of slavery.
14. In which field did the Athenians make the most lasting contributions to Western civilization? (1) industry (2) literature (3) militarism (4) religion.
15. Following Alexander's conquests, Greek and Middle Eastern civilizations blended to form the (1) Hellenic (2) Hellenistic (3) Aegean (4) Babylonian culture.

MATCHING QUESTIONS

Column A	Column B
1. Governed Athens during its "Golden Age"	a. Themistocles
	b. Solon
2. Expanded the Athenian navy to fight Persia	c. Demosthenes
	d. Draco
3. Ordered invasion of Greece by Persian army	e. Leonidas
	f. Pericles
4. First codified Athenian laws	g. Philip
5. First granted commoners the vote in the Athenian Assembly	h. Alexander
	i. Darius
6. Led Macedonian and Greek troops to conquer Persia	

IDENTIFICATION QUESTIONS: WHO AM I?

Archimedes	Epicurus	Phidias	Socrates
Aristophanes	Herodotus	Pindar	Sophocles
Aristotle	Hippocrates	Plato	Thucydides
Democritus	Homer	Pythagoras	Zeno

1. I am considered the first "scientific historian" because of my study of the Peloponnesian War.
2. A philosopher, I urged not a democracy but an aristocracy of intelligence in my book *The Republic*.
3. Because I taught youths to seek truth through persistent questioning, I was accused of corrupting their minds and was condemned to death.

4. I discovered significant mathematical relationships still studied in geometry.
5. I influenced European thinking for many centuries by my encyclopedic works on government, science, and philosophy.
6. I insisted that disease results from natural, not supernatural, causes and composed an oath of medical ethics.
7. A philosopher, I urged man to seek happiness and pleasure within a balanced moral life.
8. I was the sculptor who carved the statue of the goddess Athena for the Parthenon.
9. I portrayed the conflict between man and fate in plays of tragedy, such as *Oedipus Rex*.
10. I presented the theory that matter is composed of small indivisible particles called atoms.
11. I founded Stoicism, the philosophic school that urged man to be indifferent to pleasure or pain.
12. A blind poet, I wrote two epics, the *Iliad* and the *Odyssey*, which portrayed the life of the early Greeks.

MULTIPLE-CHOICE QUESTIONS

Select the number of the item that does *not* belong in the corresponding group.

1. *Geographical features of Greece:* (1) sharply indented coastline (2) high mountain ranges (3) small arable land areas (4) numerous navigable rivers.
2. *Areas settled by Greek colonists:* (1) shores of the Persian Gulf (2) southern France (3) shores of the Black Sea (4) Sicily.
3. *Greek bonds of union:* (1) Olympic games (2) fear of Persia (3) common language (4) loyalty to the central government.
4. *Fields of Greek civilization of which much has survived:* (1) sculpture (2) architecture (3) drama (4) painting.
5. *Evidences of Athenian democracy:* (1) jury system (2) election of officials (3) right of citizens to vote (4) representative legislative body.
6. *Greek contributions to the theater:* (1) the chorus (2) seats grouped around a stage (3) elaborate scenery (4) tragic plays.

Part 2. Ancient Rome: An Enduring World Empire

THE FOUNDING OF ROME

The *Latins*, an Indo-European-speaking *Italic* people from central Europe, crossed the Alps about 1500 B.C. and invaded Italy. Attracted by the warm climate and fertile land, the Latins settled in central Italy. On the seven hills overlooking the *Tiber River*, they founded the city of Rome.

(According to Roman legend, the city was founded in 753 B.C. by the twin brothers *Romulus* and *Remus*.)

LIFE AMONG THE EARLY LATINS

The early Latins, a simple and hardy people, (1) earned their living chiefly by farming and cattle-raising, (2) maintained close family ties, the father exercising absolute authority, (3) worshipped tribal gods (*Jupiter*, the chief god; *Mars*, god of war; *Neptune*, god of the sea; and *Venus*, goddess of love), and (4) defended Rome against frequent attacks.

ROME: FROM ETRUSCAN RULE TO INDEPENDENCE (750-500 B.C.)

Rome was captured about 750 B.C. by her northern neighbors, the *Etruscans*. From these more advanced people, the Latins, or *Romans*, learned to (1) construct buildings, roads, and walls around the city, (2) make metal weapons, and (3) apply new military tactics. The Romans in 500 B.C. drove out the Etruscans and established an independent republic.

THE EARLY REPUBLIC: AN ARISTOCRACY

The Roman Republic at first was an *aristocracy*, with power in the hands of the wealthy landowning nobles, the *patricians*. Only they could serve (1) as *consuls* (heads of state), and (2) as members of the hereditary *Senate*, which passed laws, approved appointments, and controlled foreign affairs. Largely excluded from government were the small farmers and city workers, the *plebeians*.

THE ROMAN REPUBLIC BECOMES MORE DEMOCRATIC (5TH-3RD CENTURIES B.C.)

The plebeians clamored for democratic reforms. Over the course of two centuries, they gained the right to (1) elect *tribunes* empowered to veto actions of the consuls and the Senate, (2) enact laws in the *people's assemblies*, and (3) hold all government offices, including those of consul and senator.

The plebeians' demands also resulted in codification of Roman law into the *Twelve Tables*. This prevented judges—who were nobles—from twisting unwritten laws to favor their own class.

The Romans achieved these reforms rather harmoniously, because both the patricians and the plebeians willingly compromised their differences for the good of the Republic. (Later, when willingness to compromise disappeared, civil wars destroyed the Republic.)

ROME GAINS CONTROL OF ITALY (340-270 B.C.)

In a series of wars, Rome conquered the Italian peninsula. The Romans (1) in central Italy, overwhelmed the other Latins as well as the Samnites and Etruscans, (2) in northern Italy, repulsed the Gauls, and (3) in southern Italy, captured the Greek colonies. (See map, page 50.) Rome succeeded in conquering and uniting Italy because of her:

1. **Powerful Armies.** Roman citizen-soldiers felt deeply responsible to their

Republic. They fought, not for a despot but for their own freedom, land, and government. The well-trained and strictly disciplined Roman legions were the ancient world's most effective fighting force.

2. Ability to Move Troops. The *Apennine Mountains*, running north and south through Italy, did not obstruct Roman troop movements appreciably.

3. Wise Treatment of Conquered Peoples. The Romans secured the friendship and allegiance of their conquered peoples by granting them either partial or full citizenship. From these allies, Rome received troops and support for her foreign policy.

Italy Under Roman Control

ROME CONQUERS THE WESTERN MEDITERRANEAN (264-146 B.C.)

After subjugating the Greek colonies in southern Italy, Rome sought to control western Mediterranean trade. Her chief rival, located across the Mediterranean in northern Africa, was *Carthage,* originally a Phoenician colony and now a powerful commercial empire. Rome defeated Carthage in three *Punic* (Phoenician) *Wars* and gained mastery of the western Mediterranean.

1. The First Punic War (264-241 B.C.). Fighting chiefly on the island of Sicily and in the Mediterranean Sea, Rome's citizen-soldiers eventually defeated Carthage's mercenaries (hired foreign soldiers). Rome annexed Sicily, and both sides prepared to renew the struggle. Carthage acquired part of Spain and recruited Spanish troops. Rome consolidated her position in Italy by conquering the Gauls, thereby extending her rule northward from the Po River to the Alps.

2. The Second Punic War (218-201 B.C.). *Hannibal,* Carthage's great general, led an army from Spain across the Alps and into Italy. At first, he won numerous victories, climaxed by the *Battle of Cannae.* However, he was unable to seize the city of Rome. Gradually, the tide of battle turned in favor of Rome. The Romans destroyed a Carthaginian army sent to reenforce Hannibal, then conquered Spain, and finally invaded northern Africa. Hannibal withdrew his army from Italy to defend Carthage but, in the *Battle of Zama,* was at last defeated. Rome annexed Carthage's Spanish provinces and reduced Carthage to a second-rate power.

Reasons for Rome's victory: (a) superior wealth and manpower, (b) the loyalty of most of her allies, and (c) the rise of capable generals, notably Fabius and Scipio. *Fabius* was called the *Delayer* because he did not commit his troops to decisive battle. Believing that time would help Rome, he merely harassed the enemy in Italy. *Scipio* was named *Africanus* because he triumphed over Hannibal in northern Africa.

3. The Third Punic War (149-146 B.C.). Some Romans believed that Carthage remained a threat. *Cato,* a Roman Senator, ended his speeches, regardless of subject, with the statement "Carthage must be destroyed." Rome finally attacked Carthage, destroyed the city, and annexed the territory.

ROME CONQUERS THE EASTERN MEDITERRANEAN (BY THE 1ST CENTURY B.C.)

After the Second Punic War, Rome conquered (1) Macedonia, including Greece, and (2) Syria, including most of southwestern Asia. Egypt, recognizing Rome's might, accepted Roman leadership in the eastern Mediterranean. In 30 B.C. Rome annexed Egypt. Rome was now master of the entire Mediterranean region.

THE MEDITERRANEAN CONQUESTS AFFECT ROME

1. Conquests Introduce Greek Culture. The Romans enthusiastically accepted the advanced Hellenistic culture of the eastern Mediterranean (see pages 45-46). They (a) shipped Greek treasures—books, statues, and vases—to Rome, (b) enslaved educated Greeks to serve as tutors, actors, writers, and scientists, and (c) imitated Greek culture extensively. Roman arms conquered Greece, but Greek culture conquered Rome.

2. Conquests Bring Wealth to Some Romans. (a) *Nobles* cheaply acquired huge estates in the provinces and in Italy. They often seized public lands illegally. (b) *Merchants and businessmen* prospered by filling army contracts, buying booty, supplying slaves, and trading with the provinces. (c) *Government officials* in the provinces amassed huge fortunes at the expense of their subject peoples.

These wealthy classes enjoyed lives of ease and luxury. Hard work, discipline, and patriotism—early Roman virtues—disappeared.

3. Conquests Ruin Small Farmers and Workers. Small farmers and city workers could not compete with slave labor employed by huge estates and in industry. As a result, farmers abandoned their lands and migrated to the cities; city workers suffered serious unemployment.

To gain the support of landless farmers and unemployed workers, Roman politicians sponsored programs of *bread and circuses* (food and entertainment).

4. Conquests Change the Character of the Army. The small farmer had been the backbone of the Roman army. As he disappeared, the nature of the army changed. Citizen-soldiers, loyal to the state, were replaced by professional soldiers, fighting for pay and booty, loyal to their own commanders.

FROM REPUBLIC TO DICTATORSHIP

By the 2nd century B.C. the common people were again demanding economic and political reforms. The aristocracy, controlling the Senate, bitterly opposed measures that threatened their wealth and power. Since the spirit of compromise of the early Republic was dead, peaceful reform failed. In a series of civil wars, rival Roman generals battled for supremacy. The entire conflict, lasting more than 100 years, wrecked the Roman Republic and its many democratic features. In 27 B.C. the Republic was replaced by an absolute monarchy, the Roman Empire.

1. The Gracchi Brothers Vainly Seek Peaceful Reform (133-121 B.C.). First, *Tiberius Gracchus* and, later, *Gaius Gracchus*, nobles favoring the common people, were elected tribunes. The Gracchi obtained laws that would (a) recover public lands wrongfully seized by the nobles, and (b) distribute these lands to landless Romans. Gaius further proposed to weaken the stronghold of aristocratic power, the Senate. Both brothers were killed in riots led by Senatorial opponents of reform.

2. Civil War: Marius vs. Sulla. Beginning in 88 B.C. two generals—*Marius,* the popular leader, and *Sulla,* the Senatorial leader—vied for control of Rome. Their clashes killed thousands of soldiers and civilians. Sulla prevailed and temporarily restored Senatorial power.

3. Civil War: Caesar vs. Pompey. In 60 B.C. three men—*Julius Caesar,* a popular leader; *Pompey,* a famous general; and *Crassus,* a wealthy noble— formed the *First Triumvirate.* This political alliance enabled the three men to dominate Rome. Caesar became a general and, through military victories in Gaul (France), won his army's loyalty. Caesar's book, *Commentaries on the Gallic War,* helped spread his fame.

In 49 B.C. the Senate, fearing Caesar's popularity and power, ordered him to disband his army. Caesar refused, and, taking an irrevocable step by crossing the *Rubicon River,* invaded the Senatorial portion of Italy. He defeated Pompey's Senatorial army and became dictator of Rome.

Caesar, a farsighted statesman, planned to establish stable government, reform provincial rule, provide land for the poor, and beautify the city of Rome. But he lacked time. In 44 B.C. a group of conspirators, some envying his power and others hoping to restore the Republic, assassinated Caesar.

4. Civil War: Octavian vs. Antony. After Caesar's death, civil war again erupted. The army, led by the chief conspirators, Brutus and Cassius, was defeated by forces led by Caesar's friend, *Mark Antony,* and Caesar's grand-nephew, *Octavian.* In the final conflict for power, Octavian defeated Antony at the *Battle of Actium* (31 B.C.), ending the era of civil wars. Octavian then became absolute ruler of the Roman Empire.

THE ROMAN EMPIRE: A DICTATORSHIP (27 B.C.-476 A.D.)

The Roman Empire, existing about 500 years, was a military dictatorship. Of the many Roman Emperors, some dominated the army; others were its puppets. Some devoted themselves to the Empire's welfare; others sought personal advantages. However, only a few were highly qualified to meet imperial problems.

The outstanding Roman Emperors were:

1. Augustus (27 B.C. 14 A.D.). From the Senate, Octavian accepted the title *Augustus,* meaning "Sacred Majesty." Just and capable, Augustus (a) maintained peace, (b) stabilized the government, (c) reformed provincial administration, (d) established fair taxation, (e) developed trade and industry, (f) encouraged science, art, and literature, and (g) constructed many roads and buildings. Augustus boasted, according to legend, that he transformed Rome from a city of brick to a city of marble.

During Augustus' reign, *Jesus* was born in the Roman province of Judea.

The *Augustan Age* began a 200-year period of peace and progress in the Mediterranean world (see Pax Romana, page 56).

2. Claudius (41-54 A.D.) established Roman authority in the southern part of Britain.

3. Vespasian (69-79 A.D.) dispatched an army, led by his son Titus, to Palestine. Titus suppressed a Hebrew revolt, destroyed Jerusalem, and expelled the Jews from Palestine.

4. Trajan (98-117 A.D.), through conquest, expanded the Empire to its greatest limits. His most important territorial acquisition was Dacia (Rumania).

5. Hadrian (117-138 A.D.), to repel barbarians, built defensive walls in northern Britain and central Europe.

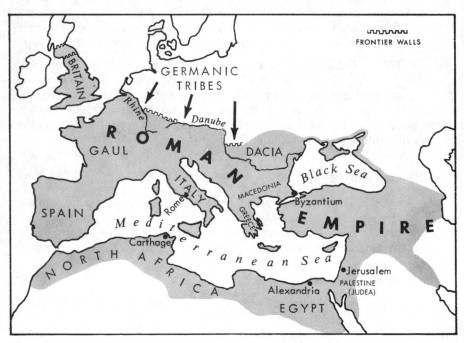

The Roman Empire at Its Greatest Extent

6. Marcus Aurelius (161-180 A.D.) was a conscientious ruler concerned with the people's welfare. He was also a Stoic philosopher who wrote a famous book, *Meditations*. His death marked the end of the Pax Romana (see page 56).

7. Diocletian (284-305 A.D.) became Emperor after a period of incompetent rule and internal strife. To simplify government, he divided the Empire into East and West—each portion administered separately. To prevent civil war, he established a system of succession to the throne. Nevertheless, his death led to renewed civil wars.

Diocletian was the last Roman Emperor who actively persecuted Christians (see page 71).

8. Constantine (312-337 A.D.) united the Empire by military force and moved his capital from Rome to *Constantinople* (formerly Byzantium). By the *Edict of Milan* (313 A.D.), he ended the persecution of Christians. Just before his death, Constantine himself was converted to Christianity.

BARBARIC TRIBES DESTROY THE ROMAN EMPIRE

1. Germanic (Teutonic) Tribes Exert Pressure (1st-4th Centuries). The primitive, warlike *Teutons*, or *Germans*, lived in central and eastern Europe. They were attracted by Rome's fertile land, great wealth, and advanced civilization.

Early Germanic efforts to enter the Empire were thwarted by Roman troops. Later, Rome permitted some Germans to settle within her borders and enlisted German soldiers in her armies.

2. The Huns Invade Europe (4th and 5th Centuries). The *Huns*, savage invaders from central Asia, terrorized Europe, causing many Germanic tribes to flee into the Roman Empire. Led by *Attila*, the "Scourge of God," the Huns later ravaged the Empire. Although a combined Roman-German force stopped them at the *Battle of Châlons* (451 A.D.), the Huns weakened Rome militarily and hastened her downfall.

3. The Germanic Tribes End the Roman Empire (4th and 5th Centuries). The full-scale Germanic migrations into Roman territory could not be stemmed by the enfeebled Roman government. Gradually the Germanic tribes established kingdoms within the Empire: the *Visigoths* in Spain, the *Ostrogoths* in Italy, the *Vandals* in North Africa, the *Franks* in Gaul, and the *Angles* and *Saxons* in Britain.

In 476 A.D. the Germans overthrew the last Emperor in Rome, thus ending the Western Roman Empire. (For a discussion of the Eastern, or Byzantine, Empire, see pages 77-79.)

REASONS FOR THE FALL OF THE ROMAN EMPIRE

Why could the Germanic hordes crush Rome, so long the master of the Mediterranean world? The answer lies not in German strength but in Roman weakness. By the 4th and 5th centuries A.D. the Roman Empire had declined because of the following internal conditions:

1. Political. (a) The dictatorial government, frequently inefficient and corrupt, did not command the people's loyalty. (b) The vast Empire, having primitive transportation and communication, could not be governed efficiently from one central city. (c) Rivalry over succession to the throne often resulted in destructive civil wars.

2. Economic. (a) Small farmers had abandoned their lands, and many had become workers on large estates. No longer independent, they lost the incentive to improve farming methods or to increase production. (b) The self-sufficiency of the large estates hampered trade and curtailed industry, thus causing an economic decline. (c) Heavy, often unjust, taxation burdened the people and destroyed their ambition to work and progress. (d) The widespread use of slaves in industry and agriculture caused great unemployment among the freemen.

3. Social. (a) People were interested mainly in pleasure and luxury. The early Roman ideals of patriotism, service, and morality had almost vanished. (b) Sharp class distinctions existed. The upper classes were wealthy and educated; the lower classes were poor and ignorant.

4. Military. (a) The warlike spirit of early pagan Rome was weakened by Christian teachings of peace and brotherhood. (b) The Roman armies included many Germanic mercenaries of uncertain loyalty. (c) The armies, considering themselves masters of the state, not its servants, often chose the Emperors and determined government policy.

ROMAN CONTRIBUTIONS TO CIVILIZATION

1. Pax Romana (27 B.C.-180 A.D.). For over 200 years, Roman military might enforced the *Pax Romana*, or "Roman peace," in the Mediterranean world. During this period, trade and commerce expanded, and the arts and sciences thrived. Greco-Roman, or classical civilization, reached everywhere in the Empire. Man's achievements under the Pax Romana prove that peace means progress.

2. Roman Law. The Romans developed bodies of law on business matters, family relationships, individual rights, and international affairs. *Justinian*, Roman Emperor at Constantinople (527-565 A.D.), directed jurists to codify these laws. The *Justinian Code* influenced the legal systems of western Europe and, less directly, the United States.

Roman law was intended to be impartial and humane. Two of its principles of justice were: (a) All persons are equal before the law. (b) Accused persons are guaranteed legal protection. For example, forced confessions are invalid.

3. Architecture. The Romans built military roads, aqueducts, bridges, and majestic marble buildings, effectively using the arch, the dome, and the column.

During the reign of Emperor Vespasian, the Romans erected the famous stone amphitheater, the *Colosseum*. In its arenas, gladiators and wild beasts battled to entertain spectators.

Ruins of the Colosseum in Rome

4. Language. Latin, the Roman language, is (a) the root of the *Romance* languages: French, Italian, Spanish, Portuguese, and Rumanian, and (b) the source of about one-half of the words in the English language.

5. Literature

a. Cicero (106-43 B.C.), a renowned orator and writer, is often called the "father of Latin prose." He wrote extensively on ethical, religious, and political subjects, and delivered famous orations in defense of the Roman Republic.

b. Vergil (70-19 B.C.) wrote Rome's famous epic poem, the *Aeneid*. In relating the adventures of Aeneas, whose descendants supposedly founded Rome, Vergil extolled Rome's greatness.

c. Horace (65-08 B.C.), in his *Odes*, wrote charming poetry about every-day life. He was a moralist who praised the early Roman virtues of simplicity, courage, and reverence.

d. Seneca (3 B.C.-65 A.D.), a Stoic philosopher, wrote essays on morals.

6. Historical Writing

a. Livy (59 B.C.-17 A.D.) wrote an encyclopedic history of Rome from its founding to the Augustan Age. Livy's patriotism prejudiced his writings.

b. Plutarch (100 A.D.) compared Roman and Greek heroes in his book of biographies, *Parallel Lives*.

c. Tacitus (55-120 A.D.), in his work *Germania*, vividly described life among the Germanic barbarians.

7. Science. The Romans were applied scientists, specializing in sanitation, public health, and engineering. The research scientists of the Empire were generally non-Romans.

a. Galen (131-201 A.D.), a Greek physician, summarized the medical information of his time and performed experiments regarding the nervous and circulatory systems.

b. Ptolemy (2nd century A.D.), a Greek astronomer, erroneously taught that (1) the earth is the center of the universe, and (2) the sun revolves about the earth. (This *Ptolemaic theory* was corrected in the 16th century A.D. by the *Copernican theory* (see page 114).

MULTIPLE-CHOICE QUESTIONS

1. Rome is situated on the (1) Po River (2) Tiber River (3) Adriatic Sea (4) Mediterranean Sea.
2. The mountains directly north of Italy are the (1) Alps (2) Apennines (3) Himalayas (4) Pyrenees.
3. The aristocratic class that controlled the Roman Senate in the days of the Republic was the (1) plebeian (2) priestly (3) military (4) patrician.
4. Carthage and Rome became bitter rivals because the Carthaginians (1) refused to worship Roman gods (2) threatened to drive the Romans out of Gaul (3) competed with Rome for commercial supremacy in the Mediterranean (4) were allied with Alexander the Great against Rome.
5. Rome's conquest of the Mediterranean world (1) strengthened democracy in Rome (2) reduced the supply of slaves (3) guaranteed land for every Roman citizen (4) led to internal conflict which eventually destroyed the Republic.
6. Soon after the Punic Wars, the redistribution of land in Rome was urged by (1) Nero (2) Mark Antony (3) Tiberius Gracchus (4) Vespasian.
7. Caesar's great rival for supremacy in Rome was (1) Pompey (2) Marius (3) Octavian (4) Hadrian.
8. Who ruled Rome at the time of the birth of Jesus? (1) Augustus Caesar (2) Sulla (3) Brutus (4) Diocletian.

9. Latin is the basis of the (1) Danish (2) French (3) Russian (4) German language.
10. The Roman orator known as the "father of Latin prose" was (1) Galen (2) Hadrian (3) Cicero (4) Cato.
11. The greatest contribution of Rome to Western civilization was her (1) practice of giving free grain to the unemployed (2) legal system (3) invention of the arch (4) medical knowledge.
12. A famous Roman historian was (1) Livy (2) Horace (3) Galen (4) Claudius.
13. The great expansion of commerce in the Mediterranean area during the first two centuries A.D. is best explained by the (1) adoption of protective tariffs (2) introduction of money (3) invention of the compass (4) maintenance of peace.
14. Roman law (1) was never written down (2) accepted confessions secured by torture (3) considered all persons equal before the law (4) neglected business matters.
15. The Roman poet who wrote the *Aeneid* was (1) Trajan (2) Horace (3) Vergil (4) Fabius.
16. An important reason why the Roman Empire declined was that the (1) Punic Wars weakened the Empire (2) Senate became too powerful (3) middle class was weakened (4) slaves revolted.
17. Which of the following pairs of modern nations occupy areas that were once included in the Roman Empire? (1) India and Egypt (2) Norway and Denmark (3) Spain and England (4) China and Germany.
18. Two outstanding contributions of Rome to Western civilization were in (1) literature and medicine (2) painting and drama (3) engineering and law (4) music and military tactics.

COMPLETION QUESTIONS

1. The author of *Commentaries on the Gallic War* was _____.
2. The military leader who defeated Antony and became first ruler of the Roman Empire was _____.
3. Roman civilization made its greatest progress during the 200-year period known as the _____.
4. In 313 A.D. the Christians were granted freedom of worship by the Roman Emperor _____.
5. The Roman Empire astronomer who mistakenly taught that the earth is the center of the universe was _____.
6. German barbarians invaded the Roman Empire in the 4th century A.D. because they were being pushed westward by the _____.

TRUE-FALSE QUESTIONS

If the statement is correct, write the word *true*. If the statement is incorrect, substitute a word or phrase for the *italicized* term to make the statement correct.

1. The lowest class of citizens in Rome was the *plebeian*.
2. *Scipio,* the great Carthaginian general, was unable to capture the city of Rome.
3. The Roman laws were collected and codified during the reign of the Emperor *Claudius*.
4. The Huns, who invaded the Roman Empire in the 5th century A.D., were led by *Xerxes*.
5. The people who most influenced Roman culture were the *Egyptians*.

Section Two. Medieval History

UNIT IV. THE MIDDLE AGES:
IN EUROPE AND THE MIDDLE EAST

Part 1. Barbaric Invasions and the Age of Feudalism in Europe

THE MIDDLE AGES

The *Middle Ages* cover the 900-year period from the destruction of the Roman Empire in the 5th century to the beginnings of modern times in the 14th century.

This era in the history of western Europe is often divided into (1) the *Dark Ages* (5th to 10th centuries), a period of disorder and decline, and (2) the *Later Middle Ages* (11th to 14th centuries), a period of advance toward a higher level of civilization.

THE DECLINE OF CIVILIZATION IN THE DARK AGES

The Germanic invasions resulted in the political collapse of the Roman Empire and the ruin of its highly developed economic and social system, thus bringing on the Dark Ages.

1. Decline of Trade and Industry. Merchants, fearing the seizure of their goods by bandits, stopped shipping to distant points and confined their trade to the local marketplace. The excellent Roman roads deteriorated. Lacking sufficient markets, industry shut down. Many unemployed workmen moved to rural areas. Cities declined in population, and many disappeared. As trade and industry dwindled, money fell into disuse.

2. Decline of Learning and Culture. During these unsettled times, (*a*) Roman schools, libraries, and museums were destroyed, (*b*) arts and sciences were neglected, and (*c*) reading and writing were forgotten. People were concerned not with learning and culture, but with remaining alive.

3. Decline of Strong Central Government. Government was now controlled by weak Germanic kingdoms: the Visigoths in Spain, the Ostrogoths in Italy, the Angles and Saxons in England, and the Franks in Gaul (France).

Their rulers generally failed to provide protection, insure justice, and maintain order. Such weaknesses existed because the Germanic kingdoms: (*a*) **Lacked manpower** to control their large territories and populations. Only a few hundred thousand Germans governed millions of other peoples. (*b*) **Lacked large armies** to subdue ambitious nobles. A noble sometimes commanded military forces stronger than those of his king. (*c*) **Lacked roads and bridges** to transport armies to trouble spots. Because the Germans knew little about engineering, they could not maintain the Roman transportation facilities. (*d*) **Lacked rules of succession** to the throne to prevent civil war after a ruler's death.

The only strong Germanic government was the Frankish kingdom in the 8th and early 9th centuries.

THE FRANKISH KINGDOM

1. Created by Clovis. Late in the 5th century invading Frankish warriors completed the defeat of the Roman armies in Gaul. Leading these Franks was a capable King, *Clovis.*

Seeking to rule all Gaul, Clovis (*a*) removed possible Frankish rivals, (*b*) subdued other Germanic tribes in Gaul, and (*c*) converted the Franks to Catholic Christianity, thereby gaining support of the Pope and of Gaul's large Christian population. By these measures, Clovis created a powerful Frankish kingdom.

2. Ruled by "Do-Nothing" Kings. Clovis' descendants, who ruled for more than two centuries, were incompetent and became known as "do-nothing" Kings. Their reign was marked by recurrent outbreaks of civil war and by a sharp increase in the power of the nobles at the expense of the King. Control of the government eventually passed into the hands of the *Mayor of the Palace,* a powerful noble.

3. Provided Leadership for Western Europe. During the 8th and early 9th centuries the Frankish kingdom dominated western Europe. It was governed successively by three outstanding individuals: Charles Martel, Pepin, and Charlemagne.

a. Charles Martel, as Mayor of the Palace, led the Frankish army that defeated the invading Moors at the *Battle of Tours* (732). This battle ended the Moslem thrust into Christian Europe (see page 80).

b. Pepin in 741 became Mayor of the Palace upon the death of his father, Charles Martel. In 751, with the Pope's approval, Pepin removed the last "do-nothing" King and assumed the Frankish throne. Grateful for Papal support, Pepin defeated the *Lombards,* a Germanic people in central Italy, and ceded their lands to the Pope. This *Donation of Pepin* gave the

Catholic Church political control over part of central Italy. (The Church ruled this area—the *Papal States*—for over 1,000 years, until Italy was unified.)

c. Charlemagne in 768 succeeded to the Frankish throne upon the death of his father, Pepin.

CHARLEMAGNE RULES A MEDIEVAL EMPIRE (768-814)

Charlemagne was the outstanding ruler in medieval Europe. During his 46-year reign, he demonstrated extraordinary ability in:

1. Warfare

a. Charlemagne's Conquests. Charlemagne conquered (1) the *Lombards* in northern Italy, (2) the *Moslems* in the Spanish March, a strip of land just south of the Pyrenees Mountains in Spain, (3) the *Slavs* in Bohemia (now part of Czechoslovakia), and (4) the *Saxons*, a pagan Germanic people in northwestern Germany.

b. Effects of Charlemagne's Conquests. Charlemagne increased the power of the Catholic Church by ending the Lombard threat to the Papal States and by converting pagan peoples to Catholicism. He also expanded the Frankish realm into an Empire that included most of western Europe. (See map, page 63.)

c. "Emperor of the Romans." At Rome in 800, Pope Leo III, recognizing Charlemagne's services to the Church and mastery of western Europe, crowned him "Emperor of the Romans." (For the subsequent political significance of this act, see pages 75-76.)

Charlemagne's "Roman" Empire differed from the original Roman Empire in that (1) it encompassed chiefly central and western Europe, whereas the original Roman Empire had centered about the Mediterranean, and (2) it crumbled upon Charlemagne's death, whereas the original Empire had endured many centuries.

2. Government.
Charlemagne divided his vast Empire into provinces, each administered by a noble responsible to him. To maintain the authority of the central government, Charlemagne sent official messengers, *missi dominici*, to the provinces to report on the nobles' loyalty and ability. This system of continuous investigation, coupled with Charlemagne's tremendous prestige, temporarily halted the shift of power from the central government to the nobles.

3. Education.
Charlemagne, unlike most Germanic rulers, valued education. He (a) established schools in monasteries and cathedrals to instruct both the clergy and the common people, (b) encouraged the collecting and

copying of Latin manuscripts to preserve ancient learning, and (c) maintained a *palace school* at his capital, *Aix-la-Chapelle,* to educate the nobles' children. To head this school, Charlemagne appointed the famous English scholar, *Alcuin.*

BREAKUP OF CHARLEMAGNE'S EMPIRE

Charlemagne's death (814) was followed by years of incompetent rule and civil war. Charlemagne's successors lacked his ability and were unable to keep the Empire intact. By the *Treaty of Verdun* (843), his three grandsons agreed to divide the territory as follows: *Louis* received the eastern part, the basis of modern Germany; *Charles* received the western part, the basis of modern France; and *Lothar* received the central part, which included the basis of modern Italy.

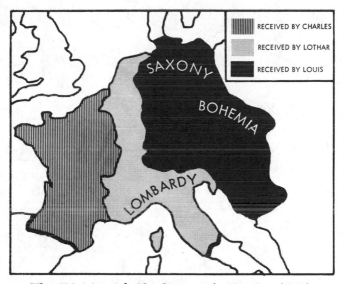

The Division of Charlemagne's Empire (843)

Charlemagne's successors proved unable to control the nobles, prevent local warfare, and suppress piracy and highway robbery. Most important, they were unable to repel new invasions of western Europe.

NEW INVASIONS OF EUROPE (9TH AND 10TH CENTURIES)

1. The **Northmen,** also known as **Norsemen** or **Vikings,** were Germanic barbarians from the north European region of Scandinavia (Norway, Sweden, Denmark). Poor soil and a coastline with many natural harbors encouraged them to become sailors. Attracted chiefly by western Europe's wealth, the Northmen at first raided and plundered only coastal and river cities. Later, faced with overpopulation at home, they settled in England, Ireland, France, Italy, and Sicily. They also settled in Russia and Iceland. (From Iceland, *Leif Ericson* sailed west and, long before Columbus, reached the New World.)

2. The **Magyars,** a wild people from central Asia, settled in Hungary. From this base, they attacked France, southern Germany, and northern Italy.

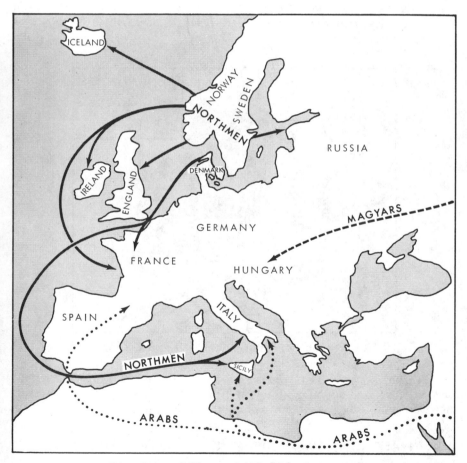

Invasions of Europe (9th-10th Centuries)

3. The **Arabs,** or **Moors,** although stopped in 732 at the Battle of Tours, retained control of Spain and North Africa. From these bases, they continued to raid southern France and Italy.

Since the governments of western Europe failed to withstand these various invaders, the people were inadequately protected. Their effort to safeguard their lives and property hastened the development of a new political, economic, and social system—*feudalism.*

DEFINITION OF FEUDALISM

Feudalism may be considered (1) a *social* system of rigid class distinctions, (2) a *political* system of local government and military defense, and (3) an *economic* system of self-sufficient agricultural manors. Feudalism varied in detail according to regional conditions.

REASONS FOR THE RISE OF FEUDALISM

1. Weakness of Central Government. The central government could not protect its subjects from foreign invasions and local warfare. Landholders consequently surrendered their lands to the powerful local noble in exchange for his promise of protection.

2. Land Policy of the Germanic Kings. In return for pledges of military assistance, the Germanic kings granted landed estates to the nobles. Possession of these large tracts of land substantially increased the nobles' power.

FEUDAL SOCIETY

1. Rigid Class Distinctions. Feudal society was sharply divided into (*a*) a relatively small number of landholding nobles—the privileged upper class, and (*b*) the great mass of peasants, or *serfs*—the unprivileged lower class. Position in feudal society was determined by birth. Regardless of ability or hard work, the serf could not advance to higher social status.

2. The Feudal Social Pyramid

a. The **King,** at the apex of feudal society, nominally owned all the land in the kingdom. Actually, the King controlled only his own estates, the *royal domain.*

b. The **powerful lords,** few in number, stood immediately below the King as his *vassals.* These lords received *fiefs* (grants of land) from the King and pledged him allegiance and military service. The vassal pledged to fulfill his obligations in a ceremony called *homage.* He was granted his fief in a ceremony called *investiture.*

c. The **lesser lords,** a more numerous group, were vassals of the powerful lords and received fiefs in exchange for pledges of allegiance and military service. The lesser lords could in turn grant fiefs to other nobles, and this process of *subinfeudation* could be repeated several times.

d. The **knights,** the lowest and most numerous group of nobles, constituted the bulk of the feudal armies.

e. The **serfs,** far outnumbering the entire nobility, constituted the broad base of the feudal pyramid.

3. Complicated Vassal-Lord Relationships. Feudal relationships of the nobility were quite complicated. When lesser lords and knights received fiefs from different superiors, they were vassals to several lords. The question of the vassal's primary allegiance led to many bitter disputes.

4. Feudal Hereditary Relationships. (*a*) The mutual obligations between lord and vassal or between noble and serf were usually *hereditary*—binding upon the heirs of both parties. (*b*) A noble's title and property could be legally inherited only by his first-born son. This restriction, awarding to the first-born son a status superior to his younger brothers, is called *primogeniture*.

FEUDAL GOVERNMENT

1. Weak Central Government. Although the central government or King theoretically administered the entire kingdom, the King could not generally exercise authority beyond the royal domain. Supposedly the supreme ruler, he was in reality only one of several powerful lords.

2. Vigorous Local Government. Because the King was weak, the local nobles completely controlled their own territory. The nobles made laws, levied taxes, dispensed justice, and waged war, thereby assuming the functions of government. Thus, feudal government was decentralized.

MILITARY ASPECTS OF FEUDALISM

1. During Wartime. When an invasion or major war threatened, the powerful lord would summon his vassals to military service. In turn, the vassals would enlist their subvassals, and then all the nobles would unite into a single army to repel the invasion or prosecute the war. At other times, minor feudal lords fought among themselves for prestige or land.

Invasions and feudal wars destroyed crops and property. However, such defenses as heavy armor and strong castle walls minimized casualties.

2. The Castle. Dominating the lord's estate, or *manor,* was his castle. A cold, dark, damp home, lacking comfort and simple conveniences, it nevertheless constituted an excellent fortress. It was (*a*) located on elevated ground, (*b*) constructed of heavy wood or (after the 11th century) thick stone, and (*c*) surrounded by a deep, wide, water-filled trench, called a *moat*. A drawbridge was lowered across the moat for access to the outside world. During attacks, the lord, his vassals, and serfs found protection in the castle.

3. During Peacetime. When peace prevailed, the lord (*a*) hunted wild animals, (*b*) held mock battles called *jousts* and *tournaments*, and (*c*) trained young nobles for knighthood.

The young noble received extended military schooling in horsemanship, in wearing armor, and in using the sword, lance, and battle-ax. At age 21, he became a warrior on horseback, or *knight*.

The knight was expected to observe a code of honorable conduct called *chivalry*. This code stressed (*a*) loyalty to God and to the knight's lord, (*b*) protection of the oppressed and helpless, (*c*) support of justice, (*d*) defense of Christianity, and (*e*) courage, courtesy, gallantry, and generosity. Unfortunately, these chivalrous ideals were frequently violated.

FEUDAL ECONOMIC CONDITIONS

1. The Self-Sufficient Agricultural Manor. The manor, or lord's estate, consisted of (*a*) the farm and pasture lands, (*b*) the lord's castle or manor house, and (*c*) the village buildings: church, blacksmith and carpenter shops, serfs' huts, and the lord's wine press, flour mill, and baking oven. The manor was largely self-sufficient economically. Its inhabitants raised crops and livestock for food, spun wool for clothing, tanned leather for shoes, and cut lumber for furniture and buildings. However, some essential items, such as salt for preserving and seasoning food, and iron for making tools and weapons, had to be secured from outside sources.

On the manor, the lord directed the activities; the serfs performed the physical labor.

2. The Serf

a. Neither Slave Nor Freeman. The serf was not a slave, since he could not be sold apart from the land and since he could claim the lord's protection. Nonetheless, the serf was not a freeman, for he was "bound to the soil" and could not leave without the lord's permission.

b. Obligations of the Serf. In return for protection and the right to live on the manor, the serf owed the lord (1) *services*—several days of labor each week on the lord's farmlands, and (2) *payment in kind*—a portion of the grain and other crops raised on the serf's land. The serf also had to give the lord a share of the goods he prepared in the lord's wine press, flour mill, and baking oven.

c. An Impoverished Life. After meeting his obligations, the serf had little left for his own family. He lived a hard, tedious life and had little opportunity for recreation and education.

3. Low Agricultural Output. In proportion to its size and labor force, the manor raised insufficient crops. (*a*) Each serf was assigned scattered strips of land rather than a compact farm. Although ensuring a fair distribution of fertile land, this arrangement wasted working time. (*b*) The serfs had only wooden plows, and crude sickles and hoes. (*c*) Little was known about crop rotation or fertilizer. To restore soil fertility, the manor followed the inefficient *three-field system,* annually leaving one-third of the land fallow (uncultivated).

4. Disappearance of Trade. At the height of feudalism (9th to 11th centuries), trade was at a virtual standstill. As manors became more self-sufficient, the need for outside products declined. In addition, feudal wars and inadequate roads and bridges made commerce unsafe and difficult. Moreover, heavy taxes imposed by each feudal lord on goods transported across his domain raised the cost of the goods.

FACTORS LEADING TO THE DECLINE OF FEUDALISM

1. The Crusades. During a 200-year period (1095-1291), western Europe undertook many *Crusades*, religious wars intended to recover the Holy Land from the Moslems. The Crusades weakened the economic basis of feudalism by awakening European demand for Eastern goods. Trade revived, towns grew, the merchant class prospered, serfs fled to the towns, and the self-sufficiency of the manor ended. (For a further discussion of the Crusades, see pages **84-85**.)

2. The Rise of National States and Absolute Monarchy. From the 14th to the 17th centuries the rise of national states weakened political and military feudalism. As the Crusades and feudal wars decimated the nobility, the King or central government gradually regained absolute power. (For a further discussion of national states and absolute monarchy, see pages **123-134**.)

Long after the feudal period ended, the French Revolution (**1789**) helped destroy the remaining traces of feudalism in western Europe. Even today, however, parts of Asia, Africa, and Latin America retain certain feudal aspects: rigid class distinctions, landless peasants, and landowning by the wealthy few.

MULTIPLE-CHOICE QUESTIONS

1. The Dark Ages in western Europe refers to the period (1) before the dawn of history (2) soon after the assassination of Julius Caesar (3) following the collapse of the Roman Empire (4) directly following the end of the Pax Romana.

2. Which was *not* a result of the Germanic invasions of the Roman Empire? (1) raising the level of civilization (2) overthrowing the Roman government (3) curtailing trade (4) destroying many fine Roman buildings.

3. Clovis was ruler of the (1) Franks (2) Britons (3) Romans (4) Saxons.

4. The Frankish leader who defeated the Moors at the Battle of Tours was (1) Clovis (2) Charlemagne (3) Pepin (4) Charles Martel.

5. Charlemagne was able to dominate western Europe successfully because he (1) controlled the commerce of this area (2) allied himself with Anglo-Saxon England (3) maintained an efficient military force (4) developed the sea power of the Franks.

6. In 800 A.D. the Pope conferred on Charlemagne the title of (1) Emperor of the Romans (2) King of the Franks (3) Mayor of the Palace (4) Master of the Royal Domain.

7. Areas that Charlemagne united within his Empire are now part of (1) France and Germany (2) England and Spain (3) Spain and Portugal (4) Austria and Russia.

8. An important result of Charlemagne's conquests was the (1) spread of Christianity (2) union of the Eastern and Western Roman Empires (3) expulsion of the Moslems from Europe (4) decline of feudalism in central Europe.

9. One people that did *not* invade medieval Europe were the (1) Northmen (2) Magyars (3) Arabs (4) Persians.

10. A basic reason for the rise of the feudal system in Europe was the (1) increase in population (2) influence of the Crusades (3) end of the manorial system (4) lack of effective central governments.

11. Feudalism served a useful purpose because it (1) encouraged education (2) eliminated warfare (3) gave the people some protection and security (4) encouraged the development of industry.

12. In western Europe during the Middle Ages, the basic economic unit was the (1) shop (2) town (3) factory (4) manor.

13. The serf was (1) bound to his master (2) the property of the state (3) free when he reached the age of 21 (4) bound to the land.

14. A characteristic of agriculture on a medieval manor was the use of (1) contour plowing (2) artificial fertilizers (3) migrant workers (4) the three-field system.

15. Unlike a serf, a vassal under the feudal system owed his lord (1) military service (2) labor on his estate (3) fees for the use of his mill and wine press (4) one-fifth of his income.

16. A basic reason for the decline of feudalism was that the (1) serfs revolted successfully (2) lesser nobles refused to honor their military obligations (3) Crusades revived trade and ended manor self-sufficiency (4) Church opposed feudal warfare.

MATCHING QUESTIONS

Column A	Column B
1 Person who pledged military service in return for land	a. Chivalry
2. Right of the first-born son to inherit his father's entire estate	b. Primogeniture
3. Estate of feudal lord	c. Royal domain
4. Presentation of fief to lesser lord	d. Vassal
5. Feudal code of conduct	e. Moat
	f. Manor
	g. Investiture

Part 2. The Roman Catholic Church: Dominant Institution of the Middle Ages

JESUS AND THE IDEALS OF CHRISTIANITY

Jesus was born in Bethlehem in the Roman province of Judea (part of Palestine) during the reign of the Emperor Augustus. Jesus received a thorough Jewish religious education and became a preacher. Emphasizing religious morals and ethics, he taught the following principles:

1. A single God is the Father of all men. Therefore all men are brothers.

2. Love God above all; love your neighbor as yourself.

3. The worthy man practices charity, justice, and the Golden Rule: "Do unto others as you would have others do unto you."

4. All persons may be cleansed of sin and may achieve eternal salvation in heaven. The meek, the oppressed, and the forgiving will receive special heavenly rewards.

Jesus' disciples (followers) believed that He is the Son of God sent to mankind as the Savior, or *Christ*. His teachings, presented in the *New Testament*, became the basis of a new religion, *Christianity*.

THE SPREAD OF CHRISTIANITY WITHIN THE ROMAN EMPIRE (1ST TO 4TH CENTURIES)

1. Early Church Leaders

a. St. Paul (1st century A.D.), a missionary, envisioned Christianity, not as merely a Jewish sect, but as a universal religion. He therefore directed Christian missionaries to emphasize the conversion of non-Jewish peoples.

b. St. Peter (1st century A.D.), the first Bishop of Rome, began to shape the internal structure of the Christian Church.

c. St. Jerome (340-420) translated the Bible from Hebrew and Greek into the first Latin, or *Vulgate*, edition.

d. St. Augustine (354-430), a philosopher, related the story of his conversion to Christianity in his autobiographical *Confessions*. He described how Christianity could lead to a world of peace and perfection in his book *The City of God*.

2. Favorable Factors. Christianity gained many converts throughout the Roman Empire.

a. People were dissatisfied with the old pagan religions.

b. People were attracted by the ideals of Christianity: one God, brotherly love, and eternal salvation. The concept of equality of man appealed especially to the poor and oppressed.

c. Christian missionaries could travel and preach with relative ease throughout the Roman Empire, a political and cultural unit.

d. Early Churchmen displayed courage, sincerity, and ability.

e. People were impressed by many early Christians who, rather than renounce their faith, suffered persecution and died as *martyrs*.

3. Opposition and Persecution. Christianity was opposed within the Roman Empire.

a. Pagan priests feared that the success of Christianity would doom their religions.

b. The upper classes considered Christianity a "slave religion" because it appealed to the lowly by preaching equality and brotherly love.

c. The government of Rome accused the Christians of treason because they (1) refused to worship the Roman Emperor, (2) refused to serve in the Roman armies, and (3) disapproved of gladiatorial combats and pagan feasts.

For 300 years Christians were persecuted by the Roman government, most severely under the Emperors Nero and Diocletian. The Christians suffered the loss of Roman citizenship, confiscation of property, torture, and death. Nevertheless, Christianity continued to grow stronger and gain converts.

4. Christianity Triumphs. In 313 the Christians gained freedom from persecution when the Emperor *Constantine* ordered religious toleration in the *Edict of Milan.* After Constantine later became a Christian, the faith grew in public esteem. In 392 the Emperor *Theodosius* proclaimed it the official state religion. Christianity was then overwhelmingly accepted by the people of the Empire.

THE SPREAD OF CHRISTIANITY OUTSIDE THE ROMAN EMPIRE (4TH TO 11TH CENTURIES)

1. Western Europe. The *Roman Catholic Church*, centered in Rome, gradually converted the Germanic peoples and other west Europeans. Outstanding landmarks of such progress were the conversion of (*a*) Clovis and the Franks in 5th-century France, (*b*) the Irish in the 5th century (by the missionary *St. Patrick*), (*c*) the Angles and Saxons in England at the end of the 6th century (by the missionary *St. Augustine of Canterbury*), and (*d*) the Saxons in 8th-century Germany after their subjugation by Charlemagne (see page 62). By the 11th century the Roman Catholic branch of Christianity dominated western Europe.

2. Eastern Europe. The *Greek Orthodox Church,* centered in Constantinople, gradually converted certain Slavic peoples (Serbs, Bulgars, and Russians) and other east Europeans. By the 11th century the Greek Orthodox branch of Christianity dominated eastern Europe.

SPLIT IN THE CHRISTIAN CHURCH

During the early Christian era, Rome and Constantinople vied for religious power. The *Pope,* or Bishop of Rome, claimed supremacy over the whole Church; the *Patriarch,* or Bishop, of Constantinople asserted authority over Church affairs in the East. They also had conflicting views on Church language, religious beliefs, and rituals. As a result of these disagreements, the Christian Church in 1054 split into two distinct parts: the Roman Catholic Church at Rome and the Greek Orthodox Church at Constantinople. (The Greek Orthodox Church later split into a number of Eastern Orthodox Churches.) The Roman Catholic and Greek Orthodox Churches retain separate identities to this day.

The Roman Catholic Church proved to be more influential.

1. It was free from political control, whereas the Greek Orthodox Church was controlled by the Byzantine Emperors.

2. It was the dominant factor in western Europe during the Middle Ages, whereas the Greek Orthodox Church was less significant in eastern Europe.

3. After the Middle Ages, as western Europe assumed greater importance in world affairs, the Roman Catholic Church expanded its missionary and other religious activities throughout the world.

STRUCTURE OF THE ROMAN CATHOLIC CHURCH

1. Secular Clergy. These Church officials live and work in the everyday world. They constitute the Church *hierarchy.*

a. The *Pope,* who resides at the *Vatican* in Rome, is the supreme leader of the Roman Catholic Church. He is considered to be in direct line of succession from St. Peter, the first Bishop of Rome. Since the 11th century, each Pope has been elected for life by the College of Cardinals.

b. The *cardinals,* called the Princes of the Church, are clergymen, usually bishops or archbishops, appointed by the Pope as his chief advisers.

c. The *bishops* head religious districts, or *dioceses.* An important diocese, called an *archdiocese,* is headed by an *archbishop.*

d. The *priests* direct local communities, or parishes. They serve and guide their parishioners, the *laity,* or *laymen.*

2. Religious Orders or Societies. The Church structure also includes those men and women who withdraw from ordinary pursuits to enter *religious orders,* or *societies.* Each society lives according to a special set of rules (*regula*). The members normally take vows of *poverty, chastity,* and *obedience.*

a. The men, designated by such names as *monks* and *friars,* live in buildings generally known as *monasteries.* Monks and friars who are also priests comprise the *regular clergy.*

b. The women are called *nuns.* Their residences are usually known as *convents.*

IMPORTANT RELIGIOUS ORDERS FOUNDED DURING THE MIDDLE AGES

1. Benedictines. The monks of the Benedictine order, founded in the 6th century, lived according to the *Rule of St. Benedict.* It introduced the vows of poverty, chastity, and obedience. These monks devoted themselves to prayer and hard work. They farmed, provided food and medical care for needy persons, extended hospitality to travelers, and maintained schools chiefly for prospective clergymen. By copying ancient manuscripts, they preserved the classical Greek and Roman literature.

2. Templars and Hospitalers. Founded during the Crusades, these orders combined the functions of monks and knights. They cared for the sick and injured, and they fought the Moslems for the Holy Land.

3. Franciscans and Dominicans. These orders were founded in the 13th century by *St. Francis of Assisi* and *St. Dominic,* respectively. These orders consisted of *mendicant* (begging) *friars,* who originally wandered from place to place, living on alms and preaching Christianity. The Franciscans ministered to the lower-class people, whereas the Dominicans concentrated chiefly upon the educated upper class. Moreover, the Dominicans often combatted heresy.

ACTIVITIES OF THE MEDIEVAL CHURCH

The most powerful institution in medieval western Europe was the Roman Catholic Church. Supreme in religious matters, it also undertook many nonreligious functions that were beyond the power of the weak feudal governments.

1. Religious Activities

a. The Church completely supervised the religious needs of the people, dispensing such *sacraments* as baptism at birth and final rites at death. Moreover, the Church taught that faith, good works, and Church membership assure eternal salvation.

b. The Church used the power of *excommunication* against those persons, including kings and powerful lords, who flagrantly violated Church laws or trampled on its rights. By excommunication, the Church expelled a person from its membership and banned him from taking part in its rites and services. By being deprived of the sacraments, the excommunicated person ran the risk of eternal damnation. If he was a king or a powerful noble, excommunication freed his subjects from all obligation to him.

c. In the 13th century, the Church established the *Holy Inquisition* to deal with heresy by uncovering and trying *heretics*—those Christians whose religious views the Church considered false and therefore dangerous. Sometimes, suspected heretics were tortured to secure confessions and repentance. Unrepentant heretics were handed over to the civil authorities for punishment—usually death.

2. Economic Activities

a. The Church derived a considerable income from its properties, gifts, and various assessments, including the *tithe*, amounting to about 10 percent of each person's income.

b. The Church maintained hospitals and asylums for the sick, aged, orphaned, and poor.

c. The Church encouraged the monks who farmed monastery lands to follow the best agricultural practices and thereby to set a good example for nearby farmers.

d. The Church prohibited *usury*—then considered as any interest charged for a loan of money.

e. By the 13th century, the Church owned 30 percent of the land of western Europe. These holdings represented gifts of land for the establishment of monasteries, convents, and cathedrals, as well as land that Church officials had received from powerful lords as feudal fiefs.

3. Cultural Activities

a. The Church promoted learning by maintaining schools, chiefly to educate young men for the priesthood. (Talented boys, even from the lower class, could thus become priests and rise in the Church hierarchy.) Although the general public was illiterate, the clergy could read and write.

b. By copying ancient books and manuscripts, the monks helped preserve Greco-Roman culture.

c. The Church influenced literature and architecture. Medieval authors, usually churchmen, wrote about religious themes (see page 90). Medieval architects designed magnificent cathedrals (see page 89).

4. Political Activities

a. The Church governed the Papal States in Italy.

b. The Church maintained its own courts for cases involving marriages, wills, contracts, orphans, widows, and clergymen. (The privilege of clergymen to be tried in Church courts rather than civil courts is called *benefit of clergy*.) The legal system developed in Church courts is called *canon law*.

c. The Church proclaimed the *Truce of God*, which prohibited feudal warfare during certain days of the week and on special holidays. This truce was often violated by feudal lords.

d. The Church claimed supremacy over civil government. This claim led to disputes between medieval Popes and civil rulers.

MEDIEVAL POPES BESTOW CROWNS UPON CIVIL RULERS

In 800 Pope Leo III crowned Charlemagne "Emperor of the Romans." Upon Charlemagne's death, his Empire collapsed and his title of "Emperor" remained unused. In 962 Pope John XII crowned Otto I, a ruler in central Europe, as Emperor. Thus began the *Holy Roman Empire*.

On the basis of these Papal crownings, the medieval Church asserted that (1) Popes may dethrone as well as crown Emperors, and (2) Popes are superior to civil rulers, including Kings and Emperors. These claims led to many disputes between Church and states.

STRUGGLES BETWEEN CIVIL RULERS AND POPES

During the Later Middle Ages, a number of civil rulers challenged Papal authority. Since the Popes often triumphed, these conflicts demonstrated the strength of the medieval Church.

1. The Investiture Struggle

a. The Issue. For many years, both civil rulers and Popes claimed the right to appoint major Church officials. Civil rulers claimed this right because they invested Church officials with feudal fiefs. The Popes also claimed this right because they invested Church officials with religious authority. (*Invest*, used in this sense, means "endow" with power.)

b. The Papal Triumph at Canossa (*1077*). Pope Gregory VII (Hildebrand) ordered civil rulers *not* to appoint Church officials. When Henry IV, King of Germany and Holy Roman Emperor, defied the order, Gregory excommunicated and deposed him. This action freed Henry's subjects from allegiance to him and encouraged his feudal lords to revolt. Acknowledging defeat, Henry journeyed to Canossa (in northern Italy) where, reputedly barefoot in the the snow, he did penance before the Pope for three days. Gregory then forgave him. This episode is a dramatic illustration of the power of the medieval Church.

c. The Concordat of Worms (*1122*). Despite Canossa, the investiture struggle continued, not only between Henry and Gregory, but also between succeeding Emperors and Popes. Finally, a compromise agreement was reached in the *Concordat of Worms.* (1) The Church alone could appoint Church officials and invest them with religious authority. (2) The civil rulers retained the right to invest these officials with feudal fiefs, thus exercising, for all practical purposes, a veto power over the selections of the Church. This settlement resolved the question of investiture, but it did not, end the rivalry between Popes and civil rulers.

2. The Archbishop of Canterbury Struggle. In 1206 Pope Innocent III appointed Stephen Langton as *Archbishop of Canterbury*, leader of the Catholic Church in England. This Papal choice was rejected by King John, who preferred his own candidate. As a result, Innocent first excommunicated John and then ordered him deposed (1212), thereby encouraging John's feudal lords to revolt. These events forced John to (*a*) accept Langton as Archbishop, and (*b*) acknowledge the Pope as his superior lord. Innocent III, who so humbled John, is considered the most powerful medieval Pope.

MULTIPLE-CHOICE QUESTIONS

1. The events described in the New Testament took place in the (1) Golden Age of Greece (2) Pyramid Age of Egypt (3) early Roman Empire (4) Middle Ages.
2. Which contributed to the early spread of Christianity? (1) its adoption by the Roman upper classes (2) its offer of hope in a world of fear and uncertainty (3) its spread by Roman conquests (4) its acceptance of polytheism.
3. The first Bishop of Rome, from whose office evolved the Papacy, was (1) St. Paul (2) St. Peter (3) St. Patrick (4) St. Augustine.
4. The chief reason why Rome persecuted the Christians was that they (1) refused to pay taxes (2) would not worship the Emperor (3) converted the pagans (4) persecuted the pagans.
5. Roman persecution of Christianity was ended by (1) Emperor Nero (2) the Edict of Milan (3) the Patriarch at Constantinople (4) the Holy Inquisition.
6. Roman Catholic missionaries were *least* active in (1) France (2) England (3) Spain (4) Russia.
7. The monastic order that introduced the vows of poverty, chastity, and obedience was the (1) Franciscans (2) Benedictines (3) Templars (4) Dominicans.
8. The Pope is elevated to office following election by (1) all Catholic believers (2) the College of Cardinals (3) the people of Rome (4) the residents of the Vatican.

9. The Pope's power to deny a person Church sacraments is called (1) benefit of clergy (2) hierarchy (3) excommunication (4) investiture.
10. The courts of the Inquisition were established to (1) combat heresy (2) stamp out corruption (3) convert Germanic barbarians (4) punish traitors to the King.
11. Heretics are persons who (1) lead lives of luxury (2) refuse to pay taxes (3) disagree with Church doctrine (4) live in solitude.
12. The Church attempted to limit feudal warfare by means of (1) chivalry (2) the Concordat (3) the Inquisition (4) the Truce of God.
13. During the Middle Ages, the lending of money for interest was prohibited by the Church and was called (1) homage (2) usury (3) donation (4) tithe.
14. The coronation, in 962, of Otto I as Holy Roman Emperor was important because it (1) gave support to the Crusades (2) made possible a strong defense of Europe against the Ottoman Turks (3) led to a struggle for power between Emperors and Popes (4) ended feudalism.
15. During the Middle Ages, the Kings and the leaders of the Church most often disagreed over the (1) use of the Latin language (2) establishment of monastic orders (3) appointment of Church officials (4) control of education.
16. Emperor Henry IV of Germany went to the Pope at Canossa to (1) enjoy a vacation (2) beg forgiveness (3) secure military aid (4) urge a Crusade.
17. A compromise in the investiture struggle was reached by (1) the Archbishop of Canterbury (2) Pope Gregory VII (3) the Benedictine Rule (4) the Concordat of Worms.

Part 3. The Byzantine and Moslem Empires: Advanced Civilizations

While medieval Europe consisted mainly of small states, the Middle East contained two large realms: the Byzantine Empire and the Moslem Empire. They brought stable rule to their people and made important contributions to Western culture.

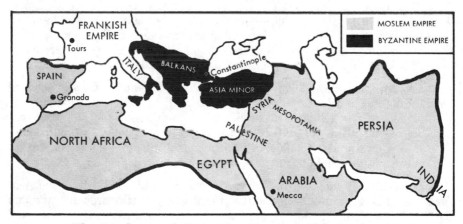

The Moslem and Byzantine Empires (8th Century)

A. THE BYZANTINE EMPIRE

BRIEF HISTORY OF THE BYZANTINE EMPIRE

1. Origin. By the 4th century A.D. the Roman Empire was divided into two parts: the West governed from Rome and the East governed from Constantinople. Although the Western Roman Empire fell to the Germanic invaders by 476 (see page 55), the eastern part survived independently until 1453, an additional thousand years. It became known as the *Byzantine Empire*, a name derived from Byzantium, the ancient Greek colony that served as the site of Constantinople. The Byzantine Empire displayed predominantly Middle Eastern and Greek cultures.

2. Greatest Extent. Under the Emperor *Justinian* (ruled 527-565), the Byzantine Empire expanded westward. Justinian, ambitious to restore the former Roman Empire, conquered northern Africa, southern Spain, and Italy.

3. Decline and Fall. From Justinian's reign to the 15th century, a 900-year period, the Empire battled continuously against various invaders. Despite occasional successes, the Empire gradually yielded the following territories: Italy to the Lombards; southern Spain to the Visigoths; Egypt, the rest of northern Africa, Syria, and Palestine to the Arabs; the Balkan provinces to the Bulgars, Serbs, and other Slavs; and Asia Minor and some Balkan provinces to the Turks.

The Byzantine Empire ended in 1453 when the Ottoman Turks captured Constantinople.

ASPECTS OF BYZANTINE LIFE

1. Autocratic Government. The Emperor, regarded as God's earthly representative, lived in splendor and maintained a lavish court. He exercised absolute power over all Empire affairs. For defense against invaders, he kept the imperial army and navy at instant readiness. He regulated the economy, derived a large income from taxes, and dominated the Byzantine Church.

2. Eastern Christianity. The *Patriarch of Constantinople*, usually selected by the Emperor and subservient to him, headed the Greek Orthodox Church. It attended to the religious needs of the Byzantine people and also sent missionaries into Europe, converting the Russians and many Balkan peoples to eastern Christianity. In 1054, after centuries of dispute, the Greek Orthodox and Roman Catholic Churches formally separated (see page 72).

3. Prosperous Trade and Industry. Agriculture was limited by insufficient farmland; nevertheless, the Byzantine Empire grew rich through trade and industry. Merchants imported Far Eastern luxuries: raw silk, spices, and precious stones. Craftsmen produced other luxuries: silk cloth, tapestry, gold and silver jewelry, perfumes, and fine glass. Constantinople, the great trade center of the Empire, exported these luxuries to Italian cities and Russia, and imported furs and agricultural products.

4. Constantinople, a Magnificent City. Constantinople contained (a) paved streets that were lighted at night, (b) beautiful homes, churches, and palaces, (c) recreational facilities: parks, playgrounds, and the *Hippodrome*, a famous chariot-racing arena, and (d) museums, libraries, and schools. Large, populous, wealthy—Constantinople surpassed any city in medieval western Europe.

BYZANTINE CONTRIBUTIONS TO CIVILIZATION

1. Codified Roman Law. Under Emperor Justinian, Byzantine legal experts collected and arranged Roman law (see pages 56-57).

2. Preserved Ancient Greek Civilization. Byzantine culture represented a continuation of classical knowledge, especially its Greek and Hellenistic aspects. The Byzantines spoke Greek. At the University of Constantinople, scholars cherished ancient manuscripts and studied classical literature, philosophy, and science. Thanks to Byzantine scholars, writings of the ancient Greeks, such as Homer, Plato, and Aristotle, were preserved for future generations.

Byzantine culture spread outside the Empire. It fascinated people in Russia and in much of the Balkans, and formed the foundation of their civilizations. In western Europe, Byzantine classical knowledge helped stimulate the revival of learning during the Later Middle Ages and the Renaissance.

3. Fostered Architecture and Art. In construction and decoration, the Byzantines made many original contributions. Their architects combined features of Greco-Roman and Persian architecture by devising a new structure—a rectangular building topped by a round dome. Their artists adorned building interiors with brilliant *mosaics*—decorations consisting of small colored pieces of glass, stone, or tile fitted together to form pictures or designs. Great skill and artistry went into the portrayal of Biblical stories and historical episodes. *Santa Sophia*, the famous church erected in the 6th century at Constantinople by the Emperor Justinian, is a noteworthy example of Byzantine architecture and art. Its plain but massive exterior contrasts with its sparkling and magnificent interior. Byzantine craftsmen also produced gold, silver, and glass objects that rank as works of art.

4. Shielded Western Europe. Because of its location, the Byzantine Empire received the first blows of invaders from the east, especially from the Arabs and Turks. By resisting these invaders, Byzantine forces indirectly were defending western Europe.

B. THE MOSLEM EMPIRE

MOHAMMED AND THE IDEALS OF ISLAM (MOHAMMEDANISM)

Mohammed (570-632) was born in the city of *Mecca*, in Arabia. He became a religious reformer who condemned his people's idol worship and urged a new religion. Because his attacks on idolatry aroused hostility in Mecca, he fled for his life to *Medina*, where the people accepted his religion, *Islam*. Mohammed's flight, or *Hegira*, in 622 marks the first year of the *Moslem* (Mohammedan) calendar.

Islam embodies the following principles:

1. There is no God but *Allah*, and Mohammed is His prophet. Man must submit to, praise, and glorify God.

2. Man must observe the following religious duties: (*a*) praying daily, (*b*) fasting during the Moslem month of Ramadan, and (*c*) if possible, making at least one pilgrimage to the Holy City of Mecca.

3. Man must follow a code of behavior that includes (*a*) giving alms to the poor, (*b*) shunning gambling and alcoholic beverages, (*c*) revering one's parents, and (*d*) treating all Moslems as brothers.

4. The faithful will be rewarded by luxurious eternal life. Moslems who die fighting for the faith are assured entrance to paradise.

Mohammed's teachings became the basis of the Moslem Bible, the *Koran*. (Some Islamic precepts—monotheism, a high moral code, and life after death—were drawn from Judaism and Christianity.)

THE ARABS SPREAD ISLAM (7TH AND 8TH CENTURIES)

The Arab tribes rapidly adopted the new Moslem religion, became unified, and prepared for conquest. The promise of paradise made the Arabs courageous warriors. In a short time, they carved out a great empire.

1. Northward. They annexed Palestine and Syria but were unable to destroy the Byzantine Empire and seize Constantinople.

2. Eastward. They subjugated Mesopotamia, Persia, and part of northwestern India.

3. Westward. They overwhelmed Egypt, the rest of northern Africa, and most of Spain. The Arabs also invaded France but were defeated by the Franks led by Charles Martel at the Battle of Tours (732). This clash halted Moslem expansion into western Europe.

As the Arabs acquired their Empire, they introduced the Moslem religion to their conquered peoples. Although the Arabs generally did not forcibly convert these peoples, many accepted Islam (*a*) to avoid special taxes on nonbelievers, and (b) because its ethical code and promise of eternal life appealed to them. Those persons who did not adopt Islam were usually allowed to pursue their own religion.

THE MOSLEM EMPIRE

1. Extent (in the 8th Century). The Moslem Empire, the largest and most populous empire of its time, extended from India to Spain. (See map, page 77.) Unified by Islam and the Arabs' military might, it was ruled by a *Caliph,* who served as both the religious and political leader. The Empire had its capital first at *Damascus* and later at *Bagdad.* These large, magnificent cities far surpassed those of western Europe in cleanliness and beauty.

2. Breakup of the Empire (by the 10th Century). Over a period of 200 years, the Moslem Empire gradually disintegrated, as rival chieftains gained absolute control of their own domains. By the 10th century, the Empire had been divided into a number of independent Moslem kingdoms.

3. Moslem Loss of Spain (by the 15th Century). Over a period of 400 years, the Moslem kingdoms in Spain were attacked and slowly conquered by the Christian states in Spain. In 1492, *Granada,* the last Moslem stronghold in Spain, fell to the Christians (see page 129).

THE TURKS CREATE A MOSLEM EMPIRE

By the 10th century many Turkish tribes of central Asia had adopted Islam. In the 11th century the *Seljuk Turks* seized Bagdad and for two centuries dominated the Moslem Middle East. As Seljuk Turkish power waned, the *Ottoman Turks* achieved Moslem leadership. In the 14th century they conquered part of the Balkans. In the 15th century, led by *Mohammed II,* they captured Constantinople (1453), ending the Byzantine Empire. (In the 16th and 17th centuries the Turks advanced deep into central Europe, twice failing to take Vienna, the capital of Austria. At the naval battle of *Lepanto* in 1571, the Turks were crushed by allied Christian fleets. After the 17th century Turkish power declined, and eventually the Turks were driven almost entirely out of Europe. See pages 217-218.)

MOSLEM CONTRIBUTIONS TO CIVILIZATION

While Christian European culture declined in the Dark Ages, the Arabs developed a flourishing civilization which spread throughout the Moslem world.

1. Education. The Moslems founded great universities, especially at Cairo in Egypt, Bagdad in Mesopotamia, and Cordova in Spain. These universities preserved and taught Greco-Roman culture. Classical learning provided a foundation for further advances by Moslem scholars, who were permitted to study and write with considerable freedom.

2. Mathematics. The Moslems (a) introduced *Arabic numerals* (adopted from India), which replaced the clumsy Roman numbering system, and (b) furthered the studies of algebra, geometry, and trigonometry.

3. Physical Science. The Moslems (a) prepared chemical compounds such as sulfuric acid and alcohol, (b) improved metal refining and cloth dyeing, and (c) gained new knowledge about the relationship between light and vision.

4. Medicine. The Moslems (a) used anesthetics (drugs that ease pain), (b) performed difficult surgery, particularly progressing in eye operations, and (c) compiled medical textbooks.

5. Agriculture. The Moslems improved farming methods by rotating crops and using fertilizer.

6. Industry. The Moslems excelled in making Cordovan leather, Damascus steel (especially swords), damask cloth, crystal glass, smooth paper, and exquisite rugs.

7. Navigation. The Moslems used the *mariner's compass* (probably adopted from China) to determine direction at sea. They believed the world to be round.

8. Literature. The Moslems esteemed books and maintained extensive libraries. Their famous literary works include the *Thousand and One Nights* (*Arabian Nights*) and the *Rubaiyat of Omar Khayyam*.

9. Language. The Moslems spread the Arabic language, which helped to culturally unify the Moslem world. Arabic is the source of some English words: alcohol, algebra, almanac, cipher, coffee, cotton, syrup, and sofa.

10. Architecture. The Moslems designed graceful *mosques* (temples) and palaces typified by rounded domes, tall slender minarets, and delicately carved lacelike decorative patterns, called *arabesques*. The *Alhambra* in Granada, Spain, is an outstanding example of Moslem architectural style.

11. Outstanding Scholars

  a. Avicenna (980-1037), Arabian philosopher and physician, utilized ancient Greek sources for his encyclopedic medical textbook, *Canon of Medicine*.

  b. Averroës (1126-1198), Spanish-Arabian physician and philosopher, wrote highly regarded commentaries upon Aristotle.

c. Maimonides (1135-1204), Jewish philosopher of the Moslem world and court physician to the Sultan of Egypt, attempted to reconcile Judaic faith with Aristotelian reason in his work, *Guide for the Perplexed.*

COMPLETION QUESTIONS

1. The capital of the Byzantine Empire, a city of paved streets and beautiful buildings, was _____.
2. The Byzantine Emperor who codified Roman law and extended the Empire to its greatest extent was _____.
3. The founder and chief prophet of Islam was _____.
4. "Praise be to Allah, Lord of the worlds" is the beginning of a prayer found in the Moslem bible, called the _____.
5. The last Moorish stronghold in Spain and site of the palace Alhambra was _____.

MULTIPLE-CHOICE QUESTIONS

1. Which was true of the Byzantine Empire? (1) It was established during the Augustan Age. (2) It was conquered by Charlemagne. (3) It lasted a thousand years after the "fall" of Rome. (4) It ended with the rise of Islam.
2. The culture of the Byzantine Empire was based chiefly upon the civilization of (1) India (2) Russia (3) Greece (4) China.
3. The wealth of the Byzantine Empire resulted from (1) agriculture (2) rich gold mines (3) trade and industry in luxury products (4) plunder seized in wars of conquest
4. The Byzantine Empire contributed to civilization by (1) utilizing ancient Greek democratic practices (2) transmitting Indian mathematical knowledge to Europe (3) shielding western Europe from Arab and Turkish invaders (4) originating the column.
5. The birthplace of Christianity, Judaism, and Islam was in (1) Africa (2) Asia (3) Europe (4) North America.
6. From which two cities did the religion of Islam spread? (1) Rome and Athens (2) Mecca and Medina (3) Constantinople and Damascus (4) Tours and Vienna.
7. In its original teachings, Islam differed from Judaism and Christianity in that Islam (1) lacked a high moral code (2) was not monotheistic (3) appealed strongly to the warrior class (4) did not believe in life after death.
8. Which battle is significant because it checked the spread of Islam in Europe? (1) Crécy (2) Dunkirk (3) Tours (4) Waterloo.
9. A country in which Moslem civilization did *not* develop was (1) Syria (2) Persia (3) Egypt (4) Denmark.
10. An Asiatic people who conquered the Arabs, accepted Mohammedanism, and swept into southeastern Europe were the (1) Turks (2) Russians (3) Magyars (4) Bulgarians.
11. Which of these was *not* a contribution of Arabic culture? (1) *The Thousand and One Nights* (2) masterpieces of stone sculpture (3) medical textbooks (4) architecture featuring minarets.
12. A significant contribution of Islamic culture to western Europe was (1) the introduction of important land reforms into feudal Europe (2) the establishment of the principle of separation of Church and State (3) advancements in mathematics and geography (4) placing of women in a superior position in society.
13. Avicenna, Averroës, and Maimonides—the three outstanding scholars of the Moslem world—were *not* all (1) philosophers (2) physicians (3) interested in ancient Greek writings (4) believers in Islam.

Part 4. The Later Middle Ages in Europe

THE CRUSADES (1095-1291)

1. Background. Late in the 11th century, the Byzantine Emperor at Constantinople appealed to the Roman Catholic Church for military aid against the Moslem Turks. The Catholic Church sympathized, partly because the Turks threatened Greek Orthodox Christianity, but mainly because the Moslems controlled Palestine, the Holy Land, and molested Christian pilgrims. Consequently, *Pope Urban II,* at the Council of Clermont in 1095, summoned western Christiandom to a religious war, or *Crusade,* to wrest the Holy Land from the Moslems.

The Pope's plea aroused enthusiasm among (a) religious persons who believed that "God wills it," (b) Christians who desired Papal forgiveness of their sins, (c) nobles who expected to acquire new lands and great riches, (d) middle-class merchants who wanted increased trade, (e) serfs who sought escape from feudal oppression, and (f) adventurers who welcomed travel and excitement.

2. Leading Events. Of seven major Crusades over a period of almost 200 years, the most significant were the First and Third Crusades.

The First Crusade, started in 1096, was a well-organized military expedition. Its outstanding leader was *Godfrey of Bouillon.* This Crusade drove the Moslems from part of Palestine, established a Christian kingdom in the Holy Land, and gained control of Jerusalem.

Nearly 100 years later, in 1187, Jerusalem was retaken by the Moslems, led by *Saladin.* The loss of the Holy City caused western Europe to undertake the Third Crusade.

The Third Crusade, started in 1189, was led by three Kings: *Frederick Barbarossa* of Germany, *Philip Augustus* of France, and *Richard the Lion-Hearted* of England. Although this Crusade failed to recapture Jerusalem, Richard persuaded Saladin to grant safe passage to Christian pilgrims.

Subsequent Crusades likewise failed to establish Christian rule in Palestine. By 1291 the Moslem Turks again completely controlled the Holy Land. They retained it until after World War I (1918).

3. Effects. Because the Crusades wrought great changes in western European life, they mark the beginning of the end of the Middle Ages.

a. Broadened the People's Outlook. The Crusaders were exposed to the Moslem and Byzantine civilizations, which were considerably superior to their own. They observed powerful governments, great cities, flourishing trade, prosperous industry, and progress in the arts and sciences. The

Crusaders also gained increased geographical knowledge. Upon returning home, they introduced new ideas and tastes.

b. Stimulated Trade and Towns. The Crusades increased European demand for Eastern products: spices, sugar, silk, rugs, paper, glassware, and precious stones. Accordingly, throughout western Europe, but especially in Italy, (1) trade increased, (2) money replaced barter, (3) towns grew in number and size, and (4) the bourgeoisie (middle class) acquired wealth and influence. (The Italian cities also grew richer by furnishing supplies to the Crusaders.)

c. Strengthened the Kings or Central Governments. The Crusades increased the kings' powers by: (1) *Weakening the nobility.* Some nobles sold their lands to raise money for their expeditions, thereby losing feudal power. Moreover, many powerful nobles were killed in the Crusades, thus removing a threat to royal power. (2) *Stimulating trade.* Since trade requires law and order, the rising merchant class opposed the feudal lords and supported the kings.

d. Weakened Serfdom. The Crusades enabled many serfs to escape from feudalism. (1) Some serfs gained freedom by joining the Crusades. (2) Other serfs paid for the use of the lord's land in money rather than in products and services. The lords preferred money to buy equipment for the Crusades or to purchase Eastern luxuries; the serfs earned money by selling surplus crops in nearby cities. Slowly, the feudal relationship between serf and lord evolved into the modern relationship of tenant and landlord. (3) Still other serfs fled to the growing cities. After spending a year and a day in a city, a serf became legally free.

e. Encouraged Learning. The Crusades stimulated European interest in education by showing that the Moslems had (1) preserved and utilized Greco-Roman knowledge, (2) maintained great universities, and (3) advanced in mathematics, science, literature, and art.

THE REVIVAL OF TRADE AND TOWNS

Starting in the 10th century, trade gradually revived as the ending of barbarian invasions permitted more settled conditions and safer transportation for persons and goods. Later, the Crusades heightened European demand for Eastern luxury products. Increased trade stimulated the growth of favorably located towns.

Since they provided facilities for storage, marketing, transportation, and production of goods, towns were essential to commerce. Medieval towns, first controlled by nearby feudal lords, later secured their freedom (1) by purchasing charters from a lord or king, or (2) more rarely, by successfully fighting for independence.

THE RISE OF THE BOURGEOISIE

As trade increased and towns grew, a new economic and social class evolved, the *bourgeoisie*, or townspeople. It consisted of enterprising persons: merchants, shopkeepers, bankers, and professional men. Since it stood between the lowest (serfs) and highest (lords) feudal classes, the bourgeoisie came to be known as the *middle class*.

LEADING MEDIEVAL TRADE CENTERS

1. In Italy. The cities of *Venice, Genoa, Pisa,* and *Naples* soon dominated trade between Europe and the eastern Mediterranean. These cities had the advantages of (*a*) Mediterranean location, and (*b*) a commercial tradition dating back to the Roman Empire. Italian ships carried European wheat, wine, lumber, and wool to such cities as *Alexandria* and *Constantinople,* and returned with valuable Eastern luxuries.

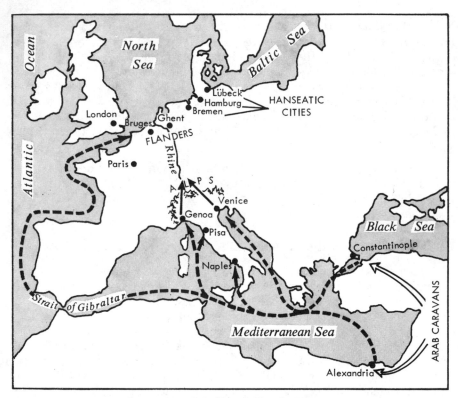

Important Medieval Trade Routes

2. In Belgium. *Bruges* and *Ghent,* cities in the Belgian province of Flanders, became the leading north European commercial centers. These Flemish cities were advantageously situated at the crossroads of the trade routes from northern Europe and Italy. The main trade routes from Italy went (*a*) across the Mediterranean, through the Strait of Gibraltar, and along the the Atlantic coast, and (*b*) across the Alps and down the Rhine River. (See map, page 86.)

The Flemish cities imported Eastern products from the Italian cities for sale throughout northern Europe. They also produced and exported their own woolen cloth.

3. In Northern Germany. *Bremen, Hamburg, Lübeck,* and other north German cities controlled trade in the Baltic and North Seas. In the 13th century these cities organized the *Hanseatic League.* In the 14th century, at the height of its power, the League included, not only German, but other north European cities. To promote the commercial interests of its members, the League (*a*) drove pirates from the northern seas, (*b*) banned non-League cities from trading in the area, and (*c*) maintained regulations for fair trade. The Hanse cities dealt chiefly in timber, grain, iron, leather, and salted fish.

TRADE FAIRS IN MEDIEVAL TOWNS

To foster trade, the Flemish cities, and later other northern European cities, sponsored fairs. These exhibitions, common by 1200, attracted (1) buyers and sellers of goods, (2) merchants from distant places who exchanged information and introduced new ideas, (3) entertainers who provided fun and frolic, and (4) common people who welcomed the relief from monotony.

THE GUILDS IN MEDIEVAL TOWNS

1. Merchant Guilds. These associations of merchants regulated *trade* within the town. They (*a*) taxed nonmember merchants to discourage competition, (*b*) encouraged fair business practices, such as honest weights and measures, exact quality standards, and uniform prices, (*c*) participated actively in town government, and (*d*) functioned as social clubs.

2. Craft Guilds. These associations of skilled craftsmen regulated *industry* within the town. A separate guild existed for each craft or occupation, such as bakers, candlemakers, weavers, tailors, and carpenters. The craft guilds undertook economic, educational, political, and social activities.

a. Economic Activities. They established wages and hours, quality of materials, standards of workmanship, production quotas, and prices. The guilds endeavored to set a *just price,* that is, a fair price for both producer and consumer.

b. Educational Activities. The craft guilds strictly regulated the training and advancement of workers. (1) The *apprentice*, or beginning worker, bound himself, generally without pay and for a seven-year period, to a master craftsman. The master supported him and taught him the craft, social manners, and morals. After this period, the apprentice might be promoted to the journeyman class. (2) The *journeyman*, or intermediate worker, could be employed in any shop in return for a daily wage. If he passed a test by producing a "masterpiece," he advanced to the master class. (3) The *master craftsman* could open his own shop, where he was both worker and owner.

c. Political and Social Activities. The craft guilds (1) were active in town government, (2) supported hospitals and provided special benefits for widows, orphans, and the sick, and (3) arranged holiday entertainment.

In summary, the craft guilds combined features of our modern labor unions, employer associations, political parties, and mutual aid societies.

LIFE IN MEDIEVAL TOWNS

1. Disadvantages. (*a*) Town streets were narrow, unpaved, unlighted, and unguarded. A citizen out alone at night faced danger. (*b*) Most town buildings were dark, dingy, constructed of wood, and close together. Fires spread rapidly from building to building. (*c*) Town walls, although providing protection against pirates, highwaymen, and feudal lords, prevented the town's physical expansion. (*d*) Town sanitation scarcely existed. Garbage dumped into streets or nearby rivers caused pollution. The towns suffered greatly from epidemics and plagues. The *Black Death* (1347-1350), a bubonic plague, alone killed about one-third of western Europe's population.

2. Advantages. In the Later Middle Ages, the towns attracted able and enterprising persons, mainly from the lower class. Towns offered (*a*) freedom from feudal restrictions, (*b*) a fuller, richer, more varied life than at the manor, (*c*) cultural and educational facilities, and (*d*) opportunities for economic advancement.

CULTURAL ACHIEVEMENTS OF WESTERN EUROPE DURING THE MIDDLE AGES

In the Dark Ages (5th to 10th centuries) western European culture retrogressed as a result of barbarian invasions, feudalism, and people's concern for the barest essentials of life. In the Later Middle Ages, western European culture began to progress because (1) the Catholic Church provided leadership and support, (2) the Crusades spread knowledge of the advanced Byzantine and Moslem civilizations, and (3) the new towns provided centers of culture and learning.

1. Architecture. Medieval people expressed their intensely religious spirit by constructing awe-inspiring cathedrals.

a. Romanesque Style. Before the 12th century architects designed cathedrals in the massive *Romanesque* style, derived from ancient Rome. This style featured thick walls, few windows, rounded arches, and strong columns. A famous example is the Cathedral in Pisa, Italy.

b. Gothic Style. Starting in the 12th century architects employed the more graceful *Gothic* style, originating in medieval France. This style utilized thin walls, flying buttresses, pointed arches, tall spires, gargoyles, and many stained-glass windows. Some notable Gothic cathedrals are *Notre Dame* in Paris and *Westminster Abbey* in London.

Romanesque Architecture:
The Cathedral at Pisa

Gothic Architecture:
The Cathedral of Notre Dame
in Paris

2. Higher Education. In the 11th and 12th centuries scholars founded many important universities: in France, the University of Paris; in Italy, the Universities of Bologna and Salerno; in England, the Universities of Oxford and Cambridge. Medieval universities taught geometry, astronomy, music, grammar, and logic—the basis of our modern liberal arts education. Students were prepared for careers in theology (religion), philosophy, law, and medicine. Except in religion, the universities relied chiefly on the writings of Aristotle, the ancient Greek scholar.

University students faced difficulties because they (*a*) were taught, not in their own tongue, but in the Church language, *Latin,* and (*b*) lacked books, libraries, laboratories, and comfortable classrooms.

3. Science and Invention. Medieval scientists were, in our modern sense, quite unscientific. They rarely experimented or questioned, mainly accepting popular superstitions and Aristotle's writings.

a. Alchemists, while attempting to transform less valuable metals into gold, gathered information that served as a basis for modern chemistry.

b. Astrologers, while seeking to foretell the future, furnished records of the planets and stars helpful to modern astronomy.

c. Inventors developed magnifying lenses, mechanical clocks, and glass windows.

d. Roger Bacon (1214-1294), alone of the medieval scientists, insisted that science requires experimentation and observation. Bacon's ideas were not accepted for several centuries.

4. Philosophy and Theology. Churchmen wrote books on philosophical and theological issues. Their method of using pure reason in the defense of faith is called *scholasticism.*

a. Peter Abelard (1079-1142), a famous medieval teacher, wrote *Sic et Non (Yes and No)*, which quoted differing views of Church leaders on many religious questions.

b. St. Thomas Aquinas (1225-1274), the greatest medieval philosopher, wrote *Summa Theologica,* which summarized Christian doctrine and denied any conflict between reason and religious faith. His philosophy was influenced by Aristotle.

5. Literature. Although few books were written, many kinds of literature flourished. Epic poems celebrated gallant heroes and stirring adventures. The outstanding medieval epics are *Beowulf,* an Anglo-Saxon (Old English) poem; the *Song of Roland,* a French epic; the *Niebelungenlied,* a German tale; and the *Song of Cid,* a Spanish work.

Beginning in the 11th century wandering musical entertainers, or minstrels —called *troubadours* in southern France and *minnesingers* in Germany— composed lyrical poems, mostly about love. Later medieval poets wrote *romances,* stories about love and adventure.

IDENTIFICATION QUESTIONS: WHO AM I?

Innocent III	Philip Augustus	Saladin
Mohammed II	Richard the Lion-Hearted	Thomas Aquinas
Peter Abelard	Roger Bacon	Urban II

1. I was the Pope who first issued the call for the Crusades.
2. As King of England, I played a leading part in the Third Crusade.
3. I was the medieval scientist who urged the method of experimentation.
4. I was the Moslem leader who drove the Christian forces from the Holy City.
5. A philosopher, I summarized Christian doctrine in the book *Summa Theologica.*

MULTIPLE-CHOICE QUESTIONS

1. The ancient city famous for religious shrines and chief goal of the Crusaders was (1) Constantinople (2) Rome (3) Jerusalem (4) Mecca.
2. An important result of the Crusades was that (1) the Turks lost interest in Constantinople (2) serfdom declined in western Europe (3) the Roman and Greek Churches were united (4) Italy was united into one nation.
3. An important result of the Crusades was (1) the permanent recovery of the Holy Land from the Moslems (2) a decrease in the number of cities in Europe (3) the beginning of the feudal period in Europe (4) an increase in trade between Europe and Asia.
4. An important effect of the Crusades upon western Europe was that the (1) kings lost power (2) Church lost power (3) kings gained power (4) feudal lords gained power.
5. The growth of trade in medieval Europe resulted in (1) invasions by German barbarians (2) the decline of banking (3) an increase in the power of the nobles (4) the rise of a middle class.
6. Which term generally refers to the merchant class? (1) bourgeoisie (2) journeymen (3) landed gentry (4) plebeians.
7. In the Later Middle Ages, merchants generally supported attempts of their monarchs to establish strong national states because the merchants (1) were assured a voice in the government (2) were forced by the Church to support the King (3) had become members of the aristocracy (4) favored a strong central government to preserve law and order.
8. A leading trade center of medieval times in southern Europe was (1) Athens (2) Madrid (3) Rome (4) Venice.
9. In the Middle Ages, Europe's main highway of trade was the (1) Atlantic Ocean (2) Mediterranean Sea (3) Indian Ocean (4) North Sea.
10. The Hanseatic League was established to (1) capture the Holy Land from the Turks (2) send trade expeditions to the Far East (3) turn back the Moslem invasion of western Europe (4) protect trade and commerce in the North and Baltic Seas.
11. A city *not* a member of the Hanseatic League was (1) Paris (2) Bremen (3) Lübeck (4) Hamburg.
12. Bruges and Ghent, the famous medieval trade centers, are located in (1) Italy (2) Germany (3) England (4) Belgium.
13. Medieval fairs were held chiefly for the purpose of (1) exchanging goods (2) buying and selling serfs (3) observing religious holidays (4) exhibiting famous works of art.
14. One purpose of a medieval merchant guild was to (1) drive nonmember merchants from its town (2) provide relief for the sick in its community (3) develop trade on a national scale (4) decorate its local cathedral.
15. An important function of the medieval craft guilds was to (1) encourage mass production of goods (2) encourage competition (3) promote free trade (4) establish an apprentice system to train craftsmen.
16. An important contribution of the medieval craft guilds was that they (1) encouraged the invention of machinery (2) set a just price for products (3) encouraged trade between nations (4) united the workers against the masters.
17. In the Middle Ages, which language did scholars in western Europe generally use? (1) English (2) French (3) Latin (4) Spanish.
18. An ancient Greek on whose science and philosophy medieval universities relied heavily was (1) Plato (2) Aristotle (3) Pericles (4) Herodotus.
19. Which feature identifies a Gothic cathedral? (1) tall spires (2) rounded arches (3) graceful minarets (4) gilded domes.

UNIT V. THE MIDDLE AGES: IN THE FAR EAST

Part 1. India: From Moslem Invasion to British Rule

INTRODUCTION

Following the destruction of the Gupta Empire in 535 (see page 24), northern India consisted of a large number of independent warring states. India's continuing political disunity and her great wealth attracted Moslem invaders.

By the 8th century the Moslem Arabs had extended their power and spread their religion to India's western neighbors, Persia and Afghanistan. For almost one thousand years thereafter, various Moslem peoples crossed India's northwest mountain passes, invaded the northern plain, and at times expanded into the Deccan. The Moslem conquests greatly influenced India's political and cultural development.

EARLY MOSLEM INVASIONS OF INDIA (8TH TO 10TH CENTURIES)

The Arabs conquered territories in the Indus River region of northwest India. These lands, at first part of the Moslem Empire, later became independent Moslem states.

EXPEDITIONS OF MAHMUD (998-1030)

Mahmud, a Turkish Moslem, who ruled in Afghanistan, led seventeen raids into India's northern plain—from the Indus to the Ganges—supposedly to spread the Islamic religion. Mahmud killed and enslaved Hindu natives, destroyed Hindu temples and artistic works, looted rich cities, and carried away much plunder. However, except for annexing the Punjab, a province of northwest India, Mahmud achieved no permanent conquests.

MOSLEM SULTANATE AT DELHI (LATE 12TH TO LATE 14TH CENTURIES)

Kutb-ud-din Aibak, a Turk and ex-slave, leading the Moslem forces from Afghanistan, destroyed the Hindu armies and conquered India's entire northern plain. Aibak established his capital at strategically located Delhi and ruled as Sultan, thus founding the Delhi Empire. Later Sultans extended Moslem power southward into the Deccan.

Despising Hinduism as idolatry, the Delhi Sultans tried to convert their conquered subjects to Islam. By persecuting Hindus and by offering tax benefits and social equality to converts, the Moslems gained new adherents, especially from the lowest castes. However, Hinduism survived as the religion of the overwhelming majority in India.

In the 14th century the Delhi Sultanate weakened, and portions became independent states, usually under Moslem rulers.

INVASION OF TAMERLANE (1398-1399)

Tamerlane, a Mongol warrior chieftain of central Asia, was one of history's great empire-builders. He ruled from Mesopotamia to Afghanistan. In 1398 he overran India's northern plain. Although Moslem, Tamerlane sacked Delhi and, it is estimated, slaughtered 100,000 persons, Moslems as well as Hindus. Inexplicably, Tamerlane soon withdrew from northern India, leaving that region physically desolated and politically disunited.

THE MOGUL EMPIRE (16TH TO 18TH CENTURIES)

Established by Mongol invaders from Afghanistan, the Mogul Empire was the last Moslem Empire in India. The outstanding Mogul Emperors were Babar and his grandson Akbar.

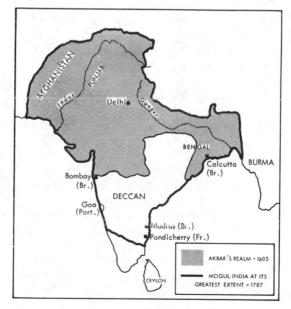

Mogul India

1. Babar (ruled 1526-1530), a descendant of Tamerlane, founded the Mogul Empire by conquering much of northern India, including Delhi.

2. Akbar (ruled 1556-1605), sometimes called "Akbar the Great," invigorated the Mogul Empire by a long, wise, and successful rule. (*a*) He extended the Empire's boundaries throughout the northern plain and southward into the Deccan. (*b*) To provide good government, he established a strongly centralized rule and a competent civil service. (*c*) Akbar supported religious tolerance and treated his realm's Hindu majority fairly. He removed the special tax upon non-Moslems, forbade slave raids upon the Hindus, and himself married a Hindu princess. (*d*) He encouraged learning and furthered art, architecture, and literature. He is rated one of history's outstanding monarchs.

Under Akbar's successors, the Empire continued to flourish but eventually declined. By the close of the 18th century, the Moguls no longer exercised power over most of India.

MOSLEM INFLUENCES UPON INDIA

1. Government. By conquest, the Moslem leaders became the ruling aristocracy, chiefly in northern and central India. (Hindu princes retained control mainly in the south.) Moslem rulers exercised absolute power over their own people and over the more numerous conquered Hindus.

2. Religion. The Moslem invasions greatly increased religious diversity in India. Some Hindus were converted to Islam; and by the 17th century Moslems in India totaled about 20 percent of the population. They were concentrated in two unconnected territories, the western (Indus) and eastern (Ganges) extremities of India's northern plain. Scattered Moslem communities existed elsewhere in India. The Moslems remained a distinctly separate group from India's overwhelming Hindu majority.

Moslems and Hindus generally regarded each other with hostility. (*a*) Islamic and Hindu beliefs conflicted with each other. For example, the Islamic belief in the brotherhood of all Moslems contradicted the caste system; the Moslem paradise in heaven contradicted the Hindu cycle of reincarnations; and the Moslem prohibition against the representation of humans clashed with the Hindu use of religious statues. (*b*) Most Moslem rulers tolerated Hinduism, but considered Hindus to be infidels. Some Moslem rulers inflicted oppressive taxes and forced labor upon the Hindus. The two peoples therefore remained antagonistic.

In 1947, when India became independent, Moslem-Hindu hostility resulted in the partition of the land into two states: Pakistan, chiefly Moslem; and India, chiefly Hindu.

3. Language. Arabic and Persian were introduced to India by the Moslem invaders. Persian served as the official language of the Mogul Empire. With the passing of time, elements of these two tongues and the native Hindi combined to form a hybrid language, *Urdu*. Today, Urdu is a national language of Pakistan.

4. Architecture. The Moslems constructed mosques, palaces, gateways, and tombs. In contrast with Hindu ornateness, Moslem structures had greater simplicity and showed the extensive use of the Moslem arch and dome.

The *Taj Mahal*, a marble edifice built in the 17th century by a Mogul Emperor as his wife's tomb, is an outstanding example of Moslem architecture. It conveys a sense of beauty, dignity, and grandeur.

Moslem Architecture in India: The Taj Mahal

COMING OF THE EUROPEANS (LATE 15TH TO 18TH CENTURIES)

In 1498, a few years before the Moguls invaded northern India, a Portuguese merchant ship under *Vasco da Gama* reached southwest India. This contact between western Europe and India was part of Europe's overseas expansion, called the *Commercial Revolution* (see pages 135-141). For many years, the Portuguese enjoyed a near-monopoly of the profitable India trade.

In the 17th century England and France—the leading European powers —each chartered East India companies and founded trading posts in India. The two nations quickly became rivals for India's trade and territory. Both trained native armies to add to their own forces and acquired allies among the native princes. By 1763, after a series of wars (see page 140), the English ended French power in India. Thereafter, the English, encountering no effective opposition from the decrepit Mogul Empire or the disunited princes, rapidly expanded their rule throughout the country.

The British conquest was unique, for, unlike previous conquerors of India, the British (1) came by sea, not by land, and (2) ultimately established their control over the entire country, not over only part. From the late 18th century onward, the history of India merges with the history of British imperialism (see page 317).

Part 2. China: Continued Rule by Dynasties

T'ANG DYNASTY (618-906)

1. **Strong Government and Revival of Confucianism.** T'ang rulers ended the four centuries of disunity and disorder that had followed the downfall of the Han Dynasty (see page 30). The T'ang Dynasty established a strongly centralized state based upon a revived Confucianism. To recruit government officials, T'ang rulers stressed civil service examinations and provided schools to train scholars. Examinations and schools created a demand for books. Not surprisingly, the T'ang Period witnessed the invention of block printing.

2. **Extent of Empire.** T'ang warriors expanded the Chinese Empire to its then greatest territorial extent: almost all of China proper; parts of Indo-China, Manchuria, Mongolia, and Tibet; and a vast region in central Asia.

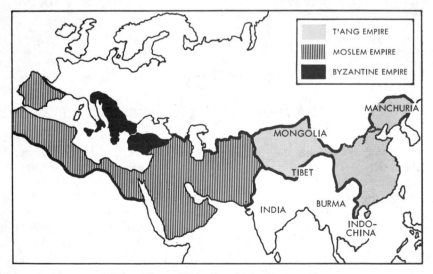

The T'ang Empire (8th Century)

The Chinese came in contact with most Asian peoples and even with eastern Europeans. The Chinese developed a flourishing international commerce. They also transmitted their culture, most notably to the Japanese.

3. Great Cultural Era. The T'ang Emperors encouraged a revival of scholarship and the arts. T'ang writers produced a great literary outpouring, especially of poetry. T'ang artists excelled in portrait and landscape paintings. They often decorated pottery, examples of which are highly prized in Western museums.

In governmental stability, territorial extent, economic prosperity, and cultural progress, the T'ang Era rivaled the Han. Many Chinese consider the T'ang Era their country's most brilliant period.

SUNG DYNASTY (960-1279)

1. A Maritime Nation. Out of the half century of political turmoil that followed the downfall of the T'ang, emerged the Sung Dynasty. Surrounded by powerful warlike neighbors, Sung rulers never controlled all of China proper and, in their later period, retreated southward below the Yangtze River.

Since land trade routes were in hostile hands, Sung China became a maritime nation. Her merchant ships sailed southward in the Pacific as far as Java, and westward in the Indian Ocean and the Arabian Sea as far as Africa. By the 11th century, Chinese seamen were navigating by means of a mariner's compass.

2. Social and Economic Reforms. In the 11th century, under Chief Minister *Wang An-shih*, the Sung state imposed a program of reform that (*a*) centralized the control of finances, commerce, and transportation, (*b*) spread the tax burden more equitably among all classes, (*c*) employed hired hands, instead of conscript labor, on state projects, (*d*) provided government loans at low interest rates to needy farmers, and (*e*) stored food surpluses for distribution during periods of shortage. The reform program, encountering upper class opposition and generating fear of too much government, was soon abandoned.

3. Continuation of Chinese Culture. In many respects, the Sung Period continued along T'ang lines. (*a*) Sung rulers centralized government, promoted education, and retained the Confucian civil service examinations, although adding many practical questions. (*b*) Sung artists and writers maintained high standards in painting and literature.

CHINA: PART OF THE MONGOL EMPIRE

1. The Mongol Empire. *Genghis Khan* (meaning "Universal Ruler"), a cruel and destructive military genius, founded the Mongol Empire. By the

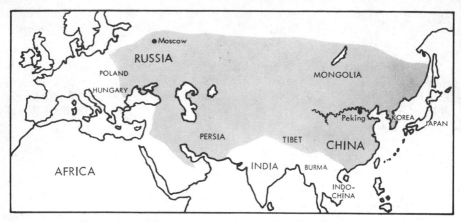

The Mongol Empire at Its Height (13th Century)

early 13th century he had united his people, the nomadic tribes of Mongolia, into a powerful military force. Then, within a 25-year period, Genghis Khan conquered vast areas: Korea and northern China, central Asia, Persia and the Middle East, and part of European Russia. The great Khan's immediate successors extended Mongol power into central Europe: Hungary, Poland, and Austria. His grandson, *Kublai Khan,* subjugated Sung China. The unified Mongol Empire, the largest known up to that time, was short-lived. By the late 13th century it had disintegrated into a number of independent states.

2. The Mongol Dynasty in China (1279-1368)

a. The Wars of Kublai Khan. This conqueror of the southern Sung state reunited the Chinese Empire. However, his efforts to annex Indo-China, Burma, Java, and Japan failed. He sent two unsuccessful naval expeditions against Japan.

b. A Period of Cultural Interchange. As part of the Mongol Empire, China entered upon a great cultural interchange with the rest of Asia and with Europe. At this time, Europeans probably learned of China's gunpowder and printing. The Chinese imported the sorghum (cereal) plant, probably from India, adopted the Arab method of sugar refining, and used Persian techniques in ceramic arts. China's wealth and culture attracted many foreign travelers, including Persians and Arabs, and some Europeans. From western Europe came Catholic missionaries and Italian merchants, most notably *Marco Polo.* His book describing his visit to prosperous Cathay (China) aroused great European interest in the Far East.

c. Mongol Rule and Decline. Kublai Khan and his successors improved roads and canals, provided care for the orphaned and sick, and generally allowed religious tolerance. Although the Mongol Emperors tried to rule in the Chinese tradition, the Chinese always regarded the Mongols as aliens. In the early 14th century Mongol power in China declined rapidly. In 1368, after a series of rebellions, the Mongols were forced to withdraw from China.

MING DYNASTY (1368-1644)

1. Prosperity and Maritime Activity. The Ming Era experienced a high level of economic prosperity. Chinese architects erected city walls, temples, and palaces to beautify the southern capital, *Nanking,* and the northern capital, *Peking.* Chinese naval designers constructed great armadas. Between 1405 and 1431 seven expeditions carried Chinese manpower and goods, and Chinese culture, to the lands of the Pacific and Indian oceans.

2. A Holding Period: Militarily and Culturally. The Ming did not attain the grandeur or brilliance of the Han or T'ang Periods. Ming domains were smaller, and Ming warriors generally were on the defensive against Mongol land attacks and Japanese sea raids. Ming rulers retained the previous governmental organization, law codes, and civil service examinations. They made

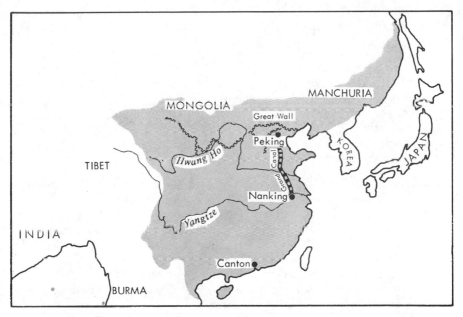

Ming China

little effort to adjust to new conditions. Ming painters and writers imitated past works and preserved past thoughts but produced little that was original.

3. Renewed Contacts With Europe. Contacts between China and Europe were renewed during the Ming Era and have continued unbroken to this day. Russian adventurers traversed the vast Siberian lands and contacted northern China. From western Europe came Roman Catholic missionaries. West European merchants, under the impetus of the Commercial Revolution (see pages 135-136), sailed halfway around the world to southern China. In 1514 the first Portuguese merchant ship arrived; Spanish, Dutch, and English ships followed. The west Europeans, confined to trade in the Canton area, introduced important New World plants: Indian corn, sweet potatoes, peanuts, and tobacco. Nevertheless, the total European impact upon Ming China remained small.

CHINESE ACHIEVEMENTS DURING THE MIDDLE AGES

1. Art and Architecture. Chinese artists during the Middle Ages painted on walls, ceramics, and silk rolls using brush pens, ink, and water colors. They depicted religious themes and nature studies, especially of landscapes. A favorite landscape scene portrayed majestic mountains and seas against which man appeared insignificant. During the T'ang Period lived the man who is often considered China's outstanding painter, *Wu Tao-hsüan*.

Chinese architects planned cities, and constructed impressive temples and vast palaces with beautiful gardens.

2. Literature. Chinese writers, encouraged by the invention of printing, produced extensive literary works: poetry, drama, and prose. The prose dealt with such subjects as history, government, geography, architecture, medicine, commerce, and everyday life, as well as fiction. The Chinese prepared many dictionaries and encyclopedias. The T'ang Period claims two outstanding Chinese poets. (*a*) *Li Po*, a master of words, created an imaginary world of lyric beauty. (*b*) *Tu Fu*, more of a realist, depicted human suffering.

3. Inventions. (*a*) In the 6th century the Chinese invented gunpowder, which they first used for festive fireworks. By the 12th century they were employing gunpowder for military purposes. (*b*) In the 7th century the Chinese printed books from carved wooden blocks. China's earliest known printed books, from the T'ang and Sung eras, are beautiful works of art. In the 11th century the Chinese evolved printing by movable type. (*c*) In the 11th century Chinese navigators determined direction from the magnetic needle enclosed in a mariner's compass. (*d*) Some sources credit the Chinese with developing an inoculation against smallpox.

However, these advances did not result from the methodical application of scientific principles. Despite their practical-mindedness, the Chinese did not develop theories of science and logical methods of scientific research.

4. Engineering. Chinese engineers built roads, bridges, and city walls, dredged river channels, erected sea and river dikes, and expanded irrigation and canal systems. China's man-made waterways, extending over hundreds of miles, were known as the *Grand Canal*.

MANCHU DYNASTY (1644-1912)

1. Introduction. Although coming after the Middle Ages, the Manchu Period is included in this section because the Manchus were China's last dynasty. Manchu China was followed by the Chinese Republic and, more recently, by Communist China. The Manchus received the full impact of European overseas expansion, first felt in China during the Ming Era. Manchu policies toward Westerners help explain modern China's history.

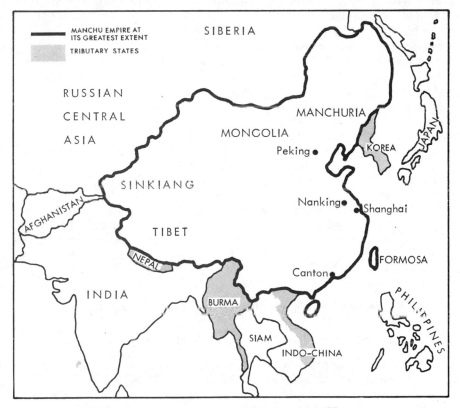

The Manchu Empire at Its Greatest Extent

2. Manchu Power and Government. With Ming China torn by rebellion, Manchu invaders swept down from Manchuria and seized the country. The invaders required Chinese men to show their loyalty by adopting the Manchu headdress: a shaved head with a *queue* (pigtail). The Manchus ruled the largest Chinese Empire ever: China proper, the island of Formosa, and the outlying provinces of Manchuria, Mongolia, Sinkiang, and Tibet. The first Manchu rulers also received tribute from Korea, Burma, Nepal, and part of Indo-China. To prevent uprisings, the Manchus stationed garrisons in strategic cities.

The Manchus ruled as Chinese Emperors, using Chinese officials and observing Chinese traditions. Until 1800 the Manchu Dynasty provided strong rule, maintained peace, and furthered prosperity. During these years, China's population expanded to an estimated 300,000,000. During the 19th century, however, the Manchu Dynasty lost its vigor and began to decline.

3. Policies Toward Westerners (Into the 19th Century). During the Manchu Era, China attracted an ever-increasing number of Westerners—missionaries, diplomats, and merchants. Overland came the Russians; by sea came the west Europeans, especially the French and English; and, in 1784, the first American merchant ship arrived in China.

The Manchus pursued the following policies toward the Westerners: (*a*) Manchu rulers viewed the Occidentals as inferior beings and denied diplomatic recognition to Western governments, since that would imply equality. (*b*) Manchu scholars held Chinese civilization as superior, considered Western culture as barbarous, and refused to see what they could learn from it. (*c*) Manchu officials restricted Western merchant ships to the port of Canton, imposed import duties unfairly, openly demanded bribes, and subjected the Western merchants to personal indignities. Despite these difficulties, Western merchants continued to come and reap great profits from cargoes of Chinese tea, silk, and porcelains.

When the European nations became aware of China's weakness, however, they used force to impose their will upon China. From the 1840's onward, the history of China merges with the history of European imperialism (see page 307).

Part 3. Japan: From Earliest Days to Nineteenth Century

GEOGRAPHIC FACTORS INFLUENCING JAPAN

1. Location. Japan consists of four major and many smaller islands in the northern Pacific, with a land area about the size of California. The islands extend in an arclike shape off the Asian mainland, some 100 miles from Korea and 500 miles from China. Even before modern transportation, Japan was

Japan: Geographic Factors

close enough to China to be affected by her history and culture, but still distant enough to develop a distinct Japanese way of life and retain a sense of isolation. Until World War II Japan was never occupied by an enemy, and the Japanese considered their homeland to be divinely protected.

2. Mountains. The mountains of Japan provide great natural beauty but limit the farming area to less than 20 percent of the land surface. The mountains are poor in mineral resources except for a meager supply of coal. The geography of Japan encouraged the Japanese to become a seafaring people, interested in fishing and trade. In the last century Japan has turned to industry.

HISTORY OF JAPAN (TO THE 19TH CENTURY)

1. Prehistoric Japan (to the 6th Century A.D.). Japan's early history is little known because the Japanese developed writing at a late date and until the 6th century A.D. left no accurate written records.

According to legend, the gods created Japan, and their descendant, *Jimmu,* became the first Emperor of Japan in 660 B.C.

According to modern research, the ancestors of the modern Japanese were probably immigrants who came from northeastern Asia by way of Korea.

Also, some immigrants probably came from southern China and the Malayan Peninsula. These early Japanese formed a number of petty states, each headed by a ruling family, or clan. By the 4th century A.D. the *Yamato* clan established a vague leadership over the other clans and became Japan's imperial family.

2. Japan Adopts Chinese Culture (6th to 9th Centuries). For three centuries, the primitive Japanese enthusiastically absorbed the advanced Chinese civilization, mainly of China's brilliant T'ang Era (see pages 96-97). All aspects of Japanese life were affected.

a. Religion. Buddhist missionaries, coming from the Asian continent, gained converts, especially among the aristocracy. By the 8th century Buddhism was widespread in Japan. Also brought from China to Japan was the philosophy of Confucius. Japanese society approved the Confucian ideal of strong family ties.

The Bronze Buddha at Kamakura in Japan

b. Art. Buddhist missionaries introduced many Chinese artistic achievements: Buddhist temple architecture, sculptured figures, and religious paintings.

c. Writing and Literature. The Japanese adapted the complex Chinese writing system to their spoken tongue. Also, they shared in China's rich literary heritage and imitated Chinese writings: poetry, history, and especially the Confucian classics.

d. Government. Following the example of T'ang China, the Japanese exalted the position of the Emperor, established a centralized government, and adopted a modified civil service examination system.

3. Feudalism in Japan Under the Shogunates (12th to 19th Centuries).
By the 12th century Japan's imperial central government proved too weak to maintain law and order. The country thereupon entered upon a 700-year feudal period of rule by the warrior class.

a. Organization of Feudal Japan. (1) The **Mikado,** or Emperor, ruled in theory but in reality was powerless. (2) The **shogun,** or most influential lord, controlled military affairs, as well as justice, lawmaking, and finance. (3) The **daimios,** or local lords, held landed estates and maintained private armies. (4) The **samurai,** or warriors, served in the lords' armies. They observed a warrior's code, *bushido.* This code of chivalry emphasized compliance with daily etiquette, contempt for physical danger, and loyalty to the feudal lord. (5) At the bottom of society were the **peasants,** who worked the land. Commoners could not advance to aristocratic status because of rigid class distinctions.

The feudal government and society of Japan in many ways resembled those of feudal Europe. (See pages 65-68.)

b. Major Shogunates. (1) *Kamakura Shogunate (1192-1333).* The Kamakura shoguns, representing various aristocratic families, ruled from the military capital of *Kamakura.* They shaped Japan's feudal system of land grants in exchange for military services. (2) *Ashikaga Shogunate (1338-1573).* The shoguns of the *Ashikaga* family exercised only vague control and proved unable to prevent recurring civil wars. (3) *Tokugawa Shogunate (1603-1867).* The shoguns of the *Tokugawa* family maintained peace and furthered prosperity. *Tokyo,* their political capital, became the nation's leading economic and cultural center. The Tokugawa accustomed the people to centralized military control, but their strong rule delayed Japan's evolution from a feudal structure to modern nationhood.

c. Important Foreign Developments of Feudal Japan

(1) *Withstood the Mongols.* In the late 13th century Japanese warriors withstood two separate Mongol invasion attempts. The second invasion fleet, in 1281, was destroyed with the help of a typhoon. The Japanese hailed this typhoon as the *kamikaze,* the "divine wind," the protector of their sacred homeland.

(2) *Failed to Conquer the Mainland. Hideyoshi,* a feudal general, gained control of Japan in the late 16th century and determined to conquer China. As a first step, Hideyoshi invaded Korea, but his death soon ended Japan's first attempt at overseas conquest.

(3) *First Welcomed but Then Excluded Western Influence.* In the last half of the 16th century Western ships reached Japan. First came Portuguese merchants. Then the Spanish, Dutch, and English followed. In 1549 came a group of Jesuit missionaries led by *St. Francis Xavier.* Japanese converts to Catholicism soon numbered many thousands, and Japanese feudal lords and European merchants developed a mutually profitable trade.

In the first half of the 17th century Japanese leaders became fearful that European missionary and trade activities would result in foreign conquest. Consequently, Japan withdrew into isolation. Japanese rulers expelled the missionaries, wiped out Christianity among the Japanese, and, except for a single Dutch station, closed all European trading posts. Until the middle of the 19th century, Japan remained isolated from Western civilization. (For the opening of Japan in 1853-1854 and subsequent developments, see pages 312-316.)

ASPECTS OF JAPANESE CULTURE

1. Importance of Foreign Influence. The Japanese talent for learning from foreign civilizations first evidenced itself from the 6th to 9th centuries when primitive Japan accepted the superior culture of China. (This capacity to learn reappeared (*a*) in the 19th century, when feudal Japan transformed herself into a modern, unified, industrialized nation along Western lines, and (*b*) in the 20th century, when Japan seemingly shed her militarist dictatorship for the democratic institutions of her World War II conqueror, the United States.)

The medieval Japanese did not merely imitate. By gradually modifying and building upon the borrowed Chinese culture, Japan created her own unique civilization.

2. Language and Literature. The Japanese used the complex Chinese characters both in their original Chinese meaning and for a simpler, phonetic system. From the 8th century onward, the Japanese developed their own literature: poetry, drama, history, and the novel. A favorite romantic theme extolled Japanese military valor. In the 11th century the court lady *Murasaki* wrote a world-famous novel of love and adventure, the *Tale of Genji.*

3. Arts. Japanese artists, following the style of the Chinese, created Buddhist religious paintings as well as landscapes, especially scenes of Japan's snow-topped mountain, *Fujiyama.* Japanese architects constructed beautiful palaces and temples set in elaborate gardens. Japanese sculptors carved impressive statues of Buddhist divinities.

4. Government Officials. Although they borrowed the Chinese method of selecting government officials by civil service examinations, the Japanese conformed to their rigid class distinctions by restricting the examinations to the aristocracy.

5. Religion. While accepting Buddhist and Confucian doctrines from China, the Japanese retained their native religion, *Shintoism*. This was a form of nature worship inspired by awe in the presence of natural wonders. However, it lacked significant moral content. For many centuries, Shintoism was blended with Buddhism and was not a separate religion. Then, in the 18th century, it was revived as a national religion with many temples, shrines, and formal ceremonies. (In the 19th century, after Japan became a modern nation, state Shintoism extolled Japanese nationalism. It was then that great emphasis was given to ancestor worship and to the belief that the Emperor descended from the gods.)

6. Good Manners and Aesthetic Appreciation. In vivid contrast to their military emphasis, the Japanese displayed a sensitivity in human relations and a love of beauty. They prized good manners and respected personal dignity, a trait that Westerners have often termed "face."

IDENTIFICATION QUESTIONS: WHO AM I?

Aibak	Genghis Khan	Marco Polo
Akbar	Hideyoshi	Tamerlane
Babar	Jimmu	Tu Fu
da Gama	Kublai Khan	Wang An-shih
Francis Xavier	Li Po	Wu Tao-hsüan

1. As ruler of the Mogul Empire in India, I extended its boundaries, provided good government, enforced religious tolerance, encouraged culture, and earned the title "the Great."
2. A great conqueror, I led a single Mongol invasion of northern India, caused much destruction of life and property, and then withdrew.
3. As chief minister during the Sung Era, I introduced a program of social and economic reform that encountered much opposition and was soon abandoned.
4. I united the Mongol tribes and led them in wars of conquest, founding a vast Empire.
5. I conquered the southern Sung state and reunited it with the rest of China—all within the Mongol Empire.
6. An Italian merchant, I traveled overland to China and, upon my return home, described my experiences in a book.
7. I lived during the T'ang Period, and my works have earned me the title of China's outstanding painter.
8. I was a Japanese feudal lord whose efforts to conquer Korea and China ended with my death.
9. A Jesuit missionary, I introduced Catholicism to Japan and won many converts.

MULTIPLE-CHOICE QUESTIONS

1. The invaders who entered northern India from the 8th to the 15th centuries were all (1) Arabs (2) Huns (3) Mongols (4) Moslems.
2. The attitude of the 13th-century Delhi Sultans toward Hinduism was one of (1) active support (2) persecution (3) indifference (4) tolerance.

3. By the 17th century much of the Moslem population in India was concentrated in the (1) southernmost tip (2) Deccan (3) Ganges Valley (4) Himalaya Mountains.

4. Many Moslem rulers accused the Hindus of idolatry because the Hindus (1) accepted caste (2) believed in reincarnation (3) considered the cow sacred (4) carved religious statues.

5. By the 17th century, of India's total population, the Moslems constituted (1) 5 percent (2) 20 percent (3) 50 percent (4) 70 percent.

6. The Taj Mahal was a famous (1) Hindu temple (2) Hindu palace (3) Moslem mausoleum (4) Moslem victory arch.

7. The European nation that first reached India by sea and monopolized India's trade for many years was (1) Portugal (2) England (3) France (4) Holland.

8. Unlike previous conquerors of India, the British (1) won the Indians' loyalty by prohibiting Mohammedanism (2) sought no profits (3) won control over the entire country (4) declined to introduce foreign ways.

9. A period of Chinese history that compared favorably with the Han Period in military power, economic prosperity, and cultural achievement was the (1) T'ang (2) Sung (3) Ming (4) Manchu.

10. Most similar to the 11th-century economic reforms under the Sung is today's United States law (1) establishing minimum wages (2) providing social security (3) authorizing the government to purchase agricultural surpluses (4) prohibiting false labeling.

11. At its greatest extent, the Mongol Empire stretched westward from the Pacific Ocean to (1) Persia (2) Sinkiang (3) European Russia (4) central Europe.

12. Under Mongol rule, China (1) conquered Japan (2) exchanged ideas with the rest of Asia and Europe (3) destroyed Confucianism (4) withdrew into isolation.

13. Which was *not* a contribution of China to civilization? (1) Gothic architecture (2) gunpowder (3) the mariner's compass (4) movable type printing.

14. The Communist Chinese today, to buttress their claims to additional territories in Asia, would use a map of (1) 13th-century Sung China (2) 16th-century Ming China (3) early 19th-century Manchu China (4) 10th-century Sung China.

15. The attitude that Manchu China first adopted toward Western merchants and culture was one of (1) welcome (2) tolerance (3) indifference (4) hostility.

16. The geographic relationship of the Asian continent to Japan is similar to the relationship of Europe to (1) Spain (2) England (3) Denmark (4) the United States.

17. By the 9th century A.D. the Japanese had (1) developed an inbred culture (2) borrowed heavily from China's culture (3) adopted Hinduism from India (4) driven Catholic missionaries from their country.

18. Feudal Europe's closest counterpart to the shogun of feudal Japan was the (1) Mayor of the Palace (2) Pope (3) knight (4) King.

19. Japan's last, or Tokugawa, Shogunate (1) failed to maintain law and order (2) caused economic ruin (3) drove out Buddhist priests (4) delayed Japan's development as a modern nation.

20. Japanese suicide pilots in World War II were called "kamikaze" after a (1) Japanese military leader who invaded Korea (2) Shinto god (3) typhoon that helped destroy a Mongol invasion fleet (4) awesome Japanese mountain.

21. Why did Japan isolate herself from Western civilization in the 17th century? (1) Few Japanese had converted to Catholicism. (2) The Japanese resented the poor quality of European goods. (3) The Japanese discovered their own deposits of iron ore. (4) The Japanese feared that European missionary and trade activities would lead to military conquest.

22. Which was *not* an aspect of Japanese culture? (1) a complex system of writing (2) equality of all classes (3) Shinto emphasis on nature worship (4) respect of good manners and personal dignity.

Section Three. Modern History

UNIT VI. THE TRANSITION:
FROM MEDIEVAL TO MODERN EUROPE

Part 1. The Renaissance: A Rebirth of Learning

THE RENAISSANCE PERIOD (14TH THROUGH 17TH CENTURIES)

The *Renaissance,* meaning rebirth or revival, was a period of approximately 300 years marking the transition between medieval and modern western Europe.

DISTINCTIVE FEATURES OF THE RENAISSANCE

The Renaissance (1) began with the rediscovery of the pagan Greco-Roman civilization, which had been generally neglected by the religious-minded Christian medieval world, (2) emphasized reason, a questioning attitude, and free inquiry—in contrast to the medieval concern with faith, authority, and tradition, (3) viewed life not as preparation for the hereafter, but as worthwhile for its own sake, and (4) featured great achievements in literature, art, and science.

THE RENAISSANCE STARTS IN ITALY

The Renaissance arose in the Italian cities because: (1) The center of Greco-Roman culture, Italy contained sculpture, buildings, roads, and manuscripts that excited curiosity about classical civilization. (2) Located on the Mediterranean, Italy had absorbed stimulating new ideas from the advanced Byzantine and Moslem worlds. (3) Benefiting from the revival of trade, Italy had wealthy, influential people who became *patrons* (supporters) of literature, art, and science. The leading Renaissance patrons were certain Popes in *Rome,* wealthy merchants in *Venice,* the *Sforza* family in *Milan,* and the *Medici* family in *Florence.*

THE RENAISSANCE SPREADS

In the 15th century Renaissance ideas began to spread from Italy to France, the German states, Holland, and England. This cultural diffusion resulted from religious, military, and commercial contacts. Also, many northern scholars traveled to Italy to absorb Italian art and learning.

HUMANISM ILLUSTRATES THE RENAISSANCE SPIRIT

Humanism, a literary movement started in 14th-century Italy, typified the Renaissance spirit.

1. Humanism concerned itself, not with religious matters, but with everyday human problems.

2. Humanism drew its inspiration from classical civilization. Humanists eagerly sought, studied, and publicized ancient Greek and Roman manuscripts.

3. Humanism revived interest, chiefly among educated people, in literature and writing.

4. Early humanists were the following:

a. Petrarch (1304-1374), an Italian, wrote beautiful sonnets expressing romantic love and appreciation of nature. He studied the classics and, in longer works, imitated the style of classical poets.

b. Erasmus (1466?-1536), a Hollander, was a brilliant classical scholar. In his book *Praise of Folly,* he ridiculed superstition, prejudice, upper class privileges, and Church abuses. By satirizing social evils, Erasmus encouraged people to think about reforms.

c. Sir Thomas More (1478-1535), an Englishman, wrote *Utopia,* a book that portrayed an ideal country—free from war, injustice, poverty, and ignorance. (The word *utopia* now refers to any ideal state.)

THE VERNACULAR REPLACES LATIN IN LITERATURE

In the Middle Ages Latin was the language of literature, of the Church, and of educated people in western Europe. Over the centuries, however, other tongues had been evolving through everyday usage. These were the *vernacular,* or *national,* languages, such as French, Italian, Spanish, German, and English.

At the end of the Middle Ages, writers began to use these vernacular languages, and later writers discarded Latin entirely. Two early great writers of the vernacular were Dante and Chaucer.

1. **Dante** (1265-1321), the "father of modern Italian," was the first to write an important work in that language. His *Divine Comedy,* a long poem, ranks among the greatest literary masterpieces. It describes Dante's imaginary trip through Hell, Purgatory, and Heaven, during which one of his guides is the Roman poet Vergil.

2. Chaucer (1340?-1400) used English in his *Canterbury Tales*, a collection of stories in verse supposedly related by pilgrims journeying to the religious shrine at Canterbury.

THE INVENTION OF PRINTING ENCOURAGES LITERATURE

About 1450 printing with movable type was invented by a German, *Johann Gutenberg*. As compared to medieval hand-copying of books, printing tremendously increased output and accuracy, and decreased cost. Inexpensive printed materials afforded all people opportunities for literacy and learning. Moreover, the availability of printing encouraged talented men to write.

RENAISSANCE LITERARY ACHIEVEMENTS

1. Machiavelli (1469-1527), an Italian, discussed ethics and government in his book *The Prince*. It describes how rulers maintained their power by methods that ignored right or wrong. Their philosophy was that "the end justifies the means." (Our word *Machiavellian* signifies "cunning and unscrupulous.")

2. Rabelais (1494?-1553), a Frenchman, wrote *Gargantua* and *Pantagruel*, portraying a comic world of giants whose adventures satirized education, politics, and philosophy.

3. Montaigne (1533-1592), a Frenchman, wrote *Essays*, expressing skepticism toward accepted beliefs, condemning superstition and intolerance, and urging man to live nobly. This work is sometimes judged the best example of the essay form.

4. Cervantes (1547-1616), a Spaniard, ridiculed feudal society, especially knighthood and chivalry, in his masterpiece, *Don Quixote*.

5. Shakespeare (1564-1616), an Englishman, is often considered as the greatest poet and playwright of all time. With sublime poetic insight and superb dramatic technique, he probed deeply into human character. Shakespeare's best-known plays include *Romeo and Juliet*, *A Midsummer Night's Dream*, *Hamlet*, *Julius Caesar*, and *Macbeth*.

6. Milton (1608-1674), an Englishman, retold the Biblical story of the Creation and the Garden of Eden in his epic poem, *Paradise Lost*. He also strongly advocated freedom of the press in an essay, *Areopagitica*.

7. Molière (1622-1673), a Frenchman, was the leading comic dramatist of French literature. Among his notable plays are *The Misanthrope* and *The Imaginary Invalid*.

CHARACTERISTICS OF RENAISSANCE ART

1. Renaissance art was considerably influenced by the artistic achievements of classical Greece and Rome. Particularly in sculpture and architecture. Renaissance artists often imitated classical works.

2. Renaissance painting emphasized realism, attention to detail, and desire for perfection.

3. Early Renaissance painters treated religious themes with a lifelike approach. Later Renaissance painters, also employing a realistic style, chose worldly subjects—landscapes, portraits, and scenes of everyday life—as well as Biblical events.

4. Renaissance art evokes admiration even today. It attracts tourists to western Europe, visitors to art museums, and collectors to art auction sales. A da Vinci painting was purchased in 1967 by Washington's National Gallery of Art for a reputed record price of $5 million to $6 million.

RENAISSANCE ARTISTIC ACHIEVEMENTS

ITALIAN

1. **Giotto** (1266?-1337), a painter, realistically portrayed religious themes in his many frescoes (paintings on walls), such as *St. Francis Preaching to the Birds.*

2. **Ghiberti** (1378-1455), a sculptor, created exquisite bronze doors for a church in Florence.

3. **Donatello** (1386?-1466), a sculptor, carved many figures of men on horseback. He is famous for his life-size statue of St. George in armor.

4. **Leonardo da Vinci** (1452-1519) was the ideal Renaissance man, a versatile genius skilled as a painter, sculptor, architect, musician, engineer, and scientist. He excelled in military engineering and devised equipment for scaling walls. He studied anatomy thoroughly and from his observations of animals sketched a parachute and a flying machine. He painted such masterpieces as *The Last Supper* and the *Mona Lisa.*

5. **Michelangelo** (1475-1564) was another many-sided Renaissance genius, talented as a painter, sculptor, poet, and architect. He painted beautiful Biblical scenes and figures on the ceiling of the *Sistine Chapel* in the Vatican; carved the *Pietà*, showing the dead Christ and His mother, Mary; carved massive statues of Old Testament figures, *David* and *Moses;* and designed the dome of *St. Peter's Cathedral* in Rome.

6. **Titian** (1477-1576), a painter, used vivid colors in his portraits of famous people and in his *Assumption of the Virgin.*

St. Peter's Cathedral, Rome   The *Mona Lisa* by Leonardo da Vinci

7. Raphael (1483-1520), a painter, captured tranquil beauty in many religious works, such as the *Sistine Madonna.*

8. Palestrina (1526?-1594), a composer, wrote church music still played today.

SPANISH

1. El Greco (1547-1614), a Greek who settled in Spain, painted many religious scenes, such as the *Crucifixion.*

2. Velasquez (1599-1660), official painter to the court of Spain, did many portraits of royalty. He commemorated a Spanish victory against the Dutch in his *Surrender of Breda.*

DUTCH

1. Hals (1580?-1666) painted scenes of everyday life, such as the *Laughing Cavalier.*

2. Rembrandt (1606-1669), often considered the greatest painter of northern Europe, effectively used contrasts of light and shadow in portraying everyday life and the common people. Among his best known works are *The Night Watch, The Anatomy Lesson,* and *Aristotle Contemplating the Bust of Homer.*

FLEMISH

1. Rubens (1577-1640) employed brilliant colors and vigorously depicted action in religious and historical paintings. One of his outstanding compositions is the *Adoration of the Magi.*

GERMAN

1. Dürer (1471-1528) is famous for his paintings, engravings, and woodcuts.

2. Holbein (1497?-1543) painted lifelike portraits of famous persons, notably of Erasmus and More.

CHARACTERISTICS OF RENAISSANCE SCIENCE

Renaissance science (1) built upon the extensive scientific writings of the Greeks and Romans, (2) developed the scientific method of observation and experimentation, (3) challenged medieval superstition and the general acceptance of Aristotle's theories, (4) uncovered much knowledge about the physical world, (5) at first encountered considerable opposition because its findings were thought to conflict with medieval religious and popular beliefs, and (6) established a firm foundation for modern scientific progress.

RENAISSANCE SCIENTIFIC ACHIEVEMENTS

1. Copernicus (1473-1543), a Polish astronomer, concluded that (*a*) the sun is the center of our solar system, and (*b*) the earth is merely one of several planets revolving about the sun. (Copernicus' conclusions disproved the Ptolemaic theory, which claimed that the earth is the center of the universe. See page 58.)

2. Vesalius (1514-1564), a Flemish physician, founded the science of anatomy as a result of his careful dissections of the human body.

3. Francis Bacon (1561-1626), an English writer, popularized the new scientific method of observation and experimentation.

4. Galileo (1564-1642), an Italian astronomer and physicist, propounded the law of falling bodies and greatly improved the telescope. His observations of the heavens confirmed the Copernican theory.

5. Kepler (1571-1630), a German astronomer, determined that the planets follow an elliptical, not a circular, orbit in revolving about the sun. Kepler's findings help explain the paths followed by man-made satellites today.

6. Harvey (1578-1657), an English physician, demonstrated that blood circulates through the body. His researches furthered the study of medicine.

7. Descartes (1596-1650), a French mathematician and philosopher, is often considered the founder of analytic geometry. His philosophy is summed up in his words "I think, therefore I am."

8. Boyle (1627-1691), an English chemist, discovered a law of gases that is fundamental to modern chemistry.

9. Leeuwenhoek (1632-1723), a Dutch naturalist, perfected the microscope. With this instrument, Leeuwenhoek studied a heretofore invisible world of bacteria, protozoa, and animal and plant cells.

10. Newton (1642-1727), an English mathematician and physicist, invented calculus and formulated the laws of motion and the law of gravitation.

IDENTIFICATION QUESTIONS: WHO AM I?

Cervantes	Galileo	Molière
Chaucer	Giotto	Newton
Copernicus	Gutenberg	Petrarch
Dante	Harvey	Rembrandt
Donatello	Michelangelo	Shakespeare

1. I am famous for my statues of David and Moses and for my frescoes on the ceiling of the Sistine Chapel in the Vatican.
2. My scientific achievements brought me great fame and many honors. I am remembered especially for my discovery of the laws of gravitation.
3. By my invention of movable type for printing, I encouraged the literary Renaissance.
4. I was a poet and playwright in the days of Queen Elizabeth I of England. My plays are produced on the modern stage.
5. I was an early humanist in Italy, and in my larger works I imitated the style of classical poets.
6. When I described my hero Don Quixote tilting at a windmill, I was poking fun at feudalism.
7. In my poem *Divine Comedy,* I portrayed an imaginary trip into the hereafter and meetings with famous persons of the past.
8. I am often considered the greatest painter of northern Europe. In the 20th century my painting *Aristotle Contemplating the Bust of Homer,* commanded a price of over $2 million.
9. I advanced the theory, forgotten since the days of the ancient Greeks, that the earth is not the center of the solar system but revolves about the sun.
10. A physicist and astronomer, I determined the speed at which objects fall and used my telescope to observe the heavens.

MULTIPLE-CHOICE QUESTIONS

1. The Renaissance in western Europe is best described as a period marked by (1) unquestioned reliance on the teachings of Aristotle (2) an advance of Moslem culture (3) Christian unity throughout western Europe (4) a spirit of questioning of formerly accepted authority.
2. An important feature of the Renaissance was an emphasis on (1) alchemy and magic (2) the literature of Greece and Rome (3) chivalry (4) the teachings of St. Thomas Aquinas.

3. Which helped cause the European Renaissance? (1) the Crusades (2) the discovery of the New World (3) the Mongol invasions of Europe (4) the Black Death.

4. Two early centers of European Renaissance culture were (1) London and Prague (2) Madrid and Berlin (3) Paris and Copenhagen (4) Venice and Florence.

5. The Medicis and Sforzas played a significant part in the Renaissance as (1) painters of everyday scenes (2) rulers of Italian cities and patrons of culture (3) scientists who furthered medical research (4) military leaders whose conquests spread the Renaissance to northern Europe.

6. The most famous works of Dante, Cervantes, and Chaucer were written (1) in Latin (2) in the language of the people (3) on scientific subjects (4) on religious subjects.

7. The term "a da Vinci of today" would best describe a person who seems to be (1) behind the times (2) a genius in many fields (3) a conformist (4) only seeking pleasure.

8. In his book *Utopia,* Sir Thomas More (1) portrayed an actual country in southeast Asia (2) described a visionary and ideal state (3) praised conditions under feudalism (4) urged the world to accept English leadership.

9. If you referred to a person as "Machiavellian," you would mean that he is (1) extremely rich (2) a heavy contributor to charitable organizations (3) interested chiefly in his own pleasures (4) not bound by moral considerations in gaining his objective.

Part 2. The Reformation: Beginning of Protestant Christianity

THE PROTESTANT REFORMATION

The *Reformation* was a religious revolt, started in 1517, against the Roman Catholic Church. The Reformation established many *Protestant* sects. (A Protestant is generally considered a Christian not of the Roman Catholic or Eastern Orthodox Churches.) Thus, in western Europe, the Reformation shattered Catholic religious unity and led to diversity in Christianity.

CAUSES OF THE REFORMATION

1. Political. Some rulers resented the Church courts and the Church claim of supremacy over civil authority. Nationalist-minded persons, except in Italy, considered the Pope a foreign ruler.

2. Economic. Some rulers opposed the Church's tax exemption, envied the Church's wealth, and desired to confiscate the vast Church properties. Some business people viewed Church taxes and the Church prohibition of interest on loans as restrictions on economic enterprise. Nationalist-minded persons resented the flow of Church taxes from their countries to the Papacy in Rome.

3. Intellectual. Some educated persons, imbued with the Renaissance questioning attitude, doubted Church authority. These persons prepared the way for a religious revolt by challenging Church teachings on astronomy, history, and Bible interpretation.

4. Church Abuses. Some persons were critical of the following Church practices, which seemed unworthy of religious leaders:

a. Worldliness—the luxurious and materialistic life of certain Popes and high clergy.

b. Nepotism—appointing relatives to Church offices regardless of ability.

c. Simony—selling appointments to Church offices.

d. Sale of indulgences—accepting money for Church pardons, called *indulgences*, without requiring true repentance. These pardons were granted to reduce punishment in the hereafter for certain sins.

5. Decline of Church Prestige. Some persons lost respect for the Church because of the Babylonian Captivity and the Great Schism.

a. The *Babylonian Captivity* (1309-1377) was a period during which the Popes lived at Avignon, France, under the domination of French kings.

b. The *Great Schism* (1378-1417) was a period during which rival Popes —at Avignon and at Rome—each claimed to be the true Pope and struggled for Church supremacy.

UNSUCCESSFUL EARLY ATTEMPTS AT REFORM (14TH-15TH CENTURIES)

1. John Wycliffe (1328?-1384), an English priest, condemned the wealth and worldliness of the Catholic Church. Denying the Pope's religious supremacy, Wycliffe argued that the Bible is the highest religious authority. To enable people to guide themselves in religious matters, he translated the Bible into English. Wycliffe was denounced by the Pope; Wycliffe's followers, the *Lollards*, were harshly persecuted.

2. John Huss (1369-1415), a Bohemian (Czech) religious leader, advocated ideas similar to those of Wycliffe. Arrested and tried as a heretic, Huss was burned at the stake. His followers, the *Hussites*, rebelled but were suppressed by the armies of the Holy Roman Emperor.

3. Desiderius Erasmus (1466?-1536), the great humanist scholar, attacked Church abuses but remained a faithful Catholic. His pleas for internal reform went unheeded.

MARTIN LUTHER STARTS THE REFORMATION (1517)

1. Luther's Background. *Martin Luther* (1483-1546), a German, received an excellent education and entered a Catholic monastic order. At age 25, Luther was appointed professor of Christian theology at the University of Wittenberg.

2. Luther Attacks the Church. Luther condemned the sale of indulgences and denounced Papal agents selling them in Germany. (The funds obtained were to be used for building St. Peter's Cathedral in Rome.) In 1517 Luther nailed to the door of the church at Wittenberg a statement of his religious beliefs, the *Ninety-Five Theses*. The theses aroused tremendous popular support, further encouraging him to attack the Church. Luther denied the Pope's supremacy; proclaimed the Bible as the final authority; translated the Bible into German; urged each individual to read and understand the Bible; and criticized a number of Catholic practices. He developed the doctrine of *justification by faith*, that faith alone ensures salvation. Excommunicated by the Pope, Luther faced punishment from Charles V, the Holy Roman Emperor.

3. North German Rulers Support Luther. Powerful northern German rulers welcomed revolt against Rome. In addition to having religious reasons, they desired to seize Church properties, weaken the Holy Roman Emperor, and end their submission to a non-German Pope. Consequently, they protected Luther against punishment. Throughout northern Germany, these rulers accepted Luther's ideas as a new religion, *Lutheranism*.

SCANDINAVIA RAPIDLY ACCEPTS LUTHERANISM

Scandinavian rulers in Norway, Sweden, and Denmark were converted to Lutheranism, established it as the official state religion, and confiscated Catholic Church properties. By the end of the 16th century Scandinavia had become almost entirely Lutheran.

OTHER PROTESTANT REFORMERS

Encouraged by Lutheran success in northern Germany and Scandinavia, Protestant reformers elsewhere challenged Catholic Church authority.

1. Ulrich Zwingli (1484-1531), a Swiss priest, taught that the Bible, not the Pope, is the supreme religious authority. Zwingli converted certain Swiss cantons (districts) to Protestantism.

2. John Calvin (1509-1564), a French religious reformer, fled from Catholic France to safety in Geneva, Switzerland. Author of the *Institutes of the Christian Religion*, Calvin became a leading Protestant spokesman. He taught the doctrine of *predestination*, that only those elected beforehand by

God would achieve salvation. He founded a simple form of worship, frowned upon such pastimes as dancing and cardplaying, and extolled a serious, moral, and hardworking life.

Calvinism spread rapidly. (a) In Switzerland, Calvinism became the *Swiss Reformed Church*. (b) In Holland, Calvinism became the prevailing faith, the *Dutch Reformed Church*. (c) In Scotland, Calvinism became the official state religion, the *Presbyterian Church*. (d) In France, Calvinism became the faith of a small, influential group, the *Huguenots*. (e) In England, Calvinism became the religion of the *Puritans*. In the 17th century a number of Puritans migrated to Massachusetts where they introduced the Calvinist *Congregational Church*.

3. **John Knox** (1505-1572), a Scottish reformer and follower of Calvin, helped establish *Presbyterianism* as the official Scottish religion.

ANGLICANISM IN ENGLAND

Henry VIII, King of England (1509-1547), at first a loyal Catholic, later broke with the Church because (1) the Pope refused to grant him a divorce from his Spanish wife, Catherine of Aragon, and (2) Henry desired the extensive Church properties in England. He induced Parliament to pass the *Act of Supremacy* (1534), which instituted an independent *Anglican Church* of England with the King as religious leader.

Henry's actions won the support of nationalistic Englishmen, who considered the Pope a foreign ruler, and of many people who opposed certain Church practices. After Henry's divorce was granted by the Anglican Church, he married an English girl, *Anne Boleyn*. Their daughter later became Queen Elizabeth I. During her reign (1558-1603), Anglicanism became firmly entrenched as the English religion.

THE CATHOLIC REFORMATION OR COUNTER-REFORMATION

To defend itself against the Protestant movement, the Catholic Church took a number of actions, known as the *Catholic Reformation*, or *Counter-Reformation*.

1. **Effective Leadership.** A succession of capable, energetic Popes provided strong leadership for Church reform. From all clergymen, they demanded devotion to duty and the highest religious standards.

2. **The Council of Trent (1545-1563).** This Church council (a) reaffirmed such basic Catholic doctrines as Papal supremacy and exclusive Church authority to interpret the Bible, (b) prohibited Church abuses—nepotism, simony, and sale of indulgences, (c) required the clergy to renounce worldly

pleasures, and (*d*) authorized an *Index*, a list of heretical books forbidden to Catholics.

3. The Holy Inquisition. These Church courts (see page 74) vigorously combatted heretics. In Italy and Spain, the Inquisition helped stop the spread of Protestantism.

4. The Society of Jesus. This monastic order was founded in 1534 by *Ignatius Loyola*. Its members, called *Jesuits*, became the leading spiritual soldiers fighting Protestantism. By serving as priests and teachers, they helped preserve Catholicism in Poland, southern Germany, and Belgium. They also won new converts in India, China, Japan, and North America.

RESULTS OF THE REFORMATION

1. Immediate Effects

a. End of Religious Unity. The religious unity of western Europe had been destroyed. Henceforth, Europe was divided according to religion, as follows:

(1) Predominantly *Catholic* were Italy, Spain, France, Belgium, Ireland, southern Germany, Austria, Poland, and Hungary.

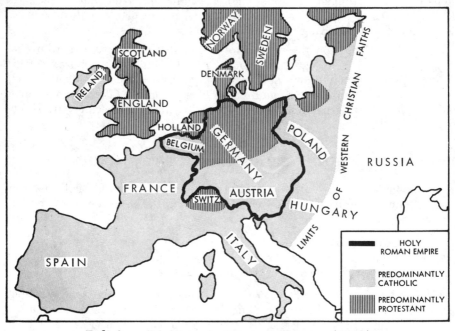

Religious Divisions in Western Europe (1648)

(2) Predominantly *Protestant* were England, Scotland, Holland, northern Germany, Switzerland, Denmark, Norway, and Sweden.

The Protestant world at first consisted of the Lutheran, Calvinist, and Anglican denominations. Later, Methodists, Baptists, and other Protestant sects arose.

b. Religious Wars. In the 16th and 17th centuries Europe endured a series of wars, caused partly by religious differences.

(1) *Civil Wars in Germany.* Catholic and Lutheran rulers in Germany fought several civil wars. The compromise *Peace of Augsburg* (1555) permitted each German ruler to choose for himself and his people either Catholicism or Lutheranism.

(2) *Dutch War Against Spain.* The Protestant Dutch revolted against their Catholic ruler, *Philip II* of Spain, after he ruthlessly tried to suppress Protestantism in Holland. Led by *William of Orange,* the Dutch drove out the Spanish forces and in 1581 declared their political and religious independence. In 1648, after more fighting, Spain recognized Dutch independence.

(3) *Spanish Naval War Against England.* Philip II desired to (a) safeguard Spanish merchant ships and colonies against English raids, (b) depose Elizabeth I, the Protestant Queen of England, and (c) restore Catholicism in England. To invade England, he organized a huge war fleet, the *Spanish Armada.* In 1588 the Armada was destroyed by the English, and Philip's plans were ruined.

(4) *Civil Wars in France.* Protestant and Catholic claimants to the French throne engaged in a series of civil wars. In 1589 *Henry of Navarre,* a Protestant, became King *Henry IV.* Seeking to end religious strife, he (a) adopted Catholicism, the predominant French religion, and (b) issued the *Edict of Nantes* (1598), which granted religious freedom to the Protestant minority, the Huguenots.

(5) *Thirty Years' War* (*1618-1648*). This war, the bloodiest of the period, originated as a religious struggle in central Europe between Protestant and Catholic rulers. The outstanding Protestant military leader was *Gustavus Adolphus,* King of Sweden. The Catholics throughout the war were led by the *Hapsburg* rulers of Austria. In the final stage of the conflict, the Catholic *Bourbon* rulers of France opposed the Catholic Hapsburg rulers of Austria and Spain. The Bourbons, hoping to extend their power, supported the Protestant cause.

Fought almost entirely in Germany, the Thirty Years' War ended in 1648 with the *Treaty of Westphalia:* (a) Catholic France obtained most of Alsace. (b) Protestant Sweden acquired territory in northern Germany. (c) Calvinist as well as Lutheran and Catholic rulers in Germany gained the right to determine the religion of their people. (d) Holland and Switzerland, both Protestant, received recognition of their independence.

(Shocked by the behavior of nations in resorting to and callously prosecuting the Thirty Years' War, *Hugo Grotius,* a Dutch scholar, wrote *Law of War and Peace,* a book considered the foundation of modern international law.)

c. Strengthening of Civil Authority. The state gained power at the expense of the Church. In Protestant countries, the governments (1) confiscated Catholic Church properties, (2) abolished Catholic Church courts, and (3) assumed control of the new Protestant churches. Even in Catholic countries, civil rulers asserted some control over the Church, especially regarding the appointment of Church officials.

2. Long-Term Effects

a. A Step Toward Religious Tolerance. During much of the Reformation, Europe, torn by contending religious groups, experienced great intolerance. Later, since many persons realized that intolerance threatened their own as well as other faiths, governments permitted some religious diversity. Catholic France granted a degree of toleration in the Edict of Nantes (1598); Anglican England extended religious freedom to most other Protestants in the *Toleration Act* (1689). However, these measures were only a first step toward religious tolerance.

b. Encouragement of Education. Protestantism, stressing individual Bible reading in a person's own language, encouraged widespread teaching of reading.

COMPLETION QUESTIONS

1. The Bohemian (Czech) religious reformer who was tried as a heretic and burned at the stake was _____.
2. The German religious reformer who started the Reformation by posting his *Ninety-Five Theses* on the church door at Wittenberg was _____.
3. The founder of the order of the Jesuits and an outstanding defender of Catholicism was _____.
4. The English King who broke with Rome and established Anglicanism was _____.
5. The French religious reformer who fled to Switzerland and wrote the *Institutes of the Christian Religion* was _____.

MULTIPLE-CHOICE QUESTIONS

1. The Protestant Reformation was (1) delayed by the questioning attitude engendered by the Renaissance (2) a complete surprise to Catholic leaders (3) supported by many rulers who desired Church properties (4) hastened by the election of an Englishman as Pope.
2. The authority of the Catholic Church was strengthened by (1) the Great Schism (2) the Babylonian Captivity (3) nepotism (4) the Council of Trent.
3. The *immediate* reason for Luther's protest against the Catholic Church was (1) simony (2) the sale of indulgences (3) the Papal refusal to permit Luther to marry (4) German nationalism.

4. Luther and Wycliffe (1) lived at the same time (2) were German (3) won immediate success as religious reformers (4) translated the Bible into the vernacular.
5. Calvinism was brought to the New World by the (1) English Puritans in Massachusetts (2) French in Canada (3) Swedes in Delaware (4) Spanish in Mexico.
6. Most effective in stopping Protestantism in Italy and Spain was the (1) Index (2) Holy Inquisition (3) work of Erasmus (4) work of John Knox.
7. The Protestant Reformation made its greatest gains in (1) Germany (2) Spain (3) France (4) Austria.
8. In which country did Protestantism attract the *fewest* followers? (1) England (2) Holland (3) Italy (4) Sweden.
9. The Thirty Years' War was fought almost entirely in (1) Italy (2) England (3) Germany (4) Spain.
10. By the Edict of Nantes, France granted religious toleration to the (1) Huguenots (2) Catholics (3) Mohammedans (4) Jews.
11. The Treaty of Westphalia in 1648 indicated that in western Europe (1) Catholicism was victorious (2) Lutheranism was victorious (3) religious unity had ended (4) a Bourbon-Hapsburg alliance had been formed.
12. The Reformation (1) weakened civil authority (2) prevented the growth of religious tolerance (3) encouraged the movement for popular education (4) prevented Catholicism from spreading outside of Europe.

Part 3. The Rise of Absolute Monarchs and National States

RISE OF THE ABSOLUTE MONARCH

1. **From Weak Medieval King to Absolute Monarch.** During the Middle Ages the weak king, exercising little power over feudal lords, usually ruled only the royal domain. Near the end of the Middle Ages, the king—particularly in England, France, Spain, Russia, Prussia, and Austria—began to extend his rule at the expense of the nobles. By the 17th century the king had become an *autocrat*, or *absolute monarch*. His supremacy was acknowledged by commoners and lords. (In England, however, only the Tudor monarchs approached absolutism. See pages 125-126.)

2. **Factors Strengthening Royal Power.** (*a*) The Crusades and other wars killed many feudal lords. (*b*) The rising middle class supported the king to assure protection of property and trade. (*c*) The introduction of gunpowder equipped the king with a powerful weapon that could destroy castles of feudal lords. (*d*) The Reformation provided the king with power formerly held by the Catholic Church. (*o*) The awakening spirit of nationalism made the king the symbol of national unity.

3. **"Divine Right of Kings."** This theory attempted to justify unlimited royal power. (*a*) The king ruled by God's authority as His earthly representative. (*b*) Obedience to the king was obedience to God. (*c*) The king could do no wrong. The divine right concept contrasts with our democratic belief that those who govern derive their authority from the people.

BEGINNING OF THE NATIONAL STATE

The independent *national state* (nation state), familiar to us today, arose when a strong ruler expanded his power from his feudal domain to a larger area. Eventually, the king ruled a nation free from external political or religious control.

In England, France, and Spain, the king united people of a common *nationality*—those sharing similar language, history, and customs. Gradually, the people transferred their loyalty from local lord and province to king and nation. Thus, in these countries, strong monarchs molded unified national states.

In Russia, Prussia, and Austria, however, the king ruled diverse nationalities, though one predominated. These monarchs, therefore, established powerful states, but their peoples did not all develop a feeling of national unity.

DEVELOPMENTS IN ENGLAND: STRONG MONARCHS AND WORLD POWER

1. Early History. (*a*) By the 6th century B.C. England was inhabited by the *Celts*. (*b*) From the 1st to the 5th centuries A.D. England was ruled by the *Romans*. (*c*) In the 5th century England was settled by various Germanic peoples, the *Jutes, Angles,* and *Saxons*. (*d*) In the 9th century England was settled by Northmen, the *Danes*. (*e*) In the 11th century England was invaded by the *Normans* led by William the Conqueror. (The Normans were the last to invade England.)

Over the course of many years, the Anglo-Saxons, Danes, and Normans assimilated (blended together) through (*a*) intermarriage, (*b*) creation of the English language, a mixture of Anglo-Saxon and Norman-French, and (*c*) development of common laws, traditions, customs, and ideas. Thus, an English nationality slowly evolved. (A similar process of assimilation occurred in most other European nations.)

2. William the Conqueror (Ruled 1066-1087)

a. Becomes King of England. William, Duke of Normandy in northern France, claimed the English throne. His claim was opposed by the English Saxon nobles who supported their lord, *Harold*. In 1066 William led his army across the English Channel and defeated the Saxons at the *Battle of Hastings*. Thereafter, he was crowned king in Westminster Abbey.

b. Strengthens Royal Power. (1) *Domesday Book*. William ordered a survey of England's landed property and other wealth. He used this information, recorded in the *Domesday Book*, for levying and collecting taxes. (2) *Salisbury Oath*. William compelled all feudal lords—from highest vassals to lowest knights—to pledge him direct allegiance and military service. Previously, English kings had received such direct pledges only from their top vassals.

3. Early Norman Kings. William's successors likewise strengthened the central government. Gradually, they assumed national powers: making and enforcing laws, establishing royal courts, and controlling foreign affairs.

4. Hundred Years' War (1337-1453)

a. Causes. The Norman kings of England were feudal lords over much French territory, which the French rulers coveted. Furthermore, Edward III of England claimed the French throne. War began when French forces advanced into English landholdings, and Edward invaded France. The resulting long intermittent struggle was called the *Hundred Years' War.*

b. Military Highlights. English forces invaded France and won notable battles at *Crécy* (1346), *Poitiers* (1356), and *Agincourt* (1415). Late in the war, however, the English lost their military advantage. They met final defeat when the French armies, inspired by Joan of Arc (see pages 126-127), ended the English siege of the city of Orléans and drove the enemy from France. By 1453 the English retained in France only the port of Calais.

c. Effect on England. The Hundred Years' War spurred English national patriotism. (1) Englishmen took pride in their notable victories. (2) They were compelled by the loss of their French territory to devote their energies solely to England.

5. Wars of the Roses (1455-1485)

a. Cause. These civil wars resulted from conflicting claims to the English throne by two families of nobles, the House of *York* (whose badge was a white rose) and the House of *Lancaster* (whose badge was a red rose). After thirty years of bitter strife, the Lancastrians triumphed and had *Henry Tudor* crowned *Henry VII.*

b. Results. The Wars of the Roses furthered a powerful monarchy in England. (1) Many nobles died in the war, thus removing rivals for royal power. (2) The Crown increased its wealth by confiscating properties of deceased nobles who had been hostile. (3) The middle class, having suffered wartime disruption of trade, rallied to Tudor support. (4) The victorious Tudor family provided England with strong, capable rulers.

6. Tudor Rule (1485-1603)

a. Henry VII (ruled 1485-1509) reestablished the King's authority over the nobles, and furthered trade and prosperity.

b. Henry VIII (ruled 1509-1547) replaced the Catholic Church with the Anglican Church controlled by the King (see page 119).

c. Elizabeth I (ruled 1558-1603) preserved Protestantism in England and achieved world power for England by humbling Catholic Spain. Elizabeth (1) aided the Dutch revolt against Spain, (2) encouraged such sea captains as *Drake* and *Hawkins* to raid Spanish merchant ships and New World colonies, and (3) organized a navy that defeated the Spanish Armada.

d. Summary of Tudor Rule. (1) Tudor rulers expanded central governmental authority and ruled as almost absolute monarchs. Although Parliament held sessions, it was effectively dominated by the Tudors. (2) They transformed England into a leading world power. (3) They aroused nationalism. (4) They enjoyed immense popularity.

7. Beginning of Stuart Rule (1603). James Stuart, King of Scotland and distant cousin to Elizabeth, became the English King, *James I.* He and his descendants, the *Stuart* rulers, proved unpopular. Eventually the people rebelled (see pages 145-147).

DEVELOPMENTS IN FRANCE: ABSOLUTISM AND WORLD POWER

1. Early History. (*a*) By the 7th century B.C. France was inhabited by the *Gauls.* (*b*) In 58-50 B.C. France was conquered by *Julius Caesar.* (*c*) Until the 5th century A.D. France was ruled by the *Romans.* (*d*) In the 5th century France was settled by the *Franks* and other Germanic tribes. (*e*) From the 8th to 10th centuries France was ruled by Pepin, Charlemagne, and their descendants, the *Carolingian* family.

2. Capetian Rule (10th-14th Centuries)

a. Hugh Capet Becomes King. In 987 Hugh Capet, a French lord, was elected to the throne. Since he controlled only his feudal domain around Paris, his authority elsewhere in France was effectively excluded by powerful feudal nobles.

b. Capetian Kings Extend Governmental Power. The Capetian kings struggled to weaken the nobles, expand royal territories, and build a strong central government. The outstanding Capetian kings were (1)*Philip Augustus* (ruled 1180-1223), who seized Normandy and other provinces from their feudal lord, King John of England, and (2) *Philip the Fair* (ruled 1285-1314), who taxed the clergy and forced the "Babylonian Captivity" (see page 117) upon the Catholic Church.

3. Hundred Years' War (1337-1453)

a. Joan of Arc Saves France. In 1429 Joan of Arc, a peasant girl from Lorraine, declared that divine voices had directed her to save France from English conquest. From King Charles VII, Joan demanded and received command of an army. Her faith and courage inspired the French soldiers. They (1) immediately raised the English siege of Orléans, and (2) eventually drove the English from France. Meanwhile, Joan was captured by the English. In 1431 she was condemned as a witch and burned at the stake.

b. Effect on France. The war (1) *spurred nationalism* by giving the French people a national heroine and a great military triumph, and (2) *strengthened royal power* by killing many nobles and enriching the Crown with the former English territories.

(For a fuller discussion of the Hundred Years' War, see page 125.)

4. Consolidation of Centralized Power (Late 15th Century). After the Hundred Years' War, French kings sought to increase their power. *Louis XI* (ruled 1461-1483), the most successful of these monarchs, curbed feudal anarchy, set up efficient central government, and is often considered the architect of French absolute monarchy.

5. Religious Civil Wars (16th Century). These civil wars were caused by opposing Catholic and Protestant claims to the throne. The conflict ended in 1589 when *Henry of Navarre* became King *Henry IV*. By following wise religious policies (see page 121), he successfully maintained power.

For 200 years, France was ruled by Henry and his descendants, the *Bourbon* family.

6. Cardinal Richelieu Guides France (1624-1642). *Richelieu*, a Cardinal of the Church and minister to King *Louis XIII*, skillfully directed French affairs to attain supremacy for the King and world power for France.

a. Supremacy for the King. Richelieu (1) destroyed the nobles' fortified castles, (2) transferred local governmental functions from the nobles to royal officials, the *intendants*, and (3) levied taxes without consent of the French lawmaking body, the *Estates-General*.

b. World Power for France. Richelieu led France into the Thirty Years' War in support of the Protestant cause. France defeated her Hapsburg rivals, Austria and Spain (see page 121).

7. Louis XIV: The Grand Monarch (Ruled 1643-1715)

a. The Absolute Monarch. Louis XIV represented the height of absolutism. Proclaiming that he ruled by divine right, Louis considered himself the *Sun King*. Near Paris, he built the magnificent *Palace of Versailles*, where he maintained an extravagant court. At Versailles, the nobles fawningly waited upon him and courted his favor. Louis exercised unlimited political powers. Not once during his long reign did he convene the Estates-General. To illustrate his attitude, tradition ascribes to Louis the statement, "L'état, c'est moi," meaning "I am the state."

b. Economic Affairs. Louis entrusted economic matters to his able finance minister, *Colbert*. To further prosperity, Colbert promoted good farming methods, built roads and canals, protected existing industries with tariffs, aided new industries with subsidies, and helped establish French trading posts in India and colonies in North America.

In 1685, to compel Catholic religious uniformity, Louis revoked the Edict of Nantes. This action damaged the economy because thousands of Protestant Huguenots (mostly skilled workmen and enterprising businessmen) fled France. Many settled in England, Holland, and America.

c. Foreign Affairs. Louis pursued an ambitious, aggressive foreign policy. He sought for France her "natural boundaries," especially the Rhine River. Fighting three major wars, he acquired some territory but failed to achieve the Rhine boundary. In a fourth major war, Louis lost some overseas possessions but placed a Bourbon relative on the Spanish throne.

At Louis XIV's death, France was the leading nation on the European continent. But the French people had wearied of wars, taxes, and despotism. Louis XVI, a descendant of the Grand Monarch, was to experience the people's extreme reaction in the French Revolution (see pages 154-162).

Territory Gained by Louis XIV

DEVELOPMENTS IN SPAIN: ABSOLUTISM AND WORLD POWER, THEN DECLINE

1. Early History. (*a*) Since prehistoric times Spain was inhabited by the *Iberians.* (*b*) To the 3rd century B.C. Spain was colonized by *Phoenicians, Greeks,* and *Carthaginians.* (*c*) In 201 B.C. Spain was annexed by Rome. (*d*) For over 600 years Spain was ruled by the *Romans.* (*e*) In the 5th century A.D. Spain was settled by Germanic tribes, the *Visigoths.* (*f*) In the 8th century Spain was invaded by North African Moslems called *Moors.*

After the Moorish invasion, the Iberian Peninsula was divided into a number of Moslem states and Christian kingdoms.

2. Unification of Spain (11th to 15th Centuries). The Christian kingdoms warred intermittently against the Moslems and slowly expanded Christian rule in Spain. In 1469 *Ferdinand* of Aragon married *Isabella* of Castile, thus uniting Christian Spain. In 1492 their armies finally conquered Granada, thereby ending Moorish rule on the peninsula.

3. Ferdinand and Isabella Rule a United Spain

a. Absolutism. Ferdinand and Isabella increased royal power considerably. They weakened (1) the *nobility* by destroying the nobles' fortified castles, (2) the *Catholic Church* by nominating important Church officials, and (3) the *Cortes,* the Spanish legislature, by enacting laws without its approval.

b. Religious Unity. Hoping to promote Catholicism, Ferdinand and Isabella persecuted Jews and Moslems, and eventually expelled them from Spain. Spain thus lost energetic merchants and skilled workmen.

c. Foreign Affairs. Ferdinand and Isabella laid the foundation for Spain's brief period of world power. (1) They financed Columbus' expedition, which discovered the New World and encouraged further exploration. As a result, Spain acquired a large colonial empire with great wealth in silver and gold. (2) For their three daughters, they arranged political marriages to strong allies. The most important marital alliance, Joanna to Philip of Hapsburg, produced an heir who became *Charles V.*

4. Reign of Charles V (1519-1556)

a. Rules an Empire. Charles of Hapsburg, absolute monarch of Spain and leading ruler of Europe, controlled not only Spain and her colonial empire, but also the Netherlands, Sicily, southern Italy, Austria, and other lands in central Europe. In 1520 he became Holy Roman Emperor.

b. Dominates European Affairs. To defend his domains, Charles repeatedly fought the French, the Moslem Turks, and the Protestant Germans. A devout Catholic, he most regretted his failure to halt Protestantism in Germany. In 1556 a weary Charles renounced his throne to withdraw into a monastery. His brother Ferdinand became ruler of Austria and Holy Roman Emperor. Charles' son became King *Philip II* of Spain.

5. Reign of Philip II (1556-1598): Spanish Power Declines. Philip hastened Spain's military and economic decline. In foreign affairs, he expended manpower and money but (a) was unable to suppress the Protestant Dutch revolt, (b) could not halt English raids on Spanish merchant ships and colonies, and (c) failed to conquer England with the Spanish Armada (1588).

In Spain, Philip's autocratic rule produced inefficient government, a crushing tax burden, and a stagnant economy. His reign began Spain's decline in world prestige and power.

DEVELOPMENTS IN RUSSIA: ABSOLUTISM AND TERRITORIAL EXPANSION

1. Early History. (*a*) By the 8th century A.D. Russia was inhabited by the *Slavs*. (*b*) In the 9th century Russia was settled by the *Northmen*. (*c*) In the 10th century Russia was influenced by Byzantine culture and converted to *Eastern Orthodox Christianity*. (*d*) In the 13th century Russia was conquered by fierce Asians, the *Mongols*, or *Tartars*. (*e*) For over 200 years Russia was controlled by the Mongols, who introduced Asian ways of living.

2. Moscow Leads Russia (15th and 16th Centuries). *Ivan the Great* (ruled 1462-1505), Slavic Grand Duke of Moscow, ended Tartar domination. Thereafter, he struggled to extend his territories, subdue the nobles, and attain absolute power. So too did his grandson, *Ivan the Terrible* (ruled 1533-1584), who often employed great cruelty. Ivan the Terrible was the first ruler to assume the title "Czar and autocrat of all Russia."

After Ivan the Terrible died, Russia endured foreign invasions and civil wars, as the nobles fought for control of the throne. In 1613 an assembly of nobles chose a new Czar, *Michael Romanov*. For over 300 years, the Romanov family ruled Russia.

3. Reign of Peter the Great (1682-1725)

a. Furthers Autocracy. *Peter*, the outstanding Romanov ruler, strengthened absolutism by (1) creating a strong army loyal to him, (2) ruthlessly crushing a revolt of the nobles, (3) appointing royal governors to replace local officials, and (4) extending government control over the Russian Orthodox Church.

b. Tries to Westernize Russia. Peter wanted to model Russia after European culture, rather than Byzantine or Asian culture. Having traveled through western Europe, he greatly admired its civilization. He introduced into Russia Western ideas on science, education, military training, and industry. To imitate Western social customs, Peter ordered his subjects to shave their long beards and discard their Oriental garments.

c. Gains a Seaport. Peter sought "windows" (seaports) to provide his landlocked country with water routes for trade with western Europe. In a long war against Sweden, he won territories adjoining the Baltic Sea. Here, he built his new seaport and capital, *St. Petersburg* (now Leningrad).

4. Reign of Catherine the Great (1762-1796): Russia Gains More Territory. *Catherine the Great,* also an autocratic ruler, extended Russia's boundaries southward and westward.

a. Southward. Warring against the Turks, Catherine gained (1) the northern coast of the Black Sea, and (2) the right of Russian ships to sail from the Black Sea into the Mediterranean Sea via the Turkish-controlled Dardanelles.

b. Westward. Catherine joined with Austria and Prussia in three partitions that completely eliminated independent *Poland.* (See map, page 133.)

Catherine, building on Peter's accomplishments, ruled an Empire consisting of Russians, Ukrainians, and Poles, as well as Baltic and Asian peoples. She made 18th-century Russia a major European power.

DEVELOPMENTS IN PRUSSIA: ABSOLUTISM AND TERRITORIAL EXPANSION

1. Early Hohenzollern Rule (15th to 18th Centuries). The *Hohenzollerns,* a family of German nobles from Brandenburg (the Berlin area), acquired Prussia, a land inhabited by Slavs and Germans. The early Hohenzollern rulers (*a*) established autocratic government, (*b*) created a well-trained army, and (*c*) by war, marriage, and diplomacy, expanded their territory.

For 500 years, the Hohenzollern family ruled Prussia; in 1871, when Prussia unified the German states, the Hohenzollern King of Prussia became Emperor of Germany.

The Growth of Hohenzollern Domains (1415-1786)

2. Reign of Frederick the Great (1740-1786): Prussia Gains Territory. *Frederick the Great,* the most famous Hohenzollern absolute monarch and a military genius, pursued an aggressive foreign policy. In 1740 he seized from Austria the province of Silesia. His action culminated in a major European conflict, the *Seven Years' War* (1756-1763), in which he was pitted against a powerful European coalition of Austria, Russia, and France. Frederick, aided only by England, barely managed to retain Silesia. In 1772, sharing in the first partition of Poland, he annexed western Poland.

Frederick thus converted 18th-century Prussia into an important European power.

DEVELOPMENTS IN AUSTRIA: ABSOLUTISM AND VAST EMPIRE

1. The Hapsburgs Acquire Austria (13th Century). The *Hapsburgs* originated as lesser feudal lords with minor territories in Alsace, Switzerland, and southern Germany. In 1273 *Rudolf I* of Hapsburg became Holy Roman Emperor and, soon afterwards, ruler of Austria. Rudolf laid the foundation for future Hapsburg power. For over 600 years, his descendants governed Austria; moreover, with few exceptions, they headed the Holy Roman Empire until its extinction (1806).

2. Highlights of Hapsburg Rule (13th-18th Centuries)

a. Reverses. Hapsburg rulers proved unable (1) in the late 15th century to prevent their Swiss subjects from winning virtual independence, (2) in the 16th century to halt the Protestant movement in Germany, and (3) in the 17th century to defeat France in the Thirty Years' War (see page 121).

b. Achievements. Despite such setbacks, strong Hapsburg monarchs greatly expanded the family domains. Their methods emphasized political marriages, territorial inheritance, and alliances. In the late 17th century Hapsburg forces, aided by other Christian troops, raised the Turkish siege of Vienna and drove the Moslems from central Europe.

By the 18th century the Hapsburg rulers exercised absolute power over a vast Austrian Empire of many nationalities: Austrians, Germans, Hungarians, Belgians, Czechs, Poles, Rumanians, Serbs, Slovenes, and Italians.

3. Leading Hapsburg Rulers (18th Century)

a. Maria Theresa (Ruled 1740-1780). As prescribed by Charles VI's will, his daughter Maria Theresa secured the Austrian throne. Despite the *Pragmatic Sanction,* a document in which most European rulers agreed to guarantee her inheritance, Maria Theresa endured numerous attacks. Eventually, she lost Silesia to Prussia but gained part of Poland. A conscientious ruler, Maria Theresa sought to govern efficiently and further prosperity.

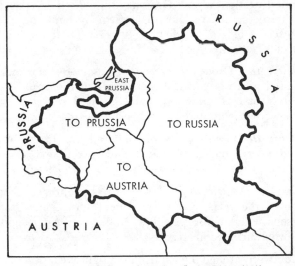

The Partitions of Poland (1772-1795)

b. Joseph II (Ruled 1780-1790). To increase royal authority, Joseph (1) subjected the Catholic Church to state control and seized Church lands, (2) weakened the nobles by taxing them and by canceling many obligations of their serfs, and (3) abolished local self-government. Joseph's policies aroused intense opposition and were later revoked. (For his reforms as an "enlightened despot," see page 134.)

ABSOLUTE MONARCHY: A SUMMARY

1. Achievements. Absolute monarchs (a) weakened the forces tending to disunite a country, (b) provided strong central government, and (c) generally furthered the growth of national states.

2. Weaknesses. Absolute monarchs (a) made a nation's welfare depend on the ability of one man, (b) often sacrificed the national interest for the autocrat's personal wishes, (c) led their nations into countless wars, and (d) disregarded the needs of the common people.

3. Absolutism Attacked by Intellectuals. Absolute monarchy was attacked by certain 18th-century philosophers who advocated ideas typical of the *Intellectual Revolution* (the *Enlightenment,* or the *Age of Reason*). According to these writers, autocracy (a) stemmed from a tradition of brute force that violated all reason, (b) perpetuated despotic government, legal and social inequality, serfdom, ignorance, and religious intolerance, and (c) prevented progress.

4. Enlightened or Benevolent Despots. Influenced by these intellectuals, certain rulers tried to justify their absolutism by claiming to govern in the people's interest. Called *enlightened* or *benevolent despots*, these monarchs introduced various reforms.

a. Frederick the Great of Prussia supported literature, music, and science, furthered new agricultural methods, ordered equal legal treatment for all persons, promoted education, and granted religious freedom. Frederick's reforms were largely undone by his successors.

b. Catherine the Great of Russia fostered art, literature, and science, permitted greater local self-government, and encouraged legal reforms. Her reforms, however, proved to be of little value to most Russians.

c. Joseph II of Austria, the most sincere enlightened despot, improved the conditions of the serfs, expanded educational facilities, attempted to make all persons equal before the law, and advanced religious toleration. Few of his reforms survived his reign.

5. Failure of Enlightened Despotism. Enlightened despots did not curb resentment against absolute monarchy. They (*a*) did not remove the basic causes of discontent—autocracy, class distinctions, unfair taxation, and frequent wars, and (*b*) could not assure good government by their successors. In time, most European peoples rebelled against absolutism.

IDENTIFICATION QUESTIONS: WHO AM I?

Charles V	Hugh Capet	Peter the Great
Elizabeth I	Joan of Arc	Philip II
Frederick the Great	Joseph II	Richelieu
Henry IV	Louis XIV	Rudolf I
Henry VIII	Maria Theresa	William the Conqueror

1. Although a peasant girl, I inspired the French armies to victory at the siege of Orléans and later witnessed the coronation of my King at Rheims Cathedral.
2. I introduced Western ideas into Russia and, by war, secured a Baltic "window" for my country.
3. Originally a feudal lord in Alsace and southern Germany, I became Holy Roman Emperor. Later, I acquired Austria as the base of power for my family, the Hapsburgs.
4. Although King of Spain and Holy Roman Emperor, I was unable to halt the spread of Protestantism in Germany.
5. During my reign in England, my sea captains humbled Spanish naval power and established England's mastery of the seas.
6. Known as the Sun King, I built the Palace of Versailles and ruled France at a time of great splendor.
7. In accordance with my father's will and the Pragmatic Sanction, I ascended the throne of Austria, but I had to defend my territories against attack.
8. I crossed the English Channel from France in 1066 and took the throne of England by defeating the Saxon ruler.
9. As ruler of Prussia and military genius, I was fond of war and yet sought to govern as a benevolent despot.

MULTIPLE-CHOICE QUESTIONS

1. Which contributed to the rise of national states in western Europe? (1) the rise of a feudal nobility (2) the need for protection from barbarian invasions (3) the widespread use of the Latin language (4) the growth of the middle class.
2. In 18th-century Europe, autocratic rulers based their claim to rule on (1) the consent of the Church (2) the support of the nobility (3) the theory of divine right (4) the support of the middle class.
3. A result of the Norman conquest of England was the (1) fusion of French and Anglo-Saxon customs (2) beginning of the English navy (3) loss of the English throne to Danish kings (4) introduction of Christianity to England.
4. Which nations were rivals in the Hundred Years' War? (1) England and Holland (2) England and France (3) France and Portugal (4) France and Spain.
5. The great aim of Louis XIV was to (1) preserve the balance of power in Europe (2) annex the German states (3) establish colonies throughout America (4) acquire territories up to France's natural boundaries.
6. The Asiatic invaders who ruled in Russia from the 13th to the 15th centuries were the (1) Mongols (2) Chinese (3) Turks (4) Huns.
7. Which one of these countries does *not* have natural boundaries for protection? (1) England (2) Italy (3) Poland (4) Spain.
8. At the end of the 18th century Poland was partitioned by Prussia, Russia, and (1) Austria (2) Belgium (3) France (4) Sweden.
9. Which royal family is correctly paired with the country it ruled? (1) Prussia—Hapsburgs (2) Spain—Tudors (3) Russia—Romanovs (4) England—Bourbons.
10. *Not* a legislative body was (1) the Cortes (2) the House of Lancaster (3) the Estates-General (4) Parliament.
11. Writers of the Intellectual Revolution urged people to (1) rely upon faith (2) obey their rulers without question (3) retain feudal ways (4) change society to conform to reason.
12. Which was characteristic of enlightened despots during the 18th century? (1) They gave their subjects a voice in the government. (2) They used their absolute power to make some reforms. (3) They united to defeat Louis XIV of France. (4) They encouraged the Renaissance.

Part 4. European Expansion Overseas: The Commercial Revolution

FACTORS ENCOURAGING OVERSEAS VOYAGES

The geographical knowledge of Europeans during the Middle Ages was limited to Europe, northern Africa, and western Asia. Beginning in the 15th century western European nations first Portugal and Spain, then England, Holland, and France—undertook expeditions that discovered new regions in Africa and the Far East, as well as the Americas. The main factors that encouraged these voyages were:

1. Trade With the East. Substantial trade between Europe and the East began during the Crusades (see pages 84-85). This profitable business became the monopoly of (*a*) Asian middlemen who brought Far Eastern goods by overland caravan to Constantinople, Alexandria, and other east Mediterranean ports, and (*b*) Italian merchants from Venice and Genoa who shipped the products from the eastern Mediterranean area to western Europe. In the 15th century the lucrative Eastern trade attracted the attention of two nations on the Atlantic coast, Portugal and Spain. To smash the monopoly of the Asian middlemen and Italian city-states, Portugal and Spain financed expeditions seeking an all-water route to the Far East.

2. European Curiosity About the Far East. Europeans were interested in the Far East because of (*a*) the reports of travelers to eastern Asia, particularly *Marco Polo*, a 13th-century Venetian who visited Cathay (China) and then wrote about his adventures and China's great riches, and (*b*) the Renaissance quest for information about the world's size, shape, and people.

3. Wealth and Ambitions of the New National States. By the 16th century the wealthy western European nations could finance expensive voyages of exploration. Furthermore, their rising middle classes desired increased trade, and their absolute monarchs sought colonial empires.

4. Scientific Progress. Scientific achievements reduced the hazards of ocean travel. These advances were (*a*) Renaissance geographical knowledge, especially the realization that the earth is round, *not* flat, (*b*) improved maps, (*c*) a better compass for determining direction, and (*d*) the greater use of the astrolabe for determining latitude.

PORTUGAL IS THE FIRST TO REACH THE EAST

Inspired by Prince *Henry the Navigator*, Portugal began to search for an all-water route around Africa to the East. Gradually, Portuguese sea captains pushed southward along the Atlantic coast of Africa. In 1488 *Bartholomew Diaz* reached the southern tip of Africa, the Cape of Good Hope. In 1497-1498 *Vasco da Gama* rounded the Cape and sailed on to India. Because he returned with a cargo worth 60 times the cost of the voyage, his trip excited western Europe.

SPAIN FINANCES TWO SIGNIFICANT EXPEDITIONS

1. Columbus. In 1492 *Christopher Columbus*, an Italian navigator, sailed from Spain. Convinced that the earth is round, Columbus planned to reach the East by sailing westward across the Atlantic Ocean. He failed because his ships were blocked by two continents hitherto unknown to Europe. Although Columbus thought he had reached islands off the coast of Asia, he had actually discovered a new world. Because this region was publicized by the Italian explorer *Amerigo Vespucci*, it was later named the *Americas*.

2. Magellan. In 1519 *Ferdinand Magellan,* a Portuguese sea captain, led several ships from Spain. He rounded the southern tip of South America and crossed the Pacific, but was killed in the Philippine Islands. In 1522 one ship arrived in Spain, thereby completing the first *circumnavigation* of the world. This daring navigational exploit, covering about 44,000 miles, proved concretely that the world is round.

EUROPEANS EXPLORE NEW LANDS (15TH TO 18TH CENTURIES)

Spurred by these discoveries, the leading western European nations sent explorers to the New World and the Far East to (*a*) seek a "northwest passage" through or around North America to the Far East, (*b*) secure gold, silver, gems, and other valuable products, (*c*) convert the natives to Christianity, (*d*) establish claims to the new lands, and (*e*) start trading posts and settlements.

IMPORTANT EXPLORERS AND THEIR ACHIEVEMENTS

Explorers	Dates	Achievements
For Spain		
Balboa	1513	Discovered the Pacific Ocean.
Ponce De Leon	1513	Discovered Florida.
Cortez	1519–1521	Conquered the Aztec Indians in Mexico.
Pizarro	1532	Conquered the Inca Indians in Peru.
De Soto	1541	Discovered the Mississippi River.
For France		
Verrazano	1524	Explored the Atlantic coast of North America; first sailed into New York Harbor.
Cartier	1535	Discovered the St. Lawrence River.
Champlain	1603–1608	Explored eastern Canada and northern New England; founded Quebec.
Marquette and Joliet	1673	Explored the upper Mississippi River valley.
For England		
Cabot	1497	Discovered Labrador and the northeast coast of North America.
Drake	1577–1580	Led the second expedition to circumnavigate the world.
Cook	1768–1770	Explored New Zealand, other southern Pacific islands, and Australia.
For Portugal		
Cabral	1500	Discovered Brazil.
For Holland		
Hudson	1609	Entered New York Harbor and sailed up the Hudson River.

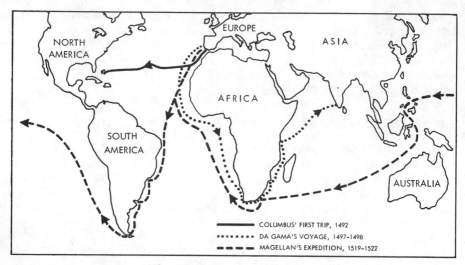

The First Voyages Overseas

COLUMBUS' FIRST TRIP, 1492
DA GAMA'S VOYAGE, 1497–1498
MAGELLAN'S EXPEDITION, 1519–1522

EUROPEAN NATIONS ESTABLISH COLONIAL EMPIRES (16TH TO 18TH CENTURIES)

1. In Asia

a. Portugal established an important trading post at *Goa* in India, and others in the East Indies.

b. Spain annexed the Philippine Islands.

c. Holland, by capturing the Portuguese posts and establishing her own trading stations, won control of the East Indies.

d. France established trading posts in India, such as *Pondicherry.*

e. England established trading posts in India at Bombay, Madras, and Calcutta. In a major war against France, she gained dominance over India (1763). England also settled Australia.

2. In the New World

a. Portugal settled Brazil.

b. Spain settled the West Indies, Florida, Texas, California, Mexico, Central America, and South America (except for Brazil).

c. Holland founded the colony of *New Netherland.* This colony, centered on Manhattan Island (now part of New York City), extended northward along the Hudson River to Albany and southward to Delaware Bay. Later, the Dutch seized the Swedish colony of Delaware.

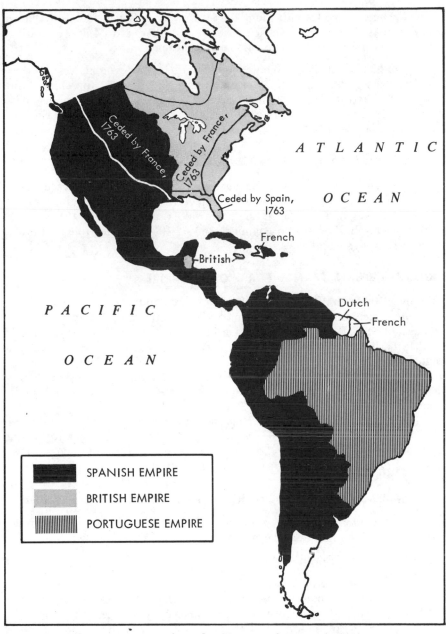

The Americas After the Treaty of Paris (1763)

d. France settled Canada along the St. Lawrence River, founding Quebec and Montreal. France also settled the Great Lakes and Mississippi River regions, founding Detroit, St. Louis, and New Orleans.

e. England settled ten colonies and seized Delaware and New Netherland from the Dutch. New Netherland was divided into New Jersey and New York. These *thirteen English colonies* bordered the Atlantic seaboard from New Hampshire to Georgia. In a major war against France, England acquired Canada (1763).

COLONIAL RIVALRY CAUSES WARS (16TH TO 18TH CENTURIES)

The western European powers engaged in a number of wars, caused partly by colonial rivalry, in which England achieved victory. (1) England raided Spanish colonies and destroyed the Spanish Armada (1588). (2) England seized the Dutch New World colonies (1664). (3) England fought France, her chief rival in several wars.

ENGLAND DEFEATS FRANCE FOR WORLD EMPIRE

For over 100 years, England and France fought many bitter wars for European dominance and colonial supremacy. The victor was finally decided by the *Seven Years' War* (1756-1763). On battlegrounds in Europe, India, and North America, the English triumphed. In India, *Robert Clive*, a brilliant English leader, crushed the French in 1757 at the *Battle of Plassey*. In the North American struggle, called the *French and Indian War* (1754-1763), the English were also victorious. They invaded French Canada and, under General *James Wolfe*, captured the stronghold of Quebec.

In the *Treaty of Paris* (1763), England acquired French Canada and all French territory east of the Mississippi. France also agreed not to impede English control of India. By adding these lands to her other possessions, England in 1763 became the world's leading colonial power.

THE COMMERCIAL REVOLUTION: RESULTS OF EUROPEAN EXPANSION

The term *Commercial Revolution* summarizes the effects that European overseas expansion had upon both Europe and the rest of the world.

1. Effects Upon Europe

a. Expanded World Trade

(1) Europe imported many commodities from the New World and the Far East: potatoes, Indian corn (maize), tobacco, chocolate, cane sugar, tea, and quinine. Some of these items were new to Europe. Others, though previously known, became cheaper and more plentiful. Their availability helped improve European living standards.

(2) Large quantities of gold and silver received from New World mines substantially affected Europe's economy. Since these metals served as currency, consumers had more money to spend for goods. Vigorous bidding for these goods raised prices, thus causing inflation. Workers therefore required higher wages. Moreover, the increased supply of currency made possible more banks, which provided funds for business investment.

(3) Limited by guild restrictions, European textile production proved insufficient to meet the demand both in Europe and overseas. To increase output, manufacturers employed the *domestic system*—sending out raw materials to be worked on in the home—and, later, the *factory system*—speeding production by using machinery (see page 229).

(4) To reduce the risk of loss to ships and goods from storm, fire, and piracy, merchants originated insurance. Each merchant contributed a specified sum, called a *premium*, to a common fund, from which an unfortunate businessman was fully compensated. A noted insurance company, founded in the 17th century, was *Lloyd's of London*.

b. Shifted Economic Power

(1) Europe's major trade routes shifted from the Mediterranean and Baltic to the Atlantic. The western European nations, bordering the Atlantic, increased their commerce, wealth, and power; the Italian city-states and north German cities declined in importance.

(2) Europe's middle class—merchants, bankers, capitalists—grew in number and achieved greater economic power. However, it was not content. Considered inferior to the landowning nobility and ruled by absolute monarchs, the middle class lacked social status and political power.

c. Adopted Mercantilism.
To further their national prosperity, Europe's governments applied the economic theories of *mercantilism*. The mercantilists argued that a nation must (1) attract the maximum amount of gold and silver, since wealth is measured in these metals, (2) export more than it imports and receive payment for the difference in gold and silver, (3) increase exports by stimulating domestic industries with bounties (subsidies), (4) discourage imports of foreign manufactures by levying tariffs, (5) acquire colonies to assure markets for manufactured goods and to guarantee sources of raw materials, (6) restrict colonial manufacturing, and (7) forbid colonies to trade with any country except the mother country. Mercantilists held that colonies exist for the benefit of the mother country.

2. Effects Upon the Rest of the World.
(a) Europeans obtained Negroes in Africa (often from Arab slave traders) for transport to New World plantations and mines. (b) Many Europeans migrated to overseas colonies, either to escape religious persecution or to improve their economic condition. (c) Trade and emigration spread European civilization throughout the world.

MULTIPLE-CHOICE QUESTIONS

1. The Crusaders hastened the discovery of America by (1) taking Jerusalem from the Mohammedans (2) stimulating European demand for goods of the East (3) driving the Turks out of Constantinople (4) increasing the power of the Church.
2. The new national states along the Atlantic undertook overseas explorations (1) as a substitute for war (2) to prove that the earth is round (3) to profit from colonies and trade (4) to reach the New World before the Chinese.
3. Which nation was the first to establish trading posts in India? (1) England (2) France (3) Holland (4) Portugal.
4. Which two European countries led in exploration and colonization during the early 15th and 16th centuries? (1) England and Germany (2) France and Russia (3) Italy and Holland (4) Portugal and Spain.
5. Two nations that successfully established colonies in North America were (1) France and Portugal (2) Russia and Denmark (3) Spain and England (4) Sweden and Prussia.
6. The eastern part of South America, encompassing Brazil, was once part of the Empire of (1) France (2) Holland (3) Portugal (4) Spain.
7. A new bridge, spanning part of New York Harbor, has logically been named in honor of the explorer (1) Balboa (2) Verrazano (3) Champlain (4) Cabot.
8. In the 18th century the major colonial rivals were (1) France and England (2) England and Russia (3) France and Prussia (4) England and Spain.
9. By the 16th century the center of commercial activity had shifted from the Mediterranean to the (1) Black Sea (2) Atlantic Ocean (3) Red Sea (4) Indian Ocean.
10. By the 17th century the chief export from Africa to the New World was (1) gold (2) rubber (3) slaves (4) spices.
11. To which of the following pairs of nations did the Commercial Revolution bring the greatest increase in wealth and power? (1) Spain and Germany (2) Portugal and Italy (3) England and Holland (4) France and Russia.
12. Mercantilism attempted to (1) maintain guild restrictions upon production (2) place tax restrictions on the merchant class (3) increase national wealth through the control of trade and industry (4) transform base metals into gold.
13. Which is *not* an aspect of 18th-century mercantilism? (1) The mother country's exports should be greater in value than its imports. (2) The mother country should encourage manufacturing in its colonies. (3) Industry within the mother country should be encouraged by the national government. (4) Colonies should exist for the benefit of the mother country.

TRUE-FALSE QUESTIONS

1. A medieval Italian traveler whose book about his visit to China aroused tremendous interest in Europe was *Leonardo da Vinci*.
2. The Portuguese sea captain who first reached India by sailing around Africa was *Prince Henry the Navigator*.
3. The Spanish expedition one ship of which was first to circumnavigate the world was originally led by *Christopher Columbus*.
4. A famous insurance company founded in the 17th century to reduce the risk of merchant ship loss is *Lloyd's of London*.
5. The first settlement on the present site of New York City was made by the *English*.
6. The military leader who won control of India for England was *Robert Clive*.
7. The decisive 18th-century war that established England as the world's greatest colonial power was the *Thirty Years' War*.
8. The many results of European expansion overseas are together known as the *Intellectual Revolution*.

UNIT VII. THE GROWTH OF DEMOCRACY

Part 1. Introduction

MEANING OF POLITICAL DEMOCRACY

The political principle that underlies democracy is that government is created by, derives its powers from, and exists to serve the people. In practice today, political democracy means a system of government characterized by the following features: (1) Governmental powers are limited by a written or unwritten constitution. (2) Governmental officials are chosen by secret ballot in free and frequently held elections. (3) The legislature passes laws by majority vote. (4) More than one political party exists, each free to present its views in seeking to become the majority party. (5) Minority groups, regardless of race, color, religion, or national origin, have the right to full and free existence. (6) The people are protected against possible governmental tyranny by constitutional guarantees of basic civil liberties, especially (*a*) freedom of speech, press, religion, and assembly, and (*b*) the right to bail, impartial trial, and equal treatment under the law.

To summarize, in a democratic government, the majority rules, and the liberties of the minority are protected, especially the liberty peaceably to become the majority.

POLITICAL DEMOCRACY THROUGH THE AGES

The democratic form of government (1) *appeared* first in the ancient Greek city-states and in the Roman republic, (2) *was replaced* by autocracy —the rulers of the Roman Empire, feudal lords of the Middle Ages, and absolute monarchs of the transition period to modern times, (3) *reappeared* as a result of the 17th-century English Revolution and the 18th-century American and French Revolutions, and (4) *developed* into the political systems democratic peoples enjoy today.

In the following chapters, we shall trace western European and American history relating to the reappearance and development of democratic government.

Part 2. England (to 1750): Democratic Gains

FOUNDATIONS FOR DEMOCRATIC GROWTH

During the later Middle Ages, England established a foundation upon which her people would erect a democracy.

1. Jury System. King *Henry II* (ruled 1154-1189) replaced feudal justice with royal courts, grand jury investigations, and, in certain cases, jury trials. Although he intended to strengthen royal authority rather than to further democracy, his reform evolved into our modern system of trial by jury.

2. Magna Carta (1215). King *John* was accused by the nobles of being a despot and of violating their feudal rights. At Runnymede, outside London, John was compelled by the nobles to sign the *Great Charter*, or *Magna Carta*. This document limited royal power by stating that the King (*a*) may *not* imprison any freeman except by judgment of his peers (equals) and in accordance with the laws, and (*b*) may *not* levy taxes without consent of the *Great Council*. (This body consisted of the higher clergy and nobility.)

Originally, Magna Carta protected the feudal nobility against royal tyranny; in time, the Charter's protections were extended to all Englishmen. Magna Carta came to mean that (*a*) the king is not an absolute ruler but is subject to the laws, (*b*) all persons are guaranteed trial by jury, and (*c*) the Great Council, which later evolved into Parliament, alone may levy taxes. Magna Carta is therefore usually considered the cornerstone of English democracy.

3. Model Parliament (1295). King *Edward I* expanded the Great Council's membership to include middle-class representatives. His purpose was to ensure the loyalty of the wealthy middle class, not to further democracy. Because the enlarged Great Council served as a model for England's future legislature, it is called the *Model Parliament*.

By providing representation for both aristocrats and commoners, Edward hastened the division of Parliament into two Houses: the hereditary *House of Lords* and the elected *House of Commons*.

4. English Common Law. By the late 13th century English judges had established the practice of basing their decisions on similar cases decided previously. These legal precedents collectively formed a body of judge-made law called the *common law*. The English common law, both civil and criminal, applied to all the people equally. To protect the individual against possible governmental tyranny, the common law held that life, liberty, and property may not be taken by illegal and arbitrary action. The common law later became the basis of the American legal system.

5. Parliamentary Lawmaking (14th Century). By threatening to withhold tax laws, Parliament compelled the English kings to accept its legislation, not only on taxes, but on all matters. Henceforth, all laws required the consent of both Houses of Parliament and the approval of the King.

THE POPULAR TUDORS: UNCHECKED BY PARLIAMENT (1485-1603)

The leading Tudor rulers, particularly *Henry VII, Henry VIII,* and *Elizabeth I,* (1) governed capably and intelligently, (2) followed a popular foreign policy by opposing Catholic Spain, (3) aided the middle class by encouraging trade and overseas expansion, and (4) outwardly appeared to consult Parliament but actually dominated it. Although forceful monarchs, the Tudors enjoyed tremendous popularity both with the people and Parliament.

THE UNPOPULAR STUARTS: CONFLICTS WITH PARLIAMENT (1603-1642)

1. Reasons for Stuart Unpopularity. The early Stuart kings, *James I* and *Charles I,* (a) ruled arrogantly and tactlessly, claiming "divine right," (b) followed an unpopular foreign policy of friendship for Catholic Spain, (c) discriminated against the *Puritans,* a powerful Calvinist sect that considered Anglicanism too close to Catholicism and tried to "purify" Anglican practices, (d) harmed the middle class by taxing it heavily while neglecting to further trade, (e) violated English law by imprisoning opponents without fair trial, and (f) raised money by various means not approved by Parliament.

Popular resentment against Stuart policies encouraged Parliament to reassert its authority.

2. Parliament Issues the Petition of Right (1628). In the *Petition of Right,* Parliament protested the despotism of Charles I. In this document, Parliament reaffirmed that according to English law the King may *not* (a) levy taxes without Parliament's consent, (b) imprison persons without a specific charge and without provision for jury trial, and (c) quarter (board) soldiers in a private home without the owner's permission. By withholding new tax laws, Parliament finally compelled Charles to sign the Petition of Right.

3. Charles I Rules Without Parliament (1629-1640). Charles disregarded the Petition of Right and denied Parliament's authority to curb his "divine right" rule. For eleven years, Charles did not convene Parliament. Ruling autocratically, he (a) illegally raised money, (b) illegally imprisoned his opponents, (c) strengthened the *Star Chamber Courts,* where accused persons often were compelled by torture to testify against themselves, and (d) antagonized the Puritans by demanding their conformity to Church practices similar to Catholicism.

4. Charles I Calls and Clashes With Parliament (1640-1642). Desperate for additional funds to suppress a Scottish rebellion, Charles summoned Parliament into session. He soon realized that the House of Commons was controlled by his enemies, the Puritans. Charles' demand for new taxes was resisted by the Puritans, who insisted that he first abandon his autocratic policies. In 1642 his attempt to arrest the Puritan leaders of Commons caused the outbreak of civil war.

THE PURITAN REVOLUTION (1642-1660)

1. Parliament Wins the Civil War (1642-1645). Parliament rallied the middle class, the small landowners, and the Puritans—groups collectively called the *Roundheads*. Parliament also had the support of the Scots, who had rebelled against Charles' interference with their Presbyterian religion. Charles had the support of the nobility, the wealthy landowners, the high Anglican clergy, and the Catholics—groups collectively called the *Cavaliers*. The Parliamentary forces, led by *Oliver Cromwell*, an ardent Puritan, decisively defeated the Royalist armies.

2. Charles I Is Beheaded (1649). Charles was captured by his enemies. His most bitter foes in Parliament accused him of treason, murder, and tyranny, and placed him on trial. Charles was convicted and executed. Although this extreme measure shocked many people, it reaffirmed that English kings rule, not by "divine right," but in accordance with the law.

3. Oliver Cromwell Rules England (1649-1658). England was declared a republic, or *Commonwealth*, and Cromwell, the victorious Puritan general, ruled as a military dictator. In 1653 he took the title of *Lord Protector* of England. A highly capable leader, Cromwell furthered prosperity and maintained a successful anti-Spanish foreign policy.

Nevertheless, Cromwell's Puritan rule did not gain popular support because many Englishmen objected to (*a*) his dictatorial government and heavy taxes, (*b*) the Puritan role in the execution of Charles I, (*c*) Puritan intolerance of the Anglican religion, and (*d*) the severe Puritan moral code, which prohibited dancing, athletic games, theatrical performances, and other amusements.

Shortly after Cromwell's death in 1658, Puritan rule ended.

THE STUARTS RULE AGAIN IN ENGLAND (1660-1688)

1. Charles II Defers to Parliament (1660-1685). Upon Parliament's invitation, *Charles II* (the exiled son of Charles I) returned to England and assumed the throne. He pledged to observe Magna Carta and the Petition of Right, and to respect the authority of Parliament. Ever mindful of his father's fate, Charles II avoided antagonizing Parliament or the people.

In 1679 Charles yielded to Parliament's wishes and approved the *Habeas Corpus Act*. This act limited the King's powers by providing that (*a*) an arrested person may secure from a judge a court order called a *writ of habeas corpus*, and (*b*) by this writ, the prisoner is entitled to a prompt statement of charges, release on bail, and a speedy jury trial.

(Today, in both England and the United States, habeas corpus protects the individual against arbitrary arrest and imprisonment.)

2. James II Antagonizes Parliament (1685-1688). Upon Charles II's death, his brother assumed the throne as *James II*. A convert to Catholicism, James outraged the people and Parliament by (*a*) his pro-Catholic acts, and (*b*) his efforts to dominate Parliament and revive "divine right" rule. Moreover, the birth of his son aroused fear of continuing Catholic rule in England.

THE GLORIOUS REVOLUTION (1688-1689)

1. Parliament Overthrows James II. Parliament secretly offered the English crown to *William,* Protestant ruler of Holland, and his wife *Mary* (Protestant daughter of James II). They accepted. When William arrived in England, James fled the country. Parliament declared the throne vacant and proclaimed William and Mary the new King and Queen.

By this bloodless revolution, Parliament (*a*) finally ended "divine right" in England, and (*b*) reaffirmed its supremacy over the King.

2. Parliament Passes Laws Furthering Democracy. As part of this Glorious Revolution, Parliament passed the following laws:

a. The **Bill of Rights** (1689) provided that (1) the King may *not* make or suspend laws, levy taxes, or maintain an army without the consent of Parliament, (2) the King may *not* interfere with Parliamentary elections and debates, (3) Parliament must meet frequently, (4) the King must be Anglican in religion, and (5) the people are guaranteed basic civil liberties: the right to petition the government and to an impartial, speedy jury trial; and protection against excessive bails and fines, and against cruel and unusual punishments.

(A hundred years later, this great document served as a model for the first ten amendments of our Constitution—the American Bill of Rights.)

b. The **Toleration Act** (1689) granted freedom of worship to non-Anglican Protestant sects.

JOHN LOCKE: PHILOSOPHER OF THE GLORIOUS REVOLUTION

In his *Two Treatises of Government* (1689), John Locke justified the Glorious Revolution by a democratic political theory. He asserted that the people (1) possess natural rights to life, liberty, and property, (2) create government and grant it authority for the sole purpose of protecting these rights, and (3) may replace, by revolution if necessary, a government that fails in this purpose.

Locke's ideas greatly influenced later thinkers, especially (1) Thomas Jefferson, who wrote the American Declaration of Independence, and (2) Jean Jacques Rousseau, who wrote the *Social Contract,* a book that contributed much to the French *Declaration of the Rights of Man.*

FURTHER DEMOCRATIC GAINS IN ENGLAND

1. Political Parties. Political parties arose shortly before the Glorious Revolution. Each party consisted of people of similar interests who banded together to gain control of Parliament. The *Tories,* later known as *Conservatives,* represented the wealthy landowners. The *Whigs,* later known as *Liberals,* represented the middle class. Political parties further democracy by offering the voters a choice of candidates and ideas.

2. Cabinet Responsibility to Parliament. *Cabinet responsibility,* originating during the reign of William and Mary, means that the *cabinet,* or King's chief ministers, is chosen from and is responsible to the majority party in Parliament. Cabinet responsibility (*a*) insures harmony between the King's ministers and the legislature, and (*b*) is democratic, since the cabinet holds office only as long as it retains the support of an elected majority in Parliament.

3. Cabinet Executive Power. Cabinet executive power developed during the rule of King *George I* (1714-1727), a German prince who inherited the English throne. (His descendants have ruled England to this day and are known as the *House of Windsor.*) Since George I spoke no English and was unfamiliar with the workings of the English government, the cabinet, and its leader, the *Prime Minister,* assumed full direction of executive affairs. (England's first Prime Minister was a Whig statesman, *Robert Walpole.*)

Cabinet executive power proved to be a democratic gain, as the English King became a mere figurehead.

SUMMARY: ENGLAND AS A LIMITED MONARCHY (1750)

1. Democratic Gains. (*a*) The King did not rule by "divine right" but was subject to English law and tradition. (*b*) Parliament controlled the government and was supreme over the King. (*c*) The government featured political parties, cabinet responsibility to Parliament, and cabinet executive power. (*d*) The people were guaranteed basic civil liberties.

2. Undemocratic Features. (*a*) Property qualifications prevented 90 percent of the people from voting for members of Parliament. (*b*) Elections were marked by bribery and corruption. (c) The hereditary House of Lords was as powerful as the elected House of Commons. (d) The government was controlled by the upper classes.

The outbreak of the French Revolution (1789) delayed further English democratic reforms.

Part 3. The American Revolution (1775-1783): Independence and Democracy

ENGLAND'S POLICY TOWARD HER THIRTEEN AMERICAN COLONIES

1. **Neglect (Before 1763).** For a long time, England neglected her American colonies. They (a) enjoyed considerable self-government and, (b) disregarded English mercantilist laws, the *Navigation Acts*. These acts, in accordance with mercantile doctrine (see page 141), sought to restrict colonial industry and to discourage colonial trade with all countries except the mother country.

2. **Effect of the French and Indian War (1754-1763).** Although England won the French and Indian War (see page 140), the English government considered the aid received from the American colonies greatly inadequate. King *George III* and the Tory party determined to (a) reestablish control over the colonies, and (b) compel the colonies to bear part of the war's cost.

3. **Strict Control (After 1763).** England then (a) vigorously enforced the Navigation Acts, (b) combatted colonial smugglers by authorizing *writs of assistance* for unlimited search of private buildings and by denying accused smugglers a jury trial, (c) subjected colonists to an import tax, particularly on tea and sugar, and a stamp tax on printed materials, (d) prohibited westward migrations beyond the Allegheny Mountains, and (e) stationed English troops in the colonies, often quartering them in private homes.

COLONIAL DEFIANCE OF STRICT ENGLISH CONTROL

The colonial patriots (1) smuggled goods to evade import taxes, (2) boycotted English goods, (3) demonstrated against English soldiers, (4) organized committees to coordinate anti-English efforts, and (5) spoke and wrote against England's colonial policy.

OUTBREAK OF THE AMERICAN REVOLUTION

In 1773 Massachusetts colonists, protesting the import tax, dumped British tea into Boston Harbor—an event called the *Boston Tea Party*. This action provoked Parliament to punish Massachusetts by restricting self-government and temporarily closing Boston Harbor—laws that the colonists called "intolerable." The other colonies rallied to support Massachusetts and united in their action against England by forming the *First Continental Congress*. Tension increased between patriots and British officials. In 1775, at *Lexington* and *Concord*, colonial *minutemen* fired upon British troops marching from Boston to seize colonial military supplies and leaders. This was the start of the American Revolution.

BASIC CAUSES OF THE AMERICAN REVOLUTION

1. Economic. (*a*) Colonial manufacturers and merchants were indignant over the English mercantilist laws, which hampered their industry and trade. They rejected the doctrine that colonies exist only to enrich the mother country. (*b*) Plantation owners and frontiersmen, eager for new land, disliked the prohibition against westward expansion. (*c*) Professional people opposed the stamp tax on printed matter, such as newspapers, pamphlets, and legal documents. (*d*) Consumers resented import taxes, which raised living costs.

2. Political. (*a*) The colonists maintained that they could be taxed only by their colonial legislatures; therefore, they considered taxes voted by Parliament as "taxation without representation." They dismissed the English argument that Parliament legislates for the entire Empire. (*b*) The colonists regarded the quartering of English soldiers, the writs of assistance, and the denial of jury trials as violations of their "rights as Englishmen." The colonists claimed that, as 17th-century Englishmen had revolted against the tyranny of the Stuarts, they were revolting against the tyranny of George III.

3. Social. (*a*) Many colonists of English stock no longer considered themselves Englishmen; after several generations, the New World environment had transformed them into Americans. (*b*) The non-English colonists—such as the Irish, Dutch, and French—came from countries traditionally hostile to England.

4. Misunderstanding. The colonies were separated from England by the Atlantic Ocean, a body of water 3,000 miles wide and bridged only by slow-moving ships. This great distance proved a barrier to understanding, negotiation, and compromise.

REASONS FOR DECLARING AMERICAN INDEPENDENCE

In 1776 the *Second Continental Congress* decided that the colonies were fighting for complete independence from England. Colonial patriots (1) complained of brutal British military behavior, (2) considered independence a logical goal, a point of view skillfully argued by *Thomas Paine* in his popular pamphlet *Common Sense*, and (3) hoped that a declaration of independence might secure foreign allies, especially France.

THE DECLARATION OF INDEPENDENCE (JULY 4, 1776)

The *Declaration of Independence*, written chiefly by *Thomas Jefferson*, was a great democratic document. It reflects Jefferson's thinking, based on the ideas of the English philosopher John Locke (see pages 147-148). In the Declaration, Jefferson outlines the basic principles that underlie democratic governments:

1. "All men are created equal" and "are endowed by their Creator with certain unalienable Rights" (rights that cannot be taken away), including "Life, Liberty and the pursuit of Happiness."
2. To secure these rights, governments are instituted among men, "deriving their just powers from the consent of the governed."
3. "Whenever any Form of Government becomes destructive of these ends, it is the Right of the People to alter or to abolish it, and to institute new Government."

After stating these democratic principles, the Declaration lists grievances against George III and concludes that the colonies have the right to independence.

DISAGREEMENT BETWEEN COLONISTS: PATRIOTS VS. TORIES

Not all colonists supported the revolution. Of the total population (1) one-third, the well-organized *patriots*, favored independence, (2) one-third were undecided, and (3) one-third, the unorganized *Loyalists*, or *Tories*, were loyal to England. The more prominent Tories consisted of wealthy landowners and government officials. During the war, many Tories fled to Canada and England, whereupon the patriots broke up the large Tory estates. Also, the patriots removed royal authority in state governments and took steps to provide more democratic state constitutions.

REASONS FOR THE AMERICAN VICTORY

The American patriots (1) were fighting on their own soil, (2) were experienced wilderness fighters, (3) were led by courageous, able men, notably the Commander-in-Chief, *George Washington*, (4) were aided by such capable foreign volunteers as the Frenchman *Lafayette*, and (5) were joined in the conflict by France in 1778 and later by Spain and Holland. Thus, the American Revolution became part of a larger war, in which the colonists, with foreign assistance, achieved victory.

By the *Treaty of Paris* (1783), the thirteen American colonies secured their independence from England.

DEMOCRATIC EFFECTS OF THE AMERICAN REVOLUTION

1. In the United States. In 1789 the *Constitution* established the present government of the *United States of America.* Representing many democratic gains, this written Constitution (*a*) created a federal republic headed by an elected *President,* (*b*) stated the powers of, and limitations upon, the government, (*c*) separated governmental powers among three branches—executive, legislative, and judicial—to prevent any one branch from dominating, and (*d*) in 1791 included a *Bill of Rights* which protected the people from possible government tyranny.

The Bill of Rights (1) guaranteed freedom of speech, press, and religion; and the right to assemble peaceably, to petition the government, and to speedy, impartial jury trial, and (2) prohibited unreasonable searches, excessive fines, cruel punishments, the forcing of a person to be a witness against himself, and the quartering of troops in homes.

2. In Latin America. The American Revolution inspired the New World colonies of Spain and Portugal to revolt in the early 19th century and achieve self-government.

3. In England. The American Revolution (*a*) discredited George III and his efforts to revive royal executive power, and (*b*) led to a gradual change in England's colonial policy. To prevent colonial rebellion, England eventually granted self-government to most of her possessions, starting in 1867 with Canada.

4. In France. The American Revolution, by encouraging Frenchmen to replace their absolute monarchy with a more democratic government, helped inspire the French Revolution of 1789.

MULTIPLE-CHOICE QUESTIONS

1. Which one of these is the best evidence of democracy? (1) The government is headed by a president. (2) Elections are held. (3) Trials are conducted. (4) Civil liberties are protected.
2. The democratic form of government first appeared in (1) the Roman Empire under Augustus (2) the Middle Ages (3) the ancient Greek city-states (4) England under Henry VIII.
3. An immediate effect of Magna Carta was to (1) establish the English Parliament (2) give equal rights to all persons (3) create a cabinet system (4) limit the King's power over the nobles.
4. Magna Carta is considered the cornerstone of English democracy because it (1) limited the power of the Church (2) limited the powers of Parliament (3) was forced upon the King by the workers in the towns (4) later became a basis for English political liberties.

5. During the 16th century the main reason for the increase in the power of the monarch in England was the (1) Glorious Revolution (2) ability of the Tudor rulers (3) ability of the Stuart rulers (4) marriage of Queen Mary to Philip II of Spain.

6. The Stuart rulers of England strongly believed in (1) the supremacy of Parliament (2) religious freedom (3) the divine right of kings (4) rule by the middle class.

7. In 1660 Parliament restored the Stuart monarchy mainly because the Commonwealth government had (1) sought to impose Puritan religious and moral beliefs upon the country (2) formed an alliance with Spain (3) caused economic depression (4) weakened England's naval power.

8. The Habeas Corpus Act made it unlawful for a citizen to be (1) taxed without the consent of Parliament (2) held indefinitely in prison without a hearing (3) persecuted for his religious beliefs (4) forced to be a witness against himself.

9. An immediate effect of the Glorious Revolution in England was (1) the return of the Tudors as rulers of England (2) the supremacy of Parliament over the King (3) universal manhood suffrage (4) restrictions on the Anglican Church.

10. The Bill of Rights of 1689 declared that (1) no taxes should be levied without the consent of Parliament (2) the King could worship as he saw fit (3) members of Parliament were to be elected by universal suffrage (4) the Star Chamber Court could be used only in cases of sedition and treason.

11. The Bill of Rights did *not* guarantee all the people the right (1) to a speedy trial (2) to petition the government (3) of protection against cruel punishments (4) to vote for members of the House of Commons.

12. John Locke justified the Glorious Revolution on the grounds that (1) kings hold power by divine right (2) government is unnecessary (3) government is a contract entered into between the ruler and the ruled (4) rulers are responsible to the House of Lords.

13. Natural rights, according to John Locke, include the right to (1) obtain a free education (2) possess private property (3) receive an old-age pension (4) work.

14. To show opposition to strict English control, the American colonists did each of the following *except* to (1) smuggle goods (2) defy writs of assistance (3) boycott English goods (4) pass mercantilist laws.

15. The Declaration of Independence (1) guarantees religious freedom to all (2) provides for a system of checks and balances (3) gives all men the right to vote (4) declares that all men are created equal.

16. The Declaration of Independence (1) guarantees free universal education (2) declares that governments derive their just powers from the consent of the governed (3) declares that every man's house is his castle (4) guarantees equal opportunity for all.

17. In America, the Tories were those colonists who (1) actively supported the Revolution (2) were undecided about the Revolution (3) remained loyal to the King (4) lived west of the Allegheny Mountains.

18. Which nation helped the American colonies in their revolt against England? (1) France (2) Italy (3) Sweden (4) Portugal.

19. To keep Stuart Star Chamber Court procedures from the United States, the American Bill of Rights (1) guarantees freedom of press (2) provides that no person shall be compelled to testify against himself (3) requires judges to be appointed for life (4) orders the keeping of records of court proceedings.

20. Since our chief executive secures office by election rather than hereditary right, the United States is a (1) republic (2) democracy (3) monarchy (4) nation.

21. The American Revolution is important in world history because it (1) delayed the Industrial Revolution in Europe (2) ended British influence in the Western Hemisphere (3) set an example for other colonial peoples (4) adopted reforms from the French Revolution.

IDENTIFICATION QUESTIONS: WHO AM I?

Charles I   James I   Thomas Paine
Oliver Cromwell   Thomas Jefferson   Jean Jacques Rousseau
George I   King John   Robert Walpole
Henry II   Marquis de Lafayette George Washington

1. I was leader of the Puritan army that overthrew tyrannical Stuart rule and established the Commonwealth in England.
2. In my widely read work *Common Sense* I urged the American colonists to seek complete independence from England.
3. At Runnymede in 1215, I was forced by some of my nobles to accept a document, Magna Carta, although its provisions were distasteful to me.
4. To strengthen central authority in England, I expanded royal circuit courts and, in certain cases, authorized trial by jury.
5. Although a Frenchman, I fought on the side of the American colonists and brought American democratic ideals back to my native land.
6. My persecution of Puritans and my clashes with Parliament led to a civil war, in which I was captured and beheaded.
7. I drew upon the philosophy of John Locke in writing the American Declaration of Independence.
8. I was a German prince who inherited the English throne. Since I knew little about English government, I permitted executive power to pass into the hands of the Prime Minister.

Part 4. The French Revolution of 1789: Democratic Gains

FUNDAMENTAL CAUSE OF THE FRENCH REVOLUTION: ABUSES OF THE OLD REGIME

The political, social, and economic system of 18th-century Europe was called the *Old Regime*. In France, the Old Regime was characterized by deep-rooted abuses.

1. Political. (*a*) The King was an absolute monarch, ruling by divine right. He exercised unlimited powers: made and enforced laws, conducted foreign affairs, dispensed justice, and controlled finances. (*b*) The King selected his ministers on the basis of noble birth or favoritism, not ability. Frequently, royal government was corrupt and inefficient. (*c*) The King censored speech and press to stifle what he considered dangerous ideas. (*d*) By using *lettres de cachet* (letters bearing the royal seal), the King imprisoned his enemies indefinitely, without charge, bail, or trial. (*e*) The King denied the people a voice in the government and a way to make known their grievances.

2. Social. The French people were divided into three rigid, distinct classes, called Estates. The *First Estate* consisted of the clergy; the *Second Estate*, of the nobility; the *Third Estate*, of the rest of the population: the bourgeoisie (merchants, bankers, manufacturers, professionals), city workers, and peasants.

The First and Second Estates, totaling 3 percent of the population, were the *privileged* classes. They (a) owned most of the land, (b) collected special feudal dues from the peasants, (c) received exemption from most taxes, (d) held the best government and army jobs, and (e) enjoyed special treatment before the law. (The First Estate, however, also included poor parish priests, who lived no better than the peasants.)

The Third Estate, or 97 percent of the population, was the *unprivileged* class.

3. Economic. The Third Estate bore almost the entire tax burden. The peasants, the most numerous Third Estate group, gave the following taxes: (a) to the government: the *taille* (land tax), *corvée* (forced labor on roads and bridges), and *gabelle* (tax on compulsory salt purchases), (b) to the Church: the *tithe*, and (c) to the lords: *feudal dues*. Such taxes left the peasants with only about half of their meager income.

The bourgeoisie, the most influential group in the Third Estate, were hampered in manufacturing and trade by (a) provincial tariffs, (b) guild restrictions, and (c) government mercantilist regulations.

OTHER BASIC CAUSES OF THE FRENCH REVOLUTION

Conditions in France under the Old Regime, although oppressive, were better than elsewhere in continental Europe. Nevertheless, the French led the way in revolt.

1. The French Bourgeoisie. The bourgeoisie of France was the most powerful in continental Europe: wealthy, well-educated, and ambitious. The bourgeoisie keenly resented the arrogance of the nobility. To remedy Old Regime abuses, the bourgeoisie sought a role in shaping government policies. The bourgeoisie provided many French revolutionary leaders.

The bourgeoisie wanted the government to discard the policy of mercantilism, with its restrictions on industry and trade, and adopt a policy of *laissez-faire* (leave business alone). These economic ideas had been skillfully presented in the book *Wealth of Nations* (1776) by the Scottish economist *Adam Smith*. Laissez-faire, Smith argued, not only would enable the bourgeoisie to further their own economic interests, but would also increase the national wealth.

2. The French Philosophers. In the 18th century the French philosophers led the *Intellectual Revolution* (also called the *Enlightenment*, or *Age of Reason*). Insisting that human institutions should conform to logic and reason, they challenged traditional royal and Church authority, and called for the end of the Old Regime. Despite censorship, the "enlightened" thinking of the French philosophers reached many people. The leading philosophers were Voltaire, Rousseau, Montesquieu, and Diderot.

a. Voltaire (1694-1778), in his book *Letters on the English*, praised England's limited monarchy and civil liberties, and denounced the French government's censorship, injustice, and despotism. Voltaire was especially bitter against the Catholic Church. He believed that its insistence upon authority barred human progress.

b. Rousseau (1712-1778), in his book *Social Contract*, declared "Man is born free, and everywhere he is in chains." Rousseau maintained that (1) the people have natural and inalienable rights to life, liberty, and property, (2) by contract among themselves, they may create government and grant it powers to serve the people, and (3) when dissatisfied, they may change the government.

Rousseau's ideas were patterned in great part after those of the 17th-century English philosopher, John Locke (see pages 147-148). They were also similar to Jefferson's ideas in the Declaration of Independence (see page 151).

c. Montesquieu (1689-1755), in his book *Spirit of Laws,* proposed to prevent despotism by reorganizing government. He urged that governmental powers be separated among three branches—executive, legislative, and judicial—instead of remaining concentrated in one person, the King.

Montesquieu's proposed separation of powers was adopted in the United States Constitution.

d. Diderot (1713-1784), in editing the *Encyclopedia,* included many articles vigorously attacking Old Regime abuses, such as religious intolerance, unjust taxation, and governmental absolutism.

3. Influence of the English and American Revolutions. Of all continental Europeans, the French had been most stimulated by the successful revolts in England and America. France was influenced by the Puritan and Glorious Revolutions in England because (*a*) the two countries are geographically close, and (*b*) the French philosophers praised the English parliamentary government.

France was influenced by the American Revolution (1775-1783) because (*a*) Lafayette and other Frenchmen fought for the American cause and spread liberal ideas, and (*b*) Benjamin Franklin and Thomas Jefferson, popular American envoys to Paris, inspired French thought.

4. Incompetent and Unpopular Government. King *Louis XVI* (ruled 1774-1792) was incompetent to rule France in such difficult times, for he possessed a dull mind and a weak character. Furthermore, his Queen, *Marie Antoinette,* was unpopular. She was a foreigner (from Austria), and a vain and frivolous person.

IMMEDIATE CAUSE OF THE FRENCH REVOLUTION: FINANCIAL DIFFICULTIES

1. Louis XVI Brings France to Financial Bankruptcy (by 1788). As a result of his predecessors' extravagances and wars, Louis XVI inherited an impoverished French treasury. Instead of instituting reforms, he worsened the situation as he (*a*) spent heavily to aid the American colonists against England, (*b*) maintained a lavish royal court at Versailles, and (*c*) refused to tax the privileged classes.

Louis ignored the advice of two able finance ministers—first *Turgot* and then *Necker*—to end court extravagances and tax the nobility. Heeding the courtiers, Louis dismissed these ministers without effecting any financial reforms. By 1788 France was in bankruptcy.

2. Louis Summons the Estates-General (1789)

a. Significance. To solve the financial crisis, Louis called into session the French legislature, the *Estates-General.* For 175 years (since 1614), French kings had ruled autocratically without convening the Estates-General. By breaking this precedent, Louis admitted that the King alone could not solve France's financial difficulties.

b. Undemocratic Features of the Estates-General

(1) *Representation.* The Estates-General consisted of the privileged First Estate—300 representatives; the privileged Second Estate—300 representatives; and the unprivileged Third Estate—600 representatives. The two privileged classes, constituting 3 percent of the population, thus had as many representatives as the unprivileged class, totaling 97 percent of the population.

(2) *Voting.* The Estates-General voted by Estates, not by individual members. Each Estate had one vote. Therefore, the two privileged Estates, together having two votes, could outvote the Third Estate.

REPRESENTATION IN THE ESTATES-GENERAL (1789)

CLASSES		REPRESENTATIVES IN ESTATES-GENERAL	VOTES IN ESTATES-GENERAL	PERCENT OF POPULATION
Privileged classes	First Estate	300	1	3%
	Second Estate	300	1	
Unprivileged class	Third Estate	600	1	97%

c. The Cahiers—Lists of Grievances. The Third Estate representatives brought *cahiers*, or lists of complaints, from the people. These documents demanded far-reaching reforms—an end to Old Regime abuses.

THE FRENCH REVOLUTION BEGINS (1789)

1. The Estates-General Becomes the National Assembly (1789). The Third Estate representatives were led by the *Abbé Sieyès* and *Count Mirabeau,* members of the privileged classes. The Third Estate members demanded that the Estates-General be transformed into a *National Assembly* with each *member,* not each *Estate,* having one vote. By this method of voting, the commoners, joined by some liberal clergy and nobility, would gain the Assembly majority and enact a program of basic reform.

When the King rejected the proposed National Assembly, the representatives of the Third Estate took two revolutionary actions: (*a*) They declared themselves to be the National Assembly. (*b*) In the *Tennis Court Oath,* they pledged to provide France with a constitution.

These actions were supported by Paris mobs, who demonstrated against the King. Thereupon, Louis capitulated and consented to the formation of the National Assembly.

2. The Bastille Is Destroyed (July 14, 1789). Incited by rumors that the King had ordered troops to Paris to disperse the National Assembly, Paris mobs stormed and destroyed a symbol of the Old Regime—the hated prison called the *Bastille.* When this news reached the provinces, the aroused peasants attacked nobles' castles and destroyed the records of feudal dues.

By such violence, the commoners (*a*) expressed their support for the National Assembly, and (*b*) gave warning to the King and the nobility not to resist reforms.

The French people celebrate July 14—the day of the fall of the Bastille— as their great national holiday. Bastille Day is the equivalent of July 4, our Independence Day.

WORK OF THE NATIONAL ASSEMBLY (1789-1791)

Controlled by its bourgeoisie members, the National Assembly legislated against Old Regime conditions.

1. Abolition of Special Privileges. The National Assembly abolished (*a*) payment of feudal dues by the peasants, (*b*) payment of Church tithes, (*c*) tax exemptions of the privileged classes, (*d*) all class distinctions, and (*e*) guild restrictions on trade and manufacturing.

2. Declaration of the Rights of Man. The National Assembly adopted the *Declaration of the Rights of Man.* (*a*) Men are born free and equal with rights to liberty, property, security, and resistance to oppression. (b) All citizens are entitled to a voice in making the nation's laws. (c) All persons are guaranteed equality before the law; freedom from unlawful arrest; and freedom of speech, press, and religion. (The Declaration of the Rights of Man was modeled after the English Bill of Rights and the American Declaration of Independence.)

3. Financial Measures. To solve the financial crisis, the National Assembly seized the Church lands, totaling one-fifth of France. This measure aided the government financially.

a. Church lands were used to back a new paper currency, called *assignats*. However, as the government kept printing an ever-increasing amount of assignats, they declined in value and eventually became worthless.

b. Church lands (and the domains of some nobles) were broken up and sold at low prices to the peasants. These sales transformed France into a nation of small, independent landowners.

4. Religious Measures. To deprive the Catholic Church of the special position it had held under the Old Regime, the National Assembly abolished Church tithes, seized Church lands, guaranteed religious freedom to all groups, and subjected the Church to state control by the *Civil Constitution of the Clergy.*

The Civil Constitution (a) turned the Catholic Church in France into a national church independent of the Pope, and (b) changed Catholic clergymen into paid government officials elected by the people.

This document was condemned by the Pope and by most French clergymen. Those clergymen who refused to swear allegiance to the law were called *nonjuring clergy.*

The Catholic Church—from highest clergyman to parish priest and devout layman—became the Revolution's bitter enemy.

5. Reform of Local Government. The National Assembly (a) replaced the old provinces with 83 *departments* ruled by local assemblies, and (b) replaced the old provincial tariffs, taxes, and regulations with uniform national taxes and laws. By deemphasizing traditional local loyalties and by making laws nationwide, the National Assembly stimulated loyalty to the nation.

0. Constitution of 1791. The National Assembly wrote a constitution providing for a *limited monarchy.* (a) The hereditary King retained limited executive powers and had only a temporary veto over legislation. (b) The elected *Legislative Assembly* passed the nation's laws. (c) Members of the Assembly had to be property owners elected by taxpaying citizens.

By these provisions, the bourgeoisie, in control of the National Assembly, expected to retain power in the new government.

THE LIMITED MONARCHY HAS A SHORT LIFE (1791-1792)

1. Supporters. Most of the *bourgeoisie* and many *peasants* were well satisfied with their gains under the Revolution. These groups supported the limited monarchy and wanted an end to excitement and change. This proved impossible, however, since too many groups were dissatisfied with the Revolution and opposed the limited monarchy.

2. Opponents Favoring a Republic

a. Girondists, a *moderate* political party representing some of the bourgeoisie, wanted a middle-class republic (similar to the United States).

b. Jacobins, a *radical* political party, represented the city workingmen, who, under the constitution of 1791, had no voice in the government. They opposed both the King and the bourgeoisie. The Jacobins desired a republic dominated by the poorer people.

The Jacobins got very close to the people because of (1) their many clubs throughout France, (2) their skillful use of newspapers and street demonstrations to spread their ideas, and (3) their capable leaders: *Marat, Danton, Robespierre.*

3. Opponents Favoring the Old Regime

a. Louis XVI resented the loss of his absolute power. He conspired with foreign monarchs against the Revolution. Louis and his wife, Marie Antoinette, attempted to flee the country, but were captured and brought back to Paris.

b. Devout Catholics, led by the nonjuring clergy, opposed the Revolution's treatment of the Church.

c. French nobles were indignant over the loss of their special privileges. The *émigrés*—nobles who had fled the country—urged foreign monarchs to invade France and restore the Old Regime.

d. Foreign monarchs, especially the kings of Prussia and Austria, feared that the French Revolution, if successful, would inspire revolt among their own subjects. In 1792 these rulers ordered their armies into France to suppress the Revolution.

4. End of the Monarchy. The limited monarchy did not survive the foreign invasion of France. As Austrian and Prussian armies moved toward Paris, French antiroyalists rioted. They accused the King of being in communication with the enemy. The French legislature thereupon deposed the King and called for elections to a *National Convention,* which was to draw up a new constitution.

THE NATIONAL CONVENTION PROTECTS AND PROMOTES THE REVOLUTION (1792-1795)

1. The First French Republic. The National Convention proclaimed France a republic—the *First French Republic*. The Convention then tried Louis XVI on charges of treason and sentenced him to death by *guillotine,* in defiance of the strong protests of the monarchs of Europe. Soon, France was invaded by additional foreign armies. Not only Prussia and Austria, but also England, Holland, and Spain sought to crush the Revolution.

2. Jacobin Domination: The Committee of Public Safety. In the face of foreign invasion, the radical Jacobins seized control of the Convention. They were determined to protect the Revolution against its enemies, both foreign and domestic. The Jacobins centralized all governmental powers into the *Committee of Public Safety.* This was a small dictatorial group led first by Danton and later by Robespierre.

3. Conscript Armies Repel Foreign Invaders. To protect the Revolution against *foreign* enemies, the Committee of Public Safety appealed to the *nationalism* of the French people. The Committee obligated all Frenchmen to compulsory military service, called *conscription,* or *draft.* Inspired by French Revolutionary ideals, the citizen-soldiers of the conscripted armies decisively drove out the invading mercenary forces.

4. The Reign of Terror Crushes Domestic Enemies. To protect the Revolution against *domestic* enemies, the Committee of Public Safety instituted the *Reign of Terror.* The Committee (*a*) arrested all persons suspected of treason, no matter how farfetched the suspicion, and (*b*) sentenced many thousands to death by guillotine, no matter how meager the evidence against them. This Reign of Terror brutally crushed all domestic opposition.

Eventually, the horrors of the Reign of Terror turned the French people against the Jacobins and brought an end to the Reign of Terror. In 1794, the rival Jacobin leaders, Danton and Robespierre, were both guillotined. The moderates, or anti-Jacobins, now regained control of the National Convention.

5. Noteworthy Reforms. To promote its Revolutionary goals, the National Convention (*a*) abolished imprisonment for debt, (*b*) abolished Negro slavery in French colonies, (*c*) adopted the metric system of uniform weights and measures, (*d*) planned a national system of education, and (*e*) prohibited *primogeniture,* a practice that required property to be willed, regardless of other children, entirely to the eldest son.

Also, the Convention drew up a constitution for a republic headed by a *Directory.*

SIGNIFICANCE OF THE FRENCH REVOLUTION

1. Democratic Ideals. The French Revolution proclaimed the individual's democratic rights in its slogan *liberté, égalité, fraternité*.

a. Liberty meant freedom for all persons (1) from despotism, especially absolute rule and unjust imprisonment, (2) from unnecessary and unfair economic restrictions, (3) to influence and change the government, and (4) of speech, press, religion, and other basic civil liberties.

b. Equality meant equal treatment for all persons (1) before the law, and (2) in business, society, and politics.

c. Fraternity meant the brotherhood of all persons working together to make a better world.

2. Emphasis on Nationalism. The French Revolution intensified the spirit of nationalism. Loyalty to the nation permeated all classes and influenced every aspect of life. (*a*) War became the concern of the entire nation, as conscript citizen-armies rose to defend—not their province or city, nor their feudal lord or King—but their country. (*b*) The *Marseillaise*, a patriotic song by *Rouget de Lisle*, was adopted as the national anthem. (*c*) *July 14, Bastille Day*, was proclaimed a national holiday. (*d*) State-controlled education began to serve as a major agency for preserving the nation's ideals.

3. Worldwide Influence. The French Revolution, with its ideals of democracy and nationalism, has tremendously influenced peoples throughout the world: first in western Europe, then in Latin America, and later in Asia and Africa. To this very day, peoples everywhere who seek democratic government and national independence reflect the influence of the French Revolution.

MULTIPLE-CHOICE QUESTIONS

1. Which statement describes the Old Regime in France? (1) No differences existed among social classes. (2) The burden of taxation fell almost entirely on the Third Estate. (3) Citizens enjoyed freedom of speech. (4) The Estates-General controlled the government.
2. The two privileged classes in France under the Old Regime were the (1) nobility and peasants (2) nobility and clergy (3) nobility and bourgeoisie (4) clergy and bourgeoisie.
3. Which was a *fundamental* cause of the French Revolution of 1789? (1) fear of foreign invasion (2) the attempted flight of King Louis XVI (3) the fall of the Bastille (4) unjust administration of the law.
4. Which is most nearly *opposite* in meaning to the *writ of habeas corpus?* (1) *lettre de cachet* (sealed letter) (2) assignat (3) Tennis Court Oath (4) tithe.
5. France was the first country in continental Europe to have a revolution against the Old Regime because (1) Louis XVI was an evil tyrant (2) the middle class was more advanced than in other countries (3) economic conditions were worse than in other countries (4) a Frenchman invented the guillotine.

6. In his book *Social Contract,* Rousseau supported the principle of (1) the totalitarian state (2) the divine right of kings (3) benevolent despotism (4) government by the will of the people.

7. Which was an important contribution of Voltaire and Montesquieu? (1) writing the Declaration of the Rights of Man (2) voting for the execution of Louis XVI (3) publicizing the injustices of the Old Regime (4) acting as advisers to the Girondists.

8. Supporters of Adam Smith's laissez-faire theory advocated (1) high protective tariffs (2) partial regulation of business by government (3) strict regulation of business by government (4) noninterference in business by government.

9. An important characteristic of the Intellectual Revolution of the 18th century was (1) a criticism of the Old Regime (2) the centralization of government (3) a dispute resulting in a split in the Catholic Church (4) a revival of interest in Latin literature.

10. The word best characterizing Louis XVI is (1) able (2) ambitious (3) incompetent (4) cruel.

11. The seizure of the Bastille on July 14, 1789, was important because it (1) gave the Revolutionists a strong fort (2) released thousands of prisoners who joined the Revolutionary army (3) placed the royal family in the power of the Revolutionists (4) represented a successful attack on a symbol of the tyranny of the Old Regime.

12. Louis XVI's purpose in summoning the Estates-General in 1789 was to (1) draft a new constitution (2) choose a new King (3) make a treaty of alliance with the United States (4) consider the question of government debt.

13. The representatives of the Third Estate demanded that the Estates-General be declared a National Assembly in order to (1) bar representatives of the clergy and nobility (2) please the King (3) achieve voting by members rather than by Estates (4) secure additional representatives from the bourgeoisie.

14. *The Declaration of the Rights of Man,* adopted by the National Assembly, was a (1) constitution to govern France (2) document stating the principles of the French Revolution (3) law confiscating Church lands in France (4) declaration of war against the monarchs of Austria and Prussia.

15. The Civil Constitution of the Clergy (1) placed the Church under government control (2) was advocated by the Church (3) was written by Diderot (4) was widely accepted by the French clergy.

16. During the French Revolution the Jacobins favored the establishment of (1) a republic (2) a limited monarchy (3) an absolute monarchy (4) a confederation.

17. Foreign intervention during the French Revolution resulted in the (1) suppression of the Jacobins (2) establishment of a limited monarchy (3) Reign of Terror (4) overthrow of the first French Republic.

18. As a result of the French Revolution, the Catholic Church in France (1) was strengthened (2) was permanently driven out (3) became the established church (4) had its power limited.

19. "Equality" in the slogan "liberty, equality, fraternity" meant equality (1) of income (2) of ability (3) before the law (4) in land ownership.

20. A permanent result of the Revolution for France was the (1) establishment of a two-party system of government (2) abolition of the feudal class system (3) loss of the French overseas empire (4) destruction of the bourgeoisie.

MULTIPLE-CHOICE QUESTIONS

Select the number of the item that does *not* belong in the corresponding group.

1. *Revolutions before 1789 in which Frenchmen took active part:* (1) Glorious Revolution (2) American Revolution (3) Commercial Revolution (4) Intellectual Revolution.

2. *Taxes burdening the peasants under the Old Regime:* (1) gabelle (2) taille (3) cahier (4) corvée.
3. *Jacobin leaders during the French Revolution:* (1) Robespierre (2) Danton (3) Diderot (4) Marat.
4. *The French Declaration of the Rights of Man:* (1) the model for the American Declaration of Independence (2) greatly influenced by Rousseau (3) drafted during the early stages of the French Revolution (4) based largely on Locke's theory of natural rights.
5. *Reforms of the National Assembly:* (1) abolition of special privileges (2) reform of local government (3) a constitution for a limited monarchy (4) shift of France's capital to Versailles.

Part 5. The Napoleonic Era (1799-1815): Military Dictatorship

NAPOLEON'S RISE TO POWER: REASONS

Napoleon Bonaparte, son of a poor village lawyer, was born on the Mediterranean island of *Corsica.* By 1799, at the age of 30, he had become master of France. His amazing rise was due to:

1. His Character. Napoleon possessed a brilliant mind, a keen insight into human nature, and tireless energy. Above all, he had tremendous ambition; he believed himself a "man of destiny." In his climb to power, he was ruthless and unprincipled.

2. His Military Ability. Educated in a French military academy, Napoleon became one of history's greatest generals. He devised superior combat tactics, inspired his soldiers, and won astounding victories. Napoleon's troops, who fondly called him the "Little Corporal," supported his political ambitions.

3. France's Desire for Orderly Government. By 1799 the French people had become weary of Revolutionary disorder and were displeased with the inefficient, corrupt Directory. They wanted a government which, while safeguarding Revolutionary gains, would prove competent and orderly. For such government, Frenchmen were willing to accept the popular military hero, Napoleon.

NAPOLEON'S RISE TO POWER: HIGHLIGHTS

1. First Public Recognition (1793-1795). Napoleon, as artillery officer, helped drive English troops from the French seaport of Toulon. Later, in 1795, Napoleon dispersed rioting Paris mobs that threatened the National Convention.

2. Italian Campaign (1796-1797). Napoleon was now given command of the French army in Italy and won a series of impressive victories in which he routed the larger Austrian forces. He thus became a national hero.

3. Egyptian Campaign (1798-1799). To secure a base for attacking England's valuable colony of India, Napoleon invaded Egypt. Napoleon's reports of great military victories, although highly exaggerated, enhanced his popularity. At home, the incompetent Directory was daily losing public support. French armies were suffering reverses in Europe. The French fleet in the Mediterranean was destroyed by the British under *Admiral Nelson* in the Battle of the Nile. In 1799 Napoleon left his army in Egypt and returned to France.

4. Coup d'État (1799). Napoleon ousted the Directory by a *coup d'état* (a swift overthrow of a government by force). He prepared a new constitution, and it was approved by a plebiscite (a "yes" or "no" vote of the people). The constitution retained the form of a republic but concentrated governmental power in the *First Consul*. Napoleon ruled France officially as First Consul, but in reality as military dictator.

5. Proclamation of Empire (1804). Napoleon changed the republic into an Empire and crowned himself *Emperor Napoleon I*. Impressed by Napoleon's military and governmental achievements, the people again voted overwhelming approval. The French Revolution had thus led to an undisguised dictatorship.

NAPOLEON DOMINATES EUROPE

In 1799, when Napoleon seized the government by his coup d'état, France was at war with the Allies, a coalition of Europe's hereditary rulers who were determined to crush the French Revolution. Napoleon took command of the French forces, won significant victories, and in 1802 ended the war favorably for France.

After a brief peace, Napoleon and the Allies resumed the conflict. The Allies wanted to overthrow Napoleon and destroy French power; Napoleon wanted to dominate Europe. From 1803 to 1809 Napoleon achieved great triumphs, defeating Austria and Russia at *Austerlitz*, Prussia at *Jena*, and Russia at *Friedland*. Only England, with her powerful navy, remained safe, for Napoleon lacked the sea power to invade the British Isles.

From 1810 to 1812, at the height of his power, Napoleon dominated continental Europe from the Atlantic coast to Russia. (See map, page 166.) Napoleon (1) ruled a France enlarged by the annexation of neighboring lands, (2) appointed relatives and generals to rule various territories: Spain, northern Italy, Naples, and parts of Germany, (3) controlled the newly created dependencies, the Grand Duchy of Warsaw (part of Poland) and the

Confederation of the Rhine (an organization of western German states), (4) reduced to minor status his defeated enemies, Prussia and Austria, and (5) formed an alliance with his former enemy, the only other continental power, Russia. Napoleon's domination of Europe faced serious challenge only from England.

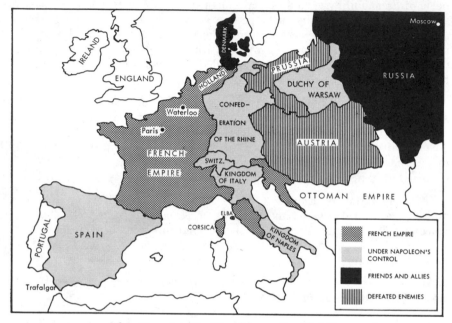

The Napoleonic Empire at Its Height

NAPOLEON'S DOWNFALL: REASONS

1. Personal Weaknesses. Napoleon's ambition caused him to overreach himself. In conquering most of Europe, he created an Empire too complex to be ruled efficiently by one man. His lust for territory and power was limitless. And as he grew older, he became stubborn and unwilling to accept advice.

2. England's Opposition to Napoleon

a. Napoleon was a symbol of the excesses of the French Revolution. The English government, a limited monarchy controlled by the upper classes, feared the shattering of tradition and the violence that had been generated by the Revolution.

b. Napoleon sought to unite Europe under his rule, whereas England wanted no one continental nation to be all-powerful. In a divided Europe,

England could shift her support from one nation to another and thereby wield the *balance of power*. (For centuries before Napoleon, Britain's continental policy had been guided by this concept.)

c. Napoleon aided French merchants and manufacturers in capturing continental markets from the British. Britain, the leading industrial and trading nation, suffered economic hardship and could not tolerate this blow at her economic well-being.

d. Napoleon planned to restore French colonial power. In the Seven Years' War (1756-1763), France had lost her major overseas territories, and England had become the leading colonial nation. Now England considered the colonial ambitions of Napoleon as a threat to her possessions.

3. England's Control of the Seas. Napoleon dominated on land, but England was "mistress of the seas." Under Admiral Nelson, the British navy overwhelmed the French fleets in the battles of the *Nile* (1798) and *Trafalgar* (1805). Naval supremacy saved Britain from invasion and shattered Napoleon's dream of an overseas empire.

(Weakness on the seas forced Napoleon to give up his largest overseas possession, the *Louisiana Territory* in North America. By treaty in 1800 he had acquired this territory from Spain. In 1803, perhaps realizing that he could not defend it against British sea power, Napoleon sold the Louisiana Territory to the United States.)

4. Napoleon's Continental System. Unable to invade the British Isles, Napoleon struck at England economically by the *Continental System*. In the *Berlin* and *Milan Decrees*, Napoleon ordered the European continent closed to English trade. Russia, his ally, at first agreed to this boycott of British goods. Napoleon despised England as a "nation of shopkeepers" and expected the Continental System to effect England's ruin.

England retaliated by the *Orders in Council*, which barred neutral nations from trading with France and her allies. Thus, England not only deprived the Continent of essential products, but also interfered with neutral trade. (England's seizure of American merchant ships bound for the Continent was one cause of the *War of 1812* between the United States and England.)

Throughout Europe, people blamed Napoleon for (*a*) a decline in trade, (*b*) an increase in business failures and unemployment, and (*c*) shortages of cloth, machinery, and foodstuffs. In place of hard-to-get imports, Napoleon proposed less popular substitutes: beet sugar (for cane sugar) and chicory (for coffee). Nevertheless, smuggling became widespread.

Although England suffered economically from the Continental System, Napoleon was harmed perhaps more by the resentment of the European people against his rule.

5. Russia's Opposition to Napoleon. As Napoleon achieved domination over Europe, Czar *Alexander I* feared that Napoleon's power threatened Russia. Also, the Russians suffered economic loss under the Continental System, which kept their grain from English markets. When, in 1812, the Czar resumed trade with England, Napoleon invaded Russia (see below).

6. Rising Spirit of Nationalism. Inspired by French example, other European peoples became nationalistic. Spaniards, Prussians, Austrians, and other peoples could no longer tolerate French domination and were ready to fight for liberation. Napoleon now faced the opposition, not of hereditary monarchs and mercenary armies, but of entire nations.

7. Exhaustion of France. After many years of warfare, France had depleted her manpower and resources.

NAPOLEON'S DOWNFALL: HIGHLIGHTS

1. Peninsular War (1808-1814). The nationalist-minded people of Portugal and Spain rebelled against French rule. By guerrilla warfare, they greatly sapped France's military strength. To aid the rebellion, England sent a British force under Sir Arthur Wellesley, who later became the *Duke of Wellington*. This *Peninsular War* resulted in the defeat of the French and their expulsion from Portugal and Spain.

2. Invasion of Russia (1812). Leading a huge army, Napoleon invaded Russia to enforce the Continental System. As the Russians at first refused battle and retreated, Napoleon overextended his lines. Then, after a costly victory at *Borodino*, Napoleon captured Moscow, but fires, probably set by the Russians, destroyed the city. Lacking shelter, food, and clothing to survive the oncoming winter, Napoleon began a long retreat. Napoleon's retreat became a rout as his forces were harassed by Russian guerrilla attacks and by the bitter cold of "General Winter." Napoleon lost three-fourths of his army in suffering his first great military defeat.

3. Wars of Liberation (1813-1814). Heartened by the success of Russia, encouraged by financial subsidies from England, and inspired by nationalism, Prussia and Austria again declared war on France. In 1813 the armies of Russia, Prussia, and Austria defeated Napoleon at *Leipzig*, in central Germany, at the *Battle of the Nations*. The following year, the Allies invaded France and captured Paris. Napoleon abdicated his throne and was exiled to the Mediterranean island of *Elba*.

4. The Hundred Days (1815). Napoleon escaped from Elba and returned to France—a return that lasted only 100 days. As he regained control of France, the Allies marshalled their forces against him. At the *Battle of Waterloo*, Napoleon met final defeat by Allied armies under the Duke of

Wellington. Napoleon was again exiled, this time to the South Atlantic island of *St. Helena*. Until his death, in 1821, Napoleon wrote his memoirs, in which he tried to justify his regime.

NAPOLEON'S ACCOMPLISHMENTS IN FRANCE

As Emperor, Napoleon exercised the powers of an absolute monarch. He made the laws, decided on war and peace, censored speech and press, ordered arbitrary arrest and imprisonment, and utilized a secret police. Nevertheless, he claimed to be a "son of the Revolution." He provided efficient government, furthered the Revolutionary principle of equality, and accomplished noteworthy reforms.

1. Centralization of Local Government. Napoleon subordinated local government to national authority. He appointed local governors (prefects), mayors, judges, and police heads, thereby strengthening his control over the country. To this day, France retains a highly centralized, or *unitary*, government.

2. Furtherance of Public Education. Napoleon organized a system of state-controlled education under the *University of France*. This was a government agency, not an institution of higher learning. It (a) controlled all levels of education from primary grades to college, (b) built new schools, (c) improved educational standards and made them uniform throughout France, and (d) prepared courses of study to extol Napoleon and stimulate French nationalism. As a result, public education progressed in France at the expense of Church schools. (The *University of the State of New York*, directed by its *Board of Regents*, resembles the University of France.)

3. Settlement of Religious Matters. Napoleon restored friendly relations between France and the Catholic Church, thus healing a rift that had taken place during the French Revolution (see page 159). The *Concordat of 1801*, a religious agreement, provided that (a) the State pay the salaries of the French clergy, (b) the Church surrender claims to lands confiscated during the Revolution, and (c) bishops be nominated by the State but confirmed by the Pope. By this agreement, Napoleon protected the peasant owners of former Church lands and pleased the French people, overwhelmingly Catholic. Although Napoleon later annexed the Papal States and was excommunicated, the Concordat remained in effect. (For later religious developments in France, see page 192.)

Napoleon also gained the support of non-Catholics. He guaranteed religious freedom and gave financial aid to Protestant and Jewish faiths.

4. Legal Reform. To establish uniform and just laws throughout France, Napoleon revised the legal system, emphasizing the Revolutionary principle of equality. The *Code Napoleon* (a) provided equal treatment before the law, (b) abolished what remained of serfdom and feudalism, and (c) guaranteed religious toleration and trial by jury. To this day, the Code Napoleon is the basis of law in France, most of western Europe, parts of Asia and Latin America, and the state of Louisiana.

5. Legion of Honor. Napoleon created a society, the *Legion of Honor*, for public recognition of distinguished military and civilian service to France. In accordance with the principle of equality, Legion membership was open to all persons regardless of social status. The Legion of Honor still exists today.

6. Improvement of Finances. By collecting taxes fairly and efficiently, paying the debts of the government promptly, and creating the *Bank of France*, Napoleon restored the government to financial health. The Bank of France, the government's financial agent, maintained sound currency and promoted economic prosperity. Napoleon's financial measures pleased the bourgeoisie and encouraged business enterprise. The Bank of France has headed France's banking system to this day.

7. Public Works. Napoleon instituted extensive public works: building roads, bridges, and canals; dredging harbors; and beautifying Paris.

NAPOLEON'S INFLUENCE UPON EUROPE

1. Map Changes. Of Napoleon's many map changes, two survived his downfall: (a) the abolition of the Austrian-dominated Holy Roman Empire, and (b) the reduction in the number of German states, which aided German unification.

2. The Legacy of the Revolution. Throughout Europe, Napoleon and his armies (a) spread French Revolutionary doctrines, especially equality, (b) ended Old Regime abuses of feudalism and serfdom, (c) introduced the Code Napoleon, and (d) encouraged state-controlled education.

3. The Legacy of War and Empire. Napoleon, through his armies and puppet governments, (a) promoted the growth of militarism, (b) aroused nationalism among the conquered peoples, (c) caused widespread destruction and a terrible loss of lives, (d) dislocated Europe's economy, (e) placed a heavy tax burden on conquered peoples, and (f) set an example of despotic rule—the first modern dictator.

MULTIPLE-CHOICE QUESTIONS

1. Which statement describes Napoleon's relation to the French Revolution? (1) He led the attack on the Bastille. (2) He helped cause the Revolution. (3) He used the ideas of the Revolution to further his own ends. (4) He was overthrown by the Revolution.

2. One reason why the French were willing to accept the leadership of Napoleon Bonaparte in 1799 was his (1) military ability (2) promise to place Louis XVIII on the throne (3) intention of building an Empire in the Western Hemisphere (4) royal ancestry.

3. Which list of titles correctly gives the steps by which Napoleon Bonaparte rose to power? (1) general, Emperor, First Consul (2) Emperor, First Consul, general (3) First Consul, general, Emperor (4) general, First Consul, Emperor.

4. The coup d'état by which Napoleon gained power was a (1) voluntary act of the legislature (2) swift and relatively bloodless revolution (3) gradual change (4) decree issued by the courts.

5. For centuries, the balance of power has been one of the fundamental principles of the foreign policy of (1) Spain (2) Great Britain (3) France (4) Russia.

6. The main reason why the rulers of other countries fought Napoleon was that he was (1) a descendant of Louis XIV (2) irreligious (3) spreading revolutionary ideas (4) of humble birth.

7. A factor contributing to Napoleon's downfall was (1) his defeat in the Egyptian campaign (2) the breakup of his alliance with Russia (3) the failure of the Napoleonic Code (4) the opposition of the Pope to the Concordat of 1801.

8. A country that Napoleon never dominated and with which he was never allied was (1) Prussia (2) Russia (3) Austria (4) England.

9. Napoleon sold the Louisiana Territory to the United States because he (1) was not interested in a colonial Empire (2) wanted American military aid against England (3) feared that he could not defend the territory against British attack (4) could not continue his war against England without the purchase money.

10. The purpose of Napoleon's Continental System was to (1) gain imports from the United States (2) restore the Holy Roman Empire (3) weaken England by an economic blockade (4) build highways of trade throughout Europe.

11. The battle that marked Napoleon's final defeat was (1) Leipzig (2) Waterloo (3) Jena (4) Trafalgar.

12. Napoleon established the University of France as an institution (1) to control all education in France (2) for advanced study (3) for military training (4) for training doctors and engineers.

13. By the Concordat between Napoleon and the Pope, (1) all Church property that had been confiscated was restored (2) the Church was given complete control of education (3) bishops were to be selected by the government and confirmed by the Papacy (4) all religions except Catholicism were prohibited.

14. The main importance of the Code Napoleon is that it (1) established democracy in France (2) is the basis of legal equality in many countries (3) suppressed the ideas of the French Revolution (4) was largely responsible for Napoleon's downfall.

15. In bringing about reforms within France, Napoleon I was attempting to (1) centralize the government (2) reestablish the Old Regime (3) safeguard freedom of the press (4) end forever the threat of absolutism.

16. An effect of Napoleon's conquests on the nations of Europe was to (1) discourage the formation of alliances (2) encourage the growth of nationalism (3) establish free trade (4) strengthen feudalism.

Part 6. The Age of Metternich (1815-1848):
Failure of Reaction

THE CONGRESS OF VIENNA (1814-1815)

1. Purpose and Leading Members. Following Napoleon's defeat, representatives from the victorious nations and France met at the *Congress of Vienna,* a peace conference to reconstruct wartorn Europe. The major figures at the conference were (*a*) England—the Duke of Wellington, (*b*) Russia—Czar Alexander I, (*c*) Prussia—King Frederick William III, (*d*) France—Prince Talleyrand, and (*e*) Austria—Prince Metternich.

2. Domination by Metternich: His Views. *Metternich,* chief minister of Austria, was a forceful and influential diplomat. An aristocrat, he hated the French Revolutionary ideals of equality, democratic government, and national states; he admired the Old Regime institutions of class distinction,

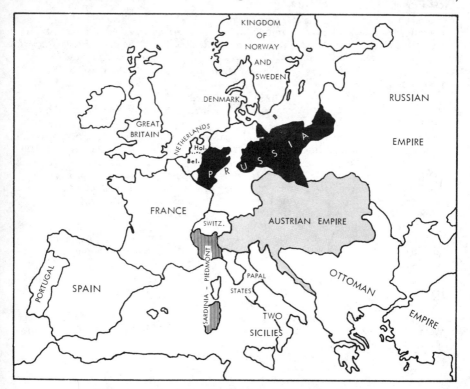

Europe After the Congress of Vienna (1815)

absolute monarchy, and multinational empires. Metternich directed the Congress toward settlements restoring the Old Regime.

3. Major Settlements

a. Principle of Legitimacy. The rightful or legitimate rulers, deposed by the French Revolution or Napoleon, were restored to power. Accordingly, a Bourbon King, *Louis XVIII,* brother of the executed Louis XVI, regained the throne of France. Other hereditary rulers returned in Spain, Holland, Sardinia-Piedmont, and the Two Sicilies.

b. Principle of Compensation. The nations that made important contributions to Napoleon's defeat were compensated (repaid) by territory. *Russia* received Finland and most of Poland. *Prussia* received part of Poland and various German territories, including some bordering the Rhine River; *England* received colonial possessions that she had occupied during the war, including Malta, Ceylon, and South Africa.

Also, victorious nations that gave up territory were compensated by other territory. Accordingly, *Holland* lost Ceylon and South Africa, but acquired Belgium; *Austria* surrendered Belgium, but obtained the Italian provinces of Lombardy and Venetia; *Sweden* lost Finland, but received Norway.

4. Contempt for Democracy and Nationalism. The political settlements of the Congress of Vienna denied the people any voice in selecting their rulers and governments. The Congress reinstated the hereditary rulers as absolute monarchs, and most of them used their power to restore the Old Regime. (In France, where Revolutionary ideals were strongest, Louis XVIII granted limited suffrage, legal equality, and freedom of speech and press.)

The territorial settlements of the Congress denied many national groups independence and unity. Belgians, Poles, Finns, and Norwegians all were handed over to foreign governments. Germans and Italians each remained disunited and divided among a number of separate states. Many different nationalities were consigned to huge Empires, such as to Russia and Austria.

THE METTERNICH SYSTEM

1. Metternich's Policies. As chief minister of the autocratic, multinational Austrian Empire, Metternich devoted his full energies to upholding the Vienna settlements and destroying French Revolutionary ideals. Because he sought to "turn the clock back" to Old Regime conditions, the *Age of Metternich* is also called the *Age of Reaction.*

(A *reactionary* wishes to return to previous conditions; a *conservative* wishes to maintain existing conditions relatively unchanged; a *liberal* wishes to make moderate changes gradually; a *radical* wishes to make basic changes rapidly. These terms became popular during the Metternich Era and survive to this day.)

To enforce his reactionary views, Metternich took stern measures. (*a*) In the Austrian Empire and in the Austrian-dominated regions of Germany and Italy, Metternich employed censorship of speech and press, secret police, spies, and arbitrary arrest. (*b*) Throughout Europe, Metternich used military force and diplomacy, especially the *Quadruple Alliance.*

 2. The Quadruple Alliance. In 1815 Metternich organized the Quadruple Alliance of Austria, Prussia, Russia, and England. (In 1818 France became a member.) For several years, the Alliance succeeded in its purposes: to enforce the Vienna settlements and suppress revolutions. This principle of cooperation among the major nations of Europe was called the *Concert of Europe.*

(By 1820 England virtually left the Alliance, finding it contrary to British trade interests and liberal traditions.)

THE HOLY ALLIANCE

In 1815 Russia's Czar Alexander I organized the well-meaning but ineffective *Holy Alliance.* It consisted of most European monarchs, who pledged to rule by Christian principles: charity, peace, and justice. Despite their pledges, the hereditary rulers continued to rule their countries in their repressive ways. (Founded in the same year and with the same leading members, the dormant Holy Alliance is often confused with the active Quadruple Alliance.)

REVOLTS AGAINST THE METTERNICH SYSTEM

Despite the expectations of reactionary statesmen, people did not forget the French Revolutionary ideals. Steadfastly, the reformers opposed autocracy, and demanded democratic government and independent national existence. Deprived of lawful means to attain their goals, they resorted to revolutions.

1. The Revolutions of 1820-1821

a. In Spain. Spanish liberals, supported by Spanish troops, revolted against their reactionary King, Ferdinand VII, and compelled him to approve a limited monarchy under a liberal constitution. The revolt collapsed in 1823 before an invading French army under Quadruple Alliance orders. The King, restored to absolute power, thereupon cruelly suppressed the Spanish liberals.

b. In Italy. Led by the *Carbonari,* a secret liberal society, the Italian people revolted in the Two Sicilies (1820) and in Piedmont (1821). They sought to replace reactionary rule by liberal, constitutional government.

Austrian armies, acting for the Quadruple Alliance, invaded Italy, suppressed the revolutions, and restored absolute monarchy.

2. The Latin American Revolutions (1810-1823)

a. Background. With Spain involved in the Napoleonic Wars, the Spanish colonies of Latin America declared their independence, adopted democratic constitutions, and established republican governments. The Latin Americans thereafter repulsed Spanish efforts to regain control. The outstanding colonial leaders were *Jose de San Martin, Bernardo O'Higgins,* and *Simon Bolivar* (the "George Washington of South America"). In 1823 Latin Americans heard rumors of a plan by reactionary European nations to reconquer the Latin American states for Spain.

b. England's Attitude. England sharply opposed this plan of reconquest. English public opinion favored Latin American independence. Furthermore, English merchants had developed a profitable trade with independent Latin America. If Spain regained control, this trade would be destroyed by Spanish mercantilist restrictions.

c. The United States' Attitude: The Monroe Doctrine. Popular sympathy and government policy in the United States also supported Latin American independence. (1) The American Revolution against England, in part, inspired the Latin American revolutions. (2) The United States preferred having weak independent republics to the south of her borders instead of a more powerful monarchical Spain. (3) American merchants and shippers had built up a profitable Latin American trade which would disappear under Spanish mercantilist control.

In 1823, despite her limited power of enforcement, the United States issued the *Monroe Doctrine.* It warned that (1) the Western Hemisphere is closed to further European colonization, and (2) any European attempt to intervene in the Western Hemisphere will be regarded as "dangerous to our peace and safety."

Since Britain also supported Latin American independence, the fear of her naval power—probably more than the Doctrine itself—influenced the reactionary European powers to abandon what plans they had for the reconquest of Latin America.

d. Significance. The maintenance of Latin American independence breached the Metternich System for the first time, and heartened other peoples seeking democracy and independence.

3. The Greek Revolution (1821-1829).

In their rebellion against Turkey, the Greek nationalists received military aid from England and, surprisingly, from France and Russia also. France and Russia temporarily ignored their distaste for revolution in order to weaken the Moslem Turks. In 1829 Greece achieved independence.

4. The Revolutions of 1830-1832

a. In France. In 1824 *Charles X* succeeded his brother, Louis XVIII, as King. Whereas Louis had followed a middle-of-the-road policy, Charles rejected compromise and attempted to restore Old Regime conditions. In 1830 the French revolted under liberal middle-class leadership. They (1) drove out Charles X, (2) enthroned *Louis Philippe*, Duke of Orleans, as a limited monarch, (3) enacted a liberal constitution, and (4) reduced property qualifications for voting in order to enfranchise more members of the middle class.

French success in 1830 ignited other European revolutions.

b. In Belgium. Rebelling against Holland, Belgian nationalists received support from England, and from France under Louis Philippe. In 1839 Belgium secured international recognition of her independence and neutrality.

c. In Italy. In a series of uprisings, Italian democrats again revolted against their absolute monarchs. The rebels were ruthlessly suppressed by Austrian armies under Metternich's orders.

d. In Poland. Polish nationalists rebelled against Russian rule, but their uprising was suppressed by the Czarist army.

The revolts in Italy and Poland failed, but those in France and Belgium succeeded. The successful revolutions of 1830-1832 proved that, even in western Europe, the Metternich System could not hold back the waves of democracy and nationalism.

5. The Revolutions of 1848

a. In France. Louis Philippe's rule eventually aroused opposition. (1) *Republicans* opposed monarchy. (2) *Liberals* deplored the government's conservative policies, press censorship, corruption, and voting restrictions. (3) *City workingmen* suffered poor economic conditions and had no vote. In 1848 rioting Paris mobs compelled Louis Philippe to flee from France.

The revolutionists proclaimed the *Second French Republic* and guaranteed universal male suffrage. *Louis Napoleon,* nephew of the former Emperor, Napoleon Bonaparte, was overwhelmingly elected President.

b. In the Austrian Empire. Inspired by French success and incited by poor economic conditions, the peoples within the Austrian Empire revolted. The Austrians demanded democracy; the Czechs and Italians claimed national independence, as did the Hungarians under *Louis Kossuth.* The avalanche of revolutions forced Metternich to flee the country. However, the revolutionary groups, belonging to different nationalities, started quarreling among themselves. Thus divided, they were conquered one at a time by the reactionary forces. The Hungarians, the last to succumb, fell when Austrian troops received help from a Russian army. Restored to full power, Austria's Hapsburg Emperor abolished serfdom, but annulled the liberal constitution that had been proclaimed.

c. In Italy and Germany. Revolutions for democracy and national unity in northern Italy and Germany were crushed. However, Sardinia-Piedmont in northern Italy retained her new liberal constitution. Prussia, the leading German state, also adopted a constitution, but it was undemocratic.

Although mainly unsuccessful, the revolutions of 1848 were noteworthy. They (1) brought about the downfall of Metternich and the collapse of the Metternich System, (2) resulted in a republic and universal male suffrage in France, a liberal constitution in Piedmont, and abolition of serfdom in the Austrian Empire, (3) marked the last effort in Europe to overthrow reactionary government by revolution *alone.* Subsequently, peoples in some European nations—for example, Austria and Italy—achieved a measure of democracy by peaceful pressure. Other national groups looked to diplomacy and war to help them achieve independence and unity.

MULTIPLE-CHOICE QUESTIONS

1. The chief purpose of the Congress of Vienna was to (1) stimulate nationalism (2) protect western Europe from autocratic Russia (3) restore the Old Regime as far as possible (4) preserve many reforms of the French Revolution.
2. The principle of legitimacy at the Congress of Vienna meant the (1) restoration of monarchs previously dethroned by Napoleon (2) extension of democracy (3) establishment of equality before the law (4) self-determination of peoples.
3. The Congress of Vienna restored the King of (1) Spain (2) Austria (3) Poland (4) Russia.
4. Which pair contains the nation that lost and the nation that gained South Africa at the Congress of Vienna? (1) Holland—England (2) Belgium—Portugal (3) Austria—Prussia (4) Belgium—England.
5. The Metternich System supported (1) independence for Belgium (2) the Greek revolution against Turkey (3) restoration of the Bourbon monarchy in France (4) a written constitution for Austria-Hungary.
6. Because Metternich attempted to "turn the clock back" to before 1789, he has been classified as a (1) reactionary (2) conservative (3) liberal (4) radical.
7. Which position would a liberal be most likely to take? (1) a return to the policies of the past (2) opposition to all change (3) moderate social and economic change (4) immediate political and economic change brought about by force.
8. The members of the Quadruple Alliance, as formed at the Congress of Vienna, were Austria, Prussia, and (1) Italy and England (2) Holland and Russia (3) Spain and Belgium (4) Russia and England.
9. The author of the Holy Alliance, by which the rulers agreed to govern according to Christian principles, was (1) Metternich (2) Talleyrand (3) Alexander I (4) Wellington.
10. Nationalism was largely responsible for the (1) French Revolution of 1830 (2) Belgian Revolution of 1830 (3) Prussian Revolution of 1848 (4) Glorious Revolution of 1689.

11. In 1820 and 1831 Austrian armies suppressed revolutions in (1) Poland (2) France (3) Italy (4) Spain.
12. The Monroe Doctrine declared that (1) the Western Hemisphere was no longer open to European colonization (2) no European country could own territory in Latin America (3) Latin America could not trade with England (4) Spain had to give up her possessions in the Western Hemisphere.
13. The Quadruple Alliance did *not* seriously challenge the Monroe Doctrine because (1) the United States was a great world power (2) Spain was willing to give up her colonies (3) Great Britain was opposed to intervention in Latin America (4) Russia was opposed to intervention in American affairs.
14. The Metternich System was most seriously challenged by the (1) Revolutions of 1848 (2) Continental System (3) Quadruple Alliance (4) Carbonari.

MATCHING QUESTIONS

For each territory in column *A,* write the letter of the nation in column *B* that acquired the territory at the Congress of Vienna.

Column A	*Column B*
1. Most of Poland	*a.* Great Britain
2. Malta	*b.* Prussia
3. Lombardy	*c.* Austria
4. Belgium	*d.* Russia
5. Norway	*e.* Italy
	f. Holland
	g. Sweden

Part 7. England: Democracy Through Evolution

UNDEMOCRATIC FEATURES OF THE ENGLISH GOVERNMENT (1750)

Although the English had taken important steps toward democracy (see pages 147-149), England in 1750 retained many undemocratic features of government.

1. Voting Restrictions. By property qualifications, voting for members of the House of Commons was limited chiefly to wealthy landowners. More than 85 percent of the adult male population could not vote. Women had no political rights.

2. Open Ballot. Voting took place by an open show of hands, not by secret ballot. The open ballot deterred many persons from voting their true beliefs, and encouraged intimidation and bribery.

3. Unfair Representation. In apportioning representation to the House of Commons, the law ignored population shifts, caused by the Industrial Revolution, from rural districts to factory cities. Whereas the newly populated urban centers, such as Manchester and Leeds, remained unrepresented in

Parliament, areas with greatly reduced populations retained their original representation. These depopulated districts were called *rotten boroughs*. A district in which a powerful landowner personally selected the representative to the House of Commons was called a *pocket borough*.

4. Officeholding Restrictions. A man could not hold public office unless he (*a*) owned considerable property, (*b*) could afford to serve without salary, and (*c*) was a member of the Church of England or of some other Protestant sect. These restrictions closed government service to Catholics, Jews, and poor people.

5. Power of the Hereditary House of Lords. Since laws required the consent of both branches of Parliament, legislation desired by the elected House of Commons could be defeated by the hereditary House of Lords.

DEMOCRATIC REFORM IN ENGLAND TEMPORARILY HALTED BY EVENTS IN FRANCE (1789-1815)

The movement for democratic reform in England was delayed during the French Revolutionary and Napoleonic Eras. Englishmen associated reform with the violence and bloodshed of the French Reign of Terror, and were too preoccupied with Napoleon to bend their efforts to domestic reform. However, after Napoleon's exile in 1815, English liberals revived the movement for democratic reform.

DEMOCRATIC REFORM IN ENGLAND: PROGRESS THROUGH EVOLUTION

In the struggle to bring political democracy to Britain, the opposing sides each gave way a little to avoid violence. They thus practiced the method of *compromise*. Reformers sought to accomplish their purpose by a gradual step-by-step approach. Opponents of reform yielded under the pressure of overwhelming public sentiment. For these reasons, we say that England achieved democracy through *evolution*. (This contrasts with France's search for democracy through *revolution*.)

THE STRUGGLE TO EXTEND THE RIGHT TO VOTE

1. The Reform Bill of 1832. The introduction of this bill constituted the first important test of the "evolutionary" method. The bill represented a moderate step forward and enjoyed widespread public approval. In Commons, it was passed by the Whig party over Tory opposition. In the hereditary House of Lords, the bill was approved only after the King threatened to appoint enough new liberal Lords to ensure its passage. (Whereas the English nobles yielded peacefully and enfranchised the middle class, at about the same time the French ruling classes employed repression, which led to the Revolution of 1830.)

This "Great Reform Bill" (a) reduced property qualifications for voting so as to enfranchise the middle class, (b) took representation away from many rotten and pocket boroughs, and (c) granted representation to many populous industrial cities. By these provisions, the bill shifted control of the House of Commons from the landed aristocracy to the commercial and industrial middle class.

2. The Chartist Movement. City workers, not enfranchised by the Reform Bill of 1832, organized the *Chartist Movement*. In the "People's Charter" they petitioned the government for (a) universal manhood suffrage, (b) equal election districts, (c) the secret ballot, (d) annual elections of Parliament, (e) removal of property qualifications for members of Parliament, and (f) salaries for members of Parliament. To rally support, the Chartists used mass meetings and parades.

The Chartist movement died out following its failure to secure reforms in 1848. In subsequent years, however, almost all Chartist demands were enacted into law.

3. The Reform Bill of 1867. This bill further reduced property qualifications for voting so as to enfranchise city workers. It was guided through Parliament by *Benjamin Disraeli*, the leader of the Conservative (formerly Tory) party. Disraeli hoped that the newly enfranchised city workers would join the landed aristocracy in the Conservative party. Together, he hoped, they could outvote the merchants and factory owners in the Liberal (formerly Whig) party. In this hope Disraeli was largely disappointed. The city workers usually supported the Liberals to obtain further democratic reforms. Later, they formed their own Labor party.

4. The Reform Bill of 1884. This bill extended the right to vote to agricultural workers. It was passed by the Liberal party under its Prime Minister, *William Gladstone*.

5. The Reform Bill of 1918. All men over 21 years of age received the right to vote, thus achieving *universal manhood suffrage*. Also, the law granted the vote to most women over 30. This reform, in appreciation of the contributions made by women during World War I, represented a triumph for the *suffragettes*. These advocates of woman suffrage were part of the *women's rights* movement for educational, professional, legal, and occupational equality with men.

6. The Reform Bill of 1928. In 1928 Parliament granted the right to vote to all women over 21 years of age. At last, England achieved the goal of *universal suffrage*.

LIMITING THE POWER OF THE HOUSE OF LORDS

1. **Undemocratic Aspects of the House of Lords.** No matter how many Englishmen were given the right to vote, Parliament could not be a truly democratic body while the House of Lords had equal powers with the House of Commons. Whereas the House of Commons is elected, the House of Lords is chiefly hereditary. As long as both Houses had to approve laws, the Lords could block any measure voted by the people's elected representatives in Commons. Furthermore, one party, the Conservatives, is assured permanent control of the House of Lords, since the Lords are mostly wealthy landowners —conservative in outlook.

2. **The Issue of the 1909 Budget.** The conflict between the House of Commons and the House of Lords came to a head over the *Budget of 1909*. In this bill, *Lloyd George*, Chancellor of the Exchequer (Treasury) in the Liberal party government, proposed to place heavy taxes on large incomes and estates. The budget was rejected by the landowners controlling the House of Lords. Parliament was dissolved and the budget issue carried to the people. In the election of January, 1910, Lloyd George's proposals won public approval as the Liberals were returned to power. The budget was reintroduced and, in view of the election results, accepted by the Lords.

3. **The Parliament Act of 1911.** The Liberals believed that public opinion was now aroused against the House of Lords. They therefore introduced a bill to weaken the Lords' legislative powers. After passage in Commons, the bill was defeated in the House of Lords. Parliament was again dissolved and the issue carried to the people. In December, 1910, the people voiced their approval of the bill by again returning the Liberals to power. When the Lords still refused to accept the bill, the King threatened to appoint enough new liberal Lords to ensure the bill's passage. Finally, in 1911 the bill was passed.

The *Parliament Act of 1911* provided that, even though the House of Lords withholds its consent, (a) money bills, approved by the Commons once, become law after thirty days, and (b) other bills, approved by the Commons three consecutive times over at least two years, become law. Thus, the act reduced the Lords' power over legislation to a temporary or *suspensive veto*. The act established the supremacy of the elected House of Commons over the hereditary House of Lords.

4. **The Parliament Act of 1949.** The Labor party government, expecting Conservative opposition to its nationalization program, proposed in 1947 to reduce the Lords' suspensive veto over general legislation to only one year. The government bill, twice rejected by the Lords, was three times passed by the Commons and became law in 1949. Thus, in the British government today, the House of Lords plays only a very minor role.

OTHER DEMOCRATIC REFORMS

1. In 1829 the *Catholic Emancipation Act* granted Catholics the right to serve in Parliament.

2. In 1833 slavery was abolished in all British possessions.

3. In 1858 Jews received the right to serve in Parliament.

4. In 1858 property qualifications for members of Parliament were removed.

5. In 1872 open voting was replaced by the secret, or *Australian*, ballot. (The secret ballot had originated in Australia.)

6. In 1885 the *Redistribution Bill* established election districts approximately equal in population.

7. In 1911 House of Commons elections were required at least once every five years.

8. In 1911 members of Commons received salaries.

THE BRITISH GOVERNMENT TODAY: AN ANALYSIS

The government of Great Britain (1) illustrates peaceful evolution from aristocracy to democracy, and (2) has served as a model for other democratic nations, including Canada, Australia, and New Zealand in the British Commonwealth, and Sweden, Norway, Denmark, Holland, and Belgium in western Europe. The major features of the English *parliamentary system* are:

1. **No Formal Constitution.** Britain, unlike other democracies, has no formal written constitution. Instead, the British consider their constitution to be made up of (*a*) *written documents and laws,* such as Magna Carta (1215), the Bill of Rights (1689), and the suffrage reform bills (1832-1928), and (*b*) *unwritten precedents* (customs and traditions), such as cabinet responsibility to Commons.

2. **The Monarch.** Great Britain is a monarchy, officially headed by a King or Queen. At one time an absolute ruler, today the British sovereign is a *figurehead*, said to "reign but not rule." The sovereign performs certain political duties, but is restricted by precedent. (*a*) He selects the Prime Minister, but by precedent must choose for this position the leader of the majority party in Commons. (*b*) He considers the bills passed by Parliament, but by precedent must approve them. (The last royal veto of a bill occurred in 1707.) (*c*) He reads the "Speech From the Throne" at the opening of Parliament, but by precedent he must advocate the program of the cabinet.

The monarch's chief duties are social and ceremonial, such as welcoming foreign statesmen and dedicating public improvements. Most important, the monarch serves as a symbol of unity for the people of Britain and the British Commonwealth of Nations.

3. Parliament. The English legislature consists of two Houses.

a. The *House of Lords,* the lesser body, may only delay legislation temporarily. Lords consists of about 1,000 members, mostly hereditary, of whom on the average some 200 attend sessions.

b. The *House of Commons,* the supreme legislative body, has unlimited power to pass laws. Commons consists of 630 members, called MP's, meaning members of Parliament. They are directly elected by the people voting by districts. (Commons is often referred to as Parliament.)

4. Cabinet Membership. The cabinet consists of (*a*) the Prime Minister, who is the leader of the majority party in Commons, and (*b*) about twenty members of Parliament selected by the Prime Minister from his party. To promote national unity during crises, the Prime Minister may include in his cabinet some members of Parliament from the opposition party, thereby forming a *coalition government.* This was done during both world wars.

5. Cabinet Powers. The cabinet exercises both executive and legislative functions.

a. Executive. (1) The Prime Minister is the head of the government, and directs and coordinates its activities. (2) Each cabinet member heads a department, such as Foreign Affairs, Exchequer (Treasury), Commonwealth Relations, and Defense. (3) The cabinet enforces laws passed by Parliament.

b. Legislative. (1) Cabinet members are also members of Commons. (Occasionally, a cabinet member is chosen from the House of Lords.) (2) The cabinet draws up the legislative program of the majority party, prepares the necessary bills, introduces them into Commons, defends them in debate, and guides them to passage.

6. Cabinet Responsibility. The cabinet remains in office as long as it commands the support of a majority in Commons. If Commons votes "no confidence" in the cabinet or rejects a major cabinet-sponsored bill, the cabinet no longer controls Commons. Then the cabinet must either (*a*) resign, whereupon the opposition majority in Commons forms a new cabinet, or, as is done more frequently, (*b*) *"go to the country"*—dissolve Commons and call for new elections. If the majority in the newly elected Commons supports the cabinet, it remains in office; if the majority is hostile, the cabinet resigns, and a new government is formed by the opposition leader.

At all times, the cabinet is directly responsible to the majority in Commons and thereby indirectly responsible to the people.

TWO DEMOCRACIES: DIFFERENCES IN GOVERNMENT

England	The United States
1. The constitution is *not* a single formal written document prepared at one time. Rather, the fundamental principles of government are contained in historic precedents, documents, and laws. These are subject to easy change.	1. A formal written constitution, drawn up at Philadelphia in 1787, established the fundamental structure and principles of government. The constitution may be amended only by a complex process.
2. Great Britain is a monarchy, headed by a hereditary ruler. The King or Queen is a *figurehead,* having no power but serving as a symbol of unity.	2. The United States is a republic, headed by an elected President. He is the chief executive and exercises great power.
3. Parliament is the legislature, consisting of (*a*) the hereditary House of Lords with minor powers, and (*b*) the elected House of Commons with unlimited legislative powers.	3. Congress is the legislature, consisting of two elected houses—the House of Representatives and the Senate—both exercising practically equal powers.
4. The House of Commons is elected for a maximum term of five years but may be dissolved earlier if the Prime Minister calls for new elections.	4. Congressional terms of office are definite. Representatives serve for two years, Senators for six.
5. The Prime Minister secures office as the leader of the majority party in Parliament.	5. The President is chosen by a nationwide vote (as expressed through the electoral college).
6. (*a*) The cabinet is selected by the Prime Minister from members of his party in Parliament.	6. (*a*) The cabinet is selected by the President from persons outside Congress, who take office with the consent of the Senate.
(*b*) The cabinet exercises both executive and legislative functions, thereby ignoring the principle of separation of powers.	(*b*) The cabinet exercises executive functions chiefly, thereby observing the principle of separation of powers.
(*c*) The Prime Minister and his cabinet remain in office as long as they command a majority in Commons. Their term of office may span the life of more than one House of Commons.	(*c*) The President serves a four-year term and is limited to no more than two terms. The cabinet remains in office at the will of the President.
(*d*) Cabinet responsibility to Parliament assures that the same party controls the executive and legislative branches. Thus, the two branches always work in harmony.	(*d*) The President (and his cabinet) may belong to one political party, while Congress (or either House) may be under control of another party. Thus, conflicts may arise between the executive and legislative branches.

POLITICAL PARTIES IN ENGLAND

1. Liberal Party. The *Liberals* (formerly called Whigs) played a leading role in English history in the 19th and early 20th centuries. As the Labor party developed, however, the Liberals lost their upper-class supporters to the Conservatives and their lower-class supporters to the Laborites. Today, the once-powerful Liberal party exists as only a minor party.

2. Conservative Party. The *Conservatives* (called Tories before the 1832 suffrage bill) remain one of England's two major parties. They draw strong support from the aristocracy and upper middle class: large landowners, prosperous farmers, industrialists, merchants, bankers, and professionals. However, their success in recent elections shows that their leadership and program appeal also to less prosperous citizens. The Conservatives (*a*) advocate free enterprise under capitalism, with government regulation to prevent abuses, (*b*) favor the continuation of existing social services, and (*c*) seek close cooperation with the United States on international affairs.

3. Labor Party. In 1901 the Labor party was created by Socialist reformers (see page 238) and practical labor union leaders. They believed that the existing parties were not representing the wishes of the working classes.

Since the 1920's Labor has been one of Britain's major parties. The Laborites draw their support mainly from the lower middle class and workers: small farmers, shopkeepers, and union members. They (*a*) believe in a socialist economy with government ownership of important industries, (*b*) urge expanding national welfare programs, and (*c*) favor cooperation (but less than the Conservatives) with the United States.

OUTSTANDING STATESMEN (19TH AND 20TH CENTURIES)

1. Liberals

a. Charles Grey, a Whig (the former name of the Liberal party), secured passage of the epochal Reform Bill of 1832.

b. William Gladstone promoted land distribution to Irish peasants and won passage for the Reform Bill of 1884.

c. Herbert Asquith won passage of the Parliament Act of 1911 and guided England at the beginning of World War I.

d. David Lloyd George fought for the Budget of 1909 and led England to victory in World War I (1918).

2. Conservatives

a. Robert Peel ended the tariff on grain imports by securing the repeal of the Corn Laws (1846). This move lowered English food costs.

b. Benjamin Disraeli sponsored the Reform Bill of 1867 and expanded British colonial power by acquiring the Suez Canal (1875).

c. Winston Churchill exemplified British courage and determination as he guided England to victory in World War II (1945). Later Churchill furthered free enterprise by returning the steel industry to private ownership.

3. Laborites

a. Ramsay MacDonald headed Labor's first government (1924).

b. Clement Attlee, Prime Minister from 1945 to 1951, nationalized important industries and expanded welfare programs.

ENGLISH POLITICAL HISTORY SINCE WORLD WAR II

1. Period of Labor Control (1945-1951). In the elections of 1945, Labor won a large majority in Commons, and *Clement Attlee* became Prime Minister. His Labor government (*a*) nationalized the electric, coal, and steel industries, (*b*) increased social security benefits and began a government program of medical, dental, and hospital service, (*c*) helped create a Western defensive alliance, the North Atlantic Treaty Organization (NATO), and (*d*) granted independence to India and Pakistan, and gave up control over Palestine. The elections of 1950 kept Labor in power, but with a bare majority. Attlee soon called for new elections.

2. Period of Conservative Control (1951-1964). In 1951 the Conservatives won a narrow majority in Commons. *Winston Churchill,* England's World War II leader, again became Prime Minister. His Conservative government (*a*) returned the steel industry to private ownership, (*b*) helped revive British industry, and (*c*) agreed to withdraw British troops from the Suez Canal. In 1955 Churchill resigned from office because of his advanced age.

Anthony Eden became Prime Minister and, in new elections, secured a majority in Commons. In 1956 Eden sent British troops into Egypt to regain management of the Suez Canal, which Egypt had seized. Under pressure from the United States, Russia, and the U.N., Eden withdrew his forces, leaving the Canal in Egyptian hands. Thereafter Eden resigned because of ill health while under severe Parliamentary criticism of his Suez policies.

Harold Macmillan succeeded Eden as the Conservative Prime Minister. In 1959 Macmillan led his party to its third consecutive election victory, winning a large majority in Commons. Although the Macmillan government maintained general prosperity, it did not solve Britain's troublesome economic problems: inflation, areas of unemployment, and an unfavorable balance of payments (that is, funds spent abroad, chiefly for foreign goods and services, exceeded funds earned from abroad, chiefly for British goods and services). In foreign affairs, Macmillan failed (*a*) to keep South Africa in the Commonwealth, and (*b*) to gain Britain's admission to the Common Market.

3. Period of Labor Control (1964-1970)

a. Political Matters. (1) In 1964 Labor won narrow control of the House of Commons. *Harold Wilson* became Prime Minister. In 1966 Wilson called for new elections and won a comfortable majority. (2) Labor lowered the voting age to 18. (3) In 1969 violence erupted in Northern Ireland (Ulster) between the Protestant majority and the Catholic minority. The Wilson government sent troops to stop the street fighting and restore order.

b. Economic and Social Matters. (1) The Wilson government renationalized the steel industry. (2) The Wilson government acted to reverse Britain's unfavorable balance of payments. It raised taxes and established controls over wages and prices. These measures were designed to lower the price of British goods in world markets and to curtail British purchases of foreign imports. Also the government lowered the value of the pound, the British monetary unit, from $2.80 to $2.40. With the pound devalued in terms of foreign currency, British consumers would find imports more costly and foreigners would find British goods less costly. The government hoped that therefore imports would decrease and exports would increase. (3) With more than one million "colored" immigrants—from India, Pakistan, the Caribbean, and Africa—having entered Britain since World War II, the country experienced racial strains. The Labor government passed laws to forbid discrimination but also tightened restrictions so as to slow the "colored" influx.

c. Foreign Affairs. (1) Britain's request for membership in the Common Market was twice vetoed by France under President de Gaulle. (2) The Wilson government branded the white breakaway regime in the British colony of Rhodesia as "illegal" and secured a U.N. vote asking all nations to apply economic sanctions against Rhodesia.

4. Period of Conservative Control (1970-   )

a. Political Matters. (1) In 1970 elections the Conservative party won an "upset" victory—a 30-seat majority in Commons and replacement of Wilson as Prime Minister by the Conservative leader *Edward Heath*. (2) Despite the stationing of British army units in Ulster, violence there continued. In 1972 Heath suspended the local Ulster government, imposed direct British rule, and appointed *William Whitelaw* to administer the province. Whitelaw's efforts to end the violence and to get the opposing groups to negotiate have so far been unsuccessful.

b. Economic and Social Matters. (1) The Heath government proved unable to restrain union-won wage increases, to reduce unemployment, to curb prices, and to slow inflation. In 1972 the government imposed a temporary wage-price freeze. (2) In 1972 the Heath government declared that Britain was morally obligated to honor requests for admission by Asians holding British passports—estimated at 55,000—who were being expelled from Uganda (a former British colony) by the black African nationalist regime of President Amin. This declaration aroused resentment, for racial and economic reasons, among many Britons.

c. Foreign Affairs. (1) With de Gaulle no longer President of France, Heath secured agreement for Britain to join the Common Market. Within Britain, Common Market membership evoked little public enthusiasm and won narrow Parliamentary approval. (2) The Conservative government was unable to settle the dispute with Rhodesia.

IDENTIFICATION QUESTIONS: WHO AM I?

Herbert Asquith	Alec Douglas-Home	Charles Grey
Clement Attlee	Anthony Eden	Ramsay MacDonald
Winston Churchill	David Lloyd George	Harold Macmillan
Benjamin Disraeli	William Gladstone	Harold Wilson

1. I was the Liberal Chancellor of the Exchequer who fought for passage of the 1909 Budget and the 1911 Parliament Act.
2. Famed as an orator and writer, I was the Conservative Prime Minister who led England to victory in World War II.
3. I was the Liberal Prime Minister who secured the vote for farm workers by the Reform Bill of 1884.
4. After a close Labor victory in the 1964 elections, I became Prime Minister.
5. As Conservative leader, I secured passage of the Reform Bill of 1867, hoping that the city workers would join with the landed aristocracy against the industrialists.
6. I took office as Labor Prime Minister immediately after World War II and nationalized several major industries.

MULTIPLE-CHOICE QUESTIONS

1. In 1800 the English government was undemocratic in that (1) Parliament lacked the power to pass laws (2) no cabinet existed (3) the King controlled Parliament (4) the House of Lords was as powerful as the House of Commons.
2. Another undemocratic feature of the English government in 1800 was that (1) the King appointed the Prime Minister (2) the King vetoed many laws (3) most citizens did not have the right to vote (4) Parliament was a hereditary body.
3. The term "rotten borough" refers to (1) an area that had lost population and was over-represented in Parliament (2) a city slum area with inadequate sanitation facilities (3) lands used for hunting (4) a large city unrepresented in Parliament.
4. The chief cause of the shift in population in England resulting in unequal representation in Parliament before 1832 was the (1) Napoleonic Wars (2) Industrial Revolution (3) Protestant Reformation (4) decline of British naval power.
5. Democracy in England developed chiefly through a process of (1) violent upheaval (2) gradual evolution (3) rapid changes (4) royal decrees.
6. The group that gained most political power as a result of the Reform Bill of 1832 was the (1) landed aristocracy (2) factory workers (3) farm laborers (4) middle-class people of the towns.
7. The Reform Bill of 1832 also (1) provided for freedom of religion (2) gave women the right to vote (3) improved representation in Parliament by abolishing many rotten boroughs (4) provided for a secret ballot.

8. One Chartist demand was (1) the right of collective bargaining (2) government ownership of industry (3) unemployment insurance for workingmen (4) the abolition of property qualifications for members of Parliament.

9. Great Britain gave women equal voting rights with men (1) shortly after the French Revolution (2) just before World War I (3) shortly after World War I (4) during World War II.

10. The Parliament Act of 1911 weakened the House of Lords by (1) discontinuing its judicial functions (2) making its membership elective rather than hereditary (3) limiting its lawmaking function to a suspensive veto (4) providing that no cabinet member may come from this body.

11. The Catholic Emancipation Act of 1829 (1) gave Catholics freedom to worship (2) gave Catholics the right to hold public office (3) disestablished the Anglican Church in Ireland (4) freed Catholics from paying certain taxes.

12. Which is true of the Prime Minister of England? (1) He is leader of the majority party in the House of Commons. (2) He is directly elected to that office by the people. (3) He is the independent choice of the King or Queen. (4) He must be a member of the House of Lords.

13. The English cabinet has (1) both executive and legislative powers (2) only legislative powers (3) only executive powers (4) only those powers assigned to it by the King.

14. Members of the English cabinet (1) are elected directly to the cabinet by the people (2) are chosen by the Prime Minister (3) hold office by hereditary right (4) are elected by a joint meeting of both Houses of Parliament.

15. The English cabinet holds office (1) for five years (2) as long as it controls a majority in the House of Commons (3) as long as it represents all shades of opinion in the country (4) until the House of Lords vetoes a bill it has proposed.

COMPARISON OF GOVERNMENTS

Consider the following statements in relationship to government in England and the United States. For each statement 1-10, write the letter of the appropriate phrase below. (A letter may be used more than once.)

(A) if the statement is true of the English government only.

(B) if the statement is true of the American government only.

(C) if the statement is true of both the English and American governments.

(D) if the statement is not true of either government.

1. The fundamental principles of government may be changed by a new law passed by the legislature only.

2. The government is a democracy.

3. The government is a limited monarchy.

4. The chief executive is elected by the members of both houses of the legislature.

5. The two houses of the legislature are approximately equal in power.

6. Cabinet members are members of the legislature.

7. The right to hold public office is not legally restricted by religious qualifications.

8. The chief executive may serve for no more than five years.

9. The chief executive remains in office even though a major law he requested of the legislature is defeated.

10. Requirements for voting meet with the approval of the suffragettes.

Part 8. France: Democracy Through War and Revolution

SECOND FRENCH REPUBLIC (1848-1852)

By the Revolution of 1848 (see page 176), France established her Second Republic and elected Louis Napoleon as President. From this nephew of Napoleon Bonaparte, the French envisioned stable government, economic prosperity, and foreign glory.

Louis Napoleon, however, used his elected position to further his personal power and popularity. He posed as the defender of democratic government, but in 1852 Louis Napoleon ended the republic and proclaimed the *Second French Empire* with himself as Emperor *Napoleon III*. In a plebiscite, the people approved these changes.

SECOND FRENCH EMPIRE (1852-1870)

1. Government. Napoleon III retained outward democratic forms: a constitution, a legislature, and universal male suffrage. In reality, his government was a dictatorship typified by secret police, censorship of the press, and state-controlled elections.

2. Early Popularity. Napoleon III gained support among (*a*) *city workers*—by legalizing unions and granting them a limited right to strike, and by providing employment on public works, (*b*) the *middle class*—by improving banking and credit facilities, by promoting railroad and canal building, and by encouraging the growth of industry, and (*c*) *nationalists*—by expanding French colonial control in Algeria, by seizing part of Indo-China, and by joining with England to defeat Russia in the Crimean War.

3. Later Discontent. Napoleon earned the hostility of (*a*) *advocates of democracy*—who realized that the Empire was a veiled dictatorship, (*b*) *Catholics*—who feared that Napoleon's aid to Italian unification was a threat to Church control of the Papal States, and (*c*) *nationalists*—who felt a loss of pride over Napoleon's humiliating failure in Mexico.

This was the *Maximilian Affair*. In 1863, with the United States engaged in the Civil War, the French invaded Mexico and enthroned their puppet, the Hapsburg *Maximilian*. By attempting to control Mexico, Napoleon violated the Monroe Doctrine (see page 175). In 1865, when the Civil War ended, the United States placed an army at the Mexican border and ordered the French to withdraw. Napoleon removed his troops. Maximilian remained, was captured by Mexican troops, and died before a firing squad.

4. Downfall. To revive his popularity and to check Prussian power, Napoleon opposed German unification. Bismarck, the chief minister of Prussia, wanted a war and goaded Napoleon into beginning hostilities. In the Franco-Prussian War (1870-1871), the French army was overwhelmed and Napoleon III was taken prisoner. French republicans, led by *Leon Gambetta*, declared the end of the Second French Empire.

ESTABLISHMENT OF THE THIRD FRENCH REPUBLIC (1871-1879)

The National Assembly, elected in 1871, contained a majority of royalists (or monarchists). They had won the election on the pledge to bring about an immediate peace; the republican minority, on the other hand, had favored continuing the war against Prussia. The royalists promptly accepted Prussia's harsh peace terms in the Treaty of Frankfurt (see page 205).

Regarding government, the National Assembly agreed to reestablish a monarchy, but was unable to decide between a Bourbon and an Orleanist king. In moves meant to be temporary, the royalists in 1871 set up a republic, and in 1875 outlined a governmental framework by four *Organic Laws*. These laws became the constitution of the *Third French Republic*. In elections between 1875 and 1879, the royalists lost control of the government to the republicans. These victories doomed royalist plans to restore monarchy.

EARLY CRISES IN THE THIRD REPUBLIC

The royalists, chiefly nobles and army officers, bitterly assailed the republic and plotted its destruction. The royalists were supported by the clericals, who included devout lay Catholics and high clergy. The clericals, remembering the Revolution of 1789, feared that a republic would weaken the Catholic Church in France.

There were two major attempts by the royalist forces to overthrow the republican government.

1. Boulanger Affair. In the late 1880's General *Georges Boulanger*, hero of the antirepublican groups, apparently planned to seize the government. To forestall a coup d'état, the republic in 1889 charged him with treason and ordered his arrest. Boulanger fled the country and soon afterwards committed suicide. By successfully handling the Boulanger threat, the Republic increased its prestige.

2. Dreyfus Affair. In 1894 *Alfred Dreyfus*—a French army captain, republican, and Jew—was court-martialed by royalist officers and declared guilty of selling military documents to Germany. Monarchists, clericals, and anti-Semites all cited the Drefyus case to discredit the Republic. To Dreyfus' defense rallied the republicans. *Emile Zola,* in an open letter, "J'Accuse," charged the army high command with "framing" Dreyfus and seeking to destroy the republic. In 1906, following several dramatic trials, Dreyfus was finally declared innocent, restored to military service, promoted, and awarded the Legion of Honor.

The Dreyfus Affair (*a*) swung public opinion strongly toward the Republic, (*b*) discredited anti-Semitism in France, (*c*) spurred the government to replace monarchist army officers with loyal republicans, and (*d*) brought about laws to weaken clerical influence.

ANTICLERICAL LAWS (1901, 1905)

1. The **Associations Law** of 1901 had the effect of closing schools conducted by religious orders. The law aimed to compel pupils to attend public schools, where they would be exposed to republican books and teachers.

2. The **Separation Law** of 1905 abrogated (ended) the Concordat of 1801 (see page 169). No longer would the government nominate bishops and pay salaries to the clergy. The law meant complete separation of Church and State.

GOVERNMENT OF THE THIRD FRENCH REPUBLIC (1875-1940)

1. Constitutional Framework. The Third Republic's constitution (the Organic Laws of 1875) established a democratic government as follows: (*a*) All men received the right to vote. (*b*) The elected legislature—the Chamber of Deputies and the Senate—passed the laws. (*c*) The President, chosen by the legislature, served as a figurehead. (*d*) The cabinet, headed by the Premier, governed the country, exercising both executive and legislative powers. The cabinet was responsible to the Chamber of Deputies and remained in power as long as it commanded a majority of the Deputies.

2. Political Parties. Many political parties arose and elected members to the Chamber of Deputies. They were seated by party: (*a*) radicals at the *left*, (*b*) moderates at the *center*, and (*c*) reactionaries at the *right*. (This seating arrangement illustrates the political meaning of the terms *Leftist*, *Centrist*, and *Rightist*.)

3. Bloc Government. Since many parties were represented in the Chamber of Deputies, no one party alone could command a majority of seats. Consequently, a cabinet was formed by a *bloc*, or coalition, of several parties. If one of the parties in a bloc disagreed with the others on a major issue, it left the cabinet. Frequently, the cabinet thereupon no longer had a majority in the Chamber. Then a new bloc, representing a new majority, formed a new cabinet. During the 65 years of the Third Republic, such cabinet changes occurred more than 100 times. Although democratic, the bloc system did not provide stable, efficient government.

4. Accomplishments. In *domestic matters*, the Third Republic (*a*) survived royalist plots aimed at its destruction, (*b*) separated Church and State, (*c*) provided free, compulsory public elementary education, (*d*) established a social security system of sickness and old age insurance, and (*e*) encouraged business growth and prosperity.

In *foreign affairs*, the Third Republic (*a*) expanded the French colonial Empire in northern Africa and Indo-China, (*b*) together with her allies, defeated Germany in World War I, and (*c*) in the late 1930's, prepared, though inadequately, to meet the threat of an armed, aggressive Nazi Germany.

5. Downfall. The Third Republic ended when German armies overran France at the beginning of World War II (see page 388). The Nazis directly ruled over northern and western France, called the *occupied zone*. The Nazis permitted a puppet French government, with its capital at the city of Vichy, to rule unoccupied France. Under Marshal *Henri Pétain*, the Vichy regime was a French version of an authoritarian state.

Meanwhile, in England, General *Charles de Gaulle* established a *Free French* government-in-exile to continue the war against Nazi Germany.

GOVERNMENT OF THE FOURTH FRENCH REPUBLIC (1946-1958)

1. Constitutional Framework. After France was liberated from German occupation, she established the *Fourth Republic*. Its constitution, modeled on that of the Third Republic, provided a similar democratic but unstable government.

a. Universal Suffrage. All men and, for the first time, women received the right to vote.

b. Weak President. Elected for a 7-year term by the legislature, the President was a figurehead.

c. Powerful Legislature. The legislature consisted of two houses. (1) The *Council of the Republic*, indirectly elected, could hold up legislation only temporarily. (2) The *National Assembly*, directly elected for a 5-year term, *alone* could pass laws. Also, it could overthrow the cabinet.

d. Responsible Cabinet. Headed by the Premier, the cabinet governed France, exercising both executive and legislative powers. The cabinet remained in office as long as it controlled a majority in the Assembly.

2. Leading Political Parties

a. Extreme Left. The *Communist party* opposed France's pro-Western foreign policy and favored a French Communist dictatorship.

b. Center. Four main parties existed in the "center": the left center *Socialists,* the center *Radicals* and *Popular Republicans* (Christian Democrats), and the right center *Independents.* These parties differed regarding business controls, labor policies, tax measures, Catholic interests, and the Algerian rebellion. However, they united in allegiance to the Republic.

c. Right. The *Rally of the French People,* founded by Charles de Gaulle, favored revising the constitution so as to strengthen the office of President and assure stable government. By 1953 de Gaulle, despairing of achieving his aims through his party, dissolved it and withdrew temporarily from political life.

3. Unstable Bloc Government. Since no one party commanded a majority in the Assembly, government was by bloc—a coalition of the center parties. However, differences on issues frequently led one center party or another to withdraw from the bloc and overthrow the government. During the 12-year life of the Fourth Republic, 25 different center-bloc Cabinets governed the country.

4. Accomplishments. The Fourth Republic (*a*) fostered France's economic recovery from destruction in World War II, (*b*) cooperated in West European moves toward economic unity, (*c*) joined pro-Western alliances against Communism, and (*d*) granted independence, although reluctantly, to the French colonies of Indo-China, Tunisia, and Morocco.

5. Downfall. The downfall of the Fourth Republic resulted from (*a*) *fundamentally*—the inability of the multiparty center-bloc system to provide stable and effective government, and (*b*) *immediately*—the failure to settle the Algerian crisis.

a. Rebellion in Algeria. Algeria was inhabited by 9 million Moslems and 1 million European (chiefly French) settlers called *colons.* In 1954 the Moslem *National Liberation Front* began guerrilla warfare to win independence from France. This Algerian rebellion tied down a large French army, drained the French treasury, and caused many cabinet crises. When a new cabinet took office in May, 1958, rumors arose that the government was ready to make substantial concessions to the Algerian rebels. French army officers and settlers in Algeria rebelled, denied the authority of the government in Paris, and demanded that all governmental power be given to General de Gaulle. In Paris, the center-bloc government resigned, an admission that it could not control the defiant army officers.

b. De Gaulle as Premier: End of the Fourth Republic. Fearing civil war as the alternative to de Gaulle, the National Assembly confirmed de Gaulle as Premier, granted him unlimited power for six months, and agreed to submit his constitutional reforms directly to the people. Premier de Gaulle reestablished the authority of the Paris government over the French army and settlers in Algeria, and prepared far-reaching constitutional reforms.

GOVERNMENT OF THE FIFTH FRENCH REPUBLIC (1958 TO THE PRESENT)

The Gaullist constitution for the *Fifth Republic* received overwhelming popular approval. The vote was a personal triumph for de Gaulle and an endorsement of his plans for a strong Presidential system. The Gaullist constitution, with later amendments, provides a government that differs markedly from that of the Fourth Republic.

1. Popularly Elected President. Instead of being elected by the legislature, the President is directly elected to a 7-year term by a majority vote of the people. It was thought that this method, authorized by a Gaullist constitutional amendment in 1962, would add prestige to the position of the President of the Republic and would weaken the parties of limited public appeal. (Previously, the President of the Fifth Republic was indirectly elected by an "electoral college.")

2. Powerful President. No longer a figurehead, the President dominates the government as a strong executive with substantial powers. The President (a) appoints his own choices to the Premiership and to other government positions, (b) serves as commander-in-chief of the armed forces, (c) negotiates treaties, (d) issues executive decrees on matters not subject to legislation, (e) after the first year of any legislature, may dissolve the National Assembly and call for new elections, and (f) in a national emergency, may temporarily assume dictatorial powers.

3. Weakened Cabinet. The cabinet, headed by the Premier, has less authority than before, since the President now exercises many of its former powers. The cabinet directs everyday governmental operations and enforces the laws. Members of the cabinet no longer sit in the National Assembly. The cabinet, although appointed by the President, is responsible to the National Assembly. However, constitutional provisions make it very difficult for the National Assembly to overthrow a cabinet.

4. Weakened Legislature. The legislature consists of the indirectly elected *Senate* and the directly elected *National Assembly*. The legislature no longer dominates the government, and its powers are severely limited. The legislature (a) meets only twice a year for no more than three months each time and (b) may pass laws only on matters specifically listed in the constitution; all other matters are handled by executive decree. Furthermore, the National Assembly (*a*) is restricted in its ability to defeat a government bill or to overthrow a cabinet by a vote of censure and (*b*) after its first year, may be dissolved and new elections ordered by the President.

5. Constitutional Council. This judicial body, an innovation of the Fifth Republic, determines the constitutionality of new laws.

OBSERVATIONS ON THE DE GAULLE CONSTITUTION

1. Democratic Aspects. Like the constitution of the Fourth Republic, the Gaullist constitution guarantees civil liberties, especially legal equality, religious freedom, and universal suffrage; provides for direct election of the National Assembly; and makes the cabinet responsible to the Assembly.

2. Strong President. Two new features of the Fifth Republic borrowed from the United States are the strong President and the separation of executive from legislative powers. The President is not responsible to the legislature and, unlike the President of the Fourth Republic, has real powers.

3. Newness and Complexity. Having many untried and involved features, the Gaullist constitution requires more time to reveal its strengths and weaknesses. The future of the Fifth Republic perturbs observers. Two questions in particular arise: (*a*) Will a President lacking de Gaulle's prestige be able to maintain a stable government? (*b*) Does the constitution have sufficient safeguards to prevent an unscrupulous President from becoming dictator?

FIFTH REPUBLIC: THE DE GAULLE ERA (1958-1969)

1. Early Years: De Gaulle Receives Strong Support. Charles de Gaulle was overwhelmingly elected as the Fifth Republic's first President. In the National Assembly elections of 1958, the *Union of the New Republic,* the newly formed rightist group of Gaullists, emerged as the largest party in the National Assembly. Together with other conservative-party support, the Gaullists held a comfortable legislative majority. The *Center* parties— *Socialists, Radicals,* and *Popular Republicans*—registered a sharp decline. The *Communists,* although polling a substantial vote, experienced a tremendous decline in Assembly seats, in part due to the new system of voting. Each district elected a single member to the Assembly. If no candidate received a majority, the two top candidates engaged in a runoff election. This permitted the other parties to join in support of one anti-Communist candidate.

In 1962 Gaullist suporters—the Union of the New Republic and its allies —won an absolute majority of National Assembly seats. This victory reflected satisfaction with de Gaulle's record: settling the Algerian crisis by granting Algeria independence, making France a nuclear power, sustaining general prosperity, and maintaining a stable, democratic government.

2. The Middle Years: De Gaulle Prevails but With Decreasing Support.
President de Gaulle sought reelection in 1965, claiming that only he could lead France to greatness. In the election, de Gaulle failed to secure the necessary absolute majority. He polled only 44 percent of the vote. In the runoff election between the top two candidates, de Gaulle secured a 55-percent majority and reelection.

De Gaulle's prestige suffered another blow in 1967 in elections for the National Assembly. Gaullist supporters fell just short of an Assembly majority. The Communists and the non-Communist Federation of the Left (Socialists and Radicals) sharply increased their representation.

The election results of 1967 were a setback for de Gaulle. Many voters, disquieted by de Gaulle's use of "personal power," felt that it was "time for a change." French workers, beset by low wages, inflation, and poor housing, complained that they were not sharing in the country's prosperity.

3. The Final Years: After a Last Victory, de Gaulle Meets Defeat.
In 1968 France was engulfed by massive sit-ins, strikes, and demonstrations, first by university students and then by over 10 million workers. The students demanded educational reforms at the government-run universities. The workers demanded higher wages and larger welfare benefits. Both groups indicated dissatisfaction with de Gaulle for his neglect of domestic affairs and his authoritarian style of government. The anti-Gaullist political parties pressed for de Gaulle's resignation. Instead, de Gaulle called for new elections for the National Assembly. In the elections, the Communists and the Federation of the Left sharply lost representation, and the Gaullists won an overwhelming majority. When faced by the possibility of anarchy, the French electorate voted for de Gaulle with his promise of orderly reform.

In 1969 de Gaulle again sought public support when he asked for a single yes-or-no vote on two issues: (*a*) to divide France into 22 regions, each to handle local affairs, and (*b*) to lessen the power of the Senate. De Gaulle warned that, if the referendum were defeated, he would step down. When 52.4 percent of the electorate voted *no*, de Gaulle resigned.

De Gaulle's defeat has been explained by the following factors: (*a*) *Economic.* Workers protested low wages, high prices, and poor housing; small merchants complained of tax discrimination. These groups resented de Gaulle's neglect of domestic reforms and his preoccupation with foreign affairs. (*b*) *Foreign Policy.* Voters were disquieted as de Gaulle's efforts to assert French influence in foreign affairs alienated France's traditional friends. De Gaulle embargoed arms to Israel, vetoed British membership in the Common Market, withdrew French forces from NATO, and opposed

American influence in European affairs. (c) **Political.** Voters saw that several capable men were available to succeed to the Presidency.

FIFTH REPUBLIC: AFTER DE GAULLE

1. Presidential Elections of 1969. (a) *Georges Pompidou,* for six years Premier under de Gaulle, was the Gaullist candidate. He vowed to maintain stable government, to allow the legislature a greater role in making policy, to foster domestic reforms, and to reconsider de Gaulle's foreign policies. (b) *Alain Poher,* President of the Senate, who led the successful fight against the de Gaulle referendum, was the "centrist" candidate. Poher promised to push domestic reforms, change de Gaulle's foreign policies, and be a modest, "down-to-earth" President. (c) Other candidates included the Socialist and Communist standard-bearers.

In the election, Pompidou, with 44 percent of the vote, was first. He faced a runoff election against Poher, who was second. In the runoff, Pompidou polled 58 percent and became the Fifth Republic's second President.

2. Pompidou Government (1969-   ). (a) In domestic matters, Pompidou inherited the basic problems caused by France's transition from small farms, stores, and factories to large enterprises in an industrialized society. Students agitated for educational reforms; workers complained of unemployment, low wages, and inflationary prices. The government (1) introduced some educational reforms but also adopted severe anti-riot regulations to curb student protests, and (2) sought to moderate union wage demands and also to battle inflation, especially by devaluating the French currency, the franc. Pompidou's policies appealed to the middle and upper classes, who feared dissent and violence and wanted law and order. (b) In foreign affairs, Pompidou maintained, with one exception, the policies of de Gaulle. French military forces remained apart from NATO, France continued to develop her own nuclear arsenal, and Pompidou reaffirmed France's independent but pro-Western foreign stance. Pompidou maintained the embargo on arms to Israel but agreed to sell Libya 100 Mirage fighter bombers, which most observers felt would end up in Egyptian hands for use against Israel. Pompidou's efforts to gain Arab friendship did not prevent Algeria from nationalizing French-owned oil companies. In 1972 Pompidou reversed one aspect of de Gaulle's foreign policy by reaching agreement with British Prime Minister Heath for Britain to join the Common Market.

In the 1973 National Assembly elections, the Gaullists faced a leftist "united front" formed by the Socialists under *François Mitterand* and the Communists under *Georges Marchais.* These two leftist parties agreed to support each other's candidates in the runoff elections. Nevertheless, the Gaullists and their allies won a comfortable majority in the new Assembly.

MULTIPLE-CHOICE QUESTIONS

1. Louis Napoleon followed in the footsteps of Napoleon Bonaparte in that Louis Napoleon (1) was a great military leader (2) completely revised the French legal code (3) donated lands in Italy to the Papacy (4) established a dictatorial Empire.

2. Napoleon III established French imperialist control over (1) Indo-China (2) China (3) India (4) Indonesia.

3. Defeated in the Franco-Prussian War, France (1) adopted the Declaration of the Rights of Man (2) restored the Bourbon monarchy (3) established a republic (4) lost her colonies in Africa.

4. The National Assembly elected in 1871 contained a majority of royalists because (1) the royalists pledged an immediate peace with Germany (2) voting was restricted to the upper classes (3) the German military commanders appointed the members of the Assembly (4) the republicans refused to stand for office.

5. Which group was charged with treason to the government by Emile Zola in his letter "J'Accuse"? (1) Jews (2) royalist army officers (3) republican politicians (4) middle-class businessmen.

6. The Dreyfus Affair in France led to (1) Napoleon's downfall (2) a scandal in regard to the Panama Canal (3) the passage of the Civil Constitution of the Clergy (4) laws separating Church and State.

7. Under the Fourth French Republic, a group of parties that acted together to form a cabinet was called (1) the center (2) an alliance (3) a bloc (4) a ministry.

8. Bloc governments under the Fourth Republic proved unstable because they (1) did not include Communists (2) failed to stop antigovernment strikes by unions (3) lost their Assembly majority when one party withdrew from the bloc (4) were limited constitutionally to six months in office.

9. The constitution for the Fifth Republic (1) allowed the President to rule by decree in emergencies (2) granted all legislative power to the Constitutional Council (3) gave independence to Algeria (4) adopted the two-party system.

10. The Fifth French Republic borrowed from American practice when it (1) made the cabinet responsible to the legislature (2) gave the President power to dissolve the legislature (3) prohibited cabinet members from serving in the legislature (4) limited legislative sessions to two 3-month sessions a year.

11. The name of the Gaullist party in the Fifth Republic is (1) Union of the New Republic (2) Radicals (3) Socialists (4) Popular Republicans.

COMPLETION QUESTIONS

1. Louis Napoleon lost French Catholic support when he aided the unification of _____.

2. Louis Napoleon failed in his attempt to gain imperialist control over _____ in the Western Hemisphere.

3. The leader of the Free French government during World War II was _____.

4. Under the Fourth French Republic, the position most similar to that of the King of England was that of the _____.

5. The immediate cause that led to the overthrow of the Fourth French Republic was the army-created crisis in _____.

6. In order to provide stability in government, the Fifth French Republic strengthened the powers of the _____.

7. Elected as first President under the Fifth French Republic was _____.

UNIT VIII. THE INFLUENCE OF NATIONALISM

Part 1. Introduction

DEFINITION OF TERMS

1. Nationality (or nation)—people united by a belief that they have social and cultural bonds: language, history, traditions, and ideals.

2. Nationalism—feeling of patriotism and supreme loyalty that a nationality has toward its own country. If a nationality lacks its own independent country, nationalism provides the driving force to create it.

3. National state (or nation-state)—an independent country containing a single nationality.

4. Subject nationality—a nationality that has not achieved independence.

5. Chauvinism—extreme nationalism that exaggerates the nation's accomplishments. Whereas nationalism makes people say "We are just as good as anyone else," chauvinism makes people say "We are far better than anyone else."

DEVELOPMENT OF NATIONALISM

1. During the Middle Ages. Until the 15th century nationalism and national states did not exist. People felt their greatest loyalty to their church, feudal lord, city-state, or province.

2. The Rise of Absolute Monarchs and National States. From the 15th to the 18th centuries moderate nationalism emerged as people became aware and proud of their own distinct nationality. They gave their loyalty to the king, the symbol of national unity. Moderate nationalism only mildly affected people's lives.

3. The French Revolution. Intense nationalism originated during the French Revolution of 1789, and spread throughout Europe and the rest of the world. People transferred their loyalty from king to country and placed the national interest above all other considerations. Intense nationalism greatly influenced the actions of men.

4. To the Present Day. In the 19th and 20th centuries intense nationalism has been fostered by a number of developments. (*a*) *State control of educa-*

tion. Public schools teach pride in the customs, ideals, and glories of a nation. (*b*) *Mass communication.* Newspapers, magazines, books, radio, and television standardize and thus unify the nation's culture and outlook on life. (*c*) *Rapid transportation.* Railroads, automobiles, and airlines unite the national state physically.

NATIONALISM: A FORCE FOR BOTH GOOD AND EVIL

Imbued with intense nationalism, people have supported movements and actions to further what they considered the well-being of their own nationality.

1. Democracy. (*a*) The nationalists of the French Revolution set up democratic institutions and defended them against invading foreign armies. (*b*) During the Metternich Era (1815-1848), Italian revolutionists aspired to both national unity and democratic government.

2. Dictatorship. (*a*) Italian patriots in the 1920's supported Mussolini in establishing a dictatorship when he appealed to the nationalism of the Italian people. (*b*) German nationalists in the 1930's rallied to Hitler's side and helped him overthrow the democratic German government and establish a dictatorship.

3. Imperialism. Nationalism provided a motive for the powerful industrial nations—England, France, Germany, Italy, Japan—to acquire colonial empires. Imperialism meant prestige, economic resources, and military bases for the mother country.

4. Anti-Imperialism. By the 20th century colonial peoples developed their own nationalism and struggled to end foreign domination. Indian nationalists, for example, ended English rule, and Algerian nationalists ended French rule.

5. Militarism and War. Modern nations have made great sacrifices when convinced that their existence was in peril. In the 20th century, Germans and Frenchmen endured peacetime conscription, tolerated heavy taxation for military expenditures, and suffered wartime hardships.

6. National Unification. (*a*) In 1815 the German people inhabited 38 independent states. By 1871 German nationalists, led by Bismarck, had unified their country. (*b*) Also in the 19th century, Italy achieved unification.

7. Disruption of Empires. (*a*) The subject nationalities in the Austro-Hungarian Empire desired independence. They plotted revolution and war. When Austria-Hungary was defeated in World War I, the various subject nationalities achieved independence. (*b*) The multinational Turkish Empire, too, came to an end following its defeat in World War I.

Part 2. German Unification by "Blood and Iron"

THE GERMAN STATES (1789-1848)

1. Factors Promoting Unity

a. Common Nationality. In the late 18th century some German people began to think of themselves as a distinct nationality and agitated for a unified fatherland. This nationalist awakening reflected the efforts of German educators, poets, writers, historians, and philosophers.

b. Napoleon's Influence. Napoleon aided German unification, although unintentionally. He aroused German nationalism against him, weakened Austrian authority in Germany by abolishing the Holy Roman Empire, and reduced the more than 300 German states to less than 100.

c. Congress of Vienna. The peace conference of 1815 helped German unity, although unwittingly. It reduced the number of German states to 38 and organized them into an Austrian-dominated league of rulers, the *German Confederation.* The Confederation proved weak and ineffective, incapable of providing Germany with a unified government. Its failure stirred the people to seek unity by other means.

d. Zollverein. In 1819 Prussia formed a German customs union, which became known as the *Zollverein.* By the 1840's it included most German states, but not Austria. The Zollverein maintained free trade between member states, but high tariffs against nonmembers. The removal of internal tariff barriers benefited German merchants and manufacturers, and promoted the country's economic unity.

2. Factors Hindering Unity

a. Differences Among the German People. In Prussia and other north German states, the people were in the main Protestant, were interested in commerce, and were turning toward manufacturing. In Bavaria and other south German states, the people were predominantly Roman Catholic and were interested chiefly in agriculture. Outnumbered by the northerners, the south Germans realized that, in a united country, they would be a minority.

b. Opposition of Austria. Austria emerged from the Congress of Vienna as an influential central European Empire containing many different peoples. Austria's rulers, committed to the Metternich System (see pages 173-174), feared that the growth of nationalism, particularly in nearby Germany, might inspire their subject nationalities to seek independence. Consequently, in 1819 Metternich induced the German Confederation to issue the *Carlsbad Decrees*. Aimed at suppressing liberal and nationalist ideas in Germany, these laws provided for (1) strict supervision of universities, teachers, and student organizations, and (2) censorship of newspapers, pamphlets, and books.

Austria's rulers also realized that, in the event of German unification, they would lose their influence over German affairs.

c. Opposition of the Lesser German States. The rulers and officials of the smaller German states feared that a unified Germany might centralize governmental power, thereby ending their authority.

d. Opposition of France. French leaders feared that a unified Germany would be sufficiently powerful to challenge France's leadership in Europe. Furthermore, the French felt militarily more secure with weak, disunited neighbors.

FAILURE OF THE 1848 REVOLUTION

German liberals led a series of revolts in 1848 aimed at ending autocracy and unifying Germany. Encouraged by early successes, they convened a parliament, the *Frankfurt Assembly*. The liberals prepared a democratic constitution, proclaimed a united Germany, and, after months of debate, offered the position of Emperor to the King of Prussia. He rejected the Assembly's offer as "a crown out of the gutter" and also because he feared that acceptance might lead to war with Austria. Since the liberals lacked the military power to enforce unification, the King's refusal spelled the failure of the Frankfurt Assembly.

The conservatives regained control throughout the German states, and the liberals experienced severe persecution. Many fled the country. A considerable number came to the United States, where they contributed to our growing democracy.

In Germany, the way was now open for the successful attempt at unity under autocratic leadership.

LEADERS OF GERMAN UNIFICATION

1. Bismarck, appointed chief minister of Prussia in 1862, belonged to the dominant, landowning aristocracy, the *Junkers*. A reactionary who despised democracy, Bismarck planned to unite Germany—not by speeches and votes as at the Frankfurt Assembly, but by "blood and iron."

2. William I, King of Prussia (1861-1888), who became Emperor of Germany in 1871, fully supported Bismarck's policies.

3. **Moltke,** Prussian general and chief of staff, contributed to Bismarck's success by building a strong army and achieving impressive military victories.

STEPS IN GERMAN UNIFICATION (1862-1871)

1. **Creation of Prussian Military Power.** In 1862 the government's request for increased military funds was defeated in the Prussian legislature, whose liberal majority opposed militarism. Thereupon, Bismarck ignored the lawmakers and, from 1862 to 1867, in violation of the constitution, governed virtually as a dictator. He and Moltke created a Prussian military machine second to none.

2. **Elimination of Austrian Influence**

a. The Danish War (*1864*). Bismarck brought about a war with Denmark over the provinces of *Schleswig* and *Holstein.* Prussia, joined by Austria, easily defeated Denmark and compelled her to cede Schleswig-Holstein.

b. The Austro-Prussian War (*1866*). Bismarck deliberately quarreled with Austria regarding the administration of the conquered provinces. Actually, Bismarck provoked war so as to end Austrian power in Germany. Most of the German states supported Austria to oppose Prussian dominance. Prussia was allied with Italy, which wanted the Italian territory held by Austria. General von Moltke's armies overwhelmed Austria so quickly that the war is called the *Seven Weeks' War.*

According to the treaty of peace, Austria (1) ceded Schleswig-Holstein to Prussia and Venetia to Italy, and (2) agreed to dissolve the Austrian-dominated German Confederation, thus withdrawing from German affairs. By treating Austria generously, Bismarck expected to gain her friendship for the emerging German state.

3. **Establishment of the North German Confederation** (1867). Following the Austro-Prussian War, Bismarck annexed several north German states and compelled the remaining ones to join in a Prussian-dominated *North German Confederation.* Only the four south German states remained outside the Confederation, but they were tied to Prussia by the Zollverein and a defensive military alliance.

4. **The Franco-Prussian War** (1870-1871). Bismarck now desired a war with France, so that the south Germans, by fighting a common enemy and experiencing wartime nationalism, would voluntarily merge into a Prussian-controlled unified Germany. When France opposed a German candidate for the Spanish throne, Bismarck seized the opportunity. He intensified Franco-German enmity by rewriting a vital telegram, the *Ems Dispatch.* Thus pro-

The Unification of Germany Under Prussian Leadership

voked, Napoleon III declared war upon Prussia, which was joined by the four south German states. General von Moltke's armies invaded France, destroyed the French forces at *Sedan*, and quickly overran the country.

In the *Treaty of Frankfurt*, France (a) ceded *Alsace-Lorraine* to Germany (these provinces, rich in coal and iron, were inhabited mostly by Frenchmen), (b) agreed to pay Germany a huge war indemnity, and (c) until final payment, consented to German military occupation. By treating France harshly, Bismarck planted the seeds of World War I.

5. Establishment of the German Empire (1871). During the Franco-Prussian War, the four south German states consented to unification with Prussia. In January, 1871, at Versailles, Bismarck proclaimed William I as Emperor (*Kaiser*) of the German Empire.

Bismarck's success—by military might and autocratic rule—established a tradition that, according to many historians, greatly impeded the development of democracy in Germany.

THE GERMAN EMPIRE: UNDEMOCRATIC GOVERNMENT

1. Autocracy. (*a*) Unlike the English King, the German ruler was no figurehead. The Kaiser commanded the armed forces, conducted foreign affairs, and appointed his choices to major government positions. (*b*) The *Chancellor* (Prime Minister) and other cabinet members were responsible to the Kaiser, not to the legislature. (*c*) In the two-house legislature, the *Bundesrat*—whose members were appointed by the heads of the various states—exercised important law-making powers; the popularly elected *Reichstag* had few powers.

2. Prussian Domination. Prussia contained almost two-thirds of the area and the population of the Empire. The King of Prussia automatically became Emperor of Germany. The chief minister of Prussia usually served as Chancellor of Germany. Prussia controlled enough votes in the Bundesrat to block any military law, tax measure, or constitutional amendment.

THE GERMAN EMPIRE UNDER BISMARCK'S DIRECTION (1871-1890)

As Germany's *Iron Chancellor,* Bismarck pursued conservative and nationalist policies.

1. Centralization of Power. To promote uniformity within Germany, the national government took away from the states their control over railways, telegraph lines, postal service, banking, and coinage. Also, national codes of law replaced the varying state legal systems.

2. Continuation of Militarism. The Empire adopted the Prussian system of compulsory, peacetime military service. Militarism was extolled by government officials, patriotic societies, and nationalist writers. In conducting foreign affairs, Bismarck emphasized military alliances.

3. Encouragement of Industrialization. Unification encouraged economic growth. Germany rapidly changed from an agricultural to a predominantly industrial nation and experienced great prosperity. The German government, eager to attain economic self-sufficiency, assisted the industrialists by (*a*) **high tariffs** to protect home industry against foreign competitors, and (*b*) **imperialism** to secure colonial raw materials and markets.

4. Persecution of Subject Nationalities. Bismarck tried to compel the Empire's minorities—Poles, Danes, and Frenchmen—to forsake their own cultures and adopt German ways. Despite persecution, these minority groups resisted *Germanization.*

5. Measures Against Catholics. The German Catholics, who inhabited chiefly the four southern states, opposed Bismarck and feared domination by Protestant Prussia. To protect their interests, Catholics organized the *Center party*, which advocated stronger states' rights. Bismarck opposed the Catholics because of their attitude on states' rights and because of their ties to the Pope. This loyalty to an international Church, Bismarck believed, evidenced a lack of German nationalism.

To weaken the Catholic Church, Bismarck in 1872 started a struggle called, by his supporters, the battle for civilization, or *Kulturkampf*. He secured laws placing the Catholic clergy under state control, ending Church influence in education, and requiring civil marriage ceremonies. These measures, denounced by the Pope and defied by clergy and laymen, intensified Catholic resistance and helped the Center party increase its representation in the Reichstag. Eventually, Bismarck permitted the repeal of most of the anti-Catholic laws as he realized their failure and desired Catholic support against another enemy, the Socialists.

6. Measures Against the Socialists. As German industry grew, city workers became more numerous and sought higher wages and better working conditions. The workers voted for the Reichstag candidates of the *Social Democratic (Socialist) party*. The Socialists pleaded the workers' cause and denounced Bismarck's policies of autocracy and militarism. Bismarck detested the Socialists because of their democratic, antimilitarist attitude and their ties to the international Socialist movement. He felt that supporters of any worldwide organization could not be true German patriots.

To combat the German Socialists, Bismarck employed: (a) **Repression.** In 1878 he secured laws which forbade Socialist meetings, banned their publications, and subjected their leaders to arrest. (b) **Social Security.** Bismarck believed that the workers would reject the Socialist party if they received government help toward economic security. Between 1883 and 1889, therefore, he secured laws to assist workers financially in case of sickness, accident, and old age. (Bismarck's social insurance program set an example later followed by most industrial nations. See pages 241-242.)

Neither repressive laws nor social legislation weakened Socialism in Germany. Even operating under severe handicaps, the Socialist party spread its ideas and even increased its Reichstag membership.

7. Foreign Policies. See page 335.

THE GERMAN EMPIRE UNDER WILLIAM II

In 1888 *William II*, a strong-willed believer in the "divine right" of kings, inherited the throne. Determined to direct German affairs personally, the new Kaiser in 1890 dismissed Bismarck from office.

Kaiser William II reversed two of Bismarck's policies: friendship for Russia and repression of Socialists. Otherwise he maintained Bismarckian conservatism and nationalism. William ruled autocratically. He favored Junker landlords, industrialists, and military officers; strengthened the army and built an imposing navy; and furthered imperialism.

The Kaiser's policies of militarism and imperialism helped bring about World War I. Still later, Adolf Hitler followed a course of militarism and imperialism, and brought on World War II.

MULTIPLE-CHOICE QUESTIONS

1. Nationalism is a (1) desire of people for self-expression (2) desire of people for democratic government (3) policy of redistributing national wealth (4) feeling that unites people of the same language, history, and tradition.
2. The term most similar to nationalism in meaning is (1) patriotism (2) internationalism (3) imperialism (4) confederation.
3. The term that means "nationalism carried to extremes" is (1) revolution (2) self-determination (3) reign of terror (4) chauvinism.
4. Nationalism became an important factor in European affairs during (1) the Middle Ages (2) the French Revolution (3) World War I (4) the Renaissance.
5. Which did *not* strengthen nationalism? (1) state control of education (2) the Old Regime (3) modern communication methods (4) improved transportation facilities.
6. At different times and in different countries, nationalism has supported conflicting ideals such as democracy and dictatorship. This proves that (1) nationalists are illogical (2) democracy and dictatorship are not too different (3) nationalists will support that form of government they identify with their country's history and interests (4) nationalists prefer war and dictatorship.
7. Nationalists would be most aroused if their country's (1) unemployment rate went up (2) flag flying before the embassy in a foreign nation was torn down (3) printing of history books increased (4) exports of manufactured goods decreased.
8. Napoleon affected German history by (1) bringing about immediate German unification (2) consolidating many small states (3) making Jerome Bonaparte Emperor of Germany (4) enlarging Prussian territory.
9. An obstacle to German unification in the period from 1815 to 1860 was the (1) lack of common language (2) rivalry between Prussia and Austria (3) power of the Holy Roman Emperor (4) territorial changes made by Napoleon.
10. The Zollverein was (1) a tariff union of German states (2) a German legislative body (3) the Prussian land-owning aristocracy (4) the cavalry unit of the Prussian army.
11. Bismarck's plan to unify Germany included (1) organizing a tariff union (2) securing the cooperation of Austria (3) compelling the other north German states to join Prussia in a confederation on Prussia's terms (4) holding a plebiscite on unification in all German states.
12. Bismarck expelled Austria from German affairs by means of (1) a diplomatic agreement (2) paying Austria a monetary indemnity (3) allowing Austria to annex Schleswig-Holstein (4) the Seven Weeks' War.
13. Bismarck completed the formation of the German Empire by means of the (1) Austro-Prussian War (2) Franco-Prussian War (3) Napoleonic Wars (4) Danish War.
14. After unifying Germany, Bismarck undertook the *Kulturkampf* to (1) encourage music and literature (2) weaken the power of the Catholic Church (3) destroy the Socialist party (4) Germanize subject nationalities.

15. Bismarck advocated social insurance in Germany because he (1) wished to compete with England in industry (2) wished to satisfy workers and to discourage socialism (3) represented the working class (4) was the leader of the Social Democratic party

16. Between 1871 and 1914 Germany became a(an) (1) democratic republic (2) highly industrialized nation (3) Fascist dictatorship (4) advocate of disarmament.

COMPLETION QUESTIONS

1. During the Revolution of 1848, German liberal groups proclaimed their country's unity at the _____ Assembly.
2. Bismarck's method of uniting Germany was expressed in the slogan _____.
3. As a result of the Franco-Prussian War, Germany annexed the provinces of _____ and _____.
4. The Prime Minister of the German Empire, appointed by the Emperor, was called the _____.
5. Under the German Empire, the cabinet was responsible to the _____.

Part 3. Unification of Italy

ITALY: A "GEOGRAPHIC EXPRESSION"

1. Factors Hindering Unity

a. Political Divisions. At the Congress of Vienna Italy was divided into many states and provinces. Most pre-Napoleonic boundaries were restored. According to Metternich, Italy would not be a united nation, but a "geographic expression." The Congress divided the country as follows: (1) The kingdom of *Sardinia-Piedmont* (also called Sardinia or Piedmont)—under Italian control. (2) The provinces of *Lombardy* and *Venetia*—annexed to Austria. (3) The duchies of *Parma, Modena,* and *Tuscany,* as well as the *Kingdom of the Two Sicilies* (also called Naples)—under local rulers dominated by Austria. (4) The *Papal States*—under Church control.

b. Opposition of Austria. The rulers of Austria fought Italian unification (1) to discourage nationalist uprisings within their Empire, (2) to retain Lombardy and Venetia, and (3) to maintain Austrian influence elsewhere in Italy.

c. Opposition of the Papacy. Church leaders believed that a united Italy would end the Pope's temporal rule over the Papal States.

d. Discord Among Nationalists. The leading Italian nationalists were in conflict on a type of government for a united Italy. *Mazzini* and *Garibaldi* sought a democratic Italian republic; *Gioberti* urged an Italian federation under the leadership of the Pope; *Cavour,* an admirer of the English government, worked for a liberal Italian monarchy.

2. Factors Promoting Unity

a. National Feeling. Beginning with the Napoleonic Era the Italians became increasingly conscious of their nationality. They recalled the past glory of Italy during the Roman Empire and the Renaissance, resented their present subjugation to Austria, and desired unity and greatness.

b. Patriotic Societies

(1) The *Carbonari*, a secret society of limited membership, conspired to overthrow tyranny. They fomented uprisings in 1820, 1821, and 1831, but the uprisings were all suppressed by Austria. Thereafter, Carbonari secrecy and intrigue lost favor among Italian nationalists.

(2) *Young Italy*, founded in 1831 by Mazzini, was a nonsecret society. It openly and successfully propagandized democratic and nationalist ideas among the people.

c. Leadership of Sardinia-Piedmont. Ruled by the *House of Savoy*, a patriotic Italian family, Sardinia aspired to unify Italy. In 1848 the King of Sardinia granted his people a liberal constitution and led his armies in support of an Italian uprising against Austria. The Sardinians were defeated, and Austria reestablished her control within Italy. Although unsuccessful in 1848, Sardinia-Piedmont won the loyalty of Italian nationalists.

LEADERS OF ITALIAN UNIFICATION

1. Mazzini, writer, orator, and founder of Young Italy, dedicated his life to securing democracy and unity for his country. Preaching through newspapers, pamphlets, and speeches, Mazzini transmitted his patriotic ardor to the masses. In the Revolution of 1848, his followers seized the Papal States, and Mazzini proclaimed the Roman Republic. When French troops crushed this uprising, he fled the country and continued his propaganda efforts from abroad. Mazzini has been called the *soul* of unification.

2. Garibaldi, a friend of Mazzini, was a military leader. He defended Mazzini's Roman Republic against the French, several times fought for Sardinia against Austria, and in 1860 conquered the Two Sicilies. Garibaldi was known as the *sword* of unification.

3. Cavour, liberal statesman appointed Prime Minister of Sardinia-Piedmont in 1852, strengthened the country by promoting industry, building railroads, improving agriculture, fostering education, and enlarging the army. Until his death in 1861, he executed a series of diplomatic moves to achieve Italian unity. Cavour has been called the *brain* of unification.

4. Victor Emmanuel II, who became King of Sardinia-Piedmont in 1849, retained his nation's liberal constitution and fully supported Cavour's policies. In 1861 he became King of Italy.

SARDINIA-PIEDMONT UNIFIES ITALY BY TERRITORIAL ANNEXATIONS (1859-1870)

1. Lombardy (1859). Shrewdly, Cavour won Napoleon III's pledge of military assistance if Austria attacked Sardinia. Thereupon, Cavour maneuvered Austria into declaring war. In a short conflict, French and Sardinian troops defeated the Austrians. As a result of the war, (a) Austria ceded Lombardy to Sardinia, and (b) following a plebiscite, Sardinia ceded Savoy and Nice to France.

Sardinia's success aroused nationalist revolts elsewhere.

The Unification of Italy Under Sardinia-Piedmont

2. The Duchies (1860). In Parma, Modena, and Tuscany, the people drove out their pro-Austrian rulers and, by plebiscites, voted annexation to Sardinia-Piedmont.

3. The Two Sicilies (1860). In 1860 Garibaldi came to the aid of the Sicilian and Neapolitan revolutionaries. He sailed from Piedmont to Sicily with a volunteer army of one thousand *Red Shirts.* Garibaldi, joined by rebels throughout southern Italy, soon gained complete control of the Two Sicilies. In the national interest, Garibaldi put aside his republican sentiments and proposed that the Two Sicilies unite with Sardinia under Victor Emmanuel II. By a plebiscite, the southern Italians so voted.

4. The Papal States (1860). While Garibaldi conquered the Two Sicilies, Cavour ordered Sardinian troops into the Papal States. The Sardinians, welcomed by nationalist groups, overran central Italy. Cavour then announced the annexation of the Papal States (except for Rome), thereby joining northern and southern Italy. In 1861 the Kingdom of Italy was proclaimed.

5. Venetia (1866). Italy allied herself with Prussia in the Seven Weeks' War against Austria. The Italians invaded Venetia but were defeated. However, the Prussian armies quickly overwhelmed the Austrians. By the peace treaty, Austria ceded Venetia to Italy.

6. Rome (1870). Because of the Franco-Prussian War, French troops supporting the Pope in Rome were withdrawn. Thereupon, Italian forces occupied the city. Following a plebiscite, Rome was annexed and designated the capital of Italy.

PROBLEMS FACING ITALY AFTER UNIFICATION

1. Government Weaknesses. Italy's limited monarchy featured a King with few powers, an elected Chamber of Deputies, and a cabinet responsible to the Chamber of Deputies. Although modeled after England's parliamentary system, the Italian government operated far less successfully. (*a*) The Italian masses, illiterate and impoverished, lacked a democratic tradition and demonstrated little public responsibility. (*b*) Until 1904, when the Pope relaxed the ban forbidding Catholics to take part in the Italian government, devout Catholics shunned government positions, and did not vote. (*c*) Until 1912, when universal manhood suffrage was adopted, only the wealthier classes could vote. (*d*) The existence of many political parties caused a number of cabinet crises. (*e*) Bribery and corruption pervaded public life.

2. Church Hostility. The Italian government sought to make peace with the Papacy. By the *Law of Papal Guarantees* of 1871, Italy (*a*) acknowledged Papal rule of an independent Vatican state within Rome, and (*b*) offered the Papacy an annual indemnity. Pope Pius IX rejected these terms, denying Italy's right to seize the Papal States. Until this dispute was settled in 1929 (see page 370), the Popes considered themselves "prisoners" in the Vatican.

3. Poor Economic Conditions. Italy lacked the coal, iron, and oil necessary for extensive industrialization; she also lacked sufficient fertile land to support her increasing population. Despite government efforts to improve economic conditions, living standards remained low. Many Italians migrated to South America and to the United States.

4. Ambitious Nationalism. Italy also weakened herself by trying to play the part of a great world power. (a) *Militarism.* Italy adopted compulsory military service and maintained a large army and navy. (b) *Imperialism.* Italy acquired the African colonies of Eritrea, Italian Somaliland, and Libya. (Italy's attempt to conquer Ethiopia in 1896 met with defeat.) (c) *World War I.* By joining the Allies and fighting Austria, Italy gained most of her *Italia Irredenta* (unredeemed Italy): *Trentino, Istria,* and *Trieste.*

Italy's nationalist policies placed heavy personal and financial burdens upon the people. Nevertheless, nationalist feeling remained strong and, after World War I, helped pave the way for Fascist rule under Mussolini (see pages 368-371).

MULTIPLE-CHOICE QUESTIONS

1. The principal obstacle to Italian unification during the 19th century was (1) domination by Sardinia-Piedmont (2) interference by foreign powers (3) lack of common traditions (4) lack of a common language.
2. The Italian who founded the Young Italy Society to arouse nationalist feeling among the people was (1) Gioberti (2) Cavour (3) Victor Emmanuel II (4) Mazzini.
3. Cavour believed that Sardinia-Piedmont could unify Italy because Sardinia-Piedmont was (1) a liberal monarchy whose ruling house was Italian (2) friendly to Austria (3) under control of the Pope (4) an enemy of France.
4. In the unification of their respective countries, both Bismarck and Cavour followed the policy of (1) winning the friendship of France (2) extending democratic reforms (3) maintaining neutrality in the Crimean War (4) provoking Austria into a declaration of war.
5. Who performed the military exploits responsible for bringing Sicily into the Kingdom of Italy? (1) Mazzini (2) Garibaldi (3) Cavour (4) Victor Emmanuel II.
6. Italy was able to annex Rome because of the (1) Seven Weeks' War (2) Franco-Prussian War (3) Austro-Sardinian War (4) Crimean War.
7. The ruling family of the Kingdom of Italy was the House of (1) Savoy (2) Bourbon (3) Hapsburg (4) Parma.
8. Both Mazzini and Garibaldi had wanted the government of a united Italy to be a(an) (1) limited monarchy (2) dictatorship (3) republic (4) absolute monarchy.
9. The attitude of Pope Pius IX toward Italian unification was (1) active support (2) encouragement (3) indifference (4) opposition.
10. After unification in 1871, the Kingdom of Italy (1) became a prosperous country (2) remained a poor country (3) discovered rich iron ore and coal resources (4) became a leading industrial nation.

Part 4. Disruption of Multinational Empires

A. THE AUSTRIAN EMPIRE

AUSTRIA IN 1815: AN EMPIRE OF MANY NATIONALITIES

1. Dominant Nationality. The German-speaking Austrians, constituting one-fifth of the population of the Empire, were the dominant nationality. They held the leading positions in government, Church, education, and army. Also Austrian was the Empire's ruling family, the Hapsburgs.

2. Subject Nationalities. These included Hungarians (or Magyars), Italians, Rumanians, and Slavic-speaking peoples: Czechs, Slovaks, Poles, Serbs, Croats, and Slovenes. (These latter three are also known as southern Slavs, or Yugoslavs.) As these subject peoples absorbed nationalist ideals—spread from France after 1789—they aspired to independence.

AUSTRIA COMBATS NATIONALISM

Until 1848 Prince Metternich directed Austrian efforts to suppress nationalist movements. He employed press censorship, spies, secret police, arbitrary prison terms, and armed forces. Nevertheless, in 1848, revolutions erupted throughout the Empire, Metternich fled the country, and several subject nationalities seemed on the verge of partial or complete independence.

By 1849, however, the Empire had regained complete control because (1) the army remained loyal to the Hapsburgs, and (2) the government succeeded in its *divide-and-rule* policy: setting one nationality against another —Austrians to suppress Czechs and Italians; Slavs to subdue Hungarians.

Austria's exertions to repress her subject nationalities sapped her military strength. In two wars—in 1859 against France and Sardinia, and in 1866 against Prussia—the Austrian armies were easily defeated.

THE EMPIRE BECOMES THE DUAL MONARCHY (1867)

To buttress their hold over the Empire, the Austrians granted an equal partnership to the Hungarians. This *Ausgleich,* or *Compromise,* of 1867, transformed the Austrian Empire into the *Dual Monarchy* of Austria-Hungary. The Hapsburg ruler now was entitled "Emperor of Austria and King of Hungary." Austria and Hungary each had her own government, independent in local matters, but joined together on common problems: foreign affairs, military defense, tariffs, and finances.

DISCONTENT WITH THE DUAL MONARCHY (1867-1914)

The Slavic peoples, as well as Rumanian and Italian minorities, remained restless and agitated for freedom because (1) unlike the Hungarians, they gained nothing from the Ausgleich, and (2) in Hungarian domains, they were oppressed even more than they had been before the Ausgleich. Following 1878, when an independent Serbia was created out of Turkish territory, the Serbs in Austria-Hungary became especially rebellious.

AUSTRIA-HUNGARY AND WORLD WAR I (1914-1918)

Serbian nationalists ignited World War I by assassinating the heir to the Austro-Hungarian throne. Austria-Hungary declared war upon Serbia, hoping to crush the Serbian threat to the Dual Monarchy. This initial conflict evolved into World War I (see page 337).

Austria-Hungary was weakened in the war by the disloyalty of her subject nationalities. Her Slavic subjects engaged in sabotage, mutiny, and, in 1918, outright revolt. Even the favored Hungarians revolted. These revolutions, coming when Austria-Hungary's military position was desperate, hastened her surrender to the Allies.

BREAKUP OF THE AUSTRO-HUNGARIAN EMPIRE (1919-1920)

By the peace treaties, the territories of Austria-Hungary were divided so that her many nationalities each achieved an independent existence. (1) Trentino, Istria, and Trieste, all having large Italian populations, were transferred to Italy. (2) Rumanian-inhabited territory was ceded to Rumania. (3) Polish-inhabited territory was combined with territories previ-

The Breakup of the Austro-Hungarian Empire
(1919-1920)

ously held by Germany and Russia to recreate a sovereign Poland. (4) Territory inhabited by southern Slavs was combined with Serbia and Montenegro to form Yugoslavia. (5) Czechoslovakia was formed out of territory inhabited mainly by Czechs and Slovaks. (6) Austria and Hungary were separated into small independent states.

PROBLEMS RESULTING FROM AUSTRIA-HUNGARY'S DISSOLUTION

1. **New Nationalist Discontent.** It proved impossible to draw boundaries that would include all the people of one nationality in one state. Consequently, a minority of Austrians and Hungarians was assigned to Czechoslovakia; some Hungarians were included in Rumania; the territory given to Italy contained some Austrians and Yugoslavs. These newly created subject nationalities agitated for further territorial revision. (When Hitler claimed the Czechoslovakian Sudetenland because of the German-speaking population that had been transferred from Austria, the fate of the Sudetenland became a matter of international concern. See page 386.)

2. **Economic Distress.** The Empire, whose industrial and agricultural regions supplemented each other's needs, had constituted a prosperous free trade area. The nations replacing the Empire adopted high tariffs, which hampered their trade relations and caused widespread economic distress.

B. THE TURKISH EMPIRE

OTTOMAN TURKEY: ANOTHER MULTINATIONAL EMPIRE

1. **Dominant Nationality.** As the 19th century opened, the Ottoman Turks, who were Moslems, governed an Empire that included parts of Asia, Africa, and Europe. The Turks themselves inhabited Asia Minor and a small European area that included Constantinople.

2. **Subject Nationalities.** These included (a) Arabs in the Middle East and North Africa, (b) Egyptians in North Africa, and (c) southern Slavs, Albanians, Rumanians, Bulgarians, and Greeks in the Balkans. Whereas the Arabs and Egyptians were Moslem, the Balkan peoples were mainly Eastern Orthodox Christian.

REASONS FOR BALKAN DISCONTENT

The Balkan peoples, inspired by nationalism, desired independence. They also detested Turkish rule. (1) *Autocracy.* Absolute power was in the hands of the Sultan. (2) *Corruption.* Money raised by heavy taxation was diverted from public use to private hands. (3) *Inefficiency.* Disorder existed in many parts of the Empire. (4) **Discrimination.** Christians were singled out for economic and religious persecution. (5) **Cruelty.** Unusual cruelty was used to suppress rebellious subjects.

TURKEY LOSES THE BALKANS

Over a 100-year period, the Balkan peoples gained freedom from an enfeebled Turkey, the *sick man of Europe*. The highlights of this struggle, often marked by atrocity and barbarism, were as follows:

1. Greek Revolution (1821-1829). Revolting against Turkey, the Greeks received aid from (a) Russia, which sought influence in the Balkans, and (b) England and France, which revered the ancient Greek heritage and wanted to restrain Russian efforts in the Balkans. By 1829 the Greeks had gained Turkish recognition of their independence.

2. Crimean War (1853-1856). From Turkey, Russia wanted Constantinople and the Straits (the Dardanelles and the Bosporus), so as to control the water route connecting the Black and Mediterranean Seas. England opposed these Russian ambitions as threatening English trade routes.

In 1853 Russia demanded the right to protect Orthodox Christians within the Turkish Empire. When Turkey refused, Russia began hostilities. England and France aided Turkey, and together their armies defeated Russia. For the time being, the Turkish Empire remained intact.

3. Russo-Turkish War (1877-1878). Supposedly enraged by Turkish atrocities against Slavic peoples, Russia declared war and defeated the Sultan's forces. Russia forced upon Turkey a peace treaty that gave Russia great influence in the Balkans. England and Austria-Hungary denounced this treaty and demanded a Balkan settlement by international conference. Under threat of a new war, Russia agreed to a conference in Berlin.

4. Congress of Berlin (1878). By this conference, Turkey (a) allowed Austria-Hungary to occupy the southern Slavic provinces of Bosnia and Herzegovina, (b) allowed England to occupy the Mediterranean island of Cyprus, (c) granted independence to Serbia, Montenegro, and Rumania, (d) granted Bulgaria self-government within the Turkish Empire, and (e) agreed that Russia receive certain Balkan territory. (In 1882, shortly after this conference, Turkey recognized English domination over Egypt.)

5. Balkan Wars (1912-1913). In the first Balkan War, Greece, Bulgaria, Montenegro, and Serbia attacked and defeated Turkey. In disposing of the ceded Turkish lands, the victors agreed, under Austrian pressure, to form an independent Albania (for Austria's reasons, see Balkan Crises of 1912-1913, pages 336-337). However, they quarreled bitterly regarding the remaining territory. In the second Balkan War, Bulgaria battled her former allies and Turkey. By the final peace treaty, Turkey retained in Europe only a small

The Breakup of the Turkish Empire in Europe (by 1914)

area including Constantinople. The Balkans now consisted primarily of independent national states.

TURKEY BECOMES A NATIONAL STATE

1. **The "Young Turks."** In 1908 this nationalist group of Turks seized control of the government. The Young Turks hoped to modernize Turkey, establish constitutional government, revitalize Turkish military power, and preserve what was left of the Empire. Some reforms were made, but the Young Turks failed to stop the breakup of the Empire: in 1908 they could not prevent Bulgarian independence; in 1911-1912 Turkey was defeated by Italy and was forced to cede Tripoli (Libya); in 1912-1913 Turkish forces were defeated by the Balkan states; in 1914-1918 Turkey joined Germany against the Allies and again met defeat.

2. Mustafa Kemal and the Nationalists. After World War I, Turkish nationalists, led by army officer *Mustafa Kemal* (later surnamed *Ataturk*) rejected the severe peace treaty offered by the Allies in 1920 and continued to fight until they secured more favorable terms. In 1923, by the *Treaty of Lausanne*, Turkey surrendered only her remaining non-Turkish territories (chiefly Arab) but retained her Turkish areas: Constantinople and Asia Minor. To prevent nationalist friction, Turks living in Greece and Greeks living in Turkey were compelled to migrate to their respective homelands. Turkey, no longer an Empire, was now reduced to a national state.

TURKEY UNDER MUSTAFA KEMAL (1923-1938)

The nationalists declared Turkey a republic, transferred the capital from Constantinople (renamed Istanbul) to Ankara, and elected Mustafa Kemal as President. Ruling as virtual dictator, he (1) modernized the country by prohibiting polygamy, outlawing Oriental dress, introducing Western law codes, encouraging industry, and (2) appealed to Turkish nationalism through press, radio, and the public school system.

TRUE-FALSE QUESTIONS

If the statement is correct, write the word *true*. If the statement is incorrect, substitute a word or phrase for the italicized term to make the statement correct.

1. The German-speaking people in the Austro-Hungarian Empire were the *Croats*.
2. Another name for the people of *Rumania* is Magyars.
3. The plan to change the Austrian Empire into the Dual Monarchy was called the *Ausgleich*.
4. The subject nationalities who gained nothing from the Dual Monarchy arrangement included the *Slavs*.
5. The heir to the Austrian throne, Archduke Francis Ferdinand, was assassinated by a *Polish* nationalist.
6. The Austro-Hungarian Empire came to an end after *the Austro-Sardinian War*.
7. In 1920 Serbs, Croats, and Slovenes were united to form the independent state of *Yugoslavia*.
8. In drawing the boundaries of Czechoslovakia, the World War I treaty-makers gave her a minority of Hungarians and *Italians*.
9. Another name for the Turkish Empire was the *Egyptian* Empire.
10. For the most part, the Christian peoples in the Balkans are members of *Eastern Orthodox* churches.
11. The Balkan people first to achieve independence in the 19th century were the *Serbs*.
12. Russia's interest in the Turkish Empire was to secure control over the *Dardanelles*.
13. In the Turkish Empire, the subject peoples of the same religion as the Turks included the *Arabs*.
14. In the Crimean War, France and England fought against *Turkey*.
15. In 1912 Turkey ceded her African territory of Tripoli to *England*.
16. During World War I Turkey fought on the side of *the Allies*.
17. Following World War I Turkey was ruled by a nationalist leader, *Mustafa Kemal*.
18. Following World War I *Greeks* living in Turkey were compelled to return to their native land.

UNIT IX. DEVELOPMENTS IN INDUSTRY, SCIENCE, AND CULTURE

Part 1. The Revolution in Production

INDUSTRIAL REVOLUTION: MEANING

1. In its narrow sense, the *Industrial Revolution* refers to the changes, beginning in the 18th century, in manufacturing methods. These were (*a*) from slower, more expensive production by hand to quicker, less costly production by machine, and, consequently, (*b*) from work in the home to work in the factory.

2. In its broad sense, the Industrial Revolution refers to the effect of machinery upon mankind's entire way of living. Our activities as citizens, workers, and consumers reflect the influence of the Industrial Revolution.

INDUSTRIAL REVOLUTION: CHRONOLOGY

1. **Old, or First, Industrial Revolution (1750-1870).** The first phase of the Industrial Revolution consisted of (*a*) the invention of the first complex machines and the building of the first factories, (*b*) the development of steam as a source of power and its application to manufacturing and transportation, (*c*) the expansion of the output of basic materials—coal, iron, and steel, and (*d*) the introduction of new methods of transportation and communication. These developments changed men's living patterns considerably.

2. **New, or Second, Industrial Revolution (1870-Still Continuing).** In the second phase of the Industrial Revolution, inventions came in greater number and brought even more sweeping changes to industry and society. This phase, still continuing, consists of (*a*) the use of new sources of power—electricity, petroleum, and atomic energy—which in turn makes possible new industries, (*b*) the deliberate application of science to industry and the development of artificial, or synthetic, products such as nylon and plastics, (*c*) the invention of newer and faster means of transportation and communication such as the airplane and radio, (*d*) the construction of machines equipped with electronic brains capable of running other machines, a process called *automation,* and (*e*) the placing of space vehicles in orbit around the earth and on flights into the solar system. Mankind has entered the *space age.*

ROOTS OF THE INDUSTRIAL REVOLUTION

1. Renaissance Spirit. By emphasizing life in this world, the Renaissance encouraged men to seek material comforts. By furthering a scientific approach to problems, the Renaissance helped pave the way for inventions.

2. Commercial Revolution. European expansion overseas uncovered new markets and created a vast demand for goods, especially textiles. Merchants acquired large sums of money, and many invested their capital in new and faster manufacturing methods.

3. The Domestic System. During the Later Middle Ages the guilds, by restricting the number of workers, hours of work, and type of tools, had limited output. In the 16th century, capitalists and workers, chiefly in the English textile industry, defied the guilds and devised a new way of producing goods, the "putting out" system, or *domestic system*. Capitalists provided the raw cotton and wool and paid the operators on a piecework basis for the finished product. The workers, usually entire families, worked at home for unlimited hours and with hand-operated tools. (Many workers supplemented their incomes by small-scale farming.) Not bound by guild restrictions, the domestic system increased the supply of textiles, but the demand for such goods increased even more rapidly. Beginning in the 18th century, the domestic system gave way to a still newer method of production, the *factory system*. The need for increased production led to new inventions, thus illustrating the familiar saying that "necessity is the mother of invention."

INDUSTRIAL REVOLUTION STARTS IN ENGLAND:
FAVORABLE CONDITIONS

1. Markets. As a prosperous nation and leading colonial power, England experienced a heavy demand for goods from both domestic and overseas markets.

2. Population. The English population included (*a*) skilled craftsmen who designed the needed machines, (*b*) wealthy capitalists who invested in such equipment, and (*c*) large numbers of workers who sought employment. With the passage of the *Enclosure Acts*, many landless peasants migrated to the cities. The Enclosure Acts legalized the practice by powerful landowners of "fencing in" open field strips and village commons. Peasants were thus deprived of their farms and had to seek work in factories.

3. Natural Resources. England had coal to provide steam power, iron ore to make machines, and good harbors to facilitate trade. Furthermore, the English colonies provided valuable raw materials, including lumber and cotton.

4. Government. The English businessman had the advantage of a government that (a) levied relatively fair and light taxes, (b) had established a stable money system and a well-organized banking system (the *Bank of England* was chartered in 1694), and (c) maintained a stable administration in a unified country.

TEXTILES: THE FIRST MECHANIZED INDUSTRY

The making of cloth was the first industry to feel the full effects of the Industrial Revolution. Cloth is made by (1) spinning raw fiber (wool or cotton) into thread, and then (2) weaving thread into cloth. To meet the urgent demand for cotton goods, spinning and weaving had to be greatly sped up and the supply of raw fiber greatly increased. By achieving these goals, England became the leading textile-producing country in the world. In devising new machines, inventors showed that "one invention leads to the next."

INVENTORS	INVENTIONS
John Kay (English)	*Flying shuttle* (1733), hand-operated, sped up weaving by loom and created a demand for thread.
James Hargreaves (English)	*Spinning jenny* (1764), hand-operated, spun eight threads at one time.
Richard Arkwright (English)	*Water frame* (1769) used water power for spinning.
Samuel Crompton (English)	*Spinning mule* (1779) combined the best features of the spinning jenny and the water frame.
Edmund Cartwright (English)	*Power loom* (1785) used water power for weaving.
Eli Whitney (American)	*Cotton gin* (1793), hand-operated at first, removed seeds from raw cotton.

STEAM: A SOURCE OF POWER

From prehistoric times to the 18th century, man secured *power*—the force, or energy, to do work—from limited and unreliable sources: his own exertions, animals, wind, and water. Man dreamed of a new kind of power to achieve freedom from fickle nature and physical drudgery. The Industrial Revolution provided the answer—*steam*. Formed by boiling water, steam exerts pressure that can be harnessed to drive engines and operate machines.

In 1705 *Thomas Newcomen* (English) devised a crude *steam engine*. It served chiefly to operate pumps draining water from coal mines.

In 1769 *James Watt* (Scottish) greatly improved upon Newcomen's work and constructed an efficient steam engine, thus opening up the *age of steam*. Watt's success illustrates the observation that "an important invention often results from the work of several men." Watt's engine was adapted for textile mills by 1785, and soon afterwards for other factories and for transportation. Tremendous industrial expansion followed.

STEAM ENGINE IN TRANSPORTATION

The horse-drawn wagon and the wind-driven sailing vessel transported goods for many centuries. When factories began producing large quantities of finished products for worldwide markets, these vehicles proved too slow and uncertain. They were replaced by steam-driven means of transportation.

1. Steamboat. In 1807 *Robert Fulton* (American) successfully launched the *Clermont*, a steam-driven side-paddle ship. Steamboats soon appeared on rivers and along coasts, and then crossed the oceans. In 1838 the *Great Western* crossed the Atlantic in 15 days, using only steam power. Today's luxury liners complete the same trip within 5 days. Tankers and freighters carry consumer goods, raw materials, and machinery to all parts of the world.

2. Locomotive. In 1814 *George Stephenson* (English) built the first successful steam locomotive. In 1830 his *Rocket* traveled at the then astounding speed of 29 miles per hour while pulling a train of cars. This achievement spurred a tremendous increase in rail-track mileage, and railroads soon became the leading means of transportation. Today's trains are safer, speedier, and more versatile. Innovations include sleepers, refrigerated freight cars, and piggyback flatcars.

COAL, IRON, AND STEEL

1. Coal. This fuel became essential to industry for supplying the heat necessary (*a*) to change water into steam, and (*b*) to remove iron from its ore. In order to reduce coal gas explosions ignited by miners' open lamps, *Sir Humphry Davy* (English) in 1815 invented the closed *safety lamp*.

2. Iron and Steel. These metals were used in the manufacture of many products, especially machines. At first, iron predominated, because steel, although stronger and less brittle, was costly to produce. In 1856 *Henry Bessemer* (English) devised the inexpensive Bessemer process of refining iron into steel. Subsequent improvements in steelmaking included the open-hearth, electric-furnace, and crucible processes. Alloys were developed for special types of steels, such as stainless steel. Steel—used to make products from watch springs to immense skyscraper structures—is the basic metal of our industrial society.

NEW SOURCES OF POWER

1. Electricity. For many years scientists conducted experiments to learn more about electricity. In 1831 *Michael Faraday* (English) moved a magnet inside a coil and generated an electric current. This discovery led to the invention of the *dynamo,* an electric generator that transforms mechanical energy into electricity. Today dynamos are driven by falling water (hydroelectric power) and by steam produced by means of coal, oil, or atomic energy. Inventors have employed electricity to run motors, to provide heat and light, and to transmit signals, sounds, and pictures.

INVENTIONS	INVENTORS	DATES
telegraph	Samuel F. B. Morse (American)	1844
telephone	Alexander Graham Bell (American)	1876
electric light bulb	Thomas A. Edison (American)	1879
wireless telegraphy	Guglielmo Marconi (Italian)	1896
radio vacuum tube	Lee DeForest (American)	1907
television	Vladimir Zworykin (American)	1934

2. Petroleum. In 1859, in the United States, *Edwin Drake* drilled the first successful oil well. At first, oil was used for lubrication and lighting, but soon it was put to other uses.

a. The Automobile. During the 1880's *Gottlieb Daimler* (German) developed a practical *internal combustion engine* powered by *gasoline,* a petroleum product. He used his engine to propel a four-wheel vehicle, thereby opening up a new and major use for petroleum as a source of power. In 1908 *Henry Ford* (American) brought automobile ownership out of the luxury class and within reach of most Americans by low-cost, mass-production, assembly-line methods. Today almost every American family owns at least one car, and automobile production is a key industry. Its growth has (*a*) stimulated related industries: oil, rubber, glass, steel, and aluminum, (*b*) created new enterprises: gasoline stations, garages, parking lots, motels, and (*c*) necessitated the building of new and improved highways.

b. The Airplane. In 1903 *Wilbur* and *Orville Wright* (American) flew, for less than a minute, the first heavier-than-air flying machine. Subsequently, aeronautical engineers designed larger and speedier aircraft. Many modern jet planes are longer than a city block and can fly at over 600 miles per hour. Today's commercial airlines, flying national and international routes, represent a major means of transportation.

c. The Diesel Engine. In 1892 *Rudolf Diesel* (German) utilized diesel oil, a fuel less expensive than gasoline, in his *diesel internal combustion engine.* Today, diesel engines power heavy machinery, buses, trucks, ocean liners, and locomotives.

3. **Atomic Energy.** See pages 253-255.

AGRICULTURAL REVOLUTION: AN ASPECT OF THE INDUSTRIAL REVOLUTION

1. **Primitive Agricultural Methods.** At the beginning of the 18th century farm methods had not progressed since feudal manor days. Farmers still relied upon a few simple tools: the wooden plow, the hoe, and the scythe. Many continued the three-field system, idling one-third of the land to restore fertility. Of fertilizers, crop rotation, and animal breeding they knew very little. Although farmers labored hard and long, they produced scanty crops.

2. **Industrial Growth Spurs Agriculture.** The revolution in industry influenced farming by (*a*) demonstrating that labor-saving machinery and science increase output, (*b*) requiring greater quantities of agricultural raw materials, such as cotton, wool, and leather, and (*c*) demanding greater food supplies for city populations.

3. **Meaning of Agricultural Revolution.** *Agricultural Revolution* refers to the change from primitive to modern farm-production methods—the use of farm machinery and scientific agriculture. The Agricultural Revolution began in England, spread to other countries in Europe, penetrated thoroughly into American farming, and to this day continues its advance in the underdeveloped areas of the world.

4. **Farm Machinery.** The following table lists some of the basic inventions that led to the "mechanization" of agriculture:

INVENTORS	INVENTIONS
Jethro Tull (English)	*Seed drill* (1701) planted seeds in rows. It improved upon "broadcast," or hand, sowing by providing space for cultivation and growth.
Charles Newbold (American)	*Cast-iron plow* (1797) turned soil deeper and more easily than the wooden plow.
Cyrus McCormick (American)	*Reaper* (1834) cut grain many times faster than a scythe.
John Deere (American)	*Self-cleaning steel plow* (1837) improved upon the cast-iron plow.

Other agricultural machines include the thresher (to separate grain from the stalk), the harvester (to cut and bind the grain), the combine (to cut, thresh, and sack the grain), the tractor (to pull equipment through the field), the corn planter, the potato digger, the electric milker, and the cotton picker.

5. Scientific Agriculture

a. Charles Townshend (English) in the early 18th century preserved the fertility of the soil by *rotation of crops*. He alternated grains with soil-enriching plants such as turnips and clover.

b. Robert Bakewell (English) in the late 18th century improved the weight of cattle by *scientific breeding*. His experiments led to better plant and animal selection.

c. Justus von Liebig (German) in the middle of the 19th century discovered that he could add fertility to the soil by using chemicals, or *artificial fertilizers*. His discovery enabled farmers to secure larger crops from the same lands.

d. George Washington Carver (an American Negro) in the late 19th century discovered many uses for a major Southern crop, the peanut. His work encouraged researchers to discover new uses for other agricultural products.

e. Other applications of science to agriculture include contour plowing to prevent soil erosion, draining swamps to augment the land supply, irrigating dry lands, combatting insect pests and plant diseases by chemicals, and improving the processes for canning, refrigerating, and freezing foods.

6. Effects of Agricultural Revolution

a. Agricultural production increased greatly, both in output per man and in total amount. The cost of foodstuffs dropped.

b. Large farms, best able to employ machines and scientific methods, began to dominate agriculture. The number of small farms has been declining.

c. The number of farmers, in proportion to total population, has decreased sharply. Many have moved to the cities.

d. Farmers found their work less laborious, since machines performed the backbreaking tasks.

e. Farming changed from a self-sufficient way of life to big business. Farmers today specialize in a few crops, sell them on national and international markets, and purchase foodstuffs for their own use.

INDUSTRIAL REVOLUTION: A SURVEY BY COUNTRY

1. England. By 1850, a century after the Industrial Revolution started, more Englishmen were employed in factories than on farms. English manufacturers produced vast quantities of cottons, woolens, shoes, cutlery, and tools for sale in domestic and foreign markets. Nineteenth-century England experienced great economic prosperity as the "workshop of the world."

Today England is faced with some difficult industrial problems. (*a*) Her coal resources are being depleted and her mining costs are rising. (*b*) Her factories need capital to replace obsolescent machinery. (*c*) Her products are meeting severe competition in world markets.

2. The United States. In 1790 *Samuel Slater*, an English immigrant, built America's first textile factory. Slater designed his equipment from memory, since at that time England prohibited the export of machines or of plans for machines. American textile manufacturing prospered, especially when the War of 1812 halted the import of English goods. After the Civil War (1861-1865), America's great industrial expansion began. Leaders were such businessmen as oil refiner *John D. Rockefeller* and steel magnate *Andrew Carnegie*. By 1914 the United States equaled England in manufacturing; today the United States is the world's leading industrial power.

3. France. After 1815, which marked the end of the Napoleonic Era, the Industrial Revolution gradually penetrated France. She built railroads, mined coal and iron, and constructed factories. However, French industry retained much handicraft labor and concentrated on such luxury items as laces, silks, wines, perfumes, and jewelry.

France did not industrialize thoroughly because (*a*) her coal resources were insufficient, and (*b*) her small farmers, chiefly independent landowners, preferred farm life to factory life. In recent years, however, France has pushed forward in the mass production of steel, automobiles, and airplanes.

4. Germany. After unification in 1871, Germany industrialized rapidly. Her progress can be attributed to (*a*) extensive coal and iron resources, (*b*) skilled workers, (*c*) talented scientists who created such new industries as dyes and chemicals, (*d*) efficient water and rail transportation, (*e*) favorable government attitudes, and (*f*) industrial leaders (such as the *Krupps*) who founded business empires. By 1914 German iron, steel, textile, and chemical products were world famous. Today, West Germany is a leading industrial power.

5. Russia. Before 1914 Russia was overwhelmingly agricultural. Her industrialization consisted chiefly of several iron and steel mills and some railroad construction. After the Revolution of 1917, Soviet rulers drove Russia toward industrialization. Today, the Soviet Union is a major manufacturing power, second only to the United States.

6. Japan. Late in the 19th century Japan started to industrialize. She was the first Asian nation to do so. Japanese manufacturers had the advantages of a large supply of cheap labor, government assistance, and nearness to Far East markets. The Japanese today export large quantities of electronic equipment, machinery, textiles, cameras, and toys.

7. Underdeveloped Countries. Many countries in Latin America, Africa, and Asia still have primitive agricultural economies. But they are eager to industrialize and raise living standards. They are hindered by their lack of capital, skilled labor, and technical "know-how." Many underdeveloped countries today receive financial and technical aid from the Soviet Union, the United Nations, and the United States.

MULTIPLE-CHOICE QUESTIONS

1. The principal cause of the Industrial Revolution was the (1) effort to eliminate child labor (2) increase in population (3) need of more manufactured goods for foreign trade (4) desire for colonies.
2. The guild system began to decline because (1) national governments taxed guilds heavily (2) guild regulations retarded business expansion (3) guilds were forbidden by law (4) apprentices were scarce.
3. In the "putting-out," or domestic, system in England (1) overseas trade was discouraged (2) piecework was done in the home (3) agriculture was the only means of making a living (4) no capital was needed.
4. A chief reason for England's leadership in the Industrial Revolution was her (1) iron and coal resources (2) nearness to a large supply of raw cotton (3) lack of good harbors (4) loss of her American colonies.
5. The 18th-century Enclosure Acts in England resulted in (1) an increase in the number of small farms (2) an increase in the number of landless farmers (3) a decrease in England's food supply (4) a deemphasis of scientific farming.
6. Which statement was true of industrial conditions in England in 1825? (1) Machinery had greatly increased production. (2) Women and children were no longer employed. (3) Fewer laborers worked in factories. (4) The number of skilled craftsmen was increasing.
7. The first machines were invented mainly by (1) trained scientists (2) skilled workers (3) capitalists (4) guild apprentices.
8. Most early inventions in the Industrial Revolution of the 18th century occurred in the field of (1) communications (2) mining (3) textiles (4) steel production.
9. The invention that made the use of electric power commercially practicable was the (1) safety lamp (2) dynamo (3) internal-combustion engine (4) radio.
10. That one invention leads to the next is shown by the relationship of (1) the steam engine to the automobile (2) the diesel engine to television (3) the power loom to the cotton gin (4) plastics to the seed drill.
11. An example of automation in the modern home is a(an) (1) electric can opener (2) vacuum cleaner (3) television set (4) oil burner thermostat.
12. The invention of machinery for spinning and weaving benefited the farmer by (1) making farm work less laborious (2) increasing the market for his goods (3) increasing government aid to the farmer (4) increasing the number of farm workers.
13. The term Agricultural Revolution refers to the (1) distribution of small farms to the peasants (2) end of taxation of farmland (3) flight of city workers to the farms (4) introduction of machinery into farming.

14. During the 19th century which was an important result of the Agricultural Revolution in England? (1) Serfdom became unprofitable. (2) It became unprofitable to own large estates. (3) Commercial farming became less widespread. (4) The proportion of the population engaged in farming declined.
15. In which one of these countries did the Industrial Revolution occur last? (1) Russia (2) France (3) the United States (4) Germany.
16. In which one of these Asian countries did the industrial revolution develop first? (1) India (2) China (3) Japan (4) Burma.

MATCHING QUESTIONS

Column A	Column B
1. George Stephenson	*a.* artificial fertilizer
2. Alexander Graham Bell	*b.* telegraph
3. Samuel F. B. Morse	*c.* airplane
4. Wilbur and Orville Wright	*d.* rotation of crops
5. Charles Townshend	*e.* telephone
6. Justus von Liebig	*f.* locomotive
7. Eli Whitney	*g.* steam engine
8. Robert Fulton	*h.* reaper
9. Sir Humphry Davy	*i.* wireless telegraphy
10. Guglielmo Marconi	*j.* steamboat
11. Cyrus McCormick	*k.* cotton gin
12. James Watt	*l.* safety lamp

Part 2. Results of the Industrial Revolution

INTRODUCTION

Now beginning its third century, the Industrial Revolution has decidedly changed our world. At first, it caused economic dislocation and many hardships. In the long run, however, the Industrial Revolution brought widespread benefits to the people of industrialized nations. Hardly a phase of life remains unaffected. Whatever we are, whatever we think, whatever we do—all are directly or indirectly traceable to the effects of industrialization.

A. ECONOMIC RESULTS

FACTORY SYSTEM

Because machines are heavy, bulky, and power-operated, only specially designed factory buildings can provide for their proper installation. Consequently, the factory rather than the home is now the center of production.

MASS PRODUCTION

Factories utilize workers and machines efficiently, economize on raw materials, and speed the output of goods by employing methods of mass production.

1. Division of Labor. The worker does not make the entire product but performs one small operation only. He can be trained for his job quickly. However, he never achieves varied skills and often finds his work monotonous.

2. Standardization. The worker turns out quantities of the same part, and the parts are standardized, or *interchangeable*. Other workers assemble the components into the finished product.

3. Assembly Line. The worker takes a position alongside a moving belt which brings him the product being processed. As the worker performs his small task, the belt moves the product to the next man for his operation. The belt moves along from worker to worker until the product is completed.

HIGHER STANDARD OF LIVING

Today we produce a greater volume and variety of goods—at lower cost—than ever before. The average American enjoys material comforts of life undreamed of by past monarchs.

MODERN CAPITALISM

1. Emergence. The new production methods of the Industrial Revolution required capital—economic wealth usually thought of as money. Capital was necessary to build factories, purchase machines, secure raw materials, and pay workers—all before any goods were sold. Consequently, the capitalist, who risked his money by investing in business, controlled the entire process of production. This economic system, based on private capital, is known as *capitalism.*

2. Laissez-Faire. In the late 18th century capitalists urged the government to abandon mercantilism (see page 141). They opposed restrictions on production and trade. They wanted to manufacture and sell their goods free from government interference, in accordance with *laissez-faire* (leave business alone), a principle advocated by Adam Smith (see page 155). In the 19th century such thinking greatly influenced England as well as other industrialized nations, but it has been sharply modified or rejected by industrial nations today.

3. Basic Principles of Capitalism. (a) *Private ownership.* Individuals (persons and corporations) own the means of production and distribution of goods. (b) *Free enterprise.* Individuals are free to choose any business and run it as they wish. (c) **Profit motive.** Businessmen direct their affairs to avoid loss and make a profit. (d) **Competition.** To outstrip his rivals, each producer strives to improve the quality and lower the cost of his goods. (e) **Market price.** Supply and demand, operating under conditions of free competition, determine the price of goods.

4. Philosophy of Interdependence. Today capitalist nations acknowledge the interdependence of capital, labor, and government. Capital provides the means of production and the managerial skills; labor provides the work; government provides law and order, and protects the people against economic abuses.

RISE OF THE CORPORATION

In the late 19th century the corporation became dominant as a form of business organization because it could best meet industry's need for capital. A corporation, operating under state charter, enables a group of individuals to engage in business as a single person. Whereas an individual businessman or a partnership has limited capital resources, the corporation can raise large sums of money by selling securities (stocks and bonds) to the public. The corporation belongs to its stockholders, each a part-owner. Nevertheless, its existence is unaffected by the death of any stockholder, for the corporation has perpetual life.

Today the individual businessman and the partnership exist chiefly in farming, the professions, small retail shops, and services. The corporation dominates the major economic areas: public utilities, transportation, communication, and manufacturing.

AGE OF BIG BUSINESS

Corporations grew to "giant" size in assets, volume of sales, and number of employees. Big business has the advantages of utilizing mass production methods, maintaining research laboratories, promoting large-scale advertising, and securing capital easily. Sometimes, big business has been criticized for certain abuses: paying low wages, selling inferior goods, competing unfairly against the small businessman, and creating monopolies to restrict competition and keep up prices.

GOVERNMENT REGULATION OF INDUSTRY

Aroused by abuses resulting from the Industrial Revolution, the people protested against laissez-faire and demanded government action. In the second half of the 19th century, governments began to pass laws designed to protect the worker, consumer, and small businessman.

ECONOMIC INTERDEPENDENCE OF NATIONS: WORLD TRADE

With the Industrial Revolution, the world became unified economically, and international trade expanded. Industrial nations exported manufactured goods and imported foodstuffs, fuels, and raw materials. Agricultural nations imported manufactured goods and exported foodstuffs. Nations rich in natural resources provided fuels and raw materials. At the same time, as different countries specialized in different manufactured goods, trade developed among industrial nations. Mutually profitable trade among nations, some statesmen believed, aided the cause of world peace.

ECONOMIC COMPETITION AMONG NATIONS

As more nations became industrialized, they engaged in bitter rivalry for world markets and for backward regions containing raw materials. Their disputes helped cause World War I.

Also, industrial nations hindered world trade by adopting *protective tariffs*. This policy, each nation contended, saved domestic manufacturers and workers from foreign competition and furthered the nation's economic self-sufficiency.

From about 1850 to 1932 England alone of the industrial nations promoted world commerce by levying no tariffs, that is, following a policy of *free trade*. The British could operate without tariffs because their industries could compete successfully against foreign imports. In 1932, as foreign competition became more intense, even England adopted a protective tariff.

LABOR PROBLEMS

For a discussion of labor problems, see pages 238-242.

B. POLITICAL RESULTS

GROWTH OF DEMOCRACY

1. Rise of the Middle Class and Working Class. Before the Industrial Revolution, the aristocracy ruled throughout Europe. With industrialization, the middle class (which included the capitalists) grew in number and economic wealth; the working class also became more numerous. Both classes desired political influence to make the government responsive to their interests. Therefore, both capitalists and workers battled for democracy, which would give them representation in government. Their efforts achieved an extension of the suffrage in many countries. In industrial nations, new parties arose and old parties changed their views to represent the wishes of businessmen and workers.

By the mid-19th century the landed aristocracy in England and France had lost its political power to the middle class. After this, the needs of the businessman, and later of the worker, determined government policy.

2. Informed Citizenry. Radio, television, newspapers, and magazines—the "mass media" of communication—have enabled citizens, as never before, to keep informed on civic matters. Modern democracy operates best with an informed citizenry.

Industrialization by itself does not guarantee the development of democracy. This lesson may be learned from the history of Germany and Japan up to World War II, and of Soviet Russia today.

AID TO NATIONALISM

The Industrial Revolution helped strengthen the feeling of nationalism. A whole nation could read the same newspapers and magazines and get the same programs on radio and television. Improved transportation encouraged nationwide travel. Thus, local points of view and customs gave way to national outlooks.

IMPETUS TO IMPERIALISM

Modern industry needs large quantities of raw materials as well as mass markets. Consequently, the leading industrial nations promoted imperialistic undertakings in Africa, Latin America, and Asia.

INDUSTRIAL NATIONS LEAD THE WORLD

Because industry creates military power and financial strength, industrial nations have come to dominate world affairs. In the late 19th century the major powers were England, Germany, and the United States; in the early 20th century Japan assumed leadership in Asia; today the world's major powers are Russia and the United States.

C. SOCIAL RESULTS

DYNAMIC SOCIETY

For centuries before the Industrial Revolution, man's way of living remained relatively the same. He viewed the future as a repetition of the present. By industrialization, man created a new world of speed, variety, change, and opportunity. He opened up new occupations and professions. No longer satisfied with present ways, man welcomed innovation and believed in the inevitability of progress.

INCREASE IN WORLD POPULATION

As a result of the Industrial Revolution, (1) productive facilities have increased the supply of manufactured goods and foodstuffs, and (2) medical science has combatted disease and prolonged man's lifespan. These developments have led to a great increase in world population.

To the mid-20th century the greatest population growth occurred in the industrialized regions: England, western Europe, and the United States. Since then, with medical care expanding throughout the world, the greatest population growth has taken place in the underdeveloped areas: Asia, Africa, and Latin America.

In 1950 world population totaled 2.5 billion; twenty years later, in 1970, it was 3.7 billion. If the current unprecedented 2-percent annual growth rate continues, world population will total 6.5 billion in the year 2000. Demographers (population experts) have named this astounding growth since the end of World War II the *population explosion*.

Some observers now question whether the world's resources will prove sufficient to provide so many people with decent living standards.

GROWTH OF CITIES

People flocked to cities to secure jobs. Also, many were attracted by the cities' social and cultural facilities: theaters, concert halls, schools, libraries, and sports arenas. Today, in the United States and England, the urban, or city, population far exceeds the rural population.

Cities face many problems: clearing slums, constructing decent housing, preventing crime, halting air and water pollution, providing mass transportation, and assuring efficient local government.

IMPROVED STATUS OF WOMEN

Before the Industrial Revolution, women occupied a status inferior to men. They directed their energies to the care of the home, while depending economically upon the men. With industrialization, women secured factory and office jobs, and became economically independent.

To better their status in society, women organized the *feminist movement*. In England, the leading feminists were *Mary Wollstonecraft* and *Emmeline Pankhurst*. In the United States, the leading feminist was *Susan B. Anthony*. Gradually, women secured equal rights to vote and hold office, to pursue an education, to engage in the professions, to own property, and to obtain justice before the law.

MORE COMFORTABLE HOMES

Industrialization has produced countless conveniences for the modern home. Our dwellings are warmed by central heating, cooled by air conditioning, cleaned by vacuum machine, and illuminated by electric light. Our foods are preserved in refrigerators and cooked on gas or electric stoves. Our entertainment comes from radio and television.

LEISURE TIME

As machine production increased, man's average working day decreased from about 15 hours in the late 18th century to 7 or 8 hours today. Workers today also receive more holidays and vacations, and many workers receive pensions that enable them to retire with an assured income. To occupy their leisure time, people have turned to education, culture, and recreation.

HUMANITARIANISM

Humanitarianism is a feeling of deep concern for the welfare of unfortunate peoples, usually coupled with a desire to improve conditions. With industrialization, humanitarians could draw upon the newly created wealth to combat many social injustices.

1. **Abolition of Negro Slavery.** In 1833 humanitarian Englishmen secured the abolition of slavery throughout the British Empire. Somewhat later, France and Holland also abolished slavery. The American Negro gained freedom as a result of the Civil War (1861-1865).

2. **Expanded Missionary Services.** Starting in the 19th century Christian missionaries who were sent to underdeveloped areas of the world expanded their activities to include educational and medical services. Famous medical missionaries include, in the 19th century, the explorer *David Livingstone,* and, in the 20th century, *Albert Schweitzer.* Also famed as a philosopher and musician, Schweitzer devoted his life to providing hospital care for the natives in Africa.

3. **Care for Sick and Wounded Soldiers.** *Florence Nightingale* (English), during the Crimean War (1853-1856), provided the first wartime nursing service. She became known as "the lady with the lamp." In 1864 *Jean Henri Dunant* (Swiss) founded the *International Red Cross.* In 1881 *Clara Barton* organized and headed the *American Red Cross.* Today the Red Cross serves not only war casualties but also peacetime disaster victims.

4. **Improved Treatment of the Insane and Criminals.** *Elizabeth Fry* (English) sought better treatment of imprisoned criminals, and *Dorothea Dix* (American) fought for better treatment of the insane. Today, the insane are

treated as mentally sick, not as possessed of the devil. Imprisoned criminals are given education and taught vocations in order to help them be restored to normal living. Reform, not punishment, is the modern-day approach.

5. Free Public Education. Humanitarians enlisted support to help school-children enjoy their youth, remain out of the labor market, and become the educated citizenry essential to a successful democracy.

In 1867 England granted suffrage to city workers, and three years later, in 1870, Parliament passed the *Forster Act*. It supplemented private schools by a system of state-supported elementary schools. In 1918 the *Fischer Act* set the age for compulsory school attendance at 14.

In the United States, *Horace Mann* and *Henry Barnard* led the movement for free public education, which, on the elementary level, became the rule by 1860.

6. Philanthropy. *Philanthropists* are persons of great fortune who devote their wealth to promote the welfare of society.

a. Alfred Nobel (Swedish), the inventor of dynamite, founded the annual *Nobel Prizes*. These awards honor individuals who make outstanding contributions to science, literature, and world peace.

b. Andrew Carnegie (American), the steel magnate, provided free public libraries and the *Carnegie Endowment for International Peace*. He also built the *Hague* (Holland) *Peace Palace*.

c. Cecil Rhodes (English), the South African diamond and gold millionaire, created the *Rhodes Scholarships*. These enable outstanding students from the United States and from the British Commonwealth (except from England) to study at Oxford University.

d. John D. Rockefeller (American), the oil magnate, through the *Rockefeller Foundation*, provided grants to colleges and universities, and encouraged research in the social sciences and humanities. He also founded the *Rockefeller Institute* (now *Rockefeller University*) for medical research.

e. Henry Ford (American), the automobile manufacturer, established the *Ford Foundation*. It grants funds to universities, medical schools, and hospitals, and finances studies of such human problems as civil liberties, democracy, and international peace.

MULTIPLE-CHOICE QUESTIONS

1. Which was an immediate result of the Industrial Revolution? (1) a decrease in population (2) an increase in the number of guilds (3) the growth of the factory system (4) less need for capital.
2. With the invention of textile machinery, more workers were employed in the industry because (1) the first machines were less efficient than hand labor (2) women and children could work the machines (3) goods were cheaper and in greater de-

mand (4) division of labor required more workers to produce the same amount of goods.

3. Which is *not* a result of division of labor? (1) quick training of workers (2) increased production (3) interesting work (4) repetitive work.

4. As a result of the Industrial Revolution, the power of the capitalist class was (1) transferred to the landed aristocracy (2) increased tremendously (3) weakened slightly (4) transferred to the working class.

5. *Not* a principle of capitalist economy is (1) the profit motive (2) competition (3) free enterprise (4) government ownership of major industries.

6. Adam Smith pointed out the advantages of (1) rule by divine right of kings (2) separation of governmental powers (3) price regulation by the laws of supply and demand (4) mercantilist regulations of trade.

7. Laissez-faire is the economic theory that government should (1) regulate all business strictly (2) not interfere in business (3) own the railroads (4) give the public lands free to the people.

8. A major reason for the formation of corporations was to (1) avoid government control (2) raise large amounts of capital funds (3) regulate labor unions (4) promote better advertising.

9. The consumer may be harmed if big business achieves (1) low prices (2) monopoly (3) greater variety of goods (4) research for new products.

10. England adopted free trade about 1850 because she (1) did not fear foreign competition (2) could grow grain more cheaply than other countries (3) opposed industrialization in the United States (4) was not interested in increasing her exports.

11. Which was an important political result of the Industrial Revolution in England in the 19th century? (1) establishment of the Bank of England (2) end of free public education (3) assembly-line production (4) suffrage for the middle class.

12. As a result of the Industrial Revolution, women have (1) become more dependent upon men (2) decreased in number (3) become heads of many large corporations (4) gained equal rights with men.

13. The "population explosion" since World War II has created serious food problems in (1) India (2) Sweden (3) France (4) Ireland.

14. *Not* a humanitarian movement is (1) abolition of slavery (2) lowering the cost of goods (3) sending medical missionaries to Africa (4) free public education.

IDENTIFICATION QUESTIONS: WHO AM I?

Susan B. Anthony	Henry Ford	Emmeline Pankhurst
Clara Barton	Horace Mann	Cecil Rhodes
Andrew Carnegie	Florence Nightingale	John D. Rockefeller
Jean Henri Dunant	Alfred Nobel	Albert Schweitzer

1. An Englishman, I made my fortune in South Africa's gold and diamond mines. I provided scholarships for outstanding students to study at Oxford University.

2. An American suffragette, I fought to give women the right to vote.

3. I organized and served as first president of the American Red Cross.

4. A noted musician and author, I devoted my life to serving as medical missionary in central Africa.

5. An American steel magnate, I sought to further international peace and provided the funds to build the Hague Peace Palace.

6. I led the fight in England to win the suffrage for women.

7. A Swiss, I founded the International Red Cross.

8. I invented dynamite and established prizes for contributions to science, literature, and world peace.

9. An Englishwoman, known as "the lady with the lamp," I began nursing services for soldiers.

Part 3. Problems of Labor and Industrialization

EARLY LABOR DISCONTENT

As workers left agriculture—and as the domestic system was replaced by the factory system—the workers became completely dependent upon the employer for their livelihood. In the early years of industrialization, workers faced many hardships. (1) Wages were low, just above the starvation level. (2) Hours were long, up to 16 per day. (3) Children from age 5 and women held jobs in factories and mines. Since they were less demanding and accepted lower wages, they often replaced men. (4) Factories were unlighted and unsanitary; machines lacked proper safeguards against accidents. (5) As invention followed invention, workers lost jobs to machines, thus causing *technological unemployment*.

A. LABOR UNIONS

WORKERS SEEK STRENGTH IN UNIONS

Workers soon found that they could not improve conditions by *individual bargaining*. A single worker appealing to the employer could be refused and discharged without disrupting production. But by *collective bargaining,* that is, acting together as a group, they were in a stronger position to secure their demands. If refused, they could all strike, and the employer would be hurt by a complete halt in production. To represent them collectively in bargaining with the employer, workers formed labor unions.

BRIEF HISTORY OF ENGLISH UNIONS

1. Legal Restrictions. Workers' efforts to unionize were hindered by (a) court decisions holding unions illegal, and (b) *Combination Laws* (1799-1800) declaring workers who joined together to improve conditions liable to imprisonment. Workers defied these restrictions until Parliament, in 1824-1825, granted them the right to form unions, but not to strike.

2. Workers' Suffrage. Unions agitated for the Reform Bill of 1867, which gave the vote to city workers. Shortly thereafter, unions secured legislation to remove the restriction upon strikes.

3. Labor Party. In 1901 the *Taff Vale Decision* held unions financially responsible for strike damages. Unions believed that this judicial ruling imperiled their existence. They decided to protect themselves by establishing the British Labor party. In 1906, with 29 Labor members in Commons, Parliament set aside the Taff Vale Decision.

4. Present Influence. The Labor party, the unions' political arm, developed into a major party and several times headed the government. In membership, English unions grew from 1½ million organized workers in 1892 to almost 10 million today. In 20th-century England, the trade unions are a powerful force in industry and politics.

UNIONS IN OTHER COUNTRIES

Unions overcame legal restrictions and emerged to defend the workers' interests. By the 20th century they were a vital force in the economic and political life of all democratic nations. In the United States, the *American Federation of Labor and Congress of Industrial Organizations* (*AFL-CIO*) now has some 13 million workers. About 4 million more workers are unionized outside the AFL-CIO. Instead of forming its own political party, American labor works to achieve legislative goals through existing political parties.

OBJECTIVES OF LABOR UNIONS

Labor unions seek (1) recognition of the union as the sole bargaining agent, (2) higher wages, (3) fewer working hours, (4) security against unemployment, (5) safe and sanitary factory conditions, (6) vacations with pay, and (7) *fringe benefits,* such as medical care, hospitalization, old-age pensions, and general welfare.

PEACEFUL SETTLEMENT OF LABOR DISPUTES

The great majority of labor disputes are settled, with little publicity, by the following peaceful methods:

1. Collective Bargaining. The union and employer meet to discuss and agree upon the terms of a labor contract.

2. Mediation. A third party, respected by both the union and the employer, secures concessions from both sides, making an agreement possible.

3. Arbitration. A third party, accepted by both sides as neutral, hears the dispute and hands down his decision, or *award.* Union and employer often pledge beforehand to accept the award. This method is used only rarely.

INDUSTRIAL WARFARE

A small minority of labor disputes erupt into industrial battles, frequently accompanied by much publicity. The union and the employer each seeks to compel acceptance of its own terms.

WEAPONS OF THE UNION

1. Strike. Employees refuse to work until union demands are met.

2. Picket. Workers parade outside the strikebound premises. They seek to enlist public support for their cause and to deter strikebreakers from taking their jobs.

3. Boycott. Workers request the consumer not to patronize the strikebound company.

4. Publicity. Unions appeal for public support through mass demonstrations, newspapers, radio, and television.

WEAPONS OF THE EMPLOYER

1. Lockout. The employer keeps the workers from their jobs until his terms are accepted.

2. Strikebreakers. The employer hires new workers to take the jobs of the strikers.

3. Injunction. Under certain conditions, the employer (or the government) may obtain a court order forbidding workers to strike, picket, or boycott. Violators of the injunction are liable to punishment for "contempt of court." (In the United States, the power of Federal courts to grant injunctions in labor disputes has been limited by the Norris-LaGuardia Act.)

4. Publicity. The employer presents his case to the public through mass communication media.

COSTS OF INDUSTRIAL WARFARE

Industrial warfare causes much hardship. (1) *Employers* suffer halted production, decreased profits, and unfavorable publicity. (2) *Workers* face unemployment and loss of income. (3) The *community* endures loss of services and shortage of products.

B. LABOR AND SOCIAL LEGISLATION

GOVERNMENTS ABANDON LAISSEZ-FAIRE IN LABOR MATTERS

Many groups have urged that governments interfere in industry to improve labor conditions. (1) Workers have demanded laws to consolidate and supplement gains achieved by unions. (2) Humanitarians have deplored factory abuses and have viewed oppressed workers as unfortunates. (3) Statesmen have argued that a healthy and contented working class strengthens the nation.

Despite strong opposition by employers, governments began in the early 19th century to enact protective labor legislation.

ENGLAND'S FACTORY AND MINE LAWS

1. The **Factory Act of 1819,** applying to cotton factories only, prohibited employers from (a) hiring children under age 9, and (b) working older children more than a 12-hour day. However, this law was inadequately enforced.

2. The **Factory Act of 1833,** applying to all textile factories, prohibited employers from (a) hiring children under age 9, and (b) working 9- to 13-year-old children more than a 9-hour day, and 13- to 18-year-olds more than a 12-hour day. In addition, the law called for strict inspection and enforcement.

3. The **Mines Act of 1842** prohibited mine employment for children under age 10 and for women.

4. The **Ten-Hour Law of 1847,** for all textile factories, limited child and woman labor to a maximum 10-hour day.

5. Subsequent laws, too numerous to list, (a) raised the factory employment age for children, (b) prohibited children and women from working in mines, (c) required safety devices on dangerous machinery, and (d) established standards of factory sanitation.

England's factory and mine legislation set an example followed by most industrialized nations.

SOCIAL SECURITY

With industrialization, workers were beset by economic insecurity. They feared unemployment resulting from technological improvement and business depression; they feared their own inability to work due to accident, sickness, and old age. Generally, they did not earn enough money to save for a "rainy day." Workers gained some protection as governments enacted social security laws.

1. Germany. Between 1883 and 1889 Germany under Bismarck led the way in social security, passing sickness, accident, and old-age insurance laws.

2. England. Between 1906 and 1911 England inaugurated accident, old-age, sickness, and unemployment insurance. In 1946, under a Labor government, England adopted a comprehensive program of social security from "cradle to grave." The *National Insurance Act* includes unemployment, sickness, accident, and maternity benefits, old-age and survivors' pensions, and death grants. The *National Health Service Act* provides for dental, hospital, and medical service. Under both acts, membership is compulsory, and costs are borne by workers, employers, and government. Because these social security acts indicate the government's concern for the welfare of its citizens, England is often called a *welfare state*.

England's comprehensive program survives despite opposition. Employers claim that it costs too much and discourages labor's incentive to work. Some doctors resent government control and protest "socialized medicine."

3. The United States. In 1935 Congress passed our first *Social Security Act,* providing old-age and unemployment insurance. This act has been revised several times to increase old-age benefits and coverage, to extend protection to totally disabled persons, orphans, and widows, and to provide medical care for the aged.

C. COOPERATIVE MOVEMENT

BRIEF HISTORY OF COOPERATIVES

A *cooperative,* or "co-op," is a business enterprise owned by its customers. In 1844 textile workers who had lost a strike for higher wages founded the first successful co-op, a grocery store at *Rochdale,* England. From retail stores, cooperatives expanded into manufacturing, housing, banking, and insurance. Today, the cooperative movement is particularly strong in England, Sweden, Denmark, and Israel. In the United States, co-ops have had only a limited influence. They exist chiefly in farm areas; since World War II, housing cooperatives have arisen in major cities.

ROCHDALE COOPERATIVE PRINCIPLES

1. Membership. Any person may join by purchasing one or more of the cooperative's shares. Shareholders are owners and receive a fixed return for having provided the capital.

2. Voting. Regardless of the number of shares owned, each member has one vote. Consequently, no small group of shareholders can dominate the cooperative.

3. Prices. The co-op charges prevailing prices and sells to both members and nonmembers.

4. Profits. Members divide the co-op's profits in proportion, not to shares owned, but to goods purchased.

D. MOVEMENTS TO DISPLACE CAPITALISM

MEANING OF SOCIALISM

Some reformers who blamed factory abuses, unemployment, and depression upon capitalism urged adoption of a new political and economic system, *socialism*.

SOCIALISM	CAPITALISM
1. *The government as representative of the people* owns and operates the means of production (farms, mines, and factories) and distribution (transportation and retail stores).	1. *Private individuals and corporations* own and operate business enterprise. The government maintains law and order, encourages private industry, and prevents abuses.
2. The government determines the needs of the people and provides goods and services for the people's *use*.	2. Private owners provide the people with goods and services in order to make a *profit*.

UTOPIAN SOCIALISM (EARLY 19TH CENTURY)

The Utopian Socialists believed that capitalists, once convinced of the merits of socialism, would discard private ownership and the profit motive. Therefore, these reformers were considered dreamers, or *Utopians*.

1. Robert Owen, a wealthy British cotton manufacturer, created a model industrial community in Scotland at *New Lanark*. Contrary to general practice, he paid high wages, reduced working hours, provided sanitary factory conditions, built decent homes for workers, established schools for their children, and permitted the workers to share in management and profits. Owen's New Lanark community prospered, but he was disappointed that other manufacturers ignored his enlightened example.

In 1825 in the United States, Owen established a model agricultural-industrial community at *New Harmony*, Indiana. This venture failed.

2. Claude Saint-Simon, a Frenchman, envisioned an ideal social order. He taught that the wealthy and educated classes should devote their energies to the benefit of the lower classes.

3. Charles Fourier, a French reformer, advocated the establishing of ideal, or Utopian, communities. Here, he believed, members working together for the common good would demonstrate the superiority of socialism. His followers established several experimental communities, which proved unsuccessful. During the 1840's American idealists, inspired by Fourier, maintained the well-known but short-lived community in Massachusetts at *Brook Farm*.

LOUIS BLANC AND NATIONAL WORKSHOPS

Louis Blanc, a French Socialist, believed that (1) every man has a right to a job, and (2) the state should provide work for the unemployed in government-financed factories, or *national workshops.*

Blanc organized a workers' party and played a major role in the French Revolution of 1848. For a while, the provisional government provided the unemployed with work: digging ditches and improving parks. However, as the middle class regained control, the government ended the work program and suppressed the subsequent workers' revolt. (During the depression of the 1930's, Blanc's ideas were applied in the United States when the government sponsored an extensive public works program.)

Blanc is considered more practical than the Utopians, since he looked for reform, not to capitalists, but to workers and the government.

"SCIENTIFIC" SOCIALISM

Karl Marx (1818-1883), German writer and economist, founded modern socialism. Exiled from Prussia after the failure of the 1848 Revolution, Marx settled in England.

Karl Marx wrote the following important works: (1) The *Communist Manifesto* (co-authored by *Friedrich Engels*), 1848, was a pamphlet outlining his socialist ideas in a simple, propagandistic style. (Marx used the term "communist" to distinguish his views from those of the Utopian Socialists, whom he scorned as dreamers.) (2) *Das Kapital* was a detailed study critically analyzing the capitalist system and expounding his theories of socialism. These works present the basic ideas of *Marxian socialism,* or *Marxism.*

1. Economic Interpretation of History. Marx argued that economic conditions determine the course of history. The class that possesses economic power controls the government and social institutions. In an industrial society based on private ownership, the capitalist class rules.

2. Class Struggle. Marx also viewed history as a struggle between conflicting economic classes, between the "have nots" and the "haves." In ancient Rome, plebeians battled patricians; in feudal society, serfs opposed lords; under private enterprise, workers (the proletariat) clash with capitalists (the bourgeoisie). This "class struggle," Marx predicted, would continue until the workers triumph and establish a socialist "classless" society.

3. Surplus Value. Capitalists exploit (take advantage of) workers by paying them just enough wages to keep them alive, that is, just above the subsistence level. The difference between their wages and the price of the goods the workers produce, Marx called *surplus value*. Although the capitalists contribute nothing to production, according to Marx, they take the surplus value as profit. Consequently, workers lack sufficient income to purchase all the goods produced, and this, in turn, Marx claimed, leads to depression.

4. Inevitability of Socialism. Marx predicted that capitalism would destroy itself as depressions became more and more serious. In time, he said, wealth would concentrate in fewer and fewer hands, while workers' conditions steadily deteriorate. Eventually the workers would be driven to overthrow the capitalists and establish a socialist state. (Marx did not make clear whether the overthrow of capitalism would come by peaceful means or by violence. However, he was certain that socialism would first come to industrial nations, not agricultural nations.)

Thus, Marx believed that socialism would be achieved not by appeals to the capitalist class, but by the working class as an inevitable result of the above "scientific" economic laws. Marxism, therefore, is known as "scientific" socialism.

CRITICISMS OF "SCIENTIFIC" SOCIALISM

Defenders of capitalism attack Marxian economics and warn against a socialist economy as follows:

1. Marxian Errors. Opponents of Marxism point out: (*a*) The economic interpretation of history neglects the vital role of noneconomic factors—for example, religion and nationalism. (*b*) The interests of capitalists and workers often coincide—for example, increased production makes possible both higher wages and greater profits. (*c*) Capitalists are entitled to profits, since they risk money and manage industry. (*d*) Under capitalism the conditions of workers have improved steadily, instead of worsening, as Marx expected.

2. Predicted Defects of Socialism. Opponents predict that under socialism (*a*) the individual will lose his incentive to work and progress, (*b*) the government, exercising economic as well as political power, will become a dictatorship controlling every phase of the citizen's life, (*c*) the government will place the needs of the state ahead of the needs of the people, and (*d*) the government will have great difficulty in managing a complex economic system and will commit serious errors in planning.

Defenders of capitalism assert that we can retain the full advantages of the free-enterprise system while remedying its defects.

BRIEF HISTORY OF SOCIALIST PARTIES

Marx's followers founded *Socialist,* or *Social Democratic,* parties to achieve (1) as the *immediate objective,* greater democracy and improved labor conditions, and (2) as the *ultimate objective,* a socialist state. During the 19th century they employed peaceful methods of publicity to gain control by the ballot.

In 1889, to coordinate world Socialist activities, the various Socialist parties formed the *Second International.* (The *First International,* founded by Marx in 1864, had been short-lived.) The Second International proclaimed the unity of all workers, regardless of nationality. Nevertheless, in World War I, most Socialist parties ignored their international ties and supported the war efforts of their respective countries. After World War I, Socialists kept their parties from being absorbed by the more aggressive Communist movement.

Since World War II, Socialist parties have exercised considerable influence in West European countries: Sweden, Norway, Italy, West Germany, France, and England. For example, the British Labor party, in office from 1945 to 1951 and again from 1964 to 1970, nationalized the Bank of England; electric power; civil aviation; railway, bus, and truck transportation; the steel industry; and coal mines.

BRIEF HISTORY OF COMMUNIST PARTIES

In Russia before World War I, the left-wing Socialists broke with the moderate Social Democrats and formed their own organization, the Bolsheviks, later called the *Communist party.* In 1917 the Bolsheviks, led by *Nikolai Lenin,* seized control of Russia by revolution (see pages 349–350). This accomplishment encouraged left-wing Socialists in other countries to establish their own Communist parties.

In 1919, to further world revolution, Russia linked the various Communist parties by the *Third International,* or *Comintern.* During World War II, to foster unity with her British and American allies, the Soviet Union dissolved the Comintern.

Today, Communist parties control Russia, much of central and eastern Europe, China, Mongolia, North Korea, North Vietnam, and Cuba. Also Communist candidates poll substantial votes in France and Italy.

COMMUNISTS VS. SOCIALISTS

Although both Communists and Socialists claim to follow Marxian ideas, they disagree on the following points:

COMMUNISTS	SOCIALISTS
1. Communism can be achieved only by *revolution*—a violent overthrow of the capitalist government and economy.	1. Socialism can be achieved by *evolution* —a peaceful and legal gaining of control by publicity and the ballot.
2. To protect the revolution, a Communist government must at first be a "dictatorship of the proletariat." It must suppress, by all available means, any movement considered procapitalist or counterrevolutionary.	2. A Socialist government, assuming power by consent of the people, must always be a democracy. It must retain the people's support by providing political liberty and economic justice.
3. Communism requires government ownership and operation of all the means of production and distribution—without exception.	3. Socialism requires nationalization only of the major industries. Small farms, small factories, and retail stores may remain under private ownership.

CHRISTIAN SOCIAL MOVEMENTS

Many devout Christians took a strong interest in social legislation but opposed "scientific" socialism, holding its economic interpretation and its doctrines of class struggle to be irreligious. Instead, they urged reform based upon religious principles, especially the Golden Rule. This movement was encouraged by religious leaders. (1) *Pope Leo XIII* in 1891 advised employers to treat workingmen in a Christian manner, and appealed to workers to form Catholic labor unions. (2) *Pope Pius XI* in 1931 proposed that workingmen share in the management and profits of industry. (3) *Pope John XXIII* in 1961 deplored low wages that condemned workers to "subhuman conditions of life." He urged that labor receive a greater share of the fruits of its industry, and preached the responsibility of society for the well-being of all its members. (4) *Pope Paul VI* in 1967 deplored the abuses of unrestrained capitalism. On behalf of the poor, both individuals and underdeveloped nations, the Pope urged a major effort to overcome misery, hunger, disease, and ignorance. (5) Some *Protestant religious leaders* called for economic and social justice.

Today the *Christian Democrats* in Italy and the *People's party* in Austria are political parties that command a considerable following for their program of protecting Catholic interests and advancing social reform.

MULTIPLE-CHOICE QUESTIONS

1. The beginning of the factory system caused (1) acute labor problems (2) a greater personal bond between employees and employers (3) equality of economic status (4) workers to turn to agriculture.

2. In 1825 English industrialists paid low wages to their employees because of (1) German competition (2) minimum wage laws (3) the absence of tariffs on food imports (4) an oversupply of labor.

3. The Industrial Revolution caused the modern labor movement because (1) workers immediately had more security (2) the standard of living improved (3) more people worked for a living (4) workers were more dependent on the capitalist.

4. The use of machines often results in (1) technological unemployment (2) decreased production (3) less need for capital (4) less need for raw materials.

5. The first labor unions in England were (1) welcomed by the employers (2) started by foreigners (3) considered illegal combinations by the courts (4) encouraged by the Combination Laws.

6. A neutral third party hands down a decision in a labor dispute under (1) collective bargaining (2) arbitration (3) mediation (4) an injunction.

7. Labor unions generally advocate (1) constant strikes to overthrow the capitalist system (2) the formation of worldwide trusts (3) social legislation for the workers (4) individual bargaining.

8. In labor disputes, unions do *not* advocate (1) picketing (2) boycotting (3) lockouts (4) publicity.

9. English legislation to end factory and mine abuses was (1) in harmony with laissez-faire doctrine (2) guaranteed in the English Bill of Rights (3) provided by the Reform Bill of 1832 (4) important to the health and welfare of the working class.

10. The purpose of social security is to (1) provide cheap life insurance (2) curtail employers' profits (3) help relieve workers from the fear of destitution (4) provide more business for the big insurance companies.

11. *Not* included in the English system of social security is protection in case of (1) old age (2) sickness (3) unemployment (4) fire.

12. The Rochdale pioneers introduced into England a form of business enterprise called a (1) utopia (2) corporation (3) cooperative (4) joint stock company.

13. According to "co-op" principles (1) shareholders do not receive dividends (2) the number of shares determines the number of votes (3) co-op prices are lower than prices in private stores (4) profits are divided in proportion to purchases.

14. Cooperatives play an important part in the economic life of (1) France (2) Italy (3) Spain (4) Sweden.

15. Socialism means (1) abolition of factory managers (2) abolition of all government (3) ownership of land by the peasants (4) ownership of the means of production by the government.

16. The early Socialists, such as Robert Owen and Charles Fourier, who wished to reform society by establishing model communities, were called (1) scientific Socialists (2) Christian Democrats (3) Utopians (4) Communists.

17. The origin of the basic concepts of world Communism may be traced to the (1) writings of Marx and Engels (2) republican uprisings in France (3) activity of Russian Bolsheviks (4) writings of Voltaire and Diderot.

18. Karl Marx believed in (1) private land cultivation (2) the right to inherit property (3) the economic interpretation of history (4) cooperation with the political party in power.

19. Which is *not* one of the beliefs of Karl Marx? (1) Capitalist countries will experience more and more serious depressions. (2) Workers' conditions will slowly improve under capitalism. (3) Labor is the most important factor in production. (4) Wealth in capitalistic countries will be concentrated in fewer and fewer hands.

20. Why would Karl Marx *not* have expected the Communist Revolution of 1917 to take place in Russia? (1) Russia was largely agricultural. (2) Most of Russia's leaders were moderates. (3) Russia retained many Oriental ideas. (4) Russia had such a large population.
21. The meaning of "a government nationalizes an industry" is that (1) branches are established throughout the country (2) the workers gain control (3) the government becomes the owner (4) all foreigners lose their jobs.
22. The Socialists disagree with the Communists on all of the following *except* (1) the need of revolution to overthrow capitalism (2) "dictatorship of the proletariat" (3) nationalization of small retail stores (4) the inevitability of socialism.
23. Christian social movements (1) are based upon the "scientific" ideas of Marx (2) seek to establish model communities (3) seek to restore production by hand (4) seek to apply the Golden Rule to economic affairs.
24. Today, a powerful Christian (Catholic) Democratic party exists in (1) Norway (2) England (3) Poland (4) Italy.

Part 4. Achievements in Science

DEFINITION OF TERMS

1. Science means a body of organized knowledge, generally relating to the world of nature. Branches of science include chemistry, physics, geology, biology, and medicine.

2. Pure, or **basic, science** is primarily concerned with gathering the knowledge for its own sake, not for its practical value. It enables us to understand ourselves and the universe.

3. Practical, or **applied, science** is concerned with converting the discoveries of pure science to daily use. Applied scientists seek the invention of new machines and the development of new products. Thus, man expands his control over his environment.

SCIENTIFIC METHOD

To investigate and solve problems, scientists (1) state the problem clearly, (2) gather data by precise observation and experimentation that includes rigid controls, (3) analyze the data to arrive at a well-reasoned conclusion—a scientific theory or law, and (4) test and retest the conclusion because a scientific law must always hold true.

The scientific method has been applied to the study of the problems of society—for example, human behavior, economic security, race relations, and world peace. In so doing, the "social scientist" (in psychology, economics, sociology, and history) tries to eliminate some variables and prejudices and strives for a factual, logical, and open-minded attitude that could lead to an improved society.

BRIEF HISTORY OF SCIENCE

1. Prehistoric Times Through the Middle Ages. Up to the Renaissance, men slowly accumulated knowledge about their physical environment. Their method was trial-and-error; their emphasis was upon practical discoveries. Peoples of many races, religions, and nationalities contributed. Prehistoric men devised the lever and wheel; other advances originated with the ancient Greeks, Indians, and Chinese, and with the medieval Moslems.

2. Renaissance Era. In the 16th century Europeans began modern science by inaugurating a "scientific revolution." Renaissance scientists employed the scientific method and made important contributions to pure science in the fields of mathematics, medicine, and astronomy (see pages 114-115).

3. Since the Industrial Revolution. Since 1750 scientists have achieved a major role in society. They have invented machines and improved farming methods. Governments, universities, and industry are eager to engage their services. Schools give high priorities to the training of scientists. The achievements of science affect our lives—at work and play, at war and peace. We live in an "age of science."

MEDICAL SCIENCE

1. Scientists and Their Contributions

a. Edward Jenner (1749-1823), English, discovered a method of preventing *smallpox* by vaccination. Jenner's approach, preventing disease by building body resistance, illustrates an important aspect of *preventive medicine*.

b. Louis Pasteur (1822-1895), French, formulated the *germ theory of disease*. He proved that certain diseases result from the invasion of the body by microscopic organisms called *germs*. Pasteur developed a vaccine that enables the body to resist the germ that causes *rabies*. He also discovered that heating such fluids as milk destroys many disease-producing bacteria. This discovery is used in the process called *pasteurization*.

c. Joseph Lister (1827-1912), English, prevented infection during surgery by the use of *antiseptics*.

d. Robert Koch (1843-1910), German, isolated the specific bacteria causing *anthrax* (a cattle disease) and *tuberculosis*.

e. Elie Metchnikoff (1845-1916), Russian, explained the disease-fighting role of *white blood corpuscles*.

f. Wilhelm Roentgen (1845-1923), German, discovered *X-rays*. By making shadow pictures of bones and internal organs, X-rays help in diagnosing illness and performing surgery.

g. Walter Reed (1851-1902), American, proved that a mosquito transmits *yellow fever*. By draining swamps where mosquitoes breed and by using insecticides, sanitary engineers have largely eradicated yellow fever.

h. Sigmund Freud (1856-1936), Austrian, pioneered the study of mental diseases and greatly influenced the growth of psychology and psychiatry.

i. Alexander Fleming (1882-1955), British, found that some harmful bacteria are destroyed by *penicillin*, an antibiotic, which has since become known as a "wonder" drug.

j. Selman Waksman (1888-   ), naturalized American, developed the antibiotic *streptomycin*.

k. Jonas Salk (1914-   ), American, created a vaccine effective against *infantile paralysis,* or *polio*.

l. Christian Barnard (1923-   ), South African, led a surgical team in performing the first human heart transplant.

2. Results of Medical Advances. (*a*) In 1900 the average lifespan of an American was about 50 years. Today his life expectancy has increased to about 70 years. (*b*) Since World War II, in the underdeveloped countries, man has significantly reduced death-causing disease and thus created a

THE GAZETTE AND DAILY—YORK, PA.

Partymiller in The Gazette and Daily, York, Pa.

"It too should be achievable."

What has man achieved in conquering space? In fighting cancer?

"population explosion" (see page 234). (*c*) In the United States and other medically advanced countries, doctors emphasize preventive medicine. They use inoculations against smallpox, diphtheria, tetanus, whooping cough, measles, and polio. Nations seek to prevent other diseases by modern sanitation, a balanced diet, and adequate exercise. People have faith that research will conquer today's major diseases: heart ailments and cancer.

GEOLOGY AND BIOLOGY

1. Scientists and Their Contributions

a. Linnaeus (1707-1778), Swedish, devised a system, still used today, for classifying plants and animals on the basis of similarities in structure. He is known as the "father of modern botany."

b. Charles Lyell (1795-1875), English, the "father of modern geology," believed that natural forces—water, wind, volcanoes—shaped the surface of the earth. Lyell estimated the age of the earth at many millions of years.

c. Matthias Schleiden (1804-1881) and *Theodor Schwann* (1810-1882), Germans, demonstrated that all living things (plant and animal) are composed of microscopic units, called *cells*.

d. Charles Darwin (1809-1882), English, in his book *The Origin of Species*, stated his *theory of evolution*. Darwin held that, during vast time eras, man and other complex forms of life evolved from simpler types by the process of *natural selection*, or *survival of the fittest*.

e. Gregor Mendel (1822-1884), Austrian, experimenting with the crossbreeding of pea plants developed the *laws of heredity*. "Mendelianism" gave impetus to scientific breeding of plants and animals.

2. Effects of These Contributions. (*a*) Man acquired a better perspective of himself and his civilization in relation to the vast age of the earth. (*b*) *Social Darwinists* applied the theory of evolution to explain the development of human institutions and used the theory of survival of the fittest to justify wars. (*c*) Farmers raised improved agricultural products and greatly increased our food supply.

CHEMISTRY AND PHYSICS (EXCLUDING ATOMIC ENERGY)

1. Scientists and Their Contributions

a. Joseph Priestley (1733-1804), English, discovered the gas *oxygen*.

b. Henry Cavendish (1731-1810), English, demonstrated that water consists of two gases, hydrogen and oxygen.

c. Antoine Lavoisier (1743-1794), French, the "father of modern chemistry," pioneered quantitative research methods. He proved that, in burning, a substance unites with oxygen.

d. Alessandro Volta (1745-1827), Italian, invented the *electric cell,* an invention that made possible many discoveries in electricity and magnetism.

e. André Ampère (1775-1836), French, made many important discoveries concerning the relationship between magnetism and electricity.

f. Michael Faraday (1791-1867), English, discovered the principle of electromagnetic induction; that is, he produced electricity by moving a magnet through a coil. This principle made possible the *dynamo* for generating electricity.

g. Dmitri Mendeleev (1834-1907), Russian, developed the *Periodic Table,* which classifies chemical elements according to their atomic weights. The Table enabled him to predict the existence of elements not then known.

2. Recent Developments. These scientists provided the foundation for two of today's giant industries, chemicals and electronics. (*a*) Chemists, usually working in research laboratories, have furnished an array of useful products: explosives, metals and alloys, building materials, and many other substances, such as synthetic dyes, flavoring extracts, drugs, synthetic fibers (rayon, nylon, orlon, dacron), synthetic rubber and leather, and a wide range of plastics. (*b*) Electronics engineers have produced automatic control devices: thermostats to regulate heating systems, the electric eye that adjusts camera lenses, instruments to guide space vehicles, and control panels to operate factories through automation. Scientists have also devised giant computers, or "electric brains," which outspeed humans in performing clerical tasks and mathematical calculations.

ATOMIC ENERGY

1. Scientists and Their Contributions

a. John Dalton (1766-1844), English, formulated the *atomic theory* to explain the structure of matter. He held that matter is composed of tiny, invisible particles, called *atoms.*

b. Marie Curie (1867-1934), Polish-born, together with her husband, *Pierre Curie* (1859-1906), French, discovered the chemical element *radium.* Physicists have used radium to help determine the structure of the atom.

c. Ernest Rutherford (1871-1937), British, discovered that the atom is largely empty space, with almost all of its mass concentrated in the tiny nucleus.

d. Lise Meitner (1878-1968), Austrian, predicted that tremendous energy would be released by splitting the nucleus of the atom. She escaped from Nazi Germany in 1938 and later communicated her findings to atomic scientists in America.

e. Albert Einstein (1879-1955), naturalized American, fled his native Germany because of Nazi religious persecution. Einstein, hailed as the outstanding modern theoretical physicist, expressed the complex relationship of matter, space, motion, and time in his *theory of relativity*. Einstein predicted that a small amount of matter could be converted into a tremendous quantity of energy according to the formula $E = mc^2$. During World War II he reluctantly urged the American government to build an atomic bomb.

f. Niels Bohr (1885-1962), Danish, described the atom as a miniature solar system. A refugee from Nazi Europe during World War II, Bohr worked on the American atomic-bomb project.

g. Enrico Fermi (1901-1954), naturalized American, employed slow-speed neutrons to split the nucleus of the atom. He fled from Fascist Italy and, while serving with the United States A-bomb research team, constructed the first nuclear reactor.

h. J. Robert Oppenheimer (1904-1967), American, directed the Los Alamos Scientific Laboratory of the Manhattan Project during World War II. At this laboratory, the first atomic bomb was designed and built.

i. Edward Teller (1908-   ), naturalized American, is considered the "father of the hydrogen bomb."

2. Atomic Energy and War. America's World War II leaders, determined to secure an atomic bomb (A-bomb) before the Germans did, inaugurated the *Manhattan Project*. They mobilized the top scientists—American, English, and Canadian, and refugees from Nazi-held Europe—and produced an A-bomb with the explosive power of 20,000 tons of TNT. In 1945 American airmen dropped the first nuclear bomb in the history of warfare on *Hiroshima*, Japan, killing or injuring 130,000 people and destroying 60 percent of the city. Subsequently, scientists developed the hydrogen bomb (H-bomb). With its explosive power (up to several thousand times the explosive power of the Hiroshima bomb), it can wipe out all life within a 60- to 100-mile radius.

The destructiveness of nuclear weapons results from their explosive blast, their tremendous heat, and their radioactivity, which can contaminate whole areas for years. Widespread fear exists that a nuclear war will mean the end of civilization. (For efforts at international control of nuclear weapons, see pages 459-462.)

3. Peacetime Uses of Atomic Energy. Scientists have devised atomic reactors that control the atom-splitting process and utilize the tremendous heat energy to change water into steam. In turn, steam can be used to propel boats and to generate electricity.

Today the United States possesses a fleet of atomic-powered surface ships and submarines, and a number of atomic-powered plants for the production of electricity. In many regions of the United States today, atomic power is competitive in cost with electricity generated by conventional fuels: natural gas, oil, and coal.

Also, atomic scientists have produced radioactive *isotopes*. These have significant uses (*a*) in medicine, to diagnose body ills, (*b*) in agriculture, to study plant growth and to preserve foods, (*c*) in industry, to uncover flaws in metal, and (*d*) in science, to explore the structure of matter.

SPACE AGE

1. The Rocket Engine. The *rocket*, an engine directly propelled by burning high-energy fuel, provides the powerful thrust necessary to lift vehicles into outer space. Following World War II both Russia and the United States began to develop rockets. In rocket thrust power, the Russians were ahead at first; however, by the mid-1960's, the Russians were overtaken and surpassed by the United States with its mighty *Saturn* rockets.

2. Beginning of the Space Age. In 1957 Russian scientists placed into orbit around the earth the first man-made satellite, *Sputnik I*. It weighed 184 pounds and carried scientific equipment to transmit data regarding outer space. In 1958 the Americans orbited their first earth satellite, the 18-pound *Explorer I*. Subsequently both nations placed weather, communications, and other satellites into earth orbit. Also they launched spaceships to the moon, to Mars, and to Venus. In 1961 the Russians placed into orbit the world's first cosmonaut, Major *Yuri Gagarin*. In 1962 the Americans launched their first orbiting astronaut, Colonel *John H. Glenn*.

In 1969 the United States achieved a historic first as the flight of *Apollo 11* enabled astronaut *Neil Armstrong* to be the first human being to set foot on the moon. Thereafter American leaders indicated further space goals: an unmanned "grand tour" of the outer planets and a manned landing on Mars. (For further details, see pages 466-472.)

SUMMARY: THE CHALLENGE OF SCIENCE

Mankind has accumulated a vast body of scientific knowledge. Until now, man has used science for both constructive and destructive purposes. With recent developments, man faces a crisis. He can take tremendous strides toward a better world or destroy his civilization. What does the future hold? The answer lies not with science but with man.

MULTIPLE-CHOICE QUESTIONS

1. The pure scientist would be most concerned with (1) purifying gasoline so as to achieve more miles per gallon (2) producing complex computers (3) writing technical manuals for operating atomic-powered ships (4) studying the basic truths of our universe.

2. A theory becomes a scientific law when it is (1) propounded by a famous scientist (2) clearly understood by the average citizen (3) proven true by repeated tests utilizing observation and experimentation (4) used in constructing machines.

3. During the last 100 years medical science has made the *least* progress in (1) reducing the strains of urban and industrialized living (2) increasing man's average lifespan (3) reducing the death rate in underdeveloped countries (4) developing preventive medicine.

4. The factor that most sped atomic energy research in the 1940's was the (1) depletion of coal reserves essential for producing electricity (2) need of an improved tool for cancer research (3) desire for more devastating weapons (4) curiosity of scientists about the structure of the atom.

5. Yuri Gagarin and John Glenn have both won fame as (1) atomic scientists (2) space travelers (3) chemists (4) physicians.

MATCHING QUESTIONS: BIOLOGY AND MEDICINE

Column A	*Column B*
1. Metchnikoff	*a.* use of antiseptics
2. Pasteur	*b.* penicillin
3. Mendel	*c.* study of white blood corpuscles
4. Jenner	*d.* transmission of yellow fever
5. Waksman	*e.* theory of evolution
6. Darwin	*f.* vaccination against smallpox
7. Lister	*g.* use of X-rays
8. Koch	*h.* germ theory of disease
9. Fleming	*i.* streptomycin
10. Roentgen	*j.* study of mental disease
	k. isolation of tuberculosis germ
	l. laws of heredity

MATCHING QUESTIONS: GEOLOGY, CHEMISTRY, AND PHYSICS

Column A	*Column B*
1. Curie	*a.* theory of relativity
2. Fermi	*b.* head of the Manhattan Project
3. Einstein	*c.* originator of atomic theory
4. Lyell	*d.* discovery of radium
5. Volta	*e.* father of the H-bomb
6. Faraday	*f.* electromagnetic induction
7. Dalton	*g.* father of modern chemistry
8. Teller	*h.* slow-speed neutrons to split atom
	i. father of modern geology
	j. inventor of electric cell

Part 5. Achievements in Literature and the Arts

CULTURAL MOVEMENTS

In any time period, writers and artists are affected by conditions in society. As a result, their works contain certain common characteristics, usually classified as cultural movements.

1. Classicism, which dominated most of the 18th century, was inspired by the classical Greek and Roman civilizations. The style and subject matter aimed to please the aristocracy, who, under the Old Regime, were the main patrons (supporters) of art. Classical works adhered to established rules and emphasized emotional restraint, formality, and dignity.

2. Romanticism, which dominated the early 19th century, expressed the spirit of revolt encouraged by the French Revolution of 1789. Romanticists rebelled against classical tradition; they asserted the individual's right to exercise imagination and express emotion. Romantic writers described the beauties of nature and the glories of past eras; romantic musicians often expressed nationalist themes.

3. Realism, which arose in the mid-19th century, describes the world as it exists, even in its less attractive aspects. Realistic writers deal with ordinary people and everyday affairs, especially problems emerging from the Industrial Revolution.

4. Victorian Age. This term refers to the years from 1837 to 1901, when England was ruled by Queen Victoria. During this age England witnessed the growth of industry, the extension of suffrage to city and farm workers, and the expansion of British imperial power. Some Victorian writers were romanticists and others realists, but generally they reflected Victorian society: middle-class domination, high moral standards, growth of democracy, and interest in social reform.

5. Impressionism. *Impressionists,* active in the late 19th century, revolted against realism. They were prominent chiefly in painting. They expressed, not "photographic" accuracy, but the artist's personal reactions.

6. Modern Tendencies. Twentieth-century writers and artists have utilized the older movements and also experimented with newer methods of expression: abstract painting such as *cubism;* nonmelodic music as well as nonharmonic music called *dissonance;* and disconnected thoughts of characters in novels, a form of writing called *stream of consciousness.* Modernists reflect the search for individuality and the complexity of our society.

BRITISH CONTRIBUTORS

1. Writers

a. Jonathan Swift (1667-1745), essayist and writer of fiction, berated mankind for its stupidity and intolerance. His *Gulliver's Travels*, intended as a biting satire, has become a children's classic.

b. Alexander Pope (1688-1744), classical poet, stated "whatever is, is right" in his often-quoted poem, *Essay on Man*.

c. William Wordsworth (1770-1850), romantic poet, acclaimed the beauty of nature and analyzed human character in *Tintern Abbey, The World Is Too Much With Us*, and *Ode: Intimations of Immortality*.

d. Walter Scott (1771-1832), romantic novelist, wrote adventure stories of the Middle Ages in *Kenilworth* and *Ivanhoe*.

e. Lord Byron (1788-1824), romantic poet, died while assisting the Greeks in their war for independence. With humor and satire, he protested the evils of society in *Don Juan*.

f. Percy Shelley (1792-1822), romantic poet, pleaded for freedom and justice in *Prometheus Unbound*. One of his most famous poems is *Ode to the West Wind*.

g. John Keats (1795-1821), romantic poet, praised beauty for its own sake in *Ode to a Grecian Urn, The Eve of St. Agnes*, and *To a Nightingale*.

h. Thomas Carlyle (1795-1881), historian of the Victorian Age, held that great men, not impersonal social and economic forces, determine history. One of his most famous works is *The French Revolution*.

i. Alfred Tennyson (1809-1892) was appointed poet laureate of England by Queen Victoria. He exalted world peace in *Locksley Hall* and extolled the glories of England in *The Charge of the Light Brigade* and *Idylls of the King*.

j. William Thackeray (1811-1863), Victorian realist, satirized the upper classes in his novel *Vanity Fair*.

k. Charles Dickens (1812-1870), Victorian novelist, was a realist and social reformer. He portrayed lower-class poverty and attacked Industrial Revolution abuses in *David Copperfield* and *Oliver Twist*. Dickens also wrote the humorous *Pickwick Papers* and a novel of the French Revolution, *A Tale of Two Cities*.

l. Robert Browning (1812-1889), Victorian poet, analyzed individuals in his dramatic poems *Rabbi Ben Ezra, My Last Duchess*, and *Andrea del Sarto*.

m. George Eliot (1819-1880) was the pen name of a Victorian woman novelist. She portrayed common people realistically in *The Mill on the Floss* and described the effect of machinery on a weaver in *Silas Marner*.

n. Thomas Hardy (1840-1928) probed character in realistic novels such as *The Mayor of Casterbridge* and *The Return of the Native*.

o. Robert Louis Stevenson (1850-1894), Victorian romanticist, wrote the adventure novels *Treasure Island* and *Kidnapped*, and the poetry collection *A Child's Garden of Verses*.

p. George Bernard Shaw (1856-1950), Socialist playwright, satirized prevailing customs and crusaded against war, poverty, and ignorance. He is witty, entertaining, and provocative in such plays as *Caesar and Cleopatra, Major Barbara, Man and Superman, Saint Joan,* and *Pygmalion*. (In 1956 *Pygmalion* was transformed into a popular musical comedy, *My Fair Lady*.)

q. Rudyard Kipling (1865-1936), the romantic "poet of imperialism," glorified the British Empire and preached the "white man's burden"—the duty to look after the world's backward peoples. He wrote the poems *The Ballad of East and West* and *Gunga Din,* and prose works such as *Soldiers Three* and *Kim*.

r. H. G. Wells (1866-1946), Socialist, envisioned the future in pseudo-scientific novels, as *The Time Machine, The War of the Worlds,* and *A Modern Utopia*. Wells deplored the waste of human resources in realistic novels such as *Tono-Bungay* and *The History of Mr. Polly*. Wells also wrote a very popular one-volume *Outline of History*.

s. John Galsworthy (1867-1933) traced the life of an English family in his series of realistic novels, *The Forsyte Saga*. Also, he dissected social and economic conflict in the plays *Strife* and *Loyalties*.

t. John Masefield (1878-1967), realistic poet, wrote of the sea in *Dauber* and the collection *Salt-Water Ballads*. In 1930 Masefield was appointed poet laureate of England.

u. T. S. Eliot (1888-1965), poet and playwright, although born in the United States, adopted British outlook and citizenship. He expressed mankind's search for spiritual values in his poem *The Waste Land* and in his poetic drama *Murder in the Cathedral*.

2. Painters

a. Joshua Reynolds (1723-1792), classical painter, specialized in portraits of the English aristocracy.

b. Thomas Gainsborough (1727-1788), classical portrait painter, won fame for *Blue Boy*.

c. Joseph Turner (1775-1851), romantic painter of landscapes and water scenes, depicted the old warship *Fighting Temeraire* and *The Battle of Trafalgar.*

FRENCH CONTRIBUTORS

1. Writers

a. Honoré de Balzac (1799-1850) realistically dissected French middle-class life in his series of novels, *The Human Comedy.*

b. Victor Hugo (1802-1885), romantic novelist, sympathized with the downtrodden in his *Hunchback of Notre Dame* and *Les Miserables.* Hugo opposed Napoleon III's dictatorship, disparaged him as "Napoleon, the Little," and was forced to flee France.

c. Alexandre Dumas (1803-1870), romantic novelist, wrote adventure stories, including *The Count of Monte Cristo* and *The Three Musketeers.*

d. Anatole France (1844-1924), realistic novelist, satirized the evils of society in *The Crime of Sylvestre Bonnard* and *Penguin Island.*

e. Marcel Proust (1871-1922), psychological novelist, provided insight into the actions of individuals and society in his cycle of novels, *Remembrance of Things Past.*

f. Albert Camus (1913-1960), philosopher and novelist, illuminated individual suffering caused by hatred, illness, and war. He is noted for his novels *The Stranger* and *The Plague.*

2. Composers

a. Charles Gounod (1818-1893) wrote romantic operas, including *Faust* and *Romeo and Juliet.*

b. Georges Bizet (1838-1875) composed the romantic opera *Carmen.*

c. Claude Debussy (1862-1918) appealed to imagination and mood in such impressionistic works as *Clair de Lune* and *The Afternoon of a Faun.*

d. Maurice Ravel (1875-1937) achieved unusual musical effects in *Rhapsodie Espagnole, Bolero,* and *Mother Goose Suite.*

3. Painters

a. Edouard Manet (1832-1883), "father of impressionism," achieved striking landscapes. He is also famous for *Lunch on the Grass.*

b. Paul Cézanne (1839-1906), impressionist, painted landscapes and still lifes. He also depicted the *Card Players.*

c. Pierre Renoir (1841-1919), impressionist, painted the popular *Canoeists' Luncheon.*

d. Paul Gauguin (1848-1903), impressionist, employed startling colors and distortions of shape. Gauguin spent his last years painting the islands and people of the South Pacific.

e. Henri Matisse (1869-1954), modernist, achieved striking effects with his primitive style in such works as *The Piano Lesson.*

4. Sculptor

a. Auguste Rodin (1840-1917) conveyed a feeling of power and intensity in his many statues, such as *The Thinker.*

ITALIAN CONTRIBUTORS

1. Composers

a. Gioacchino Rossini (1792-1868), operatic composer, is best known for *The Barber of Seville* and *William Tell.*

b. Giuseppe Verdi (1813-1901), operatic composer, expressed romantic and nationalist themes in *Rigoletto, La Traviata,* and *Aïda.*

c. Giacomo Puccini (1858-1924) was a romantic composer of operas, including *La Boheme, La Tosca,* and *Madame Butterfly.*

2. Conductor

a. Arturo Toscanini (1867-1957), orchestra conductor, fled from Fascist Italy and became a naturalized American. Toscanini won acclaim as leader of the *New York Philharmonic Orchestra* and the *NBC Symphony Orchestra.*

GERMAN CONTRIBUTORS

1. Philosophers

a. Georg Hegel (1770-1831), strong nationalist, extolled Prussia's monarchical government, equated war with progress, and placed the well-being of the state above that of its citizens. Hegel's ideas encouraged anti-democratic forces.

b. Friedrich Nietzsche (1844-1900), philosopher, condemned Christianity as a slave religion and democracy as the rule of mediocrity. He believed that a small group of "supermen" would eventually dominate the world. Nietzsche, probably unwittingly, provided the philosophical background for Germany's Nazi movement.

2. Writers

a. Johann von Goethe (1749-1832) portrayed the conflict between good and evil and held out hope for man's salvation in his dramatic poem *Faust*.

b. Friedrich von Schiller (1759-1805), romantic poet and playwright, won fame for his drama *William Tell*.

c. Heinrich Heine (1797-1856), romantic poet and essayist, attacked despotism and reaction. His most famous poem is *Die Lorelei*.

d. Gerhart Hauptmann (1862-1946) wrote realistic plays of worker and peasant discontent. He described a workers' revolt occasioned by Industrial Revolution evils in *The Weavers*.

e. Thomas Mann (1875-1955), realistic novelist, fled Nazi Germany and spent many years in the United States. He probed individual character and the problems of modern Western civilization in *Buddenbrooks, Death in Venice,* and *The Magic Mountain*.

f. Erich Remarque (1898-1970), a refugee from Nazi Germany, became an American citizen. A novelist, he attacked the stupidity and destruction of war in *All Quiet on the Western Front* and portrayed a German refugee doctor in *Arch of Triumph*.

3. Composers

a. Johann Sebastian Bach (1685-1750), church organist, experimented with new musical techniques in his many sonatas, concertos, suites, and cantatas.

b. Ludwig van Beethoven (1770-1827), one of the greatest of composers, wrote romantic music: sonatas, concertos, an opera, and nine symphonies. For the *Third (Eroica) Symphony,* it is said, he tore up a dedication to Napoleon upon hearing that Napoleon had taken the title of Emperor. Beethoven's *Fifth Symphony* is perhaps the best known of all symphonies. Beethoven combined a chorus and orchestra in his *Ninth (Choral) Symphony*.

c. Felix Mendelssohn (1809-1847), romanticist, created much delightful music. His incidental music for the play *A Midsummer Night's Dream* provided the ever-popular *Overture* and *Wedding March*. He is also known for his *"Italian"* and *"Scotch" Symphonies*.

d. Richard Wagner (1813-1883), romantic composer and German nationalist, employed Germanic themes in his operas *Lohengrin, Die Walküre, Die Meistersinger,* and *Tristan and Isolde*.

e. Johannes Brahms (1833-1897), in a romantic style, wrote symphonies, concertos, and a series of *Hungarian Dances*.

AUSTRIAN CONTRIBUTORS

1. Composers

a. Joseph Haydn (1732-1809), classical composer, wrote over 100 symphonies, including the *Clock Symphony* and the *Toy Symphony.*

b. Wolfgang Mozart (1756-1791) helped bridge classicism and romanticism by his symphonies, concertos, chamber music such as *Eine Kleine Nachtmusik,* and operas such as *The Marriage of Figaro* and *Don Giovanni.*

c. Franz Schubert (1797-1828) wrote romantic songs and the ever-popular *Unfinished Symphony.*

d. Johann Strauss (1825-1899), the "Waltz King," composed several operettas and many waltzes, such as *By the Beautiful Blue Danube* and *Tales From the Vienna Woods.*

RUSSIAN CONTRIBUTORS

1. Writers

a. Ivan Turgenev (1818-1883), realistic novelist, described the revolutionary movement in Czarist Russia in his *Fathers and Sons.*

b. Feodor Dostoyevski (1821-1881) probed human suffering in his psychological novels *The Brothers Karamazov* and *Crime and Punishment.*

c. Leo Tolstoi (1828-1910), social reformer and novelist, related Napoleon's invasion of Russia and condemned warfare and hero worship in *War and Peace.* He explored life among the aristocracy in *Anna Karenina.*

d. Anton Chekhov (1860-1904) reflected realism and pessimism in the plays *The Sea Gull* and *The Cherry Orchard.*

e. Boris Pasternak (1890-1960), poet and novelist, criticized Communist ethics and rule in his novel *Doctor Zhivago,* published only outside Russia. Awarded the 1958 Nobel Prize for literature, Pasternak rejected the award because of pressures brought by his country's Communist rulers.

f. Alexander Solzhenitsyn (1918-   ), novelist, related his experiences in a Stalinist labor camp in *One Day in the Life of Ivan Denisovich.* His later works, *The First Circle* and *The Cancer Ward,* highly critical of Soviet society, were denied publication in Russia. Awarded the 1970 Nobel Prize for literature, he accepted, and both he and the award were berated by his government's spokesmen.

2. Composers

a. Peter Tchaikovsky (1840-1893), romantic and nationalist composer, commemorated Russia's victory over Napoleon by the *1812 Overture.*

Tchaikovsky utilized Russian folk themes in his symphonies and concertos, in his opera *Eugene Onegin*, and in his ballet music such as *Swan Lake*.

b. Nikolai Rimski-Korsakov (1844-1908) wrote romantic and nationalist music based on folk themes. His works included the opera *The Snow Maiden* and the tone poem *Scheherazade*.

c. Igor Stravinsky (1882-1971) left Russia before World War I and later settled in the United States. A modernist, Stravinsky achieved striking effects in his ballet music *The Rite of Spring, Petrouchka,* and *The Firebird*.

d. Aram Khatchaturian (1904-   ) used folk themes in his ballet music *Masquerade* and *Gayne*.

e. Dmitri Shostakovich (1906-   ), noted Soviet composer, has written many nationalist works. He honored the defense of Leningrad during World War II by his *Seventh Symphony*.

OTHER EUROPEAN CONTRIBUTORS

1. Writers

a. Henrik Ibsen (1828-1906), Norwegian playwright, exposed pretense and hypocrisy in realistic plays such as *A Doll's House, An Enemy of the People,* and *Hedda Gabler*.

b. James Joyce (1882-1941), Irish novelist, experimented with stream-of-consciousness writing and innovations in his use of language. He wrote *A Portrait of the Artist as a Young Man, Ulysses,* and *Finnegans Wake*.

c. Arthur Koestler (1905-   ), Hungarian-born political essayist and novelist, by 1938 had become disillusioned with Communism. He attacked Stalinism in *The Yogi and the Commissar* and *Darkness at Noon*.

2. Composers

a. Frederic Chopin (1810-1849), Polish romanticist and nationalist, wrote delightful piano pieces, such as the *Polonaise* and the *Minute Waltz*.

b. Franz Liszt (1811-1886), Hungarian pianist, composed the melodic *Hungarian Rhapsodies*.

c. Anton Dvorak (1841-1904), Czech composer, created romantic and nationalist music, including the *New World Symphony* and the *Humoresque*.

d. Edvard Grieg (1843-1907), Norwegian nationalist, employed native folk themes in his stirring piano concerto and in his *Peer Gynt Suite*.

e. Jean Sibelius (1865-1957), Finnish composer, expressed nationalist feeling in his symphonies and in his tone poem *Finlandia*.

3. Painters

a. Francisco Goya (1746-1828), Spanish painter, excelled in portraits of nobility as well as in realistic everyday scenes. Also, he depicted the Spanish uprising against Napoleon and the French reprisals in his *The Second of May* and *The Executions of the Third of May*.

b. Vincent Van Gogh (1853-1890), Dutch impressionist, used brilliant color in still lifes and landscapes such as *Starry Night*.

c. Pablo Picasso (1881-   ), Spanish modernist, who has lived chiefly in France, was the "father of cubism." He also painted in other styles and has done sculpture, etchings, and illustrations. He achieved unusual effects in his *Three Musicians*.

MULTIPLE-CHOICE QUESTIONS

1. Classicism in music and painting (1) originated in the 20th century (2) sought to please the average citizen (3) was formal, dignified, and restrained (4) drew inspiration from primitive cultures of Asia and Africa.
2. The beginnings of the romantic movement in literature and art are sometimes associated with the (1) Protestant Reformation (2) Glorious Revolution of 1689 (3) French Revolution of 1789 (4) Russian Revolution of 1917.
3. A realistic writer would most probably choose as his subject the (1) difficulties of earning a living in a factory town (2) beauties of nature (3) battles of knights against invading barbarians (4) happy story of a poor boy's easy rise to fame and wealth.
4. *Not* an aspect of the Victorian Age in England was (1) growth of democracy (2) high moral standards (3) despair about the future (4) faith in the British Empire.
5. An impressionist landscape painting would (1) show every blade of grass (2) convey the artist's feelings about the scene (3) be best viewed standing close to the canvas (4) show nature to be ugly.

IDENTIFICATION QUESTIONS: LITERATURE

Byron	Ibsen	Nietzsche	Scott
Dickens	Joyce	Pasternak	Shaw
Goethe	Kipling	Proust	Swift
Hugo	Koestler	Remarque	Tolstoi

1. A great German literary figure, I depicted the struggle between good and evil and expressed hope for mankind in my dramatic poem *Faust*.
2. A nobleman and social reformer, I described Napoleon's invasion of Russia in my novel *War and Peace*.
3. As the "poet of imperialism," I proclaimed the "white man's burden" and extolled the British Empire.
4. A romantic poet, I protested against corruption and convention in my verse tale *Don Juan*. I died while assisting the Greeks in their war for independence from Turkey.
5. Because my writings displeased the Communist rulers of my homeland, my novel *Doctor Zhivago* was published outside of Russia and I felt compelled to reject the Nobel Prize for literature.
6. My work *Gulliver's Travels*, intended to satirize mankind for stupidity and intolerance, has become a children's adventure classic.

7. A Norwegian dramatist, I exposed pretense and hypocrisy in such plays as *An Enemy of the People.*
8. I was a French romantic novelist and author of *The Hunchback of Notre Dame* and *Les Miserables.* Because I opposed Napoleon III, I was forced to flee from France.
9. A romantic novelist, I wrote about brave knights and great adventures of the Middle Ages in such stories as *Ivanhoe.*
10. I was a Socialist and writer of satirical plays. My play *Pygmalion* provided the story for the hit musical show and movie *My Fair Lady.*
11. A German philosopher, I deprecated Christianity and democracy and predicted world domination by a group of "supermen." Years after my death, my ideas were utilized to justify Nazism.
12. A Victorian novelist, I portrayed the unfortunate effects of the Industrial Revolution in such books as *David Copperfield.*

IDENTIFICATION QUESTIONS: PAINTING AND MUSIC

Beethoven	Gauguin	Mozart	Tchaikovsky
Chopin	Goya	Picasso	Van Gogh
Debussy	Matisse	Sibelius	Verdi
Gainsborough	Mendelssohn	Strauss	Wagner

1. I composed much melodic dance music and became known as the "Waltz King." My most famous waltz probably is *By the Beautiful Blue Danube.*
2. A romantic composer whose works remain immensely popular, I wrote nine symphonies, including the *Third,* or *Eroica,* and the *Ninth,* or *Choral, Symphonies.*
3. I was a classical portrait painter, famous for my *Blue Boy.*
4. Despite my short life, I wrote many works that served to bridge classicism and romanticism in music. Among these were the operas *Don Giovanni* and *The Marriage of Figaro.*
5. An operatic composer and German nationalist, I employed Germanic themes in such operas as *Die Meistersinger* and *Lohengrin.*
6. Born in France, I gave up a business career to become a painter. Later, I left France for the South Pacific islands, where I utilized impressionist techniques in painting native scenes and peoples.
7. A Russian composer, I utilized native folk themes in many works, such as the ballet music for *The Nutcracker* and *Swan Lake.*
8. A Spanish painter known for realistic everyday scenes, I portrayed the resistance of my people against Napoleon.
9. An operatic composer and Italian nationalist, I am known for my music to the operas *La Traviata* and *Aïda.*
10. A pianist and Polish patriot, I wrote charming piano compositions such as the *Minute Waltz.*
11. Although I am known as the "father of cubism," I have experimented with many painting styles. A famous work of mine is the *Three Musicians.*
12. A French composer, I applied impressionism to music in such works as *The Afternoon of a Faun.*

MULTIPLE-CHOICE QUESTIONS

Select the number of the person who does *not* belong in the corresponding group.

1. *Writers:* (1) Galsworthy (2) Rodin (3) Hardy (4) Chekhov.
2. *Poets:* (1) Ravel (2) Heine (3) Shelley (4) Masefield.
3. *Composers:* (1) Grieg (2) Bach (3) Keats (4) Khatchaturian.
4. *Operatic Composers:* (1) Gounod (2) Bizet (3) Puccini (4) Browning.
5. *Painters:* (1) Turner (2) Tennyson (3) Manet (4) Cézanne.

UNIT X. IMPERIALISM AND COLONIAL NATIONALISM

Part 1. Introduction to Imperialism

DEFINITION

Imperialism means *control by a powerful nation over a "backward," or weaker, area.* The powerful nation is usually characterized by an advanced economy, strong government, and considerable military strength; the backward area by underdeveloped natural resources, primitive economy, weak government, and limited military power. Since World War II, imperialism has also been called *colonialism.*

OLD IMPERIALISM (16TH TO EARLY 19TH CENTURY)

1. Aspect of Commercial Revolution. During the Renaissance, western European nations, desiring trade with the Far East, pioneered direct water routes; discovered the New World; founded settlements and trading posts in the Americas, Africa, and Asia; conquered native peoples; and established European rule over them. European nations fought many wars over colonial trade and territory. By 1763 France possessed little territory; considerable empires belonged to Holland, Portugal, and Spain; and the leading colonial power was England.

2. Reasons for Decline. By the early 19th century the western European nations had lost interest in empire building. They were (a) exhausted by the Napoleonic Wars, (b) occupied with democratic and nationalist movements, (c) engaged in industrial development, and (d) convinced that the cost of colonies outweighed the benefits to the mother country.

MODERN IMPERIALISM (SINCE MID-19TH CENTURY)

1. Fundamental Cause: Industrial Revolution. Industrialized nations desired colonies to provide (a) a cheap and certain supply of *raw materials*, (b) *markets* reserved for the mother country's manufactured goods, and (c) large profits with minimum risk on investment of *surplus capital*.

2. Other Causes. The advocates of imperialism used nationalist arguments to gain public support for empire building. They claimed that the mother country would (a) gain glory and achieve "a place in the sun," (b) secure essential military bases and war materials, (c) provide an outlet for surplus population, (d) safeguard her missionaries spreading Christianity, and (e) bring to the backward areas the blessings of the superior culture of the West—a duty labeled by the poet Rudyard Kipling as the "white man's burden."

TYPES OF IMPERIALIST CONTROL

1. **Concession.** An underdeveloped country granted economic privileges, or *concessions*, to foreign businessmen. These concessions permitted them to build railroads, open mines, or drill for oil. In this way, the underdeveloped country came under the political influence of the imperialist nation. Example: Before World War I Germany, allowed to construct the Berlin-to-Bagdad railroad through Turkish territory, exercised much influence in the Ottoman Empire.

2. **Sphere of Influence.** A powerful nation secured *exclusive* economic privileges in a backward region, thereby establishing a *sphere of influence*. Usually, such an economic monopoly was respected by other imperialist nations. Example: Before World War I France, England, Germany, and Russia had exclusive control over tariffs, trade, and economic development in separate parts of China.

3. **Protectorate.** The native ruler remained in power outwardly, but the imperialist nation controlled affairs behind the scenes. Examples: French officials advised the Bey of Tunisia and the Sultan of Morocco. English authorities advised the Sheik of Kuwait.

After World War II a new form of protectorate appeared. Several countries in eastern and central Europe came under Communist control and became subject to Russian authority. These nations, which may be considered protectorates, are known as *satellites*. (For details, see pages 416-418.)

4. **Annexation.** Outright and full control occurred when a territory was formally taken over as a colony and governed by the home country. Examples: England annexed Gibraltar and Hong Kong. France annexed Indo-China.

5. **Mandate and Trusteeship: Under International Supervision.** Following World War I an attempt was made to introduce reforms in the field of imperialism. Colonies of defeated Germany and Turkey were assigned to victorious nations to be governed under League of Nations supervision as *mandates*. Following World War II the colonies of defeated Italy and Japan, together with the remaining mandates, were placed under United Nations supervision as *trust territories*. Countries administering trusteeships pledged to prepare the native peoples for self-government and to accept the supervision of the *U.N. Trusteeship Council*. (For details, see page 400.)

Examples: As *mandates*, (a) England received Palestine, Iraq, and Tanganyika, and (*b*) France received Lebanon and Syria. As *trusteeships,* (*a*) Italy retained Italian Somaliland, (*b*) Australia retained New Guinea, and (*c*) the United States received the former Japanese-mandated islands in the Pacific.

Part 2. British Empire to Commonwealth of Nations

IMPORTANCE OF THE BRITISH EMPIRE

1. Size. Within three centuries, the British assembled history's largest empire. By 1920 the British Empire had reached its greatest extent. It contained one-fourth of the world's land area and population. Its territories, found on every continent, led proud Englishmen to boast, "The sun never sets on the British Empire."

THE BRITISH EMPIRE (1920)

LOCATION	MEMBERS
Europe	Great Britain, Ireland, Gibraltar, Malta.
Africa	Egypt, Sudan, Sierra Leone, Gold Coast, Nigeria, Kenya, Tanganyika, Uganda, Zanzibar, Nyasaland, Rhodesia, Union of South Africa.
Asia 1. Middle East 2. Far East	Palestine, Iraq, Kuwait, Aden, Cyprus. India, Ceylon, Burma, Malaya, Singapore, North Borneo, Hong Kong.
Australasia	Dominions of New Zealand and Australia.
Americas 1. North America 2. South America 3. West Indies	Dominion of Canada. British Guiana. Trinidad, Tobago, Jamaica, Bahamas.

2. Resources. The British Empire was a tremendous military force: manpower, raw materials, industries, and strategic bases.

3. Governmental Variety. The British Empire illustrated (*a*) many forms of imperialist control: colonies, protectorates, and trusteeships, and (*b*) evolution into a free association of self-governing nations.

4. Independence and Commonwealth. The British pioneered in (*a*) granting colonies the status of self-governing, independent *dominions,* and (*b*) relating them to England in a voluntary association, or *Commonwealth.* Insofar as the Commonwealth nations remain loyal to England and her democratic traditions, these policies strengthen the free world.

The British Empire has been transformed into the *Commonwealth of Nations,* and the dominions are called *Commonwealth members.*

INDEPENDENT COMMONWEALTH MEMBERS

1. Brief History. Prior to the 19th century England permitted little or no colonial self-government. Usually, London appointed colonial officials, and the English Parliament enacted colonial laws. Following the successful revolt of the thirteen American colonies (1775-1783) and an unsuccessful Canadian uprising (1837), England questioned the wisdom of strict colonial rule. Thereafter, England granted Canada limited self-government; from this beginning evolved independent Commonwealth membership.

2. Self-Government of Commonwealth Members. Each member exercises full control over its own domestic and foreign affairs, such as coining money, levying tariffs, negotiating treaties, and declaring war.

3. Independence of Commonwealth Members. As stated in the 1931 *Statute of Westminster,* the Commonwealth nations and Great Britain are (a) equal in status as independent nations, (b) united by common allegiance to the British Crown, and (c) voluntarily associated as members of the Commonwealth of Nations.

STRUCTURE AND MEMBERSHIP OF THE COMMONWEALTH

1. Structure. The Commonwealth possesses no rigid organization. It is not based upon formal treaty obligations; it exercises no central control of economic or foreign policy; it cannot prevent member nations from changing their form of government or from seceding from the Commonwealth.

In essence, the Commonwealth provides its members with a means of discussing and cooperating upon issues of mutual interest.

2. Members

a. The United Kingdom. This is the official name for the union of Great Britain (England, Scotland, and Wales) and Northern Ireland.

b. Old Dominions. Canada, Australia, and New Zealand, peopled chiefly by English stock, received dominion status prior to World War I. Although independent, these members recognize the British Crown both as head of their own governments and as head of the Commonwealth. The Crown is represented in each of these members by a Governor General, who serves as a figurehead. Each has a cabinet, headed by a Prime Minister, responsible to an elected legislature.

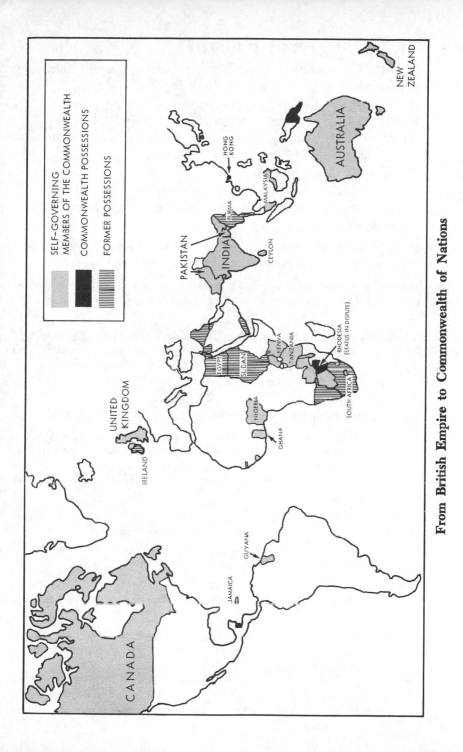

From British Empire to Commonwealth of Nations

c. New Commonwealth Nations. Many countries, peopled chiefly by native stock, received independence after World War II.

(1) *In Africa:* Ghana, Sierra Leone, Nigeria, Uganda, Kenya, Tanzania, Zambia, Malawi, the Gambia, Botswana, Lesotho, and Swaziland.

(2) *In Asia:* India, Bangladesh, Ceylon, Malaysia, and Singapore.

(3) *In the Pacific:* Fiji, Tonga, Western Samoa.

(4) *In the Indian Ocean:* Mauritius.

(5) *In the Mediterranean:* Cyprus and Malta.

(6) *In the Caribbean:* Jamaica, Trinidad-Tobago, and Barbados.

(7) *In South America:* Guyana.

These nations all acknowledge the British Crown as head of the Commonwealth. Many, however, are republics and have no Governor General.

3. Dependencies of Commonwealth Nations. England and other Commonwealth members have possessed various colonies, trusteeships, and protectorates.

4. Former Possessions Rejecting the Commonwealth. (*a*) Three former dominions—Ireland, South Africa, and Pakistan—became republics and seceded from the Commonwealth. (*b*) Two former colonies—Burma and Sudan—became republics outside of the Commonwealth.

TIES BINDING THE COMMONWEALTH

1. British Heritage. The mother country and the old dominions share a common language, a sentimental attachment to the royal family, and similar customs and traditions, especially a belief in democratic government.

The new Commonwealth members, in varying degrees, reflect British culture and political ideals.

2. Defense. In both world wars, the old dominions voluntarily fought alongside England, and the Commonwealth received protection from the powerful British navy. Today, some Commonwealth members maintain defense agreements with Britain and permit British military bases.

3. Commonwealth Conferences. To discuss Commonwealth problems, the member nations hold frequent conferences. At times, some or all members have agreed upon common action.

4. Economic Affairs. Most Commonwealth members depend to a great extent upon England to purchase their raw materials, supply manufactured goods, and provide investment capital and technical assistance.

At the 1932 Ottawa Conference, the members encouraged inter-Commonwealth trade by agreeing mutually to reduce tariff rates, a system called *preferential tariffs.* At the 1950 Colombo Conference, the more prosperous

Commonwealth members agreed to give economic aid to less developed south and southeast Asian countries. This agreement was called the *Colombo Plan*.

A. CANADA: COMMONWEALTH MEMBER

ECONOMY AND PEOPLE

Canada possesses rich natural resources: minerals (iron ore, copper, uranium, oil), forests, waterpower, and fertile soil. Predominantly agricultural, Canada is a leading producer of foodstuffs, especially wheat. Her industries —food processing, forest products, iron, and steel—are dominated by American corporations. Canada trades chiefly with the United States.

Canada's population of 22 million encompasses a large minority of French descent and a majority of English origin. The people generally support compulsory education and enjoy a high standard of living.

BRIEF HISTORY

Originally French, Canada became an English possession by the Treaty of Paris (1763) ending the French and Indian War. During the American Revolution (1775-1783), the Canadians remained loyal to England, but in 1837 they revolted unsuccessfully. In 1839 self-government for Canada was recommended in the famous *Durham Report*. By the *British North America Act* in 1867, Canada became the first dominion.

CURRENT PROBLEMS

1. French-English Friction. Since they control the province of Quebec, the French Canadians oppose any increased power for the English-dominated central government. Also, they are less enthusiastic than the English about maintaining Commonwealth ties. In the 1970 provincial elections, the Quebec party, favoring independence, polled 24 percent of the popular vote. Also, Quebec extremists carried out political kidnappings and an assassination. They were hunted down by forces of the Canadian government.

2. Small Population. Relative to her size and resources, Canada is sparsely populated. Canada restricts immigrants except from France, the United States, the old dominions, and the British Isles. Since these peoples are little inclined to migrate, Canada's population growth is slow.

3. Defense. A free world nation and NATO member, Canada coordinates her defense efforts with the United States. They cooperate in a *Permanent Joint Board of Defense* and a *North American Air Defense Command*. Since planes and missiles may attack via the North Pole region, Canada and the United States maintain, across the top of the continent, defense systems such as the radar *DEW* (*Distant Early Warning*) *Line*.

4. Latent Anti-United States Sentiment. As democratic nations, Canada and the United States have a history of close and friendly cooperation. In recent years, some Canadians have protested that the United States exerts too much influence in Canada's economic affairs and defense policies.

B. AUSTRALIA: COMMONWEALTH MEMBER

ECONOMY AND PEOPLE

Australia possesses mineral resources (gold, coal, uranium, and iron ore), fertile soil, and grazing land. A leading agricultural country, Australia exports wool, meat, and wheat. She trades chiefly with England. Australia's industries, small but rapidly developing, include iron and steel, machinery, chemicals, textiles, electrical equipment, cars, aircraft, and ships.

Australia's 13 million people, primarily of British stock, have free compulsory education and a good living standard.

BRIEF HISTORY

Explored by *Captain James Cook* in 1770, Australia became an English possession. Until 1840 the country served as a penal colony for English criminals and debtors. After the discovery of gold in 1851, Australia attracted many English settlers. In 1900 the country received dominion status.

Famed as an economic and political *experimental laboratory,* Australia pioneered in adopting government railroad and telephone ownership, universal suffrage, and the secret, or Australian, ballot.

CURRENT PROBLEMS

1. Population. In 1901 this sparsely peopled land adopted a *white Australia* immigration policy, welcoming British settlers, accepting some other white immigrants, but completely barring Asians. After 1945 racial restrictions were somewhat modified and in 1973 Australia discarded skin color as a factor in admitting immigrants. Australia's new emphasis was upon the individual's qualifications and the nation's need for skilled workers.

2. Defense. Australia strongly supports Commonwealth unity and belongs to the SEATO and ANZUS free world defensive alliances.

C. NEW ZEALAND: COMMONWEALTH MEMBER

ECONOMY AND PEOPLE

New Zealand, consisting of two large islands 1,200 miles southeast of Australia, is an agricultural country. Exporting wool, meat, and dairy products, she trades chiefly with Britain. New Zealand's 3 million people, chiefly of British stock, enjoy high literacy and comfortable living.

BRIEF HISTORY

Explored by Captain Cook and later annexed by England, New Zealand in 1907 received dominion status. The country experimented with new ideas: universal suffrage, income tax, social security, government ownership of basic industries, and compulsory arbitration of labor disputes.

CURRENT PROBLEMS

New Zealand (1) favors British settlers, (2) supports England and the Commonwealth, and (3) adheres to SEATO and ANZUS.

[Other Commonwealth members, discussed elsewhere in this unit, include India (pages 317-321), Bangladesh—formerly East Pakistan (pages 321-322)—Malaysia (page 324), and the African members (page 289).]

D. IRELAND: FORMER COMMONWEALTH MEMBER

ECONOMY AND PEOPLE

An agricultural country, raising grains, potatoes, and sugar beets, Ireland —the *Emerald Isle*—exports farm produce and imports manufactured goods. She trades chiefly with Britain. Ireland's 3 million people are Catholic.

BRIEF HISTORY

England conquered Ireland during the Middle Ages and, for several hundred years, ruled the country harshly. In the 19th and early 20th centuries the English gradually enacted reforms to eliminate major Irish grievances.

1. Religious Issue. Protestant England discriminated against Catholic Ireland by (*a*) forbidding Catholics to hold political office, and (*b*) taxing Catholics to support the Anglican Church in Ireland.

Solution. In 1829 the *Catholic Emancipation Act* declared Catholics eligible for public office. In 1869 the *Disestablishment Act* ended taxation of Irish Catholics for the support of a Church to which they did not belong.

2. Land Issue. Through conquest and rule, Englishmen gained ownership of most Irish farmlands. Chiefly *absentee landlords,* the English extorted high rents from the Irish peasants who remained as tenant farmers. (The Irish raised potatoes as their principal crop and main food. During Ireland's potato famine of the 1840's, many Irish migrated to the United States.)

Solution. From 1870 to 1903 Parliament passed several *Land Acts* providing long-term, low-interest government loans to enable Irish tenant farmers to purchase their land holdings. The leading advocate of such legislation was England's Prime Minister, *William Gladstone.*

3. Independence Issue. Britain denied Irish demands for self-government and independence. Twice in the late 19th century, Parliament defeated Gladstone's proposals for Irish *home rule.*

In 1905 Irish nationalists formed the *Sinn Fein party.* Its outstanding leader was *Eamon de Valera.* In 1916, while England was fighting World War I, the Irish revolted in the unsuccessful *Easter Rebellion.* Thereafter the Sinn Fein began guerrilla warfare to evict the British.

Solution. In 1921 Ireland (without Ulster province) received dominion status. Gradually the Irish severed their political ties to Britain. During World War II they remained neutral, extending Britain no aid. In 1949 the *Republic of Ireland* withdrew from the Commonwealth.

ULSTER: A REMAINING AND COMPLEX ISSUE

Ulster, or Northern Ireland, contains two groups hostile toward each other: (1) Scotch-Irish Protestants, descendants of 17th-century English and Scotch settlers, totaling two-thirds of the population, and (2) Irish Catholics. In 1921 Ulster voted to remain part of the United Kingdom. The vote was condemned by Ireland, which demanded the return of Ulster.

In 1969 Ulster erupted into violence. The Protestant-dominated government of Ulster pledged to remedy justifiable Catholic grievances of police brutality and of discrimination in voting, jobs, and public housing. Despite this pledge, Catholic militants in the outlawed *Irish Republican Army* (IRA) continued with bombings and shootings, demanding that Ulster be reunited with the rest of Ireland. Protestant militants organized their own paramilitary force, the *Ulster Defense Association.* Violence continued and by 1973 over 700 people had been killed. Britain sent troops to Ulster but they were unable to restore law and order; in 1972 Britain suspended the local Ulster government and imposed direct British rule exercised by administrator *William Whitelaw.* To date, Whitelaw has been unable to end the violence and to get the opposing groups to negotiate.

To the south, the Irish Republic began a crackdown on the IRA. The government argued that IRA terrorism was hindering the reunification of

Ireland by embittering relations between Catholics and Protestants in Ulster. Irish voters in 1972 strongly approved a referendum deleting from the Irish constitution the clause granting the Roman Catholic Church a "special position." Although this referendum did not remove Irish laws reflecting Catholic views on birth control, mixed marriages, and divorce, it was hailed by Irish spokesmen as a move for "peace and reconciliation."

Nevertheless, in a 1973 Ulster referendum, the Protestant majority voted overwhelmingly to remain with Britain, while the Catholic minority generally refrained from voting.

E. SOUTH AFRICA: FORMER COMMONWEALTH MEMBER

ECONOMY AND PEOPLE

South Africa is a prosperous country. Her farm and grazing lands provide corn, wheat, and wool. Her cities contain food processing, chemical, and iron and steel industries. Her mines, in addition to extracting coal and uranium, lead the world in gold and diamonds. (By dominating the diamond industry, one South African company—it is claimed—keeps world diamond prices high.) South Africa exports mineral and agricultural produce and imports manufactured goods. She trades extensively with England.

South Africa has a population of 22 million. (a) 18 percent is *European*, of Dutch and English origin. The Dutch, or *Afrikaners* (formerly called the *Boers*), outnumber the English. (b) 69 percent is *Black*, chiefly native Bantu tribes. (c) 9 percent is *Colored*, of mixed Negro and European ancestry. (d) 4 percent is *Asian*, of Indian origin.

BRIEF HISTORY

1. Boers Resent the English. In 1815 Holland ceded the Cape Colony to England. The Dutch settlers detested English rule, English abolition of Negro slavery, and English immigrants. In the 1830's the Boers left English territory in a northward mass migration, called the *Great Trek*. Eventually, they founded two republics: the *Orange Free State* and *Transvaal*. The discovery of Transvaal gold in the 1880's attracted English fortune-seekers. The Boers resented their coming and restricted their political rights.

2. Rhodes Incites the Boer War. In 1800 *Cecil Rhodes* the Kimberley (South Africa) diamond mine millionaire—became head of England's Cape Colony. Rhodes envisioned a British African Empire extending the full length of Africa from Capetown to Cairo. As a necessary step, Rhodes set out to annex the two Boer republics. In the Boer War (1899-1902) that followed, England, with considerable difficulty, defeated the resolute Dutch settlers and annexed their territories.

3. South Africa Becomes a Dominion and Supports England. In 1910 England combined her South African colonies into a self-governing dominion, the *Union of South Africa*. The Boers, who outnumbered the English settlers, assumed political control.

Louis Botha and *Jan Smuts,* former Boer generals, each of whom served as Prime Minister, urged their countrymen to uphold the dominion arrangement. During World War I Botha suppressed a Boer anti-British revolt and aligned his country with England. During World War II Smuts barely secured legislative approval for South Africa to join England against Nazi Germany. In the election of 1948, however, Smuts' *United party* (of English and loyal Dutch) lost control of the government.

4. South Africa Becomes a Republic and Leaves the Commonwealth. Since 1948 the Afrikaner (Dutch) *Nationalist party* has governed South Africa. The Nationalists secured a slim majority in 1960 authorizing South Africa to change from a dominion to a republic. At a Commonwealth Conference in 1961, South Africa's black segregation policy came under bitter attack from Asian, African, and Canadian members. Thereupon, Prime Minister *Hendrik Verwoerd* announced that his government would not remain in the Commonwealth. Later Verwoerd indicated that South Africa wished to maintain her historic friendship and economic ties with Britain.

In 1966 Verwoerd was succeeded as Prime Minister by *Balthazar Vorster.* As Minister of Justice, Police, and Prisons, he had enforced segregation.

CURRENT PROBLEMS

1. Racial Strife. South Africa has long followed a policy of discrimination against and segregation of nonwhites. Since 1948 the Nationalists have intensified their segregation, or apartness, program, called *apartheid.* City blacks are restricted to the lowest jobs, must carry identification passes, and must reside in designated sections. Rural blacks must occupy special tribal reserves. Blacks have no vote and no say in the national government.

By 1972 the Afrikaner government had granted limited self-rule to four rural areas (former tribal reserves) as black homelands or *Bantustans.* Fewer blacks, however, resided in the rural areas than in the cities.

Blacks and some whites have protested apartheid by riots, strikes, and violations of segregation laws. In turn, the government has imprisoned protest leaders and increased repressive measures.

2. International Censure. Because of her racial policies, South Africa faces the world almost alone. The other African nations, mostly black-led, have demanded full rights for South Africa's blacks. The Asian nations, especially India (concerned over the Indian population in South Africa), have protested South Africa's discriminatory practices. The Communist nations have denounced South Africa in their propaganda against the West. The free-world nations have condemned apartheid as morally wrong.

At the U.N., the African nations have secured resolutions that (a) censured the Afrikaner government for racial discrimination, (b) demanded U.N. supervision over South Africa's World War I mandate, South-West Africa (Namibia), (c) threatened to expel South Africa from the U.N., and (d) urged U.N. members to act against South Africa by severing diplomatic relations, imposing economic boycotts, and banning military shipments.

The South African government has (a) rejected U.N. control over South-West Africa (Namibia), (b) insisted that apartheid is a domestic issue over which the U.N. has no authority, and (c) argued that, in a multiracial country, the outnumbered whites would lose control to the black majority. South Africa stands almost alone but defiant.

F. COMMONWEALTH COLONIES

The Commonwealth also includes a number of British colonies. Each is headed by a Governor appointed by the British government. Some colonies control their internal affairs through locally elected legislatures.

The remaining British colonies, chiefly small military bases, include (1) in the Mediterranean—Gibraltar, (2) in Africa—rebellious Rhodesia, (3) in the Pacific—Hong Kong, (4) in the Caribbean—Bermuda, and (5) in Central America—British Honduras (Belize).

Former British colonies include (1) the independent republic of Burma, and (2) the Commonwealth members of Ceylon, Ghana, Nigeria, Cyprus, Sierra Leone, Jamaica, Trinidad-Tobago, Malta, Guyana, and Lesotho.

G. COMMONWEALTH PROTECTORATES

The Commonwealth's remaining protectorate is the Solomon Islands in the South Pacific.

Former British protectorates are (1) the independent nations of Egypt, Kuwait, and the People's Republic of Southern Yemen, and (2) the Commonwealth members of Malaya (part of Malaysia), Uganda, Malawi, Zambia, Botswana, and Swaziland.

H. COMMONWEALTH TRUSTEESHIPS

The Commonwealth's major remaining trust territory, administered by Australia, consists of part of the South Pacific island of New Guinea.

Former British mandates and trust territories are (1) Tanganyika, the major portion of the Commonwealth member Tanzania, and (2) the independent Middle East nations of Iraq, Jordan, and Israel. (For a discussion of these Middle East nations, see pages 299-305.)

Part 3. Other Empires

A. THE FRENCH EMPIRE

EXTENT PRIOR TO WORLD WAR II

As a colonial power, France before World War II ranked second only to England. In 1939 the French Empire included: (1) In Africa—Algeria, Tunisia, French Morocco, French West Africa, French Equatorial Africa, French Cameroon, French Togoland, French Somaliland, and Madagascar. (These African territories constituted the major portion of France's Empire.) (2) In the Middle East—Lebanon and Syria. (3) In the Far East—the Indo-Chinese states of Vietnam, Cambodia, and Laos. (4) In the Americas —French Guiana, and several small Caribbean and Atlantic islands. (5) In the Pacific—several groups of small islands.

The French Empire contained twenty times the area and twice the population of France.

TERRITORIAL LOSSES SINCE WORLD WAR II

Weakened by war and challenged by colonial nationalism, France granted independence to almost all her African, Middle Eastern, and Far Eastern possessions.

Today France retains only French Somaliland (renamed the Territory of the Afars and Issas), French Guiana, and some small islands, all of which are of relatively minor importance.

FRENCH COMMUNITY

By the 1958 Gaullist constitution, the Fifth Republic established the *French Community*. This organization, modeled after the British Commonwealth, serves to associate France with certain former possessions, now independent republics. Community members (1) exercise complete self-government, (2) follow common economic and defense policies, and consult regarding foreign affairs, and (3) retain the right to withdraw from the Community.

In 1960 twelve African nations, formed from the French territories of West Africa, Equatorial Africa, and Madagascar, received independence within the French Community. Today, only six remain members of the French Community—Central Africa, Chad, Congo (capital, Brazzaville), Gabon, Malagasy, and Senegal.

B. EMPIRES OF OTHER WEST EUROPEAN NATIONS

VANISHED EMPIRES

West European nations that earlier had acquired and subsequently gave up control over major colonial territories are Belgium, Germany, and Italy in Africa (see page **287**), and the Netherlands in the East Indies (see page **322**).

REMAINING EMPIRES

West European nations that acquired and still retain colonial territories in Africa are Spain and Portugal (see page **291**).

C. THE UNITED STATES EMPIRE

IMPETUS TOWARD IMPERIALISM

The United States embarked upon overseas imperialism following (1) the rapid expansion of American industry after the Civil War (1861-1865), and (2) the disappearance of cheap land with the close of the frontier (about 1900). Americans looked abroad for new markets, sources of raw materials, and opportunities for capital investment. Also, some Americans held that the United States needed foreign possessions (1) to be considered a first-class power, and (2) for strategic military reasons.

With victory in the Spanish-American War (1898), the United States emerged as an imperialist power.

AMERICAN COLONIAL POSSESSIONS: FROM ACQUISITION TO PRESENT STATUS

The United States, recalling her own colonial history, has followed an enlightened policy toward her possessions. The United States has improved economic conditions, provided health and educational facilities, and generally trained dependent peoples for self-government.

AMERICAN TERRITORIAL ACQUISITIONS AND PRESENT STATUS

Possessions	How Acquired	Present Status
Alaska	Purchased from Russia (1867).	State since 1959.
Hawaii	Annexed at request of American settlers (1898).	State since 1959.
Philippines	Ceded by Spain (1898).	Independent since 1946. Remains an ally of the United States.
Puerto Rico	Ceded by Spain (1898).	Commonwealth since 1952. Remains freely associated with the United States and exercises complete local self-government.
Guam	Ceded by Spain (1898).	Colony. Serves as a military base in central Pacific.
Some Samoan Islands	Annexed (1899).	Colonies. Serve as military bases in the Pacific.
Panama Canal Zone	Leased in perpetuity by treaty with Panama (1904).	Leased territory. Contains Panama Canal and defense installations.
Virgin Islands	Purchased from Denmark (1917).	Colonies. Serve as military bases to protect Panama Canal.
Many West Pacific Islands	Transferred from Japanese control by U.N. Security Council (1947).	Trusteeship. May be fortified for defense purposes.

D. THE SOVIET RUSSIAN EMPIRE: COMMUNIST IMPERIALISM

Since World War II the powerful, industrialized Soviet Union has extended her control over non-Russian peoples by (1) annexing territories on her borders, especially the small Baltic nations of Estonia, Latvia, and Lithuania, and (2) dominating a group of east and central European Communist nations—Bulgaria, Czechoslovakia, East Germany, Hungary, Poland, and Rumania—as protectorates, or *satellites.* The supposedly independent governments of these satellites have almost slavishly accepted Russian leadership in their domestic and foreign affairs (see pages 416-418). However, since the 1963 Chinese-Russian split destroyed world Communist unity (see pages 420-421), certain satellite nations have acted more independently of Moscow.

Also, the Russians seek to extend their influence into the newly independent Afro-Asian nations by supporting colonial nationalists against the West and by offering technical and economic aid. To thwart Russian expansion into the underdeveloped nations, the free world, led by the United States, (1) offers economic and military assistance, and (2) attempts to convince these nations not to exchange their newly won independence for Russian imperialist control.

MULTIPLE-CHOICE QUESTIONS

1. The *least* significant factor in bringing about colonial expansion in the 19th century was (1) religious persecution (2) the growth of manufacturing (3) improved transportation and communication (4) accumulation of surplus capital.
2. Regions that imperialists desire usually have (1) highly developed industries (2) great natural beauty (3) few inhabitants (4) undeveloped resources.
3. A territory nominally independent but really controlled by a foreign government is called a (1) dominion (2) protectorate (3) concession (4) colony.
4. The mandate system for international supervision of colonies originated with the (1) League of Nations (2) United Nations (3) Third International (4) Commonwealth of Nations.
5. A phrase used by Kipling to describe British imperialism is (1) "spread culture" (2) "long live the Queen" (3) "white man's burden" (4) "a place in the sun."
6. In the British Empire self-government was first extended to (1) crown colonies (2) dominions (3) mandated territories (4) naval bases.
7. Which legally established the Commonwealth of Nations? (1) the Reform Bill of 1832 (2) the Glorious Revolution (3) the Statute of Westminster (4) the Durham Report.
8. The Statute of Westminster (1931) provided for (1) abolition of slavery in colonial areas (2) land reform in Ireland (3) religious freedom in Canada (4) political equality for the dominions with the mother country.
9. Which phrase best describes the Commonwealth of Nations today? (1) an English-speaking union (2) a voluntary union of independent states (3) a confederation with equal representation in the British Parliament (4) an alliance for military self-defense.
10. The ties between the old dominions and the mother country have been strengthened by (1) heavy English migration to the old dominions since World War II (2) mutual cancellation of war debts (3) royal power to appoint old dominion cabinet officials (4) mutual trade agreements and preferences.
11. Which marked a step in the growth of self-government within the British Empire? (1) the policy of apartheid in South Africa (2) the Colombo Plan (3) the British North America Act of 1867 (4) the Parliament Act of 1911.
12. One limiting factor in the economic development of Canada is insufficient (1) mineral resources (2) exportable products (3) available foreign capital (4) population.
13. Reflecting friction between the two major population groups in Canada, the French Canadians demand (1) apartheid for Negroes (2) less industrial development in Canada (3) more power for provincial governments (4) land reform to drive out absentee English landlords.
14. The DEW line is maintained by the United States and Canada to (1) divide fishing and sealing areas between the two countries (2) gather weather data (3) provide warning against plane and missile attack across the North Pole region (4) alert North Atlantic ships to icebergs.

15. Because it first originated in that country, the secret ballot is also known as the (1) Australian (2) English (3) Irish (4) South African ballot.

16. During the 1840's many Irish migrated to the United States because (1) America lifted her immigration restrictions (2) England suppressed an Irish rebellion for independence (3) Ireland gained home rule (4) Irish farms had a series of crop failures.

17. The 19th-century English statesman who made many attempts to solve the Irish question was (1) Disraeli (2) Gladstone (3) Wellington (4) de Valera.

18. The province in northern Ireland that voted to remain under English rule was (1) Ulster (2) Eire (3) Sinn Fein (4) Kuwait.

19. Cecil Rhodes, a famous British imperialist, helped to establish England's control of (1) India (2) Egypt (3) South Africa (4) Australia.

20. South Africans of Dutch ancestry are today called (1) Trekkers (2) Afrikaners (3) Bantus (4) Rhodesians.

21. The South African Prime Minister who took his country out of the British Commonwealth in 1961 was (1) Jan Smuts (2) Paul Kruger (3) Louis Botha (4) Hendrik Verwoerd.

22. The policy of apartheid in the Union of South Africa was (1) imposed by the British after the Boer War (2) advocated by the Afrikaner Nationalist party (3) proposed by the Bantu (4) introduced by the Communists.

23. The apartheid program in South Africa calls for separation of (1) Negroes from whites (2) English from Dutch (3) farming from grazing (4) powers between the central and provincial governments.

24. After World War I Tanganyika and Palestine were made mandates of (1) France (2) Belgium (3) the United States (4) Great Britain.

25. The major portion of France's Empire before World War II was in (1) Africa (2) Asia (3) North America (4) South America.

26. Member nations in the French Community may *not* (1) join the United Nations (2) vote for the President of France (3) exercise complete self-government (4) deny equal rights to Negroes.

27. The United States emerged as an imperialist power following (1) the Civil War (2) the Spanish-American War (3) World War I (4) World War II.

28. A former American colony that has become an independent nation is (1) Puerto Rico (2) Alaska (3) Panama (4) the Philippines.

29. An aspect of Communist Russian imperialism is (1) acquiring colonies in Africa (2) sending Soviet artists to perform in the United States (3) suppressing free speech in Soviet Russia (4) acquiring satellites in eastern and central Europe.

MULTIPLE-CHOICE QUESTIONS

Select the number of the item that does *not* belong in the corresponding group.

1. *Economic causes of imperialism in the 19th century:* (1) the need for raw materials (2) the need for markets for the products of industry (3) the desire for places to invest surplus capital (4) the desire for socialized industry.

2. *Parts of the United Kingdom:* (1) Scotland (2) Wales (3) Ulster (4) Australia.

3. *Nations granted dominion status before World War I:* (1) Australia (2) New Zealand (3) India (4) Canada.

4. *Reasons for Canada's participation in World War II:* (1) the economic importance of a United Nations victory (2) her legal obligation to join England in the war (3) her loyalty to the British Crown (4) threats to vital Canadian interests.

5. *Important exports of the Republic of South Africa:* (1) gold (2) diamonds (3) wool (4) farm machinery.

6. *Similarities between Australia and New Zealand:* Both (1) are loyal to the Commonwealth (2) have experimented with economic and political reforms (3) are not on the continent of Asia (4) are approximately equal in area.

7. *Lands in the Pacific Ocean:* (1) the Bahamas (2) Malaysia (3) Australia (4) New Zealand.

8. *British Commonwealth members:* (1) Nigeria (2) Ceylon (3) Ireland (4) Ghana.

Part 4. Africa

AFRICA: LAND AND PEOPLE

1. Geography. Africa is a huge continent, three times as large as Europe. Africa's Mediterranean and Atlantic coasts had for centuries been accessible to European ships. However, until the late 19th century, her inhospitable interior—desert, mountain, and jungle—discouraged exploration and remained unknown to the outside world. Hence, Africa was called the *Dark Continent.*

2. Resources. Africa's wealth consists of (*a*) minerals: gold, diamonds, copper, bauxite, oil, uranium, and (*b*) agricultural produce: rubber, cotton, tropical woods, palm oil, cacao.

3. Population. Africa contains (*a*) in her cooler regions—the Mediterranean coast, extreme south, and interior plateaus—5 million persons of European descent, (*b*) along her northern coast, 80 million Moslems of Arab, Berber, and Egyptian stock, and (*c*) from the Sahara Desert southward, over 260 million blacks.

OLD IMPERIALISM IN AFRICA

From the 16th through the 18th centuries Europeans looked to Africa (1) for supply bases for their ships sailing to the Far East and (2) for Negro slaves. In the early 19th century, however, Europeans lost interest in imperialism (see page 267). Interest in Africa declined for two main reasons: (1) with the advent of the steamship, the need for African bases lessened, and (2) the profitable slave trade was prohibited.

MODERN IMPERIALISM: INTEREST IN AFRICA (SINCE MID-19TH CENTURY)

1. Work of Explorers. *David Livingstone,* Scottish missionary and doctor, spent many years (1840-1873) serving the natives and exploring the lands of central Africa. *Henry M. Stanley,* American newspaper reporter, headed an expedition in 1871 that "found" the presumably "lost" Livingstone. Later, Stanley undertook additional explorations. In well-publicized reports, these two men, as well as other explorers, described the geography, resources, and people of Africa.

2. Other Groups Interested in Africa. The glowing reports of explorers reawakened Europe's interest in Africa. Businessmen saw great economic opportunities. Missionaries wanted to convert the Negroes to Christianity. Nationalists dreamed of empire-building unopposed by the primitive Africans.

EUROPEAN NATIONS PARTITION AFRICA

1. England

a. To Protect Trade Routes to the East. In 1815 England acquired the *Cape Colony,* including Capetown, a port at the southern tip of Africa. In 1875 Prime Minister *Disraeli* purchased control of the *Suez Canal* from the bankrupt ruler of Egypt. By sailing through the Canal, English ships eliminated the long voyage around Africa. In 1882 England established a protectorate over Egypt. England's trade route to India—via Gibraltar, the Mediterranean Sea, the Suez Canal, and the Red Sea—became known as the *lifeline of the British Empire.*

b. To Gain a Rich Empire. *Cecil Rhodes,* foremost empire-builder in Africa, dreamed of an unbroken north-south line of British territory to be linked by a *Cape-to-Cairo* railway. Rhodes' ambition became British policy. By 1914 the British dominated South Africa, Rhodesia, Kenya,

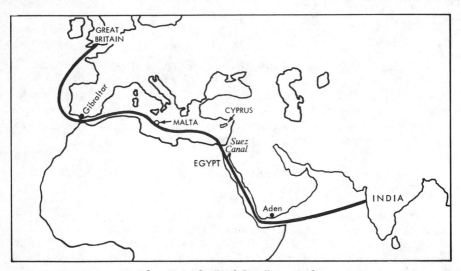

The British "Lifeline" to India

Uganda, and the Sudan, as well as Egypt. After World War I, England acquired the final link for the railroad, the former German East Africa, or Tanganyika.

Also, by the beginning of the 20th century, British control was firmly established in Sierra Leone, the Gold Coast, and Nigeria—all on the west coast of Africa.

2. France. For economic gain and nationalist glory, the French acquired a considerable African domain. By 1847 the French had subdued the Moslem tribesmen and controlled Algeria. Between 1881 and 1912 France added Tunisia, Morocco, West Africa, Equatorial Africa, and Madagascar to the French Empire.

French expansion clashed with the aims of other imperialist nations. (*a*) Italy resented French seizure of Tunisia (1881) and allied herself with Germany. (See Triple Alliance, page 335.) (*b*) Britain took over the Sudan (1898), and France surrendered her claims in order to win England's friendship. (See Fashoda Affair, page 335.) (*c*) Germany challenged France over Morocco (1906, 1911), but France retained control. (See Crises Preceding World War I, page 336.)

3. Germany. Late unification delayed Germany's imperialist ventures. Nevertheless, by 1914 Germany possessed several African colonies. But after Germany's defeat in World War I, these colonies were distributed as mandates: Tanganyika to England; Togoland and most of the Cameroons to France; South-West Africa to the Union of South Africa.

4. Italy. Another late starter was Italy. By 1914 she controlled Eritrea, Italian Somaliland, and Libya. In 1936 Italy conquered and annexed Ethiopia. Defeated in World War II, Italy surrendered her African possessions. However, until 1960, Italy retained Italian Somaliland as a trust territory.

5. Portugal. As a 16th-century maritime power, Portugal early established supply bases and trading posts on the east and west coasts of Africa. Portugal retains control over the African territories of Portuguese Guinea, Angola, and Mozambique.

6. Spain. By the early 20th century Spain controlled Spanish Morocco, opposite Gibraltar, and Spanish Sahara on the Atlantic coast of Africa. In 1956, when France granted independence to Morocco, Spain ceded Spanish Morocco to the new nation.

7. Belgium. In 1876 King *Leopold II* and a group of Belgian capitalists founded a private company to explore and manage the Congo region. The company reaped huge profits from rubber and ivory but shockingly mistreated the natives. In 1908 the Belgian government took control of the Congo.

AFRICANS OPPOSE IMPERIALISM: REASONS

The native Africans felt that any benefits of imperialism—industries, jobs, public works, improved health—were vastly outweighed by its evils.

1. Economic. (a) The Europeans seized the fertile lands and the rich mineral resources. Often, they tricked the natives. (b) The Africans worked long hours for low wages and lived in unbelievable poverty. (c) The continent's wealth benefited the foreign investors, not the natives.

2. Social. The natives were considered inferior, subjected to humiliating discrimination, and denied educational opportunities.

3. Political. The Africans received little training for self-government, their countries remained under European rule, and their nationalist demands for self-government went unheeded.

AWAKENING AFRICAN NATIONALISM

Emerging after World War I, colonial nationalism swept Africa and, especially after World War II, became a powerful anti-imperialist force. By agitating for political independence, social equality, and economic betterment, African nationalists reflected the impact of world forces.

1. Western Influences. Africans became aware of Western ideals as expressed in the American Declaration of Independence, which upheld human dignity and freedom, and the French Revolution, which inspired democracy and nationalism. They also learned of the improved living conditions that resulted from industrialization, labor unions, and government regulation. This knowledge came to Africa through colonial and missionary schools, printed materials, radio programs, movies, contacts with Europeans, and the few African leaders educated in European and American schools.

2. Communist Propaganda. Communists told Africans that they could achieve a brighter future if they drove out the imperialists. Then the Africans could utilize their natural wealth for their own betterment. Such propaganda stimulated African nationalists, most of whom were not Communists.

3. Effects of World War II. World War II sapped the military and economic strength of the major African colonial powers: Belgium, France, and Britain. They became more inclined to yield to African nationalist demands.

4. Newly Independent Asian Nations. Following World War II Africans became hopeful that they too would achieve independence when they saw one Asian nation after another free itself from European control.

5. United Nations. Africans were led to expect rapid improvements in their political status when the United Nations proclaimed the right of all peoples to self-determination, declared independence the objective of trusteeships, and provided an international forum to discuss grievances.

6. Changing World Attitude. Especially after 1945, the world came to realize the evils of imperialism and the justice of many African demands.

AFRICA TODAY

INDEPENDENT AFRICAN NATIONS IN 1945

Liberia, a Negro republic, was founded in 1822 by the United States as a haven for freed slaves. Liberia remains friendly toward the United States.

Ethiopia fell in 1936 to an invading Italian army. But with Italy's defeat in World War II, Ethiopia regained independence. A kingdom, Ethiopia is ruled by a pro-Western Emperor, *Haile Selassie.*

South Africa, granted self-government by Britain in 1910, later became an independent white-ruled republic and discriminates against her large Negro majority. (For a discussion of South Africa, see pages **277-279**.)

Egypt in 1922 ended the British protectorate and gained independence. (For a full discussion of Egypt, see page 299).

AFRICAN NATIONS GAINING INDEPENDENCE SINCE 1945

Former Colonial Power	African Nations
Great Britain	1. Outside the British Commonwealth: Sudan 2. Within the British Commonwealth: Botswana, Gambia, Ghana, Kenya, Lesotho, Malawi, Nigeria, Sierra Leone, Swaziland, Tanzania, Uganda, Zambia

France	1. Outside the French Community
	    a. In North Africa: Algeria, Morocco, Tunisia
	    b. In West and Equatorial Africa: Cameroon, Dahomey, Guinea, Ivory Coast, Mali, Mauritania, Niger, Togo, Upper Volta
	2. Within the French Community: Central Africa, Chad, Congo (capital, Brazzaville), Gabon, Malagasy, Senegal

Italy	Libya, Somalia (a union of Italian and British Somaliland)
Belgium	Congo (capital, Kinshasa), Rwanda, Burundi

REMAINING AREAS OF EUROPEAN CONTROL IN AFRICA

French Somaliland (Territory of the Afars and Issas), on the east African coast, is administered by a French governor assisted by a locally elected

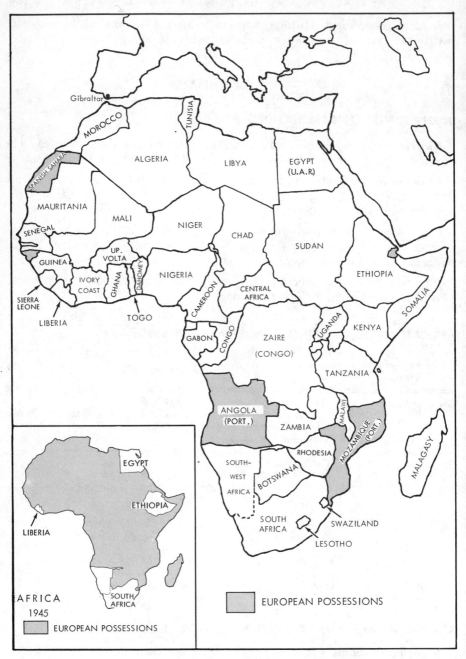

Africa Today

assembly. The Somalis, one-third of the population, favor union with Somalia; the other natives probably want to remain with France.

Spanish Sahara is administered by a governor appointed from Madrid. This territory is claimed by Mauritania and Morocco.

Angola, Mozambique, and **Portuguese Guinea** remain under strict Portuguese control, and Portugal insists upon retaining these overseas possessions. In 1961 Angolan nationalists staged a rebellion against Portuguese authority but were suppressed. However, guerrilla fighting continues.

RHODESIA: STATUS IN DISPUTE

Rhodesia has fertile soil and rich mineral resources, especially chromium. Its population is over 5 million, of whom about 5 percent are Europeans.

Until 1965 Rhodesia exercised local self-government under a white-minority regime. Her black African (mainly Bantu) population was disenfranchised. The Rhodesian government rejected England's proposal to move rapidly toward majority (meaning black) rule. In 1965 Rhodesian Prime Minister *Ian Smith,* counting upon support from Portugal and South Africa, unilaterally declared his country independent:

The British government labeled the breakaway regime as "illegal" and applied economic sanctions: suspending preferential tariffs, banning purchases of Rhodesia's sugar and tobacco, and embargoing vital oil shipments. The British expected Rhodesia to collapse economically and overthrow the Smith regime. The British government, however, rejected the demands of African nations that England crush the rebellion by force.

In 1966 Britain secured a U.N. resolution asking all members to apply sanctions against Rhodesia (see page 406). British pressure, international censure, economic sanctions, and guerrilla attacks by African nationalists all have failed to change the policies of the white-dominated regime. In 1973 Rhodesia announced that fines would be imposed, without court hearings, on native communities suspected of assisting African nationalists.

CASE STUDIES OF SELECTED AFRICAN STATES

GHANA (FORMER BRITISH COLONY OF GOLD COAST)

1. People. The people are blacks, divided into many tribes and speaking some 50 different tribal languages and dialects. Ghana's official language, however, is English.

2. Road to Independence. After many demonstrations, Ghana received independence in 1957 and became the first black nation in the Commonwealth.

3. Government. *Kwame Nkrumah,* Ghana's independence leader, headed the new government. He established a personal dictatorship, suppressed opposition, mismanaged the economy, and followed a pro-Communist foreign policy. Nkrumah was overthrown in 1966 by army leaders, who thereafter improved the economy and followed a foreign policy of neutrality. In 1969 the military returned the country to civilian rule but in 1972 they charged the civilian regime with "mismanagement" and again imposed military rule.

4. Economy. The people are engaged mainly in agriculture and also in forestry and mining. Ghana is the world's leading producer of cacao; she also exports hardwoods and minerals. She imports chiefly manufactured goods. Her chief trade partners are Britain and the United States. Ghana attracted Western capital to build a hydroelectric power plant on the Volta River and an aluminum industry.

ZAIRE (FORMER BELGIUM COLONY OF THE CONGO)

1. People. The Zairians (Congolese) are blacks divided among some 200 tribes. Few whites remain in the country. Most Zairians speak their tribal tongues, but the country's official language is French.

2. Road to Independence. After anti-Belgian riots by the Congolese people, the Congo in 1960 received independence from Belgium.

3. Government. Ill-prepared for self-government, the new republic faced army mutinies, tribal conflicts, secession by mineral-rich Katanga province, and involvement in the cold war (see page 405). Slowly and painfully, the Congo resolved these problems and established an anti-Communist central government. In 1965 General *Joseph Mobutu,* a Congo nationalist and anti-Communist, seized control and established a stable military regime. In 1971 Mobutu renamed the country Zaire and ordered the replacement of European by African names for cities, geographic features, and families. Joseph Mobutu became *Mobutu Sese Seko.*

4. Economy. The Congo's economy consists of (*a*) agriculture, which employs most of the people, many as subsistence farmers, (*b*) mining, and (*c*) light industry. Rich in mineral resources, the Congo exports chiefly copper, tin, industrial diamonds, cobalt, and uranium, but also some coffee and palm oil. She imports foodstuffs and manufactured goods. Her chief trading partners are free world nations: Belgium, Britain, and other Common Market members, and the United States. The Congo nationalized the properties of several Belgian companies, but nevertheless attracted loans and investment capital from many Western countries. Near the capital city *Kinshasa* (formerly Leopoldville), two American automobile companies are constructing motor vehicle plants.

NIGERIA (FORMER BRITISH COLONY AND PROTECTORATE)

1. People. The most populous African state, Nigeria contains many small tribes and three major ones; the Hausa, the Yoruba, and the Ibo. English is the official language, but the people speak some 250 tribal dialects.

2. Road to Independence. In a peaceful transition, Nigeria in 1960 gained independence and Commonwealth membership.

3. Government. Nigeria adopted a British-type parliamentary democracy. The government, however, was torn by tribal rivalries for control. In 1966 two army coups led to a military regime under a Hausa tribesman, *Yakubu Gowon*. Fearful of this military regime and of massacres throughout the country, the Ibo tribe, concentrated in Nigeria's eastern region, announced in 1967 its secession to form the republic of *Biafra*. The central government moved to suppress this secession, and Nigeria experienced almost three years of civil war. The central government received military equipment from Britain and Russia, while Biafra received arms from France and Portugal. In 1970, after many thousands of deaths in battle and from mass starvation in Biafra, the central government won. General Gowon's regime then faced problems of providing relief for destitute Biafrans, restoring the country's economy, and instilling a sense of nationhood.

4. Economy. The people are overwhelmingly engaged in agriculture, and also in forestry and fishing. The country contains valuable oil deposits, which are being developed by British and American companies. Nigeria exports crude oil, cacao, and peanuts; she imports manufactured goods. Her chief trading partners are Britain, the United States, and other free world nations. Since 1972, the government has moved to "Nigerianize" the oil industry, retail trade, and banks.

ALGERIA (FORMER FRENCH POSSESSION)

1. People. The people are overwhelmingly Arab, with a small percentage of Berbers. Of the 1 million French settlers in Algeria before independence, fewer than 10 percent remain.

2. Road to Independence. After nine years of guerrilla warfare, Algeria in 1962 received independence from France under de Gaulle (see page 194). Algeria was to receive French technical, cultural, and financial aid, and to permit joint French-Algerian development of the Saharan oil fields.

3. Government. Algeria immediately became a one-party state under military rule and moved toward socialism by nationalizing factories, mines, and large farms, many being French-owned. Algeria equipped her army with French and Soviet weapons and followed a pro-Communist foreign policy. In 1965 an army coup placed Algeria under the rule of a leftist Revolutionary Council headed by Colonel *Houari Boumedienne*.

4. Economy. Most Algerians are engaged in agriculture; some work in fishing, mining, and extracting oil. Algeria exports crude oil, wine, and citrus fruit; she imports foodstuffs and consumer goods. Her trade is mainly with France, but it is being oriented toward the Soviet Union by government trade pacts. In 1971 Algeria nationalized French-owned oil companies.

KENYA (FORMER BRITISH COLONY AND PROTECTORATE)

1. People. Blacks of some 40 different tribes constitute 95 percent of the people; the rest are Arabs, Indians from Asia, and British. In 1970 English was replaced as the official language by Swahili, one of many native tongues.

2. Road to Independence. In the 1950's Kenya experienced terrorism against white farmers by a secret native group, the *Mau Mau Society*. Britain restored order, began training the blacks in self-government, and in 1963 granted Kenya independence and Commonwealth membership.

3. Government. Beginning with a democratic government, Kenya chose as her first President the former Mau Mau leader, *Jomo Kenyatta*. He belonged to Kenya's largest tribe, the Kikuyu. Aware of Kenya's many races and tribes, Kenyatta advocated "Harambee," a Swahili word meaning "Let us all work together." Although torn by tribal rivalries for control, the government remained stable. In 1969 the government outlawed the major opposition party, allegedly for "subversive activities," leaving Kenya essentially with one party, the Kikuyu-dominated Kenya African National Union (KANU).

4. Economy. Although most Kenyans work in agriculture, the country also has food processing and consumer goods industries. Kenya attracts tourists to enjoy her mountains, parks, and wild game preserves. Kenya exports coffee and tea; she imports manufactured goods. Kenya's chief trading partners, which also provide her with investment capital, are Great Britain and West Germany. In 1968 Kenya moved to "Africanize" the retail trade, causing many Kenya-born Indian merchants to leave, mainly for Britain.

(Kenya's example was followed in 1972 by Uganda. President Amin expelled 55,000 Uganda-born Asians—chiefly merchants and professionals—who had retained their British passports when Uganda received independence.)

PROBLEMS BESETTING THE INDEPENDENT AFRICAN NATIONS

1. Developing National Unity. African nationalism has been largely negative—that is, it has been based more on hostility toward imperialists than on a sense of nationhood. The boundaries of most African colonies were determined by imperialist considerations rather than by related population groups. Since the new nations are based on the old colonies, most African states consist of many distinct tribes. Some of these tribes have long histories of tribal distrust and conflict, and speak a multitude of different dialects

Palmer in The Springfield (Mo.) Leader and Press

"That's strange . . . it looks easy."

and languages, some totally unrelated. African peoples face a difficult transition from primitive tribal loyalties to 20th-century nationalism.

2. Securing Professional Personnel. Europeans had provided most professional skills in Africa. Few native Africans had training as educators, doctors, scientists, engineers, and civil servants. Many skilled Europeans, fearing for their future, left Africa, especially the Congo and Algeria. Africa's shortage of professional people handicaps efforts to wipe out illiteracy, raise health standards, further industry, and provide efficient government.

3. Maintaining Popular Government. The African people lack democratic tradition and experience in running a government. Most African peoples received no political training before independence. Many African leaders are sincere and hardworking but inexpert.

In Egypt, Algeria, and many Negro nations, the people have acquiesced in army rule and one-party governments, essentially dictatorships.

4. Improving Living Standards. Most Africans live in poverty. Farmers produce scanty crops; many city workers are unemployed. African nations seek to improve agricultural methods and diversify their crops. Also, they seek to develop their mineral resources and establish industries.

Lacking capital for development, African nations need foreign aid. They have received some aid from foreign governments, mainly from the Soviet Union and the United States. However, private investors are deterred by threats of political instability, unfair taxation, and nationalization.

Independent Africa has made some economic progress, but living standards have been kept low by the continent's population explosion.

5. Determining a Foreign Policy. African nations oppose colonialism, seek to end the remaining European holdings in Africa, and resent white-dominated South Africa and Rhodesia. Toward the cold war, most African nations proclaim a policy of neutrality. In the U.N., they often vote with the new Asian states and constitute an influential Afro-Asian neutralist bloc.

Despite official neutrality, the African states have at times revealed their sympathies in the cold war. Whereas Guinea, Algeria, and Egypt have leaned toward the Communist bloc, the greater number of African states generally have adhered to pro-Western policies.

6. Seeking African Unity. In 1963 the independent African states (with the chief exception of white-dominated South Africa) met at Addis Ababa, Ethiopia, to further African unity. President Nkrumah of Ghana urged a strong union similar to that of the United States. He argued that, since no single African state is powerful enough to stand by itself economically and militarily, Africa must unite or perish. Emperor Haile Selassie of Ethiopia pointed to the vast differences—linguistic, racial, economic, and political—among the African nations and recommended a loose organization. Haile Selassie's views prevailed.

The independent African states formed the *Organization of African Unity* (*OAU*). They adopted a charter that called for the following:

a. A loose confederation. The major agencies of the OAU are (1) a Council of Ministers to meet every six months, (2) a Secretariat, or civil service, and (3) a Commission on Mediation and Conciliation to settle inter-African disputes peacefully. OAU headquarters are at Addis Ababa.

b. Far-reaching African cooperation in foreign policy, economics, education, and defense.

c. The liberation of all African territories still under foreign rule and the extension of full rights to Negroes in white-dominated lands. These provisions were directed particularly against Portugal and South Africa.

By creating the OAU, the African nations have indicated their understanding that, for them, independence from colonialism is only the beginning.

MULTIPLE-CHOICE QUESTIONS

1. In comparison with the size of Europe, the size of Africa is (1) less (2) about the same (3) slightly greater (4) much greater.
2. In addition to spreading Christianity, missionaries in Africa (1) headed white armies of conquest (2) provided capital for business ventures (3) maintained health clinics and schools (4) established the Organization of African Unity.
3. French expansion in Africa between 1875 and 1914 did *not* conflict with the ambitions of (1) Italy (2) Portugal (3) Germany (4) England.
4. The country that secured the largest part of Africa during its partition was (1) Great Britain (2) Italy (3) Germany (4) Spain.

5. Which nation was the *last* to establish a colonial empire in Africa? (1) Germany (2) England (3) France (4) Portugal.
6. Since World War II, European control in Africa has been opposed by the growth of colonial (1) nationalism (2) imperialism (3) laissez-faire (4) industrialization.
7. Colonial nationalism in Africa was (1) in part influenced by the American Declaration of Independence (2) a plot for Communist seizure of the continent (3) very different from nationalism in India (4) in favor of agriculture over industry.
8. Which two African countries were independent before World War II? (1) Egypt and Liberia (2) Algeria and Morocco (3) Libya and Sudan (4) Kenya and Guinea.
9. Which nation was conquered by Italy in 1936 and regained its independence after World War II? (1) Egypt (2) Ethiopia (3) Libya (4) Liberia.
10. Which former British colony, granted independence in 1960, has the largest native population in Africa? (1) Ghana (2) Uganda (3) Somalia (4) Nigeria.
11. Which African country gained its independence from France in 1962 following a drawn-out rebellion? (1) Tunisia (2) Algeria (3) Malagasy (4) Morocco.
12. Which of the following is still dominated by white settlers? (1) Kenya (2) Rhodesia (3) Ethiopia (4) Gabon.
13. Which problem is common to emerging nations in Africa? (1) exhaustion of natural resources (2) United Nations interference in internal affairs (3) continuing oppression by European powers (4) insufficient technically trained people.
14. The new African nations have been concerned with the continued colonial holdings in Africa of (1) Portugal (2) France (3) the United States (4) England.
15. The Organization of African Unity (OAU) is a (1) tariff union similar to the Common Market (2) loose confederation of most independent African states (3) military alliance of Africa's Negro nations (4) political union of Africa's Arab states.

TRUE-FALSE QUESTIONS

If the statement is correct, write the word *true*. If the statement is incorrect, substitute a word or phrase for the italicized term to make the statement correct.

1. The famous Scottish missionary who explored central Africa was *Henry M. Stanley*.
2. To strengthen her control over the Suez Canal, Britain established a protectorate over *Egypt*.
3. The Mau Mau Society employed terrorism against white settlers in *the Sudan*.
4. In north Africa, from Libya to Morocco, live large numbers of *Moslems*.
5. A former Italian colony in north Africa, now an independent nation, is *Libya*.
6. Zaire, rich in uranium and copper, was formerly under the control of *Portugal*.
7. Liberia, a republic in Africa, was founded by *Russia* as a haven for former slaves.

IDENTIFICATION QUESTIONS: WHO AM I?

Boumedienne	Haile Selassie	Nasser
Bourguiba	Kenyatta	Nkrumah
Gowon	Mobutu	Smith

1. I regained my throne as Emperor of Ethiopia with Italy's defeat in World War II. At the 1963 Addis Ababa meeting I urged a loose confederation of African states.
2. I led Ghana to independence and became her first President. In 1966 I was overthrown by an army coup protesting my one-man rule and pro-Communist policies.
3. In 1965 I led an army coup and seized control of Algeria. I continued the policies of my predecessor.
4. A former Mau Mau leader, I became the first President of my country after it gained independence. I urged the white settlers to remain and help build the nation.
5. To maintain white rule, I defied Britain and in 1965 declared Rhodesia independent.

Part 5. The Middle East

MIDDLE EAST: LOCATION AND IMPORTANCE

The Middle East consists of northeastern Africa and southwestern Asia (see map, page 299).

The importance of the Middle East lies in its (1) *vital waterways*—the Suez Canal and the Dardanelles, (2) *valuable oil resources*—in Saudi Arabia, Kuwait, Iraq, and Iran, and (3) *strategic location*—at the crossroads of Europe, Asia, and Africa, and on the southern flank of Russia.

IMPERIALISM IN THE MIDDLE EAST

1. England

a. To Secure Her "Lifeline" to the Far East. In the late 19th century England purchased controlling interest in the Suez Canal, established a protectorate over Egypt, and acquired the militarily valuable island of Cyprus.

b. To Restrain Other Powers. By the Crimean War (1853-1856) and the Congress of Berlin in 1878, England kept Russia out of the eastern Mediterranean and prevented her from seizing the Turkish-controlled Dardanelles. By World War I England removed German influence from the Middle East.

c. To Acquire Oil Resources. By 1914 English companies had obtained oil concessions in Iraq (then part of the Turkish Empire), Kuwait, and Persia (now Iran). During World War I England encouraged revolt among Turkey's subject Arabs. After the war, England received mandates over the former Turkish territories of oil-rich Iraq and strategically located Palestine.

2. Russia. Under both Czarist and Communist rule, Russia has sought to extend her influence into the Middle East. Before World War I Czarist Russia helped dismember the Turkish Empire and gain independence for several Balkan states, which are close to the Middle East. Since World War II the Soviet Union has dominated her Balkan satellites of Rumania and Bulgaria. Also, the Soviet Union exerts considerable influence in Egypt.

3. Germany. For investments, trade, and nationalist glory, German imperialists were attracted to the Turkish Empire. In 1899 German bankers secured Turkey's consent to complete the *Berlin-to-Bagdad* railroad. Because this railroad would enable German manufacturers to compete in Asian markets, it aroused English opposition. Germany's defeat in World War I temporarily ended her Middle East ambitions.

4. France. France in 1920 secured mandates over the former Turkish territories of Lebanon and Syria.

MIDDLE EAST OPPOSES IMPERIALISM

1. Decline of British Power

a. Egypt demonstrated against England and in 1922 gained independence. The Suez Canal remained under English control. In 1954 Egypt became a military dictatorship under *Gamal Abdel Nasser.* In 1956 Nasser defied England (and France) by nationalizing the Suez Canal. An Arab nationalist, Nasser sought to end British and French influence in the Arab world.

b. Iraq in 1932 ended the British mandate. As an independent state, Iraq experienced several revolutions. In 1968 the leftist Baath party seized control. This regime has been anti-Western, especially anti-American. In 1972 it nationalized the major Western-owned oil company in Iraq. It has

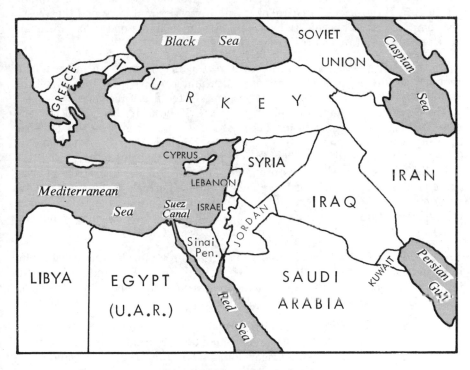

The Middle East Today

been friendly to the Communist bloc, accepting Communist loans, granting Russia oil exploration rights, and in 1972 signing a treaty of friendship and military aid with the Soviet Union.

   c. Jordan in 1946 became an independent Arab state. With the creation of Israel in 1948, Jordan annexed the Arab Palestinian territory west of the Jordan River, including the Old City of Jerusalem, and acquired a large Palestinian population. In the 1967 Arab-Israeli war, Jordan lost this territory to Israel. King *Hussein* of Jordan, maintaining a pro-Western but anti-Israeli stand, has been bitterly opposed by the Palestinian guerrillas. In 1970-1971 Hussein's army defeated the Palestine guerrillas and most fled northward into Lebanon and Syria.

   d. Israel in 1948 became an independent Jewish state (see page 301).

   e. Iran in 1951 nationalized the oil fields and refineries held by a British company. By a compromise, Iran retained ownership of the properties but permitted a group of Western companies to produce and distribute Iranian oil. In 1973 Iran took full control of its oil properties and informed the Western companies that henceforth they could be only buyers of Iranian oil. Iran nevertheless maintains a pro-Western foreign policy.

   f. Cyprus in 1960, after four years of violence, became an independent republic within the British Commonwealth and permitted Britain to retain its military bases. *Archbishop Makarios* was elected first President.
   The *Cypriotes* (inhabitants of Cyprus) are 80 percent Greek and 20 percent Turkish. Their constitution (1) guarantees many rights to the Turkish minority, and (2) provides for a Turkish Cypriote Vice President and a Greek Cypriote President, each with veto power over legislation.
   In 1963 President Makarios proposed constitutional changes. The Turks protested, fearing the loss of their rights. Greek-Turkish antagonism led to Cypriote civil war. With Turkey and Greece each threatening to intervene militarily, Britain brought the Cyprus question to the U.N. Security Council, which authorized a U.N. peace-keeping force (see page 406).

   g. Kuwait in 1961 terminated the British protectorate and became an independent Arab nation. However, Kuwait received England's pledge of military protection in case of foreign aggression. Although small in size, Kuwait is one of the world's largest producers of oil.

   2. Decline of French Power. By 1944 Syria and Lebanon, after riots, strikes, and uprisings, ended the French mandates and became independent.
   With Britain and France no longer dominant in the Middle East and with the Soviet Union exerting pressure, the United States has become increasingly involved in the area. (See cold war developments, pages 445-447.)

SURVEY OF ARAB NATIONALISM (ESPECIALLY SINCE 1945)

1. Roots. Arab peoples have become aware of their common cultural background: Arabic language, Moslem religion, and the great Arab civilization of the Middle Ages. They wish to govern themselves free of imperialist domination. They view Israel as a common enemy and seek its destruction.

2. Policies and Activities. (a) The *Arab League,* formed in 1945, seeks to unify Arab policy on world issues, especially Arab military, diplomatic, and economic action against Israel. (b) Egypt, Morocco, and Tunisia actively supported the Algerian Moslem rebellion for independence. (c) Egypt's President Nasser, the leader of Arab nationalism, dreamed of creating one united Arab nation, from the Atlantic Ocean to the Persian Gulf, as had existed during the Middle Ages. In 1958 Nasser merged Egypt and Syria to form the *United Arab Republic (U.A.R.).* In 1961 he lost Syria, which revolted and reestablished her independence. (d) In 1971 Egypt, under President Sadat, joined with Libya and Syria to form a new Arab federation. (e) In 1972 Egypt agreed to work toward a limited merger with neighboring Libya.

3. Arab Disunity. Nasser's policies, although supported by many Arab nationalists, aroused much Arab opposition. (a) His dictatorial rule was opposed by more democratically minded groups and also by the Syrian and Iraqui Socialists, the *Baath party.* (b) Nasser's pro-Soviet leanings were opposed by pro-Western Arab leaders, especially Premier *Bourguiba* of Tunisia. (c) Nasser's call for a single Arab nation aroused the fears of hereditary Arab rulers, especially of Jordan and Saudi Arabia. (d) From 1962 to 1967, Nasser clashed bitterly with Saudi Arabia regarding the civil war in Yemen. The U.A.R. provided troops for the republican forces, whereas Saudi Arabia aided the royalists. In 1967, because of the Arab-Israeli War, Nasser withdrew many troops from Yemen. (Thereupon, the Soviet Union sent massive aid—weapons, technicians, and combat pilots—into Yemen to bolster the republican regime.) In 1970 this civil war ended in compromise, with royalist supporters accepting posts in the republican government.

ISRAEL

JEWISH CLAIMS TO PALESTINE

Theodor Herzl, a journalist and Jewish intellectual, founded modern *Zionism,* the movement for a Jewish homeland in Palestine. Zionists claimed that the Jewish people (1) had lived in Palestine during ancient times, and

(2) needed a refuge in case of anti-Semitic persecution. In 1917 the British government gave support to the Zionist movement by the *Balfour Declaration,* which viewed "with favor the establishment in Palestine of a national home for the Jewish people." To fulfill the Balfour Declaration, England in 1923 received the League of Nations mandate over Palestine.

By 1938 over 500,000 Jews had migrated to Palestine. With hard work they built modern cities, established agricultural settlements, started industrialization, restored desert lands to fertility, reduced death from disease, and created an educational system.

ARAB OPPOSITION AND A NEW BRITISH POLICY

Opposition to Jewish immigration came from (1) Arab nationalists, who desired an Arab Palestine, (2) Arab ruling classes, who feared incoming Western ideas of democracy, and (3) Arab peasants and nomads, who feared the loss of their traditional ways of living. In 1939 Britain, seeking to appease the Arabs, severely limited Jewish immigration to Palestine.

During World War II six million European Jews—men, women, and children—were savagely murdered by the Nazis. Of those who survived, most sought admission to Palestine. However, England still kept the gates closed to large-scale Jewish immigration. England's policy was (1) defied by Palestinian Jews, who smuggled immigrants into the Holy Land, and (2) condemned by the United States.

PALESTINE AND THE U.N.

In 1947 England turned the Palestine problem over to the United Nations. After investigation, the U.N. General Assembly approved recommendations to (1) end the British mandate, (2) place Jerusalem under international control, and (3) partition Palestine into separate Arab and Jewish states.

Thereupon, in 1948 Israel proclaimed her independence under President *Chaim Weizmann* and Prime Minister *David Ben-Gurion.* The Israeli republic is the Middle East's only modern democratic state.

ISRAEL MAINTAINS HER EXISTENCE

1. **Israeli War for Independence (1948-1949).** The Arab states—coordinated by the Arab League—defied the U.N. decision and attacked the new Jewish state. Despite their numerical superiority, the Arabs were driven back and lost some territory to the Israelis. In 1949 the Arab states accepted armistice agreements arranged by U.N. mediator *Ralph Bunche.*

However, these agreements left unsolved (a) the precise boundaries between Israel and the adjacent Arab states, and (b) the resettlement of Arab refugees who had fled Palestine during the fighting. Furthermore, the Arab states refused to conclude permanent peace treaties and to accept the existence of Israel.

2. Continued Arab Hostility (1949-1956). (*a*) Members of the Arab League enforced an economic boycott against Israel and against private companies doing business with Israel. (*b*) Nasser defied a 1951 U.N. resolution and barred Israeli ships from the Suez Canal. (*c*) Egyptian artillery on the Sinai Peninsula blockaded ships bound for Israel's southern port of *Elath* on the *Gulf of Aqaba*. (*d*) Egypt and other Arab countries terrorized Israeli border communities by *fedayeen* (guerrilla) raids.

3. Sinai Campaign (1956). Israel feared Egypt's military buildup, which resulted chiefly from an arms deal in 1955 between Egypt and the Communist bloc. In 1956 Israel seized the initiative and invaded Egypt to wipe out fedayeen bases and end the Aqaba blockade. Israeli forces quickly scattered Nasser's armies and overran the Sinai Peninsula. (England and France also invaded Egypt, to regain control of the Suez Canal. See pages 404-405.) The United Nations condemned the attacks, secured withdrawal of the invading forces, and stationed a *United Nations Emergency Force* (*UNEF*) in the areas of tension. With the stationing of UNEF troops, Israel was free from Egyptian fedayeen raids and free to use the Gulf of Aqaba.

4. Arab-Israeli War (1967)

    a. Background. Egypt entered into military alliances with Syria and Jordan against Israel. Syria encouraged Arab guerrilla bands on her soil to raid Israeli frontier settlements. Israel threatened reprisals against Syria. Thereupon, Egypt and Syria, both heavily equipped with Soviet weapons, moved their armies toward their borders with Israel. President Nasser requested that the UNEF be removed, which was immediately done by U.N. Secretary General U Thant. Then Nasser closed the Gulf of Aqaba to Israeli shipping.

    Meanwhile, Israel called up her military reserves. The opposing armies stood face to face, and eventually war started. The Soviet Union voiced strong support for the Arabs and condemned Israel as the aggressor.

    b. The War. In a six-day war, the Israelis routed the Arab forces. The Israelis seized (1) *from Egypt*—the entire Sinai Peninsula westward to the Suez Canal and southward to Sharm el Sheikh, opening the Gulf of Aqaba to Israeli shipping, (2) *from Jordan*—all territory west of the Jordan River, including the Old City of Jerusalem, and (3) *from Syria*—the Golan Heights overlooking the Sea of Galilee.

    U.N. Security Council resolutions helped end the fighting. Israel stated that she would retain certain territories for her military security and urged direct peace negotiations with the Arab states. Egypt and Syria, having received new Soviet weapons, spoke of another "round" of fighting.

Territories occupied
by Israelis in 1967 war

MEDITERRANEAN

SEA

SYRIA

*Sea of
Galilee*

LEBANON

I S R A E L

Jordan R.

Suez
Canal

Jerusalem

*Dead
Sea*

E G Y P T
U. A. R.

NEGEV

JORDAN

Elath

SINAI
PENINSULA

Gulf of Aqaba

Sharm el
Sheikh

SAUDI ARABIA

R e d   S e a

Israel and the Bordering Arab States

3. Postwar Developments (Since 1967)

a. No War but No Peace. Arab guerrilla groups, the largest being *Al Fatah,* gave Israel no peace. Arab guerrillas increased terrorist raids against Israeli settlements and gunned Israeli commercial airplanes at airports in Greece and Switzerland. In 1972 Arab extremists employed Japanese leftists to massacre innocent civilians at the Tel Aviv airport; also the *Black September* terrorists, a faction of Al Fatah, murdered 11 Israeli Olympic athletes at Munich. In response, Israel raided guerrilla bases, most recently in Syria and Lebanon. However, the main threat to Israel was Egypt, whose leaders called for "fire and blood." Israel bested Egypt in artillery and airplane duels along the Suez Canal. Egypt increasingly became dependent upon Russia for military equipment and for over 20,000 military personnel who manned missile sites, trained Nasser's forces, and flew operational missions for Egypt. The Soviets' presence in Egypt caused the United States to voice support for Israel's right to exist. With a Russian-American confrontation possible, the United States got Egypt and Israel to accept a temporary cease-fire and a renewal of peace negotiations under U.N. representative Gunnar Jarring.

b. Egypt Under Sadat. In 1970 Nasser died of a heart attack and his position was assumed by *Anwar al-Sadat.* The new Egyptian President followed a vacillating course. In 1971 he refused to extend the cease-fire, but he did not resume the shooting duels. He offered to sign a peace treaty with Israel upon total Israeli withdrawal from occupied Arab lands, but later he proclaimed belligerently, "There will be no negotiations or peace agreement with Israel." Sadat also suppressed a conspiracy against his regime by Egyptian leaders considered pro-Soviet, but afterward he signed a 15-year Soviet-Egyptian treaty of friendship, cooperation, and military assistance.

In 1972, in a surprise move, Sadat ordered Soviet military personnel to leave Egypt. Eventually some 20,000 Soviet troops, pilots, and military advisers were withdrawn. Sadat's move probably resulted from various resentments: of the Egyptian people against increasing Soviet presence in their country, of Egyptian military leaders against Soviet advisers, and of the Egyptian government against the Soviet Union for not providing advanced offensive weapons for a new war against Israel. Sadat's move ended nearly 20 years of Egyptian military dependence upon Russia.

Soon afterward Egypt agreed—effective September, 1973—to a limited merger with neighboring Libya. Colonel *Muammar el-Qaddafi,* ruler of oil-rich Libya, favored the merger as a step toward Arab unity. Sadat hoped that the merger would mean Libyan funds for Egypt to purchase advanced offensive weapons.

CURRENT PROBLEMS FACING ISRAEL

(1) Since independence, the population of Israel has more than tripled, chiefly through Jewish immigration from Europe, North Africa, and the Middle East. Israel seeks to unite these diverse peoples culturally and to provide for them economically. (2) Israel needs capital to develop her limited natural resources, to build industries, and to bring water to her desert lands, especially the Negev region. Her plans to tap the waters of the Jordan River have aroused vehement opposition from the Arab states. (3) Israel wants a permanent peace settlement with her Arab neighbors. Three major obstacles are the future of about a million Palestinian Arab refugees; the boundaries of Israel; and the refusal of the Arab states to recognize the existence of Israel. (4) With Arab hostility undiminished, Israel spends considerable sums on military preparedness. (5) Israel, democratic and Western in outlook, must contend with the pro-Arab policy of Soviet Russia.

MULTIPLE-CHOICE QUESTIONS

1. Of Great Britain's Middle East policies, which one led to the other three? (1) purchase of the Suez Canal (2) protection of the Empire's "lifeline" (3) annexation of Cyprus (4) control of Egypt as a protectorate.
2. The Suez Canal shortened the water route between (1) New York and Istanbul (2) London and Singapore (3) Tokyo and San Francisco (4) Cairo and Venice.
3. During the 19th century Russian efforts to seek control of the straits uniting the Black and Mediterranean Seas were most strongly opposed by (1) Austria-Hungary (2) France (3) Great Britain (4) Italy.
4. A Middle Eastern country with a low standard of living despite its rich oil fields is (1) Jordan (2) Iran (3) Lebanon (4) Israel.
5. Archbishop Makarios is noted as (1) the leader of the Greek Cypriotes (2) the Prime Minister of Greece (3) the Patriarch of Eastern Christianity (4) a Roman Catholic missionary in the Middle East.
6. Which *two* countries were most concerned with the conflicts on Cyprus? (1) Israel and Egypt (2) Turkey and Greece (3) Bulgaria and Rumania (4) Italy and France.
7. Which countries were for a time joined as the United Arab Republic? (1) Egypt and Syria (2) Algeria and Jordan (3) Morocco and Yemen (4) Iran and Iraq.
8. Two nations that intervened on opposing sides in Yemen were (1) Egypt and Israel (2) Egypt and Saudi Arabia (3) Syria and Jordan (4) Algeria and the Congo.
9. By the Balfour Declaration, England announced support for (1) the Berlin-to-Bagdad railroad (2) Arab nationalism (3) Cyprus independence (4) a Jewish homeland in Palestine.
10. The first Prime Minister of the state of Israel was (1) Herzl (2) Weizmann (3) Ben-Gurion (4) Bunche.
11. One factor encouraging unity among Arab countries is (1) a common hostility toward Israel (2) similar types of government (3) common ownership of valuable oil reserves (4) the acceptance of Nasser's leadership by most Arab rulers.
12. An Israeli objective in the 1956 Sinai Campaign was to (1) gain control of the Suez Canal (2) end English power in Egypt (3) end Egyptian guerrilla raids into Israeli territory (4) establish democratic government in Egypt.

TRUE-FALSE QUESTIONS

If the statement is correct, write the word *true*. If the statement is incorrect, substitute a word or phrase for the italicized term to make the statement correct.

1. The leading natural resource of the Middle East is *uranium*.
2. Former English mandates in the Middle East are Jordan, Israel, and *Iraq*.
3. *Lebanon* was formerly a French mandate in the Middle East.
4. The country of Iran was formerly known as *Mesopotamia*.
5. In 1951 Iran terminated the oil concessions held by an *American* oil company.
6. The Arab nationalist who wanted to unite the Arab countries under his leadership was *Tunisia's Bourguiba*.
7. The Arab states vehemently oppose Israel's plan to irrigate her desert lands by utilizing the waters of the *Mediterranean Sea*.
8. The port city of Elath, at the southern tip of Israel, is on the *Persian Gulf*.

Part 6. The Far East

A. CHINA

APPEAL TO MODERN IMPERIALISTS (STARTING IN MID-19TH CENTURY)

China attracted imperialist nations for several reasons. (1) China's huge population offered a tremendous market for manufactured goods, and cheap labor to work in foreign-owned enterprises. (2) China's untapped mineral resources—coal, tin, and tungsten—attracted investors. (3) China's tea and raw silk found ready European markets. (4) China's Manchu government was inefficient and lacked military power (see pages 101-102).

VICTIM OF MODERN IMPERIALISM

1. **Britain,** by the *Opium War* of 1839-1842, (*a*) compelled China to allow imports of opium, a habit-forming narcotic, (*b*) annexed Hong Kong, and (*c*) was granted the privilege of *extraterritoriality*. This entitled an Englishman accused of a crime in China to be tried in a British court. (Extraterritoriality, soon conceded to other foreign nations, affronted Chinese justice and pride.) England later established a sphere of influence over the Yangtze River valley.

2. **France** annexed Indo-China and gained a sphere of influence in southeastern China.

3. **Germany** acquired a sphere of influence over most of the Shantung Peninsula.

4. **Russia** annexed the Amur River district, the Pacific seaport of Vladivostok, and the central Asian territory bordering Sinkiang Province; secured a lease to ice-free Port Arthur; and established a sphere of influence over Manchuria.

5. **Japan,** by the *Sino-Japanese War* of 1894-1895, annexed Taiwan (also called Formosa) and secured a sphere of influence over Korea. (In 1910 Japan annexed Korea.) By the *Russo-Japanese War* of 1904-1905, Japan took over Russia's lease to Port Arthur and Russia's sphere of influence in southern Manchuria.

The imperialist nations seemed poised to annex their respective spheres of influence, thereby threatening to dismember China.

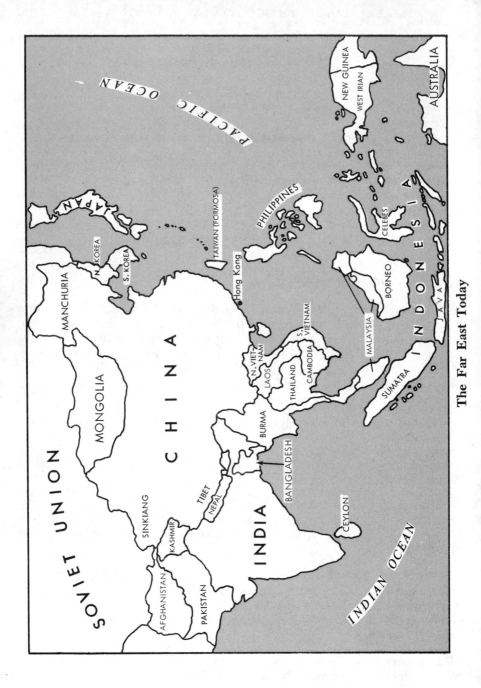

The Far East Today

OPEN DOOR POLICY (1899)

The United States was interested in China not for territory but for commerce. However, our trade was threatened by the spheres of influence and the prospect of China's dismemberment. Therefore, *John Hay,* American Secretary of State, suggested the *Open Door Policy.* It proposed equal trade rights in China for all nations. Later, it also came to mean the preservation of China's independence and territory.

The "open door" was accepted by the imperialist nations in principle, but not in practice. However, it earned us China's good will and, for many years, served as the cornerstone of American policy toward the Far East.

BOXER REBELLION (1900)

The *Boxers,* a Chinese society encouraged by many government officials, staged an uprising to drive out all foreigners and restore China to isolation. After an international military force suppressed the rebellion, the foreign nations demanded damages from China.

The United States successfully urged that China pay, not by loss of territory, but by a monetary indemnity. The other nations agreed. But when they imposed excessive indemnities, the United States returned half of her indemnity money to advance education in China and to enable Chinese students to attend American colleges.

THE NATIONALISTS ESTABLISH THE CHINESE REPUBLIC (1911-1912)

The *Kuomintang,* or *Nationalist party,* was founded by Dr. Sun Yat-sen. His program consisted of the "three principles": (1) *nationalism*—replace the weak Manchu Dynasty by a strong central government capable of freeing China from imperialist control, (2) *democracy*—elect government officials responsible to the people, and (3) *people's livelihood*—adopt Western industrial and agricultural ways in order to improve economic conditions.

As the Chinese became nationalistic and the Manchus failed to halt the imperialists, the Kuomintang attracted supporters. In 1911-1912 the Nationalists revolted, overthrew the Manchu Emperor, and proclaimed a republic.

NATIONALISTS STRUGGLE AGAINST WARLORDS (TO 1928)

The Kuomintang failed to gain control of the entire country, ruling only a small region in the south. Most of China was controlled by local warlords. For several years, Kuomintang armies made little progress in subduing the warlords. Dr. Sun asked for foreign military assistance, but only Russia—then recently turned Communist—offered help. With Soviet armaments and military advisers, Kuomintang armies became an effective fighting force.

Following Sun's death in 1925, *Chiang Kai-shek*, conservative military leader, became head of the Kuomintang. By 1928 Chiang had destroyed the power of the warlords and achieved control throughout most of China.

NATIONALISTS STRUGGLE AGAINST COMMUNISTS (TO 1937)

1. Communists Gain Supporters. The Chinese Communist party, organized in 1921, at first operated within the Kuomintang. The party steadily increased its membership and influence by winning over (*a*) some Kuomintang members who were grateful for Soviet military assistance, (*b*) landless peasants who were attracted by Communist promises to break up the estates of the rich landlords, (*c*) low-paid city workers who applauded Communist demands to seize foreign-owned businesses, and (*d*) nationalists who acclaimed Communist propaganda attacks against Western imperialists.

2. Nationalists Battle Communists. In opposing the spread of Communism within China, Chiang Kai-shek received strong support from (*a*) landlords and the emerging middle class who feared Communist economic doctrines, (*b*) democratic groups who feared Communist totalitarian rule and hoped that the Kuomintang would move toward democracy, and (*c*) nationalists who feared that the Communists would place China under the domination of the Soviet Union.

In 1927 Chiang ousted the Russian advisers, drove the Chinese Communists from the Kuomintang, and sought to destroy the Communist movement. The Communists fought back and eventually established a stronghold in northwest China, near the Russian border. For ten years China experienced inconclusive civil war. In 1937 Nationalists and Communists agreed to a truce to meet the challenge of Japanese imperialism.

CHINESE STRUGGLE FOR INDEPENDENCE AGAINST JAPAN (TO 1945)

1. Japanese Imperialism in China. Modern, industrialized Japan represented the major imperialist threat to China's independence. Japan had seized Taiwan (Formosa) (1895), Port Arthur (1905), Korea (1910), and Manchuria (1931)—all without effective Chinese opposition. In 1937 Japan invaded China proper, but this time met with considerable resistance from both Chinese Nationalists and Communists. The Japanese seized the coastal areas with their large seaport cities and occupied about one-quarter of the country, but were unable to destroy the Chinese armies. The Chinese retreated into the interior and waged guerrilla warfare. The Chinese Nationalists received armaments and loans from Britain and the United States.

2. China and World War II. In 1941 China's struggle for independence merged into World War II when Japan attacked Britain and the United

States. To strengthen China's determination to fight, the Allies (a) renounced their extraterritorial and other special privileges, (b) pledged to restore Taiwan and Manchuria to China, and (c) elevated China to United Nations "Big Five" status.

Although China fought on, her military contribution was not significant. American armed might, with some Allied help, crushed Japan by 1945 and thus saved China from Japanese conquest. As World War II ended, the Nationalists and Communists resumed their civil war.

NATIONALISTS LOSE CHINA TO THE COMMUNISTS (1949)

1. Nationalist Weaknesses. The Chiang Kai-shek regime lost public support in China because it (a) was a thinly veiled dictatorship marked by corruption and inefficiency, (b) wasted a considerable portion of the $2 billion in American loans and military supplies, (c) failed to earn the soldiers' loyalty and prevent army desertions, and (d) ignored the peasants' desire for land and the workers' demand for better living conditions. Chiang did not heed America's advice to improve political and economic conditions.

2. Communists Gain China. Following World War II Chinese Communist armies, strengthened by considerable equipment captured from the Japanese and supplied by the Soviet Union, achieved military supremacy over the Nationalists. By the end of 1949 Communist armies had driven Chiang Kai-shek to his only remaining stronghold—the island of Taiwan (Formosa). The Communists now controlled all of mainland China.

CHINA AS A COMMUNIST STATE (SINCE 1949)

At Peking, the Communists proclaimed the *People's Republic of China*, under the leadership of Premier *Chou En-lai* and Communist party head *Mao Tse-tung*. The Communists rule China's 700 million people.

1. Government. The government is a one-party dictatorship under the Communist party. By army and secret police, the government enforces its authority and deals ruthlessly with domestic opposition. In purges, the Communists executed several million Chinese as counterrevolutionists. Many others were imprisoned for "reeducation," a process labeled by non-Communists as *brainwashing*.

2. Economy

a. Industry. The government nationalized industry and inaugurated Five-Year Plans of economic development. The Plans emphasize heavy industry—iron and steel, electric power, machinery—but neglect consumer goods. Although workers' living standards may have improved slightly, wages remain low, working hours are long, and in practice strikes are forbidden.

b. Agriculture. In 1958, announcing a "great leap forward," Communist chief Mao Tse-tung compelled the peasants to transfer land to and join in *communes.* These are huge agricultural establishments in which the state owns all the equipment and land, pays wages to the workers, takes care of the children in community centers, maintains communal dining halls, and compels both men and women to work. By thus weakening the family unit, the Communists expected to increase the supply of farm workers.

Strong peasant resistance exists against the commune system, and agricultural output lags badly. Commune mismanagement and natural calamities have caused severe food shortages, and China has been forced to purchase grain from abroad. The commune system has been somewhat modified to provide individual incentive for increasing production.

Chinese agriculture, still largely unmechanized, depends chiefly on manual labor.

3. Ideology (System of Thought). The Communist government has driven out Western influence in China by closing foreign schools, expelling Christian missionaries, and banning "dangerous" books. The Communists, through mass communications media and schools, try to (*a*) promote their own ideology based upon the Chinese Communist interpretations of the doctrines of Marx and Lenin and upon the teachings of Mao Tse-tung, and (*b*) wean the people away from the ethical teachings of Confucianism. In particular, the Communists stress that the primary loyalty of the individual is to the state, not, as Confucius taught, to the family.

4. Trouble Behind the Iron Curtain: the Chinese-Soviet Split and China's "Cultural Revolution." See pages 420-422.

5. Foreign Relations. See pages 449-452.

B. JAPAN

OPENING OF JAPAN (1853-1854)

By the mid-17th century feudal Japan had withdrawn into isolation, and for 200 years she had remained unaffected by Western civilization (see page 106).

In 1853-1854 Commodore *Matthew C. Perry,* heading an American naval squadron, convinced Japan to open her ports to American trade. Soon afterwards, the leading European powers demanded and received similar trade rights. In 1864 European and American warships bombarded a Japanese seaport in retaliation against antiforeign outbreaks.

WESTERNIZATION OF JAPAN (STARTING 1867)

Impressed by Western military might, the Japanese were fearful of foreign domination. Therefore, they rapidly transformed their country from medieval feudalism to modern nationhood.

1. Government. The nobles removed the shogun from power and transferred full governmental control to the Emperor, *Mutsuhito*. In 1889 Mutsuhito granted Japan a constitution that provided an autocratic government (modeled upon that of Bismarck's Germany). The cabinet was dominated by military leaders and responsible only to the Emperor. (The Emperor's authority was further strengthened by Shintoism, the state religion, which began to preach his divine origin.)

2. Military. The government created a powerful British-type navy and Prussian-type army.

3. Education. The state began a compulsory public education system, and the Japanese became a highly literate people.

4. Agriculture. The nobles voluntarily surrendered their feudal privileges. The peasant farmers were no longer bound to the soil, and many became landowners.

5. Industry. The government encouraged a sweeping program of industrialization. Japan soon produced textiles, steel, machinery, and ships, and became a major trading and manufacturing nation.

JAPAN TURNS TO IMPERIALISM

1. Reasons. (*a*) Japanese industrialists needed raw materials—especially cotton, iron ore, and oil—and markets for their manufactured goods. (*b*) Japanese nationalists sought honor for the Emperor and glory for the military forces. They thought that colonies would raise Japan to the rank of a "big power." (*c*) Densely populated and lacking arable land, Japan wanted colonial outlets for her surplus population. (*d*) Japan's location placed her within easy reach of eastern Asia's underdeveloped nations.

2. Early Events

a. Sino Japanese War (1894 1895). Japan overwhelmed China and acquired Taiwan and a sphere of influence in Korea. (In 1910 Japan annexed Korea.)

b. Russo-Japanese War (1904-1905). Japan, to the world's surprise, defeated Russia. By the *Treaty of Portsmouth* (New Hampshire), Japan acquired the southern half of Sakhalin Island, Port Arthur, and Russia's sphere of influence in southern Manchuria. (For helping to negotiate the peace treaty, American President Theodore Roosevelt received the Nobel Peace Prize.)

c. World War I (1914-1918). Although contributing little to the Allied victory, Japan acquired Germany's concessions on China's Shantung Peninsula and mandates over the former German islands in the Pacific.

JAPAN AND THE UNITED STATES COME INTO CONFLICT

Made bold by easily won successes, Japanese militarists determined to create and dominate a *New Order* or *Co-Prosperity Sphere,* for eastern Asia. Japan's ambitions, however, clashed with the Open Door Policy of the United States. Japanese aggressions kept the two nations in conflict and led both into World War II.

1. **Washington Conference (1921-1922).** During World War I, while the Western powers were preoccupied in Europe, Japan tried to turn China into a protectorate by making the *Twenty-One Demands.* The Western powers were alarmed, and, after the war, the United States arranged the Washington Conference on naval and Far Eastern problems. Under Western persuasion, Japan joined in the *Nine-Power Treaty,* pledging to respect (*a*) equal trade rights in China, and (*b*) China's territorial integrity and independence. Also, Japan agreed to restore Chinese control over Shantung.

2. **Japanese Invasion of Manchuria (1931).** In violation of the Nine-Power Treaty, Japan invaded Manchuria, rich in coal, iron, and fertile soil. The *Lytton Commission,* investigating for the League of Nations, condemned Japan and ordered her to withdraw her troops. Instead, Japan withdrew from the League. *Henry L. Stimson,* the United States Secretary of State, informed Japan that America disapproved of the aggression in Manchuria. His statement, that the United States would recognize no territory taken by force, became known as the *Stimson Doctrine.* Neither the League nor the United States took further action.

By 1932 Japan exercised full control over Manchuria, which was now the puppet state of *Manchukuo.* In violation of the Open Door Policy, the Japanese expelled foreign business interests and monopolized the region's economic development. They built railroads, developed hydroelectric power, and created a sizable iron and steel industry, thereby increasing Japan's economic and military power.

3. **Japanese Invasion of China (1937).** Japan invaded China proper, seeking control of the entire country. Initially, Japanese armies met with success and occupied most of coastal China. By 1939, however, their advance into the interior was slowed, often to a standstill, by Chinese guerrilla resistance. Meanwhile, the United States, in support of China, (*a*) extended

government loans for the purchase of war materials, (b) permitted American volunteer pilots to fight for China as the *Flying Tigers*, (c) conducted an unofficial boycott of Japanese goods, and (d) in 1940-1941, officially embargoed the sale to Japan of scrap iron and aviation gasoline.

4. Japanese Attack on Pearl Harbor (December, 1941). To dominate the Far East, Japanese leaders held that they must drive out Great Britain and the United States. In 1937 Japan joined the Axis alliance of Fascist Italy and Nazi Germany. When World War II began in 1939, Japanese leaders believed that their opportunity was at hand. England was at war against Germany; the United States was busy supplying military equipment to the Allied nations in Europe. Consequently, in December, 1941, Japan staged a surprise attack against the American naval base at *Pearl Harbor*, Hawaii; Japanese armies invaded British-owned Malaya and the American-owned Philippines. Forced into World War II, the United States mobilized her power toward defeating the Axis nations.

JAPAN SINCE WORLD WAR II

1. Territorial Losses. Following her surrender in 1945, Japan was stripped of the territories she had acquired during 50 years of aggression. Japan lost Taiwan and Manchuria to China, the southern half of Sakhalin Island and the Kuriles to Russia, and the Japanese-mandated islands in the Pacific to the United States as a trusteeship. Korea was divided into Russian and American zones pending independence (see pages 447-449).

2. American Occupation (1945-1952). American military forces occupied Japan until 1952, when the peace treaty went into effect. General *Douglas MacArthur*, serving as Supreme Allied Commander in Japan, introduced sweeping reforms.

3. New Constitution (1947). Under MacArthur's direction, the Japanese people adopted a democratic constitution, which (a) renounced the waging of war and the maintaining of offensive armed forces, (b) denied the Emperor's divine origin but retained him as a symbol of national unity, (c) contained a Bill of Rights guaranteeing fundamental civil liberties—including freedom of speech and press, separation of church and state (ending government support for Shintoism), equality under the law (including equal rights for women), and the right to a standard of "wholesome" living, and (d) provided cabinet responsibility to an elected two-house legislature, called the *Diet*.

4. Economic and Social Reforms. MacArthur took steps by which Japan (a) dissolved the huge business monopolies, such as the *Mitsui* and *Mitsubishi*, which had controlled much of Japan's economic life, (b) encouraged free labor unions empowered with the right to strike, (c) provided farms for landless peasants, and (d) reformed education by removing ultranationalist teachers and textbooks and encouraging democratic learning.

5. War Trials. Japanese war leaders received trials before Allied courts on war crime charges: aggressive warfare and atrocities against prisoners. Found guilty, some were sentenced to long imprisonment; others were executed. Will their ill fate deter future would-be aggressors?

6. Treaty of Peace With Japan (1952). Drawn up by the United States, the Japanese peace treaty was accepted by the major Allied nations, except the Soviet Union. She refused to sign the treaty, chiefly because it confirmed Japan's position as an ally of the United States. (In 1956 Russia signed a declaration of peace with Japan.)

Considered lenient, the 1952 treaty included the following provisions:

a. Territory. Japan lost all her conquests since 1895, but retained her four large home islands. (Japan consented to American administration of the Ryukyu Islands, including Okinawa, but retained the right to claim the return of these islands. For their return to Japan, see page 453.)

b. Reparations. Japan was not required to pay reparations in money for war damages. However, Japan agreed to contribute goods and services to countries damaged by Japanese aggression in World War II.

c. Defense. Japan was recognized as an independent sovereign nation possessing the right of military self-defense. In a separate pact, the United States and Japan agreed that American troops remain stationed in Japan.

7. Limited Rearmament. The Japanese government has interpreted the constitutional prohibition against armed forces to apply to offensive—but not defensive—military units. It has therefore built up air, sea, and land units, constituting a 230,000-man "self-defense" force. These troops are insufficient to defend the nation. However, Japanese public opinion, strongly pacifist, remains unwilling to amend the constitution to permit more extensive rearmament. Meanwhile, the people are free of heavy burdens for military expenditures and depend on the United States to protect their homeland.

8. Stable, Democratic Government. Under the Japanese constitution, the people choose the two-house Diet, whose more powerful branch is the 491-seat House of Representatives. The Liberal Democratic party, the leading party, is pro-capitalist, pro-American, and anti-Communist. It has controlled postwar Japan and provided stable, democratic rule. In 1972 the Liberal Democrats secured a safe majority of 282 seats, the Socialists (the other major party) won 118 seats, and the Communists increased their representation to 38 seats. (For Japan and the cold war, see pages 452-453.)

C. INDIA, PAKISTAN, AND BANGLADESH

FACTORS ENABLING BRITAIN TO DOMINATE INDIA

By 1763 Britain had driven her chief European rival, France, from India. Thereafter, a relatively small number of English military and civilian personnel gradually expanded British control throughout vast, heavily populated India. The British conquest was facilitated by India's backwardness and disunity.

1. Military Inferiority. The Indians could not cope with the superior British military knowledge, training, and equipment.

2. Many Languages. The people were divided linguistically among more than a dozen main languages and over 200 dialects. Their many tongues reflected geographic and cultural separation.

3. Religious Divisions. Of India's total population, the Moslems constituted about 20 percent, the Hindus the overwhelming majority. Because of their divergent religious traditions and past conflicts, the Moslems and Hindus were bitterly antagonistic to each other (see page 94).

4. Caste System. Within Hinduism, the caste system rigidly divided the people and kept them from cooperating effectively (see pages 25-26).

5. Political Disunity. India was divided among more than 600 independent states, each headed by its own native prince, or *rajah*.

England's ability to extend her authority throughout all India illustrates the principle of *divide and conquer*.

INDIA AS A BRITISH POSSESSION

1. Political Control. To the mid-19th century England controlled India through a private business enterprise, the *British East India Company*. Its rule resulted in an Indian revolt in 1857, led by the British army's native soldiers, called *sepoys*. After suppressing the *Sepoy Mutiny*, the British government assumed control of the country, ruling British India directly as a colony and ruling the native states indirectly as protectorates through British "advisers" to the Indian princes. In 1876, after Prime Minister Disraeli had secured the Suez Canal, which shortened the water route to India, Parliament proclaimed Queen Victoria as Empress of India.

The English freed India of local wars, guarded her borders against invasion, and generally provided efficient administration. In response to Indian demands, England permitted the Indian people limited self-government in 1919.

2. Economic Control. England profited greatly from India, called the "brightest jewel of the British Empire." English manufacturers and workers depended upon India to purchase their textiles and machines. English merchants sought India's exports of raw jute and tea. English investors developed India's mineral resources, built railways, and established factories. By the mid-20th century India was an important Asian producer of textiles, iron and steel, and cement.

By industrializing India, the English provided employment for many Indian workers. Also, the English government improved the country by public works: schools, roads, hospitals, and irrigation and sanitation projects.

The Indian masses, however, continued to live close to the starvation level. The population almost doubled between 1850 and 1900, and job opportunities and production could not keep up with the increase in population. Handicraft workers could not compete with factories, and factory workers received extremely low wages. Farmers, the majority of the population, were beset by uncertain rainfall, crude cultivation methods, high rents, and heavy taxes.

3. Social Control. The English outlawed barbaric Indian practices: slavery, *suttee* (the Hindu practice of burning the widow on the funeral pile of her deceased husband), and *female infanticide* (killing unwanted baby girls). Also, they instituted modern health methods, thus lowering the death rate, began educational programs, and introduced the English language and English concepts of law, justice, democracy, and nationalism. However, the funds that the British made available for health and education were hardly adequate for India's massive needs.

INDIAN INDEPENDENCE MOVEMENT

By the early 20th century the Indian nationalist movement for self-government and independence centered in the *Indian National Congress party*.

1. Leaders

a. Mohandas K. Gandhi. A high-caste Hindu educated in England, Gandhi absorbed Western ideals of democracy and nationalism. He became the political and spiritual leader of the Indian masses. He was revered as a prophet and was called "saintly one," or *Mahatma*. Gandhi sought to end British rule, not with violence, but with *passive resistance*, also called *noncooperation* or *civil disobedience*. His followers boycotted British goods, shunned government service, refused to pay taxes, and disregarded British laws. Gandhi believed that passive resistance would compel England to withdraw from India.

To provide work for India's masses and to avoid the need for foreign capital, Gandhi urged India to produce goods by her ancient hand methods. Gandhi also struggled to improve the status of India's untouchables.

b. Jawaharlal Nehru. Also a high-caste Hindu educated in England, Nehru was a practical political leader with socialist leanings. He accepted Gandhi's ideas of passive resistance and aiding untouchables, but he rejected Gandhi's proposal for hand production. Instead, Nehru urged industrialization to develop India's economy and raise living standards.

c. Mohammed Ali Jinnah. A Moslem, Jinnah in the 1930's led his co-religionists out of the Congress party and into the *Moslem League.* Because he feared Hindu domination, Jinnah demanded that the Moslem sections of India become a separate independent state, *Pakistan.*

2. India Gains Independence (1947). Following World War I Indian nationalists intensified their campaign against British rule. Undeterred by repeated jail sentences, they practiced civil disobedience. Even Gandhi and Nehru were several times imprisoned.

During World War II the Congress party rejected England's offer of postwar independence, continued its policy of civil disobedience, and demanded immediate freedom. However, the Indians could not convince the British to act more rapidly. After the war, in 1947, India (chiefly Hindu) and Pakistan (predominantly Moslem) both received dominion status.

3. Moslem-Hindu Violence Accompanies Independence. With British control removed, Moslems and Hindus engaged in bloody religious riots and sought safety by mass migrations. Because Gandhi preached against such violence, he was assassinated in 1948 by a Hindu fanatic.

INDEPENDENT INDIA: DEVELOPMENTS IN GOVERNMENT

At first a dominion, India in 1950 became an independent republic but remained within the Commonwealth of Nations.

India retained a democratic government with a cabinet responsible to an elected legislature. Until his death in 1964, Nehru served as Prime Minister and led the Congress party to three overwhelming election victories.

Since 1966 India's Prime Minister has been Nehru's daughter, *Mrs. Indira Gandhi.* Her government was hampered by the split of the Congress party in 1969 into the conservative Old Congress party and Mrs. Gandhi's left-of-center New Congress party. In 1971 Mrs. Gandhi called for new elections and gained an overwhelming legislative majority. She pledged to combat unemployment and rising prices, to further land reform, and to lessen the gulf between rich and poor.

PROBLEMS FACING THE REPUBLIC OF INDIA

1. Unifying India's People. To combat the country's divisive cultural heritage, the Indian government guaranteed religious freedom, outlawed certain caste restrictions, abolished the class of untouchables and improved their economic conditions, and encouraged the use of a single official language, *Hindi*. Slowly, the people are developing a feeling of national unity.

PROBLEMS FACING INDIA

	INDIA	UNITED STATES
Population (millions)	550	210
Life expectancy (years)	50	71
Medical care (doctors per 100,000 population)	21	150
Literacy rate (percent of population)	30%	98%
Foreign trade (billions of dollars)	$4.2	$89.7
Per capita income (dollars per year)	$85	$4,150

2. Raising Living Standards by Increasing Production. India permits private and public enterprise in a mixed economy. To supplement the efforts of private businessmen, the Indian government has undertaken *Five-Year Plans:* constructing irrigation projects, electric power plants, railroads, and steel mills; distributing land to the peasants; and fostering modern farming methods. As a first goal, India seeks to raise the annual income per person to above $100. India's economic efforts benefit from some Russian and considerable American and English funds.

In improving economic conditions, India faces a challenge from certain Hindu beliefs: (*a*) that cows are sacred and not to be slaughtered for food, (*b*) that farm pests may contain reincarnated human souls and are not to be destroyed, and (*c*) that higher castes may not work alongside untouchables.

3. Wiping Out Illiteracy. Only 28 percent of the people are able to read and write. India's constitution calls for free compulsory education through the age of 14. The government is seeking to realize this goal, but must overcome a staggering shortage of schools and teachers.

4. Settling the Kashmir Dispute. India and Pakistan both claimed *Kashmir*, a native state where a Hindu prince ruled a chiefly Moslem people. Both nations agreed in principle to a U.N. plebiscite, but in practice India prevented any vote. In 1957, despite protests by the U.N. and Pakistan, Nehru annexed the Indian-occupied portion of Kashmir. (See page 404.)

5. Determining a Foreign Policy. Nehru hoped to devote India's energies to solving domestic problems. Consequently, in the cold war between Communism and the West, he set a policy of *nonalignment*, or *neutrality*.

At first Nehru expressed great fear of Western colonialism. Later, as Red Chinese troops invaded northern India in a series of border disputes, Nehru awakened to the Communist Chinese menace (see pages 453-454). After Nehru's death, Indian leaders reaffirmed their determination to protect India's borders and to maintain India's neutrality.

PAKISTAN AND BANGLADESH

1. Introduction: Pakistan Splits Into Two Nations. From independence (1947) until defeated in war (1971), Pakistan was one nation. It consisted of two nonadjacent regions separated by 1,000 miles of Indian territory. West Pakistan was larger in area but had fewer people than East Pakistan. Aside from their Moslem religion, the people of the two regions had little in common. The West Pakistanis were mostly Punjabis, who speak Urdu and look westward to the Moslem Arabs; the East Pakistanis were Bengalis, who speak Bengali and feel close to the Hindu Bengalis living in India. Despite their smaller population, the West Pakistanis controlled the central government, but in 1970 elections the Bengali *Awami League* gained a legislative majority. President *Yahya Khan* and Bengali leader Sheik *Mujibur Rahman* negotiated regarding East Pakistan's demand for autonomy but failed to agree. Thereupon the West Pakistani army seized control of the East, killing many civilians and occupying the major cities. The Bengalis declared their region's independence and retained control mostly of rural areas.

India meanwhile voiced support for East Pakistan, received over 9 million Bengali refugees—creating a tremendous relief burden—and trained Bengali guerrilla fighters. India also gained international support by signing a 20-year treaty of friendship with the Soviet Union. In late 1971 Indian military forces crossed into East Pakistan and in a two-week war defeated the West Pakistani army, making independence a reality for the new Bengali nation, *Bangladesh.* (For U.N. developments, see page 407.)

In 1972, after Britain formally recognized the new Bengali nation, Pakistan withdrew, while Bangladesh joined the Commonwealth.

2. Pakistan. (*a*) *Government.* As a result of Pakistan's disastrous defeat in the 1971 war, *Zulfikar Ali Bhutto* replaced Yahya Khan as President. Bhutto acted to remove incompetent officials, assert the authority of the central government, restore civilian rule, and draw up a new constitution. He faced many serious problems. (*b*) *Current Problems.* (1) Because of religious antagonisms, the Kashmir issue, disputes over water resources, and the 1971 war, Pakistan's relations with India remain strained. (2) The Pakistani people themselves are divided into a number of distinct linguistic and cultural groups. With the example set by the Bengalis, the Pathans of Pakistan's northwest frontier region have agitated for independence. (3) The Pakistanis are mainly farmers, especially in the Indus River valley. They use primitive agricultural methods and have a low standard of living. Many are tenants on large estates and do not have their own lands. Bhutto has begun a moderate land reform program. (4) The country is beset by inflation and rising prices, the loss of its markets for cotton textiles and cement in the former East Pakistan, and heavy defense expenditures to rebuild its military strength. (5) Although the United States had "leaned" toward Pakistan in the 1971 war, Pakistan resigned from SEATO, diluted its pro-Western foreign policy, and turned for friendship to Red China.

3. **Bangladesh.** (a) *Government.* The first Prime Minister of the new Bengali nation was Sheik Mujibur Rahman. He acted to establish the authority of the central government, to create a national army, to restore law and order, and to provide a constitution. He also faced many other problems. (b) *Current Problems.* (1) Bangladesh must recover from the wounds of war. The war resulted in considerable loss of life, hatred for the Pakistanis, razing of cities and villages, disruption of transportation, and serious food shortages. (2) Aside from the fertile land in the Ganges River valley, Bangladesh has few natural resources. Most of its large population are farmers who use primitive methods to raise chiefly jute and tea. They also face hostile weather conditions: monsoon rains that cause the rivers to flood and violent cyclone storms that bring much destruction. The Bengalis have an extremely low living standard and poor health conditions. (3) Bangladesh depends upon India—herself impoverished—for food and other economic aid. Bangladesh has been recognized by the United States, but massive American economic aid has not been forthcoming. The Bengali nation still feels the hostility of Red China, which vetoed Bangladesh's application for U.N. membership.

D. INDONESIA

LAND AND PEOPLE

Formerly the Netherlands East Indies, Indonesia consists of several thousand Pacific islands, notably Sumatra, Java, Celebes, most of Borneo, and West New Guinea (West Irian). The islands, extending about 4,000 miles from east to west, possess great wealth in (1) mineral resources: oil, coal, and tin, and (2) agricultural produce: rubber, quinine, sugar, pepper, and copra. Nevertheless, the people, chiefly farmers, have a low standard of living. The Indonesians, numbering 120 million, are predominantly Moslem.

FROM DUTCH COLONY TO INDEPENDENT NATION

For over 300 years Holland ruled the islands and developed their resources.

During World War II Dutch colonial forces fell before Japanese invaders. After the war, Indonesian nationalists set up a republic. When the Dutch tried to win back Indonesia by force, the U.N. Security Council secured a cease-fire. In 1949 Holland granted independence to Indonesia.

INDONESIA SINCE INDEPENDENCE

The Republic of Indonesia was first headed by President *Achmed Sukarno*. He faced problems of providing stable government, improving economic conditions, and replacing skilled Dutch personnel who fled the country.

In 1964-1965 Sukarno displayed friendship for Communist Russia and China and enmity toward the West. He antagonized Britain by claiming the Borneo territories of Malaysia. After Malaysia was elected to the U.N. Security Council, Sukarno withdrew Indonesia from the United Nations.

In late 1965 the Indonesian Communist party attempted a military coup. The Communist rebels were defeated by the Indonesian army, which emerged as the major power. With General *Suharto* replacing Sukarno as President,

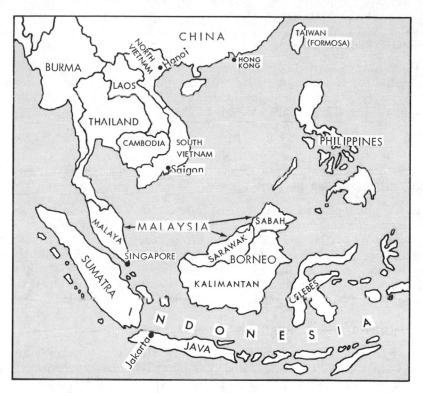

Southeast Asia Today

the military government ended the "confrontation" with Malaysia, returned to the United Nations, and welcomed Western investors.

E. MALAYSIA

BRIEF HISTORY

In 1957 the Malay States (excluding Singapore) received independence from Great Britain and joined the Commonwealth. They formed the *Federation of Malaya*. In 1963 Malaya joined with British North Borneo (now called Sabah) and Sarawak to form the new *Federation of Malaysia*.

ECONOMY AND PEOPLE

The Malay States, rich in tin and rubber, enjoy a relatively high living standard. However, agricultural North Borneo and oil-producing Sarawak are far less prosperous. Of Malaysia's 11 million people, 45 percent are Malayan and 35 percent are Chinese.

CURRENT PROBLEMS

(1) Malaysia needs to improve economic conditions in her poorer territories and to achieve political stability by integrating her diverse peoples. (2) Malaysia's Chinese minority dominates the Federation economically but resents the political control by the Malayans.

F. THE NATIONS OF INDO-CHINA

INDO-CHINA UNDER FRENCH RULE

In the 19th century, France annexed Indo-China. This was an agricultural country in Southeast Asia with a predominantly Buddhist population. During World War II, while France was overrun by the Nazis, Indo-China was occupied by the Japanese. Indo-Chinese nationalists, opposed to both Japan and France, joined an independence movement called the *Vietminh*. Although this movement contained some non-Communist nationalists, it was controlled by Communists and led by Moscow-trained *Ho Chi Minh*.

COMMUNISTS SEEK CONTROL (1946–1954)

After the war, France promised partial independence to the three states of Indo-China: Laos, Cambodia, and Vietnam. The Vietminh rejected the French offer and gained popular support by appealing to (1) *nationalism*, with promises to drive out the French completely, and (2) *land hunger*, with promises to distribute land to the peasants. For eight years, civil war raged in Indo-China. The Vietminh received aid from Red China. The French and their Indo-Chinese allies received equipment from the United States. In 1954 the Vietminh won the crucial *Battle of Dien Bien Phu.*

GENEVA CONFERENCE: TRUCE FOR INDO-CHINA (1954)

Britain and the Soviet Union (as co-chairmen), the United States, Red China, France, and the states of Indo-China sent representatives to Geneva to negotiate a settlement. The Geneva Agreements, not signed by the United States or South Vietnam, provided as follows: (1) *Laos* and *Cambodia* were recognized as independent and were expected to observe neutrality in the cold war. (2) *Vietnam* was divided at the 17th parallel: the North under a Communist government in *Hanoi,* the South under a French-sponsored anti-Communist government in *Saigon.* The people in both the North and the South were to vote by mid-1956 for a single all-Vietnam government.

DEVELOPMENTS IN VIETNAM

1. **Communist North Vietnam.** Ho Chi Minh established a Communist dictatorship, increased the army's manpower, eliminated most private enterprise, and received considerable Russian and Chinese aid. The Communists seek to gain control of South Vietnam.

2. **South Vietnam Under President Diem (1955-1963).** (*a*) *Independent and Anti-Communist Regime.* President *Ngo Dinh Diem* made his country fully independent of France. Diem rejected plans for all-Vietnam elections. He argued that honest elections were impossible in the Communist North. (*b*) **Communist Guerrilla Warfare.** Diem's regime was under growing pressure from the Communist *National Liberation Front* and its military arm, the *Vietcong.* With support from the North, the Vietcong waged guerrilla warfare throughout South Vietnam, terrorized villages, killed government supporters, and established Vietcong control over considerable rural areas. (*c*) **American Aid.** Saigon requested American aid, and this was first granted by President Eisenhower and later expanded by President Kennedy. American leaders feared that a Communist take-over in South Vietnam might cause the neighboring nations in Southeast Asia to fall to the Communists like a row of "falling dominoes." (*d*) **Diem's Downfall (1963).** In South Vietnam Diem faced opposition because of his autocratic rule, and because Buddhist priests charged Diem, a Roman Catholic, with persecuting them. In 1963 the Diem regime was overthrown by a military coup.

3. **Escalation of the War.** In 1964 limited numbers of American troops and military advisers were in South Vietnam, and American naval units patrolled the international waters of the Gulf of Tonkin. When North Vietnamese tor-

pedo boats attacked American destroyers, President Johnson ordered an air strike against North Vietnam's naval bases. By the *Gulf of Tonkin Resolution,* Congress almost unanimously supported the President's action. (In 1970 Congress repealed the Gulf of Tonkin Resolution.)

In 1965 major American bases in South Vietnam were attacked by the Vietcong. Calling these attacks provocations "directed by the Hanoi regime," President Johnson ordered continuous air strikes against North Vietnamese military targets. The United States increased its forces in South Vietnam, eventually to over 500,000 men. In accordance with the SEATO treaty, some troops from Australia, New Zealand, the Philippines, and Thailand augmented the South Vietnamese and American forces.

The Communist nations increased their support for the Vietcong. Employing the "Ho Chi Minh Trail" running through Laos, Hanoi sent more supplies and more regular army troops into the South. Moscow increased its supplies of heavy military equipment for North Vietnam. Peking assigned engineering and service troops to maintain transportation links in the North.

4. Debate in America Regarding Vietnam. American public opinion divided sharply regarding Vietnam. (*a*) The "hawks" argued that increased military action is necessary to halt aggression and contain Communist expansion in Asia. Many hawks demanded that we win the war by drastically stepping up military pressures on Hanoi even at the risk of further enraging Red China and the Soviet Union. (*b*) The "doves" urged the United States to seek peace by reducing its military activities in Vietnam. They argued that America (1) has no vital interests in Vietnam, (2) is risking war with Red China, and (3) is expending funds needed for domestic programs. The doves further argued that the South Vietnamese people have no loyalty for the Saigon government. (This government, chosen by the voters in 1967, was dominated by the military leader *Nguyen Van Thieu* as President. In 1971 Thieu ran unopposed and won a second term.)

5. The Move to Peace Talks

a. Unsuccessful Peace Efforts. From 1965 to 1968 President Johnson made several efforts to move the Vietnam issue from the battlefield to the conference table—all unsuccessful. His most notable effort came in 1965 when he halted air strikes against North Vietnam and asked Hanoi to begin peace talks. Hanoi rejected Johnson's peace offensive as a "fraud." After a 37-day pause, Johnson ordered a resumption of the air strikes.

b. Paris Peace Talks. In 1968 President Johnson ordered a halt in the bombing of most of North Vietnam and again appealed to Hanoi to agree to peace negotiations. The two nations began talks in Paris. Later, after an "informal understanding" with Hanoi setting limits on Communist military activity, Johnson halted all bombing of the North. Thereafter, the Paris peace talks were expanded to include the Saigon government and the Vietcong.

6. Nixon Administration and Vietnam

a. Diplomatic Stalemate Continues. President Nixon sought to end the Vietnam war by an honorable settlement that would free American prisoners of war and enable the South Vietnamese people to decide their own future by honest, internationally supervised elections. Following the death of Ho Chi Minh, Communist leaders in Hanoi held fast to their demands for complete withdrawal of American forces, the end of the "puppet" Thieu government, and the unification of Vietnam under Communist control. The Paris talks remained deadlocked and at times suspended.

b. Vietnamization. Nixon spurred *Vietnamization* of the war: shifting more of the burden of the fighting to South Vietnamese forces. He began the reduction of American troop strength in Vietnam, so that by late 1972 he had withdrawn over 500,000 men, leaving there only 27,000 American troops. American casualty lists grew much shorter. (However, American airmen in Thailand and naval personnel in the South China Sea increased somewhat.)

c. The War Spills Over Into the Neighboring Indo-Chinese States

(1) In *Cambodia* in early 1970, military and civilian leaders ended the rule of neutralist but leftist-leaning Prince *Norodom Sihanouk*. The new rightist-leaning regime reaffirmed Cambodia's neutrality and demanded the withdrawal of North Vietnamese and Vietcong forces maintaining bases in Cambodia as sanctuaries. Instead, the Communist forces attacked Cambodian towns, thereby arousing American fears of Communist control of the 600-mile Cambodian-South Vietnamese border. Thereupon President Nixon ordered American forces to join with South Vietnamese troops in a limited "incursion" into Cambodia to destroy the Communist sanctuaries.

(2) In *Laos* in 1970, North Vietnamese and local Pathet Lao (Communist) forces mounted an offensive against the neutralist regime headed by *Souvanna Phouma*. Despite American air support for the Laotian troops, the Communists overran much of southern Laos. In 1971 South Vietnamese ground forces with American air support began an "incursion" into southern Laos to capture enemy stockpiles and to disrupt enemy supply routes on the "Ho Chi Minh Trail." At first, the South Vietnamese moved ahead easily, but eventually they ran into heavy resistance and withdrew from Laos.

Both incursions aroused much controversy in the United States, again between the "hawks" and the "doves."

d. Hanoi's Military Offensive. In 1972, with American military strength in Vietnam sharply down, the North Vietnamese began a massive offensive in the South. Their aims were to discredit the Nixon Vietnamization policy, to overthrow the Thieu regime, and to gain a military victory. Strongly armed with Soviet tanks and heavy artillery, the North Vietnamese occupied considerable territory before they were slowed by more effective resistance.

President Nixon called North Vietnam's offensive an aggression and a violation of the 1968 "understanding"—to limit Communist military activity—that marked the beginning of the Paris peace talks. Thereupon Nixon expanded American air support for South Vietnamese forces, resumed American bombing of military targets in the North, and later mined North Vietnamese harbors, notably *Haiphong,* so that Communist vessels could no longer bring in military supplies. In the United States, critics condemned Nixon for expanding the war and risking a confrontation with the Soviet Union and China. Nixon explained that North Vietnam had expanded the war by its massive offensive and that the mining of harbors was unlikely to lead to a confrontation with the major Communist powers.

e. Secret Peace Talks. In early 1972 President Nixon revealed that for almost 30 months Washington and Hanoi had held, in and around Paris, a series of secret peace talks. The American negotiator was President Nixon's national security adviser, *Henry Kissinger;* the chief Hanoi negotiator was a member of the Politburo (the Communist party's ruling body), *Le Duc Tho.* The secret meetings continued, later were broken off, and then resumed. In January, 1973, Kissinger and Tho completed an agreement to end the war.

7. The Paris Peace Agreement for Vietnam (1973)

a. Provisions. (1) *Military.* (a) All four parties to the Paris peace conference—the United States, North Vietnam, South Vietnam, and the Vietcong—agree to an internationally supervised cease-fire. (b) The United States shall withdraw its remaining forces and dismantle its remaining military bases in South Vietnam. (c) Hanoi and the Vietcong shall return all American prisoners of war and provide the fullest possible accounting for persons missing in action. (d) All foreign troops shall be withdrawn from Laos and Cambodia and these countries shall not be used as bases for attacks upon South Vietnam. (e) No troops and no additional military supplies shall be introduced into South Vietnam. (2) *Reunification.* (a) The reunification of Vietnam shall be achieved only by peaceful means. (b) Pending reunification, both North Vietnam and South Vietnam shall respect the provisional military demarcation line at the 17th parallel. (3) *Political Arrangements for South Vietnam.* (a) Each of the two South Vietnamese parties (Saigon and the Vietcong) shall retain the areas under its control at the time of the cease-fire. (b) The two South Vietnamese parties shall end hatred, prohibit reprisals, and insure the democratic liberties of the people. (c) The people of South Vietnam have a sacred right to decide their own political future through free and democratic elections under international supervision. (d) The two South Vietnamese parties shall establish a Council of National Reconciliation and Concord—composed of Saigon, Vietcong, and neutralist members—to promote mutual respect and to organize elections. Its decisions shall be unanimous. (4) *International Control and Supervision.* An International Commission of Control and Supervision of four nations—Canada, Hungary, Indonesia, and Poland—shall oversee the cease-fire and other provisions of the agreement. For these purposes, it shall employ a 1,160-man force. (5) *Postwar Reconstruction.* The United States agrees to help the postwar reconstruction of Indo-China, including North Vietnam.

b. Observations. (1) The agreement was a compromise, with neither side gaining all its objectives. The United States did *not* secure (*a*) the withdrawal of an estimated 145,000 Hanoi troops out of the South and back to the North, (*b*) a cease-fire for Laos and Cambodia. Hanoi did *not* secure (*a*) the overthrow of the Thieu regime in Saigon and (*b*) the establishment of a Communist-dominated coalition government in the South. (2) Some observers fear that the cease-fire may be short-lived since the hatred between Saigon and the Communists has been of such long duration that their military forces may again clash and reactivate the war. (3) The agreement, if observed, would transform the struggle for South Vietnam from a military to a political conflict. (4) The Vietnam war cost the United States over an eleven-year period $140 billion, more than 300,000 wounded, and 46,000 killed. It was one of the costliest wars in American history. It was also costly in that it caused deep divisions among the American people.

c. Comments. (1) President Nixon welcomed the agreement as providing "peace with honor." It met, he claimed, the basic American conditions of assuring the return of Americans held as prisoners of war and of guaranteeing the South Vietnamese the right to determine their own political future. (2) President Thieu of South Vietnam labeled the agreement a cease-fire but not a guarantee of a long-lasting peace, expressed doubt as to whether the Communists would observe the agreement, and warned his countrymen that the new "political struggle phase, although not as bloody, will be as tough and dangerous as the military struggle phase." (3) Le Duc Tho, the North Vietnamese negotiator, hailed the agreement as "a great victory for the Vietnamese people" and also for the socialist countries. He predicted that the "Vietnamese people will advance to the reunification of the country."

THE NIXON DOCTRINE (1969)

President Nixon asserted that the United States would continue to play a major role in the Pacific but would seek to avoid involvement in another war like Vietnam. Nixon told our Asian friends that the United States would honor its treaty commitments, including military and economic aid, but would look to any Asian nation threatened by internal subversion or non-nuclear aggression to provide the manpower for its own defense. The *Nixon Doctrine,* said the President, meant a "more responsible role for the Asian nations" and also an American policy that could "be sustained over the long run."

Part 7. Imperialism and Nationalism: Evaluation and Summary

Modern imperialism has spread Western civilization to peoples all over the world. Some of its effects have been beneficial, others harmful.

EFFECTS OF IMPERIALISM UPON COLONIAL POWERS

1. Good Effects. Imperialism (a) provided manufacturers with cheap raw materials and with protected markets, investors with profitable business opportunities, exporters and importers with increased trade, and factory workers with more steady employment, (b) raised the mother country's living standards, (c) opened up colonial careers for government officials and military men, and (d) gave the imperialist nation military bases and greater manpower, and enhanced its world prestige.

2. Bad Effects. Imperialism (a) burdened taxpayers to finance colonial improvements and defense, (b) caused colonial rivalries that threatened war, (c) perpetuated the antidemocratic belief that colonial peoples are inferior, and (d) aroused colonial ill will toward the ruling peoples.

EFFECTS OF IMPERIALISM UPON COLONIES

1. Good Effects. Imperialist nations (a) developed their colonies' natural resources, improved transportation and communication, furthered agriculture, and established industries, (b) trained workers in new skills and provided the colonial peoples with employment, (c) constructed educational and health facilities: schools, hospitals, and sanitation projects, (d) halted native warfare and prohibited barbarous practices, (e) introduced Western culture: Christian ethics, democracy, science, and the belief in progress, and (f) trained the colonial peoples in self-govenment.

2. Bad Effects. Imperialist nations (a) drained wealth from the colonies, (b) maintained unbalanced economies in many colonies by emphasizing mineral and agricultural production and discouraging colonial manufacturing, (c) exploited the native workers by requiring long hours for little pay, (d) assumed an attitude of racial and cultural superiority, discriminated against the colonial peoples, and degraded their native cultures, (e) introduced previously unknown vices and diseases, and (f) aroused the colonies to feel antagonistic and to consider the imperialist peoples as oppressors.

COLONIAL NATIONALISM AND THE DECLINE OF WESTERN IMPERIALISM

1. Factors Encouraging Colonial Nationalism. Emerging in the 20th century, especially after World War II, colonial nationalism resulted from (a)

Western ideals of democracy and nationalism, (b) Communist propaganda against "capitalist exploitation," (c) exhaustion of the West European colonial powers following World War II, (d) United Nations support of self-determination, and (e) revived native pride in their own cultures.

Colonial nationalists—many of whom were educated in Europe and the United States—led the struggle against imperialist rule.

2. Extent of Imperialist Decline. Greatly weakened by World War II, the West European powers have yielded to colonial nationalism. They have relinquished control, willingly or unwillingly, over the major portions of their empires. Since 1945 over 40 new nations in Africa and Asia have achieved independence.

PROBLEMS FACING NEWLY INDEPENDENT NATIONS

1. Economic Problems: (a) Raise living standards from the poverty level. (b) Secure foreign capital to develop natural resources and further industry. (c) Decrease economic dependence upon the former mother country. (d) End reliance upon a single agricultural or mineral product. (e) Provide employment for factory workers and land for peasants.

2. Social Problems: (a) Instill in the people a sense of national pride and unity. (b) Eliminate illiteracy. (c) Improve health conditions. (d) Train personnel for professional, industrial, and governmental service.

3. Political Problems: (a) Maintain stable, efficient, and possibly democratic government. (b) Develop civic responsibility among their peoples. (c) Break down tribal organizations and loyalties. (d) Suppress army revolts and secessionist movements. (e) Combat Communist attempts to gain control.

4. Foreign Problems: (a) Aid peoples still subject to imperialist rule. (b) Maintain adequate military defenses against hostile neighbors. (c) Determine a policy toward the cold war. (d) Obtain foreign aid—from the Communist bloc or the free world or both.

PROBLEMS FACING FORMER IMPERIALIST POWERS

The former colonial powers face these problems: (1) Assuage their national pride that was wounded by military defeats and territorial losses. (2) Absorb the European settlers who fled the newly independent countries and returned to their homeland. (3) Establish mutually satisfactory relations with their former colonies so as to maintain cultural and economic ties. (4) Secure new foreign outlets for manufactured goods and capital investment. (5) Help former colonies escape Communist domination, and provide them with technical and economic aid.

THE AFRO-ASIAN NATIONS IN WORLD AFFAIRS

1. At the First Bandung Conference (1955). The Afro-Asian nations, many newly independent, met at Bandung, Indonesia. The conference condemned imperialism—whether practiced by Communist or capitalist nations—urged independence for all remaining colonies, deplored racial discrimination, and pledged continued Afro-Asian cooperation. This conference indicated Afro-Asian determination to help shape the future of the world.

2. In the U.N. General Assembly. The Afro-Asian nations tend to vote as a bloc in the General Assembly. Since they total over half the membership, their votes are essential to approve any General Assembly resolutions. Because they are against colonialism, the Afro-Asians have-demanded U.N. action against Portugal; because they are against racial discrimination, the Afro-Asians have voted to censure South Africa. On cold war issues, most—but not all—Afro-Asian nations support a policy of neutrality.

3. Cancellation of the "Second Bandung" Conference, Scheduled for Algiers (1965). With colonialism largely dead, the Afro-Asian nations lacked a unifying force. Divided by different interests and ideologies, the Afro-Asians canceled this conference.

MULTIPLE-CHOICE QUESTIONS

1. The Western powers were interested in China during the 19th century because China (1) had a large supply of oil (2) was a good market for farm machinery (3) served as an outlet for Europe's surplus population (4) offered opportunities for profitable trade.
2. As a result of the Opium War (1) the United States issued the Open Door Policy (2) Britain acquired Hong Kong (3) Russia annexed the Amur River area (4) Japan seized Formosa.
3. By granting extraterritorial rights to the foreign powers, China permitted them to (1) build railroads (2) establish tariff rates (3) lease seaports (4) try in their own courts their citizens accused of crimes in China.
4. The Open Door Policy meant that (1) all nations were equally free to trade in China (2) Britain gave up her lease holdings in China (3) Russia had a "free hand" in China (4) American missionaries were free to establish churches in China.
5. An important aim of the Open Door Policy was to (1) prevent the imperialist powers from dividing up China (2) encourage the Chinese to emigrate (3) speed China's industrial development (4) introduce democratic government into China.
6. The Boxers of China favored the (1) creation of a democratic government (2) overthrow of the Manchu Dynasty (3) expulsion of foreigners (4) opening of all Chinese ports to foreign trade.
7. As a result of the Boxer Rebellion, (1) Japan paid an indemnity to China (2) the United States withdrew her Open Door Policy (3) China paid an indemnity to the imperialist powers (4) the United States annexed the Philippines.
8. A basic aim of the Kuomintang in China was to (1) eliminate foreign domination (2) declare war against Japan (3) prevent industrialization (4) expel American missionaries.
9. Which best accounts for the lack of political unity in China before World War II? (1) religious diversity (2) lack of natural resources (3) the refusal of foreign countries to recognize China (4) the growth of the Chinese Communist movement.
10. What important iron-producing area was seized by Japan in 1931 and is now a part of Red China? (1) Tibet (2) Sinkiang (3) Mongolia (4) Manchuria.

11. As a result of her invasion of China proper in 1937, Japan (1) gained control of all China (2) failed to capture any key Chinese cities (3) captured many important cities but failed to gain absolute control of China (4) completely wiped out Communism in China.

12. One factor enabling the Communists to seize control of China after World War II was that (1) Japan had wiped out the Kuomintang armies (2) the United States refused to aid the Nationalists (3) Russia had never been imperialist toward China (4) the Chinese Communists promised to drive out the imperialist powers.

13. The communes in Communist China are (1) the basic membership units of the Communist party (2) huge housing projects in the major cities (3) newly constructed industrial communities (4) huge farms on which the peasants labor for wages.

14. Where does the government of Nationalist China maintain its headquarters? (1) Cambodia (2) Taiwan (3) Hong Kong (4) Korea.

15. Japanese ports were opened to world trade as a result of (1) Commodore Perry's expedition (2) World War I (3) the Opium War (4) the Washington Conference.

16. Japan withdrew from the League of Nations because (1) the United States refused to recognize Manchukuo (2) the Lytton Report condemned Japan's actions in Manchuria (3) Germany urged her withdrawal (4) she feared the power of Russia.

17. Before 1945 modern Japan and Great Britain were similar in that both (1) exported large quantities of wheat (2) needed raw materials and markets (3) discouraged tenant farming (4) wanted to maintain China's territorial integrity.

18. An important reform in Japan following World War II was the (1) return to the Emperor of the powers he had lost during the war (2) recognition of Shinto as the state religion (3) nationalization of industry (4) adoption of a democratic constitution providing a Bill of Rights.

19. Since World War II Japan's government has (1) been dominated by the Socialists (2) advocated pro-American policies (3) been unstable because of many small parties in the Diet (4) been controlled by the military.

20. India was valuable to Great Britain especially as a (1) place for surplus population (2) means of lowering taxes in England (3) field for missionary work (4) place for investment of English capital.

21. The British government assumed control of India after (1) the sepoy troops mutinied (2) Gandhi started a movement to free India (3) the East India Company's charter expired (4) the French threatened to take control.

22. Under English rule in the 19th century, India's population (1) declined slightly (2) remained about the same (3) increased slightly (4) increased considerably.

23. Pakistan is referred to as an underdeveloped nation today because it (1) is divided into two parts by India (2) is predominantly Moslem (3) has a poorly equipped army (4) has an agricultural economy and a low standard of living.

24. Before gaining independence in 1949, Indonesia belonged to (1) Belgium (2) China (3) France (4) the Netherlands.

25. Following Sukarno's loss of power, Indonesia improved relations with (1) Communist China (2) India (3) Malaysia (4) France.

26. The large minority group that dominates Malaysia economically consists of (1) Indians (2) Japanese (3) Chinese (4) Filipinos.

27. Which European country was directly involved in the 1946-1954 civil war in Indo-China? (1) Great Britain (2) France (3) Italy (4) the Netherlands.

28. Which American President began the United States policy of aid to South Vietnam? (1) Truman (2) Eisenhower (3) Kennedy (4) Johnson.

29. The 1955 Bandung Conference (1) reflected the desire of Afro-Asian nations to play a larger role in world affairs (2) settled the civil war in Vietnam (3) established an economic aid program for southeast Asia (4) conceded that imperialism had brought some benefits to former colonies.

30. Which is the most highly industrialized nation in the Far East? (1) China (2) India (3) Japan (4) Korea.
31. Religion was an important factor in the post-World War II partition of (1) Vietnam (2) China (3) India (4) Korea.
32. Which member of the Commonwealth of Nations is a major source of tin and rubber? (1) Ceylon (2) Malaysia (3) Indonesia (4) Pakistan.

MULTIPLE-CHOICE QUESTIONS

Select the number of the item that does *not* belong in the corresponding group.

1. *Nations that had spheres of influence in China in the 19th century:* (1) France (2) the Netherlands (3) Russia (4) Germany.
2. *Chinese territories seized by Czarist Russia:* (1) the Amur River district (2) part of central Asia (3) the Yangtze River valley (4) Vladivostok.
3. *Policies of Communist China:* (1) development of heavy industry (2) encouragement of foreign investments (3) purges of counterrevolutionists (4) weakening of family ties.
4. *Territories acquired by Japan between 1890 and 1945:* (1) Korea (2) Port Arthur (3) Formosa (4) Sinkiang.
5. *Problems facing India:* (1) strengthening the feeling of national unity (2) countering the hostility of Great Britain (3) developing industry (4) reducing illiteracy.
6. *Chief products of Indonesia:* (1) radios (2) quinine (3) rubber (4) oil.
7. *Nations carved out of Indo-China:* (1) Burma (2) South Vietnam (3) Laos (4) Cambodia.

IDENTIFICATION QUESTIONS: WHO AM I?

Chiang Kai-shek	Mohammed Ali Jinnah	Lal Bahadur Shastri
Chou En-lai	Douglas MacArthur	Souvanna Phouma
Mohandas Gandhi	Mao Tse-tung	Henry L. Stimson
John Hay	Mutsuhito	Achmed Sukarno
Ho Chi Minh	Jawaharlal Nehru	Sun Yat-sen

1. I founded the Kuomintang and led the revolution that overthrew the Manchu Dynasty.
2. Known as the "saintly one," I combatted British rule by passive resistance and secured independence for my country.
3. As Supreme Allied Commander in the Pacific, I accepted the surrender of Japan in World War II. I occupied that country and introduced democratic reforms.
4. A neutralist, I hoped to end civil war in Laos by agreeing to head a three-faction coalition government.
5. As leader of the Chinese Nationalists, I fought the warlords, the Japanese, and the Chinese Communists. By 1950 I had lost the mainland to the Communists and ruled only a small island off the China coast.
6. A Communist trained in Moscow, I successfully combatted French rule and became head of North Vietnam.
7. Fearful of Hindu domination after independence, I secured the creation of the Moslem state of Pakistan.
8. I was head of the Communist party when it gained control of China. In 1958 I proclaimed a "great leap forward" to develop China economically.
9. Opposed to Japan's conquest of Manchuria, I stated that the United States would recognize no territory taken by force.
10. As first President of Indonesia, I proclaimed a policy of neutrality in the cold war. However, I frequently antagonized Western nations by my actions.
11. As leader of the Congress party and first Prime Minister of India, I sought to set my country on the road to economic development and political democracy.

UNIT XI. WORLD WARS AND DICTATORSHIPS IN A TROUBLED WORLD

Part 1. World War I

FORMATION OF EUROPEAN ALLIANCES

1. **Triple Alliance (Germany, Austria-Hungary, and Italy).** Germany, under Bismarck's leadership, had triumphed in the Franco-Prussian War and had imposed a humiliating peace treaty on France (see page 205). To deter the French from a "war of revenge," Bismarck pursued policies to isolate France and gain allies for Germany. Bismarck sought an alliance with Austria-Hungary, whose expansion into the Balkans conflicted with Russian ambitions. In 1879 Germany and Austria-Hungary, Europe's *Central Powers,* joined in a defensive military alliance.

Italy was enraged at France, whose seizure of Tunisia in 1881 thwarted Italian plans. In 1882 Italy agreed to a defensive military alliance with Germany and Austria-Hungary, thereby completing the *Triple Alliance.*

The weakness of the Triple Alliance was Italy's historic enmity for Austria-Hungary and Italy's desire for the remaining Italian-inhabited Austrian territories.

2. **Triple Entente (France, Russia, and England).** France aspired to regain European leadership and win back her "stolen provinces" of Alsace and Lorraine from Germany. France therefore sought allies, particularly Russia. However, France could not overcome Bismarck's skillful diplomacy, which kept Russia friendly to Germany. In 1890, however, after Bismarck had been dismissed as Chancellor, Germany refused to renew her treaty of friendship with Russia. France thereafter extended military and industrial loans to Russia and gained her confidence; in 1894 the two nations entered into the *Dual Alliance.*

England considered her industrial leadership and colonial Empire threatened most by Germany. Nevertheless, in 1898 England clashed with France over control of the Sudan, in the *Fashoda Affair.* Because both nations feared Germany more than each other, they agreed to a peaceful settlement. Eventually, England gave France a free hand in Morocco, and France confirmed England's dominance in the Sudan. By this settlement in 1904, England and France began a close diplomatic understanding, the *Entente Cordiale.*

In 1907 England and Russia settled differences over spheres of influence in Persia and China. This agreement completed the *Triple Entente.*

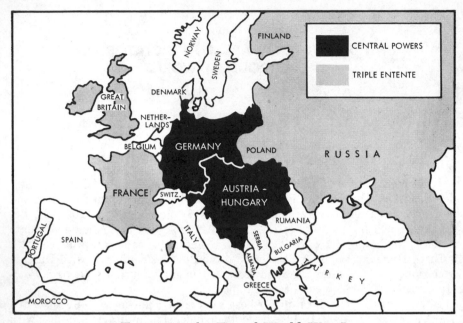

Europe on the Eve of World War I

CRISES PRECEDING WORLD WAR I

The rival alliances confronted each other in a series of diplomatic clashes.

1. Moroccan Crisis of 1905. Germany challenged France's sphere of influence in Morocco. The German Kaiser visited Morocco and pledged his support for that country's independence. Not ready for war, France agreed to submit the question of Morocco to an international conference. The *Algeciras Conference* (*a*) reaffirmed the independence of Morocco, but (*b*) recognized France's special interests in that country.

2. Moroccan Crisis of 1911. Germany challenged France's attempt to convert Morocco into a protectorate. War was averted when both nations agreed to a compromise. Germany withdrew her objections to a French protectorate over Morocco in exchange for a small area of the French Congo.

The Moroccan crises of 1905 and 1911 (*a*) constituted diplomatic setbacks for Germany, (*b*) drew France and England into closer alliance, as England supported French claims, and (*c*) intensified hostility between the Entente and the Central Powers.

3. Balkan Crises of 1912-1913. Russia supported the expansion plans of her Balkan ally and kindred Slavic state, Serbia. With Russian approval, four Balkan nations—Serbia, Montenegro, Bulgaria, and Greece—warred against, defeated, and seized territory from Turkey.

Austria thereupon intervened to force the creation of Albania out of former Turkish lands and thus deny Serbia an outlet to the Adriatic Sea. Austria's attitude reflected her (*a*) opposition to Russian influence in the Balkans, and (*b*) fear that a powerful Serbia would cause unrest among Serbians and other Slavic peoples in the Austro-Hungarian Empire. In the Second Balkan War (1913), Serbia gained some territory from defeated Bulgaria but *not* an outlet to the sea.

The Balkan crises of 1912-1913 (*a*) brought Russia and Serbia closer together, and (*b*) intensified the hatred of Russia and Serbia for Austria-Hungary.

IMMEDIATE CAUSE OF WORLD WAR I: ASSASSINATION OF THE AUSTRIAN ARCHDUKE

Serbian nationalists, both in Serbia and in Austria, plotted the breakup of the Austro-Hungarian Empire and wanted to establish a strong Serbian state. In June, 1914, a Serbian nationalist assassinated Archduke *Francis Ferdinand*, heir to the throne of Austria-Hungary. The assassination took place in the Serbian-populated region of the Austrian Empire, at *Sarajevo*. Although several Serbian government officials had been aware of the plot, no one had warned the Austrian government.

The assassination sparked a chain reaction that led Europe into World War I.

1. Austria decided to deal harshly with Serbia and obtained from Germany a promise of unconditional support—a diplomatic "blank check." Thus fortified, Austria presented an ultimatum demanding that Serbia (*a*) stop anti-Austrian propaganda, (*b*) dismiss anti-Austrian government officials, and (*c*) permit Austria to investigate, within Serbia, the assassination plot. Austria denounced Serbia's reply as unsatisfactory and declared war on Serbia.

2. Germany, seeing Russia mobilize her forces, seized the initiative and declared war against Russia and France.

3. Germany's armies moved toward France, not by crossing the mountains on the fortified Franco-German border, but by going through the Belgian level plain. By invading Belgium, Germany violated her pledge to respect that country's neutrality.

4. England feared German control of Belgium—opposite the British Isles —as a threat to her security. When Germany rejected an English ultimatum to withdraw from Belgium, England declared war on Germany.

FUNDAMENTAL CAUSES OF WORLD WAR I

All the European powers were to blame for World War I, although not in equal measure. The major causes were the following:

1. Nationalism. (*a*) France was determined to recover the French-inhabited provinces of Alsace and Lorraine. (*b*) Serbia wanted Austro-Hungarian territory inhabited by Yugoslav peoples. (*c*) Subject nationalities—Yugoslavs, Czechs, Slovaks, and Poles—sought independence, even at the price of war. (*d*) Intense patriotism assured popular support for warlike measures.

2. Imperialism. (*a*) France and Germany clashed over Morocco. (*b*) Russia and Austria-Hungary were rivals in the Balkans. (*c*) England and Germany, both highly industrialized, competed for imperialist control in Africa and the Middle East, and for world markets.

3. Militarism. (*a*) By conscripting (drafting) soldiers, lengthening their training period, and providing them with modern equipment, the continental European nations each sought military superiority. (*b*) Germany had a military tradition and extolled armed might. (*c*) Armament manufacturers—Krupp in Germany and Schneider in France—encouraged increased production of military equipment. (*d*) England, which relied heavily upon her navy for protection of her island homeland, considered Germany's huge naval building program a threat to English security.

4. International Anarchy. (*a*) No strong international organization existed with facilities to enable nations to settle disputes peacefully. (*b*) The *Hague Court of Arbitration* (also called the Hague Tribunal), established in 1899, was ineffective. It could not compel nations to submit their quarrels to its judgment or to accept its decisions.

OTHER NATIONS ENTER THE WAR

1. The Central Powers (Germany and Austria-Hungary) were joined by two nations: (*a*) Turkey in 1914—to combat her traditional enemy, Russia, and (*b*) Bulgaria in 1915—to secure revenge against Serbia (see Balkan Wars, pages 217-218).

2. The Allied Powers (England, France, Russia, Serbia, and Belgium) were joined by more than 25 nations. Most notable were (*a*) Japan in 1914—to acquire German territories in the Pacific, (*b*) Italy in 1915—won over by secret Allied promises of territory at the expense of Turkey and Austria-Hungary (previously, Italy claimed that the Central Powers were the aggressors and therefore refused to honor her defensive alliance with Germany), and (*c*) the United States in 1917.

AMERICAN ENTRANCE INTO WORLD WAR I: REASONS

When war started in 1914, President *Woodrow Wilson* urged the American people to be "neutral in fact as well as in name" and issued a *Proclamation of Neutrality*. However, confronted by world events, neither Wilson nor the American people could remain neutral. In April, 1917, Wilson asked Congress to declare war on Germany. The main reasons were the following:

1. German Unrestricted Submarine Warfare. To blockade England and to counteract British superiority in surface vessels, the Germans resorted to *unrestricted submarine warfare*. German submarines, called *U-boats*, attacked without warning and without attempting to save crews and passengers. They torpedoed ships of neutral nations as well as of belligerents. In 1915 over 100 American lives were lost when a German U-boat sank the British passenger vessel *Lusitania*. The American people were outraged as German U-boats took an increasing toll of American ships and lives.

(Although, in spite of our protests, English warships searched and seized our vessels, Americans were less angered, since such interference did not endanger American lives.)

2. Allied Propaganda. Americans were receptive toward Allied propaganda because (*a*) we felt a kinship for England, based upon common language and culture, and (*b*) our friendship for France went back to France's support of the colonial cause in the American Revolution.

3. Hostility Toward Germany. The American people became increasingly hostile toward Germany because the Germans (*a*) invaded neutral Belgium, (*b*) waged unrestricted submarine warfare, (*c*) attempted sabotage of American industries, and (*d*) tried to draw Mexico into a plot against the United States.

4. American Economic Interests. Because England effectively blockaded the Central Powers, Americans sold foodstuffs and manufactured goods almost entirely to the Allies. When the Allies exhausted their funds, American investors extended them substantial loans. Americans feared that, if Germany won the war, American loans to the Allies might never be repaid.

5. American Idealism. Americans felt that a better world would emerge if the Allied nations triumphed over the autocratic Central Powers. President Wilson called World War I "a war to end all wars" and proclaimed that "the world must be made safe for democracy."

6. American Security. Germany, if victorious, would replace democratic England as the dominant European power on the Atlantic. From this location, aggressive, militaristic Germany might threaten the security of the United States.

AMERICAN ENTRANCE INTO WORLD WAR I: SIGNIFICANCE

It (1) turned the tide of battle in favor of the Allies, (2) broke sharply with America's traditional avoidance of foreign entanglements—that is, a *policy of isolation,* and (3) marked America's emergence as a world power and to eventual world leadership.

MILITARY ASPECTS OF THE WAR

1. Worldwide Involvement. For the first time in history, all major nations throughout the world were involved in the same war. Peoples from every continent provided troops for combat.

2. New Weapons. The following military devices were used for the first time in warfare: dirigibles, submarines, giant artillery guns, tanks, and poison gas. Also used for the first time in warfare was the airplane. It was employed at first mainly for observation purposes, but later for small-scale bombings and for attacks on ground forces.

3. Naval Warfare. On the high seas, the British navy, aided by the French and later the American navies, maintained control of the Atlantic shipping lanes, dealt successfully with the German submarine menace, and effectively blockaded the Central Powers. In 1916 Germany attempted to break the blockade but was halted by England in the famous North Sea naval battle of *Jutland.*

4. Europe: Major Theater of Warfare

a. Eastern Front. From 1914 to 1917 Russian forces suffered crushing defeats, inflicted chiefly by German armies. Russia experienced two revolutions in 1917 (see pages 349-350), and, under a Communist government, withdrew from the war in early 1918 after accepting the harsh *Treaty of Brest-Litovsk.*

b. Southern Front. By 1917 the Central Powers had overrun most of the Balkans but had won no decisive battle in Italy. In 1918 an Allied force won back much of the Balkans, and an Italian offensive compelled Austria-Hungary to surrender.

c. Western Front. In 1914 German armies overran Belgium and northern France until halted by desperate French and British resistance at the battle of the *Marne.* Then the opposing armies dug into the ground for *trench warfare;* the western front became deadlocked. In 1916 the Germans attempted to smash the Allied defenses but were thrown back at *Verdun* and the *Somme* In 1918 Allied forces were reinforced by fresh American troops and unified under the command of the French *Marshal Foch.*

5. American Military Contribution. The *American Expeditionary Force* (*AEF*) of 2 million men was led by General *John J. Pershing*. In 1918 American soldiers helped halt a German offensive at *Château-Thierry* and *Belleau Wood*. Later they led the Allied end-the-war counteroffensive at *St. Mihiel* and the *Argonne Forest*.

6. German Surrender. By late 1918 the German High Command under Generals *von Hindenburg* and *Ludendorff* realized that the German armies, although still fighting on foreign soil, had lost the war. Germany sued for peace and on November 11, 1918, ended hostilities by accepting an *armistice*.

PRESIDENT WILSON'S FOURTEEN POINTS

In 1918, before the end of the war, President Wilson addressed Congress on American war aims. His program for a lasting peace consisted of the *Fourteen Points:* (1) open covenants (treaties) of peace openly arrived at, (2) freedom of the seas, (3) removal of international trade barriers (such as tariffs), (4) reduction of armaments, (5) impartial adjustment of colonial claims with due regard for the interests of the native peoples, (6-13) adjustment of European boundaries in accordance with the principle of nationality, and (14) establishment of a League of Nations.

Other Allied statesmen approved Wilson's Fourteen Points only with significant reservations. In particular, they upheld their nations' claims to territorial gains as agreed on in secret treaties.

THE TREATY OF VERSAILLES WITH GERMANY (1919)

1. Different Allied Objectives. The Allied leaders, called the "Big Four," who dominated the peace conference, each sought different objectives.

a. David Lloyd George, Prime Minister of England, sought to expand England's colonial empire, preserve her naval and industrial supremacy, and "make Germany pay for the war."

b. Georges Clemenceau, Premier of France, sought to ensure France's security against future German invasion and to weaken Germany by imposing military limitations, financial payments, and territorial losses.

c. Vittorio Orlando, Premier of Italy, sought to enlarge Italy's territory in Europe and expand her Empire overseas.

d. Woodrow Wilson, President of the United States, sought to provide a just peace and create a better world by implementing the Fourteen Points.

Out of these different and often conflicting objectives emerged the Treaty of Versailles, the result of months of struggle and compromise.

Europe Following World War I

2. Major Treaty Provisions

a. Territorial. Germany surrendered (1) Alsace-Lorraine to France, (2) the Saar Valley to League of Nations authority, and Saar coal mines to French control with the provision that, after 15 years, the Saar inhabitants decide their political future by a plebiscite (in 1934 they voted for union with Germany), (3) minor border regions to Denmark and Belgium, (4) parts of Posen and West Prussia, including a corridor to the Baltic Sea, to the new Polish Republic (this "Polish Corridor" cut off East Prussia from the rest of Germany), (5) Danzig, a Baltic seaport bordering on Poland, placed under League of Nations authority as a *free city* for Polish use.

The Saar and Danzig, predominantly German-inhabited, were transferred for economic considerations. Saar coal mines compensated France for property destruction caused by the German invasion. Danzig provided Poland with her only seaport.

The other territorial changes were more in accord with the principle of nationality. The territory granted Poland, however, contained a considerable German minority.

b. Colonial. Germany ceded all her colonies to the Allies to be held as League of Nations mandates.

c. Disarmament. The German army was limited to 100,000 volunteers. Conscription was forbidden. The Rhineland, in western Germany, was demilitarized. The German navy was reduced to a few small ships. Submarines, military aircraft, and war industries were prohibited.

These military restrictions were intended to prevent Germany from again waging war.

d. War Guilt and Reparations. Germany accepted sole responsibility for causing the war and agreed to pay reparations for all damages. (The *Dawes Plan*, 1924, provided for an orderly payment of the reparations; and the *Young Plan*, 1929, reduced the debt substantially. Germany made a few payments until 1931, but afterwards repudiated the remainder of the debt.)

e. League of Nations. The first article of the treaty provided for the establishment of the League of Nations (see pages 381-383).

3. Differing Views of the Treaty

a. Arguments Against: A Harsh Treaty That Planted the Seeds of World War II. The treaty transferred German-inhabited territory, seized all colonies of Germany, and compelled her to accept sole war guilt. It forced Germany to be unarmed while other nations remained armed, and it wounded German pride. By attacking the treaty, the Nazi party gained the support of the German people, achieved power, and brought on World War II.

b. Arguments For: A Fair Treaty That Was Not Enforced. The treaty transferred German territory chiefly on the basis of nationality, assigned German colonies as League of Nations mandates with the objective of eventual independence, disarmed Germany as a start toward world disarmament, and provided a League of Nations. The treaty alone cannot be blamed for the German people's support of Nazism. Furthermore, if the military provisions of the treaty had been enforced, Nazi Germany would not have been able to wage war.

TREATIES WITH THE OTHER DEFEATED NATIONS

1. The **Treaty of St. Germain** (1919) with Austria and the **Treaty of Trianon** (1920) with Hungary ended the Hapsburg Empire. (*a*) Austria and Hungary became independent national states. (*b*) Czechoslovakia, a new republic, was created entirely out of Austro-Hungarian territories. (*c*) Italy,

Rumania, the recreated Poland, and Yugoslavia (the enlarged former Serbia) each secured areas inhabited by her own nationals.

Both Austria and Hungary were required to limit their armies and pay reparations. Also, Austria was forbidden *Anschluss,* union with Germany.

2. The **Treaty of Neuilly** (1919) with Bulgaria provided that she cede minor territories, limit her army, and pay reparations.

3. The **Treaty of Lausanne** (1923) with Turkey contained slightly better terms than the original **Treaty of Sèvres** (1920), which she had rejected. In the Lausanne settlement, Turkey lost her non-Turkish territories but retained Asia Minor, Constantinople, and the Dardanelles. Turkey was exempted from arms limitations and payment of reparations.

RESULTS OF WORLD WAR I

1. Social. (*a*) Almost 10 million soldiers were killed and over 20 million wounded. (*b*) Millions of civilians died as a result of the hostilities, famine, and disease. (*c*) The world was left aflame with hatred, intolerance, and extreme nationalism.

2. Economic. (*a*) The total cost of the war was over $350 billion. Paying for the war brought heavy taxation and lower living standards to European peoples. (*b*) International trade suffered because nations raised tariffs and sought economic self-sufficiency. (*c*) In Russia, the Communists seized power and introduced a new economic system. (*d*) Economic dislocations caused by the war helped bring on the depression of 1929.

3. Political. (*a*) The United States emerged as a leading world power. (*b*) Three major European dynasties were dethroned: the Hohenzollerns of Germany, the Hapsburgs of Austria-Hungary, and the Romanovs of Russia. (*c*) New national states arose in central Europe. Several contained subject nationalities, especially the German-speaking populations of Poland and Czechoslovakia. (*d*) The League of Nations was established to solve international problems and advance world peace. (*e*) Many European nations, beset by economic and political discontent, turned to dictatorship—notably Russia, Italy, and Germany.

COMPLETION QUESTIONS

1. The members of the Triple Alliance were Italy, Austria-Hungary, and _____.
2. The members of the Triple Entente were France, England, and _____.
3. Before World War I Germany twice challenged French claims to the North African territory of _____.
4. The new Balkan state created after the First Balkan War to block Serbia's access to the sea was _____.
5. In 1914 Archduke Francis Ferdinand, heir to the Austro-Hungarian throne, was assassinated by a _____ nationalist.

6. President Wilson's statement of war aims, issued in January, 1918, as a basis for peace, was the _____.
7. The English Prime Minister who represented his country at the World War I Peace Conference was _____.
8. Two provinces taken by Germany from France in 1871 but restored after World War I were _____ and _____.
9. By the Treaty of Versailles, the German army was limited to no more than _____ men.
10. The nation that had control of the Dardanelles according to its peace treaty after World War I was _____.

MULTIPLE-CHOICE QUESTIONS

1. Italy entered the Triple Alliance because (1) Germany had aided her in the Austro-Sardinian War (2) she was angered by France's seizure of Tunisia (3) she was promised territory (4) she was afraid of the Triple Entente.
2. Great Britain joined the Triple Entente prior to World War I because (1) she feared rebellion in India (2) the member nations were Great Britain's traditional allies (3) the ruling families of the member nations were all related (4) she feared Germany's trade and naval policies.
3. In the decade before World War I, the two chief rivals for control of the Balkans were (1) Russia and Italy (2) Italy and France (3) Austria-Hungary and Great Britain (4) Russia and Austria-Hungary.
4. During World War I both Italy and Japan (1) joined forces with Germany (2) participated in the war to gain territory (3) were forced into the war by direct attack on their land (4) declared their position in the last year of the war.
5. Which nation withdrew from the Triple Alliance and entered World War I to fight on the other side? (1) Germany (2) Austria (3) Italy (4) Russia.
6. The country whose neutrality was violated by Germany during World War I was (1) Switzerland (2) Denmark (3) Holland (4) Belgium.
7. One aim of the United States in World War I was (1) colonial expansion (2) collection of indemnities (3) freedom of the seas (4) dismemberment of Germany.
8. President Wilson's ideals were best expressed in the provision of the Treaty of Versailles concerning (1) reparation payments by Germany (2) division of Germany's colonies among the Allies (3) war guilt (4) the League of Nations.
9. Which was true of both the Congress of Vienna (1815) and the Versailles Conferences (1919)? (1) Many of the boundaries of Europe were changed. (2) France attended both conferences as a victorious nation. (3) Small nations had as much influence as the large powers. (4) The principle of self-determination was an important basis for deciding issues.
10. Two nations created following World War I were (1) Belgium and Denmark (2) Czechoslovakia and Poland (3) Siberia and Yugoslavia (4) Sweden and Bulgaria.
11. The treaties ending World War I created a new minority problem of (1) French in Alsace-Lorraine (2) Magyars in Hungary (3) Germans in Poland (4) Serbs in Yugoslavia.
12. The treaty of peace with Austria after World War I forbade Anschluss, which meant (1) establishment of war industries (2) maintenance of a submarine fleet (3) government by dictatorship (4) union with Germany.
13. One result of World War I was that (1) the United States became a world power (2) Italy annexed Tunisia (3) France and Germany became allies (4) England lost her colonial empire.
14. An important result of World War I was that in many European nations (1) living standards rose (2) foreign trade increased (3) nationalism became less intense (4) dictators seized control.

Part 2. Russia: From Czarist Absolutism to Communist Dictatorship

RUSSIA: GEOGRAPHIC SETTING AND POPULATION

1. Tremendous Size. The world's largest country, Russia contains two and one-half times the area of the United States, or one-sixth of the world's land surface. Russia extends 7,000 miles from central Europe eastward across Asia to the Pacific Ocean. At easternmost Siberia, bordering on the Bering Strait, Russia approaches within a few miles of the United States at Alaska.

2. Rich Natural Resources. Russia possesses extensive natural wealth: fertile soil, forests, and minerals—coal, iron ore, oil, manganese, aluminum, and copper. By utilizing these resources, Russia today is a leading nation in both agriculture and industry.

3. Limited Transportation Facilities. (*a*) *Inland.* Russia's 77,000 miles of railroad, much of it single-track, is equal to about one-third of the railroad mileage in the United States. Russia's 18,000 miles of paved highways constitutes an even more extreme shortage. Russia also utilizes about 82,000 miles of natural and man-made inland waterways. (*b*) *Seaports.* The ports of Leningrad on the Baltic Sea and Vladivostok on the Pacific Ocean are icebound part of the year. Odessa on the Black Sea is a warm-water port serviceable the whole year. However, ships from the Black Sea must sail through the Turkish-controlled Dardanelles to reach the Mediterranean.

4. Many Peoples. Russia's 250 million population, chiefly Slavic, consists of (*a*) Great Russian, over 50 percent, (*b*) Ukrainian, or Little Russian, about 20 percent, (*c*) Byelorussian, or White Russian, almost 5 percent, and (*d*) about 100 other nationalities totaling about 25 percent, including a variety of Asian peoples and a number of recently annexed peoples in eastern Europe.

CONDITIONS IN CZARIST RUSSIA

Up to World War I Russia in many respects resembled 18th-century France under the Old Regime. Unlike west European nations, Czarist Russia had made little progress away from absolutism, inequality, and poverty.

1. Political Conditions

a. Absolutism of the Czar. The Czar ruled as an unlimited monarch and exercised all powers. Through the secret police, he vigorously suppressed demands for reforms and punished reformers by imprisonment, execution, or exile to penal colonies in Siberia.

b. Terrorism by Reformers. Denied lawful means of expressing discontent, reformers turned to underground activity and terrorism. They spread anti-Czarist propaganda among the people, and, turning to violence, they assassinated a number of government leaders including, in 1881, Czar Alexander II.

2. Social Conditions

a. Rigid Class Distinctions. (1) *Privileged classes.* The clergy of the state-controlled Russian Orthodox Church preached obedience to the Czar. The nobility owned much land and held important army and government positions. (2) *Unprivileged classes.* The peasants, constituting the masses, lived impoverished lives and worked hard without prospect of advancement. The conditions of city workers were hardly better. The unprivileged classes remained mostly illiterate, for the Czar's government feared that education would teach the common people "dangerous" ideas.

b. Russification. Subject peoples—such as Poles, Finns, Estonians, Latvians, Lithuanians, and Armenians—were pressured to adopt the Russian language, culture, and religion. They bitterly resisted the government's attempts to destroy their national heritages.

c. Persecution of Jews. Jews were forbidden to own land, were almost completely barred from educational institutions, and were required to live in restricted districts, called the *Pale of Settlement.* They were victimized recurrently by government-inspired outbursts of violence, called *pogroms.* (By anti-Jewish riots, the Czar's government tried to divert the attention of the people away from their own deplorable conditions.) Starting in the 1880's, many Jews fled Russia, migrating chiefly to the United States.

3. Economic Conditions

a. An Agricultural Country. Russia raised much sugar beet and grains. Her peasants, using primitive methods and lacking sufficient land, eked out a wretched living.

b. Beginnings of Industrialization (Late 19th Century). With former peasants providing cheap labor and French investors supplying capital, Russia began her Industrial Revolution. The Russians constructed iron and steel mills, textile factories, and railroads. An ambitious project, spanning the width of Russia from St. Petersburg (now Leningrad) to Vladivostok, was the *Trans-Siberian Railroad.*

Russia's industrial beginnings created two new economic classes: workers and capitalists. The workers resented their low wages and slum conditions. The businessmen resented the privileged position of the nobility. Both groups desired a voice in the government and opposed Czarist absolutism.

REFORMS IN CZARIST RUSSIA

Fearing unrest that accompanied military defeats, two Czars made concessions to the people. However, Czarist reforms proved of little permanent gain.

1. Emancipation of the Serfs (1861)

a. Background. Although serfdom had long ago disappeared in western Europe, the peasants in Russia remained serfs. They were bound to the soil, required to pay feudal dues and services, and subjected to the will of the nobles. Peasant discontent led to occasional and easily suppressed uprisings. However, after Russia's defeat in the Crimean War (1853-1856), the peasants intensified their complaints and gained many intellectuals as their spokesmen. The movement for reform began to frighten the government.

b. Reform Measures. Finally, in 1861 Czar *Alexander II,* by edict, freed the serfs, purchased land from the nobles, sold this land to peasant village communities, called *mirs,* and instructed the mirs to assign plots to their members, who would pay for the land over a period of 49 years.

c. Weaknesses. The peasants remained dissatisfied because (1) the nobles retained more than half the land, and the peasants therefore received inadequate acreage, (2) not the peasants but the mirs held title to the land, and (3) the peasants were compelled to make land payments they could not afford.

In 1906, following Russia's defeat by Japan, Czar *Nicholas II* cancelled all debts on land, permitted peasants to abolish the mirs, and transferred land titles to the peasants. These measures failed to calm the peasants. They needed more land and hungered for the extensive fertile fields in the nobles' estates.

2. Establishment of a Legislature (1905)

a. Background. In the Russo-Japanese War (1904-1905), Russia met defeat amidst evidence of government inefficiency and corruption. The people demanded reforms in a series of strikes, demonstrations, riots, and scattered uprisings. A group of workers, trying to deliver a petition to the Czar, were fired upon by troops, an event called "Bloody Sunday." These developments, reflecting widespread discontent, became known as the *Revolution of 1905.*

b. Reform Measures. Czar Nicholas II (1) guaranteed certain personal liberties, (2) established a lawmaking body, the *Duma,* and (3) permitted Duma elections by universal male suffrage.

c. Absolutism Restored. As the revolutionists quarreled among themselves, the Czar used the soldiers returning from the war to spread terror and reestablish his control. Thereafter, he restricted suffrage to the upper classes and limited the power of the Duma, making it no more than a "debating society."

FOREIGN AFFAIRS OF CZARIST RUSSIA

1. Imperialism and Pan-Slavism. Czarist Russia pursued imperialist policies toward China and Persia (Iran), and in the Balkans. Because many Balkan peoples—Bulgars, Serbs, Croats, and Slovenes—spoke Slavic languages related to Russian, the Czars justified Russian expansion into the Balkans by claiming Slavic unity, *Pan-Slavism.* Up to 1914 Russia helped many Balkan peoples gain independence from Turkey (see page 217).

2. Triple Entente and World War I. Russia came in conflict with Austria-Hungary over the Balkans and Pan-Slavism. To counter the alliance between Austria-Hungary and Germany, Russia reached agreements with France and England, thereby forming the Triple Entente. In 1914 Russia supported Serbia in the chain of events that led to World War I.

RUSSIAN REVOLUTIONS OF 1917

1. March Revolution: The Czar Is Overthrown

a. Underlying Causes: Conditions in Czarist Russia. (1) *Political.* The people wanted an end to Czarist absolutism and repression. Especially the middle class and workers desired a voice in the government. (2) *Economic.* Peasants wanted the nobles' fertile lands. City workers wanted better economic conditions. (3) *Social.* Subject nationalities wanted an end to discrimination and Russification.

b. Immediate Cause: Czarist Wartime Incompetence. (1) *On the battlefront.* Soldiers received inadequate food, clothing, and battle equipment; officers, chiefly nobles, lacked ability; Russian armies met with defeat after defeat; casualties ran high. (2) *On the home front.* Factories proved unable to satisfy military and civilian needs; railroad transportation broke down; cities faced food shortages; prices soared.

With soldiers war-weary and deserting, peasants rioting, workers striking, and Duma members demanding reform, Russia was ripe for revolution. In March, 1917, soldiers defied government orders to fire on striking workers, and the Duma spurned Czarist commands to dissolve. Czar Nicholas II, realizing that his authority was gone, abdicated the throne.

c. The Provisional Government Fails (March-November, 1917). This temporary government was headed first by the liberal democrat Prince *George Lvov,* and later by the moderate Socialist *Alexander Kerensky.* It guaranteed civil liberties, freed political prisoners, and sought to establish a middle-of-the-road democratic regime.

Nevertheless, the provisional government (1) insisted upon continuing the war, (2) proved unable to provide the cities with food, and (3) refused to approve land seizures by the peasants. It therefore lost support among the public and especially among the newly organized *soviets* (councils) of workers and soldiers.

2. November Revolution: The Communists Seize Control. The Communist party, a small but well-organized and highly disciplined group, originated with left-wing Russian socialists, the *Bolsheviks.* They had fanatically defied Czarist rule. Hunted by Czarist police, many Bolshevik leaders had been sent to Siberian prison camps; others had fled to exile.

In 1917 the Bolsheviks gained skilled leadership by the return from exile of *Leon Trotsky* and *Nikolai Lenin.* The realistic, shrewd, iron-willed Lenin headed the party and was assisted by Trotsky, a brilliant orator and organizer. By demanding "Peace, Bread, and Land" for soldiers, city workers, and peasants respectively, the Bolsheviks appealed to the masses. The Bolsheviks attracted considerable support because the Russian people—then overwhelmingly not Communist and not aware of fundamental Communist aims—were displeased with the Kerensky regime.

The Bolsheviks quickly gained influence in the soviets, extended the authority of the soviets, and undermined the Kerensky government. Finally, in November, 1917, Red troops easily toppled the provisional government. The Bolsheviks established a regime led by Premier Lenin and War Minister Trotsky.

RUSSIA UNDER LENIN: CONSOLIDATION OF COMMUNIST POWER (1917-1924)

1. Sought Popular Support. Lenin took Russia out of World War I by accepting Germany's severe terms in the *Treaty of Brest-Litovsk.* Russia lost much territory, especially Finland, Estonia, Latvia, Lithuania, Russian Poland, and the Ukraine. In domestic affairs, Lenin (a) organized the workers to take over the factories and nationalized industry, and (b) directed the peasants to seize the nobles' estates and then nationalized all land. Thus, the Communists carried out their program of "Peace, Bread, and Land."

2. Crushed Opposition. The Communists under Lenin encountered strong enmity from the following groups: (*a*) *Within Russia* were the anti-Bolsheviks, or "Whites," who were led by former Czarist officers. (*b*) *Outside Russia* were the newly created state of Poland (which desired additional Russian territory) and the Allies (who resented Communist Russia's withdrawal from the war and her policy of world revolution).

From 1917 to 1920 the Communist regime faced attack by Polish troops, Allied intervention forces, and Russian "White" armies. To protect their revolution, the Communists acted ruthlessly. In 1918 they put to death Czar Nicholas II and his family. Communist secret police, often judging by hearsay evidence and prejudiced against the upper classes, executed thousands as counterrevolutionaries.

The Communist "Red" army smashed all military threats. Its success resulted from (*a*) Trotsky's ability as military organizer and inspirational leader, (*b*) the peasant soldiers' determination to prevent the nobles' return, (*c*) Russian nationalism, which made Russians resent foreign intervention, and (*d*) disunity and war-weariness among the "Whites" and the various foreign armies.

3. Gained Diplomatic Recognition. By 1921 the Communists had conceded the independence of Finland, Estonia, Latvia, Lithuania, and Poland but had recovered the Ukraine. They ruled Russia unchallenged. Thereafter, Lenin's government received diplomatic recognition from most foreign nations. (The United States did not recognize the Soviet Union until 1933. Our recognition meant that we acknowledged Red control over Russia; it did *not* imply approval of the Communist regime.)

4. Lenin's Death. In 1922 Lenin suffered the first of a series of strokes. His illness touched off a struggle among top Communists for the eventual leadership of Russia. Lenin's death in 1924 brought this struggle into the open.

RUSSIA UNDER STALIN (1924-1953)

Joseph Stalin, General Secretary of the Communist party, battled War Minister Leon Trotsky for supreme power. Stalin emerged victorious. In 1929 Trotsky was sent into exile; in 1940, in Mexico, he was slain by an assassin, supposedly an agent of Stalin.

Stalin's control over the party made him dictator of Russia, although he waited until 1941 to become Premier. Stalin destroyed internal opposition by brutality and terror: secret arrests, fake trials, inhuman forced-labor camps, and mass executions. On the constructive side, Stalin transformed Russia from a backward agricultural nation into a modern industrial state and guided her to victory in World War II.

RUSSIA UNDER KHRUSHCHEV (1953-1964)

When Stalin died in 1953, *Nikita Khrushchev,* then little known to the Western world, became First Secretary of the Communist party. By shrewdness, intrigue, and party manipulation, Khrushchev eliminated his chief rivals. Internal Affairs Minister *Lavrenti Beria* was denounced as a foreign agent, arrested, and executed; Premier *Georgi Malenkov* was compelled to confess blunders and resign; other important officials, including another Premier, a Foreign Minister, and a Defense Minister, were removed from office. By 1958 Khrushchev felt secure enough to assume the Premiership and openly rule the Soviet Union. Although Khrushchev halted the worst aspects of Stalinist terror, he maintained a tightly controlled dictatorship.

Khrushchev directed Russian efforts toward space flights, with considerable success. However, in economic matters, Khrushchev failed to halt the decline in the rate of Russian industrial growth and failed to spur Russian agricultural output. Toward the European satellite nations, Khrushchev somewhat relaxed Russian control. In the cold war, Khrushchev acted cautiously. He agreed to the Limited Nuclear Test Ban Treaty and advocated a policy of "peaceful coexistence" with the West. His cautious policy toward the West was one factor in the split between the Soviet Union and Red China.

RUSSIA UNDER BREZHNEV AND KOSYGIN

In a surprising development in 1964, Khrushchev was removed from his positions as First Secretary of the Communist party and as Premier. In *Pravda,* the Communist party newspaper, Khrushchev was denounced (by implication but not by name) for "harebrained scheming, immature conclusions, and hasty decisions." Khrushchev's removal, according to Western observers, was caused by his undignified personal conduct, his worsening of the dispute with Communist China, and his failure to spur industrial and agricultural output. From Khrushchev himself, the peoples of the Soviet Union and the world heard nothing. He has become an "unperson" in Russia —his writings have been removed from bookstores; his picture has been removed from public buildings; his name has not been mentioned in newspapers and on radio.

Khrushchev was succeeded by two men long associated with him. *Leonid Brezhnev,* who had been Khrushchev's deputy in the Communist Party Secretariat, became First Secretary. *Aleksei Kosygin* became Premier. The new regime (1) pledged to continue the policy of peaceful coexistence toward the West, (2) sought—so far unsuccessfully—to lessen the breach with Red China, and (3) worked to improve the Soviet economy.

GOVERNMENT OF COMMUNIST RUSSIA

Based largely upon the Constitution of 1936, the Soviet government uses the outward forms of democracy to conceal the actuality of Communist dictatorship. What the Soviet government claims to be *in theory* is very different from what it is *in fact.*

1. Federal Organization. The *Union of Soviet Socialist Republics* (U.S.S.R., or Soviet Union) is a federation of fifteen republics. Thus, the Soviet Union has (a) one central government—housed in Moscow's famous fortress, the *Kremlin*—which exercises extensive nation-wide powers, and (b) fifteen republics, which are smaller governmental units. Each republic represents a major national group.

The *Russian Soviet Federated Socialist Republic,* with four-fifths of the country's area and over half of its population, is by far the largest of these republics. Consequently, the Soviet Union is still commonly called Russia.

In theory, each republic is independent and may secede from the U.S.S.R. *In fact,* each republic is dominated by the highly centralized Communist party, views secessionist activity as treasonable, and dares not deviate from the policies set by the central government at Moscow.

2. The Central Government

a. Legislature. The *Supreme Soviet* of the U.S.S.R., the chief legislative body, consists of two houses: the *Soviet of the Union,* elected by population, and the *Soviet of Nationalities,* based upon national groups. The two houses jointly select the Supreme Soviet's *Presidium* (a small permanent committee). Between sessions of the Supreme Soviet, its powers are exercised by the Presidium.

In theory, the Supreme Soviet enacts Russia's laws. *In fact,* the Supreme Soviet—meeting no more than twice a year for about a week at a time—automatically approves laws previously issued by its Presidium and by the executive branch.

b. Executive. The *Council of Ministers,* or cabinet, the chief executive body, consists of the heads of the major ministries—such as Foreign Affairs, Defense, Trade, Agriculture, Conservation of Resources, and Culture—and its chairman, the *Premier.*

In theory, the Supreme Soviet appoints these top officials. *In fact,* it unanimously approves the men previously designated by the Communist party.

In theory, the Council of Ministers enforces the laws and directs the government. *In fact,* in addition to enforcing laws, the Council of Ministers makes laws by issuing decrees.

c. Judiciary. The *Supreme Court*, the chief judicial body, consists of about 80 judges appointed for five-year terms.

In theory, the Supreme Court, in accordance with the constitution, renders independent judgments. *In fact,* the Supreme Court may not declare laws unconstitutional, may not void ministerial decisions, and has never deviated from Communist party policy.

d. Civil Rights. In theory, Soviet citizens are guaranteed (by the 1936 constitution) freedom of speech, press, and assembly, and are protected against unjust arrest and unfair trial. *In fact,* persons who speak, print, or assemble in opposition to the government are regarded as criminals. In searching out opposition, the secret police ignores the constitutional guarantees of freedom. Political prisoners are denied the right to counsel and to witnesses. The secret police usually extort confessions from such prisoners before their trials begin.

e. Elections. In theory, the Soviet government is controlled by the voters. All Soviet citizens over 18 years of age may vote—chiefly for legislature members and judges. *In fact,* since only one slate of candidates (picked by the Communist party) is permitted, the people have no choice. Citizens who fail to vote risk being considered hostile to the regime and are treated accordingly.

3. The Communist Party

a. Membership. With nearly 10 million members, the Communist party contains about 5 percent of the total Soviet population. Most party members are recruited from Communist youth groups. Party members are carefully selected and accept iron discipline. They devote their leisure time almost entirely to party work, which may involve difficult assignments. As compensation, party membership offers special privileges and is essential for personal advancement in almost any field of work.

Party members are carefully watched. Those who do not measure up to standards or who are suspected of opposing the existing leadership are expelled by *purges.*

b. Pyramidal Organization. At its base, the Communist party consists of local units (formerly called "cells") organized within factories, farms, offices, and schools. These primary units elect representatives to higher party groups, each of which elects representatives to the next highest body up to the *All-Union Party Congress.* Since this Congress meets infrequently—supposedly every four years—it delegates its powers to its *Central Committee,* which in turn chooses the two all-powerful party organs, the Presidium and the Secretariat.

(1) The *Presidium,* or *Politburo,* consists of a small group that determines party policy.

(2) The *Secretariat* directs party work and membership. In practice, the First or General Secretary—the position held by Stalin, later by Khrushchev, and now by Brezhnev—dominates the party and thereby the country.

c. Power Over Russia. The Communist party dominates the Russian people and government. (1) The Communist party is Russia's only party. No opposition party is permitted to exist. (2) The Communist party selects all candidates for government office. Candidates for key positions usually are leading party members; candidates for less important posts may be nonmembers approved by the party. (3) The Communist party keeps a watchful eye on the government. If the party is dissatisfied with the attitude or accomplishment of any official, it will take steps to remove him from office. (4) The Communist party controls the army, the regular police, and the secret police—all instruments for destroying opposition and enforcing the party's will. (5) The Communist party controls education, the radio, the theater, and the press. These sources of information and means of propaganda are used to extol the party leaders, to glorify the party's role in Russian history, and to justify the *party line* (the Communist stand on issues).

4. Transferring Power in a Dictatorship. *In theory,* when the Russian head of government dies, his successor is selected by the Supreme Soviet. *In fact,* after the deaths of Lenin and Stalin (see pages 351-352), a bitter struggle, marked by violence, took place within the Communist party. Each time, the successor was the man with the most power over the Communist party, its First Secretary. (In contrast with a dictatorship, our American democracy faces no bitter struggle for power upon the death of a President. In accordance with the provisions of the United States Constitution, the elected Vice President assumes the office of President.)

Khrushchev's removal in 1964 was probably engineered by a small group of Communist leaders, including Leonid Brezhnev, Khrushchev's deputy in the Secretariat.

ECONOMIC SYSTEM OF COMMUNIST RUSSIA

1. War Communism (1917-1921). Immediately upon seizing power, the Communists sought to transform Russia's economic system from capitalism to communism. While fighting civil war and foreign intervention, the government nationalized mines, factories, railroads, and land, and prohibited most private ownership.

War Communism proved a failure. Many factories and farms had been destroyed during wartime; government officials lacked economic management skills; factory workers failed to maintain production schedules; and farmers curtailed output because the state seized their surplus crops without payment. With manufactured goods scarce, foodstuffs lacking, and famine widespread, Russia by 1921 was in economic chaos.

2. New Economic Policy (1921-1928). To restore Russia's economic health and safeguard Communist rule, Lenin in 1921 announced the *New Economic Policy (NEP)*. Under this *temporary retreat* from communism, (*a*) private owners were permitted to operate retail stores and small factories for profit, (*b*) farmers were allowed to sell surplus crops in the open market, (*c*) foreign capitalists were encouraged to invest in Russia, and (*d*) foreign engineers and technicians were offered liberal salaries. These represented only small concessions to capitalism, since over 80 percent of Russia's economy—including railroads, iron and steel mills, coal mines, banks, and public utilities—remained in government hands.

The NEP, operating in peacetime, revived Russia's economy. By 1928 agricultural and industrial output had reached pre-World War I levels.

3. Five-Year Plans (1928-1958). Under Stalin in 1928, the Communists began five-year programs of all-inclusive economic planning. Russia experienced six Five-Year Plans, the sixth and last one being scrapped in 1958 as a failure, two years before its scheduled end.

a. Overall Objectives. The Five-Year Plans called for rapid and sustained economic growth. Although they sought increased agricultural output, the Plans placed major emphasis upon expanding *heavy industry,* such as iron and steel, aluminum, chemicals, electric power, and machinery. Heavy industry received top priority in order to produce weapons and thereby strengthen the country militarily.

The Plans gave low priority to *light industry*—just enough to provide the people with minimal living conditions. The Communists viewed a higher standard of living as an ultimate, not an immediate, goal. Unlike the American economy, which is consumer-oriented, the Russian economy under the Five-Year Plans was geared to the needs of the state.

b. Special Objectives. The First Five-Year Plan (1928-1932) also called for the elimination of the remnants of capitalism—namely, the owners of private stores and factories (*nepmen*) and the well-to-do peasants (*kulaks*). The Fourth Five-Year Plan (1946-1950) repaired the destruction wrought by the German invasion during World War II. The Fifth Five-Year Plan (1951-1955) provided for Russian economic aid to Communist-bloc and underdeveloped nations.

c. Industry. The *State Planning Commission (Gosplan)* established master plans for each industry and factory. The planners determined the wages and hours of workers, the kind and location of new factories, and the type and amount of goods to be produced.

To achieve ever-increasing production goals, the Communists (1) employed propaganda, stressing the needs of the country and the promise of a better life in days to come, (2) rewarded outstanding workers with pay differentials and social approval, and (3) punished unsuccessful plant managers by demotion and sometimes arrest as saboteurs.

d. Agriculture. Russia's farmland is divided approximately as follows: (1) 30 percent is in *state farms*, which are vast agricultural factories whose workers receive fixed wages. (2) 65 percent is in *collectives*, which are compulsory farm communities whose peasant members are paid in produce and in money. (In many ways, the collectives resemble the Czarist mirs.) (3) 5 percent is in *garden plots*, which are essentially private-enterprise farms permitted industrial workers and collective farmers, as a sideline, to raise food for family use and for sale in the open market. Although the garden plots utilize only 5 percent of the acreage, they are most carefully cultivated and account for over 20 percent of the agricultural production in the U.S.S.R.

During the First Five-Year Plan collectives arose as the government forced farmers to pool their land, livestock, and equipment and to work the total area together. However, members of collectives are permitted small garden plots. The collectives pay the government a portion of the harvest as land taxes and for government services: bank credit, rental of farm machinery, and technical help. The collectives must sell a portion of the harvest to the government at low government-set prices and may sell the remainder on the open market. The collectives make possible large-scale production and strict government control over farming.

During the First Five-Year Plan the kulaks, or prosperous farmers, slaughtered their livestock and wrecked their equipment rather than join collectives. They received harsh treatment from the Communist regime; they were driven from their lands and starved to death, sentenced to forced labor, or killed. By 1932 the kulaks as a class had been eliminated at the cost of several million lives.

e. Accomplishments. The Five-Year Plans transformed Russia from an agricultural to a leading manufacturing nation. Russian industrial output increased twenty-fold. The Communists created new industrial centers deep in Siberia and central Asia. During World War II, when the Germans occupied large portions of western Russia, these new centers helped sustain the economy and the war effort.

Russia developed a pool of skilled technicians and engineers, and produced the most complex space vehicles and the most modern military equipment. She became the world's second largest industrial power, surpassed only by the United States.

Compared to Czarist days, the Russian people enjoyed improved living standards. These standards, however, remained below those of most West European nations and far below those of the United States.

f. Weaknesses

(1) *In Industry.* Centralized planning and management resulted in bureaucracy, waste, and error. Costs of production were high. Quality was often poor. Consumer goods were scarce. A housing shortage existed.

(2) *In Agriculture.* Although Russia employed almost half of her labor force in agriculture, the increase in food output barely kept up with the increase in population. (By contrast, the United States, with less than one-tenth of her workers in agriculture, produced huge surpluses.) Some problems were crude farm equipment, meager irrigation facilities, shortage of fertilizers, and outmoded production methods. Serious food shortages occurred periodically. The peasants resented collectivization. Whenever possible, they neglected work on the land of the collectives and devoted their energies to their own small garden plots. Agriculture was the weakest link in the Russian economy.

g. End of the Five-Year Plans.

As the Sixth Five-Year Plan failed to achieve agricultural and industrial production goals, Khrushchev took the following steps: (1) *Agriculture.* Farm prices were raised in order to spur output. (However, collective farmers had little use for additional income as long as few consumer goods were available.) (2) *Labor.* Compulsory schooling was reduced by two years, and most youngsters were ordered to go to work at the age of 16. (3) *Capital.* The $65 billion worth of Soviet bonds —which the people had been pressured to purchase—would neither earn interest nor be redeemed for 20 years. (4) *The Plan.* The Sixth Five-Year Plan was replaced by a new Seven-Year Plan.

4. The Seven-Year Plan (1958-1965)

a. Specific Goals.

The Plan aimed to catch up to and eventually surpass the United States. It called for an 80-percent increase in industrial production. The Plan set ambitious goals for heavy industry. It set only modest goals for consumer goods. For example, auto production was scheduled to increase to 225,000 by 1965 (compared to an annual American output of 9 million). The Plan also promised to alleviate the housing shortage, raise wages, and reduce the 45-hour workweek.

b. Obstacles Facing the Plan.

(1) It set opposing goals. Increasing production conflicted with reducing hours of work; expanding heavy industry conflicted with easing the housing shortage. (2) The Plan called for tremendous capital investment, more than the Communist economy could provide. (3) The Plan disappointed the Russian people by not giving greater priority to consumer goods and better working conditions. (4) Because of the declining birth rate during World War II, Russia faced a labor shortage.

c. The Seven-Year Plan Is Scrapped. The Plan failed to achieve its goals. (1) Capital investment and labor supply proved inadequate, and Russia's industrial growth slowed. (2) Agricultural output lagged badly, and Russia bought wheat from capitalist nations: Canada, Australia, and the United States. In 1963 Khrushchev scrapped the Seven-Year Plan and ordered a special two-year plan for 1964-1965.

Following Khrushchev's removal in 1964, his successors sought economic improvement: (1) *Agricultural Reforms.* First Secretary Leonid Brezhnev announced plans for (*a*) doubling the capital investment in agriculture, presumably to provide additional farm machinery and fertilizer, (*b*) raising prices paid by the government for compulsory grain deliveries and leaving more grain for collectives to sell on the open market, (*c*) lowering prices on manufactured goods, electricity, and foodstuffs in the rural areas down to levels already effective in the cities, and (*d*) lowering the income tax on collective farms so as to leave more income for the collective farm members. The Soviets hoped that these "bread and butter" incentives would spur agricultural output. (2) *Industrial Reforms.* Premier Aleksei Kosygin announced plans to grant factory managers in consumer goods industries greater freedom to increase production and improve quality. They would

Hesse in The St. Louis Globe-Democrat

"But my stomach doesn't have ears."

receive incentive bonuses based upon their performance—judged not only by volume of output but by ability to satisfy consumer wants and to generate profits (a capitalist concept). These reforms were labeled *Libermanism* after their chief proponent, Soviet economist *Yevsey Liberman*.

6. The Five-Year Plan for 1971-1975. (*a*) *For Consumers.* The Plan promised "a considerable growth of the people's living and cultural standards" and scheduled a slightly higher growth rate for light industry than for heavy industry. (The Plan, however, did not speed up capital investment for housing.) It pledged no price rises for consumer goods. This Plan thus reiterated promises made but not kept by previous plans. (*b*) *For Heavy Industry.* Production by heavy industry was already at a substantially higher level than by light industry. Therefore heavy industry was allotted 75 percent of the Plan's total investment capital. (*c*) *For Industrial Workers.* The Plan pledged moderate wage gains but called for sharply increased labor productivity—output per worker. By offering more consumer goods, the Plan hoped to give workers an incentive to work harder so as to earn more money with which to buy such goods. (*d*) *For Agriculture.* To overcome food shortages, the Plan called for an increase in agricultural output of 20 percent. The Plan sharply raised the capital investment for agriculture and projected a sharp increase in farmers' earnings.

For 1972 Kosygin disclosed that the growth rate (4 percent) of the Soviet economy was the lowest of the past 10 years. The planned growth rate was not achieved especially because of (*a*) agriculture—where the basic weaknesses of Soviet farming were augmented by a harsh winter and a summer drought, and (*b*) Soviet labor productivity—which is one-half that of American industrial workers and one-fifth that of American farmers.

To remedy these conditions, the Soviets (*a*) purchased some $2 billion of grain from capitalist nations and signed a three-year order to buy from the United States at least $750 million of grain, (*b*) revised 1973 economic goals by cutting back the growth rate for heavy industry slightly and for consumer industry sharply, and (*c*) demanded the elimination of waste and inefficiency.

(For Soviet efforts to increase trade with the United States, see pages 479-480.)

THE WORKING CLASS IN COMMUNIST RUSSIA

The Communists boast that Russia is the "workers' state" and that her government is a Communist party-led "dictatorship of the proletariat." The Soviet Constitution of 1936 guarantees each worker the right to (1) employment, (2) leisure time, including annual paid vacations, and (3) social security, including old-age, accident, and sickness insurance, as well as medical and hospital care. Soviet workers, however, are subjected to working conditions far less desirable than those of American workers.

1. Labor Conditions

a. Choice of Employment. The Soviet government denies most beginning workers any choice of occupation and channels them into those jobs considered essential to the state.

b. Labor Discipline. The state requires workers to have official *workbooks*, containing full educational and employment records. Under Stalin, workers guilty of unexcused lateness and absence, or leaving a job without approval, could be heavily fined or even sent to a slave labor camp. Under Khrushchev, lateness and absence penalties were lightened, and most workers were permitted to leave their jobs without approval. Under Brezhnev and Kosygin, workers have faced a tightening of labor discipline.

	New York	Moscow		New York	Moscow
Beef (1 pound)	20 min.	88 min.	Haircut, men	46 min.	39 min.
Milk, fresh (1 quart)	7 min.	29 min.	Refrigerator	32 hours	343 hours
Eggs (1 dozen)	17 min.	162 min.	Washing machine	53 hours	204 hours
Toilet soap (small bar)	2 min.	25 min.	Medium-sized car	762 hours	7,907 hours

Adapted from *The New York Times.* © 1971 by *The New York Times Company. Reprinted by permission.*

Cost of Selected Items Affecting Living Standards in New York and Moscow

Costs are expressed in time spent on the job by an average industrial worker. Figures reflect differences in wages and prices in the two cities.

c. Factory Conditions. Although the newer plants generally provide good working conditions, the older plants remain substandard, having poor lighting, insufficient ventilation, and inadequate protection against accidents.

d. Wages. The state determines pay scales. These vary greatly according to the importance of the industry and the worker's skill and output. Wherever possible, the pay is based upon piecework, which compels the worker to speed up production in order to earn a better living. For most workers, wages remain low. In 1957 Russia introduced her first minimum wage law; in 1972 the minimum was raised to $85 per month. (While comparisons are not exact, American workers have a minimum wage of over $250 per month.) Although the standard of living of Russian workers is higher than in Czarist times, it remains low by Western standards.

2. Labor Unions. Russian workers belong to large labor unions under Communist party domination. The unions administer welfare programs and promote social and cultural activities: health resorts, libraries, theaters, sports, and dances. The unions' chief function, however, is to serve the state by spurring the workers to greater productivity. Unlike American labor organizations, Russian unions have no say in determining wages and no right to strike for better conditions.

3. Slave Labor. Under Stalin, Communist Russia utilized a large labor force, estimated in the millions, consisting of persons arbitrarily arrested by the secret police as enemies of the state. Political prisoners, as well as ordinary criminals, were sentenced to *corrective labor camps,* located in desolate and inhospitable regions, especially northern European Russia and Siberia. As *forced,* or *slave, laborers,* they were harshly treated and assigned to backbreaking work in mines and forests, and on construction projects.

After Stalin, the Khrushchev regime ended mass political arrests, freed most political prisoners, and abolished many corrective labor camps. It retained some camps as penal work colonies for ordinary criminals. The Brezhnev-Kosygin leadership reverted to a crackdown on dissenters, sending some outspoken writers and other intellectuals to labor camps.

SOCIAL AND CULTURAL CONDITIONS IN COMMUNIST RUSSIA

1. Status of Women. The Soviet government grants women full legal equality with men. Few women, however, have achieved top government and party positions.

The Communist regime fosters community kitchens, laundries, and nurseries so as to free women from household tasks and enable them to fill regular jobs. Women work as doctors, teachers, clerks, and factory hands; many even perform hard manual labor as construction workers and tractor drivers. Women comprise half the total Soviet labor force. By means of bonuses and medals, the state encourages women to raise large families.

2. Education. The Communist government uses education to fashion loyal Soviet citizens and to train manpower for industrial and scientific tasks. Under the 1958 educational reorganization, most students receive compulsory primary schooling for eight years and then must find employment. These young workers may complete their secondary education by a three-year, part-time course. Thereafter, capable students, generally selected by examination, may attend technical institutes and universities. Most students at these higher levels receive salaries from the government and are exempt from military service.

In the primary and secondary grades, Soviet children study (*a*) Russian language and literature, (*b*) Russian and world history as viewed by Marxist-Leninist theory—condemning capitalism, praising the Communist party, and glorifying Russia, (*c*) a foreign language, most often English, (*d*) mathematics, and (*e*) science—biology, chemistry, and physics. Compared to Americans, Russian students receive much more rigorous schooling: longer hours, more schooldays, more homework, and far greater stress on foreign languages, mathematics, and science.

The Communist educational system has practically wiped out illiteracy. Because the emphasis is on science rather than on the humanities, it produces many more engineers and technicians than does the United States. These graduates, in part, help explain Russia's tremendous strides in missile and space developments.

However, Communist education aims primarily at developing specialists. In the humanities, Russian students are not trained to think and decide for themselves, but must give unquestioning acceptance to the "party line."

3. Religion. At first the Communists considered the Russian Orthodox Church a Czarist agent, ended its control over education and marriage, seized its buildings and lands, and persecuted its leaders. In World War II, however, the government used the Orthodox Church to arouse the people in defense of "Mother Russia." Since then the regime has tolerated the Orthodox Church but strictly limits its activities. Minority religious groups—especially Jews, Roman Catholics, and Moslems—have been special targets for Soviet propaganda. All three have been charged with having loyalties outside the Soviet Union and have been subjected to varying degrees of oppression.

Officially, the Soviet constitution permits both freedom of religious worship and freedom of antireligious propaganda. However, the regime actively supports antireligious museums, demonstrations, and publications. The "party line" proclaims that no true Communist can be religious and denies the existence of God—a view called *atheism*. Nevertheless, the Communists have been unable to drive all religious feeling from the people, especially among the older generation.

4. Russian Nationalism and the Treatment of National Minorities. At first, insisting that all workers are united by common bonds, the Communists gave equal rights to all national groups. Within the Soviet Union, the Communist authorities (a) prohibited discrimination against non-Russian peoples, and (b) permitted each national group its own culture.

Since the mid-1930's, however, the Soviet government has pursued policies of (a) Russian nationalism—praising Russian heroes, even of Czarist days, and celebrating Russian national holidays, and (b) Russification—requiring all students, regardless of nationality, to study Russian language and history, and supplanting native minority cultures by the dominant Russian culture.

5. Treatment of Jews. Russian Jews—considered both a national and religious minority—were subjected to widespread anti-Semitism in Czarist Russia. Following the Communist Revolution, anti-Semitism abated somewhat. However, during Stalin's last years, Russian Jews suffered severely. Jewish newspapers and theaters were closed; Jewish artists, writers, and doctors were arrested and disappeared; the entire Jewish population experienced bitter anti-Semitism. However, Jews were not allowed to emigrate. Since Stalin, the Soviet regime has maintained a pro-Arab and anti-Israeli foreign policy. Soviet anti-Semitism has continued as the regime keeps most synagogues closed, restricts the supply of prayer books, prohibits teaching the Hebrew language, and spreads anti-Zionist propaganda. The Communists seek to destroy the Jewish cultural and religious heritage.

With the Israeli victory over the Arabs in the 1967 war, the 2.6 million Jews in Russia felt a surge of ethnic pride. By the thousands, Jews—especially young ones—claimed the right to emigrate to Israel. After applying for visas, they faced considerable harassment: loss of their jobs and apartments, threats of arrest for not working, waiting to see if their applications would be approved, and payment of an exit fee of over $1,000 per person. Nevertheless, the number of Jews permitted to leave for Israel rose from 2,000 in 1969 to over 30,000 in 1972. To stem emigration by Jews—the most highly educated ethnic group in the Soviet Union—the Soviet regime in 1973 set a new requirement: each emigrant must pay an additional exit fee based upon the education received from the state. This "brains tax," which could go as high as $50,000 per person, brought protests from militant Jews inside Russia and from organizations and governments throughout the world, especially the United States.

6. Culture. The Soviet regime affords the people many cultural opportunities: libraries, theaters, museums, operas, concerts, and ballets. Since literature and art are expected to propagandize for Communism, the regime encourages writers and artists by providing generous pay and granting them honors and awards. The Communists demand that literary and artistic works strive for popular appeal and support the Soviet state. Many Soviet cultural works are dull and undistinguished, but they conform to the "party line" and praise life under Communism. The Communist party hails such works as "Socialist realism."

Under Stalin, the party ruled the cultural world heavy-handedly; suspected or open dissenters were sent to slave labor camps. Khrushchev slightly relaxed controls, but the Brezhnev-Kosygin leadership reverted to demanding strict conformity to official standards. Defying the authorities, many writers and artists struggle for their right to produce works in freedom.

FOREIGN RELATIONS OF COMMUNIST RUSSIA

1. 1917-1933: Hostility Toward the World. The Communists resented the Allies' aiding counterrevolutionary forces during the Russian civil war. They believed also that capitalist nations would seek to destroy Communist Russia. To promote revolutions in capitalist nations, Russia in 1919 organized the *Third International,* or *Comintern* (see page 246). The Soviet government thereby reaped the ill will of other nations.

2. 1933-1939: Cooperation With Capitalist Democracies. After the Nazi party seized power in Germany, the Soviet Union feared Germany as aggressive, warlike, and anti-Communist. In 1934 Russia joined the League of Nations, and urged the "peace-loving" nations to protect themselves against aggression by united action, called *collective security.* In 1935 Russia and France joined in a military alliance.

However, in 1938 Russia bitterly denounced England and France for signing the Munich Agreement with Germany without consulting Russia. This pact allowed Hitler to take part of Czechoslovakia (see page 386).

3. 1939-1941: Non-Aggression Pact With Nazi Germany. Claiming that England and France would not help Russia in case of a German attack, the Soviets in 1939 signed a *Non-Aggression Pact* with Germany. The pact gave Russia time to strengthen her defenses. It gave Germany protection against a two-front war and served the Nazis as the "go-ahead signal" for aggression against Poland, thus bringing about World War II.

While the west European nations were at war, Russia annexed eastern Poland, part of Finland, and all of Lithuania, Latvia, and Estonia.

4. 1941-1945: Wartime Alliance With the Democracies. In June, 1941, Russia was attacked by Germany and forced into World War II. Thereafter, Russia (*a*) received considerable military equipment from the United States, (*b*) abolished the Comintern to show friendship toward her allies, (*c*) took part in top-level allied conferences to plan military strategy and arrange postwar settlements, and (*d*) helped create, and joined in, the United Nations. In 1945 Russia and her allies achieved complete military victory.

5. 1945-Present: Expansion and Cold War. As a result of World War II, Russia enlarged her boundaries and helped local Communist parties seize control of countries in eastern Europe and Asia. This expansion of Communist power angered and frightened the free world nations and led to the *cold war*—a diplomatic, economic, and ideological struggle, accompanied by localized military encounters. (See The Cold War Era, page 415 on.)

MULTIPLE-CHOICE QUESTIONS

1. In area, Russia is (1) equal to (2) smaller than (3) slightly larger than (4) much larger than   the United States.

2. Before 1914 Russia's economy was dependent predominantly on (1) mining (2) agriculture (3) fishing (4) industry.

3. Russia's international trade has been hampered by the lack of (1) sufficient natural resources (2) a large laboring class (3) a sufficient number of ice-free ports (4) areas suitable for agriculture.

4. In 1914 the Czar of Russia was (1) an absolute ruler (2) less powerful than the King of England (3) controlled by the Duma (4) controlled by the Communists.

5. The Russian serf was dissatisfied after his emancipation in 1861 because he (1) could not move to the city (2) was required to buy his land in one payment (3) could not acquire enough land (4) was required to pay feudal dues to his former lord.

6. A major aim of Russian foreign policy during the 19th century was to (1) strengthen Poland as an ally against Germany (2) expand to the south and east (3) encourage the working peoples of the world to revolt (4) maintain friendship with Turkey.

7. Which factor contributed most to the Revolutions of 1917 in Russia? (1) The Allied powers favored the revolutions. (2) The Czar was willing to abdicate. (3) Tolstoi organized the revolt. (4) The Russian people were discouraged with their defeats in World War I.

8. Which of the following did the Bolsheviks in 1917 emphasize *least* in their efforts to win over the Russian people? (1) immediate peace (2) reform of land ownership (3) redistribution of wealth (4) abolition of religion.

9. The official name of Russia is the Union of Soviet Socialist Republics. *Soviet* means (1) democratic (2) dictatorial (3) a responsible ministry (4) a council.

10. Soviet elections are marked by (1) the campaigning of many political parties (2) restriction of the vote to men only (3) one slate of candidates (4) voting by Communist party members only.

11. The death of Stalin was followed by a(an) (1) period of brief rule by his son (2) immediate outbreak of international conflict (3) bitter struggle for power among his important followers (4) return to the previous form of government.

12. Which method was used to suppress liberty in both Czarist Russia and Communist Russia? (1) indoctrination through public education (2) rigid class distinctions (3) maintenance of a secret police (4) establishment of a single political party.

13. Of the total Russian population, Communist party members number about (1) 90 percent (2) 50 percent (3) 25 percent (4) 5 percent.

14. The Stalinist Five-Year Plans emphasized (1) investments by foreign capitalists (2) agriculture over industry (3) production of household appliances and automobiles (4) development of steel mills and electric power plants.

15. An important effect of the Five-Year Plans on Russian agriculture was (1) the establishment of collective farms (2) the growth of small farms (3) an increase in the number of farm workers (4) a decrease in farm production.

16. Wages of Russian workers are (1) where possible, based on piecework (2) higher than wages in the United States (3) set by collective bargaining (4) tied to the profits of industry.

17. Under Stalin, Russia maintained corrective labor camps as (1) health centers for workers (2) schools for learning new technical skills (3) scientific research centers (4) work prisons for "enemies of the state."

18. Under both Czarist and Communist regimes, Russian Jews were (1) given preferential treatment (2) treated equally with the other Russian peoples (3) especially singled out for discrimination (4) denied education.

19. A cultural aspect of Communist Russia has been to (1) keep women in the home (2) emphasize literature and art at the expense of physics and chemistry (3) discourage Russian nationalism (4) restrict free creative effort by writers and composers.

MATCHING QUESTIONS

Column A	*Column B*
1. Khrushchev's successor as Premier of Russia	*a.* Stalin
2. Inaugurator of First Five-Year Plan	*b.* Nicholas II
3. Moderate Socialist head of 1917 provisional government	*c.* Brezhnev
4. Organizer of Red Army who later fled to Mexico	*d.* Molotov
5. Liberator of the serfs	*e.* Lenin
6. First Communist dictator of Russia	*f.* Alexander II
7. Last hereditary ruler of Russia	*g.* Kosygin
8. Khrushchev's successor as First Secretary of the Soviet Communist party	*h.* Beria
	i. Malenkov
	j. Kerensky
	k. Trotsky

TRUE-FALSE QUESTIONS

If the statement is correct, write the word *true*. If the statement is incorrect, substitute a word or phrase for the italicized term to make the statement correct.

1. The village communities which owned the land following emancipation of the serfs in 1861 were the *Dumas*.

2. The Revolution of 1905 was an aftermath of the *Crimean* War.

3. The Russians who fought the Communists from 1917 to 1921 were known as *Nepmen*.

4. The Communists have developed new industrial centers in central Asia and *Siberia*.

5. The official Communist stand on issues is called the *party line*.

6. The signal for the outbreak of World War II was Russia's Non-Aggression Pact in 1939 with *Poland*.

Part 3. Italy: Fascist Dictatorship to Democratic Republic

FASCISM IN ITALY: BASIC IDEAS

Following World War I *Benito Mussolini* organized the *Fascist* movement. He derived the word "Fascist" from the symbol of authority in ancient Rome, the *fasces,* a bundle of rods enveloping an ax. Fascism in Italy served as the model for similar movements in other countries, most notably Nazism in Germany. Fascists favored dictatorship and nationalism; they opposed democracy and Marxism.

1. Against Democracy. The Fascists (*a*) denounced democratic government as weak and inefficient, (*b*) ridiculed the idea that the state exists to serve the people, and (*c*) scoffed at civil liberties and multiparty systems of government.

2. For Dictatorship. The Fascists (*a*) praised dictatorship as strong and efficient, (*b*) claimed that "the people are nothing; the state is everything," (*c*) advocated Fascist seizure of power by force and violence, and (*d*) indicated that, under Fascism, the government would control every phase of human activity, thus forming a *totalitarian state.*

3. For Extreme Nationalism. The Fascists (*a*) exaggerated the accomplishments of the nation, (*b*) advocated imperialism, so that the nation could rule an empire, (*c*) hailed military might as a demonstration of the nation's strength and vitality, and (*d*) glorified war, claiming that it brought out the best qualities in a people and enabled the "superior" nations to rule the world.

4. Against Marxism. The Fascists (*a*) opposed the Marxist goal of a socialist economy, (*b*) condemned Marxist efforts that belittled nationalism and fostered international unity among workers, and (*c*) claimed that only Fascism could save a nation from being taken over by Socialists and Communists.

FACTORS EXPLAINING THE FASCIST RISE TO POWER IN ITALY

1. Economic Distress. After World War I the Italian people saw their already low living standards decline further. They suffered from (*a*) ruinous inflation that drove prices high, (*b*) heavy taxes to pay the war cost, and (*c*) widespread unemployment. By promising to improve economic conditions, the Fascists won support among low-paid workers, the unemployed, the impoverished middle class, and landless peasants.

2. Fear of Communism. In some areas, Italian workers seized factories, and peasants seized lands—in imitation of what was then happening in Russia. To conservative Italians, these seizures foreshadowed a Communist revolution in Italy. By fighting against Italian Socialists and Communists, the Fascists won widespread support of factory and land owners. From these wealthy and influential persons, Mussolini secured funds for his party, arms for his private military bands, and jobs for his followers.

3. Appeal to Nationalism. Although Italy had received Italia Irredenta (territory containing Italians) from Austria following World War I, Italian nationalists were disappointed. They had expected more territory, especially colonies in Africa and the Middle East and Balkan lands that would have permitted Italy to dominate the Adriatic Sea. Fascist boasts to restore the ancient Roman Empire appealed to nationalists: youths, veterans, and professional army officers.

4. Weak Government. Because no one political party commanded a majority in Parliament, Italy had a series of bloc, or coalition, governments. Unstable and weak, they proved unable to solve Italy's economic problems, to maintain law and order, and to overcome the threat of Fascism.

5. Lack of Democratic Tradition. The Italian people, many of them illiterate and poverty-stricken, were primarily occupied with earning a living. They showed little concern for governmental matters and had little training in civic responsibilities. When faced by the threat of a Fascist dictatorship, the people did little to defend their democracy.

6. Leadership of Mussolini. Unscrupulous and ambitious, Mussolini changed from Socialist to extreme nationalist during World War I and served in the Italian army. Following the war, he created the Fascist party, organized Fascist military bands called *Black Shirts*, and ordered violence and brutality against his opponents.

FASCISTS SEIZE POWER IN ITALY

The Fascist party quickly attracted considerable support, and the Fascists grew bold. In 1922 Mussolini felt powerful enough to demand control of the government. He threatened to use force and ordered his supporters to "march on Rome." The King, Victor Emmanuel III, refused to declare martial law. Unopposed by the army, Black Shirt bands poured into the capital, and the King requested Mussolini to form a government. Thus, with neither a popular vote nor a Parliamentary majority, Mussolini seized power.

ITALY UNDER FASCISM (1922-1943)

1. Government. The Fascists transformed Italy into a totalitarian dictatorship with Mussolini as the leader, *Il Duce*. They permitted the existence of only one political party, the Fascist party, and limited legislative elections to a yes-no vote on a single Fascist-chosen list of candidates. The Fascists denied civil liberties and, to suppress opposition, used secret police, violence, and imprisonment. Mussolini exhorted the people to "believe, fight, obey."

2. Labor. The Fascist government strictly controlled the Italian workers. The Fascists (*a*) determined wages, hours, and working conditions, (*b*) dominated the labor unions, and (*c*) prohibited strikes. In spite of lavish promises, the standard of living of the working class continued to be among the lowest in Europe.

3. Industry. Although the Fascists left most industry under private ownership, they did not permit genuine free enterprise. To the disappointment of their capitalist supporters, the Fascists strictly regulated economic matters—production, prices, capital investment—to further government objectives. To insure Fascist control, Mussolini organized both industry and labor into a small number of Fascist-led economic associations, called *corporations*. Consequently, Fascist Italy became known as a *corporate state*.

The Fascists built hydroelectric plants and armament factories and encouraged industrial development. They boasted that Fascist efficiency made the railroads run on time.

4. Public Works. The Fascists relieved unemployment by a program of public works: clearing slums; building roads, bridges, and public buildings; and draining swamplands. The *Pontine Marshes* were drained and restored to agricultural use, after having been unfarmed for 25 centuries.

5. Religion. To end the long dispute over Italy's seizure of Church lands during Italian unification (see pages 212-213), Mussolini and the Catholic Church in 1929 concluded the *Lateran Pacts*. (*a*) Italy recognized the Pope as sovereign ruler of Vatican City (located within Rome). (*b*) Italy retained, but made financial payment for, the rest of the Papal States. (*c*) Italy agreed to establish Catholicism as the state religion. These pacts strengthened Mussolini's influence over Italian Catholics, who constituted 99 percent of the population.

Following the formation of the Rome-Berlin Axis, Fascist Italy in 1938 began persecuting her small minority of 70,000 Jews. In this way, Italy was deprived of the talents of Italian citizens of Jewish faith.

6. Militarism. Seeking military grandeur, Mussolini (*a*) expanded Italy's armed forces by conscripting men to four years of military service followed by eleven years in the reserve, (*b*) required military training in Fascist youth groups and in schools, and (*c*) granted bonuses to large families, whose sons would eventually swell the ranks of his armies.

Mussolini's efforts to make Italy a great military power were severely hindered by Italy's lack of essential raw materials: coal, iron, and oil.

7. Imperialism and War. To dominate the Adriatic and Mediterranean Seas and to acquire colonies, Fascist Italy embarked on a policy of aggression. (*a*) In 1935-1936 despite League of Nations opposition, Italian troops invaded and conquered Ethiopia (see page 385). (*b*) In 1936 Italy and Nazi Germany reached an understanding that soon became a military alliance, the *Rome-Berlin Axis*, later expanded into the *Rome-Berlin-Tokyo Axis*. (*c*) In 1936, by supplying massive military aid, Italy and Germany enabled Spain's General Francisco Franco to overthrow the republican Spanish government and establish a Fascist type of regime (see page 385). (*d*) In 1939 Italy strengthened her position on the Adriatic Sea by invading and conquering Albania. (*e*) In 1940, when France was at the point of collapse, Italy joined with Germany in World War II against France and England. Mussolini expected a quick and easy victory—but he was wrong.

ITALY AND WORLD WAR II

1. Overthrow of the Fascist Regime (1943). Italian armies met with defeat after defeat. Fascist forces were driven back in Greece; they were wiped out in Ethiopia and North Africa; and in 1943 they were routed by Allied armies invading Sicily.

Stunned by military defeat, bombings, and invasion, the Italian people turned against Mussolini and his Fascist government. In 1943 the King and leading army officers forced Mussolini to resign and arrested him. A non-Fascist government took office and surrendered unconditionally to the Allies. Meanwhile, Mussolini escaped from imprisonment and fled to northern Italy where, protected by German armies, he proclaimed an Italian Fascist Republic. In 1945 Mussolini was captured and executed by Italian anti-Fascists.

2. The Treaty of Peace With Italy (1947). Italy (*a*) ceded border areas to France and Yugoslavia, (*b*) ceded the Dodecanese Islands (in the Aegean Sea) to Greece, (*c*) agreed to pay minor reparations and to limit her military forces, (*d*) surrendered her colonies, and (*e*) gave the United Nations the Adriatic seaport of Trieste as a Free Territory (available for Yugoslav use). (In 1954 Italy, by agreeing to permit unrestricted Yugoslav access to the port facilities, regained Trieste.)

ITALY BECOMES A REPUBLIC AND ADOPTS A DEMOCRATIC CONSTITUTION

By referendum, in 1946 the Italian people deposed the monarchy that many persons associated with the discredited Fascist regime. Accordingly, King Humbert II left the country, and Italy became a republic.

Italy's new constitution, effective in 1948, provided for (1) a Parliament of two houses—Chamber of Deputies and Senate—each with equal legislative powers, (2) a Premier and a cabinet able to command a majority in Parliament, and (3) a President elected by Parliament and serving chiefly as a symbol of unity.

The constitution (1) provides for universal suffrage—male and female, (2) guarantees civil liberties and economic rights, (3) prohibits the reestablishment of the Fascist party, and (4) recognizes the special position of the Catholic Church by granting state subsidies to the Church and by requiring state-supported schools to provide Catholic religious instruction.

PROBLEMS FACING THE ITALIAN REPUBLIC

1. **Government Instability.** Since 1948 the Italian government has been controlled chiefly by the *Christian Democratic* (Catholic) *party*. This center party advocates (a) further industrialization by such means as government subsidies, (b) social and economic reforms to improve living conditions, (c) protection of the interests of the Catholic Church, and (d) cooperation with the Western democracies against aggressive Communism.

Since the elections of 1953, the Christian Democrats, although Italy's largest political party, have lacked a majority in Parliament. Therefore, they have formed coalition governments to attract the votes of minor center parties—Liberals, Republicans, and right-wing Socialists—and, more recently, of left-wing Socialists. Because such center coalitions disagree frequently, Italy experiences recurrent cabinet crises. The government has been frequently reorganized but remains under Christian Democratic leadership.

2. **Communist Movement.** The *Italian Communist party*, seeking a Communist dictatorship, has considerable influence among anticlerical persons, intellectuals, workers, the unemployed, and peasants. The Communists are Italy's second largest political party. Despite outspoken opposition by the Catholic Church, they consistently poll one out of every four or five votes.

The Communists have failed to gain left-wing Socialist support for a Communist-dominated alliance, or *Popular Front*. Nevertheless, the Communists are powerful enough to represent an ominous threat to Italian democracy.

3. **Revival of Fascism.** Because Fascism is outlawed, persons holding Fascist views named their party the *Italian Social Movement*. This *neo-Fascist* group, over the last decade, has doubled its popular vote from 5 per-

cent to 10 percent. Although still relatively small, the Italian Social Movement constitutes a nucleus for a possible Fascist revival.

4. Foreign Policy. Under the Christian Democrats, the Italian government follows a strongly pro-Western foreign policy and favors close military and economic cooperation with the other nations of Western Europe. In 1949 Italy joined the Western nations in the North Atlantic Treaty Organization (a military alliance) and contributed troops to the NATO army.

5. Economic Improvement. To better living conditions, the Italian government (*a*) joined the Marshall Plan and received almost $2 billion in American economic aid (*b*) began land reform by distributing land from the large estates to the peasants, (*c*) undertook public works: building roads, houses, and schools, (*d*) joined with other West European nations in programs of economic cooperation, most notably the Common Market (see page 428), and (*e*) promoted tourist trade and encouraged industrial expansion.

Following World War II Italy experienced tremendous economic progress. Once mainly farmers, Italians have become workers overwhelmingly in service occupations, commerce, and industry. Italy's industries have changed from small handicraft shops to mass-production factories. They produce textiles, chemicals, and machinery. The middle class has grown, and workers in the industrial North have enjoyed considerable prosperity. From the end of World War II to the 1970's, Italy's *gross national product* (GNP) — a measure of the money value of goods and services—has quadrupled.

Nevertheless, Italy remains a relatively poor country. She is hampered by limited natural resources, high unemployment (about 10 percent of the working force), inflation and labor unrest, great poverty in the agricultural South, painfully slow progress in land reform, and a wide disparity between rich and poor.

6. Social Issues: (*a*) In the 1970's Italians divided sharply regarding a law, narrowly passed, which, under certain conditions, permits divorce. Devout Roman Catholics, whose religious teachings prohibit divorce, oppose the law; anticlerical groups favor it. The opponents of divorce secured signatures to a petition to force a public referendum on the law. To this writing, the referendum has not been held. (*b*) In the 1970's Italy experienced a sharp increase in crime, especially by juvenile offenders, and in politically inspired violence and the international drug traffic.

Part 4. Germany: Nazi Dictatorship

DEMOCRATIC GERMANY: THE WEIMAR REPUBLIC (1919-1933)

As World War I ended, the German people revolted against Kaiser William II, overthrew his autocratic regime, and established a democratic republic. Its constitution, drawn up at the town of *Weimar,* provided for (1) a weak President elected by popular vote, (2) a two-house legislature, with the Reichstag—the more powerful house—directly elected by the people, (3) a powerful Chancellor and cabinet responsible to the Reichstag, (4) a bill of rights, (5) civil and political equality of men and women, and (6) protection of minority groups.

The *Weimar Republic* provided Germany with democratic government from 1919, when it signed the Treaty of Versailles, until 1933, when the Nazis came into power.

FASCISM APPEARS IN GERMANY: THE NAZI PARTY

Following World War I a small group of extremists led by Adolf Hitler formed the *National Socialist party,* or *Nazi party.* Like the Fascists in Italy, the Nazis attacked democracy, promised to save Germany from Marxism, advocated extreme nationalism and militarism, and called for a dictatorship.

FACTORS EXPLAINING THE NAZI RISE TO POWER

1. Economic Distress. (*a*) Until 1923 the German government, instead of raising taxes, printed excessive quantities of paper money. The purchasing power of the German mark declined to almost nothing. This inflation harmed especially the middle class, which saw its savings accounts, life insurance policies, and pensions become worthless. (*b*) Starting in 1929 the worldwide depression caused business failures, falling wages, and rising unemployment. In 1932 over six million Germans were out of work.

By promising to improve the economy, the Nazis gained a strong following among the middle class, the workers, and the unemployed. Some observers hold that the Nazis rose to power "on the empty stomachs of the German people."

2. Fear of Communism. Many Germans, driven by economic distress, supported the German Communist party. In 1930 the Communists polled nearly five million votes, almost 15 percent of all the votes cast. Conservative groups now feared a Communist revolution. By battling the Communist movement, the Nazis, like the Fascists in Italy, gained the support of property holders, bankers, and industrialists. These people provided the Nazis with money, military equipment, and jobs.

3. Appeal to Nationalism. German patriots, who had gloried in the power of Germany before 1914, were emotionally unable to accept defeat in World War I. The Nazis exploited such nationalist feeling. They (a) pledged to tear up the Treaty of Versailles and denounced the German war-guilt clause, (b) demanded the return of Germany's colonies and European territories, (c) defended Germany's right to rearm, and (d) claimed that the German armies had been "stabbed in the back," mainly by Jews and Communists— *not* defeated by the Allies. Nazi chauvinism (extreme nationalism) won support of students, veterans, and army officers.

Hitler also proclaimed that the Germans were destined to rule the world because they constituted a "pure Aryan" race, physically and mentally superior to all other people. Although the Nazi doctrine of German racial superiority is contrary to all scientific evidence, many Germans chose to believe that they were the *master race.*

4. Attack Upon Jews. Hitler personally hated Jews, blamed them for Germany's ills, and pledged to drive them from German life. Hitler's anti-Semitic policies won widespread support. (a) Prejudice against Jews had always been strong in Germany. In Bismarck's time, religious bigots frequently attacked Jews and discriminated against them. (b) Many Germans readily accepted Nazi propaganda making Jews the *scapegoats* for Germany's troubles. If Jews were to blame for Germany's military defeat and economic woes, then the German people were not responsible. (c) Unprincipled persons anticipated the looting and seizing of Jewish businesses and homes.

5. Weaknesses of the Weimar Government. Of Germany's several political parties, no single one could command a Reichstag majority. The leading moderate parties—Catholic Center and Social Democrat—differed on economic and religious matters and did not cooperate effectively. Furthermore, by 1932 the antirepublican extremists—Nazis on the right and Communists on the left—together had more Reichstag votes than the moderate parties working for the republic's survival. Consequently, Germany's democratic government was unstable and could not cope with Germany's pressing problems.

6. Lack of a Democratic Tradition. The main heritage of the German people was not democracy, but autocracy. Under the autocratic leadership of Bismarck and the Kaiser, Germany had achieved unification, economic growth, and world power. In contrast, under the democratic Weimar Republic, Germany had accepted the hated Treaty of Versailles and fallen into economic distress. Hence, to many Germans, autocracy meant success, democracy failure. Furthermore, the German people had little experience in the functioning of a democratic government. Many Germans were willing to exchange their freedom for Nazi promises of economic security and nationalist glory.

7. Leadership of Hitler. Born in Austria, Adolf Hitler was an unsuccessful artist who served in the German army during World War I. He helped form the Nazi party and rose to leadership by his organizational ability. While briefly imprisoned for an unsuccessful rebellion in 1923 (see below), Hitler outlined his plans for a Nazi Germany in the book *Mein Kampf* (*My Struggle*). By means of private armies of *Storm Troopers*, violence to terrorize the opposition, spectacular mass rallies, and his own ability to sway German audiences, Hitler led the Nazis to control of Germany.

THE NAZIS SEIZE POWER IN GERMANY

In 1923 the Nazis, then a small group, joined with other extreme nationalists in Munich in a petty rebellion, or *putsch*. They were easily suppressed, and Hitler was briefly imprisoned.

After 1929, as economic conditions in Germany worsened, the Nazis attracted increasing support. In 1932 they polled nearly 12 million votes—37 percent of the total—and became the largest party in the Reichstag. However, they lacked a majority. In 1933 Hitler was appointed Chancellor, after he swore to President Hindenburg that he would maintain the constitution. He immediately called for new elections. In voting marked by intimidation, violence, and deceit, the Nazis and their supporters achieved a narrow margin of control of the Reichstag. Thereupon, they ended the Weimar Republic, and Hitler assumed dictatorial powers.

THE THIRD REICH: NAZISM IN POWER (1933-1945)

1. Government. The Nazis transformed Germany into a dictatorship. (*a*) As *Der Führer*, or *The Leader*, Hitler exercised supreme power. The Reichstag was infrequently summoned and was expected only to applaud and approve Hitler's decisions. (*b*) All parties except the Nazi party were outlawed. The Nazis permitted Reichstag elections but limited the choices to a yes-no vote on a single list of Nazi-selected candidates. (*c*) Under *Heinrich Himmler*, the *Gestapo*, or secret police, brutally suppressed all opposition. Anti-Nazis—whether democrat, liberal, Socialist, Communist, Catholic, Jew, or Protestant—suffered unbelievable tortures and often death in concentration camps. The Third Reich deprived the individual of both human dignity and civil liberties. (*d*) By extending government control over every aspect of human activity, the Nazis established a totalitarian state.

2. Propaganda. An elaborate Propaganda Ministry, headed by *Joseph Goebbels,* utilized all media of information and education, and operated within Germany and throughout the world. Goebbels used the technique of the *big lie.* Nazi propagandists operated on the theory that any lie—if stated authoritatively, repeated incessantly, and guarded from critical analysis—will eventually be accepted by most people.

3. Education. The Nazis used the schools to instill blind obedience to the Führer. Only Nazis were permitted to teach, and the courses of study were changed to foster Nazi purposes. Only Nazi textbooks were used. On the high school level, chemistry courses included the making of poison gases; mathematics courses, the calculating of bombing distances. In social studies, the stress was upon the evils of democracy and the "superiority of the Aryan race." Nazi education was described by an anti-Nazi writer as a "school for barbarians."

4. Science and Culture. The Nazis harnessed science and culture to serve the state. (*a*) Scientists worked on weapons of war. (*b*) Anthropologists attempted to "prove" Aryan supremacy. (*c*) Writers extolled Hitler and Nazism. (*d*) Censors held public book-burning ceremonies to destroy works by anti-Nazis. (*e*) The government banned the reading or performance of works by persons of Jewish origin, such as the poetry of Heine and the music of Mendelssohn.

5. Persecution of Jews. The Nazis deprived German Jews of citizenship; burned their synagogues; and ousted them from jobs, businesses, and homes. Nazi Storm Troopers subjected Jews to physical violence and sent them to forced labor, torture, and starvation in concentration camps. Only a few Jews escaped from Germany and found refuge in other lands.

During World War II, as German armies overran most of Europe, Jews in the conquered lands fell under the Nazi yoke. The Nazis now intensified their anti-Semitic program with a barbarism unmatched in history. Special Nazi forces herded Jews into infamous concentration camps such as *Buchenwald, Auschwitz,* and *Dachau.* Employing specially constructed gas chambers and crematoria, the Nazis exterminated six million men, women, and children. These human beings were murdered not because they had committed any crime but because they were of Jewish faith or origin.

6. Religion. The Nazis realized that their doctrines were contrary to the ethical concepts of Christianity. Nazi violence and aggression conflicted with the "Golden Rule." Nazi "master race" propaganda conflicted with the "brotherhood of man."

Consequently, the Nazis sought to control Christianity. Nazi officials directed the activities of the Protestant Churches. Those ministers who failed to cooperate were sent to concentration camps. Also, Hitler tried to weaken the Catholic Church. The Nazis discouraged attendance in Catholic schools, tried many priests and nuns on various trumped-up charges, and imprisoned clergymen who challenged Nazism.

7. Women. The Nazis assigned women to an inferior position in German society. Women were excluded from politics and were ordered to devote themselves to kitchen tasks and childbearing. Hitler wanted an increasing population that he could mold to Nazi ideas and draft into his armies.

8. Labor. The Nazi regime determined wages, hours, and working conditions, dominated the labor unions, and prohibited strikes. The Nazis almost completely eliminated unemployment by driving anti-Nazis and married women from jobs, furthering public works, spurring the production of armaments, and enlarging the armed forces.

9. Industry. The Nazis permitted private ownership of industry subject to strict regulation. Instead of allowing free enterprise, the state controlled prices, production, profits, capital investment, foreign trade, and banking.

In 1936 *Hermann Goering* headed a Nazi Four-Year Plan to prepare the German economy for war. He sought economic self-sufficiency, or *autarchy*, and emphasized the production of armaments. Goering's slogan was "guns not butter."

10. Militarism. The Nazis (*a*) created a large conscript army and a powerful air force, (*b*) remilitarized the Rhineland, (*c*) shifted German industry into war production, and (*d*) gave military training to children in schools and in Hitler Youth Organizations. By rebuilding Germany's military might, Hitler violated the Treaty of Versailles, but the Allies took no action. Meanwhile, the Nazis sang "Today we rule Germany, tomorrow the world."

11. Aggression and War. Hitler planned territorial expansion in Europe, claiming that Germany needed *Lebensraum* (living space). (*a*) In 1936 Germany and Italy reached an understanding that later became a military alliance, the *Rome-Berlin Axis*. (*b*) In 1936 Germany and Italy gave men and equipment to General Franco of Spain, enabling him to overthrow the Spanish republican government and establish a Fascist type of regime. (*c*) In 1938, in violation of the World War I peace settlement, Germany invaded and annexed Austria. (*d*) In 1938 Germany, having secured the reluctant approval of England and France, seized the *Sudetenland*, the region of Czechoslovakia bordering on Germany and Austria. Hitler's pretext was that the Sudetens were a German-speaking people. Six months later, however, Hitler seized the rest of Czechoslovakia, inhabited by Slavic-speaking peoples. (*e*) In 1939 Hitler demanded the return of Danzig and the Polish Corridor. When Poland, backed by England and France, did not yield, Hitler invaded that country, thereby starting World War II. (For details, see Fascist Aggression, pages 385-386.)

WORLD WAR II AND THE COLLAPSE OF THE NAZI REGIME

At first, German armies achieved great triumphs, overrunning most of Poland, western Europe, and the Balkans. After June, 1941, Nazi armies penetrated deep into Russian territory.

In late 1942 the tide of battle turned against the Nazis. By 1945 German forces had been routed in Russia, wiped out in North Africa, and driven from France, and the Nazis were fighting on German soil. Germany was being invaded from both east and west. German cities, factories, and railroads lay ruined by Allied bombings. In April, 1945, Hitler died in Berlin, apparently by suicide. Shortly thereafter, Germany surrendered unconditionally, and the Nazi regime ended.

GERMANY SINCE WORLD WAR II

The Allies divided Germany into four zones, with Russia, England, France, and the United States each occupying one zone. By quarreling over Germany's future, the Western powers and Russia soon linked German postwar history to the cold war (see pages 436-444).

MULTIPLE-CHOICE QUESTIONS

1. In a totalitarian state (1) all industry is owned by the government (2) the state controls every aspect of the lives of its people (3) the state guarantees civil liberties to loyal citizens (4) a complete revolution occurs about every twenty years.

2. In general, a dictator (1) furthers critical thinking on political matters by students (2) encourages free labor unions (3) suspends military service (4) controls the means of communication.

3. Dictatorships do *not* accept the principle that (1) might makes right (2) strict censorship is necessary (3) one party should be supreme (4) the state exists for the individual.

4. A major difference between dictatorship and democracy is that a dictatorship does *not* have a (1) multiparty system (2) cabinet (3) parliament (4) written constitution.

5. One reason for Mussolini's rise to power in Italy was that he (1) promoted the annexation of Rome (2) promised Italians a republican form of government (3) conquered Ethiopia (4) had the support of industrial leaders.

6. Mussolini gained control of the Italian government following (1) a national election (2) a majority vote in the Italian legislature (3) his threat to use force (4) the depression of 1929.

7. The Fascist government of Italy was similar to the Communist government of Russia in that it (1) was controlled by the proletariat (2) was democratically elected (3) was controlled by capitalists (4) suppressed opposition.

8. The controversy between Italy and the Pope over state seizure of Church lands was settled by the (1) abdication of the Italian King (2) Law of Papal Guarantees (3) Lateran Pacts with the Pope (4) elevation of Pope Paul VI.

9. Under Fascism workers could *not* (1) belong to labor unions (2) go out on strike (3) vote in national elections (4) belong to the Fascist party.

10. Under Fascism industrial prices were generally set by the (1) capitalists (2) state (3) consumers (4) workers.

11. Which was supported by Mussolini? (1) an alliance with Nazi Germany (2) a policy of free trade (3) nonintervention in the Spanish Civil War (4) nationalist movements in Ethiopia and Libya.

12. The constitution of the Italian Republic does *not* guarantee (1) civil liberties (2) universal suffrage (3) separation of Church and State (4) cabinet responsibility to Parliament.

13. Today, the Italian Republic faces the problem of (1) securing workers for new mass-production industries (2) gaining allies in the cold war (3) regaining ownership of Sicily (4) maintaining stable government.

14. Immediately after World War I Germany became a (1) dictatorship (2) constitutional monarchy (3) republic (4) Communist satellite.

15. For the period 1920-1940, which is considered a result of the other three? (1) rise of the Nazi movement (2) rise of unemployment in Germany (3) German tradition of militarism (4) Treaty of Versailles.

16. In post-World War I Germany, the savings of the middle class were wiped out by (1) inflation of currency (2) government confiscation (3) bank failures (4) payment of reparations.

17. The Nazis blamed Germany's defeat in World War I upon (1) the German General Staff (2) Allied superiority in manpower and equipment (3) German scientists for failing to develop new weapons (4) traitors in the German civilian population.

18. In matters of religion, the Nazis (1) permitted freedom of worship (2) forced all Germans to become Protestants (3) sought to make the churches serve the nation (4) made Catholicism the official religion.

19. A policy of Nazi Germany was (1) self-determination for the peoples of Europe (2) adoption of laissez-faire (3) establishment of collective farms (4) maintenance of concentration camps.

20. German Nazism differed most from Russian Communism with respect to the (1) ownership of property (2) existence of secret police (3) political party system (4) censorship of newspapers and radio.

21. Hitler's territorial demand immediately preceding the outbreak of World War II was (1) Alsace-Lorraine (2) the Sudetenland (3) the Polish Corridor (4) Albania.

MATCHING QUESTIONS

Column A	*Column B*
1. Head of the Gestapo	*a.* Benito Mussolini
2. General who became President of the Weimar Republic	*b.* Heinrich Himmler
3. Leader known as "Il Duce"	*c.* Hindenburg
4. Last Kaiser of Germany	*d.* William II
5. Composer whose music was banned in Nazi Germany	*e.* Humbert II
6. Author of *Mein Kampf*	*f.* Adolf Hitler
7. Minister of Nazi Propaganda	*g.* Joseph Goebbels
	h. Felix Mendelssohn
	i. Hermann Goering

Part 5. Failure of the Peace Movement and World War II

THE LEAGUE OF NATIONS

Following World War I, mankind hoped for an era of world peace. Woodrow Wilson, wartime American President, believed the League of Nations to be the single most important step toward this goal. At President Wilson's insistence, the League of Nations Covenant (Constitution) was made part of the Treaty of Versailles. In 1920 the League started operations; its headquarters were at Geneva, Switzerland.

PURPOSES OF THE LEAGUE OF NATIONS

The League was created (1) to provide a world organization and thus eliminate international anarchy, (2) to prevent war by encouraging disarmament and by settling international disputes peacefully, and (3) to solve economic and social problems through international cooperation.

ORGANIZATION OF THE LEAGUE OF NATIONS

1. The **Assembly,** consisting of all member nations, discussed international issues and made recommendations by *unanimous* vote.

2. The **Council,** consisting of selected permanent and nonpermanent members, was chiefly concerned with threats to world peace. Its recommendations also required *unanimity*.

3. The **World Court** was to settle legal disputes between nations on the basis of international law.

4. Specialized **commissions** and **agencies** dealt with economic and social problems. For example, the *Permanent Mandates Commission* supervised colonies held as mandates, the *International Health Organization* combatted disease, the *Minorities Commission* protected the rights of minority groups, and the *International Labor Organization* (*ILO*) gathered labor statistics and worked to improve world labor conditions.

THE LEAGUE SEEKS TO PREVENT WAR

To settle disputes peacefully, League procedures called for (1) arbitration by neutral third parties, or (2) judicial decision by the World Court, or (3) inquiry and recommendation by the Council.

If an aggressor nation refused to submit to peaceful settlement, the League could advise (but could not force) its member nations to employ coercive measures, called *sanctions*. These might be *diplomatic*, such as withdrawing ambassadors; *economic*, such as halting trade; and, finally, *military*. (The League, in its brief existence, never attempted military sanctions.)

THE UNITED STATES REFUSES TO JOIN THE LEAGUE

In 1919 President Wilson presented the Treaty of Versailles with its provision for League membership to the Republican-controlled Senate. Leading Republican Senators, favoring isolation and personally hostile to Wilson, a Democrat, led a long, bitter fight against the League. Wilson countered by an extensive speaking tour, but his efforts ended abruptly when he suffered a paralytic stroke. The Senate, by a wide margin, rejected the Treaty of Versailles.

The isolationists argued as follows: (1) The League might involve the United States in a war, thereby violating the American Constitution, which gives only Congress the power to declare war. (2) The League might interfere in domestic matters, such as tariff and immigration policies. (3) The League would be dominated by England and her dominions, which had a total of six Assembly votes. (4) League membership would involve us in the problems of the entire world and thus violate America's traditional policy of isolation. The United States never joined the League.

THE UNITED STATES COOPERATES WITH THE LEAGUE

The United States cooperated, in a limited way, with the League by (1) joining the International Labor Organization, (2) working with League agencies to wipe out disease, suppress slavery, and establish standards in communication and transportation, and (3) supporting the League during the crisis over Manchuria (see Stimson Doctrine, page 314).

LEAGUE SUCCESSES

In the 1920's the League peacefully settled boundary disputes between small nations, such as disputes between Finland and Sweden, Yugoslavia and Albania, and Greece and Bulgaria. Also, the League achieved economic and social progress by aiding nations financially, combatting disease, and curtailing opium traffic.

LEAGUE WEAKNESSES

1. Membership. The League did not include all major nations. The United States never joined. Russia entered the League in 1934 but was expelled in 1939. Germany and Japan withdrew in 1933, and Italy withdrew three years later.

2. Voting. League decisions required unanimous votes.

3. Powers. The League constituted an association of independent nations wherein each retained complete freedom of action, that is, *national sovereignty*. The League lacked the power to tax, to draft an army, and to enforce its decisions. Although it could request money, men, and support from its members, each state was free to respond according to its own national interests. The League was not a strong world government, but a very weak *confederation*.

LEAGUE FAILURES

The League's outstanding failures were its inability to (1) halt the Japanese invasion of Manchuria (1931), (2) halt the Italian conquest of Ethiopia (1935), and (3) oppose German rearmament and territorial seizures (1935-1938) in violation of the Treaty of Versailles. In 1946 the League voted itself out of existence and transferred its properties to the new world organization, the United Nations.

NAVAL DISARMAMENT

1. Early Agreements. Realizing that the armaments race had helped cause World War 1, the naval powers sought disarmament.

    a. Washington Conference (1921-1922). England, the United States, Japan, France, and Italy agreed to stop building capital ships (large warships) for 10 years and to maintain capital ships in a ratio of 5:5:3:1.67:1.67, respectively.

    b. London Naval Conference (1930). England, the United States, and Japan agreed to a ratio of 10:10:7, respectively, for five years, for cruisers and destroyers as well as capital ships.

2. Eventual Failure. At the *London Conference* (1935), Japan demanded a 10:10:10 ratio, or *parity*, with England and the United States. The democracies refused on the ground that Japan had no need of such naval power unless for aggression. No agreement was reached; soon afterwards Japan started a new naval race.

Also in 1935 Nazi Germany denounced the disarmament provision of the Versailles Treaty and began to rearm on land and sea. German remilitarization encountered no serious opposition from the other signatories of the treaty.

INTERNATIONAL PACTS

1. Nine-Power Treaty at the Washington Conference (1921-1922). Japan, the United States, England, France, and five smaller nations agreed to respect equal trade in and the independence of China. By thus reaffirming the Open Door Policy, these nations hoped to prevent imperialist conflict over China.

2. Locarno Pacts (1925). Germany agreed (*a*) to accept as permanent her boundaries with Belgium and France, (*b*) to keep the Rhineland demilitarized as required by the Treaty of Versailles, and (*c*) to submit to peaceful settlement any disputes concerning her boundaries with Czechoslovakia and Poland. The Locarno Pacts were guaranteed by the nations involved and by Italy and England.

3. Kellogg-Briand Pact (1928). *Frank Kellogg,* American Secretary of State, and *Aristide Briand,* French Foreign Minister, proposed a pact to settle all disputes peacefully and to outlaw war "as an instrument of national policy." Most nations, including Germany, Japan, and Italy, signed this idealistic statement, also called the *Pact of Paris.*

4. Failure of International Pacts. In the 1930's militarist Japan, Fascist Italy, and Nazi Germany began aggressions in defiance of these pacts. When Germany under Hitler first violated the Locarno Pacts, the other signatory powers failed to take effective action, and the Locarno agreements became worthless. The Nine-Power Treaty and the Kellogg-Briand Pact contained no provision for enforcement.

THE UNITED STATES AND THE PEACE MOVEMENT (1919-1939)

Following World War I, the American people desired peace, but they could not decide on the road to follow—*international cooperation* or *isolation.*

Toward international cooperation, the United States government (1) supported certain activities and decisions of the League, (2) joined in naval disarmament, and (3) signed the Nine-Power Treaty and the Kellogg-Briand Pact.

Many Americans, however, still rejected international cooperation and held that we could ensure peace for ourselves only through isolation. Their views dominated American foreign policy in the years between World Wars I and II. Pursuing a policy of isolation, the United States (1) refused to join the League of Nations and the World Court, (2) discouraged international trade by raising tariff barriers, and (3) adopted neutrality legislation.

AMERICAN NEUTRALITY ACTS (1935, 1937)

Sensing that Europe was again headed toward war, Congress passed two *Neutrality Acts* which (1) prohibited the sale of war implements to belligerents, (2) banned loans to belligerents, (3) prohibited Americans from sailing on ships of belligerents, and (4) forbade American merchant ships to enter war zones. This last provision surrendered traditional American claims to *freedom of the seas*—the right of a neutral nation to trade with belligerents in goods not intended for war use.

Congress hoped that these laws would prevent the economic and emotional entanglements that, many believed, had involved the United States in World War I. However, these American efforts to assure peace for ourselves weakened the world peace movement and overlooked the fact that aggression elsewhere might endanger our own security.

FASCIST AGGRESSION (1931-1939)

Japan, Italy, and Germany (1) engaged in one act of aggression after another, thereby violating, without any effective opposition, the major international peace agreements: Treaty of Versailles, Covenant of the League of Nations, Nine-Power Treaty, Locarno Pacts, and Kellogg-Briand Pact, (2) withdrew from membership in the League, and (3) joined together to form a military alliance, the *Rome-Berlin-Tokyo Axis*. The record of aggression follows.

1. Manchuria. In 1931-1932 Japan invaded and conquered China's northern province of Manchuria. Japan flouted League of Nations efforts to halt her aggression and thus, for the first time, revealed the League's weaknesses. (For details, see page 314.)

2. Ethiopia. In 1935 Italy invaded Ethiopia. The League of Nations named Italy the aggressor and voted minor economic sanctions but failed to recommend an embargo on Italy's most essential import—oil. Undeterred by such feeble opposition, Mussolini conquered and annexed Ethiopia.

3. German Remilitarization. Nazi Germany violated the Treaty of Versailles in 1935 by reintroducing conscription and in 1936 by remilitarizing the Rhineland. Hitler encountered no serious Allied opposition despite Germany's then limited military strength.

4. Spain. In 1936 General *Francisco Franco* began a revolt against the legally elected left-of-center government of Spain. While the Loyalist government received limited aid from Russia, Franco received extensive support of troops and military equipment from Italy and Germany. After three years of civil war, Franco won complete control and established a Fascist type of dictatorship friendly to Germany and Italy.

5. China. In 1937 Japanese forces from Manchuria invaded China proper. The Japanese overran China's coastal areas but failed to penetrate far into the interior. The Chinese continued their resistance and received limited aid from Britain and the United States.

6. Austria. In 1938 Hitler invaded and annexed Austria on the ground that all German-speaking people belonged within one German nation. *Anschluss* (union) of Germany and Austria violated the World War I peace treaties. Furthermore, anschluss was never approved by the Austrian people in an honest plebiscite.

7. Czechoslovakia. Later in 1938 Hitler demanded the *Sudetenland*, a region in Czechoslovakia bordering on Germany and inhabited by German-speaking people. Although the Sudeten people were not oppressed, Nazi propagandists manufactured stories of "Czech atrocities," and Hitler promised "help." The Czech government, a democracy under President *Eduard Benes*, refused to yield. It counted on its alliance with Russia and France and expected English support. However, England and France decided not to risk war but to appease Hitler.

At the *Munich Conference*, English Prime Minister *Neville Chamberlain* and French Premier *Edouard Daladier* agreed to let Hitler seize the Sudetenland. Deserted by her friends, Czechoslovakia yielded. Chamberlain returned to England and proclaimed that he had preserved "peace in our time." Hitler announced that this was his last European territorial demand.

Six months later, however, Hitler seized the Slavic-inhabited remainder of Czechoslovakia. In England, the Chamberlain government at last realized that Hitler could not be trusted to keep his promises. England and France joined in a military alliance and guaranteed protection to Germany's next probable victim, Poland.

8. Albania. In 1939 Mussolini invaded and annexed Albania, giving Italy control of the Adriatic Sea.

9. Poland. In 1939 Hitler demanded the return of Danzig and the Polish Corridor on the ground that they were inhabited by German-speaking people.

Before Poland responded, Nazi Germany and Communist Russia announced a 10-year *Non-Aggression Pact*. The world was surprised because Hitler had always preached hatred of Communism, and Stalin had always condemned Fascism. (*a*) The pact **enabled Russia** to avoid (for the time being) involvement in a major war and, by its secret clauses, gave Stalin a free hand over eastern Poland and the Baltic states. (*b*) The pact **protected Germany** against a two-front war and secretly promised Hitler foodstuffs and war supplies from Russia.

On September 1, 1939, German troops invaded Poland; two days later, England and France honored their guarantee to Poland and declared war on Germany. World War II had started.

BASIC CAUSES OF WORLD WAR II: AXIS PHILOSOPHY AND AGGRESSION

1. Axis Totalitarianism. With Japan ruled by the military and Germany and Italy each dominated by a Fascist party, the Axis nations were totalitarian dictatorships. They scorned the democratic ideals of civil liberties, of the dignity of the individual, and of world peace, and they openly declared their intent to destroy democracy.

2. Axis Militarism. The Axis nations spent vast sums on armaments, devised new weapons and battle techniques, built huge military organizations, and psychologically prepared their peoples for war. They proclaimed war a glorious adventure and death for the Fatherland the highest honor.

3. Axis Nationalism. Japanese Shinto teachings, Italian dreams of a revival of the Roman Empire, and German "master race" doctrines all fostered a narrow and bigoted nationalism. The Axis nations considered themselves superior and destined to rule over "lesser peoples."

4. Axis Imperialism. The Axis powers embarked upon imperialism with the excuse that they lacked land and resources and were *have-not* nations. Japan expanded into Manchuria and China proper to establish a Japanese-dominated "New Order in Asia." Italy enlarged her African empire and planned to make the Mediterranean an "Italian lake." Germany annexed Austria and Czechoslovakia as first steps toward European domination and eventually, perhaps, world domination.

SUBSIDIARY CAUSES OF WORLD WAR II

1. Failure of Appeasement. England and France followed a policy of *appeasement*—that is, making concessions to the dictators in the hope that the dictators would eventually be satisfied and stop their aggression. Anxious for peace, democratic peoples failed to understand that each concession strengthened the aggressors and emboldened them to make further demands. The chief advocate of appeasement was Neville Chamberlain, and its final application was the transfer of the Sudetenland by the Munich Conference.

2. Failure of Collective Security. Peace-loving nations, by coordinating their military strength and acting collectively, might have protected each other from aggression. However, the democratic peoples shrank from any kind of military action. The United States was determined to remain neutral; England and France delayed the formation of a firm alliance until 1939.

Communist Russia urged collective security because she feared attack by Nazi Germany. Democratic nations, however, were reluctant to enter into collective security pacts with the Soviet Union because they (*a*) did not believe Communist sincerity, (*b*) feared Communist plans for world revolution, and (*c*) were not eager to protect the Soviet Union. Indeed, some people felt that a Russo-German war would lessen both the Communist and Fascist threats to Western democracy. In 1939, however, Russia saw an opportunity to turn the Nazi war machine against England and France. Thereupon, Russia terminated her support of collective security and concluded the Stalin-Hitler Non-Aggression Pact.

3. American Neutrality Legislation. By prohibiting loans and the sale of war implements to all belligerents, the Neutrality Acts actually favored the well-armed aggressor nations over their ill-equipped victims. Furthermore, these laws implied that Americans would "stay on their side of the street" and would not intervene to check Axis aggression in Asia and Europe.

THE SECOND WORLD WAR (1939-1945)

1. Initial German Successes (1939-1940)

a. Conquest of Poland. German armies, employing massive air bombings and tank assaults, unleashed a new "lightning war," or *blitzkrieg*. They speedily rolled across the open plains of Poland and destroyed all resistance. Germany annexed western Poland. (As agreed in the Hitler-Stalin Pact, Russia seized eastern Poland. Russia also annexed the Baltic countries of Estonia, Latvia, and Lithuania and, after a four-month war, secured territory from Finland.)

b. Conquest of Denmark and Norway. Nazi armies next overran neutral Denmark and Norway. In Norway, Nazi armies received assistance from traitors, called *fifth columnists*, led by *Vidkun Quisling*. Germany thus gained valuable submarine bases on the Atlantic Ocean.

c. Conquest of France. Nazi armies invaded northern France in 1940 by going through the plains of neutral Holland and Belgium. The Germans thus bypassed the Franco-German border with its mountainous terrain and French defensive fortifications, the *Maginot Line*. Nazi armies easily defeated the Allied defenders. The British retreated to *Dunkirk* and miraculously evacuated most troops to England. French resistance collapsed, and French forces fled southward. With Mussolini confident that victory was already won, Italy entered the war. As the German forces continued their advance southward, France surrendered.

The Germans occupied over half of France, including the whole Atlantic and Channel coasts. For unoccupied France, they permitted an antidemocratic government at *Vichy*, headed by Marshal *Henri Pétain*. In England, General *Charles de Gaulle* proclaimed a *Free French* movement determined to continue the war and liberate France.

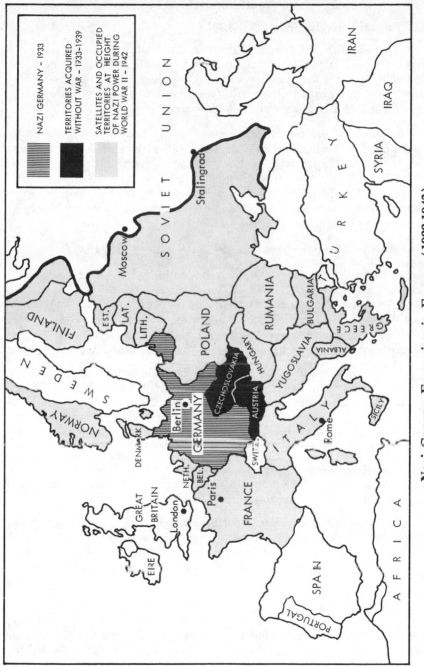

Nazi German Expansion in Europe (1933-1942)

2. England Stands Alone (1940-1941)

a. Leadership of Churchill. *Winston Churchill,* who had repeatedly opposed appeasement of the Nazis, replaced Chamberlain as Prime Minister. Churchill inspired the English people to courage and determination, as he called upon them to save the world from the "abyss of a new dark age." "I have nothing to offer," he said, "but blood, toil, tears, and sweat."

b. Battle of Britain. Hitler ordered his *Luftwaffe* (air force) to soften England for invasion. For three months England was subjected to devastating air attacks. The *Royal Air Force (RAF),* however, drove off the Luftwaffe. By maintaining control of the air lanes, the RAF compelled the Nazis to shelve their plans for an invasion of England. Instead, the Nazis turned southward, overrunning the Balkans and placing an army in North Africa to support the Italians.

3. American Preparedness and Aid to the Allies (1939-1941)

a. Neutrality Act of 1939. Soon after World War II started, President *Franklin D. Roosevelt* requested Congress to pass the Neutrality Act of 1939. This law permitted belligerents to purchase war materials, provided they paid cash and carried the goods away in their own vessels. *Cash and carry* was designed to give limited assistance to the Atlantic sea powers (France and England) and, at the same time, maintain American neutrality.

b. Changes in Public Opinion. President Roosevelt labored to awaken the American people to the threat to their national security. When France fell in 1940, Americans finally realized that England alone stood between them and a hostile Fascist world. For America's self-defense, Congress supported a vast military build-up and aid to England by *all measures short of war.*

c. Military Preparedness. Congress authorized a two-ocean navy and a huge air force, and passed the 1940 *Selective Service Act.* It provided for America's first peacetime conscription (draft).

d. Destroyer-Naval Base Deal of 1940. President Roosevelt traded 50 "over-age" destroyers to England in exchange for military bases on British territory in the Western Hemisphere from Newfoundland to British Guiana. England needed the destroyers to combat German submarines; the United States used the bases as defensive outposts.

e. Lend-Lease Act of 1941. Realizing that Britain's cash was almost exhausted, President Roosevelt requested new legislation to maintain the United States as the "arsenal of democracy." Congress passed the *Lend-Lease Act* authorizing the President to lend or lease goods to any nation whose defense he deemed necessary for the defense of the United States. Immediately, Roosevelt extended substantial aid to England; he later gave aid to other Allies, including Russia. (Total lend-lease aid amounted to $50 billion.) Also, Roosevelt ordered that merchant ships carrying lend-lease materials be convoyed by the United States Navy part way across the Atlantic.

f. Embargo on Strategic Materials to Japan. As an advocate of the Open Door Policy, the United States opposed Japan's plans for an east Asian empire. In 1940-1941 the United States protested Japanese occupation of French Indo-China. Since protests proved ineffective, President Roosevelt embargoed the sale of aviation gasoline, scrap iron, and other strategic materials to Japan and "froze" Japanese assets in the United States.

4. The Axis Makes Two Mistakes (1941)

a. German Attack Upon Russia. Despite the Russo-German Non-Aggression Pact, Hitler ordered a blitzkrieg against Russia (June, 1941) to acquire the grain, coal, and iron of the Ukraine and the oil of the Caucasus. Hitler expected a quick victory, but Russia proved to be a formidable foe. Russian armies retreated slowly, "scorching the earth," and Communist guerrilla bands harassed the invaders. The Nazis occupied much territory, stretching their supply lines, but were unable to crush the Soviet armies.

b. Japanese Attack Upon the United States. On December 7, 1941, Japan staged a "sneak attack" upon the American naval base at *Pearl Harbor,* Hawaii, forcing the United States actively into the war. Under General *Hideki Tojo,* the Japanese government planned to humble the United States and assure Japanese domination of eastern Asia. Japan's Axis partners (Germany and Italy) immediately declared war on the United States.

Axis strategists hoped that, if they forced the United States into a Pacific war, the United States would be unable to complete her military preparations and would be forced to curtail lend-lease aid to England and Russia. However, the Axis reckoned without the American people. They closed ranks behind President Roosevelt with eager determination to "win the war and the peace that follows."

5. Victory in Europe (1942-1945)

a. From North Africa to Italy. In October, 1942, a British army under General *Bernard Montgomery* defeated the Germans and Italians at *El Alamein,* Egypt, and began pursuing them westward. In November, 1942, an Anglo-American army under General *Dwight D. Eisenhower* invaded French North Africa and moved eastward. By thus placing the enemy in a vise, the Allies destroyed the Axis African armies. In 1943 the Allies crossed the Mediterranean and invaded Sicily and southern Italy. Mussolini's Fascist government collapsed, and Italy surrendered unconditionally. To resist the Allied advance northward, Germany rushed troops into Italy.

b. Russian Counteroffensive. In early 1943, following a six-month battle, the Russians annihilated a 300,000-man Nazi army deep inside the Soviet Union at *Stalingrad.* Following this great victory Russian armies seized the initiative, materially assisted by huge amounts of American lend-lease, especially motor vehicles and airplanes. The Communists drove the Nazis from Russia and pursued them through Rumania, Bulgaria, Yugoslavia, Hungary, Austria, Czechoslovakia, and Poland. In 1945 the Russians reached eastern Germany and stormed into Berlin.

c. Anglo-American Invasion of France. To prepare the way for invasion, American and British airmen bombed Nazi-held Europe, and underground patriots sabotaged Nazi factories and harassed Nazi forces. On June 6, 1944, American and British forces, commanded by General Eisenhower, crossed the English Channel and landed in *Normandy* in northern France. This greatest waterborne invasion in history established a major *second front.* The invading forces met a powerful German army, which had been kept from the Russian front in anticipation of the attack. Allied forces pushed back the Nazi army and drove the Germans from France.

d. Surrender of Germany. In 1945 Anglo-American armies crossed the Rhine River in Germany and continued to the Elbe. Here they met the Russians driving in from the east. After Hitler committed suicide, Germany surrendered unconditionally. President *Harry S. Truman,* along with British Prime Minister Churchill, officially proclaimed victory in Europe on May 8, 1945—*V-E Day.*

6. Victory in the Pacific (1942-1945)

a. Initial Japanese Offensive. In 1942 Japanese forces, pushing southward, overran the Philippines, the Malay States, the Dutch East Indies, and part of New Guinea. Poised just north of Australia, they were halted by the American naval victory in the *Coral Sea.* Soon afterwards, American forces won a naval victory in the Central Pacific at *Midway.*

b. Allied Counteroffensive. In August, 1942, General *Douglas MacArthur* moved the Allied forces (chiefly American) northward in "island-hopping" offensives on the road to Japan. Overcoming fierce resistance, Allied troops seized *Guadalcanal* in the Solomon Islands; the *Gilbert, Marshall,* and *Caroline* Islands; and *Guam.* In 1944, while the American navy was winning a decisive victory at *Leyte Gulf,* American forces returned to the Philippines. In early 1945 they also captured *Iwo Jima* and *Okinawa.* From these island bases, American airmen launched destructive raids upon Japan.

c. The Atom Bomb and the Surrender of Japan. In August, 1945, the United States dropped a single atom bomb—the first to be used in war—on the Japanese city of *Hiroshima.* It killed or injured 130,000 people. Two days later Russia declared war against Japan and invaded Japanese-held Manchuria. The following day the United States dropped a second atom bomb, this time on *Nagasaki*. Defenseless against atomic bombings and without allies, Japan surrendered unconditionally. President Truman officially declared September 2, 1945, as *V-J Day*.

SIGNIFICANT FACTS DESCRIBING WORLD WAR II

1. Total War. The war was fought not only by armed forces at the battle-front but also by civilians in factories and in the home. Even schoolchildren took part, collecting scrap metal, rubber, and newspapers; helping air-raid wardens; and assisting in War Bond drives.

2. Global War. This most extensive war was fought on all major seas and in Africa, Asia, and Europe. It involved almost 60 nations, seven of them on the side of the Axis. To plan global military strategy, top Allied leaders held a series of conferences, such as the ones at Teheran, Yalta, and Potsdam.

3. Scientific Progress. Scientists and engineers devised or adapted for war purposes such inventions as radar, guided missiles, jet-propelled planes, magnetic mines, and atom bombs. World War II witnessed the use of blood plasma, penicillin, and sulfa drugs to save lives.

4. Major Role of the Airplane. Great fleets of airplanes attacked troop and naval units, destroyed railroads and industrial centers, and prepared the way for invasion. Control of the air was essential to offensive action on land or sea.

RESULTS OF WORLD WAR II

1. Economic. (*a*) The war—the most costly in history—exacted military expenditures of over $1,100 billion and caused property damage of over $230 billion. The military expenditures of the United States alone were over $330 billion. (*b*) European and Asian nations, ravaged by military action, faced difficult problems of economic recovery. (*c*) The Communist economic system spread from Russia to eastern and central Europe, and to several Asian nations.

2. Social. (*a*) The war—the most destructive in history—left over 22 million servicemen and civilians dead, and over 34 million wounded. For the United States alone, the dead and wounded totaled over one million. (*b*) Several million *refugees* and *displaced persons*, uprooted by the war, needed assistance to rebuild their shattered lives.

3. Political. (*a*) Germany, Italy, and Japan met complete military defeat, and their totalitarian systems were overthrown. (*b*) The United States and

Russia emerged as the major world powers and soon came into conflict, the *cold war*. (*c*) Russia acquired an empire of Communist satellite nations. (*d*) The Asian and African colonial peoples embraced intense nationalism and hastened the downfall of Western imperialism. (*e*) Great Britain and France declined as world powers and gradually relinquished major portions of their Empires. (*f*) The atomic age brought the problem of achieving international control of atomic energy. (*g*) To preserve peace, the Allies formed a new international organization, the *United Nations*.

MULTIPLE-CHOICE QUESTIONS

1. One reason for the failure of the peace movement between World War I and World War II was the (1) absence of an international court of justice (2) weakness of the League of Nations (3) invention of the atomic bomb (4) conflict between the members of the Triple Alliance and the Triple Entente.

2. Which was the most serious cause of the ineffectiveness of the League of Nations? (1) international Communism (2) the predominance of national sovereignty (3) rivalry among British Commonwealth countries (4) the underdeveloped state of the Asian members of the League.

3. Which nation was *never* a member of the League of Nations? (1) Italy (2) Soviet Russia (3) Germany (4) the United States.

4. The first blow to the prestige of the League of Nations was (1) France's seizure of Syria and Lebanon (2) Italy's conquest of Ethiopia (3) Hitler's occupation of the Sudetenland (4) Japan's invasion of Manchuria.

5. *Not* an accomplishment of the League of Nations was (1) enforcing the disarmament of Germany (2) establishing the World Court (3) curtailing the opium traffic (4) establishing the International Labor Organization.

6. In the Italo-Ethiopian dispute, the League of Nations (1) ineffectively attempted to apply sanctions (2) showed a sympathetic attitude toward Italy (3) refused to take any action (4) brought about a settlement through World Court action.

7. *Not* a concern of the Washington Conference (1921-1922) was (1) the burden of naval armaments (2) the Far Eastern imperialistic ambitions of the great powers (3) Japan's economic penetration into China (4) the Indian nationalist movement.

8. The Kellogg-Briand Pact of 1928 recommended (1) outlawing war (2) the settlement of the Allies' war debts (3) nonintervention in the Far East (4) naval disarmament.

9. The Kellogg-Briand Pact failed to accomplish its purpose because (1) it was not signed by Germany (2) it was signed by too few nations (3) it had no provisions for enforcement (4) it was rejected by the League of Nations.

10. In the years between World War I and World War II, the United States (1) joined the League of Nations (2) formed an alliance with England (3) attempted to return to a policy of isolation (4) agreed to naval parity for Japan.

11. The main purpose of the American Neutrality Act of 1937 was to (1) stay out of war (2) increase foreign trade (3) cooperate more closely with the League of Nations (4) protect the rights of neutrals in wartime.

12. Germany's rearmament, starting in 1935, was (1) essential to the policy of collective security (2) encouraged by France (3) in violation of the Treaty of Versailles (4) a policy of the Weimar Republic.

13. During the Spanish Civil War, General Franco received military aid from (1) Germany and Russia (2) Germany and Italy (3) Italy and France (4) the United States and England.

14. Hitler argued that Germany should annex the Sudetenland to (1) protect the German-speaking population (2) reduce French influence in central Europe (3) gain control of additional munitions factories (4) prevent Communist seizure of the area.

15. The British Prime Minister who negotiated the Munich Pact and believed that it meant "peace in our time" was (1) Attlee (2) Churchill (3) Lloyd George (4) Chamberlain.

16. The Munich Pact provided that Germany receive (1) the Sudetenland (2) Alsace-Lorraine (3) the free city of Danzig (4) Austria.

17. Today, the word *Munich* is used to mean (1) a vacation town (2) a successful international conference (3) the surrender of vital interests because of the threat of force (4) a military victory.

18. The Non-Aggression Pact of 1939, preceding the outbreak of World War II, was between (1) Germany and Poland (2) Germany and the United States (3) Germany and Russia (4) England and the United States.

19. A condition prior to the outbreak of both World War I and World War II was (1) acts of appeasement by England (2) a series of international crises (3) the nonexistence of international peace organizations (4) Communist imperialism.

20. What physical feature, which has influenced the history of Poland, was significant in the early months of World War II? (1) many natural seaports (2) an eastern mountain range (3) flat plains (4) large reserves of petroleum.

21. After the fall of France to the Nazis in World War II, a Free French movement was started by (1) Pétain (2) Clemenceau (3) Daladier (4) de Gaulle.

22. The man who became British Prime Minister during the darkest days of World War II and held that post until victory was achieved was (1) Chamberlain (2) Attlee (3) Eden (4) Churchill.

23. In a speech in 1940, the people of England were offered nothing but "blood, toil, tears, and sweat" by (1) Churchill (2) Hitler (3) Stalin (4) Roosevelt.

24. The Lend-Lease Act of 1941 provided that the United States could (1) declare war against Germany (2) trade destroyers for English naval bases in the Western Hemisphere (3) supply the countries fighting the Axis nations with the necessary equipment (4) send an expeditionary force to Europe.

25. Hitler invaded the Soviet Union and seized the Ukraine because the Ukraine had (1) Russia's only outlet to the Baltic Sea (2) much fertile land (3) a large supply of oil (4) many large cities, including Moscow.

26. Which represents a similarity in the careers of Napoleon Bonaparte and Adolf Hitler? (1) death in exile (2) an invasion of Russia (3) lasting legal reforms (4) a program of anti-Semitism.

27. The first city in the history of warfare to be atom-bombed was (1) Hiroshima (2) Tokyo (3) Munich (4) Nanking.

28. The two nations that emerged as major world powers following World War II were (1) the United States and England (2) the United States and the Soviet Union (3) the Soviet Union and Germany (4) the Soviet Union and China.

Part 6. The United Nations

HOPES FOR A BETTER WORLD

In 1941 President Roosevelt stated that the goal of the United States was a world whose people would enjoy the *Four Freedoms:* (*a*) freedom of speech, (*b*) freedom of religion, (*c*) freedom from want, and (*d*) freedom from fear. To achieve these goals, the Allied powers moved to create the United Nations.

STEPS TOWARD THE UNITED NATIONS

1. The Atlantic Charter (1941). President Roosevelt and Prime Minister Churchill, meeting on board ship in the Atlantic, issued a complete statement of principles, the *Atlantic Charter*. Remindful of Wilson's Fourteen Points, this document stated that England and the United States (*a*) desired no territorial gain, (*b*) respected the right of all peoples to choose their own form of government, (*c*) hoped that all men would live in freedom from fear and want, (*d*) believed that nations must abandon the use of force, and (*e*) would seek to establish a "system of general security," implying an international organization.

In 1942 the Allied nations met at Washington, pledged support for the Atlantic Charter, and adopted the name *United Nations* (U.N.).

2. Dumbarton Oaks Conference (1944). The United States, Great Britain, Russia, and China sent representatives to Dumbarton Oaks (in Washington, D. C.), where they drew up U.N. Charter proposals.

3. Yalta Conference (February, 1945). The Big Three—President Roosevelt, Prime Minister Churchill, and Premier Stalin—decided upon procedures for voting in the U.N. Security Council and called upon the United Nations to send delegates to San Francisco to prepare the Charter.

4. San Francisco Conference (April-June, 1945). Despite the unexpected death of President Roosevelt just before the conference, delegates representing 50 nations met as planned. They completed the U.N. Charter.

The United States became the first nation to ratify the Charter, as the Senate overwhelmingly approved American membership. Also, the United States provided the U.N. with headquarters located in New York City.

PURPOSES OF THE UNITED NATIONS

The United Nations has as its goals to (1) maintain international peace and security, (2) by collective action, remove threats to the peace and suppress acts of aggression, (3) develop friendly relations among nations, (4)

Tom Little in The Nashville Tennessean

"Where agreement is possible."

promote respect for human rights without distinction as to race, sex, language, or religion, and (5) encourage international cooperation in solving economic, social, cultural, and humanitarian problems.

ORGANIZATION OF THE UNITED NATIONS

1. General Assembly: The International Forum

a. Membership and Voting. The General Assembly consists of all U.N. member nations, now totaling over 130, each having one vote. General Assembly decisions on "important questions" require a two-thirds majority.

b. Powers. The General Assembly has the power to (1) discuss international problems fully and freely, (2) make recommendations to member nations, to the Economic and Social Council, to the Trusteeship Council, and to the Security Council, (3) elect members of other U.N. organs, (4) with the prior recommendation of the Security Council, suspend or expel any member nation persistently violating U.N. principles and admit "peace-loving" nations to membership, (5) approve the U.N. budget and apportion the expenses among the member nations, and (6) propose U.N. Charter amendments, which come into effect when ratified by two-thirds of the member nations, including all permanent members of the Security Council.

c. Sessions. The General Assembly meets in *regular* session annually, for about three months. If necessary, however, the Assembly may be summoned into *special* session.

2. Security Council: The Executive Agency

a. Membership. The Security Council consists of fifteen members: (1) Five are *permanent:* the United States, Great Britain, France, Russia, and China. (Until 1971 China's seat was held by the Nationalist regime, which since 1949 controlled only the island of Taiwan. In 1971, as the United States and Red China moved toward a better relationship, the General Assembly voted, with American support, to admit Red China as representative of the Chinese people and, despite American opposition, to expel the Nationalist delegation as representative only of Taiwan.) (2) Ten are *nonpermanent,* each elected for a two-year term by the General Assembly. Until a Charter amendment in 1965, the Security Council had included only six nonpermanent members. The increase to ten reflected the large rise in Afro-Asian membership in the U.N. and the demand for Security Council seats according to "equitable geographical distribution."

b. Voting. Decisions by the Security Council on important matters require the affirmative vote of nine members, including the five permanent members. Thus, by a negative vote, any one of the Big Five can defeat a Security Council decision, that is, exercise its *veto power.* Abstention from voting by a permanent member is not considered a veto.

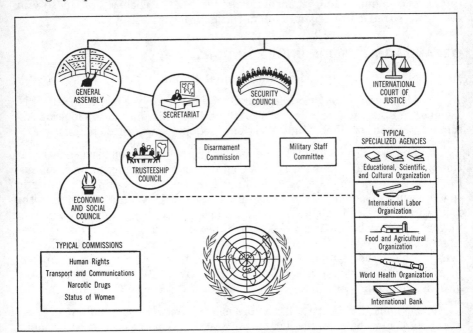

The Organization of the United Nations

c. Powers. The Security Council has the primary responsibility of maintaining international peace and security. It may (1) investigate disputes that could endanger world peace, (2) make recommendations for peaceful settlement, and (3) if necessary, call upon U.N. member nations to take economic or military action against an aggressor nation.

d. Sessions. To be able to deal instantly with any international crisis, the Security Council functions *continuously*.

e. Agencies Directly Under the Security Council. (1) The *Military Staff Committee* advises the Council regarding the use of military force to preserve international peace. (2) The *Disarmament Commission* draws up plans for the regulation and reduction of conventional armaments and for the elimination of nuclear weapons.

3. Secretariat: The Civil Service

a. Personnel and Duties. The Secretariat consists of the *Secretary General* and his staff—all charged with primary loyalty to the United Nations. The Secretary General is appointed (usually for a five-year term) by the General Assembly upon the recommendation of the Security Council. The Secretary General selects and directs his staff, numbering several thousand employees, to perform U.N. clerical and administrative work. In addition, the Secretary General is authorized to (1) bring to the attention of the Security Council any matter threatening world peace, and (2) perform other tasks assigned by major U.N. organs, such as the Security Council or the General Assembly. Such tasks have included the undertaking of special diplomatic missions, and the directing of U.N. emergency military forces.

b. Persons Serving as Secretary General. Trygve Lie of Norway served as first Secretary General. In 1953 he was succeeded by Sweden's *Dag Hammarskjold.* In 1960-1961 Hammarskjold had to defend himself against bitter Russian attacks for his efforts to bring order to the Congo (see page 405). In 1961 Hammarskjold died in an airplane crash while on a U.N. peace mission to the Congo. Hammarskjold's successor, agreed upon by Russia and the United States, was Burma's *U Thant.* After serving for 10 years, Thant declined another term. Effective 1972, the U.N. selected a new Secretary General, the Austrian statesman *Kurt Waldheim.*

4. International Court of Justice: The Court for Nations. The International Court of Justice consists of 15 judges who decide cases by majority vote. The Court has the power to (*a*) settle legal disputes between nations, and (*b*) grant U.N. organs advisory opinions on legal questions. Nations submitting disputes to the Court agree in advance to accept its decisions.

5. Trusteeship Council: For Protection of Colonial Peoples

a. Membership and Voting. The Trusteeship Council consists, in equal number, of nations administering and nations not administering trust territories (see pages 268-269). It must include all the permanent members of the Security Council. Its decisions require a simple majority.

b. Powers. The Trusteeship Council supervises trusteeships so as to safeguard colonial peoples. It has power to (1) consider reports submitted by the administering nations, (2) accept and examine petitions from the peoples of the trust territories, (3) with consent of the administering nation, send an investigating committee, and (4) submit an annual progress report to the General Assembly.

6. Economic and Social Council (ECOSOC): For Mankind's Welfare

a. Membership and Voting. The Economic and Social Council consists of 27 members, each elected for a three-year term by the General Assembly. Decisions require a simple majority, each member nation having one vote.

b. Powers. The Economic and Social Council is concerned with improving economic, social, cultural, educational, and health conditions throughout the world. ECOSOC may conduct studies and make recommendations to U.N. member nations and to the General Assembly. Through ECOSOC's efforts, the U.N. hopes to eliminate the underlying causes of war.

c. ECOSOC Commissions and Committees. To further its objectives, ECOSOC organized (1) the *Commission on Human Rights,* which seeks to encourage respect for human rights and fundamental freedoms for all persons, regardless of race, sex, language, or religion, and (2) other commissions and committees concerned with such problems as control of narcotics, prevention of crime, and the status of women. ECOSOC also receives reports from such U.N. bodies as the U.N. Children's Fund (UNICEF), the High Commissioner for Refugees, and the U.N. Development Program.

SPECIALIZED AGENCIES

The specialized agencies are independent organizations, some predating the United Nations, that came into existence by intergovernmental agreement. They include most (but not all) nations as members; they secure their funds chiefly by voluntary contributions from member nations; they directly serve only those nations that request assistance; and they coordinate their efforts with the U.N. through the Economic and Social Council.

1. The **United Nations Educational, Scientific, and Cultural Organization (UNESCO)** seeks to promote the worldwide exchange of information on education, science, and culture. UNESCO undertakes projects to raise educational standards and to combat ignorance and prejudice. UNESCO bases

Tom Little in *The Nashville Tennessean*

". . . to conquer everywhere the ancient
enemies of man."—President Johnson

*What U.N. efforts and agencies are working to conquer
these "enemies"? What factors retard such endeavors?*

its work on the belief stated in its Charter: "Since wars begin in the minds
of men, it is in the minds of men that the defenses of peace must be constructed."

2. The **International Labor Organization (ILO)** endeavors to improve
world labor conditions. ILO defines minimum labor standards and assists
countries in formulating labor laws.

3. The **Food and Agriculture Organization (FAO)** attempts to raise
world food and nutrition levels. FAO provides information to improve
methods of growing and distributing food.

4. The **World Health Organization (WHO)** seeks to improve world
health standards. WHO surveys health conditions, combats mass diseases
and epidemics, and helps nations improve public health services.

5. The **International Monetary Fund** tries to promote world trade by helping nations to maintain stable currencies.

6. The **International Bank for Reconstruction and Development** (**World Bank**) encourages economic progress by providing loans to countries for large-scale projects, such as electric power plants and railroads.

7. Other specialized agencies include (*a*) the **International Civil Aviation Organization** (**ICAO**)—to expand and improve civil aviation facilities and to standardize laws regarding use of air lanes, (*b*) the **Universal Postal Union** (**UPU**)—to provide uniform mail procedures, and (*c*) the **World Meteorological Organization** (**WMO**)—to coordinate data on weather and develop weather-forecasting services.

IMPROVEMENTS OF THE U.N. OVER THE LEAGUE OF NATIONS

1. The League included Russia for only a short time and never secured American membership. The U.N. contains these and most other world powers. (The major nonmembers are Nationalist China, Bangladesh, and the following Communist and non-Communist regimes of three former political units: East Germany and West Germany, North Korea and South Korea, and North Vietnam and South Vietnam.)

2. The League Covenant permitted members to withdraw, and Germany, Italy, and Japan did so. The U.N. Charter contains no such provision.

3. League agencies required a unanimous vote to recommend action. The U.N. Security Council requires nine out of fifteen votes (including the Big Five), and the U.N. General Assembly requires a two-thirds vote.

4. The League handled economic and social problems through minor and sometimes temporary agencies. The U.N. Economic and Social Council is a major and permanent agency.

MAJOR ACTIONS TAKEN BY THE UNITED NATIONS

ACTIONS PERTAINING TO SOCIAL AND ECONOMIC MATTERS

1. Children's Fund. In 1946 the General Assembly created the *United Nations International Children's Emergency Fund* (*UNICEF*). It provides food, vitamins, and medicine to millions of needy children; it trains nurses to help mothers in proper child care. UNICEF's activities, now permanent, are financed by voluntary contributions of governments and individuals. (American youngsters raise funds for UNICEF by making Halloween "trick or treat" collections and by selling UNICEF greeting cards.)

2. Declaration of Human Rights. In 1948 the General Assembly overwhelmingly approved the *Declaration of Human Rights,* drawn up by the Commission on Human Rights of ECOSOC. The Declaration states that all human beings are born free and equal and, without discrimination of any kind, are entitled to (*a*) *civil rights:* life; liberty; freedom of religion, speech, and assembly; and a voice in their government; (*b*) **legal rights:** freedom from arbitrary arrest and the right to a fair trial; (*c*) **economic rights:** employment, participation in labor unions, an adequate living standard, private property, and leisure time; and (*d*) **social rights:** education and a cultural life. Although these ideals will not soon be realized throughout the world, they provide a "standard of achievement for all peoples and all nations."

3. Genocide Convention. In 1948 the General Assembly adopted the *Genocide Convention,* drawn up by the Commission on Human Rights. This Convention declared illegal the deliberate extermination of any human group (as the Nazis had attempted with the Jews) and provided that violators be tried before an international court. The Convention, ratified by 63 nations, represents an attempt to rally world opinion in favor of granting all people freedom from fear.

4. Technical Assistance. In 1949 the United Nations and several specialized agencies began the *Expanded Program of Technical Assistance.* This endeavor, now part of the *U.N. Development Program,* coordinates efforts to improve social and economic conditions in over 140 underdeveloped territories and countries, chiefly in Africa, Asia, and Latin America. Technical experts have helped underdeveloped peoples increase food production, develop natural resources and industries, fight disease, and reduce illiteracy. Nationals of underdeveloped areas have received fellowships to study abroad and return to their homelands as technicians and professionals.

ACTIONS PERTAINING TO INTERNATIONAL DISPUTES

In dealing with international disputes, the U.N. has compiled a mixed record: in some cases—success; in others—failure.

1. Iran. In 1946 Iran complained that Russian troops, stationed on her soil during World War II, had not been withdrawn. The Security Council discussed the problem despite Russian objections. Shortly afterward Russia removed her troops.

2. Greece. In 1946 the Greek government charged that three Communist nations—Yugoslavia, Albania, and Bulgaria—were aiding rebel Communist guerrilla bands in northern Greece. The United Nations (*a*) established an investigating commission, which confirmed the Greek charges, and (*b*) requested the Communist nations to stop supporting the guerrilla bands. Following the split between Yugoslavia and Russia in 1948, Yugoslavia ceased aiding the Greek rebels and the rebellion collapsed. (For American efforts to help Greece, see the Truman Doctrine, page 424.)

3. Palestine. In 1947-1948 the General Assembly (*a*) took over the Palestine problem from England, (*b*) conducted an investigation, and (*c*) approved the partition of Palestine into an Arab state and a Jewish state. The U.N. decision was defied by the Arab nations, which attacked the new Jewish state, Israel, but without military success. In 1949 *Ralph Bunche,* U.N. mediator, succeeded in arranging a truce. (See pages 302-303.)

4. Indonesia. Between 1947 and 1949 the United Nations (*a*) arranged truces ending hostilities between Dutch and Indonesian forces, and (*b*) assisted in negotiations that led to Indonesia's independence. (See pages 322-323.)

5. Korea. After World War II Korea, a former Japanese possession, was divided into American and Russian zones of occupation pending reunification and independence. In 1948 a U.N. commission to unify Korea held elections in United States-occupied South Korea but was denied admission into Russian-occupied North Korea.

In 1950, when the North Korean Communists invaded South Korea, the Security Council (with Russia absent) called upon the invaders to withdraw and, when that request was ignored, asked U.N. member nations to provide military aid to South Korea. Sixteen nations sent troops to bolster South Korean forces. This first U.N. army consisted chiefly of South Koreans and Americans. In early 1951, after Communist Chinese forces had entered the Korean War, the General Assembly declared Red China guilty of aggression. In mid-1951 the U.N. command began negotiations with the Communists and, in 1953, achieved a truce. (See pages 447-448.)

6. Kashmir. Since 1948 the United Nations (*a*) helped end hostilities between India and Pakistan over Kashmir, (*b*) secured agreement of both nations to a U.N.-supervised plebiscite, (*c*) was defied when India annexed, without any plebiscite, that portion of Kashmir held by Indian troops, (*d*) declared India's action not binding upon the United Nations, and (*e*) in 1965, by a Security Council resolution, helped halt renewed Indian-Pakistani hostilities. (Also see the *Tashkent Declaration,* page 455.)

7. Hungary. In 1956 Russian troops suppressed a revolt of the Hungarian people against the Russian-dominated government of their country. The U.N. General Assembly overwhelmingly condemned Russia and demanded that (*a*) Russia cease her intervention in Hungarian affairs, (*b*) Russia withdraw her military forces from Hungary, and (*c*) U.N. observers be admitted into the revolt-torn country. Russia and the puppet Hungarian regime defied the U.N. by rejecting these demands. (See page 420.)

8. Egypt. In 1956 Egypt was invaded by (*a*) Israel, which sought to stop border raids by Egyptian forces and to end a shipping blockade by Egyptian guns commanding the Gulf of Aqaba, and (*b*) England and France, which hoped to undo Egyptian nationalization of the Suez Canal. The United States, although conceding Egyptian provocation, opposed the invasion. Russia denounced the invaders and threatened to help Egypt with troops.

The U.N. General Assembly, by a vote of 64 to 5, condemned the attack and passed resolutions demanding a cease-fire and the withdrawal of the invading forces. The resolutions were heeded. To supervise arrangements and maintain peace in the Middle East, the General Assembly requested member nations (excluding the Big Five) to volunteer troops for an international police force, the *United Nations Emergency Force (UNEF)*. (See page 445.)

9. The Congo: 1960-1961

a. Background. In 1960 the Congo received independence from Belgium. The new republic faced serious problems: rivalry between pro-Communist Premier *Patrice Lumumba* and pro-Western President *Joseph Kasavubu;* army mutinies; tribal conflicts; secession by mineral-rich Katanga province under its own leader, *Moise Tshombe;* the continued presence of Belgian troops; and involvement in the cold war.

b. The U.N. and the Congo Crisis. The U.N. Security Council (1) called upon Belgium to withdraw her troops, and (2) authorized Secretary General Hammarskjold to restore order in the Congo by means of a United Nations Emergency Force. Under Hammarskjold's direction, the UNEF helped prevent bloodshed and violence. Although Russia demanded that he support Lumumba in the Congolese power struggle, Hammarskjold remained neutral.

Meanwhile, Lumumba was removed from office, arrested by the Congo army, and slain by his political foes. Eventually, the Congo government passed into anti-Communist hands, Belgium withdrew her troops, and Katanga was brought back under central control.

c. Dispute Over Hammarskjold and the U.N. Congo Operation

(1) *Russia Attacks Hammarskjold.* Enraged by Lumumba's fall from power, Russia blamed Hammarskjold and demanded his resignation. Soviet Premier Khrushchev proposed that the duties of the Secretary General be taken over by a "troika," a three-man board of Western, Soviet, and neutralist representatives, each with veto power. (2) *Hammarskjold Receives Support.* With overwhelming support of the Western and most Afro-Asian nations, Hammarskjold refused to resign. He pointed out that the Soviet Union could prevent the election of a new Secretary General and, by insisting upon the creation of a veto-dominated three-man board, would weaken the U.N. (3) *Hammarskjold Dies.* After Hammarskjold died on a Congo peace mission, he received worldwide tribute for his devotion to the U.N. Thereupon, Russia ceased her demand for a three-member Secretary General and agreed to Burma's *U Thant* as Hammarskjold's successor.

10. Goa.

In 1961 India seized Goa, a tiny Portuguese colony on the Indian coast. At the U.N., India was defended by most Afro-Asian nations and by Russia, which vetoed a Western resolution urging India to withdraw her troops and negotiate with Portugal. The U.N. took no other action.

11. Cyprus

a. Background. In late 1963 Cyprus was torn by bitter communal strife between her majority Greek and minority Turkish populations (see page 300). Turkey's threat to aid the Turkish Cypriotes was countered by Greece's threat to help the Greek Cypriotes.

b. The U.N. and the Cyprus Crisis. In 1964 the Security Council authorized a temporary U.N. peace force to restore order on Cyprus. The U.N. force halted the communal strife, thereby possibly preventing war between Greece and Turkey. However, the Cyprus problem remains unsolved.

12. Rhodesia. In 1965 the white minority regime of Rhodesia, under Prime Minister *Ian Smith,* rejected British proposals that it move toward rule by the black majority. Instead, Smith unilaterally declared the country independent of Britain. Britain labeled the breakaway regime "illegal," applied economic sanctions, and later secured a Security Council resolution requesting all U.N. members to apply economic sanctions. This resolution was derided by most African nations, which contended that economic sanctions would not topple the Smith regime and demanded that Britain use military force. The resolution was ignored by several nations, notably Portugal, which retains colonies in southern Africa, and white-ruled South Africa.

In 1970 a Security Council resolution condemning Britain for not using force against Rhodesia was vetoed by Britain and the United States.

In a 1971 tentative agreement, the Rhodesian regime pledged to reduce discrimination against blacks over many years and Britain pledged to end sanctions and grant Rhodesia independence. When the Rhodesian blacks rejected this agreement, Britain discarded it and continued the sanctions.

13. South-West Africa. Having received this former German colony from the League of Nations as a mandate, South Africa refused to change the mandate into a U.N.-supervised trusteeship. South Africa's white supremacy and apartheid policies angered the Afro-Asian nations. In 1966 the General Assembly (*a*) declared the South-West Africa mandate at an end, (*b*) ordered U.N. control of the territory, and (*c*) created a committee to guide South-West Africa to independence. (Later the U.N. gave the territory the name of Namibia.) South Africa warned that she would resist any U.N. interference in South-West Africa.

14. Arab-Israeli War of 1967. Following the outbreak of fighting (see pages 303-305), the Security Council passed several resolutions calling for a cease-fire. These resolutions, accepted by the victorious Israelis and eventually by the three vanquished Arab states, helped end the hostilities.

Meanwhile, the Soviet Union vowed full support for the Arab cause and introduced a Security Council resolution (*a*) condemning Israel as the aggressor, and (*b*) demanding the withdrawal of Israeli forces to the 1949 armistice lines. The Soviet resolution was opposed by the United States as a "prescription for renewed hostilities," since it did not link the withdrawal of Israeli forces to steps for a durable peace. Following the overwhelming defeat of the Soviet resolution in the Security Council, the Soviets secured an emergency session of the General Assembly.

At the emergency session, the Soviets introduced their previous resolution. Receiving only 30 percent of the votes, it was decisively defeated.

The United States proposed that (a) Israel withdraw her troops, (b) the Arabs concede Israel's right to exist in peace and to use the Gulf of Aqaba and the Suez Canal, and (c) both sides begin negotiations to settle other issues, especially the Arab refugee problem. The United States, however, withdrew its resolution and supported a Latin American resolution that called only for the withdrawal of Israeli troops and the end of Arab belligerency against Israel. Although gaining almost 50 percent of the votes, this resolution also failed of adoption. The General Assembly did pass a resolution declaring Israel's unification of Jerusalem invalid.

The Security Council later adopted a resolution calling for the (a) withdrawal of Israeli forces from the conquered territories, (b) right of every Middle Eastern state to live in peace, (c) free navigation of international waterways, (d) just settlement of the refugee problem, and (e) appointment of a special U.N. representative to seek a Middle East agreement.

Gunnar Jarring, a Swedish diplomat, attempted the peace mission. Pursuing quiet diplomacy, Jarring has met with Arab, Israeli, American, and Soviet officials. To date his progress has been very slow.

15. Indian-Pakistani War (1971)

   a. Background. See page 321.

   b. At the United Nations. As the war started, the Security Council met, with Red China supporting West Pakistan and the United States condemning India. Three times Security Council resolutions, calling for a cease-fire and withdrawal of forces, were vetoed by the Soviet Union. Thereupon the General Assembly considered the issue and voted overwhelmingly for a cease-fire and withdrawal of military forces. India ignored this resolution and its chief representative called the Assembly "not very realistic." With the war over, the Security Council passed a resolution requesting observance of the cease-fire and aid for the Bengali refugees in India. Meanwhile Pakistani representative *Zulfikar Ali Bhutto,* who was to become the new President of Pakistan, denounced the U.N. as a "fraud and a farce."

AN ANALYSIS OF THE UNITED NATIONS

1. An Optimistic View: Effectiveness of the U.N.

   a. Almost Universal Membership. The U.N. is the world's most representative body of nations. It is a "parliament of man," mirroring the hopes and fears of mankind.

b. Availability of Forum. The U.N. provides a forum where member nations may discuss world problems and present their views to world opinion.

c. Uniting for Peace Resolution. This resolution enables the General Assembly to deal with a threat to world peace if the Security Council fails to act because of a veto. It states that the General Assembly (1) if not in session, may be summoned into emergency session within 24 hours, and (2) may recommend, by a two-thirds vote, that U.N. members take collective action, including the use of armed force.

The Uniting for Peace resolution, invoked during the Egyptian and Hungarian crises in 1956, has increased the importance of the General Assembly.

d. Resolving International Problems. Through the U.N., many international problems have been solved, brought closer to a solution, or at least kept from erupting into a major war. Examples of U.N. achievements include (1) independence for Indonesia, (2) the partition of Palestine, and (3) the withdrawal of invading forces in 1956 from Egypt.

e. U.N. Military Forces. The U.N. has secured the military cooperation of a number of member nations. Examples are (1) the formation of a U.N. army to repel aggression against South Korea, and (2) the creation of UNEF units to preserve peace in the Middle East, the Congo, and Cyprus.

f. Economic and Social Progress. The Economic and Social Council and the specialized agencies have worked steadfastly toward eliminating some of the economic and social causes of war. The technical assistance program has improved conditions in many underdeveloped countries.

g. Colonial Independence. The Trusteeship Council has helped colonial peoples form independent nations, including Cameroon, Togo, Somalia, Tanganyika (now part of Tanzania), Rwanda, and Burundi.

h. Preventing International Anarchy. The U.N. keeps the world from reverting to total international anarchy. It serves as a bridge between the opposing sides in the cold war and enables the neutral nations to bring their influence to bear upon world problems.

2. A Pessimistic View: Problems Besetting the U.N.

a. Blocs Within the U.N. The U.N. consists of three blocs: (1) The *Western bloc* (about 50 nations) includes the United States, Western Europe, most of Latin America, and some British Commonwealth members. This bloc generally supports American leadership. (2) The *Soviet Communist bloc* (about 10 nations) follows Russian policy. (3) The *Afro-Asian bloc* (about 70 nations) has grown tremendously and now constitutes a U.N. majority. The Afro-Asian nations are opposed to colonialism, and most are in favor of cold war neutrality. Red China, since its admission in 1971, has sought to be spokesman for the Afro-Asian bloc, but has had limited suc-

Mauldin in The St. Louis Post-Dispatch

"Shock waves."

How has nationalism resulted in defiance of the U.N.? Will nationalism lead to the ultimate failure of the U.N.?

cess in securing united Afro-Asian support. Blocs are a divisive force within the U.N. that tend to aggravate international friction.

b. Self-Seeking Use of the U.N. U.N. members often consider international problems on the basis of individual or bloc interests, rather than on the basis of U.N. principles. Most Afro-Asian nations approved India's military seizure of Goa, although the U.N. Charter prohibits the use of force.

Many U.N. members use the organization as a means for spreading propaganda. Communist Cuba has several times used the General Assembly as a forum to arouse world opinion against the United States.

c. Veto Power. Russia's use of the veto—over 100 times—has limited the effectiveness of the Security Council and decreased its importance.

The United States has used its veto only three times. (1) In 1970 it vetoed a resolution that condemned Britain for not using force to end white rule in Rhodesia. (2) In 1972 it vetoed a resolution that condemned Israel for reprisal raids against Palestinian guerrillas in Lebanon but made no mention of the provocation—the murder of 11 Israeli athletes at the Munich Olympic Games by Palestinian terrorists. (3) In 1973 it vetoed a resolution calling upon the United States to conclude a new "just and fair treaty" that would assure Panama "effective sovereignty" over the Panama Canal Zone, but making no mention of American efforts to achieve a new treaty and satisfy many Panamanian demands. The American spokesman called the resolution "unbalanced."

Red China exercised its first veto in 1972 to deny U.N. membership to the new Asian nation of Bangladesh.

d. Defiance of U.N. Resolutions. Some nations have refused to heed U.N. resolutions on the ground that the issues involved are domestic matters and therefore not subject to U.N. jurisdiction. In other cases, nations have defied the U.N. on the ground that they were protecting their national interests. Examples of defiance of the U.N. include (1) the Arab attack upon Israel, (2) Russia's refusal to permit U.N.-supervised elections in North Korea, (3) Russia's suppression of the Hungarian rebellion, (4) India's annexation of part of Kashmir, and (5) South Africa's insistence upon apartheid and upon retaining South-West Africa (Namibia).

e. Lack of Military Power. The U.N. has no permanent military force of its own. It depends upon member nations to honor resolutions requesting armed forces. Only 16 nations—at that time constituting about one-fourth of the U.N.—heeded the call for troops to aid South Korea.

f. Financial Difficulties. The U.N. secures funds for its regular budget by assessing member nations according to ability to pay. In 1970 the United States was first, being assessed 31.5 percent of the U.N. regular budget, whereas the Soviet Union was second, being assessed 14 percent; in addition the United States voluntarily contributed 45 percent of funds for U.N. special activities—such as UNICEF, WHO, and technical assistance—whereas the Soviet Union voluntarily contributed only 1.5 percent.

The U.N. has found itself in financial straits because certain nations were unwilling to pay their assessments for UNEF peace-keeping operations. The Soviet bloc and most Arab states refused to pay their share of UNEF Middle East expenses; these same nations, as well as Belgium, France, and South Africa, refused to pay their UNEF Congo assessments.

In the 1970's the United States acted to reduce its financial support for the U.N. At AFL-CIO urging, the United States withheld funds from the International Labor Organization to protest the 1970 appointment of a Soviet official as an ILO assistant director general. In 1972 the United States won General Assembly approval to reduce "as soon as practicable" its contribution to the U.N. regular budget to 25 percent.

g. Bypassing the U.N. The major nations have frequently resorted to direct diplomacy outside the U.N. The United States, Russia, and Britain

Palmer in The Springfield (Mo.) Leader and Press

"Complicating matters."

Why is the U.N. in financial difficulty? How do financial problems deter U.N. efforts to fulfill its responsibilities?

directly negotiated the nuclear test ban treaty. The United States and Russia directly concluded the SALT missile agreements. The U.N. loses prestige whenever nations ignore its facilities.

h. Withdrawal and Return of Indonesia. In 1965 Indonesia, under the leftist government of President *Sukarno,* resigned from the U.N. He claimed that the world organization was being manipulated by imperialist powers. In 1066 tho Indonocian army took control of tho government and ended Sukarno's power. Indonesia then returned to the U.N., but her withdrawal and return established an unfortunate precedent.

i. No Action Against International Terrorism. Extremist groups have employed terrorism—deliberate violence against innocent civilians—so as to further the extremists' political goals. Black revolutionaries in the United States hijacked American airplanes to Cuba and Algeria to escape from

"Time for reappraisal."

Is the U.N. following in the footsteps of the League?
What factors led to the failure of the League?

American authorities and sometimes to secure ransom and the release of other terrorists. Turkish extremists hijacked a Turkish airplane to Bulgaria and demanded that Turkey release three guerrillas sentenced to death for kidnapping and murder. Croatian separatists (opposed to Tito's Yugoslavia) hijacked a Swedish plane to Spain to secure the release of six Croatians imprisoned in Sweden for murder.

Palestinian extremist groups, notably *Al Fatah* and its *Black September* terrorist faction, seek to destroy Israel. They have planted bombs to blow up planes of pro-Western nations flying passengers to Israel; also they have hijacked pro-Western passenger planes to secure ransom or the release of captured Arab extremists. In 1972-1973 Palestinian guerrillas claimed responsibility for three particularly brutal massacres. They employed three Japanese left-wing extremists who disembarked from an Air France plane at the Israeli airport at Tel Aviv and with machine guns and hand grenades killed 25 persons (including 15 Puerto Ricans on a pilgrimage to the Holy Land) and wounded 77 others. Later, Black September terrorists murdered 11 Israeli athletes at the Munich Olympic Games. In 1973 Black September terrorists coldbloodedly executed three diplomats—two Americans and a Belgian—in the Sudan.

Secretary General Kurt Waldheim proposed that the General Assembly act to prevent international terrorism. His proposal was defeated in the General Assembly's Legal Committee by a coalition of Arab, Communist,

African, and some Asian nations. These nations claimed that terrorism was a legitimate weapon of peoples battling "alien regimes" to secure "self-determination." The United States, Britain, Canada, and other pro-Western nations were disappointed. These nations planned to cooperate in undertaking their own anti-terrorist measures, thereby bypassing the United Nations.

3. A Realistic View. The United Nations is not meant to be a world government; it is a loose confederation whose member states retain their sovereignty. The United Nations is only an instrument available for their use. Although the U.N. embodies mankind's highest hopes, its strength and influence will reflect the wishes of the world's peoples and governments.

MULTIPLE-CHOICE QUESTIONS

1. "They hope to see established a peace . . . which will afford assurance that all the men in all the lands may live out their lives in freedom from fear and want" is quoted from the (1) Atlantic Charter (2) Genocide Convention (3) United Nations Charter (4) Lend-Lease Act.

2. The conference that completed the United Nations Charter met in (1) New York (2) Geneva (3) Yalta (4) San Francisco.

3. According to the U.N. Charter, each nation's voting strength in the General Assembly is according to (1) size (2) population (3) military strength (4) the principle of one vote per nation.

4. According to the U.N. Charter, the General Assembly meets (1) in continuous session (2) at least once a year (3) only when called by the Secretary General (4) only in time of emergency.

5. Which agency of the U.N. was given primary responsibility for investigating situations that threaten world peace? (1) the Economic and Social Council (2) the Secretariat (3) the Security Council (4) the Trusteeship Council.

6. The U.N. Charter gives the Security Council the power to (1) veto decisions of the Assembly (2) cancel treaties made by member nations (3) recommend the use of force to stop aggression (4) elect the Secretary General.

7. A resolution proposed in the Security Council may be vetoed by (1) any member of the Security Council (2) the Secretary General (3) any permanent member of the Security Council (4) only the Soviet Union and the United States.

8. The country that has most often blocked action in the U.N. by use of the veto is (1) France (2) the Soviet Union (3) the United Kingdom (4) the United States.

9. The nonpermanent members of the Security Council are selected by the (1) General Assembly (2) Economic and Social Council (3) five permanent members of the Council (4) Secretariat.

10. The U.N. Secretary General is most likely to come from a neutralist nation because (1) of a U.N. Charter provision (2) his salary is paid by the neutralist bloc (3) his appointment must be recommended by the Security Council (4) of a tradition originating in the League of Nations.

11. Who succeeded Dag Hammarskold as Secretary General of the United Nations? (1) Trygve Lie (2) Ralph Bunche (3) U Thant (4) none of these.

12. One function of the Economic and Social Council is to (1) settle boundary disputes between nations (2) promote respect for human rights (3) direct the economies of underdeveloped nations (4) regulate the use of atomic energy.

13. The specialized agency that seeks chiefly to promote cultural cooperation and improve understanding among nations is (1) UNICEF (2) the Trusteeship Council (3) WHO (4) UNESCO.

14. A weakness of UNESCO in its effort to foster world understanding is that it (1) must report to ECOSOC (2) is subject to "Big Five" veto power (3) cannot work within a country unless invited (4) selects its personnel chiefly from Communist countries.

15. Since its inception, the United Nations has (1) admitted many new member nations (2) adopted a plan by which nations may withdraw from the U.N. (3) outlawed atomic weapons (4) established a permanent U.N. military force.

16. The Genocide Pact was the work of (1) the ILO (2) the Military Staff Committee (3) UNESCO (4) the Commission on Human Rights.

17. An accomplishment of the U.N. has been the (1) abolition of the veto power (2) establishment of a military government in Egypt (3) expansion of technical aid to underdeveloped regions (4) establishment of international control of atomic energy.

18. The General Assembly resolution urging Russia to cease her interference in the Hungarian revolt of 1956 was (1) unable to secure a majority of the votes (2) defeated by the use of the veto (3) accepted by Russia (4) rejected by Russia.

19. The General Assembly resolution urging Israel, France, and England to cease their invasion of Egypt in 1956 was (1) opposed by the United States (2) accepted by Israel but rejected by France and England (3) accepted by the three nations concerned (4) opposed by Egypt.

20. "Since wars begin in the minds of men, it is in the minds of men that the defenses of peace must be constructed," is a quotation from the (1) Four Freedoms (2) Yalta Conference (3) U.N. Charter (4) UNESCO Charter.

21. Until 1971 the admission of Red China to the United Nations had been vigorously opposed by (1) Egypt (2) Russia (3) India (4) the United States.

22. The Secretary General of the United Nations who was attacked by the Soviet Union for his conduct of the U.N. Congo operation was (1) Trygve Lie (2) Dag Hammarskjold (3) U Thant (4) Ralph Bunche.

23. The U.N. finances its activities chiefly by (1) charging admission to visitors (2) assessing member nations (3) placing a tax upon citizens of U.N. member nations (4) selling U.N. stamps and souvenirs.

MATCHING QUESTIONS

Column *A* lists disputes that were brought before the U.N. For each dispute in column *A*, write the letter of the nation or nations in column *B* that were *directly* involved in that dispute.

Column A	*Column B*
1. Possession of Kashmir	*a.* Greece and Turkey
2. Foreign troops in the Congo	*b.* England, France, and Egypt
3. Control of the Suez Canal	*c.* Algeria
4. Civil war on Cyprus	*d.* Belgium
5. Foreign troops in Hungary	*e.* Russia
6. Independence for Indonesia	*f.* The Netherlands
7. Possession of Goa	*g.* Communist China and Korea
	h. India and Portugal
	i. India and Pakistan

Part 7. The Cold War Era

THE COLD WAR: DEFINITION

The *cold war* began soon after World War II as a struggle between the *Western bloc* led by the United States and the *Soviet Communist bloc* led by Russia. The United States, alarmed by Communist expansion in central Europe and Asia, acted to contain Soviet power within its existing territory and influence. This policy was called *containment*.

The cold war has been fought by propaganda, diplomacy, scientific and economic competition, espionage, and localized military action, but *not* all-out war.

Today the cold war has become much more complex: (1) the Western nations have become less dependent upon the United States, (2) the Soviet bloc has been troubled by discontent and disunity, and (3) Red China has become bitterly opposed to the Soviet Union.

DIFFERENCES BETWEEN RUSSIA AND THE UNITED STATES

RUSSIA	THE UNITED STATES
1. *Dictatorial* government.	1. *Democratic* government.
2. *Communist* economic system.	2. *Capitalist* economic system.
3. *Denial* of civil liberties.	3. *Guarantee* of civil liberties.
4. *Regimentation* of social and cultural life.	4. *Freedom* in social and cultural life.

BRIEF HISTORY OF SOVIET-AMERICAN RELATIONS

1. 1917-1941: Unfriendly. The Communists resented (*a*) American aid to anti-Red forces following the Russian Revolution, and (*b*) America's refusal until 1933 to recognize the Soviet Union.

The United States resented (*a*) Russia's withdrawal from World War I, enabling Germany to concentrate her armies on the western front, (*b*) Russian efforts to spread revolution in non-Communist countries by means of the *Comintern,* and (*c*) Russia's Non-Aggression Pact of 1939 with Nazi Germany—an agreement that encouraged Germany to start World War II.

2. 1941-1945: Cooperative. During World War II, Russia and the United States found themselves fighting against a common enemy, Germany. To create amity with her democratic allies, Russia dissolved the Comintern. To assist Russia, the United States (*a*) provided her with $11 billion of lend-lease equipment, and (*b*) led the Western allies in opening second fronts in Europe by invading southern Italy and northern France. Also, Russia, the United States, and Britain coordinated military strategy and made postwar plans at several top-level conferences: *Teheran, Yalta,* and *Potsdam.*

3. 1945-Present: Unfriendly. As World War II ended, Russia reverted to her prewar attitude of hostility toward non-Communist countries, especially the United States. Soviet leaders declared that (a) "warmongers" in America were plotting against the Soviet Union, (b) the spread of Communism is necessary for the security of the Soviet Union, and (c) Communism inevitably must triumph over capitalism throughout the world. Until his death in 1953, Stalin pursued a "hard line" toward the West, but his successors have urged *peaceful coexistence*. They have not, however, abandoned the Soviet goal of communizing the world.

American leaders (a) denied the warmongering charge by pointing to America's devotion to peace, (b) held the expansion of Russian power a threat to the safety of the free world, and (c) predicted victory for the American way of life in peaceful competition with Communism.

A. THE COMMUNIST WORLD

THE RECORD OF COMMUNIST EXPANSION SINCE 1939

OUTRIGHT ANNEXATIONS	LOCAL COMMUNIST PARTIES SEIZE CONTROL
BY RUSSIA 1. *Countries:* Estonia, Latvia, and Lithuania. 2. *Territories:* from Czechoslovakia, Finland, Germany, Japan, Poland, and Rumania. BY CHINA 1. *Country:* Tibet	1. *In Europe:* Albania, Bulgaria, Czechoslovakia, East Germany, Hungary, Poland, Rumania, and Yugoslavia. 2. *In Asia:* China, North Korea, and North Vietnam. 3. *In America:* Cuba.

RUSSIA DOMINATES HER SATELLITES

1. Meaning of Satellites. The *satellites* are the Communist-dominated nations of eastern and central Europe that, in most important matters, accept Russian authority. Communist satellites are Bulgaria, Czechoslovakia, East Germany, Hungary, Poland, and Rumania. Their relationship to Russia is similar to that of protectorates and a mother country.

The satellite nations (self-proclaimed *people's republics*) have governments that essentially imitate Russian domestic practices. (a) They are dictatorships, each controlled by its own Communist party. (b) They have nationalized industry, tried to collectivize agriculture, and proclaimed master economic plans. (c) They have denied many civil liberties and restricted free cultural expression. (d) In Poland and Hungary, both predominantly

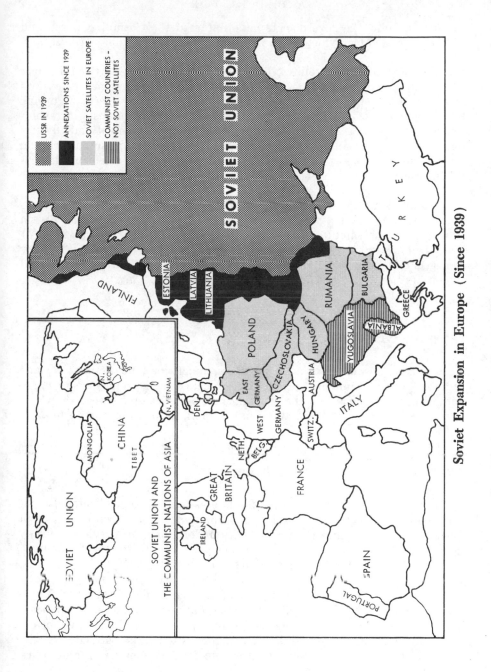

Soviet Expansion in Europe (Since 1939)

Roman Catholic, the governments have harassed the Catholic Church and at times arrested clergymen, most notably Hungary's Cardinal *Mindszenty*.

2. Establishment of Satellites. To help local Communist parties take over and maintain control, Russia (*a*) fostered Communist regimes in eastern and central Europe as her armies pursued the retreating Germans during the closing year of World War II, (*b*) trained local Communists in revolutionary tactics and leadership, (*c*) provided military equipment and advisers for local Communist forces, (*d*) maintained Russian troops in eastern and central Europe, and (*e*) violated the Yalta Conference agreement by thwarting free elections in Soviet-occupied nations.

3. Methods of Russian Control. (*a*) Russian specialists in political, economic, and military matters "advise" the satellite governments. (*b*) Russia tries to keep the satellite economies tied to her own by trade treaties. (*c*) Russian military forces are stationed in some satellite countries. (*d*) Russian generals head a unified military command coordinating Soviet and satellite armed forces within an alliance, the *Warsaw Pact*.

THE IRON CURTAIN

By restrictions on visitors, newspapers, magazines, books, movies, and radio programs, Communist regimes have blocked their peoples from contact with democratic ideas. This barrier that had been set up between the Communist nations and the West, Winston Churchill named the *iron curtain*.

TROUBLE BEHIND THE IRON CURTAIN

The Russians have tried to give the impression (1) that Communist nations enjoy complete unity of thought and purpose and willingly accept Russian dominance, and (2) that peoples under Communist rule are firmly devoted to Communist methods and objectives. In truth, the Communist world has been troubled by disunity and discontent, as follows:

1. Yugoslavia Since 1945. *Marshal Tito*, Communist dictator of Yugoslavia, defied the wishes of Stalinist Russia and pursued nationalist policies. Tito was emboldened to act independently because Yugoslavia was not occupied by Russian troops and does not border Russia. In 1948 Tito was denounced by the world Communist leadership for following "a hateful policy in relation to the Soviet Union."

Stalinist Russia and the satellites sought to overthrow the nationalist-minded Tito by (a) ending economic relations and friendship treaties with Yugoslavia, (b) utilizing press and radio for anti-Tito propaganda, and (c) encouraging subversion within Yugoslavia. These efforts proved unsuccessful. Since Stalin's death, Russia has somewhat repaired relations with Yugoslavia. Nevertheless, Tito remains free of Russian domination.

The Western democracies were cheered by this rift in the Communist bloc, resulting from Tito's independence of Russian control and his advocacy of *national Communism*. The democracies hoped that other satellites would follow Tito's example. To enable Tito to resist Russian pressure, the democracies extended Yugoslavia widespread aid: loans, food, trade treaties, diplomatic support, and military equipment. The West fully realizes that Yugoslavia is a Communist nation, but not a Russian satellite.

2. Power Struggle Following Stalin's Death in 1953. The death of Joseph Stalin signaled a bitter struggle for power among the top Russian Communists. *Nikita Khrushchev* became First Secretary of the Communist party, a position that Stalin had used to rise to absolute power. Khrushchev eliminated his chief rivals in Russia. One was executed; others were deposed from positions of importance. In 1958 Khrushchev assumed the Premiership, thus becoming the official head of the Soviet government (see page 352).

The struggle for power after Stalin's death gave the world an unusual glimpse of the conflict that can exist within the Russian dictatorship—a conflict that is usually kept well hidden below the surface.

3. Downgrading of Stalin (1956). Stalin had used every means of propaganda to encourage hero-worship of himself as a great teacher, leader, and military genius. In 1956 Khrushchev began an all-out attack to downgrade Stalin in the eyes of the Soviet people. Khrushchev condemned Stalin for (a) purges of military and political leaders on false charges, (b) blunders in foreign affairs, (c) terror against innocent Soviet citizens, and (d) personal cowardice during World War II. After Khrushchev's denunciation of Stalin, the Communist party spread the new anti-Stalin line.

In the satellite nations, the anti-Stalin campaign strengthened the Titoist doctrine of national Communism and helped set off upheavals, especially in Poland and Hungary.

4. Uprising in Poland (1956). The Polish people engaged in strikes and demonstrations (a) to achieve better living conditions, and (b) to end Russian domination. *Wladyslaw Gomulka*, who had been imprisoned as a Titoist, regained the leadership of the Polish Communist party and announced that Poland would seek her own road to socialism. Khrushchev was alarmed by Poland's trend toward independence, but Gomulka reassured him that Poland would remain Communist and allied with Russia. Khrushchev thereupon pledged not to interfere in Poland's internal affairs.

By this bloodless revolution, Poland under Gomulka achieved (*a*) a measure of independence in domestic matters, enabling Gomulka to end the forced collectivization of agriculture, and (*b*) expulsion of Russian agents from positions of authority over the Polish army, economy, and government.

5. Revolution in Hungary (1956). The Hungarian people revolted for (*a*) better living conditions, (*b*) the withdrawal of Soviet troops, and (*c*) full national independence. *Imre Nagy*, a Titoist, became head of the government, appointed non-Communists to his cabinet, and demanded the immediate withdrawal of Soviet forces. Nagy announced Hungary's neutrality in the cold war and withdrawal from the Warsaw Pact.

Such anti-Russian moves were more than Khrushchev would permit. Russian troops seized all of Hungary and suppressed the Hungarian *freedom fighters*. Thousands of Hungarians were killed or deported to Siberia; almost 200,000 fled their native land. The Soviets smashed the Nagy government, replacing it with a puppet Hungarian regime under *Janos Kadar*. The Soviets thus defied condemnation by the United Nations (see page 404).

6. Chinese-Soviet Split. Despite their 1950 treaty of alliance, China and Russia gradually became hostile and by 1963 openly disagreed as follows:

a. Ideological Conflict. (1) **Russia.** Khrushchev asserted that world Communism can be achieved through *peaceful coexistence*. He claimed that people, impressed by Soviet economic and scientific achievements, will turn to Communism. Meanwhile, Communist nations will subject the West to unremitting economic competition, propaganda, and probably subversion. However, Communists must make every effort to avoid nuclear war. A Communist paradise cannot be built upon millions of corpses. Russian support of peaceful coexistence has been reaffirmed by Khrushchev's successors, Brezhnev and Kosygin. (2) **China.** Mao Tse-tung derided peaceful coexistence as a myth and held the view that war against capitalism is inevitable. Communists must support the revolutionary struggles of oppressed peoples even at the risk of nuclear war. If war does come, it will prove the United States to be a "paper tiger," will end capitalism, and will usher in a glorious Communist future.

b. Russian Atomic Aid to China. (1) **Russia.** Until 1959 the Soviets trained Chinese atomic scientists, sent Russian technicians to China, and provided China with an atomic reactor to produce nuclear materials. As the ideological conflict became acute, Russia terminated her aid. (2) **China.** Peking at first complained that Soviet aid was not enough and after 1959 deplored its termination.

c. Chinese-Soviet Borders. (1) **Russia.** Nineteenth-century treaties established the borders between Russia and China and must be respected. (2) **China.** The treaties by which Czarist Russia seized the Amur River

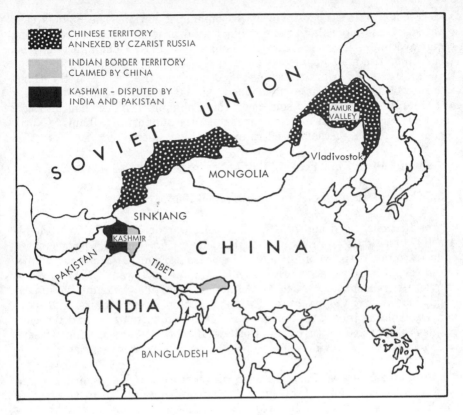

CHINESE TERRITORY
ANNEXED BY CZARIST RUSSIA

INDIAN BORDER TERRITORY
CLAIMED BY CHINA

KASHMIR – DISPUTED BY
INDIA AND PAKISTAN

Border Disputes on the Asian Mainland

*Communist China is said to covet Mongolia and the territory
annexed from China by Czarist Russia.*

valley, the port of Vladivostok, and central Asian territory bordering Sinkiang province were imperialist-imposed and are not valid now. In 1969
Chinese and Russian forces clashed at a border point north of Vladivostok.

d. China-India Border Dispute. (1) *Russia.* The Soviets blamed China
for this border dispute (see pages 453-454) and extended aid to India. (2)
China. The Chinese denounced Moscow for failing to act "fraternally" toward a Communist nation engaged in a dispute with a non-Communist
country.

e. World Communist Leadership. (1) *Russia.* As the oldest and most
advanced Communist nation, Russia claimed the leadership of the Communist bloc. Khrushchev conceded that there are many roads to Communism

and accepted Tito's Yugoslavia as a Communist nation. The Soviets condemned Chinese appeals to yellow, black, and brown peoples as containing racial overtones. Russia retained the support of most Communist nations. (2) *China.* The most populous Communist nation, China claimed to be the true interpreter of Marxist-Leninist doctrine and the leader of the Communist world. The Chinese condemned the Yugoslavs as renegades. They also charged that Russia "sold out" the Communist movement in Latin America, Africa, and Asia. The Chinese had the support of Albania. (North Korea and North Vietnam tried to avoid taking sides.)

7. Removal of Khrushchev (1964). See page 352.

8. "Cultural Revolution" in China (1966-1969)

a. Reasons. Aged and ill, Mao Tse-tung was determined that after his death China would continue his policies: (1) *within the country,* increased collectivization despite opposition by the peasants, and (2) *in foreign affairs,* world revolution even at the risk of war. Mao did not want China to adopt "Soviet revisionism," by which he meant the use of the profit motive in economic matters and the loss of revolutionary zeal in foreign affairs. Mao's opponents, holding important positions in the Communist party and the government, supported pay rises for workers and private acreage for farmers, and considered Mao's views inappropriate for building the nation.

b. Three Years of Turmoil. Mao moved to crush his opponents by a "great proletarian cultural revolution." He mobilized millions of youths into the *Red Guard* groups. The Red Guards denounced "revisionism" and terrorized the opposition. The "cultural revolution" fragmented China's Communist party, undermined industrial and agricultural production, disrupted transportation, closed educational institutions, and shattered Chinese society.

c. Return to Stability. By 1970 China returned to stability: the Red Guards were disbanded and order was restored by realistic and increasingly powerful army leaders; industrial and agricultural production recovered to 1966 levels; and the government reflected control of moderate political leaders under Premier Chou En-lai.

9. Invasion of Czechoslovakia (1968). *Alexander Dubcek* became head of the Czechoslovak Communist party and pledged a program of "liberalization." Dubcek lifted censorship of press, radio, and television and permitted non-Communists to assemble and form political groups. Dubcek also indicated that Czechoslovakia would seek trade and loans from the West.

To reassure the Soviet Union, Dubcek asserted that Czechoslovakia remained a Communist nation and a loyal Warsaw Pact member.

Russian leaders, however, feared that the Czechoslovak reforms might spur similar movements in the other satellite nations. In 1968, after Russian pressures failed to halt "liberalization," overwhelming Soviet forces, supported by troops of four Warsaw Pact nations—East Germany, Poland, Hungary, and Bulgaria—invaded Czechoslovakia. The invaders encountered not military resistance, but disdain and defiance from the Czechoslovak people. Unable to establish a puppet regime, the Soviets allowed Dubcek to remain in office but at the price of enforcing Soviet demands for "normalization." Czechoslovakia reestablished censorship, banned non-Communist political organizations, removed officials disliked by the Russians, accepted Soviet advisers, and consented to the stationing of Soviet troops on Czechoslovak soil. In 1969 the Russians pressured Dubcek out as head of the Czechoslovak Communist party and replaced him by a more amenable man, *Gustav Husak.*

The Russian invasion of Czechoslovakia, condemned by many Western and neutral nations, was also condemned by three Communist states—Yugoslavia, Rumania, and China—and by many Communist parties, notably those in Italy and France. These Communist groups rejected the Russians' claim that they had saved Czechoslovakia from "counter-revolutionary forces." They also rejected the *Brezhnev Doctrine* that whenever a Communist nation endangers socialism at home or in other Communist countries, the Soviet Union has the duty to intervene with military force.

10. Unrest in Poland (1970-1971). Polish workers, smoldering over food shortages, felt their earnings threatened by a new wage incentive system. When the government, just before Christmas, increased prices of food, fuel, and clothing, workers in coastal cities began riots and demonstrations. As the rioting spread to other cities, Wladyslaw Gomulka resigned as head of Poland's Communist party and was replaced by *Edward Gierek.* This change was approved by Russia, which feared that the Polish disturbances might infect the other satellite nations. The Gierek regime moved to quiet discontent by providing funds to assist the lowest income families, shelving the wage incentive system, and revoking the price increases. However, the regime rejected demands for higher wages and called for "law, order, and discipline."

B. THE COLD WAR: FOREIGN AID

THE TRUMAN DOCTRINE

1. Purpose. In 1947 Greece was under attack from Communist guerrilla bands (see page 403), and Turkey was under pressure from Russia for concessions over the Dardanelles. If successful, these Communist efforts would have expanded Russian influence into the eastern Mediterranean. President Truman therefore announced that "it must be the policy of the United States to support free nations" against direct and indirect Communist aggression. Congress supported this *Truman Doctrine* by overwhelmingly approving economic and military aid for Greece and Turkey.

2. Effects. The Greek government welcomed the Truman Doctrine. Greece was in economic chaos as a result of Axis occupation during World War II. American economic aid helped revive the Greek economy. American military aid helped Greece put down Communist guerrilla attacks. (Furthermore, Yugoslavia had halted aid to the Greek guerrillas following Tito's split with Russia.)

The Turkish government, bolstered by American economic and military aid, has withstood Russian demands for control of the Dardanelles.

THE MARSHALL PLAN

1. Reasons for Offer. In 1947 Secretary of State *George C. Marshall* offered American economic aid to *all* European nations (including Russia and her satellites) to enable them to recover from the destruction of World War II. He said, "Our policy is directed not against any country or doctrine but against hunger, poverty, desperation, and chaos." World War II had crippled the economies of European nations, victor and vanquished alike. Cities were wrecked, factories and mines destroyed, transport facilities disrupted, and agricultural yields reduced.

The United States wanted to help Europe in order to (*a*) improve the living conditions of the people, (*b*) end the need for continued American relief funds, (*c*) revive a mutually profitable trade between the United States and Europe, and (*d*) lessen the danger of Communism in Western Europe. People enjoying good living standards, it was thought, are unlikely to heed Communist propaganda.

2. The European Recovery Program (ERP). The Marshall Plan, officially the *European Recovery Program*, aided most non-Communist nations of Europe: Great Britain, France, Austria, Belgium, Denmark, Greece, Iceland, Ireland, Italy, Luxembourg, the Netherlands, Norway, Portugal, Sweden, Switzerland, Turkey, and West Germany. They cooperated with each other and with the United States to achieve "recovery not relief." The United States provided $12.5 billion, most of which was spent in this country for foodstuffs, raw materials, and machinery—all deemed essential for economic recovery.

3. Achievements. During its four years (1948-1951), the Marshall Plan helped strengthen the forces of freedom in Europe. It (a) promoted strong economic recovery, permitting many countries to surpass prewar levels of production, (b) furthered political stability, (c) reduced Communist influence, and (d) encouraged West European countries to move toward economic unity (see pages 427-429).

4. Russian Opposition. Russia condemned the Marshall Plan as a scheme of American capitalists to gain economic and political control over Europe and announced that she would exert every effort to defeat the Plan. (a) Russia and her European satellite nations refused America's offer of Marshall Plan aid. (b) Russia initiated an economic aid program of her own, the *Council of Mutual Economic Assistance* (COMECON). This program competed with the Marshall Plan by bringing about closer economic relations between Russia and her satellites.

POINT FOUR PROGRAM

In his 1949 Inaugural Address, President Truman reaffirmed America's opposition to Russian expansion. As *Point Four* in America's effort to contain Communism, Truman proposed a "bold new program" to utilize our scientific and industrial knowledge to give *technical assistance* to underdeveloped nations.

Under the Point Four Program, Congress annually has appropriated considerable sums of money to meet the requests of developing nations—in Latin America, the Middle East, Africa, and Asia. The United States has sent technical specialists to help increase agricultural and industrial output, further urban development, improve government administration, promote public health, and advance education. The Point Four Program has made gratifying contributions in bettering conditions in underdeveloped lands.

EISENHOWER DOCTRINE

In 1957 President Eisenhower warned that the economic and political instability of the Middle East made it vulnerable to Communist infiltration. Eisenhower offered the Middle East nations (1) a multimillion dollar program of economic and military aid, and (2) armed assistance, upon request, to repel open Communist aggression. The *Eisenhower Doctrine* was welcomed by Lebanon and Saudi Arabia but was denounced by Egypt and Syria as an American plot to dominate the Arab world.

PEACE CORPS

In 1961 President Kennedy inaugurated a new foreign aid agency, the *Peace Corps*. It enrolls idealistic volunteers who receive token pay, work in underdeveloped countries that request aid, and live as do the native peoples. Peace Corps volunteers fill the gap between the highly skilled technical advisers of the Point Four Program and the relatively unskilled local labor. For example, they might follow up a Point Four malaria-control demonstration by remaining with the villagers and assisting in the day-by-day work.

Peace Corps volunteers have performed laudably in about 50 nations and have won friends for the United States.

AMERICAN FOREIGN AID: AN OVERVIEW

The United States continues to spend substantial sums for foreign aid. Currently, American military aid is administered by the Defense Department, and economic aid by the State Department's *Agency for International Development (AID)*.

From 1945 to the present the United States has extended about $120 billion in military and economic aid to more than 100 countries. Of this total, about 80 percent has been in the form of grants (outright gifts) and about 20 percent in the form of loans. At the beginning, our foreign aid was chiefly economic assistance for Europe, especially England, France, and West Germany. As Europe recovered from the war, the United States extended economic and technical aid to the developing nations of the world. As a result of Communist aggression in Korea in 1950, the foreign aid program has since placed greater emphasis upon military aid for the Far East, especially South Korea, Japan, Taiwan, and South Vietnam.

CRITICISMS OF OUR FOREIGN AID PROGRAM

Americans overwhelmingly recognize the necessity of foreign aid for the *mutual security* of both the United States and the recipient nations. For foreign aid, Congress annually appropriates several billion dollars—varying from 1 to 3 percent of our national budget. Nevertheless, a small but vocal minority opposes foreign aid claiming that it (1) is too great a burden on the American taxpayer, (2) diverts funds that could be used for improvements within the country, (3) is characterized by inefficient administration, waste, and corruption, (4) creates competition for American manufacturers and farmers by building up foreign industry and agriculture, and (5) has failed to lessen the danger of Communism.

FOREIGN AID PROGRAMS OF WEST EUROPEAN NATIONS

The United States has urged the more prosperous free-world nations—notably England, France, and West Germany—to cooperate with us in extending aid to underdeveloped lands. These nations accepted the idea of joint responsibility and have initiated their own modest foreign aid programs.

THE COMMUNIST ECONOMIC OFFENSIVE SINCE 1954

The Russians have repeatedly boasted that the Communist economic system will outstrip capitalism in peaceful economic competition. The Communist bloc has challenged the free world by offering economic and military assistance to most underdeveloped nations, both neutral and pro-Western. More than 20 countries—notably Argentina, India, Indonesia, Iraq, and the United Arab Republic—have accepted Communist bloc aid, chiefly in the form of loans. Since 1954 aid from the Soviet Union and her European satellites has totaled about $6 billion. Also, the Communists have provided technical assistance by sending abroad large numbers of skilled personnel. By this offensive, the Communists expect to increase their influence in the underdeveloped countries.

In recent years the Chinese Communists have offered aid to Latin American and Afro-Asian nations in competition with the Russian-led program of assistance.

To date American foreign aid remains far greater than that extended by the Communist nations.

C. WEST EUROPEAN ECONOMIC UNITY

THE INNER SIX

Encouraged by their cooperation under the Marshall Plan, six Western European nations moved toward economic unity. They were Belgium, France, Italy, Luxembourg, the Netherlands, and West Germany—collectively called the *Inner Six.*

1. **European Coal and Steel Community (Schuman Plan).** In 1952 the Inner Six, accepting the proposals of French Foreign Minister *Robert Schuman,* agreed to (*a*) abolish tariffs on coal, iron, and steel, (*b*) establish a supranational (above any nation) *High Authority* to administer these resources in the interests of the entire community, and (*c*) grant the High Authority power to control prices, production, wages, and working conditions.

2. European Atomic Energy Community (Euratom). In 1957 the Inner Six agreed to form a supranational *European Atomic Energy Commission* to (a) coordinate atomic research, (b) pool nuclear materials, and (c) increase the production of electric power by atomic installations.

3. European Economic Community (EEC or Common Market). In 1957 the Inner Six agreed to join in a tariff union. They established a supranational *European Economic Commission* which would gradually (a) eliminate internal tariff barriers and (b) establish a unified tariff system on goods imported from outside the tariff union area. The European Economic Community was to be a free trade area—that is, a *Common Market* without man-made barriers to the movement of goods, capital, and labor.

4. Objectives. European Community moves toward economic unity aimed to (a) provide more coal, iron, steel, electric power, farm produce, and consumer goods at lower prices, (b) raise living standards, (c) reduce both domestic and foreign Communist threats, and (d) expand foreign trade.

THE OUTER SEVEN

In 1959 seven West European nations (Austria, Denmark, Great Britain, Norway, Portugal, Sweden, and Switzerland—collectively called the *Outer Seven*) formed the *European Free Trade Association (EFTA)*. The EFTA proposed gradually to eliminate tariff barriers among its members.

The existence of two trade blocs—the Inner Six and the Outer Seven—aroused fears of economic rivalry.

AN ENLARGED COMMON MARKET

Britain twice applied for Common Márket membership but each application was vetoed by France under President de Gaulle. He viewed Britain's membership as a threat to his hopes for French leadership in Western Europe. With de Gaulle's retirement in 1969, Britain again applied for membership. In 1971 Prime Minister *Edward Heath* and French President *Georges Pompidou* agreed that Britain was to enter the European Community as follows: (1) to mid-1977 Britain and the six Common Market members would reciprocally reduce tariffs so as to achieve a customs union, and (2) special protection would be provided for dairy products from New Zealand and sugar from other British Commonwealth nations. Also, Britain's entry would be accompanied by membership for Ireland, Denmark, and Norway.

In Britain the House of Commons approved European Community membership. In the other three nations, the people balloted in popular referendums. The Irish and the Danes voted overwhelmingly for membership; the Norwegians by a close vote rejected membership. (The five remaining EFTA members—Austria, Norway, Portugal, Sweden, and Switzerland—concluded

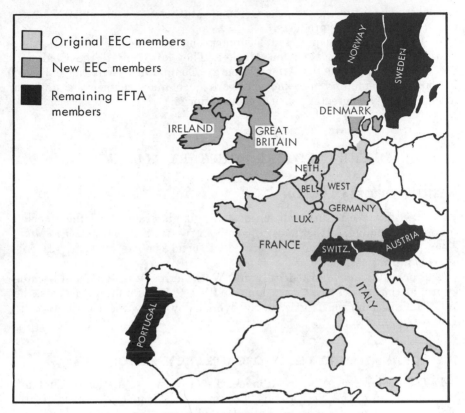

West European Economic Unity

A COMPARISON: EEC vs. THE THREE MAJOR ECONOMIC NATIONS

	Nine-Nation EEC	U.S.A.	U.S.S.R.	Japan
Area (sq.mi.)	590,000	3,600,000	8,800,000	143,000
Population (millions)	253	205	243	104
G.N.P. (billions of dollars)	$626	$991	$200	$196
Imports (billions of dollars)	$116	$40	$12	$19
Exports (billions of dollars)	$112	$43	$13	$19

Source: Commission of the European Communities (1970 figures)

special trade agreements with the Common Market to permit by 1977 tariff-free trade in industrial products.)

In 1973 Britain, Ireland, and Denmark officially became members, thus making a nine-nation Common Market. They also joined the Coal and Steel Community and the Atomic Energy Community. Will the enlarged European Community later move toward a common currency, a uniform foreign policy, and greater political cooperation?

D. THE COLD WAR: MILITARY ALLIANCES

WESTERN EUROPEAN UNION

In 1948 five West European nations—England, France, and the Benelux countries (*B*elgium, *N*etherlands, *Lux*embourg)—formed the *Western Union*. They pledged (1) economic, cultural, and social cooperation, and (2) collective military assistance.

This organization admitted Italy and West Germany in 1955, and became known as the *Western European Union* (*WEU*). In its military aspects, the WEU has accomplished little, being overshadowed by the North Atlantic Treaty Organization.

THE NORTH ATLANTIC TREATY ORGANIZATION (NATO)

1. **The Defensive Military Alliance.** In 1949 twelve nations—England, France, Belgium, the Netherlands, Luxembourg, Denmark, Iceland, Italy, Norway, Portugal, Canada, and the United States—signed the *North Atlantic Pact*. They declared that (a) they would consider an attack on any one of them as an attack on all, and (b) they would come to the defense of the attacked member nation with armed force if necessary. The American Senate, by overwhelmingly ratifying the Pact, again showed that the United States had abandoned her past isolationism.

NATO admitted the eastern Mediterranean countries of Greece and Turkey in 1952 and West Germany in 1955, bringing its total membership to 15 nations. (For West German admission, see pages 440-441.)

Russia vigorously attacked the North Atlantic Pact, claiming that it was (a) aggressive in character and a threat to the Soviet Union, and (b) a violation of the United Nations Charter, which pledged the member nations to work together for peace. The United States dismissed these Russian charges by claiming that the Pact was (a) defensive in character—a warning to would-be aggressors, and (b) in accordance with the United Nations Charter —which permitted regional agreements for the maintenance of peace and security.

The North Atlantic Pact Countries

2. The NATO Army. In 1950 the North Atlantic Pact nations further strengthened themselves against Communist aggression by authorizing "an integrated military force adequate for the defense of the freedom of Europe," that is, a NATO army. The head of the NATO army, called the *Supreme Allied Commander in Europe* (*SACEUR*), has always been an American general. The first Supreme Commander was Dwight D. Eisenhower. NATO headquarters, located in Belgium, are known as the *Supreme Headquarters of the Allied Powers in Europe* (*SHAPE*).

To fulfill her obligations, the United States has assigned several divisions to Europe as part of the NATO army and has given billions of dollars in military equipment to our NATO allies.

Since 1950 the North Atlantic Treaty nations have created (a) a NATO army, navy, and air force, (b) NATO air bases, and (c) unified NATO military commands for Europe.

It is hoped that NATO will deter the Communists from undertaking any aggression in Europe. But in the event of open conflict, the free world expects NATO to serve as a military *shield* to withstand the initial Communist attack until NATO members can bring into action their *sword*, that is, their massive retaliatory strength.

3. Problems Facing NATO. The alliance has faced many strains: (a) Several disputes have occurred among members. Greece and Turkey have disagreed over Cyprus; the United States and England have disagreed with West Germany over the division of NATO costs. (b) Many NATO members have been reluctant to equip West German soldiers with nuclear weapons.

NATO's most serious problem was posed by President de Gaulle of France. A nationalist, jealous of French sovereignty, de Gaulle resented American influence in NATO and created an independent French nuclear force. In 1966 de Gaulle claimed that NATO, as a military shield, was obsolete because of the (a) development of nuclear missiles, and (b) Soviet policy of

Le Pelley in The Christian Science Monitor

"Parlez-vous NATO—I say—Parlez-vous NATO?"

Does France "talk NATO"? What is France's defense policy? Is it realistic?

peaceful coexistence. Accordingly, de Gaulle withdrew all French forces from NATO and demanded the removal of all NATO troops, chiefly American and Canadian, from French soil. De Gaulle, however, pledged that France would remain in the North Atlantic Pact.

De Gaulle's military withdrawal was deplored by the 14 other NATO members, who stressed the value of an integrated military organization. Nevertheless, they yielded to de Gaulle's demands. By 1967 all NATO troops had left French soil, and SHAPE headquarters had been transferred from near Paris to Belgium. Under President Pompidou, successor to de Gaulle, France's military forces remained outside of NATO.

SOUTHEAST ASIA TREATY ORGANIZATION (SEATO)

1. The Defensive Military Alliance. In 1954 eight nations—the United States, Great Britain, France, Australia, New Zealand, Thailand, Pakistan, and the Philippines—established SEATO. Each member nation (a) agreed that armed aggression against any other member would "endanger its own peace and safety" and pledged to "meet the common danger in accordance with its constitutional processes," (b) recognized that civil wars might involve foreign aggression, and (c) offered to aid, upon request, the nonsignatory Southeast Asian states of Cambodia, Laos, and South Vietnam.

2. Weaknesses of SEATO. (a) SEATO lacks a unified armed force and military command. (b) SEATO specifically excludes Taiwan (Formosa) from its protection, although Taiwan was a major danger spot in Asia. (Taiwan was excluded because Great Britain and some other member nations disagreed with the United States on the advisability of protecting the Nationalist Chinese stronghold from the Communists.) (c) SEATO's main strength comes from its non-Asian members. (d) Four important Southeast Asian nations—India, Burma, Ceylon, and Indonesia—refused to join SEATO. These nations seek to remain neutral in the cold war, want to avoid antagonizing Communist China and Russia, and are suspicious of the Western powers because of past imperialism. (e) France has indicated her disapproval of SEATO by refraining from active participation in SEATO gatherings. (f) Displeased by lack of SEATO support in her quarrels with India, Pakistan has accepted military aid from Communist China. After her defeat in the 1971 Indian-Pakistani War, Pakistan withdrew from SEATO.

CENTRAL TREATY ORGANIZATION (CENTO)

1. The Defensive Military Alliance. In 1955 five nations—England, Turkey, Pakistan, Iran, and one Arab state, Iraq—signed the *Bagdad Pact* establishing the *Middle East Treaty Organization (METO)*. In 1959 Iraq, under a new regime, withdrew from METO. The four remaining allies chose

The Cold War

a new name—*Central Treaty Organization (CENTO)*—to emphasize their central position, linking NATO to the west with SEATO to the east.

2. Weaknesses of CENTO. (*a*) No Arab state is a member. (*b*) Except for England, CENTO members are not major military nations. (*c*) No unified military command exists. (*d*) The United States is not formally a member, although she strongly supports the alliance.

ADDITIONAL AMERICAN MILITARY ALLIANCES

Today, the United States has military alliances with over 40 nations of the free world. In addition to NATO and SEATO, the United States has entered into the following military commitments:

1. The **Rio Inter-American Defense Treaty** (1947) between the United States and the Latin American nations of the Organization of American States (OAS) provided for the common defense of the Western Hemisphere.

2. The **Anzus Pact** (1951) between Australia, New Zealand, and the United States provided that each nation (*a*) consider an attack upon one of the others as dangerous to its own safety, and (*b*) act to meet the common danger.

3. Bilateral **Mutual Defense Treaties** with Taiwan, Japan, the Philippines, and South Korea pledged the United States to consider an attack on any one of these nations as a common danger and to assist the nation attacked.

Also, the United States maintains military bases in Spain.

The United States hopes that her system of military alliances—which provides for over 200 American bases in countries ringing the Soviet bloc—will deter the Communists from further aggression.

COMMUNIST MILITARY ALLIANCES

1. Chinese-Soviet Treaty. In 1950 Soviet Russia and Communist China signed a treaty of "friendship, alliance, and mutual aid" providing for (*a*) mutual military aid in case of attack by Japan or by an ally of Japan (meaning the United States); and (*b*) consultation on all international matters of mutual concern. Russia provided considerable military equipment to strengthen Red China's fighting power.

Although relations between the Soviet Union and China became openly strained by 1963, Chinese Premier Chou En-lai has insisted that the alliance remains intact.

2. Warsaw Pact. In 1955 Russia and her European satellites formed an alliance providing for a unified Communist military command. This was designed as a counterweight to NATO, which had been strengthened by West German membership.

E. THE COLD WAR: IN GERMANY

THE ALLIED DECISIONS REGARDING GERMANY (1945)

At the Yalta and Potsdam Conferences, and in other agreements, the United States, Britain, and Russia made several decisions concerning Germany.

1. Territory. The eastern provinces were detached from Germany with part occupied by Russia but most under Polish control (see map below). These territorial changes were meant to be temporary, pending determination—in a formal peace treaty—of Germany's final boundaries. (Russia and Poland now insist that these changes are permanent.)

2. Occupation Zones. The rest of Germany was divided into four zones, with each of the Big Four powers—Russia, Britain, the United States, and France—governing one zone. Berlin, lying 110 miles inside the Russian zone, was likewise divided into four sections, with each of the Big Four controlling one section. The three Western Allies were guaranteed access to Berlin by surface and air routes across the Russian zone. These divisions of Germany were meant to be temporary, pending a formal peace treaty.

Germany Following World War II

The highway, the railroad, and the air lanes shown on the map are the military access routes between West Germany and Berlin.

3. Economy. The German economy was to be directed toward agriculture and peaceful industries. War industries were barred. Certain German factories and industrial equipment were to be dismantled and removed, chiefly to the U.S.S.R., as partial reparation.

4. Disarmament. Germany was to be thoroughly disarmed so as to render her unable to wage aggressive warfare again.

5. Education. German schools were to work for the "development of democratic ideas." The Allies recognized that reeducation of the German people would be a long and difficult task.

6. Denazification. Nazism was to be wiped out completely. All Nazi organizations, including the Nazi party, Storm Troopers, and the Gestapo, were dissolved. Former Nazis were not to be allowed to hold public office or other positions of influence. War criminals were to be brought to trial.

Partymiller in The Gazette and Daily, York, Pa.

"Will we learn the lessons?"

What are "the lessons" of the Nazi war crimes trials? Has mankind, by today, learned "the lessons"?

WAR TRIALS

1. Nuremberg Trials. An *International Military Tribunal* met at Nuremberg (1945-1946) and tried Hermann Goering and other top Nazi leaders. They were charged with crimes against humanity, violations of international law, and waging aggressive warfare. These trials, it was hoped, would serve to democratize Germany, to expose the evils of Nazism, to further international law, and to discourage future aggressors. The Tribunal found 19 of the 22 defendants guilty; it sentenced 12 to death and the others to prison.

2. In the American Zone. A special *United States Military Tribunal* held a series of trials for secondary Nazi leaders. *Alfred Krupp,* head of the Krupp munitions works, was sentenced to prison for exploiting slave labor and plundering Nazi-occupied countries. The United States later permitted West German *denazification courts* to try less important Nazis. These courts were quite lenient, and many former Nazis regained positions of influence.

3. In the Russian Zone. At first, the Communists severely punished Nazi war criminals. Soon, however, the Communists abandoned denazification trials and treated former Nazis leniently in order to gain their support.

THE WEST AND RUSSIA DISAGREE ON GERMANY

Soon after the end of World War II, the West and Russia came into conflict over Germany. Fundamentally, each side sought German support for itself and against the other. Western plans for German reunification that would swing Germany toward the West were rejected by Russia. Soviet plans for German reunification that would bring Germany into the Communist camp were rejected by the West (see pages 442-443).

THE BERLIN BLOCKADE (1948-1949)

Under Stalin, Russia tried to drive the Western Allies out of Berlin by blockading the surface routes—roads, rails, and canals—between Berlin and the Western zones of Germany. To thwart this *Berlin blockade,* the Allies supplied the West Berliners with food, medicine, and other necessities by means of an *airlift.* The Soviets could not halt the airlift except by shooting down Allied planes, a course they were unwilling to take for fear of starting an all-out war. The Russians therefore abandoned the blockade.

DEVELOPMENTS IN WEST GERMANY

1. Establishment of the German Federal Republic. Despairing of reaching an agreement with Russia for German reunification, the three Western Allies in 1949 combined their zones to form the *Federal Republic of Germany* with its capital at *Bonn.* In 1955 West Germany was granted full sovereignty.

2. Government of West Germany. The West German constitution provides for a democratic government with (*a*) a guarantee of civil liberties and free elections, (*b*) a two-house Parliament consisting of a Bundestag and a Bundesrat, and (*c*) a Chancellor responsible to the Bundestag.

Germany's two major parties are the *Christian Democrats* and the *Social Democrats*. Although they differ in details, both parties support a welfare state, NATO membership, and a pro-Western foreign policy. The Christian Democrats for many years were the largest party in the Bundestag. Until 1963 *Konrad Adenauer,* their leader, served as Chancellor.

In 1969 elections, the Christian Democrats remained the largest party in the Bundestag, but the Social Democrats in coalition with the minor Free Democratic party secured a narrow legislative majority. *Willy Brandt,* Social Democratic leader, became Chancellor, and *Walter Scheel,* Free Democratic head, became Foreign Minister. Brandt pledged to improve relations with East Germany, Poland, and Russia, and to support West European political and economic unity.

In 1972 elections, Brandt's coalition government won a strong vote of confidence and gained a substantial majority in the Bundestag.

DEVELOPMENTS IN EAST GERMANY

1. Establishment of the German Democratic Republic. In opposition to the Federal Republic, Russia in 1949 transformed her zone into the *German Democratic Republic* with its capital at *East Berlin.* This East German state is a Russian satellite occupied by Soviet troops.

2. Government of East Germany. A self-proclaimed "democratic republic," East Germany is a typical Communist dictatorship with restrictions on civil liberties, a secret police, and only one political party. For 25 years *Walter Ulbricht* headed the East German Communist party and controlled the country. In 1953 anti-government riots were suppressed by Soviet forces. In 1971 Ulbricht resigned because of old age and was replaced by *Erich Honecker.* The Western powers have refused to recognize East Germany.

A COMPARISON OF THE TWO GERMANYS

1. Area. West Germany comprises 70 percent of the total area of postwar Germany as compared to 30 percent for East Germany.

2. Population. West Germany contains over 75 percent of the German people as compared to less than 25 percent for East Germany.

3. Industrialization. West Germany, the more industrial of the two Germanys, contains the industrial heart of Europe, the *Ruhr Valley.* The East German economy is more agricultural than that of West Germany.

4. Economic System. West Germany has a capitalist economy, typified by private enterprise, free labor unions, and government regulation only to prevent economic abuses. East Germany has a Communist economy, typified by government ownership of industry and collectivization of agriculture.

5. Economic Developments Since World War II. Aided by Marshall Plan funds, West Germany made a remarkable recovery from the devastation of World War II. Her cities, transportation system, and industry were all rebuilt. Today, West Germany is the leading industrial nation of Western Europe and enjoys a high standard of living.

In contrast, East Germany made a far slower recovery. For years, its cities —notably East Berlin—were not rebuilt, and its people suffered serious shortages of food and other consumer goods. In search of better living standards, many East Germans fled to West Germany. To stop this flow, the Communists in 1961 built the *Berlin Wall.* Having thus halted the flight of skilled workers and also having relaxed economic controls, East Germany in the 1960's experienced considerable economic growth, but its living standard remains below that of West Germany.

THE ISSUE OF WEST GERMAN REARMAMENT

In the 1950's, to further strengthen the defenses of Western Europe, the NATO nations debated the rearming of West Germany.

The following were the chief arguments *in favor:* (1) West Germany's manpower, natural resources, and industry would greatly strengthen the military might of the West. (2) West Germany's geographic position in central Europe makes her the West's first line of defense against Communist attack. (3) The West German people are reliably anti-Communist and willing to defend themselves in case of Communist aggression.

	POPULATION (millions)	GROSS NATIONAL PRODUCT (billions of dollars)	STEEL (millions of metric tons)	CEMENT (millions of metric tons)
WEST GERMANY	58	132	37	32
FRANCE	50	117	20	25
GREAT BRITAIN	55	87	24	18
ITALY	53	75	16	26

Germany's Role in Western Europe

Why does West Germany demand greater influence in West European matters? Do you approve?

The following arguments were raised *against* rearming West Germany: (1) West Germany's manpower and strategic location will be of little importance in a future global war. Victory will depend upon air power and nuclear might. (2) The West German people are not reliable allies, since they are principally interested in reunification and might be reluctant to fight against the East Germans. (3) Should there be a revival of the Nazi type of nationalism, a rearmed Germany may again embark upon aggression.

The chief advocate of rearming West Germany was the United States; the chief Western opponent was France, which had suffered severely from German invasions in 1870, 1914, and 1940. Nevertheless, in the face of the Communist menace, the Western powers agreed to rearm West Germany, but with safeguards.

THE PARIS AGREEMENTS OF 1955

1. **West German Sovereignty.** West Germany was restored to complete control over her domestic and foreign affairs (except for negotiations regarding German unification and West Berlin). Germany agreed to let Allied troops remain in West Germany and West Berlin for the defense of the free world.

2. **West German Rearmament.** (*a*) West Germany was admitted to NATO (see pages 430-432). (*b*) West Germany's army, assigned to NATO, was limited to 12 divisions—about 275,000 men. (*c*) West Germany was not to manufacture atomic, biological, or chemical weapons, guided missiles, or large warships. (*d*) West Germany pledged not to resort to force to achieve the reunification of Germany.

RUSSIA OPPOSES REARMAMENT AND NATO MEMBERSHIP FOR WEST GERMANY

1. **Propaganda.** Russia denounced the Paris Agreements as evidence of "aggressive Western militarism" and warned that West German membership in NATO would doom German reunification.

2. **Soviet Military Measures.** To counteract the rearming of West Germany, the Communists increased the army of East Germany by introducing conscription. Also, the Soviet Union signed the Warsaw Pact with her European satellites (see page 435).

3. **Austrian Peace Treaty: An Example for Germany.** Like Germany, Austria had been divided into four zones after World War II. In 1955, after ten years of deliberate delay, Russia agreed to a treaty granting Austria reunifi-

cation and independence. In return, Austria pledged herself to cold war *neutrality*. Pointing to Austria as an example, Soviet leaders warned that Russia would permit German reunification only at the price of German neutrality.

CONFLICTING PROPOSALS FOR GERMAN REUNIFICATION

Both the Western powers and Russia claim to favor German reunification. However, the current outlook for uniting the two Germanies is bleak, because each side in the cold war will permit reunification only in accordance with its own proposals.

Kuekes in The Cleveland Plain-Dealer

"Maybe there is no solution."

Why will the West not accept Soviet proposals? Why will the Soviet Union not accept Western proposals?

1. Western Proposals. The Western nations propose that the World War II Allies sign a German peace treaty that would (*a*) reunify Germany in a democratic fashion by U.N.-supervised elections in both East and West Germany, and (*b*) permit reunited Germany to join in any alliance, including NATO. Russia rejects these proposals because (*a*) free elections would probably result in a pro-Western government for all of Germany, and (*b*) NATO membership for a reunited Germany would strengthen the military power of the West at the expense of the Communist camp.

Both major parties of West Germany approve the Western proposals for German reunification.

2. Russian Proposals. Russia proposes that (a) the World War II Allies sign a peace treaty with each of the two Germanys, thereby enabling East Germany to retain her "socialist gains," (b) the East German and West German governments negotiate with each other regarding reunification, and (c) a reunited Germany remain neutral in the cold war. The Western powers reject these proposals because they would (a) perpetuate the East German satellite regime, and (b) weaken the West's military power by requiring West Germany to withdraw from NATO.

As a satellite state, East Germany supports the Russian proposals for German reunification.

RUSSIA PROVOKES ANOTHER CRISIS OVER BERLIN (1958-1961)

1. The Russian Challenge on Berlin. In 1958 Soviet Premier Khrushchev announced his determination to drive the Western powers out of Berlin.

2. Khrushchev's Probable Objectives. (a) Eventually West Berlin would be absorbed by East Germany, thereby expanding Communist rule and closing down a "showcase" of democracy and capitalism behind the Iron Curtain. The freedom and prosperity of West Berlin contrasted sharply with the repression and drabness of East Berlin. (b) West Berlin would no longer serve as an escape route for refugees fleeing from Communist East Europe. (In 1961 the Communists closed this escape route by erecting a barbed-wire and concrete barrier, the *Berlin Wall*.) (c) The West's prestige would be shattered, thereby undermining the NATO alliance.

3. Western Responses to the Soviet Challenge. The Western nations (a) stated their determination to remain in Berlin, (b) condemned the Berlin Wall for disrupting the lives of Berlin citizens, and (c) indicated willingness to negotiate regarding Berlin. Although negotiations failed, the Soviets did not act to threaten Allied rights in West Berlin.

STEPS TO REDUCE TENSIONS OVER BERLIN AND GERMANY (SINCE. 1970)

1. West Germany Improves Relations With Communist East Europe (1970-1972). While affirming West Germany's strong adherence to the Western world, Chancellor Willy Brandt moved in 1970 to "normalize" his country's relations with the Communist nations of Eastern Europe. (1) He met with East German Prime Minister Willi Stoph—the first such meetings of leaders of the two Germanys—but they failed to resolve any issues. (2) Brandt traveled to Moscow and later to Warsaw, paying homage to the Soviet Unknown Soldier, the Polish Unknown Soldier, and the Jews who battled in the Warsaw Ghetto uprising—all victims of Nazi aggression in World War II. Brandt signed two separate treaties—with the Soviet Union and with Poland—by which (a) West Germany accepted the existing Soviet and Polish borders, with the *Oder-Neisse Line* as Poland's boundary with Germany, thereby conceding sizable areas taken from prewar Germany (see map, page 436), and (b) the signatories renounced the use of force and agreed to strive for economic, scientific, and cultural cooperation.

These treaties were hailed by Brandt as leading to a new era of peace for Europe, but they were opposed by many Germans for accepting the territorial losses to Poland and Russia. In 1972 the treaties secured a minimal approval in the Bundestag.

2. The Big Four Reach Another Berlin Agreement (1971). In 1971 the Big Four powers reached a new Berlin agreement (a) providing for unimpeded road and rail traffic, and continued commercial and cultural ties, between West Berlin and West Germany, (b) permitting personal and business visits by West Berliners to East Germany, (c) accepting West German responsibility for, but limiting her political activity in, West Berlin, and (d) allowing Russia to open a consular office in West Berlin.

3. West Germany and East Germany "Normalize" Their Relations (1972). West Germany and East Germany signed a treaty that (a) confirmed the existence of two Germanys and established formal relations between them, (b) allowed additional visits by West Germans to relatives living in East Germany, (c) called for the two Germanys to cooperate in such areas as sports, environmental control, airlines, and technical knowledge, (d) proposed that both Germanys be admitted to the U.N., and (e) left unanswered the question of German reunification.

F. THE COLD WAR: IN THE MIDDLE EAST

EGYPT AND THE COMMUNIST WORLD (1955)

In 1955 Premier Gamal Abdel Nasser of Egypt, the major leader of Arab nationalism, failed to secure arms from the United States because he refused to pledge not to use them for aggression. Thereupon, he turned toward the Communist bloc. Egypt concluded an agreement exchanging Egyptian cotton for Communist planes, tanks, and other equipment. Also, Egypt received Communist technicians and military personnel. Nasser's speeches became increasingly friendly toward the Communist bloc and increasingly hostile toward the West.

EGYPT SEIZES THE SUEZ CANAL (1956)

To increase Egypt's irrigated land area and electric-power facilities, Nasser planned a high dam on the Nile River at *Aswan*. Nasser needed foreign aid, but his anti-Western attitude caused the United States to withdraw her offer of assistance. Thereupon, Nasser proclaimed the nationalization of the Suez Canal Company, owned by English and French stockholders. He explained that the profits from the operation of the canal would be used to build the Aswan Dam. (Subsequently, Nasser secured Russian financial and technical aid for construction of the dam.)

Nasser's nationalization of the Suez Canal was strongly opposed by England and France. These two countries depended upon the Suez Canal for trade with the Orient and especially for transporting oil from the Middle East to European markets. They therefore wanted to maintain control over the canal.

THE INVASION OF EGYPT (1956)

In 1956 Britain, France, and Israel invaded Egypt. Britain and France sought to regain control of the Suez Canal. Israel sought to end Egyptian guerrilla attacks and economic blockades. Most nations, including Russia and the United States, condemned the attack. Russia, seeking to extend her influence in the Arab world, denounced the invaders as aggressors and threatened to intervene with force on the side of Egypt. President Eisenhower stated that, although Nasser had been guilty of provocation, the invasion had been "taken in error." By taking a stand against the invasion, the United States outraged France and England but won the approval of other nations, especially the neutral Asian-African bloc, which had rallied to Egypt's support. The crisis ended when the U.N. General Assembly brought about the withdrawal of the invading forces (see pages 404-405).

LEBANON AND JORDAN REQUEST WESTERN AID (1958)

Egypt and Syria combined in 1958 to form the *United Arab Republic*. This union aroused Arab nationalists in other states. The pro-Western governments of Lebanon and Jordan feared uprisings by Nasser sympathizers seeking to merge their countries with the United Arab Republic. Lebanon and Jordan therefore requested and received military assistance from the United States and England respectively. President Eisenhower explained that America sought only to preserve the independence of Lebanon. Both the United Arab Republic and the Soviet Union denounced the Anglo-American actions as aggressive. When Lebanon and Jordan announced that the danger of revolution had diminished, the American and British troops were withdrawn. (See the Eisenhower Doctrine, page 425.)

ARAB-ISRAELI WAR (1967)

See page 303.

POSTWAR DEVELOPMENTS (SINCE 1967)

See pages 304-305.

FOREIGN INFLUENCE IN THE ARAB WORLD: AN OVERVIEW

1. Decline of British Influence. Once predominant in the Arab world, English power has dwindled greatly. England has granted independence to her Arab possessions, yielded the Suez Canal to Egypt, and lost influence over Jordan and Iraq. (For details, see pages 298-300.)

2. Factors Aiding Communist Influence. (*a*) The Arabs mistrust the West because of past British and French imperialism. (*b*) Russia supports the Arabs' anti-Israeli stand. (*c*) The Arab masses subsist close to the poverty level. Even in the oil-rich states, although the ruling classes have amassed great wealth, the people have scarcely benefited. (*d*) The Communist bloc has extended foreign aid to the Arab states, especially to Syria, Iraq, and Egypt. In 1960 Communist technicians, working with Egyptian labor, started on the construction of the Aswan High Dam. In 1970 it began full operations.

3. Factors Opposing Communist Influence. (*a*) Moslem leaders realize that Communism is antireligious. (*b*) Arab upper classes fear the loss of their wealth and power. (*c*) Within Egypt, the government suppresses the local Communist movement. (*d*) Arab nationalists seek the goal of Arab unity, not the Communist objective of international working class unity. (*e*) Oil-rich Arab states are economically tied to the West. They depend chiefly upon American and British oil companies to discover, refine, and market their oil.

4. American Policies. With the decline of British influence, the United States assumed a greater role in the Middle East. American goals are to reduce Communist influence, to improve living standards, to achieve permanent peace between the Arab states and Israel, and to win Arab friendship. The United States has extended technical assistance to several Arab nations, but our offer of more extensive aid under the Eisenhower Doctrine (see page 425) was welcomed only by Lebanon and Saudi Arabia. The United States supports the CENTO alliance (see pages 433-434), but no Arab state is a member. American efforts to achieve permanent peace between the Arab states and Israel have had few positive results. In 1967 America was blamed by the Arabs for their defeat in the war against Israel. In summary, American policies toward the Arab world have met with little success.

G. THE COLD WAR: IN THE FAR EAST

KOREA

1. Korea After World War II. In 1945 Korea (a colony of Japan since 1910) was divided at the 38th parallel: the North occupied by Russian troops, the South by American troops. Russia and the United States failed to agree regarding Korean reunification, and Russia defied U.N. attempts to unify the country by free elections. The Russians established a Communist government in North Korea and trained and equipped a powerful Korean army. In South Korea, U.N.-supervised elections established an independent anti-Communist government headed by President *Syngman Rhee.*

2. Communist Aggression Against South Korea (1950-1953). In June, 1950, without warning, North Korean Communist forces crossed the 38th parallel and invaded South Korea. The U.N. Security Council (with Russia absent) promptly recommended that U.N. members furnish military assistance to South Korea. The U.N. army consisted chiefly of American and South Korean units, with contingents from 15 other anti-Communist nations. It was headed by United States General Douglas MacArthur.

At first, the U.N. forces retreated before the Communist assault. After reinforcements arrived, General MacArthur launched a counterattack which drove the North Korean armies back across the 38th parallel and deep into North Korea close to the Manchurian border. In November, 1950, powerful Communist Chinese armies crossed into North Korea and attacked the U.N. forces, inflicting heavy losses and compelling MacArthur to retreat. By the summer of 1951 the battle line had become stabilized near the 38th parallel.

Meanwhile, the U.N. General Assembly voted (with opposition only from the Soviet bloc) to declare Red China guilty of aggression in Korea and to embargo the shipment of war goods to Red China.

3. The MacArthur-Truman Controversy. In April, 1951, President Truman, as commander-in-chief of the American armed forces, dismissed General MacArthur for insubordination. Truman charged that the general had repeatedly disregarded instructions to refrain from making foreign policy statements that criticized government policies.

The two men had disagreed sharply. MacArthur advocated carrying the war to Red China, especially Manchuria. He urged that the United States fight an all-out war to win complete victory over Communism in Asia. Truman feared that an invasion of Manchuria would lead to war with Russia and held that the United States must fight a limited war in Asia so as not to leave Western Europe—the key to American security—defenseless.

4. Truce in Korea (1953). Meeting mainly at Panmunjom, U.N. and Communist truce representatives took two years to reach an agreement for halting hostilities. The conference was long deadlocked regarding the return, or *repatriation*, of prisoners. The U.N. claimed that many of its prisoners did not want to return to their Communist homelands; the Communists insisted upon compulsory repatriation. Finally, the conference agreed that prisoners be given freedom of choice. (Eventually, two of every five prisoners held by the U.N. refused to return to Communist rule.)

The truce (*a*) was hailed by the U.N. as a victory against aggression, (*b*) was criticized by the South Korean government for failing to unify the country under anti-Communist leadership, and (*c*) was greeted by most Americans with relief. The Korean struggle cost the United States $18 billion, 103,000 wounded, and 33,000 killed.

5. Korean Developments Since the Truce

a. Continued American Interest. In support of South Korea, the United States extended considerable economic and military aid, kept 40,000 troops there, and signed a bilateral Mutual Defense Pact. In turn, South Korea sent a fighting force to aid the Americans in South Vietnam.

b. Continued Communist Interest. In 1961 Soviet Russia signed a defense treaty pledging to assist North Korea "with all forces and by every means." Communist China also made a similar defense pledge to North Korea.

c. Renewed Communist Pressures Upon South Korea and the United States. From 1967 to 1971, North Korea sent raiding parties into the South to commit sabotage and spread terror. For example, in 1968 North Korean commandos slipped into the Southern capital of Seoul to assassinate President Park, but they were captured before they could carry out their plans.

Also in 1968, North Korean patrol boats seized the American intelligence ship *Pueblo*. The Communists claimed that the *Pueblo* had intruded into North Korean waters on a criminal and hostile mission. The United States answered that the *Pueblo* had been in international waters and condemned the seizure.

To secure the release of the *Pueblo* crew, the United States negotiated with the North Koreans. After almost a year, the chief American negotiator signed a document confessing intrusion into North Korean waters, while publicly repudiating the confession, and North Korea freed the *Pueblo* crew.

In 1969 North Korean fighters shot down an unarmed American intelligence plane off the North Korean coast, killing its 31-man crew. North Korea charged that the plane had intruded into her air space. This charge was denied by President Nixon, who asserted that the United States would continue its reconnaissance flights and would protect its planes.

d. Korea Remains Divided. South Korea and North Korea are separated by a neutral zone near the 38th parallel. The Communists have rejected U.N. proposals to unify Korea by free elections, probably fearing that the South Korean government would win control over all Korea.

In 1972 in a startling agreement, South Korea and North Korea announced that they would (1) not provoke each other by armed attacks, (2) replace suspicion of each other by mutual trust, (3) help the Red Cross reunite divided Korean families, and (4) seek reunification by peaceful means.

e. Changes in Government. In 1960 South Korea was swept by anti-government riots protesting rigged elections, police terror, corruption, and autocratic rule. Syngman Rhee ended his 12-year presidency by resigning. In 1961 General *Chung Hee Park,* leading a military junta (council), seized power. Three times thereafter Park was elected President. He improved economic conditions and maintained a pro-American foreign policy.

In 1972 Park claimed that the reunification talks with North Korea required a "reform" of South Korea's political structure. He imposed martial law, dissolved the National Assembly, prohibited political activities, and imposed press censorship. Under these conditions, Park conducted and won a public referendum for a series of constitutional amendments enabling him, in effect, to remain President for life and to dominate the other branches of government. Park's actions were expressly disapproved by the United States, which felt that Park was attempting to assure his own continued political power and not to further a Korean dialogue on reunification.

COMMUNIST CHINA

1. **Border Dispute With India.** Despite India's recognition of Red China, Peking has been antagonistic toward this nation. In 1951 the Communists annexed Tibet and placed Chinese troops at the Indian border. In 1959 they

brutally suppressed a Tibetan revolt and invaded northern India in a border dispute. In 1962 the Chinese resumed their invasion of India. (See pages 453-454, and map, page 421.)

2. Relations With England. Communist China received British recognition and has not yet moved to drive the British from Hong Kong. Nevertheless, Red China has been basically hostile toward England.

3. Relations With the United States (to 1971). The Communists harshly treated American officials, missionaries, and businessmen caught in China during the civil war. They directly intervened in the Korean War and fought American troops. Communist China was most hostile toward the United States, claiming that "American imperialism" was China's unceasing enemy.

In opposition to Red China, the United States (a) recognized the Nationalist government on Taiwan as the legal government of China (b) refused to recognize the Peking regime, (c) successfully opposed Red China's bid for admission to the U.N., (d) maintained an embargo on trade with Communist China, and (e) signed *Mutual Defense Treaties* pledging to defend South Korea and Taiwan.

4. Dispute Over Taiwan (Formosa). The *United States* viewed Taiwan as a vital Pacific military base, the Nationalist armies as a dependable anti-Communist force, and the Chiang Kai-shek government as an ally. Consequently, the United States extended economic and military aid to Taiwan and vowed to defend Nationalist China according to a 1955 bilateral Mutual Defense Treaty.

White in The Akron Beacon Journal

"Never mind that . . . we may be invaded!"

At what is the Communist leader pointing? Will this answer satisfy the masses of Communist China?

Red China was determined to annex the island and destroy the Nationalist government. The Chinese Communists warned the United States that nothing would deter them from "liberating" Taiwan.

5. Red China Develops Nuclear Weapons. Having refused to sign the limited nuclear test ban treaty (see pages 460-461), China in 1964 set off her first atomic bomb. In 1967 China exploded a hydrogen bomb and in 1970 sent up its first earth satellite, indicating sufficient thrust power to launch ICBM's. China's speed in developing nuclear weapons and missiles created a major new world problem.

To meet the possibility of a Red Chinese missile attack by the mid-1970's, the United States began to construct an antiballistic missile (ABM) system. (See pages 464-465.)

6. Relations With Russia. See pages 420-422.

7. Recent Developments

   a. "Cultural Revolution" in China (1966-1969). See page 422.

   b. Stability and a New Foreign Policy. By 1970 China had ended the "cultural revolution" turmoil and returned to stability. Thereupon China turned from preoccupation with internal matters to a more active foreign role, especially steps to end a 20-year "freeze" in Chinese-American relations.

China resumed ambassadorial talks with the United States in Warsaw and arranged a visit by the American table tennis team. Their visit, Premier Chou stated, "opened a new page in the relations of the Chinese and American people." President Nixon, who had made several overtures to "normalize" relations, was pleased by these Chinese responses and relaxed our trade embargo on exporting nonstrategic goods to China. Thereafter Chou En-lai invited President Nixon to visit China. Nixon accepted, expressing the hope that this "will become a journey for peace."

   c. The Nixon Visit to China (1972). Accompanied by his national security adviser *Henry Kissinger* and Secretary of State *William Rogers*, President Nixon visited Communist China. Warmly received, Nixon spent a hectic week that included sight-seeing, entertainment, banquets, a meeting with Mao Tse-tung, and numerous negotiating sessions with Chou En-lai. The visit concluded with the issuance of a communiqué in which (1) the United States and China each stated their differences regarding Vietnam, Korea, and Taiwan, (2) the United States agreed that Taiwan is part of China, urged peaceful settlement of the Taiwan issue by the Chinese themselves, and agreed ultimately to withdraw all American forces from Taiwan (but did not renounce its mutual defense pact with Taiwan), and (3) the United States and China agreed to peaceful coexistence and to improve and expand their contacts.

This historic visit, analysts believed, may signify the following: (1) *for China*—realization that the major threat to its national interests comes from the Soviet Union rather than the United States, (2) *for the United States*—less fear that China seeks to export revolution and dominate Eastern Asia, and (3) *for both nations*—an attempt, after so many years of bitterness and hostility, to build a bridge of better understanding.

In 1973 the United States and China moved closer toward formal diplomatic relations by agreeing that each nation would establish a "liaison office" in the other's capital.

JAPAN

1. American Friendship for Japan: Since the Cold War

a. Reasons. (1) With the reforms introduced in Japan during the American occupation (see pages 315-316), the United States considers Japan as an Asian "bulwark of democracy." (2) Japan represents a counterbalance to the growth of Communist power in Asia—notably in China, North Korea, and North Vietnam. (3) Japan is a valuable ally because of her industrial capacity, her large manpower, and her strategic location off the Asian coast.

b. Evidences. The United States (1) treated Japan generously in the 1952 treaty of peace, (2) extended economic and military aid to Japan, (3) stationed American forces in Japan to maintain peace in the Far East, (4) developed close commercial and cultural ties with Japan, and (5) in 1972 returned the Ryukyu Islands, including Okinawa, to Japan but retained limited use of American military bases there.

2. Important Developments

a. Economic Recovery. Under her free-enterprise economic system, postwar Japan achieved remarkable economic growth. Industrial production regained prewar levels by 1951 and since then has more than tripled. Japan ranks among the world's top manufacturers of steel, synthetic fibers, electrical products, and cotton yarn; she is first in shipbuilding. Japan is the world's third greatest economic power, and her people enjoy a standard of living approaching that of Western Europe. However, with limited farmland and mineral resources, Japan must "export or die."

b. Trade With the United States. Japan provides the second largest market for American exports and, in turn, finds the United States her best customer. Americans purchase Japanese textiles, toys, cameras, radios, and television sets. These imports have harmed American manufacturers, who complain that Japanese wages are far below those paid American workers, protest this competition, and request adequate tariff protection. To quiet American complaints, Japan has voluntarily limited certain exports.

c. Issue of Trade With Red China. Before World War II, Japan traded extensively with China. Today Japan still views mainland China as a potentially large source of raw materials and a market for manufactured goods. During the Korean conflict, Japan cooperated with the free world in a strict trade embargo against China. Thereafter some Japanese leaders protested the embargo, arguing that trade with Red China is essential to Japan's economic well-being. In 1957 Japan somewhat eased restrictions, but trade between the two countries has not increased significantly.

d. Japanese-American Strains (Since 1971). (1) *Economic.* As the Nixon administration, in 1971-1973, twice devalued the American dollar, the Japanese yen was revalued upward. Japanese products would now cost American consumers more and Japanese leaders feared a decline in Japan's exports to the United States. Japan had achieved economic recovery, American spokesmen replied, and should now help America decrease its imports and increase its exports so as to correct its unfavorable balance of trade. (2) *Diplomatic.* Japanese leaders feared that President Nixon's 1972 visit to Red China might lead to Sino-American agreements harmful to Japanese interests. Japan was reassured by President Nixon that "no secret deals" had been made and that Japan remained a key American friend and ally. Thereafter Japan moved independently of the United States, establishing diplomatic relations with Red China and ending diplomatic (but not economic) ties with the Chinese Nationalist regime on Taiwan.

INDIA

1. Red Chinese Aggression Affects India. Until 1959 Prime Minister Nehru of India followed a policy of friendship for Communist China. Thereafter, Nehru's sympathy for Red China was severely shaken—if not destroyed—by Chinese actions in Tibet (India's northern neighbor) and on the Indian border.

a. Tibet. In 1959, after eight years of Chinese Communist occupation and rule, the Tibetan people revolted. The Chinese Communists (1) suppressed this revolt, taking many Tibetan lives, and (2) accused India of having aided the revolt—a charge which Nehru indignantly denied. Nehru condemned Red China's brutality in Tibet and granted asylum to thousands of Tibetan refugees, including that country's civil and spiritual head, the *Dalai Lama.* The Indian people were angered at Red China, especially because Tibet and India have a history of close commercial and spiritual ties.

b. The Indian Border. For many years China had disputed her boundary with India. In 1959, following the Tibetan revolt, Communist Chinese troops crossed India's northern frontier, attacked Indian border patrols, and occupied large areas of territory claimed by India. In 1962 the Chinese renewed their attack, overpowered Indian resistance, and occupied additional territory. Nehru warned that his country would resist Communist aggression. He requested and received military aid from England and the United States. (See map, page 421.)

2. American Relations With India. The United States hoped that India would side with the free world because India (*a*) in the words of former Prime Minister Nehru, is "firmly wedded to the democratic way of life," (*b*) is menaced by aggressive Chinese Communism, and (*c*) needs American aid to raise the living standard of her people. To date, India has received American economic aid worth billions of dollars.

In 1959, during the India-China border dispute, President Eisenhower Indian history. In 1962, when Chinese troops resumed their attack, President Kennedy airlifted weapons for India's border forces. In 1966 President

Bimrose in The Portland Oregonian

"Backbreaker."

What peacetime problems face India? What wartime problems?

Johnson authorized substantial wheat shipments to prevent starvation in parts of India.

In 1971, however, President Nixon condemned India for sending its troops into East Pakistan and forcibly gaining independence for Bangladesh.

3. Russian Relations With India. Russia seeks to win India to the Communist side or, at least, to keep her neutral in the cold war. (*a*) Russia granted loans for the development of India's heavy industry. Russia's economic aid to India, however, is far less than that extended by the United States. (*b*) In 1963, as the split between Russia and Red China widened, Soviet leaders voiced support for India in her border dispute with China. (*c*) In 1966 Russia hosted an Indian-Pakistani conference at the Soviet city of Tashkent in central Asia. India and Pakistan, having recently fought over Kashmir, agreed to observe the U.N. cease-fire, to restore diplomatic relations, and to settle disputes by peaceful means—all items constituting the *Declaration of Tashkent*. (*d*) In 1971 Russia signed a 20-year treaty of friendship with India; thereafter, as the Indian-Pakistani war started, Russia supported India by vetoing three Security Council resolutions for a cease-fire and withdrawal of Indian forces to their own soil. (See page 407.)

THE NATIONS OF INDO-CHINA

For a discussion of the cold war in Laos, Cambodia, and Vietnam, see pages 324-329.

THE SITUATION IN THE FAR EAST: AN OVERVIEW

1. Communist Strength. (*a*) Russia herself is a Far Eastern power, possessing Siberia and a long Pacific coastline. (*b*) Communists control the Chinese mainland, North Korea, North Vietnam, Mongolia, and Tibet. (*c*) The Communist bloc has extended economic aid to non-Communist countries in the Far East, especially India and Indonesia. (*d*) Communists have won the support of many Asians by promising to improve living standards and distribute land to the peasants.

2. Free World Strength. (*a*) The United States is geographically tied to the Far East, possessing a long Pacific coastline, the states of Alaska and Hawaii, and many central and western Pacific islands. (*b*) The United States has an extensive series of Far Eastern military alliances—SEATO, the Anzus Pact, and bilateral Mutual Defense Treaties with Nationalist China, Japan, the Philippines, and South Korea. (*c*) Among the friends of the free world, the United States counts Malaysia and South Vietnam. (*d*) The United States has extended considerable aid to neutral and pro-Western nations in the Far East.

3. Neutral Nations. Four important Far Eastern nations—Burma, Ceylon, India (all former British colonies), and Indonesia (a former Dutch colony) —desire neutrality in the cold war. All four nations have been suspicious of the West because of past Western imperialism. They have also been suspicious of Communist China because of her brutal suppression of the Tibetan revolt and her aggression on the Indian borders.

Burma, Ceylon, India, and Indonesia seek neutrality so that they may devote themselves to domestic problems, especially raising the living standards of their people.

4. India vs. China: Which Way for Asia? In her approach to domestic problems, India represents a major challenge to China. India has a democratic government with a mixed economy of private and public enterprise; Red China has a totalitarian government with a Communist economy. If India can successfully raise her standard of living, she will teach the people of underdeveloped nations an important lesson: that, to improve living conditions, it is *not* necessary to resort to Communist totalitarian methods.

H. THE COLD WAR: OVER CUBA

CUBAN-AMERICAN RELATIONS UNTIL 1959

The United States has long had a special interest in Cuba, located some 90 miles off the Florida coast. By the Spanish-American War in 1898, the United States compelled Spain to free Cuba. In 1901 the United States secured Cuban consent to the *Platt Amendment*. It made Cuba a virtual protectorate by granting the United States (1) the right to intervene militarily in Cuba to preserve Cuban independence and to protect life, liberty, and property, and (2) the naval base in eastern Cuba at *Guantanamo Bay*. In 1934, under the *Good Neighbor Policy*, the United States abrogated (abolished) the Platt Amendment but was permitted to retain the Guantanamo base under a lease that could be ended only by mutual consent.

Until 1959 the United States dominated the Cuban economy. American investors placed large sums in Cuban public utilities, iron and nickel mines, and sugar and tobacco plantations. The United States provided the chief market for Cuban agricultural and mineral exports, and was the chief source of Cuban imports of manufactured goods. Cuban vacation resorts attracted American tourists. The American people considered Cuba as a friend and ally.

THE CASTRO REGIME (SINCE 1959)

In 1959 *Fidel Castro,* on the promise to restore democracy, received widespread Cuban support and overthrew the corrupt military dictatorship of *Fulgencio Batista.* Once in power, Castro forbade elections, violated civil liberties, expropriated American investments without compensation, demanded the return of the Guantanamo naval base, denounced the United States as imperialist, negotiated trade agreements with Communist-bloc nations, and received Communist military equipment for his armed forces. In 1961 Castro admitted being a "Marxist-Leninist" and proclaimed his intention to transform Cuba into a Communist state.

THE UNITED STATES AND RUSSIA DISPUTE OVER CASTRO'S CUBA

The Soviet Union has given full support to the Castro regime. In 1960 Soviet Premier Khrushchev threatened to launch Russia's rockets against the United States if she intervened militarily in Cuba. For the United States, President Eisenhower warned that we would never permit "the establishment of a regime dominated by international Communism in the Western Hemisphere."

BAY OF PIGS INVASION (1961)

In 1961 American-trained Cuban exiles launched a small-scale invasion of Cuba at the *Bay of Pigs*. Although easily crushed by Castro's military forces, the invasion sparked a bitter argument between Russia and the United States. Premier Khrushchev demanded that the United States halt the "aggression" against Cuba and warned that the Soviet Union would assist Castro. In reply, President Kennedy proclaimed American admiration for the Cuban invaders and warned Russia that the United States would "protect this hemisphere against external aggression."

SOVIET MISSILE BASES IN CUBA (1962)

1. The Crisis. In October, 1962, President Kennedy charged that Russia secretly was constructing offensive bomber and missile bases in Cuba—a threat to the security of the Western Hemisphere. The President ordered a *quarantine* by American naval and air forces on shipments of offensive arms bound for Cuba. He demanded that Russia dismantle the Cuban missile bases and withdraw the bombers and missiles. Furthermore, the President warned that, if any nuclear missiles were launched from Cuba, America would reply with a full retaliatory blow against the Soviet Union. This firm United States stand won the support of our NATO and Latin American allies.

How would Russia respond? At first, Russia called the American charges false and labeled the American quarantine "piracy." Then, after several suspenseful days, Khrushchev agreed to dismantle the missile bases and withdraw the offensive weapons. In turn, Kennedy agreed to lift the quarantine and pledged that the United States would not invade Cuba. War was averted.

2. Reactions to the Settlement. (*a*) President Kennedy considered the settlement an honorable accord, not a victory. The President felt relieved that the Soviet offensive weapons were withdrawn in peace. However, the United States is aware that Cuba remains Communist, heavily armed with defensive weapons, and bolstered by Soviet military and technical personnel. (*b*) Premier Khrushchev called the settlement an example of his policy of "peaceful coexistence." He claimed that the American pledge not to invade Cuba had ended the need for the Soviet missile bases. (*c*) Castro resented the settlement and protested that Cuba had not been consulted. (*d*) Mao Tse-tung denounced the Soviet Union for betraying the Communist cause by yielding to the "imperialists." (*e*) Other nations hoped that, after this narrow escape from war, both Russia and the United States would undertake new efforts to improve East-West relations.

I. THE COLD WAR: SCIENTIFIC DEVELOPMENTS

1. Nuclear Energy

THE ISSUE OF INTERNATIONAL CONTROL

1. Nations Possessing Nuclear Power. The United States led the way in developing nuclear energy, exploding the first atomic bomb in 1945. (For a fuller discussion of nuclear energy, see pages 253-255.) Other nations followed: Russia in 1949, Great Britain in 1952, France in 1960, and Communist China in 1964. Today the United States and Russia each have more than enough nuclear weapons and delivery systems to cause unbelievable death and destruction.

Scientists believe that a number of other nations possess the technical know-how to become nuclear powers.

2. Failure to Achieve International Control

a.. The Baruch Plan. In 1946 the *United Nations Atomic Energy Commission* was instructed to prepare an effective system of international control of nuclear weapons. At that time, the United States held a monopoly over such weapons. Nevertheless, *Bernard Baruch,* America's representative to the Commission, proposed the following plan: The United States would destroy its atom bombs and share its technical know-how with other nations on condition (1) that an international authority be created to insure that atomic energy was being used only for peaceful purposes, and (2) that this international authority have the right of unlimited inspection and the power to punish violators without the restrictions of the Big Five veto in the U.N.

b. Russia Rejects the Baruch Plan. Russia violently criticized the Baruch Plan, especially the proposals (1) to eliminate the veto power, and (2) to provide unlimited inspection. Instead, Russia proposed an international treaty to outlaw the atom bomb, but made no provision for effective enforcement. The United States therefore rejected the Russian proposal as unrealistic.

When the Baruch Plan came before the Security Council in 1948, Russia prevented its passage by exercising her veto. The United Nations Atomic Energy Commission halted its work—a result probably desired by Russia. Unrestricted by any international control system, Russia exploded her own atom bomb in 1949, thereby ending the United States' monopoly. Thereafter, both nations continued to develop nuclear weapons and to explode a considerable number of bombs.

THE ATOMS-FOR-PEACE PLAN

1. Proposed by President Eisenhower. In 1953 President Eisenhower proposed that (*a*) the "have" nations in atomic energy contribute atomic materials and know-how to an international atomic pool, and (*b*) the "have not" nations draw upon this pool for the peaceful uses of atomic energy—in industry, agriculture, and medicine. The *atoms-for-peace* plan won the unanimous approval of the U.N. General Assembly.

2. The Plan Becomes a Reality. An *International Atomic Energy Agency* (*IAEA*) was empowered to (*a*) encourage nuclear research, the exchange of technical knowledge, the training of scientists, and the establishment of health and safety standards, (*b*) accept atomic materials from the "have" nations, and (*c*) exercise strict inspection over materials granted "have not" nations to ensure the use of these materials for peaceful, not military, purposes.

In 1957 the IAEA began operations from its permanent headquarters at Vienna, Austria. To date, the IAEA has had few requests for atomic fuel. Its main work has been in encouraging research, holding scientific meetings, and establishing safety regulations.

HALTING NUCLEAR BOMB TESTS

In the mid-1950's the people of the world were increasingly fearful of the rising level of radioactivity resulting from nuclear weapons testing. Their fears moved Russia, the United States, and Britain to seek agreement for halting nuclear tests. From 1958 to 1963 the three nuclear powers held a series of conferences at Geneva.

1. Conflicting Proposals for Halting Nuclear Tests. Russia proposed the immediate cessation of nuclear tests without any provision for enforcement. The Western powers rejected an unpoliced ban. Instead, they proposed a test ban coupled with a system of inspection and control. Russia vehemently rejected the Western proposal as a plot to establish spy rings on Soviet territory.

In 1961 the United States offered a treaty to ban nuclear tests that could be detected without on-site inspection, but to exclude underground blasts from the ban. These could be confused with earthquakes and could therefore not be detected from far away. The Russians rejected this proposal at first, but in 1963 Premier Khrushchev reversed Russia's position and indicated that the Soviet Union would accept a limited test ban.

2. Limited Nuclear Test Ban Treaty (1963)

a. Provisions. The Big Three powers (1) agreed not to conduct nuclear tests in the atmosphere, in space, and under water (these tests can be detected, by air-sampling and monitoring devices, without on-site inspection), (2) excluded underground tests from the ban but agreed to continue negotiations on this matter, (3) invited all other nations to sign the treaty, and (4) provided an escape clause permitting each signatory to withdraw from the treaty if it feels that the test ban jeopardizes its national interests.

b. France and Red China Abstain. Although about one hundred nations joined the Big Three in signing this treaty, two key nations did not. (1) *France.* President de Gaulle insisted that France continue atmospheric testing and develop her own H-bomb. De Gaulle wanted to restore France to world prestige and to end her dependence upon the United States' nuclear deterrent. (2) *Red China.* Chinese leaders denounced the treaty as an attempt by a few powers to monopolize nuclear weapons and called Russia's support of the treaty a capitulation to United States imperialism.

Pratt in The Sacramento Bee

"Color picket line."

Why are France and China picketing the Nuclear Test Ban Treaty? Are they thinking of the welfare of humanity or of national glory?

c. The United States Senate Ratifies the Treaty. The Senate ratified the treaty by an 80-19 vote. American ratification was quickly followed by Russian and British ratification. President Kennedy warned that the treaty did not eliminate the danger of war.

FURTHER EFFORTS TO HALT THE NUCLEAR ARMS RACE

1. Outlawing Nuclear Weapons in Outer Space. In 1966 the U.N. General Assembly approved a treaty on the peaceful uses of outer space. The treaty prohibited any nation from claiming sovereignty over the moon, and forbade nations to place nuclear arms or other weapons of mass destruction in outer space or on any heavenly body. The treaty, signed by more than 80 nations, became effective in 1967 after ratification by Britain, Russia, and the United States.

2. Outlawing the Spread of Nuclear Weapons. From 1963 to 1968, the *United Nations Disarmament Committee* of 18 nations—including Britain, the United States, and Russia—met at Geneva to draft a treaty outlawing the spread, or *proliferation,* of nuclear weapons. The Committee's work was based on the belief that the more nations gain nuclear weapons, the more difficult it will be to prevent their accidental or deliberate use. In 1968 the United States and Russia agreed upon a draft treaty which provided that (*a*) nations without nuclear weapons agree not to develop such weapons and that they accept a system of inspection, administered by the International Atomic Energy Agency, to ascertain that their nuclear activities are not being diverted from peaceful to military purposes, (*b*) the nuclear powers help other nations develop peaceful uses of atomic energy, and (*c*) the nuclear powers seek further agreements to halt the arms race.

The *Nuclear Non-Proliferation Treaty* was overwhelmingly approved by the U.N. General Assembly. However, some nations without nuclear weapons expressed reluctance to sign the treaty. These reluctant nations included Australia, India, Israel, Japan, and West Germany. They were being asked to forgo atomic weapons, which could be vital to national defense. Further, they feared that the treaty would inhibit their development of peaceful atomic energy. To encourage nations without nuclear weapons to sign, America, Russia, and Britain each pledged to assist any signatory nation attacked by an aggressor using nuclear weapons.

In 1970 the treaty, ratified by 40 nations without nuclear weapons plus Britain, the United States, and Russia, went into effect.

3. Outlawing Nuclear Weapons on the Seabed. In 1970 the U.N. General Assembly overwhelmingly approved a treaty prohibiting any nation from placing nuclear weapons on the seabed outside its 12-mile limit. In 1972 this treaty, signed by over 85 nations, went into effect.

4. Strategic Arms Limitation Talks (SALT). See pages 464-465.

2. Missiles and Satellites

MISSILE DEVELOPMENTS

Since World War II the United States and Russia have developed rocket-propelled missiles capable of delivering conventional or nuclear warheads. The smallest are tactical missiles—short-range, low-yield—used, for example, as battlefield artillery for close support of troops. The most significant missiles are the *intermediate range ballistic missile (IRBM)*, the *intercontinental ballistic missile (ICBM)*, and the *antiballistic missile (ABM)*.

1. Intermediate Range Ballistic Missile (IRBM). These missiles soar into space and then descend to earth hitting a target up to 2,500 miles away from the launching site. The United States has relied chiefly on the *Polaris* and on its newer version, the *Poseidon*. Both missiles can be launched from a surface ship or from a submerged submarine. American missile-carrying submarines, patrolling Norwegian and Mediterranean waters, are close enough to the Soviet Union to expose Russia's major military targets to IRBM attack.

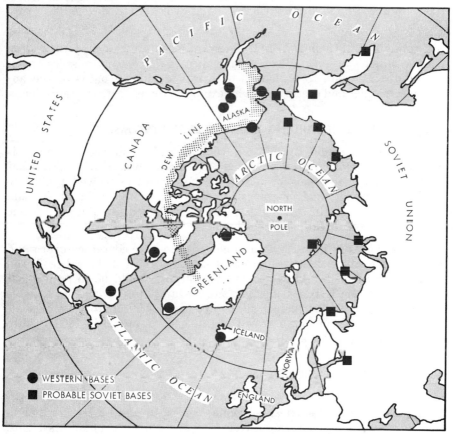

Western and Soviet Bases Facing the North Polar Region

Russia also has IRBM's ready for use (*a*) from land-based sites against our European allies, and (*b*) from missile-carrying submarines in the North Atlantic against major American targets.

2. Intercontinental Ballistic Missile (ICBM). These missiles soar into space, travel at a speed up to 20,000 miles per hour, and descend to earth, hitting a target over 6,000 miles away from the launching site. The earliest ICBM's carried a single warhead. More recent models are capable of carrying multiple warheads, with each warhead aimed at a different target. These are named *multiple individually targetable reentry vehicles* (*MIRV's*).

The ICBM has been called the "ultimate weapon" because its speed and its nuclear explosive power make any defense against it extremely difficult. The United States relies chiefly on the solid-fuel *Minuteman*. Russia also has ICBM's, which can be launched from sites in the Soviet Union to attack targets in the United States. China too is working to develop her own ICBM's.

3. Antiballistic Missile (ABM). These missiles are designed to destroy offensive missiles in space. When radar indicates that enemy missiles are en route, the ABM's are to be launched to explode in the paths of the approaching missiles and destroy them by explosive force, heat, and radiation.

CONSIDERATIONS REGARDING ABM DEFENSE SYSTEMS

1. In the Soviet Union. By 1967 the Russians had begun installing an antiballistic missile system around Moscow. Western observers surmised that Russian ABM's were meant for defense against American as well as Chinese missiles. The Soviets had long considered the United States as their main enemy. However, as Russo-Chinese relations worsened, the Soviets became concerned with the threat posed by China.

2. American ABM Plans. American officials too were concerned over rapid Chinese strides in nuclear weapons and missiles. In 1969 President Nixon proposed the *Safeguard* ABM system. Its purpose would be to protect not our cities, but our ICBM launching sites, against any Soviet or Chinese initial attack, or first strike, so as to preserve our retaliatory, or second-strike, capacity. Nixon won narrow Congressional approval in 1969-1970 to begin work on four ABM sites.

TWO SALT ACCORDS—SIGNED IN 1972

After almost three years of *Strategic Arms Limitation Talks* (*SALT*), held alternately at Helsinki and Vienna, American and Soviet negotiators completed two accords covering certain aspects of nuclear missiles systems. The accords, signed at the Moscow summit meeting by President Nixon and Communist party leader Brezhnev, provided as follows:

1. The Treaty on ABM's. The United States and the Soviet Union (a) agreed to protect by ABM defense systems only two sites each, (b) defined the two sites to be protected as each nation's capital and one ICBM launching site each, (c) accepted a ceiling of 200 ABM launchers per nation—100 for each site, (d) pledged not to build nationwide ABM defense systems, and (e) provided that the treaty be of unlimited duration but allowed each nation, upon six months notice, to withdraw from the treaty if "extraordinary events . . . have jeopardized its supreme interests."

This treaty, observers pointed out, (a) contains a withdrawal clause in apprehension of future Chinese developments and (b) reflects the belief that the United States and the Soviet Union each have the ability to absorb a "first strike" and to retaliate powerfully upon the other nation, thereby making the outbreak of a nuclear war between them improbable. This treaty was overwhelmingly ratified by the United States Senate.

2. The Interim Agreement on Offensive Missiles. The United States and the Soviet Union "froze" at the current level their offensive-missile systems: (a) for the United States—1,054 land-launched ICBM's and 656 submarine-launched missiles, and (b) for the Soviet Union—1,618 land-launched ICBM's and 710 submarine-launched missiles. This agreement was to last for five years unless replaced sooner by a more comprehensive accord.

This agreement on offensive missiles (a) did *not* cover the number of warheads per missile, thereby giving the United States with its advanced MIRV technology the advantage of 5,700 warheads as compared to 2,500 for the Soviet Union, (b) did *not* cover the explosive power of each warhead, thereby giving the Soviet Union with its larger warheads a 3 to 1 lead in explosive power over the United States, (c) did *not* cover the number of long-range bombers capable of delivering nuclear bombs, thereby giving the United States a lead of 460 strategic bombers to 140 for the Soviet Union, (d) did *not* limit the construction of strategic bombers and did *not* prevent the replacement of existing missiles and submarines by more destructive models, and (e) did *not* provide for on-site inspection to prevent violations although both nations pledged not to interfere with other methods of verification.

Supporters of the interim agreement pointed out that it (a) reflects the opinion that both nations are roughly equal in offensive missile power, (b) may encourage a feeling of friendship and cooperation between the two nations, and therefore (c) may arrest the arms race.

Critics of the interim agreement pointed out that it (a) will not reduce the current offensive missile arsenals, (b) will shift the arms race from competition in missile numbers to competition in technology and in areas not covered by its provisions, and therefore (c) will make highly improbable any significant reduction in arms defense spending.

Although the offensive missiles accord was an executive agreement and therefore did not require ratification, it was submitted by Nixon to both houses of Congress and received an overwhelming "concurrence."

"From the sublime to the ridiculous."

How do Soviet results in space compare with results in
agriculture? How do you explain the difference?

RUSSIA LAUNCHES HER SPUTNIKS

The *International Geophysical Year* (1957-1958) was an international cooperative effort to increase man's knowledge of his physical environment. As part of the program, the United States and Soviet Russia each announced plans to orbit rocket-launched satellites equipped with recording instruments. The Soviet Union was first to fulfill this promise. In 1957 Russian scientists placed into orbit around the earth the first man-made satellite, the 184-pound *Sputnik I,* and later the 1,120-pound *Sputnik II.*

EFFECT OF RUSSIA'S SATELLITES UPON THE UNITED STATES

Russia's initial lead in the space race perturbed the American people. Why had the United States fallen behind? (1) As a dictatorship, the Russian government was able to concentrate all necessary resources toward achieving its space goals. As a democracy, the United States had to heed demands for other goals, such as more consumer goods and lower taxes. (2) Soviet education, critics said, was ahead of that in the United States in science, mathematics, and technical subjects. (3) The Soviets channeled their ablest students into the fields of science, mathematics, and engineering by offering incentives of higher pay and community approval. In the United States, capable students had a choice of many other lucrative fields.

THE UNITED STATES SPEEDS UP ITS SPACE PROGRAM

1. Congress approved additional funds for missile and satellite research, development, and production.

2. Congress passed the *National Defense Education Act* of 1958 to strengthen American defenses by improving education. The act provided federal funds to be used for (*a*) grants to states to purchase textbooks and equipment for the teaching of science, mathematics, and foreign languages, and (*b*) loans and fellowships to aid college students interested in technical subjects and in teaching. This act has been extended several times.

3. Congress also established a new agency to direct nonmilitary space projects—the *National Aeronautics and Space Administration* (*NASA*).

INITIAL AMERICAN SPACE FLIGHTS

In 1958, from *Cape Canaveral* (now called *Cape Kennedy*), Florida, the United States orbited its first satellite, the 18-pound *Explorer 1*, and then the 3-pound *Vanguard 1* and the 18-pound *Explorer 3*. Russian Premier Khrushchev gibed at the American satellites, calling them "grapefruits" in relation to the much larger Russian Sputniks.

MAJOR SOVIET EFFORTS IN SPACE

1. Unmanned Flights

a. Around the Earth. Starting in 1962 the Soviets have launched a considerable number of flights in their *Cosmos* series. Cosmos satellites have many scientific and military purposes.

In 1967 Soviet scientists used radio control from earth to direct two spacecraft, *Cosmos 186* and *Cosmos 188*, into docking, then into flying together, and finally into resuming their separate orbits. The Soviets hailed this feat as a step toward the "creation in orbit of big scientific space stations." In 1968 *Cosmos 218* probably tested a system of delivering bombs from space. In 1970 the Soviets launched over 70 Cosmos flights.

b. To the Moon. In 1959 *Luna 1* passed within 5,000 miles of the moon; *Luna 2* hit the moon's surface; *Luna 3* sent back pictures of the previously unseen, or dark, side of the moon. In 1966 *Luna 9* achieved the first "soft landing" on the moon and transmitted about 30 pictures. In 1970 *Luna 16* landed on the moon, scooped up 3½ ounces of lunar soil and returned with this cargo to earth. *Luna 17*, which also landed on the moon, carried a self-propelled vehicle, *Lunokhod 1*. It roamed short distances on the lunar surface, collecting and analyzing lunar soil, and relayed the data back to earth. In 1972 *Luna 20* returned to earth with a cargo of moon rocks. (These Soviet unmanned moon explorations contrasted with the American manned moon landings and raised the issue of which method was more advantageous in terms of costs and results.)

   c. To the Planets. (1) *Mars.* Two Soviet spaceships to Mars, launched in 1962 and 1964, failed to transmit any data about that planet back to earth. In 1971 the *Mars 3* spaceship parachuted to the surface of Mars a capsule which transmitted data regarding the temperature, atmosphere, and surface material of Mars. (2) *Venus.* In 1961 the Soviets launched a Venus probe, but the craft sent back no signals. In 1966 *Venus 3* completed a 106-day, 175-million-mile trip by crashing onto the planet Venus. In 1967 *Venus 4* neared Venus and parachuted an instrumented capsule toward the planet's surface. The capsule radioed back data regarding the temperature, pressure, and composition of the atmosphere of Venus. From 1969 to 1972 Venus probes *5* through *8* gathered further scientific data about Venus.

   2. Manned Flights. In 1961 the Soviets achieved a historic first in space flights. *Vostok 1* orbited the earth once, carrying the world's first cosmonaut, *Yuri Gagarin.* In 1964 *Voskhod 1,* which carried three men on 16 orbits of the earth, became history's first multipassenger space capsule. In 1965 *Voskhod 2,* which carried a two-man crew and completed 17 orbits of the earth, achieved another first. *Aleksei Leonov,* dressed in a special spacesuit and tied to a safety line, left the craft and floated in space.

   In 1967 *Soyuz 1,* on its return to earth, crashed when its parachute lines snarled, and the fall killed cosmonaut *Vladimir Komarov.* His death was the first known casualty on any space flight. In 1968 *Soyuz 3* achieved a rendezvous with an unmanned spacecraft. In 1969 *Soyuz 4* and *Soyuz 5* docked in space, and two cosmonauts transferred from one craft to the other; later three *Soyuz* ships carrying seven cosmonauts orbited the earth at the same time. In 1970 *Soyuz 9,* carrying two cosmonauts, remained in orbit for almost 18 days.

   In 1971 the Soviets orbited the first unmanned space station, the huge *Salyut,* and sent three cosmonauts in *Soyuz 11* to live in the station and perform varied scientific experiments. The men set a new space endurance record—almost 24 days. Returning to earth, their Soyuz capsule made a normal landing, but the three men were found dead. A Soviet investigation concluded that the deaths were due to a rapid drop in the capsule's air pressure but stated that the ship's structure was undamaged. Unofficially, observers reasoned that the cosmonauts had failed to close the capsule's hatch tightly.

MAJOR AMERICAN EFFORTS IN SPACE

1. Unmanned Flights

a. Around the Earth. (1) Starting in 1958, the United States launched a number of flights in its *Explorer* series. Explorer satellites have increased our scientific knowledge of space regarding meteors, radiation, and magnetic fields. (2) Beginning in 1960, the United States launched several *Transit* navigational satellites designed to help airplane and ship pilots locate their position. (3) In 1960 *Echo 1* relayed radio messages throughout the world. In 1962 *Telstar 1*, a privately developed communications satellite, transmitted television signals between the United States and Western Europe. In 1965 *Early Bird*, launched for the private Communications Satellite Corporation (Comsat), transmitted telecommunications signals across the North Atlantic. In 1970 three *Intelsat* satellites, launched for Comsat, became part of a global telecommunications network. (4) From 1960 to 1965 the United States launched ten *Tiros* satellites to gather data about the weather. In 1966 the United States launched several improved Tiros-type weather satellites, the *ESSA* series, and in 1970 *Nimbus 4*, an advanced weather satellite. (5) In 1972 the United States launched its first *Earth Resources Technology Satellite—ERTS—*to photograph continuously the earth's surface, thereby providing data for checking food crops, locating mineral deposits, protecting the environment, and monitoring glaciers and icebergs.

b. To the Moon. In 1962 the United States hit the moon's surface with *Ranger 4.* In 1964 *Ranger 7*, before striking the moon, transmitted thousands of detailed pictures of the lunar surface. In 1966 *Surveyor 1* achieved a "soft landing" on the moon and sent back over ten thousand pictures; also *Lunar Orbiters 1* and *2* orbited the moon and provided a photographic survey of the moon's surface.

c. To the Planets. (1) *Mars.* In 1964 *Mariner 4* began a successful 325-million-mile flight to Mars. It transmitted some 20 pictures of the Martian surface. In 1969 *Mariner 6* and *Mariner 7* flew past Mars and sent back pictures and scientific data. In 1971 *Mariner 9* went into orbit about Mars and sent back excellent pictures of the planet's surface. (2) *Venus.* In 1962 *Mariner 2* traveled 180 million miles in 3½ months to within 21,000 miles of Venus and sent back much scientific data. It reported the surface temperature of Venus to be 800 degrees Fahrenheit, too hot for life as we know it. In 1967 *Mariner 5* passed within 2,500 miles of Venus and radioed back data regarding the planet's atmosphere. (3) *Jupiter.* In 1972 *Pioneer 10* began a 21-month journey that would bring it, by December 1973, near the distant planet Jupiter. This spacecraft is expected to provide data regarding Jupiter and the outer fringes of our solar system. Thereafter Pioneer 10 will leave our solar system. It carries a pictorial plate which, if seen by scientifically minded inhabitants of another star system, would enable them to figure out when the spacecraft was launched, from where, and by what kind of beings.

2. Manned Flights

a. Project Mercury (1961-1963). In 1961 *Freedom 7* carried *Alan Shepard* on a suborbital flight, rising into outer space and then falling back to earth without going into orbit. In 1962 *Friendship 7* circled the earth three times, carrying America's first orbiting astronaut, *John Glenn.* Compared with the first Russian manned orbital flight, Glenn's spacecraft weighed 60 percent less, his rocket thrust power was 50 percent less, and his flight took place 10 months later.

Eric in The Atlanta Journal

"War of the words."

Lunacy or necessity—what is your opinion?

In 1963 Project Mercury came to an end. It had inaugurated America's program of manned space flights by successfully launching two suborbital and four orbital flights, all of single-passenger vehicles.

b. Project Gemini (1964-1966). In 1965 *Gemini 3,* the world's first maneuverable manned spacecraft, completed 3 orbits, carrying America's first two-man space team. *Gemini 4* achieved the first space walk by an American. *Gemini 7,* also carrying two astronauts, proved man's ability to endure space flight for 14 days—considered the time necessary for a flight to the moon and back. *Gemini 6* was maneuvered to within a few feet of Gemini 7, and the two spacecraft flew in close formation for four hours— man's first space *rendezvous* (meeting). In 1966 *Gemini 8* locked onto an *Agena* vehicle, achieving man's first *docking* in space.

In 1966 Project Gemini came to an end. It had orbited ten two-man spacecraft, and American astronauts had practiced rendezvousing, docking, and space-walking.

c. Project Apollo (1967-1972). Project Apollo orbited still larger spacecraft and in 1969 sent the first space teams to the moon and back.

(1) *Preliminary Flights. Apollo 8,* launched by the mighty *Saturn 5* rocket, carried three astronauts across 240,000 miles of space to within 70 miles of the moon's surface. After 10 orbital flights around the moon, Apollo 8 returned to earth. *Apollo 10* successfully tested, in the vicinity of the moon, the capability of the lunar module, or landing craft, to leave and then return to the command or "mother" ship.

(2) *Moon Landings.* In 1969 *Apollo 11* achieved mankind's first landing on the moon. While *Michael Collins* orbited the moon in the "mother" ship *Columbia, Neil Armstrong* and *Edwin Aldrin* descended in the lunar module *Eagle* to the moon's surface. Armstrong, the first man to set foot on the moon, spoke the historic words "That's one small step for a man, one giant leap for mankind." The two astronauts gathered rock samples, set up scientific experiments, stationed a plaque saying "we came in peace for all mankind," and then ascended to the "mother" ship. The three men then returned safely to earth. *Apollo 12* repeated the moon-landing triumph.

In 1970 *Apollo 13* ruptured an oxygen tank en route to the moon, but the three astronauts returned safely to earth in their crippled ship. (Thereafter American and Russian scientists reached an agreement to develop compatible systems for rendezvous and docking so that, in case of trouble, spacemen could help each other regardless of country.) In 1971 *Apollo 14* completed a successful moon-landing trip. Its astronauts positioned scientific instruments, performed intricate tests on the moon's surface, and brought back large quantities of moon rocks. *Apollo 15* astronauts traveled the moon's surface in an electric car. In 1972 *Apollo 16* astronauts explored the moon's mountainous highlands. *Apollo 17* astronauts concluded the program with, in

NASA's words, "the last, longest, and most successful of seven manned lunar landing missions."

The entire manned flight program, from 1961 to 1972, cost the nation $25 billion.

3. Future Space Goals. President Nixon received the report of a special task group proposing post-Apollo space programs. The President endorsed proposals for an unmanned "grand tour" of the "outer," or more distant, planets by the late 1970's and for a manned landing on Mars by the mid-1980's. Nixon asserted that in the making of space history "this nation means to play a major role."

Meanwhile NASA, faced with a leveling-off of federal funds after 5 years of cutbacks, slowed work on post-Apollo space projects. As a result, many scientific and technical workers were dismissed, and experienced space research and production teams were broken up. Nevertheless, NASA planned to launch *Skylab*, a manned earth-orbiting scientific laboratory, and to develop a reusable space shuttle for carrying men and supplies between earth and the space station.

J. THE COLD WAR: MAJOR DIPLOMATIC DEVELOPMENTS

SUMMIT MEETING OF 1955

No meeting between top Communist and Western leaders took place from the time of the Potsdam Conference (1945) until after Stalin's death (1953). The new leaders of Russia urged a summit meeting, claiming that it would ease international tensions. In 1955, after much preparation, the United States, England, France, and Russia held a "meeting of the heads of government" at Geneva. Their top leaders discussed East-West problems in a calm, friendly atmosphere but reached no settlements. Many persons hailed this conference for fostering a new spirit of international understanding. President Eisenhower, however, warned that only history could tell the true worth of the conference. Subsequent events indicated that the 1955 summit meeting had failed to resolve any cold war problems.

STEPS TOWARD A NEW SUMMIT MEETING

After launching her Sputniks in 1957, Russia proposed a "top-level meeting of representatives of capitalist and socialist countries" to settle all important East-West issues. President Eisenhower and Secretary of State John Foster Dulles were skeptical, recalling that the 1955 conference had solved no problems but had served the Russians in their propaganda that the Communists desired peace. After Khrushchev visited the United States and met with President Eisenhower in 1959, the Western Big Three and the Soviet Premier agreed to a 1960 summit conference in Paris.

SUMMIT MEETING OF 1960: A FIASCO

1. Spying and the Summit Meeting. Two weeks before the meeting, a U-2 (an unarmed, high-altitude American reconnaissance plane) was brought down deep inside Russian territory. The United States considered U-2 flights as essential for protection against surprise missile attack and to counterbalance the extensive Communist espionage system throughout the free world. Furthermore, such American flights had been known to Russian officials, but they had not previously protested.

2. Collapse of the Summit Meeting. Now Soviet Premier Khrushchev seized upon the U-2 incident for propaganda. He charged the United States with an "act of aggression" and threatened America's allies with Soviet rocket attacks upon bases used for spy plane flights. He rejected the American reply that the flight had no aggressive intent.

In this suddenly embittered atmosphere, the Big Four leaders arrived at Paris. Immediately, Khrushchev announced that he would not participate in the meeting unless the United States would (a) end all U-2 flights over Russia, (b) admit that past flights had been acts of aggression and would apologize for them, and (c) punish those persons responsible for the flights. President Eisenhower replied that the flights had been suspended, but he rejected the other terms. Macmillan and de Gaulle pleaded with Khrushchev not to wreck the summit meeting, but Khrushchev remained adamant. He publicly vilified Eisenhower, withdrew an invitation for Eisenhower to visit the Soviet Union, and hurled insults at the United States. The summit meeting was dead—even before it had started.

3. After the Summit Meeting. Although further strained, East-West relations underwent no fundamental change. President Eisenhower stated that, despite the collapse of the summit meeting, the United States would seek businesslike dealings with the Soviet Union on all major issues. Premier Khrushchev reaffirmed that his foreign policy toward non-Communist nations, including the United States, remained "peaceful coexistence."

NIXON'S JOURNEY TO MOSCOW (1972)

In early 1972 Soviet-American tensions rose over Vietnam, as North Vietnamese forces with heavy Soviet equipment massively attacked the South and as Americans mined North Vietnamese harbors to keep out Soviet supply ships. Nevertheless, as per schedule, President Nixon journeyed to Moscow to a summit meeting with Soviet Premier Kosygin and party chief

Brezhnev. Nixon received a restrained but correct welcome and his time was occupied chiefly with businesslike negotiations. Nixon and the Soviet leaders signed a number of significant accords: (1) *on space*—to cooperate in 1975 in a joint Soviet-American docking and flight of manned spacecraft, (2) *on health*—to coordinate Soviet-American research on cancer, heart disease, and public health, (3) *on incidents at sea*—to set rules so that Soviet and American naval vessels operating near each other will avoid collisions, (4) *on environment and technology*—to cooperate in the study of pollution problems and in other scientific research, (5) *on trade*—to establish a joint commission to resolve trade problems so as to increase Soviet-American trade, and (6) *on nuclear arms*—to limit ABM sites and "freeze" current offensive missile arsenals. Both the United States and Russia, despite their sharp disagreements on many world problems, seemed determined to improve their relationship and to prevent nuclear war.

K. RECENT TRENDS IN WORLD AFFAIRS: AN OVERVIEW

EMERGENCE OF THE AFRO-ASIAN NATIONS

Since World War II some 70 independent nations have arisen in Africa and Asia out of the former colonial empires of the Western powers. Their emergence has had a significant impact upon world affairs.

1. Political. The emergence of the new nations presented a challenge to both the Soviet Union and the Western world. Both have worked hard to win and retain the friendship of the Afro-Asians. The new nations have achieved special importance in the U.N., where, together with previously independent Afro-Asian nations, they form a bloc totaling a majority of U.N. membership. They have the votes necessary to prevent passage of any General Assembly resolution of which they disapprove. They oppose colonialism and demand support for this policy from both the Communist and the Western blocs. In the cold war, the Afro-Asian nations are predominantly neutralist. They seek to moderate tensions between the Communist and Western worlds and to prevent the outbreak of a nuclear holocaust.

2. Economic. The Afro-Asian nations have primitive economies and face widespread poverty. They blame these conditions on their dependent economic status as suppliers of raw materials and buyers of manufactured goods; they desire to achieve more balanced economies by developing natural resources, improving agriculture, and, above all, building industry. They are receiving economic and technical assistance through the U.N. Also, the Western bloc, the Russian bloc, and Communist China are engaged in a three-way competition to promote trade with the Afro-Asian nations and to improve their economies.

FRENCH PLANS FOR WESTERN EUROPE AS A "THIRD FORCE"

Following World War II Western Europe depended greatly upon the United States, and welcomed American economic aid under the Marshall Plan and American military assistance through NATO. Today Western Europe has recovered economically, has moved toward internal unity through the Common Market, and is far less dependent upon the United States. Europe's progress has cheered American leaders, who seek an equal partnership between the United States and an integrated Europe. This partnership, they believe, will prove of mutual benefit economically and will assure adequate military defense for the free world.

However, President de Gaulle of France held a conflicting viewpoint. De Gaulle, a nationalist, envisioned Europe as a French-led "third force," opposed to the Soviet Union and allied to, but independent of, the "Anglo-Saxon" powers: England and the United States. To achieve his goal of "European independence," de Gaulle (1) vetoed English membership in the Common Market, claiming that it would lead to American domination, (2) rejected American proposals for a multinational nuclear force in NATO and insisted upon building an independent French nuclear deterrent, and (3) opposed American policy in the Far East by recognizing Red China and urging neutrality for South Vietnam.

De Gaulle's plans for a European "third force" met with no support from the other Western European governments. The other Common Market members deplored his veto of English membership, and the British accused him of trying to dominate Europe. The other NATO members favored the general idea of European nuclear defense through NATO. The United States

Pierre in Aux Ecoutes, Paris

"Your universal key only seems to be able to take things apart."

Why did American and British statesmen feel that de Gaulle could only "take things apart"? What did he want to put together?

was disappointed in French foreign policy under de Gaulle and fearful of its effect upon free world unity.

Nevertheless, de Gaulle believed that his dream of a "third force" would yet come true. As the nations of Western Europe continue their close economic cooperation, they may also achieve some form of political union. This union would be equal in power to the United States and be able to assert considerable independence in its foreign policy.

STRAINS IN THE COMMUNIST WORLD

Under Stalin, the Soviet Union demanded conformity, and even subservience, from the nations in the Communist bloc. When Tito pursued national Communism for Yugoslavia, Stalin condemned him as a renegade and sought unsuccessfully to crush him. Since Stalin's death, the Soviet Union conceded that there are many roads to Communism, revived her friendship for Yugoslavia, and allowed Gomulka, a Titoist, to remain in power in Poland. The Soviet Union also reluctantly permitted its European satellites to exhibit considerable independence in economic matters. For example, Rumania defied COMECON plans that she remain a producer of raw mate-

Ellinwood in The Arizona Daily Star, Tucson

"Having trouble keeping them in orbit."

What events have affected relations between Russia and her European satellites? How? Why?

rials and insisted upon industrialization. However, the Soviet Union has resorted to military force and invaded two of its satellites: Hungary in 1956 to suppress an anti-Russian uprising, and Czechoslovakia in 1968 to halt a Communist-led "liberalization" program.

The greatest blow to Communist unity resulted from the split, which had become open and bitter by 1963, between the two giants of the Red bloc, the Soviet Union and China. The Chinese have challenged Russian leadership of the world Communist movement and have proposed militancy against the West in place of Khrushchev's policy of "peaceful coexistence."

For the free world, the split in the Communist bloc represents both a danger and an opportunity. The *danger* is that Russia will be forced to adopt a more militant position in order to compete with the Chinese Communists. The *opportunity* is that Russia will seek to prove the success of "peaceful coexistence" by easing world tensions.

With the improvement of Chinese-American relations, evidenced by President Nixon's 1972 visit to China, the Soviet Union became alarmed. Although Nixon had stated that his visit "is not directed against any other nation," the Russians feared the possibility of a Chinese-American understanding or alliance aimed at them. They consequently took steps to assure the military security of their long border with China and also to improve Russian-American relations.

IMPROVEMENT IN RUSSIAN-AMERICAN RELATIONS

Since the beginning of the cold war, Russian-American relations have varied from comparative calm to great tension. Relations *deteriorated* during the Berlin blockade of 1948-1949 and the Korean War of 1950-1953. They *improved* with the Austrian Peace Treaty in 1955, the summit conference of 1955, the inauguration of scientific and cultural exchange programs in 1958, and Khrushchev's visit to the United States in 1959. They *deteriorated* with the U-2 incident and the summit conference of 1960, the building of the Berlin Wall in 1961, and the Cuban missile crisis of 1962.

Following the peaceful settlement of the Cuban crisis and the deepening of the Soviet-Chinese split, Russian-American relations took a turn for the better.

1. Limited Nuclear Test Ban Treaty. In 1963 the United States and Russia agreed to a ban on all but underground nuclear tests. This was the first agreement to emerge from 18 years of East-West disarmament negotiations. It was followed in 1964 by announcements, in the United States and the Soviet Union, of cutbacks in their production of nuclear explosive materials.

2. Hot Line. In 1963 Russia and the United States established a "hot line" emergency communications link between Washington and Moscow to reduce the risk of war by blunder or miscalculation.

3. Wheat Sale. With Russia suffering from a poor grain harvest in 1963 and again in 1972, the United States sold substantial quantities of wheat to the Soviet Union.

4. Cultural and Scientific Exchanges. The two nations have encouraged "people to people" contacts. Reciprocal visits have been made by athletes, scholars, concert artists, orchestras, ballet groups, writers, and scientists.

5. Consular Treaty. In 1964 the United States and the Soviet Union negotiated their first bilateral treaty. It (*a*) permitted negotiations for establishing consulates outside of Washington and Moscow, (*b*) granted diplomatic immunity to consular officials, and (*c*) required that consular officials be informed of and granted access to any of their country's citizens placed under arrest. This treaty was ratified by both nations.

6. Nuclear Non-Proliferation Treaty. In 1968 the United States and the Soviet Union agreed on a draft treaty to outlaw the spread of nuclear weapons. Both powers hoped that the treaty would reduce the danger of nuclear war. In 1970 the treaty went into effect.

Justus in The Minneapolis Star

"The second step."

How far have we gone on the road to disarmament? What might be the next steps?

7. Nixon's Journey to Moscow (1972). See pages 473-474.

8. Soviet-American Trade Agreement. In 1972 Soviet and American negotiators concluded a sweeping trade package that provided as follows: (*a*) The Soviets agreed to pay, in yearly installments until 2001, the sum of $722 million for nonmilitary lend-lease materials kept by Russia after World War II. (*b*) The United States agreed that the government's Export-Import Bank would grant credits and guarantees for the sale of goods to Russia. (*c*) The United States agreed to tax Soviet imports at the lowest regular tariff rate— such treatment being known as "most-favored nation" status.

The Soviets gained a promise of substantial credits with which to purchase American machinery and technology so as to improve their industrial output, to pay for imports of American grain, and to develop Siberian oil and gas resources.

The United States gained a promise of payment of the World War II lend-lease debt, and foresaw huge exports of American agricultural and industrial products to Russia and significant imports of Soviet energy and mineral resources to the United States. Secretary of State Rogers considered the treaty a step toward a "better political relationship."

Mauldin in The St. Louis Post-Dispatch

"?"

Is it spring or just a temporary thaw? What factors argue for a thaw in the cold war? Against a thaw?

Congress, however, indicated that it would not approve the trade package as long as the Soviets maintained an exorbitant "education tax" to deter persons, chiefly Jews, wishing to emigrate from the Soviet Union. Senator Henry Jackson and Representative Wilbur Mills, with overwhelming Congressional support, each branch sponsored similar legislation to bar government credit and "most-favored nation" treatment to any country that denies its citizens the right to emigrate and that charges more than "nominal" exit fees. In early 1973 the Soviets indicated that the "education tax" had been suspended indefinitely although the law remained on the books. Senator Jackson held this "suspension" insufficient since the Soviets could reimpose the tax at any time and could use other methods to harass would-be emigrants.

To this writing, the fate of the sweeping Soviet-American trade package remains in doubt.

MATCHING QUESTIONS

Column A	*Column B*
1. Russian proponent of "peaceful coexistence" doctrine	*a.* Marshal Tito
2. Chancellor of West Germany	*b.* John F. Kennedy
3. Communist leader of Poland	*c.* Dwight D. Eisenhower
4. Proponent of "atoms-for-peace" plan	*d.* Edward Gierek
5. Communist leader of Cuba	*e.* Janos Kadar
6. President of South Korea	*f.* Joseph Stalin
7. American President who journeyed to Peking and Moscow	*g.* Richard Nixon
8. American author of plan for international control of atomic energy	*h.* Fidel Castro
	i. Chung Hee Park
9. Communist leader of Yugoslavia	*j.* Nikita Khrushchev
10. Communist leader of Hungary	*k.* Bernard Baruch
	l. Willy Brandt

TRUE-FALSE QUESTIONS

If the statement is correct, write the word *true*. If the statement is incorrect, substitute a word or phrase for the italicized term to make the statement correct.

1. The Truman Doctrine was intended to keep Russian influence out of Greece and *Italy*.
2. President Truman's offer of economic aid to underdeveloped areas is known as the *Fourteen-Point* Plan.
3. The nation that joined NATO after the Paris Agreements of 1955 was *Austria*.
4. The NATO member having a common frontier with the Soviet Union is *Turkey*.
5. The two nations, now NATO partners, that have fought each other twice in this century are France and *Italy*.
6. Hong Kong now belongs to *Nationalist China*.

7. Relations between India and Red China were strained by Red China's suppression of the revolt in *Kashmir.*

8. *France* refused to sign the 1963 Limited Nuclear Test Ban Treaty and subsequently exploded her first atomic bomb.

9. The nation that desires to lead a European "Third Force" independent of the Anglo-Saxon powers is *France.*

MULTIPLE-CHOICE QUESTIONS

1. Before 1941 relations between the United States and Russia were (1) very friendly (2) based on similar ideals (3) unfriendly (4) improved by the Soviet-German Non-Aggression Pact of 1939.

2. Which group consists entirely of Russian satellites? (1) Austria, Poland, Turkey (2) Czechoslovakia, Greece, Turkey (3) Czechoslovakia, East Germany, Poland (4) Hungary, Israel, Poland.

3. Estonia, Latvia, and Lithuania are (1) islands forming part of Indonesia (2) territories seized by Communist armies in the Balkans (3) neutralist nations (4) former independent nations now part of the Soviet Union.

4. The Communists seek to keep democratic ideas from their people by means of (1) containment (2) the iron curtain (3) coexistence (4) COMECON.

5. Which European Communist country has most successfully resisted Russian domination? (1) Hungary (2) Yugoslavia (3) Bulgaria (4) Rumania.

6. An issue in the dispute between the Soviet Union and Communist China is the (1) superiority of Communism over capitalism (2) need for censorship of newspapers (3) method of achieving world Communism (4) value of atomic weapons.

7. Originally the Marshall Plan was an offer made to (1) all European nations (2) all U.N. members (3) only English-speaking nations (4) only anti-Communist nations.

8. An important purpose of the Marshall Plan was to (1) limit European armaments (2) establish a United States of Europe (3) improve economic conditions in European nations (4) prevent Soviet Russia from securing raw materials.

9. The Marshall Plan helped (1) end Communist influence in Italy (2) increase industrial production in Europe by more than 50 percent (3) restore democratic government in Czechoslovakia (4) decrease industrial production in Europe by 10 percent.

10. "The United States is prepared to use armed forces to assist . . . such nations requesting assistance against armed aggression from any country controlled by international Communism" is a quotation from the (1) Korean Truce (2) Eisenhower Doctrine (3) Warsaw Pact (4) Potsdam Declaration.

11. The chief purpose of the Schuman Plan for Western Europe was to (1) build an international military force (2) establish high tariffs (3) promote the Point Four program (4) abolish tariffs on coal and iron.

12. A step already taken toward a united Western Europe has been the (1) selection of Geneva as its capital (2) creation of a common market (3) adoption of a single currency system (4) adoption of a single constitution.

13. The Common Market is essentially a (1) military alliance (2) federal form of government (3) tariff union (4) communications corporation.

14. England's application for membership in the Common Market was twice vetoed by (1) Russia (2) France (3) West Germany (4) the United States.

15. A major reason for creating the North Atlantic Treaty Organization (NATO) was to (1) supervise the West German government (2) protect member nations against Communist aggression (3) distribute Point Four funds (4) regulate world trade.

16. NATO was weakened when a member nation withdrew all its troops from the integrated military command. This member nation was (1) Italy (2) France (3) West Germany (4) Turkey.

17. A major difficulty in providing NATO with nuclear weapons for the defense of Western Europe has been the (1) refusal of the United States to cooperate (2) refusal of West Germany to permit missile bases on her soil (3) reluctance of many NATO members to give nuclear arms to West German troops (4) reluctance of England to use nuclear weapons even for self-defense.

18. The countries *not* a party to any military pact include (1) Portugal, Spain, the United Kingdom (2) Sweden, Switzerland, Yugoslavia (3) Greece, Italy, the Netherlands (4) Poland, Rumania, Spain.

19. Which was the first major clash between the Western powers and the Soviet Union? (1) the Berlin airlift (2) the defense of Hong Kong (3) the Hungarian revolt against Soviet Russia's domination (4) the invasion of South Korea.

20. An important similarity between the governments of Great Britain and West Germany in the 20th century is that both have (1) a written constitution (2) a king (3) a "responsible" prime minister (4) an elected "upper house."

21. The city of Berlin is located (1) within East Germany (2) within West Germany (3) on the border between East Germany and West Germany (4) on the border between East Germany and Poland.

22. The capital of West Germany is (1) Bonn (2) Berlin (3) Nuremberg (4) Strasbourg.

23. The Western nation most fearful of the revival of German power is (1) England (2) France (3) Italy (4) the United States.

24. The top Nazi leaders were tried at Nuremberg on charges of (1) losing the war (2) destroying the Weimar Republic (3) inventing rockets (4) committing crimes against humanity.

25. The United States gave economic aid to West Germany after World War II chiefly to (1) help stop the spread of Communism (2) strengthen Germany against French power (3) help Germany socialize her industry (4) raise the German standard of living above the prewar level.

26. Khrushchev demanded that the Western powers withdraw from West Berlin because that city is (1) his birthplace (2) a valuable seaport (3) still in ruins caused by World War II bombings (4) a showcase of democracy and capitalism behind the iron curtain.

27. The withdrawal of troops from Austria in 1955 illustrated that (1) the United Nations had the power to settle disputes (2) agreement was possible between the Western Allies and the Soviet Union (3) Anglo-French influence dominated central Europe (4) small nations held the balance of power in Europe.

28. Which nation in the Middle East has received substantial military aid from the Communist bloc? (1) Israel (2) Saudi Arabia (3) Egypt (4) Turkey.

29. In 1958 President Eisenhower heeded a request for American troops by the Middle East country of (1) Israel (2) Lebanon (3) Egypt (4) South Vietnam.

30. The event that occurred *first* in Korea was (1) North Korea's invasion of South Korea (2) the creation of the Republic of Korea (3) intervention of Chinese Communist troops in Korea (4) division of Korea at the 38th parallel.

31. Which issue was the chief cause of delay in negotiating a truce in Korea? (1) the U.N. resolution calling Red China an aggressor (2) the boundary line between North and South Korea (3) the exchange of war prisoners (4) the status of Formosa.

32. Following the Korean War (1) Korea was unified (2) Nationalist China obtained control of Korea (3) Communist influence in Korea was ended (4) Korea remained divided in two sections.

33. Which is characteristic of Red China's foreign policy? (1) voting with Russia in the U.N. General Assembly (2) spreading Communist propaganda in Southeast Asia (3) offering aid to SEATO (4) compromising with Nationalist China over off-shore islands.

34. Which group pairs a country with a territory that it is demanding? (1) Italy—Cyprus (2) France—Madagascar (3) Communist China—Taiwan (4) Japan—Korea.

35. The policy of neutralism is best shown in (1) Japan's economic recovery since 1945 (2) Great Britain's withdrawal from Palestine (3) the Soviet Union's attempt to control Yugoslavia (4) India's policy in the East-West controversy.

36. Which is a basic cause of unrest throughout Asia? (1) complete control by European powers (2) lack of important natural resources (3) manpower shortage (4) low standard of living for the majority of the people.

37. President Kennedy viewed the settlement of the 1962 missile base crisis over Cuba as a(an) (1) American victory (2) Russian victory (3) honorable accord (4) proof of the value of the U.N.

38. The Baruch Plan for international control of atomic energy did *not* propose (1) elimination of the veto power (2) unlimited inspection by an international authority (3) stockpiling of atom bombs (4) sharing American atomic know-how with other nations.

39. The U.N. did *not* adopt the Baruch Plan for international control of atomic energy because of (1) the U.N.'s lack of interest in the problem (2) American opposition to international control (3) a Russian veto (4) English refusal to cooperate.

40. The 1963 limited nuclear test ban, negotiated by the United States, the United Kingdom, and the Soviet Union, permits testing (1) in the atmosphere (2) in space (3) below the ground (4) under water.

41. In 1957 the first man-made satellite was placed into orbit around the earth by (1) a U.N. team of scientists (2) Russia (3) the United States (4) England.

42. By Project Apollo, the United States proposed to (1) send space teams to the moon and back (2) find ways of utilizing frozen Arctic lands (3) establish a worldwide tele-communications system (4) train India's pilots to fly the newest jets.

43. The Summit Conference of 1960 (1) temporarily decreased East-West tensions (2) never really discussed vital East-West issues (3) marked a change in Khrushchev's policy toward German reunification (4) marked a change in Eisenhower's policy toward West Berlin.

WORLD LEADERS

Algeria	Col. Houari Boumedienne, President
Australia	Gough Whitlam, Prime Minister
Bangladesh	Sheik Mujibur Rahman, Prime Minister
Burma	General Ne Win, Premier
Cambodia	Lt. Gen. Lon Nol, President In Tam, Premier
Canada	Pierre Elliott Trudeau (Liberal), Prime Minister Robert L. Stanfield (Conservative), Minority Leader
Ceylon (Sri Lanka)	Mrs. Sirimavo Bandaranaike, Prime Minister
China (Communist)	Mao Tse-tung, Communist Party Chairman Chou En-lai, Premier
China (Nationalist)	Chiang Kai-shek, President
Cuba	Fidel Castro, Premier and Communist Party First Secretary Raul Roa, Foreign Minister
Cyprus	Archbishop Makarios, President
Czechoslovakia	Gustav Husak, Communist Party First Secretary Lubomir Strougal, Premier
Egypt	Anwar al-Sadat, President
England	Elizabeth II, Queen Edward Heath (Conservative), Prime Minister Alec Douglas-Home, Foreign Secretary Harold Wilson (Labor), Minority Leader
Ethiopia	Haile Selassie I, Emperor
France	Georges Pompidou, President Jacques Chaban-Delmas, Prime Minister Maurice Schumann, Foreign Minister
Germany (East)	Erich Honecker, Communist Party First Secretary Willi Stoph, Prime Minister
Germany (West)	Dr. Gustav Heinemann, President Willy Brandt (Social Democrat), Chancellor Walter Scheel (Free Democrat), Foreign Minister

Ghana	Col. Ignatius K. Acheampong, Chairman of the National Redemption Council
Greece	George Papadopoulos, Premier
Guinea	Sekou Touré, President
Hungary	Janos Kadar, Communist Party First Secretary
India	V. V. Giri, President Mrs. Indira Gandhi, Prime Minister
Indonesia	Lt. Gen. Suharto, President
Iran	Mohammed Riza Pahlevi, Shah
Iraq	Ahmed Hassan al-Bakr, President
Ireland	Erskine Childers, President Liam Cosgrave, Prime Minister
Israel	Ephraim Katzir, President Mrs. Golda Meir, Prime Minister
Italy	Giovanni Leone, President Mariano Rumor, Premier
Japan	Hirohito, Emperor Kakuei Tanaka (Liberal Democrat), Prime Minister
Jordan	Hussein I, King
Kenya	Jomo Kenyatta, President
Korea (North)	Kim Il-sung, Prime Minister
Korea (South)	Chung Hee Park, President
Laos	Prince Souvanna Phouma, Premier
Malaysia	Tun Abdul Razak bin Hussein, Prime Minister
Morocco	Hassan II, King
New Zealand	Norman E. Kirk, Prime Minister
Nigeria	Maj. Gen. Yakubu Gowon, Head of Military Council
Pakistan	Zulfikar Ali Bhutto, President
Philippines	Ferdinand Marcos, President
Poland	Edward Gierek, Communist Party First Secretary Piotr Jaroszewicz, Premier
Portugal	Dr. Marcello Caetano, Premier
Rhodesia	Ian Smith, Prime Minister
Rumania	Nicolae Ceausescu, President of the State Council Ion Gheorghe Maurer, Premier

Russia	Leonid Brezhnev, Communist Party General Secretary
	Aleksei Kosygin, Prime Minister
	Nikolai Podgorny, Chairman of the Presidium of the Supreme Soviet
	Andrei Gromyko, Foreign Minister
	Yakov A. Malik, Chief Delegate to the United Nations
Saudi Arabia	Faisal Abdel Aziz al Saud, King
South Africa	J. J. Fouche, President
	Balthazar Vorster, Prime Minister
Spain	Gen. Francisco Franco, Chief of State
	Adm. Carrera Blanco, Premier
Syria	Gen. Hafez al-Assad, Chief of State
Tanzania	Julius Nyerere, President
Tunisia	Habib Bourguiba, President
Turkey	Fahri Koruturk, President
	Naim Talu, Prime Minister
United Nations	Kurt Waldheim (Austria), Secretary General
United States	Richard M. Nixon (Republican), President
	Spiro T. Agnew (Republican), Vice President
	William P. Rogers, Secretary of State
	John Scali, Ambassador to the United Nations
Vatican City	Paul VI, Pope
Vietnam (North)	Ton Duc Thang, President
	Le Duan, Communist Party First Secretary
	Pham Van Dong, Premier
Vietnam (South)	Nguyen Van Thieu, President
Yugoslavia	Marshal Tito, President
Zaire	Mobutu Sese Seko, President

INDEX

Abelard, Peter, 90
Absolute monarchs, 123-134
Acropolis, 45
Adenauer, Konrad, 439
Aeschylus, 43
Africa, 285-296
Afrikaners, 277-278
Afro-Asian nations, 331-332; in U.N., 408-409; significance, 474
Age of Nobles, in Egypt, 6
Age of Reason, 133, 155-156
Agricultural Revolution, 225-226
Aibak, Kutb-ub-din, 92
Airlift, Berlin, 438
Airplane, 224; in World War I, 340; in World War II, 393
Akbar, 94
Albania, 337, 371, 386, 422
Alcuin, 63
Alexander I, Czar, 168, 172, 174
Alexander II, Czar, 347, 348
Alexander the Great, 23, 42
Al Fatah, 304
Algeciras Conference, 336
Algeria, 194, 196-197, 293-294
Alliances, before World War I, 335; in cold war, 430-435
Alphabet, 15
Alsace-Lorraine, 205, 335, 342
Amenhotep IV, 7, 8
American Expeditonary Force, 341
American Revolution, 149-152, 156
Amin, Idi, 188, 294
Angles, the, 55, 60, 71, 124
Anglican Church, 119
Angola, 291
Anschluss, 344, 386
Anthony, Susan B., 234
Antiballistic missile (ABM), 451, 464-465
Antony, Mark, 53
Anzus Pact, 435
Apartheid, 278-279
Aqaba, Gulf of, 303, 404
Aquinas, St. Thomas, 90
Arab-Israeli War of 1967, 303-305, 406-407
Arab League, 301
Arabs, 65, 301-305, 406-407
Arameans, 16
Archbishop of Canterbury struggle, 76
Archimedes, 46
Architecture, Egyptian, 8; Sumerian, 13; Chaldean, 18; ancient Indian, 26; ancient

Chinese, 32-33; Greek, 45; Roman, 57; Byzantine, 79; Moslem, 82; medieval European, 89; medieval and modern Indian, 95; medieval Chinese, 100; Japanese, 106
Aristarchus, 46
Aristophanes, 43
Aristotle, 44, 90
Art, Egyptian, 8; ancient Indian, 26; ancient Chinese, 32-33; Byzantine, 79; medieval Chinese, 100; Japanese, 104, 106; Renaissance, 112-114; and Industrial Revolution, 257-265; in Communist Russia, 364-365
Aryans, 23
Ashikaga Shogunate, 105
Asia: see *China, Far East, India, Japan, Middle East*
Asoka, 23-24
Asquith, Herbert, 185
Assembly line, 230
Assignats, 159
Associations Law, 192
Assurbanipal, 17
Assyrians, 17
Astrology, 13
Astronomy, Babylonians, 13; Chaldeans, 18; Ptolemy, 58; Renaissance, 114
Aswan High Dam, 445, 446
Athens, 37-39, 41, 43
Atlantic Charter, 396
Atomic energy: see *Nuclear energy*
Atoms-for-peace plan, 460
Attila, 55
Attlee, Clement, 186
Augsburg, Peace of, 121
Augustus, 53-54
Aurelius, Marcus, 55
Ausgleich, 214
Australia, 274, 433, 435
Australian ballot, 182, 274
Austria, absolutism and empire through 18th century, 132-133; and Congress of Vienna, 172-173; Revolutions of 1848, 176-177; opposes German unification, 202-204; opposes Italian unification, 209-212; Austrian Empire in 19th century, 214-216; in World War I, 215, 335, 337-338, 340, 343-344; composers, 263; invaded by Hitler, 386; World War II peace treaty (1955), 441-442
Austria-Hungary, 214-216